R. Gupta's®

POPULAR MASTER GUIDE

DSSSB–TEACHERS

TGT

ENGLISH

Recruitment Exam

by

RPH Editorial Board

2027 EDITION

RAMESH PUBLISHING HOUSE, NEW DELHI

Published by
O.P. Gupta *for* Ramesh Publishing House

Admin. Office
12-H, New Daryaganj Road, Opp. Officers' Mess
New Delhi-110002 ☎ 23275224, 23245124

E-mail: info@rameshpublishinghouse.com
For Online Shopping: www.rameshpublishinghouse.com

Showroom
● Balaji Market, Nai Sarak, Delhi-110006 ☎ 23282525 📱 9354373464
● 4457, Nai Sarak, Delhi-110006

Book Code: R-1321

ISBN: 978-93-5012-028-6

Price: ₹ 360

Printed at: Deepak Offset, Delhi

CONTENTS

Scheme of Examination

The selection shall be made through One Tier (objective type/MCQ) examination as given below. DSSSB will conduct One Tier Examination (Objective Type/MCQ) of 02 hour duration. The Test Components of objective Examination (In Section A and Section B) along with their number of questions and time disposition is given below:

ONE TIER EXAMINATION (OBJECTIVE TYPE/MCQ)

Section	Test Components	Number of Questions	Marks
A. (i)	General Awareness	20	20
(ii)	General Intelligence and Reasoning Ability	20	20
(iii)	Arithmetical & Numerical Ability	20	20
(iv)	Test of Hindi Language & Comprehension	20	20
(v)	Test of English Language & Comprehension	20	20
B. MCQs of one mark each from the subject concerned including questions on teaching methodology/B.Ed.		100	100
Total		**200**	**200**

Previous Years' Paper

Delhi Subordinate Services Selection Board (DSSSB)

TGT (English) Recruitment Exam, 2025

(Exam held on 31-08-2025)

POST SPECIFIC SUBJECT RELATED QUESTIONS

1. Which of the following poems by Percy Bysshe Shelley is considered his political and philosophical masterpiece?

1. Ozymandias
2. To a Skylark
3. Prometheus Unbound
4. Adonais

2. Match the authors in List-1 with their works in List-2.

List-1	List-2
A. Oliver Goldsmith	I. Evelina
B. Frances Burney	II. The Castle of Otranto
C. Horace Walpole	III. The Mysteries of Udolpho
D. Ann Radcliffe	IV. The Vicar of Wakefield

1. A-III, B-IV, C-I, D-II
2. A-I, B-II, C-III, D-IV
3. A-II, B-III, C-IV, D-I
4. A-IV, B-I, C-II, D-III

3. Select the statement that is NOT a true feature of Stream of Consciousness novels.

1. In the Stream of Consciousness novel, the writer is interested in the growth of a character from one stage to another.
2. The Stream of Consciousness novel has no tangible plot with ups and downs or a moral principle.
3. In such a work, we could see a unique drama taking place at the level of characters' imaginings, a drama in which opinions and outlooks might be in harmony with each other like a kind of internal monologue.
4. In the Stream of Consciousness, a person observes and associates life's details in a manner that, when given a sequence, it could assume a fictional shape.

4. Which of the following options indicate what the given lines from 'Sons and Lovers' might mean?

But no, he would not give in. Turning sharply, he walked towards the city's gold phosphorescence. His fists were shut, his mouth set fast. He would not take that direction, to the darkness, to follow her. He walked towards the faintly humming, glowing town, quickly.

1. A disturbed state of mind's sudden realisation and movement towards optimism
2. A disturbed state of mind that feels alienated from the world around it and yet finds courage to live within it
3. A disturbed state of mind that resorts to violence to destroy the world that was the cause of all its pain
4. A disturbed state of mind that drowns itself in hollow pleasures and materialistic pursuits

1. 3	2. 4	3. 1	4. 2

5. 'The Rime of the Ancient Mariner' is a/an ______.

1. ode 2. satire
3. lyrical ballad 4. haiku

6. In part one of Swift's novel 'Gulliver's Travels', Lilliput represents:

1. Italy 2. France
3. England 4. Greece

7. What kind of a novel is 'Frankenstein' written by Mary Shelley?

1. A combination of eastern fantasy and proletarian
2. A combination of pastoral and detective
3. A combination of Gothic horror story and science fiction
4. A combination of modern and European fiction

8. Read the following statements and select the correct option.

A. The stream of consciousness stressed the subjective field, the personal dilemmas and uncertainties of individual human beings.

B. The impressions presented in the stream of consciousness novel are based on an individual character's subjective worldview and imagination and, thus, are not verifiable in an objective manner.

1. A is true but B is false.
2. Both A and B are true but B is not the correct explanation of A.
3. A is false but B is true.
4. Both A and B are true and B is the correct explanation of A.

9. Select the genre of novel that uses the narrative technique with the following two main characteristics.

A. The very convention of sequence is discarded.

B. Characters are like walking thoughts with fluid mental states that change by the minute and may get away from or merge with others arbitrarily, with no validation from the circumstance in which they are placed.

1. Stream of Consciousness
2. Bildungsroman
3. Magical Realism
4. Speculative

10. In 'Ode to the West Wind', the poet describes the West Wind as a destroyer and a preserver. What does the 'destroyer' signify?

1. Destruction of humanity
2. Natural disasters
3. Death of the present year
4. End of the Earth

11. Read the following statements and select the most appropriate option.

Lawrence has shown through the female characters that there is pay parity in the society when it comes to remunerating the work done by both the genders in 'Sons and Lovers'. He also demonstrated the condition of women in an abusive marriage and how young girls are not allowed to indulge in intellectual pleasures of philosophy and poetry.

Assertion (A): However, these females were merely demonstrated as caricatures of their counterparts in the society while no attention has been paid to portray the complexities of their inner world and psyche along with their private struggles.

Example (E): The women characters were easily influenced by the central male figure and act against their own interests for the sake of the hero.

1. Both A and E are true but E is not an example of A.
2. A is true but E is false.
3. Both A and E are true and E is an example of A.
4. A is false but E is true.

5. 3	**6.** 3	**7.** 3	**8.** 4	**9.** 1	**10.** 3	**11.** 3

12. Which of the following is a tragedy written by John Webster that explores themes of corruption, power, and gender within a decaying aristocracy?

1. Every Man in His Humour
2. The Revenger's Tragedy
3. The White Devil
4. Tamburlaine

13. Identity the lines from Shelly's 'Ode to West Wind'.

1. "The still, sad music of humanity."
2. "O Wind, If Winter comes, can Spring be far behind?"
3. "And 'tis my faith that every flower Enjoys the air it breathes."
4. "Look on my works, ye Mighty, and despair!"

14. Which of the following is a work by Geoffrey Chaucer?

1. Paradise Lost
2. Utopia
3. The Canterbury Tales
4. Faerie Queene

15. Which notable event occurred during the lifetime of Edmund Spenser?

1. The signing of the Magna Carta
2. The establishment of the Church of England
3. The Restoration of the monarchy
4. The defeat of the Spanish Armada

16. Which of the following accurately describes an event in 'Gulliver's Travels'?

1. Gulliver leads a rebellion against the Lilliputians.
2. Gulliver travels to an island populated by giants.
3. Gulliver becomes the king of an island nation.
4. Gulliver discovers an ancient treasure.

17. In Shelley's 'Ode to the West Wind', what does 'dead thoughts' symbolise in the lines 'Drive my dead thoughts over the universe/ Like withered leaves to quicken a new birth'?

1. The poet's despair and stagnation
2. The poet's forgotten ideas
3. The poet's lost creativity
4. The poet's memories of the past

18. Select the play by John Webster from the given options.

1. The White Devil
2. Ralph Roister Doister
3. The Schoolmaster
4. Aracadia

19. Which of the following categories does the novel 'Sons and Lovers' NOT fit into?

1. Fantasy Novel
2. Regional Novel
3. Realist Novel
4. Autobiographical Novel

20. Select the option which is a characteristic of Wordsworth's poetry.

1. Hellenism
2. Sensuousness
3. Negative capability
4. Love for nature

21. Which famous line from 'Ode to the West Wind' by Percy Bysshe Shelley expresses the poet's longing for renewal and the power of transformation?

1. "A thing of beauty is a joy for ever."
2. "The mind is its own place, and in itself/Can make a Heaven of Hell, a Hell of Heaven."
3. "If Winter comes, can Spring be far behind?"
4. "Till the spell of this loneliness upon my spirit fell."

12. 3 **13.** 2 **14.** 3 **15.** 4 **16.** 2 **17.** 1 **18.** 1 **19.** 1 **20.** 4 **21.** 3

22. In the story of Bacchus, who is his mortal mother?
1. Dione 2. Europa
3. Semele 4. lo

23. Emily Dickinson's verse is often associated with common meter, which is defined by alternating lines of ______.
1. six syllables and eight syllables (6868)
2. eight syllables and six syllables (8686)
3. four syllables and six syllables (4646)
4. eight syllables and four syllables (8484)

24. Which poem by John Keats contains the line, 'A thing of beauty is a joy for ever'?
1. To Autumn
2. Ode to a Nightingale
3. Ode on a Grecian Urn
4. Endymion

25. Which poem is attributed to John Donne?
1. The Rape of the Lock
2. The Sun Rising
3. The Prelude
4. The Faerie Queene

26. What revenge does Philomela seek after her ordeal?
1. She kills the son of her captor and serves him as a meal.
2. She curses the house of her captor.
3. She calls upon the gods to destroy the city.
4. She flees to the forest and lives as a hermit for the rest of her life.

27. What is the primary theme explored in Ralph Waldo Emerson's poem 'Hamatreya'?
1. The strength of familial bonds
2. The beauty of nature
3. The fleeting nature of human ownership and the permanence of the earth
4. The joys of childhood

28. How does TS Eliot's 'Murder in the Cathedral' depict martyrdom as a religiou[s] theme?
1. As a means to gain power within the church
2. As a sacrifice for one's religious belie[f]
3. As a tragic consequence of politica[l] betrayal
4. As a divine calling that transcend[s] personal desire

29. Identify the line from John Keats 'Endymion'.
1. The landscape with the quiet of Sky
2. To strive, to seek, to find, and not t[o] yield
3. A thing of beauty is joy for ever
4. And all that's best of dark and bright. Meet in her aspect and her eyes

30. Identify the literary device used in the following lines.

"A spring of love gushed from my heart,
And I blessed them unaware:"

1. Euphemism
2. Metaphor
3. Allusion
4. Simile

31. Match the authors listed in Column 1 with their corresponding works listed in Column 2.

Column 1	Column 2
1. Daniel Defoe	(*a*) Gulliver's Travels
2. Jonathan Swift	(*b*) Elegy Written in a Country Churchyard
3. William Congreve	(*c*) Robinson Crusoe
4. Thomas Gray	(*d*) The Way of the World

1. 1-(*d*), 2-(*c*), 3-(*a*), 4-(*b*)
2. 1-(*c*), 2-(*d*), 3-(*b*), 4-(*a*)
3. 1-(*a*), 2-(*b*), 3-(*c*), 4-(*d*)
4. 1-(*c*), 2-(*a*), 3-(*d*), 4-(*b*)

22. 3 **23.** 2 **24.** 4 **25.** 2 **26.** 1 **27.** 3 **28.** 2 **29.** 3 **30.** 2 **31.** 4

32. Which poem by Shelley is an elegy written in memory of John Keats?

1. The Revolt of Islam
2. Hellas
3. Alastor
4. Adonais

33. Match the Authors with their works.

Author	Work
I. Louisa May Alcott	A. Adventures of Huckleberry Finn
II. Kate Chopin	B. Woman in the Nineteenth Century
III. Margaret Fuller	C. The Call of the Wild
IV. Jack London	D. Little Women
V. Mark Twain	E. The Awakening

1. I-A, II-C, III-D, IV-B, V-E
2. I-B, II-C, III-E, IV-D, V-A
3. I-D, II-E, III-B, IV-C, V-A
4. I-C, II-D, III-A, IV-B, V-E

34. Select the short story written by Pudhumaipithan.

1. Redemption
2. The Tiredness of Rosabel
3. The Legacy
4. The Duchess and the Jeweller

35. Which of the following is the central theme in TS Eliot's 'Murder in the Cathedral'?

1. The rise of social rebellion against authority
2. The pursuit of political dominance over the Church
3. The conflict between fate and free will
4. The spiritual struggle between personal ambition and divine purpose

36. In 'July's People', Nadine Gordimer explores the complexities of post-apartheid South Africa through the experiences of her characters. What significant aspect of Gordimer's background as a South African writer informs her narrative style and thematic concerns in this novel?

1. Her relocation to England during her formative years, shaping her views on colonialism
2. Her first-hand experiences of apartheid, providing a nuanced perspective on racial and social issues
3. Her engagement with European literary traditions, which influenced her narrative techniques
4. Her background in journalism, which allowed her to adopt a detached, observational tone in her writing

37. The name of the protagonist of the play 'The Good Woman of Setzuan' is ______.

1. Chen
2. Dongmei
3. Xiang
4. Shen Te

38. In the play 'All My Sons' written by Arthur Miller, Steve Deever's son ______ is a lawyer by profession and a veteran of World War II.

1. George Deever
2. David Deever
3. Stephen Deever
4. Michael Deever

39. What kind of a novel is 'Frankenstein'?

1. Children's literature
2. Picaresque novel
3. Bildungsroman
4. Epistolary novel

40. Which of the following poems by Nissim Ezekiel is a poignant reflection on the poet's feelings of alienation, otherness and his desire for acceptance and understanding?

1. The Patriot
2. The Professor
3. Minority Poem
4. Night of the Scorpion

32. 4	**33.** 3	**34.** 1	**35.** 4	**36.** 2	**37.** 4	**38.** 1	**39.** 4	**40.** 3

41. Match the following authors with their corresponding works of popular literature.

1. Lewis Carroll	A. The Night Train at Deoli
2. Agatha Christie	B. Alice's Adventures in Wonderland
3. Ruskin Bond	C. Maqbool
4. Vishal Bhardwaj	D. Murder on the Orient Express

1. 1-B, 2-D, 3-C, 4-A
2. 1-C, 2-A, 3-D, 4-B
3. 1-B, 2-D, 3-A, 4-C
4. 1-A, 2-C, 3-D, 4-B

42. Which of the following elements is considered essential for the effectiveness of a short story as a literary genre?
1. A lengthy exposition that provides detailed background information
2. A complex plot with multiple subplots
3. A concise narrative that focuses on a single incident or theme
4. A well-developed character arc for every character

43. What is the primary objective of deconstruction as a critical methodology?
1. To find the "true" meaning of a text
2. To analyse the author's biography
3. To challenge, subvert, and deconstruct binary oppositions and dominant interpretations
4. To understand the historical context

44. Which of the following is the main theme of 'Waiting for Godot'?
1. Hypocrisy and moral depravation
2. Existentialism and isolation
3. Capitalism and lust
4. Gender and cultural identity

45. In Alice Munro's short story 'Boys and Girls', what theme is primarily explored?
1. The dangers of technology
2. The significance of ancient myths
3. Gender roles and the expectations of society
4. The pursuit of fame and fortune

46. What happens to Pyramus and Thisbe the end of the story?
1. They both die by suicide.
2. They are saved by a benevolent god
3. They are turned into birds by the god
4. They escape to a foreign land togethe

47. How does Homer depict the concept honour in 'The Iliad' through the actio of Hector?
1. Hector's spying on the Greek camp night
2. Hector's decision to face Achille knowing he might die
3. Hector's attempt to negotiate peace wi the Greeks
4. Hector's betrayal of Trojans by fleei the battle

48. Match the following authors to the respective works:

1. RK Narayan	A. And Some Ta a Lover
2. Mulk Raj Anand	B. The Dark Ho No Terrors
3. Shashi Deshpande	C. Coolie
4. Dina Mehta	D. The Guide

1. 1–C, 2–D, 3–B, 4–A
2. 1–D, 2–C, 3–B, 4–A
3. 1–B, 2–C, 3–D, 4–A
4. 1–A, 2–C, 3–B, 4–D

49. Kate Millet has criticised 'Sons and Lover in her book 'Sexual Politics' because t novel is centred on the needs of Pa around which the female characters gath as satellites with no social or psychologic existence of their own. According to Ri Rylance, Millet interprets 'Sons and Love not as a realist novel but a ______.
1. speculative fiction
2. bildungsroman novel
3. fantasy
4. heroic male romance

41. 3	**42.** 3	**43.** 3	**44.** 2	**45.** 3	**46.** 1	**47.** 2	**48.** 2	**49.** 4

50. The main purpose of the Theatre of Absurd in Samuel Beckett's 'Waiting for Godot' is to:

1. awaken the feeling of patriotism
2. report the moral decline in modern milieu
3. discuss the religious issues in contemporary society
4. confront people with a bewildering experience

51. In Mulk Raj Anand's 'The Lost Child', which aspect of the child's character is most significantly highlighted through his reaction to the fair and his subsequent loss?

1. His disdain for parental authority
2. His independence and desire for adventure
3. His materialistic desires and greed
4. His innocence and vulnerability in a chaotic world

52. Which incident in 'The Iliad' most clearly contrasts the ideals of honour with the real horror of war?

1. The duel between Paris and Menelaus
2. Agamemnon's gift offerings to Achilles to return to battle
3. Achilles' killing of the Amazon queen Penthesilea
4. Priam begging Achilles for the body of Hector

53. The given description highlights one of the important themes of the novel 'Sons and Lovers'.

Identify the theme.

Mrs. Morel's sons do not become miners, but move into more respectable classes because of her efforts to give her children good education. Throughout the novel 'Sons and Lovers', the financial position of the Morel family continues to improve which helps them move upwards in the social hierarchy.

1. Violence inherent in the institution of family
2. The capitalist exploitation of the poor
3. Social mobility and class aspiration
4. Gender-based discrimination

54. Which of the following best describes popular literature?

1. Literature that reflects high culture and sophisticated tastes
2. Literature that is difficult to understand and analyse
3. Literature that is only studied in academic settings
4. Literature that is widely read and enjoyed by the general public

55. In which poem did Nissim Ezekiel use Indian English as a theme?

1. Goodbye Party for Miss Pushpa T.S.
2. Woman and Child
3. A Time To Change
4. Hymns in Darkness

56. Identify the lines taken from the poem 'Brahma' written by RW Emerson.

1. "Where are these men? Asleep beneath their grounds:
And strangers, fond as they, their furrows plough.
Earth laughs in flowers, to see her boastful boys
Earth-proud, proud of the earth which is not theirs;
Who steer the plough, but cannot steer their feet
Clear of the grave."
2. "They called me theirs,
Who so controlled me;
Yet every one
Wished to stay, and is gone,
How am I theirs,
If they cannot hold me,
But I hold them?"

50. 4	**51.** 4	**52.** 4	**53.** 3	**54.** 4	**55.** 1

3. "They reckon ill who leave me out;
When me they fly, I am the wings;
I am the doubter and the doubt,
I am the hymn the Brahmin sings."
4. "Mine and yours;
Mine, not yours.
Earth endures;
Stars abide—
Shine down in the old sea;
Old are the shores;
But where are old men?
I who have seen much,
Such have I never seen."

57. Which theme is central to the short story 'The Legacy'?

1. The complexities of marriage and personal identity
2. The relationship between humans and nature
3. The struggle for power in a corporate world
4. The quest for adventure and discovery

58. What does the reaction of the child's parents to his disappearance reveal about their character and the socio-economic context in which they live in 'The Lost Child'?

1. They prioritise their own struggles over their child's safety.
2. They are indifferent to the child's needs and desires.
3. They demonstrate deep love and helplessness in the face of poverty.
4. They are overly protective and fearful of the outside world.

59. Match the poets in List-1 with their poems in List-2.

List-1	List-2
A. ST Coleridge	I. Adonais
B. PB Shelley	II. She Walks in Beauty
C. John Keats	III. Christabel
D. Lord Byron	IV. Ode to Autumn

1. A-II, B-III, C-I, D-IV
2. A-IV, B-II, C-III, D-I
3. A-I, B-IV, C-II, D-III
4. A-III, B-I, C-IV, D-II

60. Which of the following themes is showcased in 'The Sleepwalkers' by Nissim Ezekiel?

1. Liberal, modern, intellectual and educated men and women of progressive America
2. Liberal, modern, intellectual and educated men and women of progressive India
3. Intolerant, modern, intellectual and educated men and women of progressive America
4. Intolerant, traditional, ignorant and uneducated men and women of India

61. Select the option which is NOT among the chief characteristics of the Romantic Age.

1. Use of Heroic Couplet
2. Subjectivity
3. Melancholy
4. Love of the Supernatural

62. What is the nationality of the author Nadine Gordimer, who wrote 'July's People'?

1. South African
2. Australian
3. Canadian
4. British

63. Who are the protagonists in the play 'The Waiting for Godot'?

1. Riccardo and Tommaso
2. Antonio and Lorenzo
3. Vladimir and Estragon
4. Andrea and Giovanni

64. Which of the following factors is NOT an active partner in the formation of stream of consciousness?

1. Power of association to recreate an older episode with imaginative effort
2. Habitual pre-disposition of living an active mental life rather than an actively physical one
3. A cluster of memories that left significant trace on the individual's mind
4. The spatial dimension of social activity

56. 3	**57.** 1	**58.** 3	**59.** 4	**60.** 2	**61.** 1	**62.** 1	**63.** 3	**64.** 4

65. Identify the theory mentioned in the given statement.

Lawrence disapproved of the way Alfred Kuttner 'reduced the complexities of fiction to schematic simplicity of the theory' while interpreting 'Sons and Lovers'. However, Kuttner was the first one to trace the association of this theory with the text.

1. Marxist theory
2. Queer Theory
3. Postcolonial Theory
4. Psychoanalytic Theory

66. Match the authors in List-1 with their works in List-2.

List-1	List-2
A. Samuel Richardson	I. The Life & Opinions of Tristram Shandy, Gentleman
B. Tobias Smollett	II. Clarissa
C. Laurence Sterne	III. Shamela
D. Henry Fielding	IV. The Adventures of Roderick Random

1. A-III, B-I, C-IV, D-II
2. A-II, B-IV, C-I, D-III
3. A-IV, B-I, C-II, D-III
4. A-I, B-II, C-III, D-IV

67. In 'Mont Blanc', what does Shelley suggest about the relationship between nature and the human mind?

1. The human mind imposes meaning on nature.
2. The mind and nature are locked in a struggle for dominance.
3. The human mind is powerless before nature's immensity.
4. Nature is subordinate to the human mind.

68. Match the authors listed in Column 1 with their corresponding works listed in Column 2.

Column 1	Column 2
1. Samuel Johnson	(*a*) The Beggar's Opera
2. Alexander Pope	(*b*) The Rape of the Lock
3. John Gay	(*c*) The School for Scandal
4. Richard Brinsley Sheridan	(*d*) The Vanity of Human Wishes

1. 1-(*a*), 2-(*c*), 3-(*b*), 4-(*d*)
2. 1-(*c*), 2-(*d*), 3-(*b*), 4-(*a*)
3. 1-(*d*), 2-(*b*), 3-(*a*), 4-(*c*)
4. 1-(*b*), 2-(*a*), 3-(*d*), 4-(*c*)

69. In a Wordsworth poem, emphasis is placed on the word 'revisiting'. This poem was composed during his revisiting of Tintern Abbey, which stands on the banks of ______, after a lapse of ______.

1. the river Severn; 10 years
2. the river Dee; 1 year
3. the river Wye; 5 years
4. the river Teme; 15 years

70. Select the theme of the poem 'After Blenheim'.

1. The destructive results of war
2. Relationship between man and nature
3. Balance and moderation
4. Romanticism and scepticism

71. Select the main theme of Tintern Abbey.

1. Life and death
2. Transition or change
3. Good versus evil
4. Childhood memories

72. In 'July's People', how does Nadine Gordimer problematise gender roles within the context of apartheid South Africa?

1. By highlighting the vulnerability and agency of women in a patriarchal society during a time of social upheaval
2. By ignoring the role of women altogether and focusing solely on male perspectives
3. By depicting all male characters as oppressive figures without any redeeming qualities
4. By presenting female characters as entirely independent and self-sufficient

65. 4	**66.** 2	**67.** 3	**68.** 3	**69.** 3	**70.** 1	**71.** 2	**72.** 1

73. Grey's 'Elegy Written in a Country Churchyard' talks about:
1. the supernatural world of Xanadu
2. the problem of poverty and unemployment
3. issues of perseverance and resolution in the face of defeat
4. the death of England's underprivileged individuals

74. Which poet is known for writing two different kinds of poems—terse and meticulous, as well as lucid and free?
1. William Wordsworth
2. Nissim Ezekiel
3. Rabindranath Tagore
4. TS Eliot

75. Match the following authors to their respective works.

1. RK Narayan	A. Untouchable
2. Mulk Raj Anand	B. That Long Silence
3. Shashi Deshpande	C. A Tiger for Malgudi
4. Dina Mehta	D. Brides Are Not for Burning

1. 1–B, 2–A, 3–C, 4–D
2. 1–C, 2–A, 3–B, 4–D
3. 1–D, 2–A, 3–B, 4–C
4. 1–A, 2–C, 3–B, 4–D

76. What do the following lines from Sons and Lovers signify?

"He [Paul Morel] was a sensitive, imaginative boy, with a deep love for his mother and a strong sense of justice. But he was also intensely passionate, and his emotions were always on the surface. He was like a child, who, having no knowledge of the meaning of things, yet feels the truth of them."
1. The psychological effects of trauma
2. Oedipus complex
3. The platonic mother son bond
4. The inner turmoil of the protagonist

77. Which of the following genres is most likely to be considered popular literature?
1. Epic poetry
2. Scholarly articles
3. Romance novels
4. Philosophical essays

78. Identify the poem from which the given line has been taken.

"O latest born and loveliest vision far"
1. Ode to Psyche
2. Ode to Autumn
3. Ode to a Nightingale
4. Ode on a Grecian Urn

79. In 'All My Sons', Arthur Miller describes the relationship between a father and his son and the disappointing reality ______.
1. that none of them visited the countryside
2. that both were satisfied with their future
3. that neither of them could meet each other's expectations
4. that their teachers were happy with them

80. In the poem 'Ode to the West Wind', why does Shelley describe the 'sea-blooms and the oozy woods' as 'sapless'?
1. To emphasise their vulnerability to decay
2. To criticise nature's inability to sustain life
3. To show the barrenness caused by the wind
4. To depict their lifelessness in winter

81. Which of the following poems was written by Kamala Das?
1. Enterprise
2. A River
3. Night of the Scorpion
4. My Grandmother's House

73. 4	**74.** 2	**75.** 2	**76.** 4	**77.** 3	**78.** 1	**79.** 3	**80.** 4	**81.** 4

82. What is the structural characteristic of Pablo Neruda's poem 'Tonight I Can Write'?

1. It consists of a single stanza with consistent line length.
2. The poem is written in free verse with varying line lengths and irregular stanza breaks.
3. It follows a traditional sonnet structure with 14 lines and a specific rhyme scheme.
4. The poem is divided into four quatrains, each with an AABB rhyme scheme.

83. Which Biblical allusion is reflected in Thomas Becket's return to Canterbury in 'Murder in the Cathedral'?

1. Noah preparing for the great flood
2. David defeating Goliath
3. Moses leading the Israelites out of Egypt
4. Jesus's entry into Jerusalem before his crucifixion

84. Identity the work of Shakespeare for which the following sentence is the explanation.

Locally, we are transported into the Highland of Scotland, where everything appears tinged with superstition, full of tangible intercommunication with the supernatural world and prognostics of the moral life by signs in the animate and inanimate kingdom.

1. Coriolanus 2. Cymbeline
3. Macbeth 4. Twelfth Night

85. In Shelley's 'Ode to West Wind', what is symbolised by 'yellow, and black, and pale, and hectic red'?

1. Changing seasons
2. Autumn leaves
3. Disease and decay
4. Fire and destruction

86. How did Philomela reveal the tragedy of rape that was committed on her?

1. She wove the entire incident on a tapestry and sent it to her sister.
2. She revealed to the court when she was charged with killing the son of the king that she murdered his son to take her revenge on Tereus.
3. She ran to the palace screaming how she was raped by Tereus.
4. She transformed into a nightingale and sang sad songs about her rape.

87. With regards to Samuel Beckett's Waiting for Godot, which of the following is NOT a characteristic of Absurd Theatre?

1. Little dramatic action
2. Traditional structure and narrative
3. Absence of plot
4. Dislocated language

88. In RK Narayan's novel 'A Tiger for Malgudi', what is the name of the tiger who becomes the central character of the story?

1. Moti 2. Sher Khan
3. Raja 4. Bhagya

89. In 'Adonais', Shelley writes, 'Life, like a dome of many-colored glass, / Stains the white radiance of Eternity'. What does this metaphor suggest?

1. Life is a beautiful but temporary experience.
2. Life distorts the purity of eternal truths.
3. Life is fragile and easily broken.
4. Life is an illusion created by human perception.

90. What theme is explored in the short story 'The Yellow Wallpaper' by Charlotte Perkins Gilman?

1. The invention of new technology
2. The effects of isolation and mental illness
3. The impact of migration on women
4. The impact of the supernatural on everyday life

82. 2	**83.** 4	**84.** 3	**85.** 2	**86.** 1	**87.** 2	**88.** 3	**89.** 2	**90.** 2

91. In aesthetic education, the principle of 'multiple perspectives' primarily encourages:
1. openness to diverse interpretations and ways of understanding experiences
2. the view that there is a single correct interpretation of a work
3. reproduction of established artistic conventions without critique
4. isolation of aesthetic inquiry from cultural context

92. Universal Design for Learning (UDL) is most accurately described as:
1. a method for identifying giftedness
2. a curriculum for remedial teaching only
3. a diagnostic tool for intellectual disabilities
4. a framework to design flexible learning environments

93. The concept of proximal development, highlighting the gap between what a child can do independently and what they can do with assistance, was introduced by:
1. John Bowlby
2. Lev Vygotsky
3. Erik Erikson
4. Jean Piaget

94. Cooperative learning method help science learners in all of the following ways, EXCEPT:
1. they provide opportunities for sharing ideas, exploration, refining, and questioning their own and others' ideas
2. they help learners construct understanding of scientific phenomena through examining, sharing, and learning from peers
3. they make learners take responsibility for their learning but depend solely on the teacher for all knowledge
4. they encourage active involvement and continuous engagement of all learners in the learning process

95. Which of the following best exemplifies interdisciplinary learning in a classroom?
1. Combining concepts from history and geography to explore the idea of colonialism
2. Teaching math and science separately, following different curricula
3. Teaching subjects without any reference to real-world issues
4. Memorising separate definitions for physics, chemistry, and biology

96. In the context of language across the curriculum, listening skills are essential because they:
1. are tested in oral interviews only
2. are unrelated to academic development
3. help learners comprehend content, instructions, and peer ideas
4. do not support learning in non-language subjects

97. Which principle ensures that the curriculum content progresses from simple to complex?
1. Principle of sequence
2. Principle of novelty
3. Principle of balance
4. Principle of utility

98. What is the primary distinction between assessment and evaluation?
1. Evaluation only applies to student work, not programmes.
2. Assessment gathers evidence of learning; evaluation interprets that evidence to make judgments.
3. Assessment focuses on assigning grades; evaluation only measures attitudes.
4. Assessment is a broader concept, while evaluation is always informal.

91. 1	**92.** 4	**93.** 2	**94.** 3	**95.** 1	**96.** 3	**97.** 1	**98.** 2

99. What is the primary purpose of subject content analysis in pedagogy?
1. To paint the classroom walls
2. To fix the class timetable
3. To align content with objectives
4. To count the number of books

100. The concept of gender as distinct from sex refers to:
1. the genetic makeup of an individual
2. socially constructed roles and behaviours of men and women.
3. only the physical and physiological differences
4. the biological characteristics of being male or female

EXPLANATORY ANSWERS

1. Shelley's Prometheus Unbound (1820) is regarded as his greatest political and philosophical work. It reinterprets the Greek myth of Prometheus as a symbol of human aspiration, liberty, and moral progress. The lyrical drama expresses Shelley's vision of human perfectibility and resistance to tyranny, making it both a political allegory and a philosophical treatise on idealism and the human spirit.

2.
- Oliver Goldsmith – The Vicar of Wakefield (IV): A sentimental novel about family virtues and rural simplicity.
- Frances Burney – Evelina (I): A novel of manners and social satire focusing on a young woman's entry into society.
- Horace Walpole – The Castle of Otranto (II): The first Gothic novel, blending romance, terror, and supernatural elements.
- Ann Radcliffe – The Mysteries of Udolpho (III): A Gothic romance known for its sublime landscapes and psychological suspense.

3. This statement is not true. Stream of Consciousness fiction (seen in works by Virginia Woolf and James Joyce) focuses on the flow of inner thoughts and perceptions rather than on external events or linear character development. The emphasis is on depicting the mind's associative processes, not the chronological evolution of character.

4. In Sons and Lovers by D.H. Lawrence, this passage reflects Paul Morel's emotional conflict after his mother's death. Though grief-stricken and alienated, he decides to move toward life and light—the "city's gold phosphorescence"—signifying resilience and a determination to live despite suffering.

5. The Rime of the Ancient Mariner by Samuel Taylor Coleridge is a lyrical ballad, combining the storytelling tradition of the ballad form with the lyrical, emotional quality of Romantic poetry. It was first published in Lyrical Ballads (1798), co-authored with Wordsworth, and exemplifies themes of sin, redemption, and harmony between man and nature.

6. In Part I of Jonathan Swift's Gulliver's Travels (1726), Lilliput symbolizes England. The petty political rivalries, bureaucratic absurdities, and moral hypocrisy of the Lilliputians mirror English society and its government during Swift's time. Through satire, Swift exposes the trivial disputes (like the Big-Endians vs. Little-Endians) as metaphors for religious and political conflicts in contemporary England.

7. Mary Shelley's Frankenstein (1818) is both a Gothic and an early science fiction novel. It blends the eerie, supernatural atmosphere

99. 3	**100.** 2

of Gothic literature with speculative scientific experimentation. Victor Frankenstein's attempt to create life reflects early 19th-century fascination with galvanism and human ambition, while its tone and imagery evoke horror and moral anxiety characteristic of the Gothic tradition.

8. The stream of consciousness technique, used by writers like Virginia Woolf and James Joyce, indeed focuses on the subjective field—the inner dilemmas, perceptions, and emotional responses of individuals (A true). These impressions stem from a character's personal and unverifiable perspective, shaped by their imagination and consciousness (B true). Hence, B correctly explains A.

9. The narrative technique described—where sequence is discarded and characters' thoughts flow freely—belongs to the stream of consciousness genre. This style seeks to capture the continuous, often chaotic movement of the mind, without logical structure or external validation. It mirrors the inner workings of human thought as seen in works like Joyce's Ulysses and Woolf's Mrs Dalloway.

10. In Shelley's Ode to the West Wind (1819), the West Wind as a destroyer signifies the end of the old year, sweeping away the decaying leaves and remnants of the past. This destruction is cyclical and necessary, preparing the way for rebirth and renewal. Thus, the wind's dual role as "Destroyer and Preserver" symbolizes nature's eternal process of death and regeneration.

11. In Sons and Lovers, D.H. Lawrence presents women like Gertrude Morel and Miriam as emotionally strong yet often subjugated by patriarchal norms. The assertion correctly points out that while Lawrence portrays women's struggles in love, marriage, and social expectations, their inner complexity is underexplored; they function as extensions of the male protagonist's development. The example fits this idea perfectly—the women are influenced by Paul Morel and act contrary to their self-interest, illustrating Lawrence's limited psychological depth in his female characterization.

12. John Webster's The White Devil (1612) is a Jacobean tragedy that delves into corruption, lust, power, and gender politics in a morally decaying aristocracy. Set in Italy, it portrays the downfall of Vittoria Corombona, whose ambition and sensuality challenge patriarchal authority. The play's dark tone, complex characters, and cynical worldview make it a classic of revenge and moral decay.

13. "O Wind, if Winter comes, can Spring be far behind?" This concluding line from Shelley's Ode to the West Wind (1819) symbolizes hope and renewal. After depicting the destructive force of the wind, Shelley ends with this prophetic optimism—implying that even after periods of death or despair, rebirth and transformation inevitably follow, just as spring follows winter.

14. The Canterbury Tales (late 14th century) by Geoffrey Chaucer is a collection of stories told by pilgrims traveling to Canterbury. It presents a vivid social panorama of medieval England, blending satire, humor, and moral reflection. Chaucer's use of vernacular English and realistic characterization established him as the "Father of English Poetry."

15. Edmund Spenser (1552–1599), author of The Faerie Queene, lived during Queen Elizabeth I's reign, a period marked by national pride and Protestant identity. One of the defining historical events of his lifetime was the defeat of the Spanish Armada in 1588, which inspired patriotic and allegorical themes in his poetry celebrating Elizabethan virtue and English supremacy.

16. In Gulliver's Travels (Part II), Gulliver visits Brobdingnag, a land inhabited by giants. Here, the size contrast between Gulliver and the inhabitants serves as satire on human pride and moral corruption. The Brobdingnagians' society, simple yet morally superior, exposes the pettiness of European politics and culture that Swift critiques through Gulliver's experiences.

17. In Shelley's Ode to the West Wind, the phrase "Drive my dead thoughts over the universe / Like withered leaves to quicken a new birth" symbolizes the poet's dead thoughts—his feelings of despair, hopelessness, and creative stagnation. Shelley appeals to the West Wind to scatter these decayed ideas so that new, revitalized thoughts may arise, suggesting a desire for intellectual and spiritual rejuvenation.

18. The White Devil (1612) by John Webster is a tragedy exploring themes of moral decay, revenge, and corruption within aristocratic society. The play portrays deceit, hypocrisy, and violence, with strong female characters like Vittoria Corombona challenging patriarchal norms, while the surrounding corruption reflects a cynical view of human nature.

19. D.H. Lawrence's Sons and Lovers (1913) is not a fantasy novel. It is a realist, regional, and autobiographical novel that reflects Lawrence's own upbringing in a Nottinghamshire mining town. The work realistically portrays working-class life, family relationships, and psychological conflicts, especially the deep emotional attachment between Paul Morel and his mother.

20. A defining feature of Wordsworth's poetry is his love for nature. He viewed nature as a living spiritual force that nurtures and elevates the human soul. In works like Tintern Abbey and The Prelude, he presents nature as a moral teacher and source of emotional and intellectual inspiration, reflecting his deep Romantic faith in its power to heal and transform the human spirit.

21. This final line from Shelley's Ode to the West Wind (1819) beautifully captures his longing for renewal and transformation. After invoking the wind as both "Destroyer and Preserver," Shelley ends with hope that decay and despair will inevitably be followed by rebirth and rejuvenation, just as spring follows winter. It reflects his deep faith in the cyclical power of nature and the human spirit's capacity for renewal.

22. In Greek mythology, Semele was the mortal mother of Bacchus (Dionysus), the god of wine and ecstasy. She was loved by Zeus, who appeared to her in his divine form at her own request—an act that caused her death. However, Zeus saved the unborn Dionysus by sewing him into his thigh until birth, symbolizing the god's dual mortal and divine nature.

23. Common Meter, often associated with hymns and ballads, is also known as the ballad stanza or hymn meter. It consists of four-line stanzas (quatrains) written in an iambic rhythm, where lines alternate between iambic tetrameter (eight syllables) and iambic trimeter (six syllables), creating the distinctive 8686 syllabic pattern. This alternating rhythm gives the verse a musical and lyrical flow, making it suitable for reflective and spiritual poetry. Emily Dickinson frequently used this meter in her poems, often introducing her own subtle variations and slant rhymes, lending her works a unique cadence and emotional resonance.

Ourselves – (8)

And Immortality. – (6)

Thus, the Common Meter alternates between iambic tetrameter and iambic trimeter, producing the balanced and melodic rhythm that defines Dickinson's verse.

24. The line "A thing of beauty is a joy for ever" opens John Keats's Endymion (1818), a long narrative poem based on Greek mythology. It expresses the Romantic belief in the eternal power of beauty to uplift the human soul, symbolizing Keats's aesthetic idealism and his faith that beauty offers transcendence beyond temporal suffering.

25. The Sun Rising by John Donne is a Metaphysical poem that personifies the sun as an intruder disturbing the lovers' private world. Through witty conceits and bold imagery, Donne elevates love above cosmic order, declaring that their bed is the center of the universe, showcasing his distinctive blend of intellect, passion, and paradox.

26. In the myth of Philomela from Ovid's Metamorphoses, after being raped and silenced by Tereus, Philomela reveals his crime to her sister Procne by weaving it into a tapestry. Together, they exact revenge by killing Tereus's son Itys and serving his flesh to Tereus at a banquet. When he discovers the truth, the gods transform them all into birds–Philomela into a nightingale, Procne into a swallow, and Tereus into a hoopoe.

27. Ralph Waldo Emerson's poem "Hamatreya" reflects the transcendentalist theme that while humans pride themselves on possessing land and property, ultimately the earth possesses them. The poem mocks human arrogance and asserts that nature endures while human achievements fade. The closing thought, "Earth laughs in flowers," epitomizes the idea that nature remains eternal and self-renewing beyond human mortality.

28. In T.S. Eliot's "Murder in the Cathedral" (1935), martyrdom is portrayed as a spiritual vocation, not an act of political defiance or personal ambition. The protagonist, Archbishop Thomas Becket, accepts death as part of divine will, symbolizing surrender to God's higher purpose. Eliot presents martyrdom as transcendence beyond ego and worldly concerns, aligning with Christian ideals of faith and sacrifice.

29. This famous opening line from John Keats's Endymion (1818) captures the Romantic belief in the enduring power of beauty. Keats asserts that beauty offers perpetual delight and spiritual upliftment, serving as an eternal source of inspiration amid the impermanence of human life.

30. The lines "A spring of love gushed from my heart, / And I blessed them unaware" from Coleridge's The Rime of the Ancient Mariner use metaphor. The "spring of love" symbolizes the sudden awakening of compassion and spiritual renewal within the Mariner's heart, marking his moral transformation as he unconsciously blesses the sea creatures he once despised.

31.
- Daniel Defoe – Robinson Crusoe (*c*): Considered one of the first English novels, it tells of a man's survival on a deserted island, symbolizing self-reliance and colonial expansion.
- Jonathan Swift – Gulliver's Travels (*a*): A satirical narrative that critiques human nature and political institutions through Gulliver's voyages.
- William Congreve – The Way of the World (*d*): A Restoration comedy exploring wit, love, and social manners.
- Thomas Gray – Elegy Written in a Country Churchyard (*b*): A reflective poem on mortality and the dignity of common life.

32. Percy Bysshe Shelley's Adonais (1821) is an elegy written in memory of John Keats, lamenting his death and celebrating his poetic spirit's immortality. The poem blends classical pastoral form with Romantic ideals of artistic transcendence.

33.
- Louisa May Alcott – Little Women (D): A domestic novel about four sisters' moral and emotional growth.
- Kate Chopin – The Awakening (E): Explores female independence and societal constraints in the 19th century.
- Margaret Fuller – Woman in the Nineteenth Century (B): A foundational feminist text advocating gender equality.
- Jack London – The Call of the Wild (C): Depicts the primal instincts of a domesticated dog in the wild.
- Mark Twain – Adventures of Huckleberry Finn (A): A picaresque novel critiquing race and society in antebellum America.

34. The Tamil writer Pudhumaipithan, a pioneer of modern Tamil short fiction, wrote Redemption. His works are known for their sharp social realism, humanism, and critique of hypocrisy, depicting ordinary lives with psychological depth.

35. In T.S. Eliot's "Murder in the Cathedral" (1935), the central conflict lies within Thomas Becket, who wrestles between ego-driven ambition and submission to divine will. The play portrays martyrdom as a test of faith, where Becket's acceptance of death symbolizes triumph of spiritual purpose over worldly desires.

36. Nadine Gordimer's July's People (1981) reflects her direct experience of life under apartheid in South Africa. Having lived through systemic racial segregation and witnessed its impact on both white and black communities, she portrays the social disintegration, shifting power dynamics, and moral ambiguities of post-apartheid transition with authenticity. Her insider's understanding lends psychological depth and realism to her characters' interactions, making her narrative a profound commentary on privilege, guilt, and change.

37. In Bertolt Brecht's play The Good Woman of Setzuan (1943), Shen Te is the central character—a kind-hearted prostitute who struggles to live morally in a corrupt society. To survive, she assumes a male alter ego, Shui Ta, revealing Brecht's exploration of capitalism, morality, and human duality. Shen Te embodies the conflict between goodness and survival in an unjust world, aligning with Brecht's concept of epic theatre and social critique.

38. In Arthur Miller's All My Sons (1947), George Deever is the son of Steve Deever, Joe Keller's former partner who was imprisoned for selling defective airplane parts. George, now a lawyer and World War II veteran, returns to confront the Kellers after realizing his father's innocence. His character symbolizes the moral awakening and disillusionment central to Miller's critique of ethical compromise in pursuit of success.

39. Mary Shelley's Frankenstein (1818) is structured as an epistolary novel, presented through a series of letters written by Captain Robert Walton to his sister. Within this frame narrative, Victor Frankenstein recounts his tragic story, and the creature narrates his own experiences. This layered storytelling enhances realism, emotional intimacy, and multiple perspectives, making it a hallmark of early Gothic and proto-science fiction writing.

40. Nissim Ezekiel's Minority Poem poignantly expresses his feelings of alienation and cultural displacement as an Indian Jewish poet writing in English. Through introspective and ironic tones, he reflects on his struggle for identity and belonging in postcolonial India. The poem captures his yearning for acceptance while acknowledging his perpetual sense of "otherness," a recurring theme in his deeply personal and urban-centered poetry.

41. • Lewis Carroll – Alice's Adventures in Wonderland (B): A children's fantasy novel blending logic, nonsense, and satire, exploring the boundaries of imagination.

• Agatha Christie – Murder on the Orient Express (D): A classic detective novel featuring Hercule Poirot, known for its intricate plot and moral questioning of justice.

• Ruskin Bond – The Night Train at Deoli (A): A short story reflecting simplicity and emotional subtlety in everyday Indian life.

• Vishal Bhardwaj – Maqbool (C): A cinematic adaptation of Shakespeare's Macbeth, set in the Mumbai underworld, blending literature and modern film realism.

42. A short story's power lies in its economy of expression and focus on one significant moment, character, or emotion. It avoids lengthy exposition or subplots, creating impact through brevity, precision, and unity of effect—qualities perfected by writers like Edgar Allan Poe, Anton Chekhov, and O. Henry.

43. Deconstruction, introduced by Jacques Derrida, aims not to uncover a single truth but to expose how texts contain contradictions and multiple meanings. It questions hierarchies such as reason/emotion, speech/writing, or male/female, revealing that meaning is unstable and contingent on language itself.

44. Samuel Beckett's Waiting for Godot (1953) reflects the existential condition of modern humanity—endless waiting, meaninglessness, and spiritual emptiness. Through Vladimir and Estragon's repetitive dialogues and inaction, Beckett portrays alienation and the futility of seeking purpose in an absurd world, central to Theatre of the Absurd.

45. In Alice Munro's Boys and Girls, the young female narrator confronts societal gender expectations that restrict her individuality. Set in a rural Canadian context, the story explores the moment when a girl realizes that society's roles are rigidly defined by gender, marking the loss of innocence and the awakening of social awareness.

46. In the myth of Pyramus and Thisbe, found in Ovid's Metamorphoses, the lovers are separated by a wall but plan a secret meeting. When Pyramus believes Thisbe has been killed by a lion, he falls on his sword in grief. On discovering his body, Thisbe takes her own life. Their deaths symbolize the tragic consequences of love constrained by societal and familial barriers, and their blood is said to have stained the mulberry fruit red.

47. In Homer's The Iliad, Hector embodies honour and heroism through his acceptance of fate. Despite knowing that confronting Achilles will lead to his death, Hector chooses to defend Troy, his family, and his people. His courage and sense of duty define Homeric honour (kleos), emphasizing glory through valour and self-sacrifice rather than survival.

48. • R.K. Narayan – The Guide (D): A novel about Raju's transformation from tourist guide to spiritual guide, exploring identity and redemption.

• Mulk Raj Anand – Coolie (C): Depicts the exploitation and suffering of the poor under colonial India through the story of Munoo.

• Shashi Deshpande – The Dark Holds No Terrors (B): Focuses on the emotional and gendered struggles of a woman trapped in a patriarchal marriage.

- Dina Mehta - And Some Take a Lover (A): A play exploring love, loneliness, and female desire in modern Indian society.

49. Kate Millett, in Sexual Politics (1970), criticizes D.H. Lawrence's Sons and Lovers for being a heroic male romance rather than a realist novel. She argues that Lawrence centers male psychological growth and sexual awakening while relegating women to passive or nurturing roles. According to Rick Rylance, Millett sees the novel as an expression of male ego and emotional dominance rather than a balanced social narrative.

50. The Theatre of the Absurd, exemplified by Samuel Beckett's Waiting for Godot, seeks to confront audiences with confusion and existential uncertainty. Through circular dialogue, inaction, and purposeless waiting, Beckett reflects the absurdity of human existence in a meaningless world. The intent is not to provide solutions but to make audiences feel the disorientation and emptiness of modern life.

51. In Mulk Raj Anand's The Lost Child, the child's excitement at the fair—his fascination with toys, sweets, and colors—reflects his innocent wonder. However, when he gets separated from his parents, his priorities shift; he no longer desires material things and cries only for his mother and father. This change highlights the pure dependence and emotional vulnerability of childhood amid the confusion and chaos of the world.

52. This powerful scene in Homer's The Iliad (Book 24) epitomizes the contrast between honour and the horror of war. King Priam, despite his grief, humbles himself before Achilles—his son's killer—to beg for Hector's body. The moment reveals the futility of vengeance and the shared humanity that transcends battlefield glory, exposing the emotional devastation that underlies the heroic ideal.

53. In D.H. Lawrence's Sons and Lovers, Mrs. Morel's ambition for her children drives them toward education and social advancement. Her determination to lift the family above their mining-class background represents aspiration for upward mobility. The novel thus explores the conflict between working-class roots and middle-class ambitions, showing how education and refinement become paths of both progress and alienation.

54. Popular literature refers to works that appeal to a broad audience through accessible language, relatable themes, and engaging storytelling. Unlike highbrow or academic literature, it aims to entertain while sometimes reflecting social issues or emotions familiar to everyday readers. Examples include detective fiction, romance, fantasy, and thrillers.

55. In this humorous poem, Nissim Ezekiel uses Indian English as both theme and medium, playfully mimicking the speech patterns of Indians speaking English. Through this linguistic satire, he captures the quirks, warmth, and cultural hybridity of Indian communication, turning local idiom into poetic expression that celebrates identity while gently exposing linguistic oddities.

56. "They reckon ill who leave me out; When me they fly, I am the wings; I am the doubter and the doubt, I am the hymn the Brahmin sings." These lines from Ralph Waldo Emerson's "Brahma" express the Hindu concept of the unity of all existence—the divine as both immanent and transcendent. Emerson, inspired by Vedantic philosophy, speaks in the voice of Brahma, the universal spirit, emphasizing that opposites like doubt and belief are part of the same divine reality.

57. In Katherine Mansfield's short story "The Legacy," the central theme revolves around self-discovery and marital alienation. The wife's secret writings, revealed after her death, force her husband to realize how little he understood her inner world. The story explores emotional distance, the limits of understanding between partners, and the quiet assertion of individuality within marriage.

58. In Mulk Raj Anand's The Lost Child, the parents' reaction to their son's disappearance reflects tender affection and emotional despair. Despite their modest socio-economic status, their grief transcends material concerns. The story highlights how love and helplessness coexist in the lives of the poor—parents who may not fulfill every desire but whose emotional bond with their child is profound and genuine.

59. • S.T. Coleridge – Christabel (III): A Gothic narrative poem blending mystery, the supernatural, and moral ambiguity.
 • P.B. Shelley – Adonais (I): An elegy mourning John Keats and celebrating artistic immortality.
 • John Keats – Ode to Autumn (IV): A meditation on transience and fulfillment in nature's cycle.
 • Lord Byron – She Walks in Beauty (II): A lyrical celebration of inner and outer feminine beauty.

60. In Nissim Ezekiel's The Sleepwalkers, the poet portrays urban, modern Indians—educated, rational, and seemingly progressive—who nonetheless live mechanically, devoid of emotional depth or moral direction. The poem critiques the spiritual emptiness beneath modern sophistication, reflecting Ezekiel's recurring theme of disconnection in postcolonial Indian society.

61. The Romantic Age (late 18th–early 19th century) rejected the rigid forms and rationalism of the Neoclassical period, which favored the heroic couplet (a hallmark of poets like Pope and Dryden). Romanticism emphasized subjectivity, emotion, nature, melancholy, imagination, and the supernatural. Hence, the use of the heroic couplet is not a characteristic feature of Romantic literature.

62. Nadine Gordimer was a South African writer and Nobel laureate (1991) whose works—like July's People and Burger's Daughter—explore the moral and social complexities of life under apartheid. Her nationality deeply influenced her themes of racial injustice, political consciousness, and ethical responsibility.

63. In Samuel Beckett's "Waiting for Godot" (1953), Vladimir and Estragon are the two protagonists. They wait endlessly for a mysterious figure named Godot who never arrives. Their repetitive dialogue and aimless actions embody the existential futility and absurdity of human life, central to Beckett's Theatre of the Absurd.

64. The stream of consciousness technique concerns the inner flow of thoughts, feelings, and memories within a character's mind. It draws on associations, psychological impressions, and emotional continuity, not on external or spatial social contexts. Hence, the spatial dimension of social activity is not an active element in forming stream-of-consciousness narration.

65. Alfred Kuttner was the first critic to apply Freudian psychoanalytic theory to Sons and Lovers, interpreting Paul Morel's relationship with his mother through the lens of the Oedipus complex. D. H. Lawrence, however, later criticized such reductionist readings, arguing that Kuttner oversimplified the novel's emotional and psychological depth by confining it to Freudian categories.

66. • Samuel Richardson – Clarissa (II): A psychological epistolary novel exploring virtue, morality, and female endurance.
   • Tobias Smollett – The Adventures of Roderick Random (IV): A picaresque novel depicting the hardships and adventures of an ambitious young man.
   • Laurence Sterne – The Life and Opinions of Tristram Shandy, Gentleman (I): A comic, digressive narrative breaking traditional storytelling conventions.
   • Henry Fielding – Shamela (III): A satirical parody of Richardson's Pamela, exposing moral pretensions and hypocrisy.

67. In Shelley's Mont Blanc (1817), the poet confronts the sublime power of nature, represented by the mountain, as something vast and incomprehensible. He reflects that the human mind, though capable of perception and imagination, remains humbled by nature's eternal grandeur and indifference. The poem thus presents nature as both awe-inspiring and beyond human control or understanding.

68. • Samuel Johnson – The Vanity of Human Wishes (*d*): A moral satire on human ambition and futility.
   • Alexander Pope – The Rape of the Lock (*b*): A mock-epic highlighting the trivialities of aristocratic life.
   • John Gay – The Beggar's Opera (*a*): A satirical ballad opera critiquing corruption in politics and society.
   • Richard Brinsley Sheridan – The School for Scandal (*c*): A Restoration-style comedy exposing gossip and hypocrisy in high society.

69. Lines Composed a Few Miles Above Tintern Abbey by William Wordsworth was written in 1798 during his revisit to the River Wye after five years. The poem reflects his spiritual growth and the transition from youthful delight in nature's beauty to mature philosophical contemplation of its moral and restorative power.

70. Robert Southey's poem After Blenheim (1798) is a powerful anti-war ballad. Through the innocent questioning of children and the evasive answers of Old Kaspar, the poem exposes the futility and devastation of war, challenging the glorification of military victories like the Battle of Blenheim.

71. The central theme of Wordsworth's "Tintern Abbey" is transition or change, particularly the evolution of the poet's relationship with nature over time. Wordsworth contrasts his youthful, passionate response to nature with his mature, reflective appreciation. The poem explores how the passage of time transforms human perception, turning nature from a source of sensory pleasure into a moral and spiritual guide that sustains the mind through life's changes.

72. In Nadine Gordimer's July's People, gender roles are re-examined against the backdrop of apartheid's collapse and shifting power structures. Gordimer portrays women—particularly Maureen Smales—as navigating between vulnerability and agency. The novel reveals how political and social revolutions also unsettle domestic and gender hierarchies, questioning both racial and patriarchal dominance within the same context.

73. Thomas Gray's Elegy Written in a Country Churchyard (1751) is a contemplative poem mourning the uncelebrated lives of the poor villagers buried in a rural churchyard. It reflects on mortality, the equality of death, and the quiet dignity of those denied fame or privilege. Through its universal tone, the elegy honors the forgotten and emphasizes the democratic truth that death spares none—neither the great nor the humble.

74. Nissim Ezekiel is known for writing two contrasting kinds of poetry—some pieces are terse, meticulously crafted, and introspective, while others are lucid, conversational, and free-flowing. His work blends irony,

realism, and philosophical questioning, often addressing themes of alienation, identity, and urban Indian life. This stylistic duality marks his distinct contribution to modern Indian English poetry.

75.
- R.K. Narayan – A Tiger for Malgudi (C): A novel blending fable and philosophy, narrated by a tiger reflecting on human greed and spiritual growth.
- Mulk Raj Anand – Untouchable (A): A stark portrayal of caste oppression and social injustice in pre-independence India.
- Shashi Deshpande – That Long Silence (B): Explores the inner life of a woman confronting patriarchal constraints and self-realization.
- Dina Mehta – Brides Are Not for Burning (D): A social drama exposing the evils of dowry and the exploitation of women in Indian society.

76. In this passage from Sons and Lovers, D.H. Lawrence reveals Paul Morel's emotional conflict and psychological sensitivity. His imagination, passion, and deep attachment to his mother cause an inner struggle between affection and independence. The description of his emotions "on the surface" and his instinctive grasp of truth reflect his turbulent inner world, torn between maternal love, personal desire, and moral awareness.

77. Romance novels fall under popular literature, as they are widely read and appreciated by the general public for their emotional appeal and accessibility. Unlike academic or highbrow works, popular literature emphasizes entertainment, relatability, and human emotions such as love, loss, and desire, making it commercially and culturally significant.

78. The line "O latest born and loveliest vision far" appears in John Keats's "Ode to Psyche" (1819). The poem celebrates Psyche, the last-born goddess of love and the soul, whom Keats vows to worship with his imagination rather than traditional ritual. It reflects Romantic ideals of creativity, beauty, and the sanctity of the human mind's imaginative power.

79. In Arthur Miller's All My Sons, the strained relationship between Joe Keller and his son Chris embodies disappointment and moral conflict. Joe expects admiration and loyalty, while Chris seeks integrity and truth. Their inability to fulfill each other's moral and emotional expectations exposes the tragic clash between familial love and ethical responsibility.

80. In Shelley's Ode to the West Wind, the phrase "sea-blooms and the oozy woods... sapless" conveys the deathlike stillness of nature during winter. The poet uses this imagery to illustrate the dormancy and lifelessness that precede renewal. By invoking the West Wind, Shelley seeks revitalization, symbolizing the cyclical process of death and rebirth in both nature and human creativity.

81. The poem "My Grandmother's House" by Kamala Das expresses her nostalgia, loneliness, and longing for lost love and warmth. Through the image of her grandmother's house, she recalls a place of unconditional affection now replaced by emptiness. The poem symbolizes the poet's emotional deprivation and search for identity and belonging, written in her confessional, intensely personal style.

82. Pablo Neruda's "Tonight I Can Write (The Saddest Lines)" is composed in free verse, reflecting the spontaneous flow of memory and emotion. The irregular line lengths and stanza breaks mirror the fragmented rhythm of grief and recollection. The structure complements the poem's theme of lost love, where longing, remembrance, and melancholy intermingle without formal restraint.

83. In T.S. Eliot's "Murder in the Cathedral," Thomas Becket's return to Canterbury parallels Christ's entry into Jerusalem before his Passion. Becket's calm acceptance of martyrdom mirrors Jesus's awareness of his impending death, emphasizing the themes of sacrifice, faith, and divine will. The Biblical allusion elevates Becket's death to a spiritual act of redemption rather than mere political resistance.

84. This description refers to Shakespeare's "Macbeth," set in the Scottish Highlands, where superstition, omens, and supernatural forces dominate. The witches' prophecies, visions, and ghostly apparitions shape the moral and psychological landscape, blending the real and the unreal. The play explores how the supernatural manipulates human ambition and moral corruption.

85. In Shelley's Ode to the West Wind, the phrase "yellow, and black, and pale, and hectic red" refers to autumn leaves. These colors symbolize the decaying yet beautiful stage of nature's cycle, where life transitions toward death. The imagery of the dying leaves scattered by the wind reflects Shelley's meditation on transience, renewal, and the creative force that follows destruction.

86. In Ovid's Metamorphoses, after being raped and silenced by Tereus (who cut off her tongue), Philomela ingeniously reveals the truth by weaving her story into a tapestry and sending it to her sister Procne. This act of nonverbal communication symbolizes women's resilience and creativity in expressing truth even under oppression, leading to their eventual revenge.

87. Samuel Beckett's Waiting for Godot exemplifies the Theatre of the Absurd, which rejects traditional plot, structure, and logical dialogue. It features circular, repetitive conversation, minimal action, and existential themes. Hence, a traditional structure and narrative is not a characteristic of Absurd Theatre, which instead emphasizes purposelessness and human despair.

88. In R.K. Narayan's "A Tiger for Malgudi", the central character is a tiger named Raja, who narrates his own story. Through his life—from captivity and exploitation to spiritual awakening under a saint's guidance—Raja symbolizes the journey from instinct and ignorance to enlightenment, reflecting Narayan's themes of self-realization and harmony between nature and spirit.

89. In Shelley's Adonais, the metaphor "Life, like a dome of many-coloured glass, stains the white radiance of eternity" suggests that earthly life and human experiences distort the pure, undivided truth of eternity. While life's diversity is beautiful, it fragments the perfect unity of the eternal. Death, therefore, releases the soul from illusion back into divine purity.

90. Charlotte Perkins Gilman's The Yellow Wallpaper (1892) explores female psychological suffering caused by isolation and patriarchal medical oppression. Confined to a room under the "rest cure," the narrator descends into madness, projecting her entrapment onto the wallpaper's patterns. The story critiques societal norms that silence women's intellect and autonomy, making it a landmark in feminist psychological fiction.

91. In aesthetic education, the principle of multiple perspectives promotes the idea that there is no single fixed meaning to an artwork or experience. Learners are encouraged to appreciate different viewpoints, cultural influences, and emotional responses. This principle develops critical thinking, empathy, and interpretive flexibility, allowing students to understand that beauty and meaning are contextually constructed rather than absolute.

92. Universal Design for Learning (UDL) is an educational framework that guides teachers to design flexible, inclusive learning environments. It ensures that curriculum goals, teaching methods, materials, and assessments are accessible to all learners, regardless of ability or background. UDL emphasizes multiple means of engagement, representation, and expression, thereby removing barriers and supporting diverse learning needs.

93. The concept of the Zone of Proximal Development (ZPD) was introduced by Lev Vygotsky, a Russian psychologist. It defines the gap between what a child can do independently and what they can achieve with guidance or collaboration. This idea underscores the importance of social interaction and scaffolding in learning, where teachers or peers provide support until learners gain autonomy.

94. In cooperative learning, students actively engage with peers to construct understanding through discussion, collaboration, and problem-solving. Dependence "solely on the teacher" contradicts the philosophy of cooperative learning, which values shared responsibility and peer interaction. Therefore, option 3 does not align with the principles of cooperative learning in science education.

95. Interdisciplinary learning integrates knowledge, methods, and perspectives from multiple disciplines to explore a common theme or problem. Studying colonialism by combining history (political events, empire building) and geography (spatial expansion, trade routes, and resource distribution) allows students to see interconnections across fields, promoting holistic understanding and critical thinking.

96. In the Language Across the Curriculum (LAC) approach, listening is a vital receptive skill that supports comprehension and learning in all subjects. Effective listening enables students to understand classroom instructions, grasp subject content, and engage meaningfully in discussions. It fosters active participation, critical thinking, and collaboration, making it foundational to both language and academic development.

97. The principle of sequence ensures that curriculum content progresses logically from simple to complex, concrete to abstract, and known to unknown. This principle helps learners build on prior knowledge systematically, facilitating gradual cognitive development and deeper understanding. It ensures that each new concept connects meaningfully with earlier learning.

98. Assessment refers to the process of collecting data or evidence about students' learning through tests, observations, or assignments. Evaluation, on the other hand, involves analyzing and interpreting that evidence to make value judgments or decisions about achievement, effectiveness, or progress. Thus, assessment is diagnostic and descriptive, while evaluation is judgmental and conclusive.

99. In pedagogy, subject content analysis ensures that the teaching material aligns with learning objectives and outcomes. It helps teachers break down topics, identify key concepts and skills, and plan instructional strategies that match the desired educational goals. This analysis ensures coherence between what is taught and what students are expected to learn.

100. While sex refers to biological and physiological differences, gender refers to the socially constructed roles, behaviours, and expectations assigned to men and women. These roles vary across cultures and time, influencing identity, opportunity, and social interaction. Understanding this distinction is key to promoting gender equality and inclusivity in education and society.

Previous Paper (Solved)

Delhi Subordinate Services Selection Board

DSSSB–TGT (English) Recruitment Exam, 2021*

POST SPECIFIC SUBJECT RELATED QUESTIONS

1. Select the most appropriate option to substitute the underlined segment in the given sentence. If no substitution is required, select 'No improvement' as your answer.

Long gone are the days when customs and excise boats patrolled the coast with the aim to prevent and catching smugglers.

A. with the aim for prevention and to catch
B. No improvement
C. with the aim of preventing and catching
D. to the aim of preventing and to catch

2. Select the most appropriate option to substitute the underlined segment in the given sentence. If no substitution is required, select 'No improvement' as your answer.

Soldiers and emergency service workers have been deployed in Germany to help with the search and rescue.

A. No improvement
B. to help with the searching
C. for helping with the search
D. helping in the search

3. Find the part of the given sentence that has an error in it. If there is no error, choose 'No error'.

(A) Neither ground or sky/ (B) was visible during the/ (C) entire one-hour flight to Baltimore./ (D) No error.

4. Find the part of the given sentence that has an error in it. If there is no error, choose 'No error'.

(A) He had passed/ (B) his life pursue crime/ (C) and in protecting the weak./ (D) No error.

5. Find the part of the given sentence that has an error in it. If there is no error, choose 'No error'.

(A) Making and to get rid of/ (B) excess food accounts for/ (C) around 8-10 per cent of greenhouse gas emissions./ (D) No error.

6. Find the part of the given sentence that has an error in it. If there is no error, choose 'No error'.

(A) Most economic and political/ (B) resources are concentrated/ (C) in the southern region of US./ (D) No error.

7. Select the most appropriate option to substitute the underlined segment in the given sentence. If no substitution is required, select 'No improvement' as your answer.

Despite of being a brighter student, I left college in my third year to pursue my dream.

A. No improvement
B. In spite been a brighter
C. Despite of being a bright
D. Despite being a bright

8. Select the most appropriate option to substitute the underlined segment in the given sentence. If no substitution is required, select 'No improvement' as your answer.

Studies say redirecting our focus from our own problems to help anothers could do wonders for our mental health.

A. No improvement
B. to helping others could do wonders to
C. to helping others can do wonders for
D. to help one another can do wonders in

*Exam held on 14-09-2021.

9. Find the part of the given sentence that has an error in it. If there is no error, choose 'No error'.

(A) I never considered myself among/ (B) the most beautiful girl or in any way/ (C) a perfect candidate for a beauty pageant./ (D) No error.

10. Select the most appropriate option to substitute the underlined segment in the given sentence. If no substitution is required, select 'No improvement' as your answer.

Big companies asked us for making our puddings cheaper.

A. No improvement
B. asking us make
C. ask us in making
D. have asked us to make

11. Find the part of the given sentence that has an error in it. If there is no error, choose 'No error'.

(A) Whenever I have needed something,/ (B) members of my extended family has/ (C) always stepped into provide it./ (D) No error.

12. Find the part of the given sentence that has an error in it. If there is no error, choose 'No error'.

(A) We embarked on these car/ (B) projects with grandiose visions, many/ (C) as unrealistic such they were ingenious./ (D) No error.

13. Select the most appropriate option to substitute the underlined segment in the given sentence. If no substitution is required, select 'No improvement' as your answer.

Messages and videos circulating in bulk did in past incited mob violence in India.

A. No improvement
B. have in the past incited
C. did in past incite
D. had in past incited

14. Find the part of the given sentence that has an error in it. If there is no error, choose 'No error'.

(A) He snatched the/ (B) letter from her and looking/ (C) for the signature./ (D) No error.

15. Select the most appropriate option to substitute the underlined segment in the given sentence. If no substitution is required, select 'No improvement' as your answer.

She found the goat and her new born kid exact where she expected them.

A. exactly where she expected
B. where she expect
C. where exact she expected
D. No improvement

16. Find the part of the given sentence that has an error in it. If there is no error, choose 'No error'.

(A) It was already the beginning/ (B) of July when on her return/ (C) journey she drove into the alpine forest./ (D) No error.

17. Select the most appropriate option to substitute the underlined segment in the given sentence. If no substitution is required, select 'No improvement' as your answer.

There are tactics leaders can use for making surity more introverted employees can continue to contribute.

A. can use for making sure much
B. can use to make sure more
C. No improvement
D. could use to make surity more

18. Find the part of the given sentence that has an error in it. If there is no error, choose 'No error'.

(A) While the month that/ (B) Esther was touring solo in the Pyrenees,/ (C) we still talked every day./ (D) No error.

19. Find the part of the given sentence that has an error in it. If there is no error, choose 'No error'.

(A) The revenue generated from mobile/ (B) ads is substantial and will being becoming/ (C) the bread and butter for many businesses./ (D) No error.

20. Find the part of the given sentence that has an error in it. If there is no error, choose 'No error'.

(A) Exposure to drugs/ (B) not only effect the/ (C) fish themselves, but their offspring also./ (D) No error.

21. Fill in the blanks to complete the given sentence by choosing the appropriate words from the given options.

We had a very ______ walk, despite getting ______ lost in Birch woods.

A. tranquil, very B. enjoyable, rather
C. lovely, quiet D. cynical, caught

22. Fill in the blank to complete the given sentence by choosing the appropriate word from the given options.

Plastic is the ______ common type of debris floating in the world's oceans.

A. very B. few
C. much D. most

23. Following are parts of a single sentence. Pick the grammatically correct parts among these and choose the combination with the numbers of these correct parts.

(*i*) There is a thing in
(*ii*) the middle of your
(*iii*) Howling Desert with an
(*iv*) Longer neck and long legs.

A. Only (*iii*) B. Only (*i*)
C. (*ii*) and (*iv*) D. (*i*) and (*ii*)

24. Fill in the blank to complete the given sentence by choosing the appropriate word from the given options.

He turned back to his father, ______ was watching him with interest.

A. who B. whom
C. which D. that

25. Fill in the blank to complete the given sentence by choosing the appropriate word from the given options.

The room was silent for ______ minutes after they left.

A. little B. fewer
C. a few D. the little

26. Choose the appropriate verbs from the given options to fill in the blanks and complete the sentence.

When it came night and they ______ their supper, they would crowd around the open fire and coax Jennie to ______ them stories.

A. had, tell B. had, say
C. have, tell D. have had, told

27. Select the sentence from the given options that conforms to Standard English Usage.

A. He did not lose sight either of the welfare of his army and of the doings of the enemy.
B. He did not lost sight either of the welfare of his army or the doings of the enemy.
C. He did not lose sight either of the welfare of his army or of the doings of the enemy.
D. He did not loose sight of either the welfare of his army or of the doing of the enemy.

28. Fill in the blanks to complete the given sentence by choosing the appropriate words from the given options.

Philosophical ______ are divided between those who approach issues by starting with ______ principles.

A. ethics, absolute
B. clemency, sober
C. recognition, random
D. deception, sonorous

29. Fill in the blanks to complete the given sentence by choosing the appropriate words from the given options.

Selection of soups and salads are ______ at the café for those who want ______ lunch.

A. secondary, fulfil
B. mandatory, maximum
C. redundant, lightest
D. available, healthier

30. Following are parts of a single sentence. Pick the grammatically correct parts among these and choose the combination with the numbers of these correct parts.

(*i*) Contraction of the heart muscle
(*ii*) Generated a force, cause pressure to
(*iii*) Rising in your blood vessels, which drive
(*iv*) The flow of blood around your body.

A. (*ii*) and (*iv*) B. (*i*) and (*iv*)
C. (*i*), (*ii*) and (*iii*) D. (*i*) and (*iii*)

31. Choose the appropriate prepositions from the given options to fill in the blanks and complete the sentence.

Everyone agrees ______ the need to reduce the amount of energy used and carbon emitted ______ our homes.

A. too, in B. for, in
C. on, from D. of, on

32. Following are parts of a single sentence. Pick the grammatically correct parts among these and choose the combination with the numbers of these correct parts.

(*i*) They need to
(*ii*) Clear the air
(*iii*) About the inheritance issue,
(*iv*) But that isn't enough.

A. (*ii*) and (*iii*) B. (*ii*) and (*iv*)
C. (*i*), (*ii*), (*iii*) and (*iv*) D. (*ii*), (*iii*) and (*iv*)

33. Following are parts of a single sentence. Pick the grammatically correct parts among these and choose the combination with the numbers of these correct parts.

(*i*) The man had taken
(*ii*) A step or two across
(*iii*) The glass roof before he notices
(*iv*) The presence of a strangers.

A. (*i*) and (*ii*) B. Only (*iv*)
C. Only (*iii*) D. (*i*) and (*iv*)

34. Fill in the blanks to complete the given sentence by choosing the appropriate words from the given options.

There is certainly no ______ of big and tall golf shirts available in the men's fashion world ______.

A. dearth, today
B. stimulation, forever
C. impunity, now
D. multitude, ever

35. Select the sentence from the given options that conforms to Standard English Usage.

A. Samay had not wanted to believe that one of his sons betrayed the rest of the Council.
B. Samay did not wanted to believe that one of his sons betrayed the rest of the Council.
C. Samay had not wanted to believe one of his son betraying the rest of the Council.
D. Samay has not wanted to believe that one of his sons betray the rest of the Council.

36. Fill in the blank to complete the given sentence by choosing the appropriate word from the given options.

It is important to know ______ or not elephants are present in protected areas.

A. either B. whether
C. rather D. while

37. Choose the appropriate prepositions from the given options to fill in the blanks and complete the sentence.

He was called ______ by the judge to bring forth the treasures of the church which had been committed ______ his keeping.

A. upon, to B. off, on
C. for, upon D. over, for

38. Choose the appropriate prepositions from the given options to fill in the blanks and complete the sentence.

That pleased smile was ______ his lips again and his eyes held a glint ______ humour.

A. on, of B. through, off
C. across, for D. in, for

39. Fill in the blank to complete the given sentence by choosing the appropriate word from the given options.

They talked over the affairs of the house exactly ______ if they were equals.

A. for B. as
C. so D. such

40. Choose the appropriate verbs from the given options to fill in the blanks and complete the sentence.

He ______ seventy-five thousand acres of land when he ______ much younger.

A. bought, was
B. has bought, was
C. had bought, were
D. did buy, have been

41. Select the sentence from the given options that conforms to Standard English Usage.

A. Allen lived at a time when botany have been a popular scientific subject for woman in highest social classes.
B. Allen lived at a time when botany was a popular scientific subject for women in the higher social classes.
C. Allen lived at time while botany was a popularly scientific subject for women in higher social classes.
D. Allen living at times when botany was a popular scientific subject for women in higher social classes.

42. In the following question, a sentence has been given in Direct/Indirect speech. Out of the four alternatives suggested, select the one which best expresses the same sentence in Indirect/Direct speech.

"Will you forgive your sister for all the mistakes?", Mr. Jones said to his son.

A. Mr. Jones said to his son if he would be forgiving his sister for all the mistakes.
B. Mr. Jones was asking his son if he will forgive his sister for all the mistakes.
C. Mr. Jones asked his son if he would forgive his sister for all the mistakes.
D. Mr. Jones asked his son that if he will forgive his sister for all the mistakes.

43. In the given question, four statements are labelled as P, Q, R and S which when logically ordered form a coherent passage. Choose the option that represents the most logical order.

P : His periods of reserve were not constitutional, but the result of moods.
Q : Sitting there beside Mrs. Baroda, his silence melted for the time.
R : Gouvernail was in no sense a diffident man, for he was not a self-conscious one.
S : He talked freely and intimately in a low, hesitating drawl that was not unpleasant to hear.

A. QSPR
B. PRQS
C. SPQR
D. RPQS

44. In the following question, a sentence has been given in Active/Passive voice. Out of the four alternatives suggested, select the one which best expresses the same sentence in Passive/Active voice.

Jhanvi wears a yellow dress on Thursday.

A. On Thursday Jhanvi wears a yellow dress.
B. A yellow dress is worn by Jhanvi on Thursday.
C. On Thursday a yellow dress is being worn by Jhanvi.
D. A yellow dress was worn by Jhanvi on Thursday.

45. In the following question, a sentence has been given in Direct/Indirect speech. Out of the four alternatives suggested, select the one which best expresses the same sentence in Indirect/Direct speech.

Fatima said. "What are we planning for tomorrow?

A. Fatima told that what we were planning for the next day
B. Fatima asked what we were planning for the next day.
C. Fatima asked that what we have been planning for the next day.
D. Fatima asked what we have been planning for tomorrow.

46. Select the sentence from the given options that conforms to Standard English Usage.

A. Mr Miller had stressed that demand cutting for sand needful to be seen as part of wide effort to reducing overconsumption of natural resources.
B. Mr Miller stresses that cutting demand for sand needs to be seen as part of a wider effort to reduce overconsumption of natural resources.

C. Mr Miller stressed that cutting demand for sand needs to be seen as part of widest effort to reducing overconsumption of natural resources.

D. Mr Miller stresses that cutting demand for sand needed to being seen as part of a wider effort to reduce overconsumption of natural resources.

47. In the given question, there is a sentence of which some parts have been jumbled up. Rearrange these parts which are labelled P, Q, R and S to produce the correct sentence. Choose the proper sequence.

The French

P : had time to fire three

Q : before the hussars got

R : rounds of grapeshot

S : back to their horses

A. PRQS B. PQRS

C. SPQR D. QPRS

48. In the following question, a sentence has been given in Direct/Indirect speech. Out of the four alternatives suggested, select the one which best expresses the same sentence in Indirect/ Direct speech.

The author said that the past cannot be changed.

A. The author said to me, "The past could not change."

B. The author said, "The past will not be changed."

C. The author said, "The past cannot be changed."

D. The author says, "The past could not be changed."

49. In the following question, a sentence has been given in Direct/Indirect speech. Out of the four alternatives suggested, select the one which best expresses the same sentence in Indirect/ Direct speech.

The said, "We were asking a rhetorical question."

A. They told that they have been asking a rheotrical question

B. They say that them asking rhetorical question

C. They said that they were asking a rhetorical question.

D. They said that they had been asking a rhetorical question.

50. In the following question, a sentence has been given in Direct/Indirect speech. Out of the four alternatives suggested, select the one which best expresses the same sentence in Indirect/ Direct speech.

She said, "I cannot eat chocolates daily."

A. She says that she could not eat chocolates daily.

B. She said that she could not eat chocolates daily.

C. She told she cannot eat chocolates daily.

D. She said that she cannot eat chocolates daily.

51. In the given question, four statements are labelled as P, Q, R and S which when logically ordered form a coherent passage. Choose the option that represents the most logical order.

P : And provide opportunities for them to do this alongside their studies.

Q : Universities should look at ways they can address the barriers of cost and time.

R : They could work with schools to look at ways they could help to get people involved in sport when they are younger.

S : It is important for universities to encourage students to take part in sport and physical activity.

A. PRSQ B. SPQR

C. QPRS D. RPQS

52. Select the sentence from the given options that conforms to Standard English Usage.

A. My ongoing research indicated that advertising practitioners is becoming more aware that the imagery they use can have an affect on society.

B. My ongoing research indicates that advertising practitioners are becoming more aware that the imagery they use can have an effect on society.

C. My ongoing research indicated that advertising practitioners is to become much aware that the imagery they used could have an effect in society.

D. My ongoing research indicates that advertising practitioners are to become most aware that the imagery they use could have an effect in society.

53. In the following question, a sentence has been given in Active/Passive voice. Out of the four alternatives suggested, select the one which best expresses the same sentence in Passive/Active voice.

My mother welcomed my friends at our farmhouse.

A. My friends had been welcomed by my mother at our farmhouse.

B. My friends are welcomed at our farmhouse by my mother.

C. My friends have been welcomed by my mother at our farmhouse.

D. My friends were welcomed by my mother at our farmhouse.

54. In the given question, there is a sentence of which some parts have been jumbled up. Rearrange these parts which are labelled P, Q, R and S to produce the correct sentence. Choose the proper sequence.

A body found buried

P : England has shed new light on

Q : in a ditch by construction workers

R : in the east Midlands of

S : Roman slavery in Britain

A. RPQS B. PRSQ

C. QRPS D. SQPR

55. In the given question, there is a sentence of which some parts have been jumbled up. Rearrange these parts which are labelled P, Q, R and S to produce the correct sentence. Choose the proper sequence.

The morning

P : was getting hot

Q : by the time they managed

R : to water the mules

S : and fill their canteens

A. PQRS B. PSQR

C. QRPS D. QPSR

56. In the following question, a sentence has been given in Active/Passive voice. Out of the four alternatives suggested, select the one which best expresses the same sentence in Passive/Active voice.

The worker has refused to work at midnight.

A. Working at midnight was being refused by the worker.

B. Working at midnight is refused by the worker.

C. To work at midnight has been refused by the worker.

D. To work at midnight had been refused by the worker.

57. In the following question, a sentence has been given in Direct/Indirect speech. Out of the four alternatives suggested, select the one which best expresses the same sentence in Indirect/Direct speech.

My teacher said, "I want to talk more about this issue."

A. My teacher said she wants to talk more about that issue.

B. My teacher said that she wanted to talk more about that issue.

C. My teacher said that she has wanted to talk more about that issue.

D. My teacher told to me that she wanted to talk more about this issue.

58. In the following question, a sentence has been given in Active/Passive voice. Out of the four alternatives suggested, select the one which best expresses the same sentence in Passive/Active voice.

I am supposed to give a speech in the evening.

A. A speech is been supposed to be given by me in the evening.

B. It is supposed that a speech would be given by me.

C. A speech is supposed to be given by me in the evening.

D. A speech in the evening will be given by me.

59. In the following question, a sentence has been given in Active/Passive voice. Out of the four alternatives suggested, select the one which best expresses the same sentence in Passive/Active voice.

Have you verified all the bank details?

A. Did all the bank details have been verified by you?

B. Have all the bank details been verified by you?

C. Has all the bank details being verified by you?

D. Were all the bank details been verified by you?

60. In the following question, a sentence has been given in Active/Passive voice. Out of the four alternatives suggested, select the one which best expresses the same sentence in Passive/Active voice.

Divya is decorating a room for her brother's birthday.

A. A room has been decorated by Divya for her brother's birthday.

B. For her brother's birthday a room was being decorated by Divya.

C. For her brother's birthday a room had been decorated by Divya.

D. A room is being decorated by Divya for her brother's birthday.

61. In Henrik Ibsen's "Ghosts", Osvald Alving came back to his house from Paris because ______.

A. he did not like Paris

B. to meet Pastor Mandors

C. to take his mother with him to Paris

D. to persuade Regina to marry him

62. Which writer is known to give birth to Detective fiction genre?

A. Edgar Allan Poe

B. Arthur Conan Doyle

C. Mark Twain

D. H.P. Lovenaft

63. Read the following lines and identify the correct author.

Born in modern day Sri Lanka, this writer was a victim of poor mental health but also one of the largest contributor to the Oxford Dictionary.

A. William Shakespeare

B. G.B. Shaw

C. Dr. James Murray

D. Dr. William Chester Minor

64. The Suitable Boy by Vikram Seth is ______.

A. the longest novel in English

B. is a work of economical literature

C. is a satirical work

D. is a six volume of poetry

65. Which period in American Literature is known as "Jazz Age"?

A. 1920-1940 B. 1890-1900

C. 1945-1960 D. 1830-1870.

66. Which of the following is NOT a work of Robert Frost?

A. Ulysses

B. Fire and Ice

C. A Boy's Will

D. The Gift Outright

67. Which of the following is NOT a work of William Faulkuer?

A. Absalom, Absalom!

B. Dry September

C. A Farewell to Arms

D. As I Lay Dying

68. "Et Tu Brute", a famous phrase from Julius Caesar showcases which emotion of the speaker?

A. Hatred B. Disbelief

C. Affection D. Sympathetic

69. Who coined the term "ratiocination"?

A. D.H. Lawrence

B. F., Scott Fitzgerald

C. Edgar Allan Poe

D. H.G. Wells

70. Which of the following are the poems written by John Donne?

I. The Canonization
II. The Faerie Queen
III. The Valediction : Forbidding Mourning
IV. Elegy : To his Mistress Going to Bed

A. II and IV B. I, II and III
C. I and II D. II, III and IV

71. All the world's a stage/And all the men and women merely players./They have their exits and their entrances,/And one man in his time plays many parts.

These lines have been taken from?

A. Romeo and Juliet by Shakespeare
B. Macbeth by Shakespeare
C. Othello by Shakespeare
D. As You Like It by Shakespeare

72. In the given question, four statements are labelled as P, Q, R and S which when logically ordered form a coherent passage. Choose the option that represents the most logical order.

P : With dogs, for example, a wagging tail is not always the sign of a happy dog.
Q : Animals have sophisticated communication systems and we need to learn about these if we are to "hear" what they're saying.
R : You have to listen for pitch, speed, spacing and volume to work out what they are saying.
S : And a bark can indicate excitement, fear, surprise, frustration and more.

A. QPSR B. SPQR
C. QSPR D. QSRP

73. Select the correct chronological order of the following Ibsen's plays.

A. Love's Comedy → The Pillar Society → Ghosts → Peer Gynt
B. The Pillars of Society → Peer Gynt → Love's Comedy → Ghosts
C. Love's Comedy → Peer Gynt → The Pillars of Society → Ghosts
D. Peer Gynt → Love's Comedy → Ghosts → The Pillars of Society

74. When was "Lyrical Ballads" published?

A. 1798 B. 1800
C. 1802 D. 1799

75. Which of the following works by Shakespeare is not a comedy?

A. As You Like It
B. Merchant of Venice
C. Macbeth
D. Much Ado About Nothing

76. Ruskin Bond is an Anglo-Indian author of British descent. Which of the following was his first novel?

A. Untouchable
B. A Flight Of Pigeons
C. Rusty
D. The Room On The Roof

77. Which of the following is the best known play by Thomas Middleton?

A. Women Beware Women
B. The Fair Maid of the West
C. The Shoemaker's Holiday
D. The Duchess of Malfi

78. In the given question, four statements are labelled as P, Q, R and S which when logically ordered form a coherent passage. Choose the option that represents the most logical order.

P : Demand for electricity is growing faster than the roll-out of renewable energies.
Q : This is leading to a surge in the use of heavily polluting coal and undermining efforts to reach carbon neutrality.
R : Electricity demand is expected to grow by 5 per cent this year.
S : This is much more than the 1 per cent drop it experienced last year as the global economy tumbled into recession.

A. PRQS B. SPRQ
C. QPRS D. RPSQ

79. The given lines by John Keats are taken from which of the following odes?

"Season of mists and mellow fruit fulness,/ Close bosom-friend of the maturing sun;/ Conspiring with him how to load and bless/ With fruit the vines that round the thatch – eaves run;"?

A. Ode to A Nightingale
B. To Autumn
C. Dejection: An Ode
D. Ode on a Grecian Uru

80. How many books does John Milton's "Paradise Lost" contains?
A. 10 B. 8
C. 24 D. 12

Directions (Qs. No. 81 to 85): *Read the following information carefully and answer the given questions.*

Plant-based diets have surged in popularity during the past few years. As a result, there is been a boom in demand for plant-based alternatives to favourite foods – including meats, such as sausages and burgers. The plant-based meat alternatives industry is projected to see massive growth over the next few years. But there is still a lot we don't know about these food products – including whether they are as healthy as some may think. Although many of these products claim to be made primarily from plants, they aren't all that different to other ultra-processed food products. They often contain many similar ingredients – including protein isolates, emulsifiers, binders and other additives – and are made using industrial processing methods, so can be considered an ultra-processed food product.

Plenty of evidence links ultra-processed foods to obesity, type 2 diabetes, cancer and other chronic diseases. This is probably due to a combination of their poor nutritional content, synthetic additives and lack of fibre, which is important for giving a feeling of fullness. These types of foods are also a reason why poor diet has become the world's top cause of death from chronic diseases, as they're readily available, easy to overeat, lack nutrients and now provide around a half or more of the calories consumed in countries such as the US, UK, Australia and Canada.

81. Choose the word that means the same as the word 'massive' as used in the passage.
A. Trivial B. Modest
C. Leverage D. Enormous

82. According to the passage, all the given statements are correct EXCEPT:
A. Popularity of plant-based diet is decreasing day-by-day.
B. Plant-based products and ultra-processed foods share many similar ingredients.
C. Ultra-processed foods can cause type 2 diabetes.
D. Ultra-processed foods have poor nutritional content.

83. What can be the suitable title for the given passage?
A. Why we eat junk food?
B. Advantages of ultra-processed food
C. Plant-based diet: Healthy or not
D. Poor diet and its consequences

84. Which of the following ingredients is NOT present in ultra-processed foods?
A. Soy Protein B. Protein isolates
C. Emulsifiers D. Binders

85. Why people are consuming ultra-processed food items?
A. They are very tasty.
B. These food items are readily available.
C. These food items improve digestion.
D. They give a feeling of fullness.

Directions (Qs. No. 86 to 90): *Read the following information carefully and answer the given questions.*

Deforestation and climate change are altering the Amazon rainforest's ability to soak up carbon, according to a new study. Significant parts of the world's largest tropical forest have started to emit more CO_2 than they absorb. The southeast is worst-affected, say, scientists, with higher rates of tree loss and an increasing number of fires. Temperatures there have risen by three times the global average during the hottest months.

Areas of our planet that absorb more carbon from the atmosphere - for example, in the form of the greenhouse gas CO_2 - than they store are known as sinks. The role played by the lands and forests of the Earth in soaking up carbon has been a critical factor in preventing faster rates of climate change. Since the 1960s, these sinks have taken in around 25 per cent of carbon emissions from the use of fossil fuels. The Amazon, home to the world's largest tropical forest, has (A) ______ a key role in absorbing and storing much of that carbon. But the growing impacts of climate change and deforestation are taking their toll on this crucial CO_2 sponge.

Earlier this year, a study showed that the rainforest in Brazil released about 20 per cent more CO_2 into the atmosphere than it took in over the period from 2010-2019. The researchers are worried that the changing climate is also interfering with rainfall, which they argue, has immediate consequences for Brazil. "This is very bad news for everybody but mainly for Brazil," said Dr. Gatti.

86. In the given passage, Dr. Gatti is referring to which bad news?
A. Inability of flora to absorb CO_2 from the atmosphere.
B. Excessive deforestation in the southeast region of the Amazon.
C. Increasing number of bushfires in the tropical forest of Brazil.
D. The impact of climate change on rainfall in Brazil.

87. According to the passage, all the given statements are correct EXCEPT:
A. The southeast part of the Amazon rain forest is worst-affected due to climate change.
B. The potential of Amazon rainforest to soak up carbon dioxide is decreasing.
C. Climate change is dependent on the number of trees in a region.
D. Before 2010, the rainforest in Brazil released no CO_2 into the atmosphere.

88. Choose the word that means the same as the word 'crucial' as used in the passage.
A. Fleeting B. Minor
C. Scarce D. Pivotal

89. According to the context of the passage, which of the following words can be placed in the blank (A)?
A. defined B. regulated
C. balanced D. played

90. The given passage mainly talks about:
A. Wildlife present in the Amazon forest.
B. Lack of precipitation in Brazil.
C. Deforestation and its negative impact on fauna.
D. Climate change in the Amazon regions.

91. An artist uses paper, canvas, clay, metal, paint etc. which can be moulded or transformed to create some physical or art object. Which of the following are those physical or art objects?
I. Drawing II. Painting
III. Sculpture IV. Design
A. II, III and IV B. I, II and III
C. I, II and IV D. I, II, III and IV

92. Which of the following statement is NOT correct about Growth?
A. Growth stops with maturity
B. A part of development is growth
C. Growth refers to physical changes
D. Growth is not totally observable and measurable

93. Beliefs and assumptions about ______ influence the actual teaching learning processes and practices.
I. modes of evaluation
II. role of teachers
A. Only I B. Both I and II
C. Only II D. Neither I nor II

94. 'Society thinks that certain types of work are meant to be done by males only and certain other by females only.' Which of the following statement satisfies this given statement?
I. We rarely see women tilling a land using a plough.
II. We rarely see males washing clothes of children and other family members.
A. Neither I nor II B. Only I
C. Both I and II D. Only II

95. Which of the following combination is correct?
I. Assessment for learning – Summative
II. Assessment of Learning – Formative
A. Only II B. Only I
C. Both I and II D. Neither I nor II

96. Which of the following are the approaches to Learning and Teaching?
I. Competency – Based Approach
II. Subject – Centered Approach

III. Constructivist Approach
IV. Learner – Centered Approach

A. II, III and IV B. I, II, III and IV
C. II and IV D. I and II

97. 'Make room for shared experiences.' Which of the following statement is correct regarding the given statement?

I. They are an invaluable source of language work.

II. They create an atmosphere of involvement and togetherness.

A. Only II B. Only I
C. Neither I nor II D. Both I and II

98. Which of the following statement is correct?

I. The idea of providing quality education by valuing the individual need in a group as a unit is called as inclusive education.

II. Inclusion is about building the inner strength and mounting confidence among children.

A. Both I and II B. Only II
C. Only I D. Neither I nor II

99. Which of the following ways of looking at language restrict the versatility of language and its usage?

I. Language only as a means of communication.

II. Language as a pairing of a grammar and a dictionary.

A. Neither I nor II B. Only II
C. Both I and II D. Only I

100. While thinking about the marks and grades several questions may come to the mind of a teacher. Which of the following are those questions?

I. Do they tell anything about the extent and pace of learning?

II. Do they provide information on the areas of strength and weakness of the student in learning?

III. Do they indicate about the difficulties a student is facing during learning?

A. I, II and III B. Only II
C. II and III D. I and II

ANSWERS

1	2	3	4	5	6	7	8	9	10
C	A	C	A	C	A	D	C	B	D
11	**12**	**13**	**14**	**15**	**16**	**17**	**18**	**19**	**20**
C	C	B	A	A	A	B	C	A	A
21	**22**	**23**	**24**	**25**	**26**	**27**	**28**	**29**	**30**
B	D	D	A	C	A	C	A	D	B
31	**32**	**33**	**34**	**35**	**36**	**37**	**38**	**39**	**40**
C	C	A	A	A	B	A	A	B	A
41	**42**	**43**	**44**	**45**	**46**	**47**	**48**	**49**	**50**
B	C	D	B	B	B	A	C	D	B
51	**52**	**53**	**54**	**55**	**56**	**57**	**58**	**59**	**60**
B	B	D	C	A	C	B	C	B	D
61	**62**	**63**	**64**	**65**	**66**	**67**	**68**	**69**	**70**
D	A	D	A	A	A	C	B	C	B
71	**72**	**73**	**74**	**75**	**76**	**77**	**78**	**79**	**80**
D	A	C	A	C	D	A	A	B	D
81	**82**	**83**	**84**	**85**	**86**	**87**	**88**	**89**	**90**
D	A	C	A	B	D	D	D	D	D
91	**92**	**93**	**94**	**95**	**96**	**97**	**98**	**99**	**100**
D	D	B	C	D	B	D	A	C	A

Previous Paper (Solved)

Delhi Subordinate Services Selection Board

DSSSB–TGT (English) Recruitment Exam, 2018*

POST SPECIFIC SUBJECT RELATED QUESTIONS

Directions (Qs. No. 1 and 2): *Change the voice of the given sentence.*

1. "They were questioning the spy".
A. The spy was questioned by them
B. The spy questioned by them
C. The spy was being questioned by them
D. The spy had been questioned by them

2. "I was obliged to do so".
A. Some one asked me to do so
B. Circumstances obliged me to do so
C. They asked me to do so
D. There was an obligation to do so

Directions (Qs. No. 3-5): *Use appropriate connecting words from the given options.*

3. You must apologise, _______ you will be punished.
A. but B. till
C. though D. otherwise

4. There was a little hope of success _______ they decided to perform the operation.
A. Where as B. So
C. Nevertheless D. Neither

5. He was _______ praised but also rewarded.
A not only B. neither
C. either D. so

Directions (Qs. No. 6-10): *Select the correct option for the underlined words:*

6. <u>What</u> did you pay for this?
A. interrogative pronoun
B. distributive pronoun
C. reciprocal pronoun
D. demonstrative pronoun

7. They keep away from <u>each other</u>.
A. Indefinite pronoun
B. Distributive pronoun
C. Reciprocal pronoun
D. Demonstrative pronoun

8. He drank <u>little</u> water.
A. verb B. adverb
C. adjective D. preposition

9. He <u>need</u> not ask my permission.
A. verb B. preposition
C. primary auxiliary D. modal auxiliary

10. They <u>seldom</u> come here.
A. preposition B. adverb
C. conjunction D. verb

Directions (Qs. No. 11-14): *Complete the sentence using correct option:*

11. We shall start early lost
A. We will miss the bus
B. We should miss the train
C. We miss the train
D. We shall miss the train

12. As soon as the thief ran out of the jail,
A. than the guard fired at him
B. when the guard fired at him
C. the guard had fired at him
D. the guard fired at him

13. Everyone will admit that:
A. he is innocent B. he was innocent
C. he will be innocent D. none of the above

14. Select the sentence which is grammatically wrong.
A. It is too good to be true
B. You are too kind
C. Sita is as tall as Sneha
D. He is a rather careless fellow

* Held on 02-09-2018.

Directions (Qs. No. 15-19): *Read the passage below and answer the questions:*

Nations, like individuals, derive support and strength from the feeling that they belong to an illustrious race, that they are the heirs of their greatness and ought to be the perpetuaters of their glory. It is of momentous importance that a nation should have a great past to look back upon. It steadies the life of the present, elevates and upholds it and lightens and lifts it up, by the memory of the great deeds, the noble sufferings and the valorous achievements of the men of old. The life of nations, as of men, is a great treasury of experience, which, wisely used, issues in social progress and improvement; or misused, issues in dreams, delusions and failure. Like men, nations are purified and strengthened by trials. Some of the most glorious chapters in their history are those containing the record of sufferings by means of which their character has been developed. Love of liberty and patriotic feeling may have done much, but trial and suffering nobly borne more than all.

(Smile)

15. What lightens and lifts the life of the present?
A. nations
B. trials
C. great past of nations
D. none of the above

16. ______ issues in dreams; delusions and failure if misused.
A. the life of nations
B. the memory of great deeds
C. the noble sufferings
D. none of the above

17. Some of the historic chapters are glorious because:
A. they contain the story of heroic characters
B. they contain the record of suffering
C. they contain great memories
D. they contain the issues of society

18. Find the synonym of 'undauntable' from the passage.
A. upholds B. glorious
C. valorous D. noble

19. Find the word from the passage which can be used as the antonym of 'verity'.
A. deeds B. delusion
C. glorious D. illustrious

Directions (Qs. No. 20-24): *Read the passage below and answer the questions:*

Death's a leveller which also doesnot discriminate on the basis of sex, colour, wealth or religion. But death sentence; at least in India is surely discriminatory in nature as the haves, the powerful and the influential may commit a murder or two but are never sent to the gallows. But Justice Bhagawati declared that the death sentence was unconstitutional and discriminatory as it strikes mostly against the poor and deprived sections of the community. "The rich and the affluent usually escape from its clutches". Death sentences, he said, is a privilege of the poor. Another jurist and activist apex/court judge V.R. Krishna Iyer in a judgement said "............... who, by and large, are the men whom the gallows swallow? .... is the white collar criminals and the corporate criminals whose wilful economic and environmental crimes inflict mass deaths or who hire assassins and murder by remote control? Rarely, with a few exceptions, they hardly fear the halter. The feuding villager, heady with country liquor, the striking workers desperate with defeat, the political dissenter and sacrificing liberator intent on changing the social order from satanic misrule, the waifs and strays whom society has hardened by neglected into street toughs; or the poor householder–husband or wife–driven by dire necessity to burst tantrums–it is this person who is the morning meal of the Macabre executioner'.

20. Find a word from the passage which is the synonym of nonconformist.
A. Deprived B. Dissenter
C. Assassin D. Householder

21. When Justice declares that death sentence is the privilege of the poor, he is being:
A. Angry B. Sarcastic
C. Jubilant D. Stoic

22. In passage, the 'haves' refer to:
A. The Indians

B. Those who do not commit a murder
C. The affluent in society
D. White collar criminals

23. According to the passage the "gallous swallow" refers to:
A. The rich and effluent
B. Any law breaker without any discrimination
C. The environmentalists
D. None of these

24. Find a word from the passage which refers to "a rope for hanging criminals'.
A. Macabre B. Halter
C. Strays D. Waif

25. "The Rape of Lucrece" is a poem written by:
A. Ben Jonson B. Thomas Middleton
C. Dekher D. Shakespeare

26. Which of the following is the best known play by Thomas Middleton?
A. Women Beware Women
B. The Fair Maid of the West
C. The Shoemaker's Holiday
D. The Duchess of Malfi

27. 'Adam' is the central character of:
A. On his Blindness
B. Paradise Lost
C. On Reaching the Age of Twenty Three
D. To the Nightingale

28. "The Holy War" by Bunyan was published in:
A. 1554 B. 1682
C. 1665 D. 1570

29. ______ was a Clergyman whose best known work is 'The Holy War'.
A. Thomas Fuller B. Sir Thomas Browne
C. Robert Burton D. Bunyan

30. Jonathan Swift's first notable work, ______ which, not published is a Keen Satire upon parties in the controversy.
A. Jew of Malta
B. Gullivers Travels
C. Tale of a Tub
D. The Battle of the Books

31. 'The Palace of Illusions' is a 2008 novel by:
A. Chitra Banerjee Divakaruni
B. Arundhati Roy
C. Amish Tripathi
D. Anita Desai

32. Which of the novels by Salman Rushdie portrays the lives of Zulfikar Ali Bhutto and General Muhammad Zia-Ul-Haq?
A. The Satanic Versus
B. The Moor's Last Sigh
C. Shame
D. Midnight Children

33. 'The Bluest Eye' is a novel by:
A. Toni Morrison
B. Frances Hodgsen Burnett
C. Bernard Shaw
D. D.H. Lawrence

34. ______ is the first novel by D. H. Lawrence published in 1911.
A. Women in Love
B. Sons and Lovers
C. The White Peacock
D. The Trespasser

35. "A bird came down the walk
He did not know I saw
He bit an angle-worm in halves .... "

The above lines are taken from:
A. Emily Dickinson B. Robert Frost
C. Hawthrone D. Whitman

36. Which of the following is a pastoral romance by Sir Philip Sidney?
A. Arcadia
B. Discoverie of Guiana
C. Organum
D. Purchas

37. "Sonnet on Milton" was written by:
A. Wordsworth B. Blake
C. Milton D. Arnold

38. 'A little learning is a dangerous thing'—this quote is taken from Essay on Criticism by:
A. Jonathan Swift B. Alexander Pope
C. Joseph Addison D. Richard Steele

39. Shakespeare's sonnets were first published in:
A. 1609 B. 1598
C. 1616 D. 1600

40. "Life is a tale, told by an idiot,
Full of sound and fury,
signifying nothing ...."
In which play do these lines appear?
A. Julius Caesar B. Hamlet
C. Macbeth D. Richard II

41. Dorothea Brooke is a 19 year old orphan in the novel _______ by George Eliot.
A. Romola B. Adam Bede
C. Middle March D. Daniel Deronda

42. Which of the following deals with the adventures of a poor clerk off on his bicycle for a holiday?
A. The Wheels of Chance
B. The Jungle Book
C. Clayhanger
D. Black Bartlemy's Treasure

43. 'The Silver Box' is a problem play by:
A. James M. Barrie B. John Galsworthy
C. H. G. Wells D. Arnold Bennet

44. 'The Jew of Malta' is a play which deals with lust for wealth written by:
A. Shakespeare B. Marlow
C. Thomas Kyd D. John Lyly

45. "Why this is hell, nor am I out of it,
Think'st thou that I; who saw the face of God..."

The above lines are from:
A. The Merchant of Venice
B. The Jew of Malta
C. Faustus
D. Paradise Lost

Directions (Qs. No. 46-48): *Fill in the blanks with correct forms of verb.*

46. I am tired I _______ to bed now.
A. go B. will go
C. am going D. goes

47. I ______ I won't be late.
A. promise B. am promising
C. will promise D. none of the above

48. It _____ for ten days.
A. rained B. has been rainy
C. is raining D. was rainy

49. He shall be given a present if he passes this year.
The underlined words indicate that the sentence is:
A. a threat B. a promise
C. a determination D. a command

50. In my younger days I _____ run four miles at a stretch.
A. can B. will
C. might D. could

51. If I could fly like a bird, I _____ be with you now.
A. would B. will
C. shall D. none of the above

Directions (Qs. No. 52-54): *Fill in the blanks with correct options.*

52. Each of the players ______ given a reward.
A. are B. were
C. have D. was

53. My sister and my mother _______ me to study medicine.
A. wants B. want
C. has wanted D. have wanted

54. He and I ______ at Oxford together.
A. am B. was
C. were D. is

Directions (Qs. No. 55-58): *Select the correct option for the underlined part:*

55. "Get out of my way, whoever you are".
A. Noun clause B. Adverb clause
C. Adjective clause D. None of the above

56. "Life is what we make of it".
A. Adjective clause B. Noun clause
C. Adverb clause D. None of the above

57. I paint because I like painting.
A. Noun clause B. Adverb clause
C. Adjective clause D. None of the above

58. We eat that we may live.
A. Adjective clause B. Adverb clause
C. Noun clause D. None of the above

Directions (Qs. No. 59-61): *Put punctuation marks for the following sentences:*

59. Solomon says of the making of books there is no end.

A. Solomon says, of the making of books there is no end.

B. Solomon say—"Of the making of books, there is no end".

C. Solomon says : "Of the making of books there is no end".

D. Solomon says : "Of the making of books; there is no end".

60. He said I won't allow it

A. He said, 'I won't allow it'.

B. He said; 'I won't allow it'.

C. He said : I won't allow it

D. He said, I won't allow it.

61. Did you hear a sound he asked

A. "Did you hear a sound". he asked.

B. "Did you hear a sound," he asked.

C. "Did you hear a sound"—he asked

D. "Did you hear a sound"? he asked.

Directions (Qs. No. 62-66): *Read the passage below and answer the questions:*

Great men of science, literature and art-apostles of great thoughts and lords of the great heart—have belonged to no exclusive class or rank in life. They have come alike from colleges, workshops and farm-houses—from the huts of poor men and the mansions of the rich. Some of God's greatest apostles have come from the ranks. The poorest have sometimes taken the highest places; nor have difficulties apparently the most insuperable proved obstacles in their way. Those very difficulties in many instances would even seem to have been their best helpers, by evoking their powers of labour and endurance and stimulating into life faculties which might otherwise have lain dormant. The instances of obstacles thus surmounted and of triumphs thus achieved are indeed so numerous, as almost to justify the proverb that 'With will one can do anything'.

62. The passage gives the message about:

A. apostles of great thought

B. great difficulties

C. God's great apostles

D. the power of will

63. Who are the best helpers mentioned in the passage?

A. Science B. Literature

C. Poverty D. Difficulties

64. Select a word from the passage which is a synonym of 'proponent'.

A. endure B. labour

C. apostle D. obstacle

65. Find the word which can be the antonym of stoppage.

A. evoke B. faculty

C. stimulate D. endurance

66. Select the meaning of the word 'insuperable'.

A. Surmountable B. Vincible

C. Superable D. Impregnable

Directions (Qs. No. 67-71): *Read the passage below and answer the questions:*

"There is little the Chinese regime does on human rights that endears itself to the West", said Barshefsky in a speech in Baltimore—one of hundreds of recent forays by senior Administration officials and their allies eager to give President Clinton an important foreign-policy victory before he leaves office. Nonetheless, this side argues, China is evolving for the letter. "Twenty years ago, China was a closed society : no private enterprise, no phones, no hope, no future", said New York Congressman John J. LaFalce. "But when China normalized relations with the United States, things began to change". The Bill's proponents cited testimony from a long list of luminaries in an attempt to show that deeper trade links would push China in the right direction. Martin Lee was quoted as saying that 1.3 billion people should not be punished economically for the sins of the regime. The son of American Evangelist Bill Graham testified that a million Bibles were distributed in China last year. And the Dalai Lama, no softly on human rights, was cited as saying that it would be a good thing for China to be in the WTO.

When the vote finally came last Wednesday faith in American trade, technology and exports as proselytizing agents won the day. Of course, the victory was greatly aided by an extensive advertising and lobbying campaign mounted by the US Corporations in key congressional districts. Normal trade ties not only would benefit China, said TV ads sponsored by major companies and trade groups, but would bring jobs to Americans who would sell more soyabeans, computers, mobile phones and Tom Cruise movies in markets newly opened by the agreement and Beijing's accession to the WTO. The battle is won. But remains to be seen whether this faith in American enterprises is well placed, whether it can actually promote change. And will Americans even sell more in China? May be, but only with a great deal of efforts by the US Companies. The US might be able to double its exports to China in the next five years. Still, American Corporations are huffing and puffing with excitement at what they view as the huge potential of the Chinese market.

67. According to the passage things changed in China:
A. With the advent of modernism
B. After the Govt's decision to open to the Wesrern World and relationship between US and China
C. Relationship between UK and China
D. None of these

68. The China—US window opened mainly for:
A. Trade and Commerce
B. Employment Opportunities
C. Foreign Policies
D. All of these

69. At the turn of events, the author is:
A. Very optimistic B. Very pessimistic
C. Altruistic D. Skeptical

70. What does "proselytizing agents" refer to in the passage?
A. Priests
B. People who convert others to their religion
C. Those who get a commission for every conversation
D. Trade, technology and exports convince people they are for their betterment

71. Select a word which means "someone who talks about something with great enthusiasm".
A. Allies B. Evangelist
C. Proponent D. None of the above

72. Which of the following poems of Chaucer written after the death of the wife of Chaucer's Patron, John of Gaunt?
A. Complaynte to Pite
B. Book of the Duchess
C. The 'ABC'
D. Troilus and Criseyde

73. The Faery Queen is the great work upon which _______ fame chiefly rests.
A. Chaucer's B. Sack Ville's
C. Spencer's D. Sidney's

74. "Hell hath no limits, nor is circumscribed
In oneself place; for where we are is hell,
And where hell is there must we ever be."

The above lines are taken from:
A. Edward II B. Faustus
C. Tamburlaine D. The Jew of Malta

75. Which of the following plays begins on a street in Venice, in the midst of an argument between Roderigo and Jago?
A. King Lear B. Henry IV
C. Othello D. Tempest

76. "Fair is foul and foul is fair"—in which play this quote occur?
A. Macbeth
B. The Merchant of Venice
C. As You Like It
D. The Winter's Tale

77. The climax of the Merchant of Venice takes place in:
A. The court of the Duke of Venice
B. The house of Shylock
C. In Belmont
D. Morocco

78. Who wrote the romance 'Rosalynde' which supplied the plot for Shakespeare's 'As You Like It'?
A. Greene B. Lodge
C. Lyly D. Nash

79. In which play does Forest of Arden figure?
A. A Midsummer Night Dream
B. Macbeth
C. As You Like It
D. The Merry Wives of Windsor

80. "The Village by the Sea" is set in a small village called:
A. Thul
B. Kasauli
C. Chandni Chowk
D. Mirpore

81. 'Latter Day Psalm' is a poetry collection by:
A. Robert Frost
B. Vikram Seth
C. Nizzim Ezekiel
D. Mulk Raj Anand

82. _____ won the Sahitya Academy Award in 1984 and returned the same award in October 2015.
A. Khushwant Singh
B. Anita Desai
C. Vikram Seth
D. K. N. Daruwalla

83. The Protagonist John Brown and his friend Janet Hayakawa are the characters from:
A. The Golden Gate
B. An Equal Music
C. A Suitable Boy
D. None of the above

84. Railway Raju is a famous character by:
A. Mulk Raj Anand
B. R. K. Narayan
C. Khushwant Singh
D. Ruskin Bond

85. 'The Secret Life of Emily Dickinson', a novel written by:
A. Walt Whitman
B. Jerome Charyn
C. Mabel Loomis Todd
D. Edwin Arlington Robinson

86. Prometheus Unbound, a ______ is the best work of Shelley's revolutionary enthusiasm.
A. Novel
B. Prose
C. Lyrical drama
D. Play

87. Yahoos are the characters of ______ in his 'Gulliver's Travels'.
A. Defoe
B. Jonathan Swift
C. Addison
D. Tylor

88. The plot of 'The Pilgrim's Progress', centres on the journey of _____, the allegory's protagonist.
A. Evangelist
B. Pliable
C. Goodwill
D. Christian

89. 'The Mill on the Floss' is a novel by:
A. Thomas Hardy
B. George Eliot
C. Charlse Reade
D. Anthony Trollope

90. _____ wrote under the pen name Currer Bell.
A. Charlotte Bronte
B. Emily Bronte
C. Anne Bronte
D. Branwell Bronte

91. Universally accepted features of distance learning are:
A. Learner is at a distance from the teacher
B. Pre-produced course consisting of presentation brought about by other means that print
C. Organized non contiguous two-way communication
D. All the above

92. Subject are characterised by:
A. Being concepts independent of how they have been studied
B. Being studied by multiple discipline
C. Having little or no overlap wtth adjacent subjects
D. All the above

93. Education is a powerful instrument of:
A. Social transformation
B. Personal transformation
C. Cultural transformation
D. All the above

94. Teacher uses visual aids to make learning:
A. Simple
B. More Knowledgeable
C. Ouicker
D. Interesting

95. The transition from formal to non formal education may basically occur in two ways, they are:
A. The founding of institutions as open universities and the gradual advance of non formal elements
B. Founding of systematic, model and administration according to a given set of laws and norms
C. The founding of institutions with minimum classroom attendance and programs that the teacher and students must observe
D. All the above

96. The formal education has:
A. Participants who are found in all age brackets
B. Well-defined set of process
C. No adopted strategy
D. None of the above

97. Which of the following are known as receptive skills?
A. Listening and Speaking
B. Listening and Reading
C. Reading and Speaking
D. Speaking and Writing

98. Which of the following are the merits of using Bilingual method in teaching English?
A. Teacher saves time and makes conversation easier
B. It doesn't require specially trained teachers
C. This method is useful at lower stages of education
D. Both A and B

99. Which of the following are special features of academic discipline?
A. Discipline have a particular object of research
B. Discipline doesn't have theories and concepts
C. Disciplines have developed specific research methods
D. Both A and C

100. A teacher can establish rapport with his students by:
A. Becoming a figure of authority
B. Impressing students with knowledge and skill
C. Playing the role of a guide
D. Becoming a friend to the students

ANSWERS

1	2	3	4	5	6	7	8	9	10
C	B	D	C	A	A	B	C	D	B
11	**12**	**13**	**14**	**15**	**16**	**17**	**18**	**19**	**20**
B	D	A	D	C	D	B	C	B	B
21	**22**	**23**	**24**	**25**	**26**	**27**	**28**	**29**	**30**
B	C	D	B	D	A	B	B	A	D
31	**32**	**33**	**34**	**35**	**36**	**37**	**38**	**39**	**40**
A	C	A	C	A	A	A	B	A	C
41	**42**	**43**	**44**	**45**	**46**	**47**	**48**	**49**	**50**
C	A	B	B	C	B	A	A	B	D
51	**52**	**53**	**54**	**55**	**56**	**57**	**58**	**59**	**60**
A	D	B	C	B	B	B	B	D	A
61	**62**	**63**	**64**	**65**	**66**	**67**	**68**	**69**	**70**
B	D	D	C	C	D	B	A	D	D
71	**72**	**73**	**74**	**75**	**76**	**77**	**78**	**79**	**80**
C	B	C	B	C	A	A	B	C	A
81	**82**	**83**	**84**	**85**	**86**	**87**	**88**	**89**	**90**
C	D	A	B	B	C	B	D	B	A
91	**92**	**93**	**94**	**95**	**96**	**97**	**98**	**99**	**100**
B	B	B	D	A	B	B	A	D	B

Previous Paper (Solved)

Delhi Subordinate Services Selection Board

DSSSB–TGT (English) Recruitment Exam, 2015

POST SPECIFIC SUBJECT RELATED QUESTIONS

1. Diagrams can be used effectively to test which one of the following skills?
A. Application B. Speaking
C. Listening D. Watching

2. Education, according to John Dewey, is
A. a professional need
B. a family need
C. a psychological need
D. a social need

3. An effective counsellor must have all the following characteristics EXCEPT
A. a genuine rapport with counselee
B. perpetual sensitivity
C. identical personal traits as the clients
D. personal security

4. Effective classroom management is when there is
A. Creation of learning environment
B. Reduction of student misbehaviour
C. Creation of an orderly environment
D. Detection of inappropriate behaviour

5. The words a learner recognizes, but does not use in her/his speech or writing are called
A. productive vocabulary
B. formative vocabulary
C. active vocabulary
D. receptive vocabulary

6. All the following are valuable pieces advice to a language teacher designing oral activities for his/her students, EXCEPT
A. If the subject matter of the listening passage is related to the learner's needs, the teacher need not worry about the type of delivery of the passage
B. A thorough rehearsal of the script should be done before delivering the material for listening activity
C. The teacher should identify the learner's need for the kind of listening skill to be focussed
D. Both A and C

7. The main objective of teaching is
A. to impart information to students
B. to ready students for examinations
C. to bring about socially desirable behavioural changes in students
D. to give a thorough knowledge of the syllabus

8. Identify the practice which cannot be called 'a faulty reading habit'
A. regression B. silent reading
C. finger pointing D. subvocalization

9. While framing a question paper, a teacher has to ensure in it, the absence of
A. subjectivity
B. no use of vague words
C. reliability
D. objectivity

10. If a child speaks unusually loudly, the teacher should understand that the child may have
A. difficulty in speech
B. hearing impairment
C. arrogance
D. repairable voice disorder

11. Who among the following is a psychologist who has contributed immensely to the study of differences across stages of human development before adulthood?
A. Jean Piaget B. Carl Jung
C. Holland D. Sigmund Freud

12. Microteaching aims at
A. developing teaching skills in teachers
B. developing students' ability

C. achieving partial command of the subject
D. developing feedback skills of students

13. One of the functions of NCTE is
A. to prescribe syllabus for secondary education
B. to promote coordinated development of teacher education
C. to conduct surveys relating to education
D. to improve the quality of planning in education

14. As part of reinforcement, a teacher can utter "Wah!", "humm", "aha!" etc. This is usually categorized as
A. Positive Verbal Reinforcement skill
B. Negative Non-Verbal Reinforcement skill
C. Extra Verbal Cues
D. Negative Verbal Reinforcement skill

15. A good teacher is one who
A. lives an altruistic life
B. has command of the subject
C. has an impressive academic record
D. has genuine interest in his students

16. Which one of the following reading tasks do you use to think up a suitable title for reading passages?
A. Reading for detail
B. Skimming
C. Scanning
D. Understanding

17. The material or passage used to test the learner's listening skill must be
A. modelled on heard speech
B. densely structured
C. formal in style
D. read out very slowly

18. In a classroom, a good introduction by the teacher to a text to be used for reading comprehension exercise
A. Is elaborate
B. Is a one-way lecture by the teacher
C. Does not tell the students what they themselves can find out in the passage
D. Provides glimpse of all the important points in the passage

19. Which of the following is a style of Programmed Instruction developed by Norman A. Crowder?
A. Linear style B. Branching style
C. Framing style D. Mathematics

20. The most effective technique a teacher may use in order to enable students to attain 'Affective Level Objective' is
A. Experimentation
B. Discussion
C. Lecturing
D. Dramatisation

21. The Kothari Commission of Education was set up in
A. 1952 B. 1986
C. 1964 D. 1970

22. When we study the influence of heredity on individual differences of learners, we usually focus more on
A. Social heredity
B. Cultural heredity
C. Institutional heredity
D. Biological heredity

23. Curriculum can be designed and organized through
A. Context-centred approach
B. Subject-centred approach
C. Social-development approach
D. Teacher-centred approach

24. Holland's theory of careers assumes six kinds of environment populated by six types of individuals. Which of the following is NOT one of these six kinds of environment?
A. Realistic B. Virtual
C. Investigative D. Enterprising

25. Which of the following combinations has ONLY the criteria determining the selection of presentation mode for the content at hand?
A. Subject matter, evaluation, time available
B. Evaluation, instructional objectives, subject matter
C. Content, teacher's qualification, time available

D. Instructional objectives, student's back-ground, teacher's teaching style

26. Awarding 'grades' in place of 'marks' is recommended as

A. Grades have greater attraction for learners
B. Differentiation among students based on marks will be removed
C. Rote-learning is minimised
D. Oral examinations can be accommodated

27. Among the stages of cognitive development, pre-operational stage is the level at which an individual accomplishes

A. Trial-error behaviour
B. Inferences
C. Perceptual reasoning
D. Goal directed behaviour

28. National Talent Search Examination is conducted by

A. NCERT B. CBSE
C. MHRD D. NIEPA

29. Teaching-learning environment in school will suffer if

A. The autonomy of the learner is not respected
B. The teacher innovates incessantly
C. There are regular Parent-Teacher meets
D. The teacher is not paid promptly

30. Identify the process that is NOT involved in comprehension

A. Interpretation B. Extrapolation
C. Translation D. Perception

Fill in the blanks to complete the following sentences by choosing the appropriate word from among options given :

31. Since many old shops have _____ across the street, the earlier directory is _______

A. come up .... out-dated
B. started ..... anachronic
C. transferred .... redundant
D. relocated ... obsolete

32. The internet is a medium where users have nearly ______ choices and ______ constraints about where to go, and what to do.

A. unlimited .... maximum
B. abundant .... minimal
C. encouraging ..... frustrating
D. sufficient .... little

33. Besides extraordinary ________ skills, Raman had a ________ voice, which held his audience in rapture.

A. oratory .... sonorous
B. speaking ..... coarse
C. gift for the gab .... gruff
D. moralizing .... chirpy

34. The plotters met _____ so as to conspire a _____ against the oppressive rule of Julius Ceaser.

A. secretively ... ban
B. clandestinely .... revolt
C. aggressively .... crime
D. hiddenly .... mutinous

35. The daily accused the leader of _______ for making promises he knew he could not _______

A. impunity .... uphold
B. double-faced ..... keep
C. deception ..... keep
D. hypocrisy .... fulfil

Choose the appropriate prepositions from among the choices to fill in the blanks and complete the sentences :

36. The latest reports received say power-babu Paneek Chatterjee, at present ______ deputation in Washington D.C., is expected _____ take over as the Prime Minister's personal secretary.

A. upon ; up B. in ; to
C. on ; to D. in ; over

37. Now, a 50-paise coin is a numismatic slice of the past _________ fond memories _______ the people who experienced the anna-paise age.

A. of ; of B. with ; in
C. with ; for D. along ; for

38. There is a similar continuum ______ the optimism/pessimism axis ______ psycho-analysts.

A. in ; in B. on ; among
C. on ; in D. in ; between

39. Some economists argue that allowing the free-market to operate _______ interference is the most efficient method of establishing prices _______ all cases.

A. without ; in B. despite ; of
C. with ; of D. with ; in

40. Formerly, coal was considered the only source of energy; now, _______ the age of coal we have moved _______ the age of electricity.

A. out of ; to
B. from ; into
C. from ; over to
D. out of ; into

Choose the appropriate verbs to fill in the blanks and complete the sentences below:

41. A recent study done in the state, _______ 20 districts, revealed that the Siddhis _______ the poorest community in the state.

A. having covered; were
B. having covered; had been
C. covering; were
D. covering; are

42. In contrast to the expansion and development of business education in the U.S., Japanese b-schools _______ no more than two hundred MBA's each year.

A. have been graduating
B. graduating
C. graduate
D. would graduate

43. The welfare of all people can be increased only if we use available human resources in the most efficient way.

A. could have been increased
B. can be increased
C. has to be increased
D. must be increased

44. Conversely, if we _______ the luminosity of stars in other galaxies, we _______ their distance by measuring their apparent brightness.

A. could know ; would have worked out
B. knew ; could work out
C. know ; can work out
D. know ; could have worked out

45. Europe _______ us the higher obligations of public good, which _______ society independent of individual caprice.

A. has been teaching ; make
B. has taught ; making
C. has taught ; made
D. will teach ; makes

Choose the sentence that conforms to Standard English usage:

46. A. Those who wish to see mankind fruitful in the work which men alone can do, will take a little account of national boundaries.

B. Those who wish to see mankind fruitful in the work which men alone could do will take a little account of national boundaries.

C. Ones who wish to see mankind fruitful in the work which ones alone can do will take a little account of national boundaries.

D. Those who wish to see mankind fruitful in the work which men alone can do will take little account of national boundaries.

47. A. The more abstract the question you ask me, the hard it becomes for me to get in touch with any feeling at all.

B. The more abstract the question you ask me, the harder it becomes for me to get in touch with any feeling at all.

C. The most abstract the question you ask me, the hardest it becomes for me to get in touch with any feeling at all.

D. The abstract the question you ask me, the harder it becomes for me to get in touch with any feeling at all.

48. A. That in the end the great development of the scientific movement occured mainly in Protestant countries is due to the impotence of the natural churches.

B. That ended the great development of the scientific movement occured mainly in Protestant countries is due to the impotence of the natural churches.

C. End of the great development of the scientific movement occured mainly due to the natural impotence of the churches.

D. The end of the great development of the scientific movement occured mainly due in part the impotence of the churches.

49. A. Traditional Chinese medicine is believed to have less side effects and is preferred to chemical drugs.

B. Traditional Chinese medicine is believed to have fewer side effects and is preferred than chemical drugs.

C. Traditional Chinese medicine is believed to have fewer side effects and is preferred to chemical drugs.

D. Traditional Chinese medicine are believed to have fewer side effects and are preferred to chemical drugs.

50. A. No visitor can miss the sight of the imposing 10 feet tall idol of Lord Shiva at the entrance.

B. No visitor can miss the sight of the imposing 10 foot tall idol of Lord Shiva at the entrance.

C. Visitors can not miss the sight of the imposing 10 feet tall idol of Lord Shiva in the entrance.

D. Visitors hardly miss the sight of the imposing 10 feet tall idol of Lord Shiva at the entrance.

Read the following passage and answer the questions given below it :

The World Bank has been pressing for the removal of restrictions on Floor Space Index (FSI) - or at least their considerable relaxation - in the inner parts of Mumbai and Bangalore. The thinking that leads to this recommendation is based on a mathematical model.

Called the monocentric-city model, this assumes the city is inhabited by a number of identical residents, each earning the same income, and who all work in the Central Business District (CBD). The inhabitants commute from their residences to the CBD on a dense radial road network, paying a certain amount per round-trip mile (including the cost of travel time). An implicit assumption is that commuting is by car, not by public transport that might lead to some preferred travel routes, and not by walking which incurs no explicit travel cost. Further, each resident is assumed to be a renter, paying a certain amount per square foot of housing, and occupying a certain amount of square feet of housing. The price naturally falls with distance from the CBD, and the housing area occupied increases.

The mathematical formulation then moves through various complexities to the consideration of FSI, and what happens when FSI is restricted (as it is in most cities). The FSI restriction tends to limit population density in the central part of the city; and so causes the city to spread out.

Studying the condition of the new resident as the city grows, the model suggests that if FSI restrictions in the inner city are removed, this accommodates more people closer to the centre and so their commuting times are reduced. This is claimed to result in a welfare gain for them, which is measured in terms of their reduced commuting costs. So the claim is that lifting FSI restrictions brings about overall welfare gain.

The first indication that something is flawed in the argument comes from consideration of where the limit lies if we allow unlimited densification. Every increment in density will result in still more saving for commuters. As the model stands, there is no limit to the saving possible, until commuting cost is reduced to zero. We are obviously missing something. There has to be a constraining parameter that would put a cap, sooner or later, on how small the city can get while being both efficient and attractive.

51. The author of the passage is to likely to agree with which of the following?

A. The monocentric-city model from the World Bank assumes homogeneity of metropolitan cities in India.

B. The World Bank has vehemently put across its emphasis on removal of restrictions on FSI, using a laudable mathematical model.

C. The monocentric-city model assumes a homogeneous life style among the residents in the inner parts of the two cities.

D. Because of the mathematical model of the World Bank, there is stunningly unlimited saving possibility, leading to zero commuting cost.

52. It can be inferred from the passage that

A. The monocentric-city model of the World Bank assumes that each resident in Mumbai earns the same income.

B. As per the monocentric-city model, every individual working in the CBD has a car to commute to the place of work.

C. The monocentric-city model does not consider the residents going to work by walking because it costs no travel charges.

D. The monocentric-city model of the World Bank unfortunately ignores the importance of public transport for a Bangolorean.

53. Which of the following is TRUE according to the first paragraph of the passage?

A. The World Bank has been demanding nothing less than total repeal of FSI in Mumbai and Bengaluru.

B. The World Bank has been flexible in allowing for even a considerable relaxation based on a mathematical model.

C. The mathematical model on which the World Bank's recommendations are based is called 'mono-centric-city model'.

D. The World Bank has preferred to demand for removal of restrictions on FSI only in some areas of Mumbai and Bengaluru.

54. The attitude of the author of the passage towards the World Bank's demand and its basis can be best described as

A. Appreciative B. Critical

C. Sceptical D. Indifferent

55. Which of the following best reflects the relationship among the distance from CBD, rent on housing space and the occupied housing area in Mumbai and Bengaluru?

A. Distance from CBD and rentals on housing are inversely related while housing area occupied increases away from CBD.

B. Both housing rentals and area occupied are inversely related to the distance from CBD.

C. All the three are inversely related to one another.

D. All the three increase proportionate to an increase in one of them.

Read the following passage and answer the questions set on it :

Pope Benedict's sudden resignation has stunned the world, and Pundits are searching for motivations beyond his plea of old age. To complicate matters, there is also a strange 900-year-old prophecy involved.

According to a famous prophecy made by St. Malachy, a clairvoyant Bishop of the 12th century, there would be 112 more Popes. Pope Benedict, who resigned, was the 111th. And whoever is elected Pope in the next few days will be the 112th. During the papacy of this final Pope, says the prophecy, Rome - and the Church - will be wiped out! To quote its ominous words : "The City of Seven Hills shall be destroyed, and the dreadful Judge shall judge the people".

Rubbish, one might say. We have heard a lot of lunatic Doomsday predictions, and the Mayan prophecy is still fresh in our minds. But this time there is one small difference: St. Malachy actually described each of the 111 Popes till date with eerie accuracy, summing up each one with a vivid Latin phrase. And so far he's never been wrong.

For example, he described Pope Paul VI as 'Flos Florum', meaning 'Flower of Flowers'. Paul VI's coat of arms, as it happened, featured three Iris blossoms. His successor, Pope John Paul I, was described as 'De Medietate Lunae', or 'Of the half moon'. This was puzzling, because the description just did not seem to fit. But one month later, when John Paul I suddenly died, one realized that he had become Pope at the time of the half moon and died by the next half moon. His successor, Pope John Paul II, was described as 'De Labore Solis', or 'Of the eclipse of the sun' : it turned out he was born during a solar eclipse!

People have been talking about the prophecy of the Popes with increasing frequency since the 1970s, as the end of the line drew closer. In 2005, when John Paul II, the 110th Pope, died, people looked at the prophecy again, in anticipation, and found the next Pope described as 'Gloria Olivae', or 'The Glory of the Olive'. But what did this mean? Some people thought it signified Israel; others said it meant the new Pople would be a Benedictine, an order symbolised by the olive. Sure enough, the conclave ultimately elected Cardinal Joseph Ratzinger, a Benedictine priest from Germany, who—to seeminly reinforce the prophecy—took the name Pope Benedict XVI, after the founder of the order.

56. St. Malachy's prediction regarding Pope John Paul I was

A. Proven and made apparent posthumously
B. Realized by the suddenness of his death
C. Considered perfect because of its timing
D. Ratified only by his becoming Pope at the time of the half moon

57. All the following reflect the author's opinions as given in the passage, EXCEPT

A. St. Malachy's predictions show a high degree of accuracy
B. The World is really shocked by Pope Benedict XVI's announcement of his resignation
C. St. Malachy's prophecy holds the same promise as the Mayan prophecy.
D. St. Malachy's prophecy has compounded the already intriguing episode of Pope Benedict's resignation and its impact

58. Which of the following best describes the author's reaction towards the accuracy of St. Malachy's predictions?

A. The author is dismayed by their accuracy
B. The author realizes gradually how accurate the predictions are
C. The author rubbishes the probability of these predictions
D. The author is surprised at the rate of accuracy of these predictions

59. According to the passage, how are the realization of the prediction for Pope Benedict XVI as 'The Glory of the Olive', and the final selection of a Benedictine priest as Pope related?

A. That Pope took the name Pope Benedict XVI
B. Benedictine Order is symbolised by the Olive
C. 'The Glory of the Olive' signified Israel
D. They are connected by the demise of Pope John Paul II in 2005

60. Chronologically, which one of the following successions of Popes is correct?

A. St. Malachy → Pope Paul IV → Pope John Paul I → Pope John Paul II
B. Pope Paul VI → Pope John Paul I → Pope John Paul II → Pope Benedict XVI
C. Pope John Paul I → Pope John Paul II → Joseph Ratzinger → Pope Benedict XVI
D. Pope Benedict XVI → St. Malachy → Pope Paul VI → Pope John Paul I

Pick the sentence that conforms to Standard English usage :

61. A. Most are of the opinion that so long as handwriting is legible and not a scrawl, one should not face any ridicule from others regarding his or her handwriting.
B. Most are of the opinion that as long as handwriting is legible and not a scrawl, one should not face any ridicule from others regarding one's handwriting.
C. Most are of the opinion that as long as handwriting is legible and not a scrawl, an individual should not face any ridicule from others regarding one's handwriting.
D. Many are of the opinion that as long as handwriting is legitimate and not a scrawl, one should not face any ridicule from others regarding his or her handwriting.

62. A. I have known no culture which is as much scornful as we of cultures that have done better.
B. I have known no culture which is as scornful as we of cultures that have done well.

C. I have known no other culture which is as scornful as we are of cultures that have done better.

D. I have known no other cultures which is as scornful as we are of cultures that have done well.

63. A. Neither it is feasible nor desirable to keep India's foodgrain sector insulated from world markets.

B. It is neither feasible nor is desirable to keep India's foodgrain sector insulating from world markets.

C. It neither is feasible nor desirable to keep India's foodgrain sector insulating from world markets.

D. It is neither feasible nor desirable to keep India's foodgrain sector insulated from world markets.

64. A. Human wildlife conflict is not new, but the reports of these incidents reflect that it is at its worst now.

B. Human wildlife conflict is not new, but the reports of these incidents reflects that is at its worse now.

C. Human wildlife conflicts are not new, but the reports of these incidents reflects that they are at their worst now.

D. Human wildlife conflict is not new, but these reports of the incidents reflect that they are at their worse now.

65. A. The impact of Tagore's ideas upon Gandhi and Nehru has perhaps been given less attention than they deserve.

B. The impact of Tagore's ideas upon Gandhi and Nehru have perhaps been given less attention than they deserve.

C. The impact of Tagore's ideas upon Gandhi and Nehru has perhaps been given least attention than it deserves.

D. The impact of Tagore's ideas on Gandhi and Nehru has perhaps been given less attention than it deserves.

Each of the following sentences is divided into four segments. Find out which of these segments is grammatically erroneous :

66. (A) I still feel/(B) that the distribution of our responsibilities/(C) is not quiet/(D) as neat as it may appear at first.

67. (A) We lived so close to the airport/(B) that, from our balcony,/(C) I could see/(D) aircrafts take off and land.

68. (A) With their comical faces/(B) and stuffed toy looks/(C) lemur is/(D) Madagascar's biggest tourist draw.

69. (A) Not only these odes/(B) convince scholars of their antiquity/(C) but they also received/(D) some fine critical acclaim.

70. (A) The recent charges/(B) levelled by a former Vice Chancellor/(C) against the highest authority of the universities/(D) is shocking.

Following are parts of a single sentence. Pick the grammatically correct parts among these and choose the combination with the numbers of these correct parts :

71. (i) The Harassed Husbands of Borivali,
(ii) One of the last suburb
(iii) On Mumbai's Western Railway line,
(iv) Used to meeting in the Sanjay Gandhi National Park.

A. (i), (ii) and (iii) B. (i) and (iv)
C. (i) and (iii) D. (iii) and (iv)

72. (i) Married Subhash
(ii) In over thirty years,
(iii) Madhu thinks
(iv) They are made for one another.

A. only (iii) B. (ii) and (iv)
C. (ii) and (iii) D. (i) and (iv)

73. (i) All language teachers
(ii) Agree in Principle
(iii) That testing student's command of spoken language
(iv) Is important to judge their overall language competence.

A. (i), (ii) and (iii) B. (i), (ii) and (iv)
C. (iii) and (iv) D. (ii) and (iv)

74. (i) Even if China's trade data
(ii) Is showing signs of a recovery,

(iii) Bilateral trade with India
(iv) Has remained at a slump.
A. (ii) and (iv) B. (i) and (ii)
C. (i) and (iii) D. (ii) and (iii)

75. (i) My grandfather and me
(ii) Were good friends
(iii) And we had been constantly together
(iv) For a long times
A. (ii) and (iv) B. only (iii)
C. only (ii) D. (ii) and (iii)

76. Which of the following works of Walter Scott is not a novel?
A. Ivanhoe
B. Kenilworth
C. The Bride of Lammermoor
D. The lady of the lake

77. Match the poems with their poets :
(*a*) Siegfried Sassoon 1. 1916 seen from 1921
(*b*) Wilfred Owen 2. Survivors
(*c*) Edmund Blunden 3. Anthem for Doomed Youth
(*d*) W.B. Yeats 4. Municipal Gallery

	(*a*)	(*b*)	(*c*)	(*d*)
A.	3	1	2	4
B.	2	3	1	4
C.	2	3	4	1
D.	3	2	4	1

78. In Hardy's 'Tess of the D'Urbervilles', who is described as "a fly on a billiard table of infinite length"?
A. Tess B. Henchard
C. Mrs. Yeobright D. Angel Clare

79. Charles Lamb wrote under the pseudonym
A. H.D.
B. Elia
C. Samuel L. Clemens
D. Alpha of the plough

80. Which of the following is not considered as a metaphysical poet?
A. George Herbert
B. Henry Vaughan
C. Robert Burns
D. Richard Crashaw

81. One of these writers below is a distinguished novelist. He has contributed a lot to the sub-genre called 'campus novel', demystifying and debunking university academics. Who is the writer being referred to?
A. James Joyce
B. David Lodge
C. J.K. Rowling
D. P.G. Woodhouse

82. The concept of 'Affective Fallacy', as identified by the new critics, is tendency to judge a work by
A. its effect on the reader
B. the intentions of its author
C. its realisation of the fictitious world
D. its affectations as shown through the characters

83. 'Astropel and Stella' is a collection of songs and sonnets by
A. Philip Sydney
B. Henry Howard
C. Edmund Spenser
D. John Milton

84. "There is sweet music here that softer falls,
Than petals from blown roses on the grass,"
These lines appear in one of Tennyson's poems. Who utter/s these words?
A. Tithonus
B. Ulysses
C. Telemachus
D. Companions of Ulysses

85. Which of the following can best reflect the subject of Nathaniel Hawthorne's 'The Scarlet Letter'?
A. hereditary evil
B. the unconscious cruelty
C. sinful passion
D. human progress

86. Which of the following works sought to explain in terms of structuralist anthropology, the presence in diverse cultures of the idea that women were subordinate to men.
A. 'Having Faith'
B. 'Is Female to Male as Nature is to Culture?'

C. 'In Search of Our Mother's Gardens'
D. 'Sexual Politics'

87. "Away ! away ! for I will fly to thee,
Not charioted by Bacehus and his Pards,
But on the viewless wings of poesy...."
These lines appear in
A. John Keats' 'Ode to a Nightingale'
B. William Wordsworth's 'To the Skylark'
C. Thomas Campbell's 'Ode to Winter'
D. P.B. Shelley's 'To a Skylark'

88. Find the correct chronological order of the following Shakespearean plays
A. Macbeth → Romeo and Juliet → The Comedy of Errors → The Tempest
B. The Comedy of Errors → The Tempest → Romeo and Juliet → Macbeth
C. The Comedy of Errors → Romeo and Juliet → Macbeth → The Tempest
D. Romeo and Juliet → The Comedy of Errors → Macbeth → The Tempest

89. Who among the following is/are the writer/s of 'The Female Spectator'?
A. Addison and Steele
B. Jonathan Swift
C. Charles Lamb and Mary Lamb
D. Eliza Haywood

90. 'Pen is mightier than the sword' is an example of
A. Oxymoron B. Synecdoche
C. Hyperbole D. Metonymy

91. A petrarchan sonnet has two parts.
The second part has six lines.
The first part of the sonnet is called
A. an octave B. a couplet
C. a quartrain D. a sestet

92. Among T.S. Eliot's works, the character of Tiresias appears in
A. 'Gerontion'
B. 'Murder in the Cathedral'
C. 'The Love Song of Alfred Prufrock'
D. 'The Wasteland'

93. "The nature found in his works is a violent, barbaric and blood-ridden one." Here 'his works' refers to the poems of
A. Roy Fisher
B. Ted Hughes
C. William Wordsworth
D. Geoffrey Hill

94. Charles Darwin's 'On the Origin of the Species' appeared in the year
A. 1880 B. 1611
C. 1859 D. 1832

95. Which of the following is not a work by Dr. Samuel Johnson?
A. 'An History of the Earth and Animated Nature'
B. 'The Vanity of Human Wishes'
C. 'Rasselas'
D. 'Lives of the English Poets.'

96. Munoo is the central character in Mulk Raj Anand's novel
A. 'Kanthapura' B. 'The Untouchable'
C. 'The Village' D. 'Coolie'

97. The play wright who has written the play 'Ulysses' is
A. Stephen Philips
B. G.B. Shaw
C. Harold Pinter
D. James Joyce

98. Fra Pandolf's name finds mention in Robert Browning's
A. 'Rabbi Ben Ezra'
B. 'The Bishop Orders His Tomb'
C. 'My Last Duchess'
D. 'Pippa's Song'

99. 'Hamartia' means
A. error of judgement
B. pride
C. reversal in fortune
D. discovery of facts

100. "The primary aim of literature is to estrange or defamiliarize"—These words sum up the essential contention of
A. Deconstruction
B. Russian Formalism
C. Eco-Criticism
D. Practical Criticism

ANSWERS

1	2	3	4	5	6	7	8	9	10
B	D	C	A	D	A	C	B	A	B
11	12	13	14	15	16	17	18	19	20
A	A	B	C	D	B	A	C	B	D
21	22	23	24	25	26	27	28	29	30
C	D	B	B	D	B	C	A	A	D
31	32	33	34	35	36	37	38	39	40
D	B	A	B	D	C	C	B	A	B
41	42	43	44	45	46	47	48	49	50
D	C	B	B	A	D	B	A	C	B
51	52	53	54	55	56	57	58	59	60
C	B	D	C	A	A	C	D	B	B
61	62	63	64	65	66	67	68	69	70
B	C	D	A	D	C	D	C	A	D
71	72	73	74	75	76	77	78	79	80
C	A	B	D	C	D	B	A	B	C
81	82	83	84	85	86	87	88	89	90
B	A	A	D	C	B	A	C	D	D
91	92	93	94	95	96	97	98	99	100
A	D	B	C	A	D	A	C	A	B

ENGLISH LANGUAGE

1 Comprehension Passages

INTRODUCTION

In the English language paper, questions on comprehension test are very important for the aspirants appearing in the competitive examinations. Therefore, you should try to learn how to solve these questions. Practice of solving these questions will greatly help you in the examination.

Comprehension means the act of comprehending or the capacity of the mind to understand. In the examination papers, questions on comprehension test are included to judge the ability of the aspirants to understand the given passage.

Directions: *In this chapter few passages for comprehension test are given. Read the passages carefully and answer the questions given after each passage. Each question is provided with four alternative answers and they are marked as 'A', 'B', 'C', and 'D'. Out of the four alternatives, choose the correct answer according to the context of the passage.*

PASSAGE-1

A need of tremendous significance, which has been discussed recurrently in educational literature, relates to the creation of a demand for education. Of course, the underlying assumption in this concern is that notwithstanding how poor people view education today, its widespread diffusion up to a minimal level is essential for national well-being. If this proposition is accepted, then it becomes, imperative that measures should be taken to create a feeling in the community that their future would be at stake if they do not look after the elementary education of their children. Because of the present apathy, there is total dependence on Government, and consequently, there is hardly any effort on the part of a village or the community leadership or at the level of block or district, to set up or even to help the proper running of schools. It is undeniable that, to a great extent, this is also because the school system is now a part of a gigantic bureaucratic set up which leaves no room for intervention at the local levels and is, in effect, equally frustrating to a teacher with some initiative. If the community is to be involved, local resources, knowledge and skills will have to help in setting up and managing the schools; school children of suitable age will have to participate in community work; and learning experience including skill development will have to be provided in other establishments where necessary, if the schools do not have the related facilities. The community will also have to assume responsibility for maintaining the school buildings and for arranging midday meals, uniforms (especially for girls) and books, etc., as these would greatly facilitate the retention of children in the schools. This would be facilitated if the community is also authorised to keep an eye on the performance of schools and specially of the teachers.

1. The community is not able to take active part in the running of schools largely because

A. the community has no interest in the school system

B. the present day school system does not allow any local intervention
C. the teachers have no initiative for community work
D. the community leaders depend on the government

2. Which of the following measures DOES NOT indicate community involvement in the school system?
A. People in the community help in the setting up and management of schools
B. Many learning experiences are provided to children in establishments outside school
C. Schools become a part of the bureaucratic system
D. People assume the responsibility of arranging midday meals, uniforms, etc.

3. "Its widespread diffusion up to minimal level is essential." Here DIFFUSION means
A. dissemination B. proclamation
C. publicity D. amplification

4. Today the most significant need in the area of education is that
A. the schools should be run properly
B. people should look after the education of their children
C. education should be provided to all
D. people should themselves demand education

PASSAGE-2

It is easy to accept Freud as an applied scientist, and indeed, he is widely regarded as the 20th century's master clinician. However, Marx is better understood for being an applied sociologist. Marx was no Faustian, concerned solely with understanding society, but a Promethean who sought to understand it well enough to influence and to change it. He was chiefly concerned with the social problems of a lay group, the proletariat, and there can be little doubt that this work is motivated by an effort to reduce their suffering, as he saw it. His diagnosis was that their increasing misery and alienation engendered endemic class struggle; his prognosis claimed that this would culminate in revolution. His therapeutic prescription was class consciousness and active struggle.

Here, as in assessing Durkheim or Freud, the issue is not whether this analysis is empirically correct or scientifically adequate. Furthermore, whether or not this formulation seems to eviscerate Marx's revolutionary core, as critics on the left may charge, or whether the formulation provides Marx with a new veneer of academic respectability, as critics on the right may allege, is entirely irrelevant from the present standpoint. In so far as Marx's or any other social scientist's work conforms to a generalised model of applied social science, and in so far as it is professionally oriented to the value and social problems of laymen in his society, he may be treated as an applied social scientist.

Despite Durkheim's intellectualistic proclivities and rationalistic pathos, he was too much the product of European turbulence to turn his back on the travail of his culture. "Why strive for knowledge of reality, if its knowledge cannot aid us in life," he asked. "Social science," he said, "can provide us with rules of action for the future." Durkheim, like Marx, conceived of science as an agency of social action, and was professionally oriented to the values and problems of laymen in his society. Unless one sees that Durkheim was in some part an applied social scientist, it is impossible to understand why he concludes his monumental study of *Suicide* with a chapter on "Practical Consequence," and why, in the Division of Labour, he proposes a specific remedy for anomie.

1. According to the author, which of the following did Marx and Durkheim have in common?
A. Regard for practical application of science
B. An interest in penology
C. A belief in the importance of class struggle
D. None of the above

2. What action did Marx prescribe for the proletariat?
A. Alienation B. Passive resistance
C. Class consciousness D. None of the above

3. Marx sought to
A. Understand society
B. Change the educational system
C. Apply science to philosophy
D. Both (A) and (B)

4. It may be inferred from the passage that the applied social scientist might be interested in all of the following except
   A. the theory of mechanics
   B. rehabilitation of delinquents
   C. reduction of social tensions
   D. industrial safety

PASSAGE-3

The social Darwinist conception of evolution is not that of the biologist but of the propagandist looking for justification for his political theories. The simplistic formulation of ferocious antisocial struggle finds no place in the theories of modern biologists. Even on the animal level the scientific picture is not that of "struggle" and ruthless elimination. If in the tropics a pigmented skin is an advantage, no one is swept to destruction in a fight for blackness. Modifications of that sort, which prove advantageous, gradually establish themselves without trouble. Even living on other animals for food does not imply savagery—fishermen are not unpleasant and aggressive persons; tribes living, as they once did, on shellfish are not haters of their kind; even pig breeders and chicken farmers can be kind to their neighbours and no worse than the rest of us. Lorenz, constantly quoted to defend innate aggression, points out that the predatory carnivores are not angry when bringing down an antelope. It is simply a matter of going to fetch the dinner. A lion can be angry, but not when going out to kill. One might go on and take the whole case to pieces bit by bit, but enough has been said to indicate that the picture of "nature red in tooth and claw" is the poet's view—the phrase was Tennyson's—not the scientist's: it is tendentious, controversial exaggeration, not objective science. Even the notion of the "survival of the fittest" begs the question. If we say that the fittest survive, we only mean that they do survive. It implies no other quality than survival ability. It holds just as well for the oyster or the flourishing flea as for the beautifully adapted camel or flying fox. It does not follow that the survivor is the fittest even in being the finest specimen of its kind, let alone of the kind that we would prefer to see flourish.

1. The instinct to kill in carnivores comes from their
   A. need to survive
   B. need to prove their might
   C. inherently brutal nature
   D. liking for flesh
2. The writer's attitude towards poets is that of
   A. awe   B. scorn
   C. anger   D. indifference
3. The term 'survival of the fittest' suggests the survival of the
   A. mightiest   B. finest
   C. best   D. prepared
4. By citing various examples the writer tries to establish the fact that savagery does not entail
   A. killing of any kind
   B. killing of lesser animals
   C. killing dispassionately to serve an end
   D. ruthless killing
5. The concept of ferocious antisocial struggle finds credence with
   A. biologist   B. scientists
   C. Lorenz   D. Darwin

PASSAGE-4

The difficulty in the education of young infants is largely the *delicate balance* required in the parents. Constant watchfulness and much labour are needed to avoid injury to health : these qualities will hardly exist in the necessary degree except where there is strong parental affection. But where this exists, it is very likely not to be wise. To the devoted parents, the child is immensely important. Unless care is taken, the child feels this and judges himself as important as his parents feel but later in life his social environment will not regard him so fondly and the habit of assuming that he is the centre of other people's universe will lead to disappointment. It is, therefore, necessary, not only in the first year, but afterwards also, that parents should be breezy, cheerful and rather matter-of-fact where the child's possible ailments are concerned. In old days, infants were too much petted, sung to, rocked and dandled. This was wrong since it turned them into helpless pampered parasities. The right rule is : encourage spontaneous activities but discourage demands on others. Do not let the child see how much you do for him or how much trouble you take. Let him, wherever possible, taste the joy of success, achieved by his own efforts, not extracted by tyrannising over the grown-ups.

1. 'Delicate balance' required in parents in sentence one refers to
   A. cautiousness B. possessiveness
   C. indifference D. matter-of-factness
2. In the past the excessively fondled children became
   A. troublesome B. mischievous
   C. parasites D. abnormal
3. For the possible ailments of the child, the writer advised the parents to be
   A. indifferent B. demanding
   C. unsympathetic D. matter-of-fact
4. The author wishes the parents to let the child
   A. manage his own things
   B. be absolutely free
   C. work under their guidance
   D. seek anybody's help if needed
5. A child pampered by his parents is likely to become
   A. disappointed B. demoralised
   C. dependent D. independent

PASSAGE-5

The world dismisses curiosity by calling it idle or mere idle curiosity—even though curious persons are seldom idle. Parents do their best to extinguish curiosity in their children because it makes life difficult to be faced everyday with a string of unanswerable questions about what makes fire hot or why grass grows. Children whose curiosity survives parental discipline are invited to join our university. With the university, they go on asking their questions and trying to find the answers. In the eyes of a scholar, that is what a university is for. Some of the questions which the scholars ask seem to the world to be scarcely worth asking, let alone answering. They asked questions too minute and specialised for you and me to understand without years of explanation. If the world inquires of one of them, why he wants to know the answer to a particular question, he may say, especially if he is a scientist, that the answer will in some obscure way make possible a new machine or weapon or gadget. He talks that way because he knows that the world understands and respects utility.

But to you who are now part of the university, he will say that he wants to know the answer simply because he does not know it, the way the mountain climber wants to climb a mountain, simply because it is there. Similarly, a historian asked by an outsider, why he studies history, may come out with the argument that he has learnt to repeat on such occasions, something about knowledge of the past making it possible to understand the present and mould the future. But if you really want to know why a historian studies the past, the answer is much simpler, something happened and he would like to know what. All this does not mean that the answers which scholars find to their questions have no consequences. They may have enormous consequences but these seldom form the reason for asking the question or pursuing the answers. It is true that scholars can be put to work answering questions for the sake of the consequences as thousands are working now, for example, in search of a cure for cancer. But this is not the primary function of the scholars. The consequences are usually subordinate to the satisfaction of curiosity.

1. The common people consider some of the questions that the scholars ask unimportant
   A. as they are too lazy and idle
   B. as they are too modest
   C. as it's beyond their comprehension
   D. as it is considered a waste of time
2. According to the passage, parents do their best to discourage curiosity in their children
   A. because they have no time
   B. because they have no patience to answer them
   C. because they feel that their children ask stupid questions continuously
   D. because they are unable to answer all their questions

3. According to the passage, the children make life difficult for their parents
   A. by their ceaseless curiosity
   B. by unceasing bombardment of questions
   C. by asking irrelevant questions
   D. by posing profound questions
4. Children whose curiosity survives parental discipline means
   A. children retaining their curiosity in spite of being discouraged by their parents
   B. children pursuing their mental curiosity
   C. children's curiosity subdued due to parents' intervention
   D. children being disciplined by their parents
5. A historian really studies the past
   A. to comprehend the present and to reconstruct the future to
   B. to explain the present and plan the future
   C. to understand the present and make fortune
   D. to understand the present and mould the future

PASSAGE-6

I do not suggest that the cultural side of education should be ignored. On the contrary, I think, it is essential to the production of the sort of adult who best fits the modern world. But I think that what is important in cultural education should be conveyed, at any rate in the early stages, by methods far more attractive than those now usually practised. History and geography should be taught at first by means of the cinema. When taught this way, they will give pleasure; attention will be spontaneous and therefore the impression will be less temporary. In spite of reforming movements, there is still among educators a feeling that what is enjoyed without effort cannot have much educational value. I would have children made aware of the manners and customs of tribes and nations utterly remote from their own. Education conducted on these lines would do more than many books 'to cure provincialism in space and time' and to make children realize that actual human beings with actual feelings can be outwardly very different from the people among whom they live, but inwardly composed of the same human material. A Zulu would not appear strange, remote or savage but one like themselves.

1. The expression 'to cure provincialism in space and time' means to get rid of
   A. regional feelings B. obscure ideas
   C. narrow views D. selfish opinion
2. The writer thinks that the cultural side of education is needed to make man
   A. appreciate one's heritage
   B. appreciate other civilizations
   C. suitable for modern civilization
   D. admire his environment
3. The writer criticised traditional educators for not
   A. using cinema as a method of teaching
   B. making learning an enjoyable activity
   C. imparting information about remote tribes
   D. imparting information about various cultures
4. The response of the learners to teaching through cinema is
   A. absorbing B. long-lasting
   C. enthusiastic D. superficial
5. One of the goals of education should be to make children realise that
   A. human culture is diverse
   B. regional cultures should not be ignored
   C. they must respect values of alien culture
   D. there is a unified system of human values underneath cultural diversity

PASSAGE-7

Both plants and animals of many sorts show remarkable changes in form, structure, growth habits, and even mode of reproduction in becoming adapted to different climatic environment, types of food supply, or mode of living. This divergence in response to evolution is commonly expressed by altering the form and function of some part or parts of the organism, the original identity of which is clearly discernible. For example, the creeping foot of the snail is seen in related marine pteropods to be modified into a flapping organ useful for swimming, and is changed into prehensile arms that bear suctorial disks in the squids and other cephalopods. The limbs of various mammals are modified according to several different modes of life—for swift running (crusorial) as in the horse and antelope, for swinging in trees (arboreal) as in the monkeys, for digging (fossorial) as in the moles and gophers, for flying (volant) as in the bats, for swimming (aquatic) as in the seals, whales and dolphins, and for other adaptations. The structures or organs that show main change in connection with this adaptive divergence are commonly identified readily as *homologous* in spite of great alterations. Thus, the finger and wrist-bones of a bat and whale, for instance, have virtually nothing in common except that they are definitely equivalent elements of the mammalian limb.

1. The author provides information that would answer which of the following questions?
   I. What factors cause change in organism?
   II. What is the theory of evolution?
   III. How are horses legs related to seals flipper?
   A. I only B. II only
   C. I and III only D. I, II and III
2. Which is the most appropriate title for the passage, based on its content?
   A. Evolution
   B. Our Changing Bodies
   C. Adaptive Divergence
   D. Changes in Organs
3. The author organises the passage by
   A. comparison and contrast
   B. general statements followed by examples
   C. hypothesis and proof
   D. definition of key terms
4. The author's style can best be described as
   A. Objective B. Humorous
   C. Esoteric D. Patronizing
5. Which of the following words, could best be substituted for 'homologous' (in bold type) without substantially changing the author's meaning?
   A. Divergent B. Corresponding
   C. Altered D. Tactile

PASSAGE-8

Shames and delusions are esteemed for soundest truths, while reality is *fabulous*. If men would steadily observe realities only, and not allow themselves to be deluded, life, to compare it with such things as we know, would be like a fairy tale and the Arabian Night's entertainments. If we respect only what is inevitable and has a right to be, music and poetry would resound along the streets. When we are unhurried and wise, we perceive that only great and worthy things have any permanent and absolute existence—that petty fears and petty pleasures are but the shadow of the reality. This is always exhilarating and sublime. By closing the eyes and slumbering and consenting to be deceived by shows, men establish and confirm their daily life of routine and habit everywhere, which still is built on purely illusory foundations. Children, who play life, discern its true law and relations more clearly than men, who fail to live it worthily, but who think that they are wiser by experience; that is by failure.

I have read in a Hindu book that there was a king's son who, being expelled in infancy from his native city, was brought up by a forester and growing up to maturity in that state, imagined himself to belong to the barbarous race with which he lived. One of his father's ministers, having discovered him, revealed to him what he was and the misconception of his character was removed and he knew himself to be a prince, "So soul," continues the Hindu philosopher, "from the circumstances in which it is placed, mistakes its own character, until the truth is revealed to it by some holy teacher and then it knows itself to be Brahma."

We think that is which appears to be. If a man should give us an account of the realities he beheld, we should not recognize the place in his description. Look at a meeting house, or a court house, or a jail, or a shop, or a dwelling house and say what that thing really is before a true gaze and they would all go to pieces in your account of them. Men esteem truth remote, in the outskirts of the system, being the farthest star, before Adam and after the last man. In entirety, there is indeed something true and sublime. But all these times and places and occasions are now and here. God himself culminates in the present moment and will never be more divine in the lapse of all ages. And we are enabled to apprehend at all what is sublime and noble only by the perpetual instilling and drenching of the reality that surrounds us. The universe constantly and obediently answers to our conceptions : whether we travel fast or slow; the track is laid for us. Let us spend our lives in conceiving, then. The poet or the artist never yet had so fair and noble a design but some of his posterity at least could accomplish it.

1. The author believes that children are often more acute than adults in their appreciation of life's relations because
   A. children know more than adults
   B. children can use their experience better
   C. children's eyes are unclouded by failure
   D. experience is the best teacher
2. The writer's attitude towards the arts is one of
   A. indifference B. suspicion
   C. admiration D. repulsion
3. The passage implies that human beings
   A. cannot distinguish the true from the untrue
   B. are immoral if they are lazy
   C. should be bold and fearless
   D. believe in fairytales
4. The author is primarily concerned with urging the reader to
   A. mediate on the meaninglessness of the present
   B. appraise the present for its true value
   C. look to the future for enlightenment
   D. spend more time in leisure activities
5. The word 'fabulous' in the passage means
   A. wonderful B. delicious
   C. birdlike D. illusion

PASSAGE-9

In this world of human affairs there is no worse nuisance than a boy at the age of fourteen. He is neither ornamental nor useful.

It is impossible to shower affection on him as on a little boy and he is always getting in the way. If he talks with childish lisp he is called a baby, and if he answers in a grown-up way he is called *impertinent.* In fact any talk at all from him is resented. Then he is at the unattractive, growing age. He grows out of his clothes with indecent haste, his voice grows hoarse and breaks, and quavers, his face grows suddenly angular and unsightly. It is easy to secure the shortcoming of early childhood, but it is hard to tolerate even unavoidable lapses in a boy of fourteen. The lad himself becomes painfully self-conscious. When he talks with elderly people he is either unduly forward, or else so unduly shy that he appears ashamed of his very existence.

Yet it is at this very age when in his heart of hearts a young lad most craves for recognition and love; and he becomes the devoted slave of any one who shows him consideration. But none dare openly love him, for that would be regarded as undue indulgence and therefore bad for the boy. So, what with scolding and chiding, he becomes very much like a stray dog that has lost his master.

For a boy of fourteen his own home is the only paradise. To live in a strange house with strange people is little short of torture, while the height of bliss is to receive the kind looks of women and never to be *slighted* by them.

1. How do grownups react to a boy of fourteen whenever he speaks?
   A. They call him impertinent
   B. They call him a baby
   C. They resent it
   D. They call him either a baby or an impertinent fellow and resent any talk at all from him
2. Point out the figure of speech in the first sentence
   A. A metaphor
   B. An alliterative sentence
   C. Hyperbole
   D. Exaggeration
3. Point out any two unavoidable lapses in a boy of fourteen
   A. He grows painfully self-conscious and talk with a lisp
   B. He craves for love and recognition and behave like a stray dog

C. His voice grows hoarse and breaks and quavers, his face grows suddenly angular and unsightly
D. He is neither antenatal nor useful

4. What does a boy of fourteen crave for?
A. Recognition
B. The height of bliss
C. Recognition and love
D. Love and indulgence

5. "He becomes the devoted slave of anyone who shows him consideration." Point out the figure of speech.
A. Simile
B. Metaphor
C. Hyperbole
D. Personification

6. "He becomes very much like a stray dog that has lost his master" is a:
A. metaphor
B. good metaphor
C. bad simile
D. good simile

7. "Impertinent" in the slang means:
A. happy-go-lucky
B. care-a-hang
C. cheeky
D. rowdy

8. "For a boy of fourteen his own home is the only paradise." Substitute another word for "Paradise".
A. Heaven
B. Shelter
C. Haven
D. Garden

9. "The height of bliss" indicates
A. excitement
B. the greatest joy and happiness
C. the greatest fear
D. the feeling of shyness

10. 'Slighted' is Synonymous with
A. insulted
B. treated with love
C. beaten
D. scolded

PASSAGE-10

Foot-racing is a popular activity in the United States. It is seen not only as a competitive sport but also as a way to exercise, to enjoy the *camaraderie* of like-minded people and to donate money for a good cause. Though serious runners may spend months training to compete, other runners and walkers might not train at all. Those not competing might run in an effort to beat their own time or simply to enjoy the fun and exercise. People of all ages, from those less than one year of age (who may be pushed in *strollers*) to those in their eighties, enter into this sport. The races are held in city streets, on college campuses, through parks and in suburban areas and they are commonly 5 to 10 kilometres in length.

The largest foot-race in the world is the 12 kilometre Bay to Breakers race that is held in San Francisco every spring. This race begins on the east side of the city near San Francisco Bay and ends on the west side at the Pacific Ocean. There may be 80,000 or more people running in this race through the streets and hills of San Francisco. In the front are the serious runners who compete to win and who might finish in as little as 34 minutes. Behind them are the thousands who take several hours to finish. In the back of the race are those who dress in costumes and come just for fun. One year, there was a group of men who dressed like Elvis Presley and another group consisted of fire-fighters who were tied together in a long line carrying a fire-hose. There was even a bridal party, in which the bride and the groom threw flowers to bystanders and they were actually married at some point along the route.

1. The word "camaraderie" could best be replaced by which of the following words?
A. Games
B. Jokes
C. Companionship
D. Views

2. The main purpose of the passage is
A. make fun of runners in costumes
B. give reasons for the popularity of foot-races
C. describe a popular activity
D. encourage people to exercise

3. As used in the passage the word "strollers" refers to:
A. carriages
B. wheelchairs
C. wagons
D. cribs

4. Which of the following is not the reason why people enter foot-races?
A. To exercise
B. To enjoy
C. As a compulsion
D. For charity

5. Which of the following is NOT implied by the author?
A. Foot-races appeal to a variety of people

B. Running is a good way to strengthen the heart
C. Workers can compete for prizes
D. Age and profession is no bar to enter footraces

PASSAGE-11

Culture is the cultivation of plant or garden, not the eradication of its roots. It is an understanding of the roots and seeds, their patient care and instructed nourishment. Culture is not knowledge, nor is it art; still less is it acquaintance with literature and art. By culture, I mean first of all what the anthropologists mean; the way of life of a particular people living together in one place. Culture is made visible in their arts, their social system, their habits, their customs and their religion. It is an aggregate of customs, institutions, manners, standards, tastes, morals and beliefs. Now these are transmitted rather by the family than by the school; hence when family life fails to play its part, we must expect our culture to deteriorate. It is a delusion to think that the maladies of the modern world can be put right by a system of instructions. On the contrary, universal education, by lowering standards, morals and tastes to a common denominator and by sharpening the wits rather than disciplining character, tends to breakdown existing checks and balances. Education should be the drawing forth of potential values; it should not be the destruction of the safeguards that tradition places around the young egos naturally inclined to willful and precarious flights.

1. According to this passage, education is
   A. the sharpening of wits
   B. tapping and encouraging the inherent values in man
   C. the substitution of old traditions with new ones
   D. the development of moral standards
2. The passage suggests that universal education
   A. is the solution to the problems in the modern world
   B. is, in fact, aggravating the existing problems of the modern world
   C. would help retain the cultural values
   D. would prevent us from transmitting culture to the future generations
3. The writer uses the term 'culture' to refer to
   A. one's acquaintance with literature and art
   B. the cultivation of a plant or garden by a community
   C. the way of life of a particular people living together in one place
   D. one's acquisition of knowledge
4. The culture of a community is said to deteriorate when
   A. there is a fall in its educational standards
   B. the family life fails to play its part
   C. there is universal education
   D. it adopts the modern system of instruction
5. The culture of a community is transmitted
   A. more by school than the family
   B. more by the family than school
   C. equally by both
   D. by the peer group

PASSAGE-12

Every survey ever held has shown that the image of an attractive woman is the most effective advertising gimmick. She may sit astride the mudguard of a new car, or step into it ablaze with jewels, she may lie at the man's feet stroking his new socks, she may hold the petrol pump in a challenging pass, or dance through woodland glades in slow motion in all the glory of a new shampoo. Whatever she does, her image sells. The *gynolatry* of our civilization is written large upon its face, upon hoardings, cinema screens, television, newspapers, magazines, tins, packets, cartons, bottles, all consecrated to the reigning deity, the female fetish. Her dominion must not be thought to entail the rule of women, for she is not a woman. Her glossy lips and matt complexion, her unfocused eyes and flawless fingers, her extraordinary hair all floating and shining, curling and gleaming, reveal the inhuman triumph of cosmetics, lighting, focussing and printing. She sleeps unruffled, her lips red and juicy and closed, her eyes as crisp and black as if newly painted and her false lashes immaculately curled. Even when she washes her face with a new and creamier toilet soap her expression is as tranquil and vacant, and the paint as flawless as ever. If ever she should appear tousled and troubled, her features are miraculously smoothed to their proper veneer by a new washing powder on a bouillon cube. For, she is a doll : weeping, pouting or sinking, running or reclaiming, she is a doll.

1. The author's primary purpose in this passage is
   A. to ridicule women
   B. to show the dominance of women in advertising
   C. to portray the obsession of women with trivial thing
   D. to depict the emancipation of women

2. What point is the writer trying to make when he says "she may lie at a man's feet stroking his new socks"?
   A. Women like being subservient
   B. Women are observed with clothes
   C. This is a typical posture of women in advertising
   D. Women enjoy this kind of intimacy

3. The 'gynolatry' of one civilization would suggest all the following except that
   A. women enjoy immense power in modern society
   B. the image of women boost sales as few other things can
   C. women worship is all pervasive in advertising
   D. glamorous and attractive women are the forte of modern advertising

4. By saying that women depicted in an advertisement is 'not a woman' the author implies that
   A. in real life women are less attractive
   B. the depiction of women in advertisement is grossly artificial and unreal
   C. in real life women are more dominant
   D. in advertisement, a woman is a mere commercial symbol

5. In the last sentence of the paragraph, the word 'doll' is meant to express
   A. tenderness B. delicacy
   C. contempt D. beauty

PASSAGE-13

Today, every major *anthology* of ninteenth century poetry includes examples of the work which Christina Rossetti produced during her long literary *career.* Born in 1830, she began composing verse at the age of eleven and continued to write for the remaining fifty three years of her life. Her brother Dante Gabriel Rossetti, himself a poet and painter, soon recognised her genius and urged her to publish her poems. By the time of her death in 1894, Christina had written more than eleven hundred poems and had published over nine hundred of them. Although her work has earned her recognition as the greatest woman poet of the Victorian Age, there is still no authoritative edition of her poetry.

1. Christina Rossetti began writing poetry
   A. only after her brother urged her to do so
   B. when she was fifty-three years old
   C. when she was very young
   D. when her genuis was recognised

2. Christina's brother was probably a good judge of her work because
   A. he loved his sister very much
   B. he himself published poems
   C. he was a poet
   D. he was a famous painter

3. At the time this passage was written, Christina Rossetti's poetry
   A. was almost unknown
   B. was rarely published
   C. had made her known as the greatest woman poet of the eighteenth century
   D. had not been collected in an authoriative edition

4. By 1894, Christina had
   A. published only a few of the many poems she had written
   B. published all the poems she had written
   C. published more than eleven hundred poems
   D. published over nine hundred poems

5. The word "anthology" probably means
   A. writer B. collection
   C. poem D. poet

PASSAGE-14

Several years ago my parents, my wife, my son and I ate at a restaurant. After a wonderful dinner, the waiter set the bill in the middle of the table. That's what it happened, my father did not reach for the bill.

Conversation continued. Finally, it dawned on me. I was supposed to pay the bill. After hundreds of restaurant meals with my parents after a lifetime of thinking of my father as the one with the money, it had all changed. I reached for the bill and my view of myself suddenly altered; I was an adult.

Some people mark off their lives in years, I measure mine in small events—in rites of passage. I did not become a young man at a particular age, like 13, but rather when a boy strolled into the shop where I worked and called me "mister". The realization hit me like a punch; I was suddenly a mister.

I never thought that I would fall asleep in front of the television set as my father did. Now it's what I do best. I never thought I would prefer to stay at home, but now I find myself foregoing parties. I used to think that people who watched birds were weird, but this summer I found myself watching them, and may be I'll get a book on the subject. I yearn for a religious conviction that I never thought I'd want to feel close to my ancestors long gone, and echo my father in arguments with my son; I still lose.

One day I became a father, and not too long after that I picked up the bill for my own father. I thought then it was a rite of passage for me. But one day, when I was little older, I realized it was one for him too.

1. Which of the following does the author consider a rite of passage for him?
   A. Becoming thirteen years old
   B. Going to a restaurant with his parents, wife and son
   C. Being called 'mister' by the boy in the shop
   D. Working in a shop as a young boy

2. The author's father expected his son to pay the restaurant bill because
   A. he did not have enough money
   B. he acknowledged that his son was now an adult
   C. it was the first time the family was eating out together
   D. the waiter had set the bill in the middle of the table

3. "Rites of passage" for the author generally refers to
   A. events that mark the passage of time
   B. imitating his father as he grows older
   C. slowing down in his pace of living
   D. the act of growing old with time

4. In the fourth paragraph, the author makes the point that as people grow older they
   A. become lazier and less adventurous in their behaviour
   B. have to take on many more financial responsibilities
   C. turn to their children more for help and advice
   D. behave in the same way as their elders even if they never thought they would

5. In the fourth paragraph, 'foregoing parties' means
   A. going early to parties
   B. hosting many parties
   C. giving up parties
   D. going to many parties

PASSAGE-15

Language, they say, is the lens through which human beings perceive the world. If so, English is perhaps the most distorting lens through which to see animals. It has perpetuated a cross-eyed view of birds, beasts, fish and fowl. The very word 'animal' connotes the brutish and the sensual. Animal instinct implies baseness and vulgarity. The language transfers negative human traits to animals, making the former appear as characteristics of the latter. Thus, the chicken is cowardly, frightened, faint-hearted; the goat lustful and foolish; the bear rough and ill-bred. Butterflies are flighty, seals slippery and foxes notorious for craftiness and cunning.

Much the worst are the reptiles particularly the snake, creeping, base, malignant, abject, ungrateful and treacherous. Always the snake in the grass.

Each species carries its denigration forever embedded in its English name giving the language as many unpleasant adjectives as it could possibly want. To be bull-headed is to be impetuous and obstinate; the cattish woman is spiteful and backbiting. An elephant's walk is ungainly, bird-brains are to be ridiculed and the herd mentality draws only contempt. You can be as blind as a bat, and batty if you are crazy as well.

1. According to the passage, the chicken is
   A. cowardly, the goat cunning and the bear ill-bred
   B. simple, the goat foolish and the bear rough
   C. cowardly, the goat lustful and foolish and the bear rough and ill-bred
   D. faint-hearted, the goat lustful and ill-bred and the bear crafty
2. According to the passage, English language is the lens
   A. through which people see a correct picture of the world
   B. that does not permit one to see a correct picture of the world
   C. through which people see a distorted animal world
   D. through which people see the beautiful animal world
3. In the English language, the animals are
   A. used for uninteresting comparisons
   B. used for unpleasant comparisons
   C. used for pleasant comparisons
   D. not used for any comparisons
4. The phrase, "Always the snake in the grass" implies
   A. the snake hiding in the grass for its victims
   B. a dangerous person
   C. a person secretly working against you
   D. a harmless person
5. According to this passage, elephant walk is
   A. ungainly, bird brains ridiculous and herd mentality contemptible
   B. beautiful, bird brains ridiculous and herd mentality contemptible
   C. ugly, bird brains beautiful and herd mentality good
   D. ugly, bird brains ridiculous and herd mentality good

PASSAGE-16

Teaching, more even than most other professions, has been transformed during the last hundred years from a small, highly skilled profession concerned with a minority of the population, to a large and important branch of the public service. The profession has a great and honourable tradition, extending from the dawn of history until recent times, but any teacher in the modern world who allows himself to be inspired by the ideals of his predecessors is likely to be made sharply aware that it is not his function to teach what he thinks, but to instil such beliefs and prejudices as are thought useful by his employers.

1. According to this passage, in modern times a successful teacher is primarily supposed to
   A. impart knowledge
   B. impart new and the latest skills
   C. toe the lines preferred by those in authority
   D. instil values he cherishes the most
2. The author seems to
   A. be against the current trend in the teaching profession
   B. approve the recent developments in the mode of teaching
   C. be a traditionalist in his views
   D. consider education as a part of public service
3. The modern teacher is not able to follow the ideals of his predecessors because
   A. of tremendous advancements in professional skills
   B. of social and financial constraints
   C. the students are not serious about studies
   D. the modern teacher has more interest in politics than in academic activity
4. What has transformed teaching into an important branch of public service is
   A. teaching skills

B. technical developments
C. utilitarian philosophy
D. the demand of the employing industry

5. In ancient times the teaching profession was
A. limited to a highly skilled minority
B. reserved for the upper class
C. reserved for a privileged few
D. open to all

PASSAGE-17

Among the natural resources which can be called upon in national plans for development, possibly the most important is human labour. Since the English language suffers from a certain weakness in its ability to describe groups composed of both male and female members, this is usually described as 'manpower'.

Without a productive labour force, including effective leadership and intelligent middle management, no amount of foreign assistance or of natural wealth can ensure successful development and modernisation.

The manpower for development during the next quarter-century will come from the world's present population of infants, children and adolescents. But we have no assurance that they will be equal to the task. Will they have the health, the education, the skills, the socio-cultural attitudes essential for the responsibilities of development?

For far too many of them the answer is no. The reason is basic. A child's most critical years, with regard to physical, intellectual, social and emotional development, are those before he reaches five years of age. During those critical formative years he is cared for almost exclusively by his mother and in many parts of the world the mother may not have the capacity to raise a superior child. She is incapable of doing so by reason of her own poor health, her ignorance and her lack of status and recognition, of social and legal rights, of economic parity, of independence.

One essential factor has been overlooked or ignored. The forgotten factor is the role of women. Development will be handicapped as long as women remain second-class citizens, uneducated, without any voice in family or community decisions, without legal or economic status, married when they are still practically children, and henceforth producing one baby after another, often only to see half of them die before they are school-age.

We can enhance development by improving "womanpower," by giving women the opportunity to develop themselves. Statistics show that the average family size increase in inverse ratio to the mother's years of education—is lowest among college graduates, highest among those with only primary school training or no education. Malnutrition is most frequent in large families, and increases in frequency with each additional sibling.

The principle seems established that an educated mother has healthier and more intelligent children and that this is related to the fact that she has fewer children. The tendency of educated, upperclass mothers to have fewer children operates even without access to contraceptive service.

The educational level of women is significant also because it has a direct influence upon their chances of employment; and the number of employed women in a country's total labour force has a direct bearing on both the Gross National Product and the disposable income of the individual family. Disposable income, especially in the hands of women, influences food purchasing and therefore the nutritional status of the family. The fact that this additional income derived from the paid employment of women provides a logical incentive to restrict the size of the family.

1. The writer made only one of the following statements; indicate which one?
A. The world's present population of infants, children and adolescents is very healthy
B. The world's present population of infants, children and adolescents is very sickly
C. The world's present population of infants, children and adolescents may not be equal to its task
D. The world's present population of infants, children and adolescents is likely to go morally bankrupt

2. Among the natural resources which can be called upon in national plans for development?
   A. The most important is certainly human labour
   B. The most important is possibly human labour
   C. The least developed is certainly human labour
   D. The least developed is undoubtedly human labour
3. Without a productive labour force, including effective leadership and intelligent middle management
   A. No productive work is possible
   B. Entrepreneurs will incur heavy losses
   C. Economic development will not keep pace with nationalist movements
   D. No amount of foreign assistance or of natural wealth can ensure successful development and modernization
4. According to the writer, we can enhance development by
   A. giving women the opportunity to develop themselves
   B. making greater capital investments in agriculture and industry
   C. establishing Ministry of Economic Planning and Development
   D. increasing wages and improving general condition of service for all workers
5. The manpower development during the next quarter-century
   A. will be adversely affected by the threat of war
   B. will come from the world's present population of infants, children and adolescents
   C. Will be well taken care of by the current emphasis on free education for women
   D. Will be adversely affected by the country's economic losses and political instability
6. The writer directly or indirectly made three of the following statements; indicate the one he didn't make
   A. many of the world's present population of infants, children and adolescents will not have the health, the education, the skills, the socio-cultural attitudes essential for the responsibilities of development
   B. a child's most critical years with regard to physical, intellectual, social and emotional development, are those before he reaches five years of age
   C. development will be handicapped as long as women remain second-class citizens
   D. in the advanced countries of the world, women are regarded as first-class citizens, but in the developing countries they are third-class citizens.

PASSAGE-18

Many of the underdeveloped countries will promote the growth of their economies in one way or another, no matter whether they receive substantial outside aid in the process or not. The character of that development, however, is likely to be strongly influenced by the types and amounts of aid available. The outcome is much more likely lo be favourable, from the standpoint of the objectives for successful development set up previously, if there is substantial international aid than if it is not.

By substantial aid I mean not only large amounts of technical assistance but also of capital. Initially, the capacity of an underdeveloped country to use capital productively may be surprisingly small-limited by lack of organisation, trained personnel and other social obstacles. At this stage technical assistance is its main need from outside, with comparatively small amounts of capital, much of which may have to be in the form of grants for non-self-liquidating projects in education, health, access, roads to rural areas and the like.

If, at this stage, substantial capital is available from outside to supplement what can be formed internally (and to stimulate internal capital formation, for it does that too), the rate of economic growth can be considerably increased and the strains, frustrations and political risks of the development process are likely to be considerably less.

It is possible for underdeveloped economies to modernise themselves with very little capital from outside. Japan's imports of capital were small, though some of it came at crucial times. The contribution of foreign direct investments to the advancement of technical know-how also was greater than would be indicated merely by the size of the investment. The erstwhile Soviet Union industrialised its economy with practically no aid from foreign investment capital except for the foreign-owned installations confiscated after the revolution, though it imported machinery in the early days on short-term or intermediate-term credits and hired services of foreign experts.

Both Japan and Russia achieved their development in an authoritarian political and social framework. The outcome in both cases, from the standpoint of the peace of the world and democratic ideals, was highly unfavourable.

In the absence of outside aid, the only way to accumulate capital is to increase production without taking much of the benefit in more consumption, or even while pushing consumption standards down. Where the people are already near the subsistence level, this may mean extreme hardship. Somehow the people must be motivated to change their accustomed ways quickly, to work hard and to forego present consumption so that capital investment can be made.

1. The passage says that

A. Japan imported substantial capital before it became modernised

B. the Soviet Union industrialised its economy with plenty of foreign investment capital

C. Japan rejected offers of substantial foreign capital investment at the early stages of its economic development

D. in the early days of its economic development the Soviet Union imported machinery on short-term or intermediate term credits and hired foreign experts

2. Which of the following points or statements did the writer actually make?

A. Japan and Russia achieved their development in a democratic framework

B. Japan and Russia achieved their development in an authoritarian socio-political framework

C. Japan and the Soviet Union would have developed faster had they relied on democratic methods

D. Japan and the Soviet Union are still among the underdeveloped countries of the world

3. The passage says

A. without foreign aid no underdeveloped country can grow

B. underdeveloped countries must refrain from seeking foreign aid

C. the economies of under-developed countries are more likely to grow faster with substantial foreign aid and than without

D. Underdeveloped countries are economically backward because their governments have not got their priorities right

4. Substantial aid in this context means:

A. technical assistance, in the form of trained personnel

B. capital, in the form of bank loans and overdrafts

C. large amounts of technical assistance and capital

D. a cheap and plentiful supply of labour

5. The availability of substantial capital from outside

A. can help to stimulate internal capital formation

B. does encourage wasteful tendencies

C. seldom helps to accelerate the rate of internal growth

D. tends to discourage local capital formation

6. In the absence of outside aid, the only way to accumulate capital is to:

A. increase tax and import duties

B. launch an internal campaign for the conservation of goods and property

C. increase production without taking much of the benefit in more consumption

D. make conditions attractive to foreign investors

PASSAGE-19

Human analytical abilities remain vastly superior to anything demonstrated elsewhere in the animal kingdom. Virtually in all studies of animal intelligence and language skills, performance plummets as more elements are added to a task and as an animal has to remember these elements for long periods. By contrast, humans can call on vast working memory.

Many evolutionary scholars suspect that as ancient human groups became larger, the need to keep track of ever more complex social interactions was what really pushed the human brain toward superiority. Both dolphins and chimps have very complex interactions, but the intricacy of their social world pales beside the lattice of entanglements that characterised human society as early. Homosapiens bonded together to gather food and defend themselves. In Somalia today, warring clans identify friend or foe by demanding that those accosted recite their ancestry going back many generations. It is easy to see how similar challenges in antiquity might have driven the development of brainpower.

It does not lessen the grandeur of the human intellect to argue that it evolved partly in response to social pressures or that these pressures also produced similar abilities in "lesser" creatures. Instead, the fact that nature may have broadly sown the seeds of consciousness, suggests a world enlivened by many different minds. There may even be practical applications. Studies of animal cognition and language have yielded new approaches to communicating with handicapped and autistic children. Some scientists are pondering ways to turn intelligent animals like sea lions and dolphins into research assistants in marine studies or into lifeguards who can save the drowning upon command.

If the notion that animals might actually think poses a problem, it is an ethical one. The great philosopher, such as Descartes, used their belief that animals cannot think as a justification for arguing that they do not have moral rights. It is one thing to treat animals as mere resources if they are presumed to be little more than living robots, but it is entirely different if they are recognised as fellow sentient beings. Working out the moral implication makes a perfect puzzle for a large-brained, highly social species like our own.

1. Does the author believe that the grandeur of the human intellect is lessened by the fact that the same evolutionary pressure produced similar abilities in animals as in humans?

A. Perhaps yes B. Perhaps no
C. Yes D. No

2. What could be some of the practical applications of animal intelligence?

A. To use dolphins for solving difficult mathematical problems
B. To use some animals for guarding and supervising other animals
C. To develop new approaches to communicate with handicapped and mentally ill children
D. All of these

3. In many studies of animal intelligence and language skills, the performance significantly drops

A. as we move from humans to animals
B. membered for long periods
C. as we move from animals with large brains to those with small brains
D. as the time allowed to develop these skills is reduced

4. What makes a perfect puzzle for a large-brained highly social species like humans, according to the author?

A. Determining the moral implications of the fact that animals might actually think
B. discovering the real reason why nature developed the ability to think in animals
C. Deciding what should be the ideal relationship between humans and animals
D. To answer the question if animals are different from humans

5. What really pushed the human brain towards superiority?

A. The need to keep track of ever more complex social interactions

B. The need to develop efficient methods of gathering food
C. The need to find better methods of defending themselves
D. The need to evolve faster than other species

6. What is the ethical problem posed by the notion that animals might actually think?
A. It is difficult to accept that humans are also animals
B. animals should perhaps not be used in laboratory experiments
C. Animals cannot perhaps be treated as mere resources
D. It has to correctly assessed as to how much can an animal actually think

7. Why did early Homosapiens bond together?
A. They formed social groups as they were social animals
B. To gather food and to defend themselves
C. To maintain genetic purity
D. They were more comfortable with similar people

PASSAGE-20

The process of economic development of underdeveloped countries differs from that of developing countries and also from that of developed countries. Developing countries, though not all but most of them expect their domestic industries to be the basis for their programme of economic development. They generally earmark the local market for the new local industry by simply prohibiting imports that might compete. Although it may not be very efficient method, local industry can be guaranteed a profit because consumers within the nation are directly or indirectly forced to purchase the domestic product because of prohibition of imports or high tariffs on imports.

Developing countries have lots of natural resources and also they have labour available in abundance. Local-market industries may utilise both these very important assets. Foreign exchange credit of these countries can be conserved, even if the production materials or parts must be bought from other countries, because these imports will usually cost less than if the finished products were imported.

There are certain disadvantages in relying on local market industries as the basis for industrial development. With unlimited protection, these industries will never have reason to be efficient in their operation. With little or no competition from the world's large manufacturers, the quality of their products will probably be inferior. Yet, the country's consumers, unable to buy the same item from foreign producers, must purchase from the local industry in effect helping to subsidise its existence.

Real competition, in most developing countries, is unlikely to exist because of an inadequate market and a limited ability of the people to purchase. Companies may flourish because the power of the state has been used to force the consumers to support them. This may mean that to provide employment for a hundred workers in the new factory and profit of the owner, thousands of people must pay extra for every soap or tooth paste they buy. This unfair type of industrial development often contributes to social and political tensions. Market growth for many products is urgently needed if there is ever to be enough sales volume; but this is often made impossible by the high prices charged for locally made products.

1. Which of the following may be a source of unrest among the common people? The industrial development in which
A. imports are allowed without any hesitation
B. consumers are forced to buy foreign goods
C. consumers are allowed to buy imported consumables
D. people have to pay extra on their purchases

2. Which of the following is the effect of meagre buying power of people in developing countries?
A. The market is not fully equipped with modern tactics
B. Companies cannot make progress for want of resources
C. Foreign exchange reserves continue to reduce significantly
D. There is a likelihood of increase in social and political tension

3. In developing countries, the expenses on employment in factories and their owners profit are
   A. shared largely by the local industries against their desires
   B. shared proportionately between local and foreign producers
   C. borne wholly by the government
   D. required to be borne ultimately by the consumers
4. Which of the following factor(s) is/are in favour of the local manufacturers?
   (*i*) Availability of country's natural resources
   (*ii*) Cheaper labour
   (*iii*) Lower cost of imported raw materials
   A. Only (*i*) B. Only (*ii*)
   C. (*i*) and (*ii*) only D. None of these
5. According to the passage relying on local market industries for industrial development is
   A. the best among all available solution
   B. helpful to make local industries self-reliant
   C. not free from major demerit
   D. None of these
6. Which of the following is true about domestic companies in developing countries?
   A. They obtain assured profit through govt. support and have access to natural resources and labour
   B. These companies are extremely efficient
   C. The quality of their products is superior
   D. None of these
7. Which of the following is/are the most favourable impact(s) of prohibiting imports?
   (*i*) Profit to local industries is assured
   (*ii*) Foreign exchange reserves are reduced
   (*iii*) Imposition of any quality is assured
   A. (*i*) only B. (*ii*) only
   C. (*iii*) only D. All of these
8. Which of the following factors compel(s) the consumers to buy the domestic products?
   (*i*) The superior quality of domestic goods
   (*ii*) Rules and regulations that prohibit imports
   (*iii*) Very high import duties levies
   A. Only (*i*) and (*ii*)
   B. Only (*i*) and (*iii*)
   C. Only (*ii*) and (*iii*)
   D. None of these
9. The author thinks that the local industries are most likely to become inefficient because
   A. Of the inferior quality of their products
   B. Of the consumers fancy for buying foreign products
   C. these local industries enjoy unrestricted protection
   D. None of these

ANSWERS

PASSAGE-1

1	2	3	4
B	C	A	B

PASSAGE-2

1	2	3	4
A	C	D	A

PASSAGE-3

1	2	3	4	5
A	D	A	C	D

PASSAGE-4

1	2	3	4	5
A	C	D	A	C

PASSAGE-5

1	2	3	4	5
C	D	A	A	D

PASSAGE-6

1	2	3	4	5
C	C	B	C	D

PASSAGE-7

1	2	3	4	5
C	C	A	B	D

PASSAGE-8

1	2	3	4	5
C	C	A	B	D

PASSAGE-9

1	2	3	4	5
A	B	C	C	B
6	7	8	9	10
B	C	B	B	A

PASSAGE-10

1	2	3	4	5
C	C	B	C	C

PASSAGE-11

1	2	3	4	5
B	B	C	B	B

PASSAGE-12

1	2	3	4	5
B	C	B	B	D

PASSAGE-13

1	2	3	4	5
C	C	D	D	B

PASSAGE-14

1	2	3	4	5
C	A	A	D	C

PASSAGE-15

1	2	3	4	5
C	C	B	C	A

PASSAGE-16

1	2	3	4	5
C	D	A	C	A

PASSAGE-17

1	2	3	4	5
C	B	D	A	B
6				
D				

PASSAGE-18

1	2	3	4	5
D	B	C	C	A
6				
C				

PASSAGE-19

1	2	3	4	5
A	C	B	A	A
6	7			
C	B			

PASSAGE-20

1	2	3	4	5
D	D	D	C	C
6	7	8	9	
A	A	C	C	

2

Spot the Error

The most common errors in English are of spellings, grammar and usage of words. By regular practice, the errors can be easily spotted and minimised.

COMMON ERRORS WITH NOUNS AND NOUN-PHRASES

	Incorrect	Correct
1.	I have bought new *furnitures.*	I have bought new *furniture.*
2.	The wages of sin *are* death.	The wages of sin *is* death.
3.	She told these *news* to her mother.	She told her mother this *news.*
4.	He took *troubles* to do his work.	He took *trouble* (or pains) over his work.
5.	The *cattles* were grazing.	The *cattle* were grazing.
6.	He showered *many abuses* on me.	He showered *much abuse* on me.
7.	I spent the holidays with my *family members.*	I spent the holidays with my *family.*
8.	There is no *place* in this compartment.	There is no *room* in this compartment.
9.	Write this new *poetry* in your *copy.*	Write this new *poem* in your *note-book.*
10.	He took *insult* at this.	He took *offence* at this.
11.	Put your *sign* here.	Put your *signatures* here.
12.	She is my *cousin sister.*	She is my *cousin.*
13.	*Sunil's* my *neighbour's* house was burgled.	*Sunil* my *neighbour's* house was burgled.
14.	I lost a *ten-rupees* note.	I lost *a ten-rupee* note.
15.	Road closed for *repair.*	Road closed for *repairs.*
16.	His house is out of *repairs.*	His house is out of *repair.*
17.	What is the *reason* of an earthquake?	What is the *cause* of an earthquake?
18.	This building is made of *stones.*	This building is made of *stone.*
19.	I disapprove of *these kinds* of games.	I disapprove of *this kind* of games.
20.	Veena's and Sheela's father is ill.	Veena and Sheela's father is ill.
21.	His *son-in-laws* are doctors.	His *sons-in-law* are doctors.

Incorrect	Correct
22. *Alms* is given to the *poor.*	*Alms* are given to the poor.
23. He always keeps his words.	He always keeps his *word.*
24. I carried the *luggages.*	I carried the *luggage.*
25. *Two-third* of the work is left.	*Two-thirds* of the work is left.

COMMON ERRORS WITH PRONOUNS

Incorrect	Correct
1. Both did not go.	Neither went.
2. We all did not go.	None of us went.
3. Each of these boys play.	Each of these boys plays.
4. Whoever does best he will get a prize.	Whoever does best will get a prize.
5. One should not waste his time.	A man should not waste his time.
6. I and she are sisters.	She and I are sisters.
7. He is wiser than me.	He is wiser than I.
8. Between you and I, Anil is not to be trusted.	Between you and me, Anil is not to be trusted.
9. Nobody was there but I.	Nobody was there but me.
10. Who is there ? It is me.	Who is there ? It is I.
11. Only he and me can use this card.	Only he and I can use this card.
12. Let you and I go now.	Let you and me go now.
13. Everyone got one's pay.	Everyone got his pay.
14. Everyone is frightened when they see a tiger.	Everyone is frightened when he sees a tiger.
15. These two friends are fond of one another.	These two friends are fond of each other.
16. I did not like him coming at that hour.	I did not like his coming at that hour.
17. Who do you think I met?	Whom do you think I met?
18. You should avail this opportunity.	You should avail yourself this opportunity.
19. When you have read these books, please return the same to me.	When you have read the books, please return them to me.
20. They that are humble need fear no fall.	Those that are humble need fear no fall.

COMMON ERRORS WITH ADJECTIVES

Incorrect	Correct
1. These all oranges are good.	All these oranges are good.
2. He held the book in the both hands.	He held the book in both hands.
3. Both men have not come.	Neither man has come.
4. That man should do some or other work.	That man should do some work or other.
5. He is elder than I.	He is older than I.

Incorrect	Correct
6. Shakespeare is greater than any other poets.	Shakespeare is greater than any other poet.
7. He is a coward man.	He is a cowardly man.
8. Many villagers cannot write his own name.	Many villagers cannot write their own name.
9. Each of us loves our home.	Each of us loves his home.
10. Much efforts bring their reward.	Much effort brings its reward.
11. He found hundred rupees.	He found a hundred rupees.
12. He had leave of four days.	He had four days leave.
13. This is a worth seeing sight.	This is a sight worth seeing.
14. He will spend his future life here.	He will spend the rest of his life here.
15. There is a best teacher in that class.	There is a very good teacher in that class.
16. Of the two plans this is the best.	Of the two plans this is the better.
17. He is becoming strong every day.	He is becoming stronger every day.
18. He is worst than I.	He is worse than I.
19. Jaipur is hot than Delhi.	Jaipur is hotter than Delhi.
20. In our library the number of books is less.	In our library the number of books is small.
21. From the three he is more clever.	He is the cleverest of the three.
22. India is the first peace-loving country in the world.	India is the foremost peace-loving country in the world.
23. Verbal instruction will not do.	Oral instruction will not do.
24. Her command over French is most excellent.	Her command over French is excellent.
25. He has not some money with him.	He has not any money with him.
26. I have visited Bombay many a times.	I have visited Bombay many a time.
27. Death is more preferable to dishonour.	Death is preferable to dishonour.
28. I gave him a few books I had.	I gave him the few books I had.
29. If he wants farther help send him to me.	If he wants further help, send him to me.
30. She is so cunning as a fox.	She is as cunning as a fox.

COMMON ERRORS WITH VERBS

Incorrect	Correct
1. He asked had we taken our luggage.	He asked if we had taken our luggage.
2. She asked what are you doing.	She asked what we were doing.
3. Rama asked to Anil why he is angry.	Rama asked Anil why he was angry.
4. He does not care for his money.	He does not take care of his money.
5. He does not care for his work.	He takes no care over his work.
6. No one cared for him after his mother died.	No one took care of him after his mother died.
7. He got angry before I said a word.	He got angry before I had said a word.

Incorrect	Correct
8. I met a man who was my tutor 20 years ago.	I met a man who had been my tutor twenty years ago.
9. I had been for walking yesterday.	I went for a walk yesterday.
10. If I shall do this I shall be wrong.	If I do this I shall be wrong.
11. I have left trekking.	I have given up trekking.
12. I came to know as to how he did this.	I learnt how he did this.
13. I came to know why he was sad.	I found out why he was sad.
14. He knows to swim.	He knows how to swim.
15. The criminal's head was cut.	The criminal's head was cut off.
16. I said to him to go.	I told him to go.
17. I told the teacher to excuse me.	I asked the teacher to excuse me.
18. He is troubling me.	He is giving me trouble.
19. I have got a hurt on my leg.	I have hurt my leg.
20. She gave a speech.	She made a speech.
21. He has given his examination.	He has sat for his examination.
22. He took out his shoes.	He took off his shoes.
23. I have ordered for a new car.	I have ordered a new car.
24. He would not hear me.	He would not listen to me.
25. I struck a blow on his face.	I struck him in the face.
26. He denied to come.	He refused to come.
27. He lived there for a day.	He stayed there for a day.
28. The book is not found.	The book is lost.
29. Shut the light.	Turn off the light.
30. I must revenge my brother.	I must avenge my brother.

COMMON ERRORS IN SUBJECT-VERB AGREEMENT

Incorrect	Correct
1. The owners of this factory *is* very rich.	The owners of this factory *are* very rich.
2. The pleasures of nature that one can experience at Shimla *is* beyond description.	The pleasures of nature that one can experience at Shimla *are* beyond description.
3. There *is* no street lights in our colony.	There *are* no street lights in our colony.
4. He and I *am* entrusted with the job.	He and I *are* entrusted with the job.
5. Rice and curry *are* his favourite dish.	Rice and curry *is* his favourite dish.
6. The honour and glory of our country *are* at stake.	The honour and glory of our country *is* at stake.
7. Time and tide *waits* for none.	Time and tide *wait* for none.
8. All the passengers with the driver *was* killed.	All the passengers, with the driver, *were* killed.

	Incorrect	Correct
9.	The teacher, with her students, *were* going out.	The teacher, with her students, *was* going out.
10.	I as well as they *am* tired.	I as well as they *are* tired.
11.	Not only the soldiers but their captain also *were* captured.	Not only the soldiers but their captain also *was* captured.
12.	Neither you nor I *were* selected.	Neither you nor I *was* selected.
13.	Either of these two applicants *are* fit for the job but neither want to accept it.	Either of these two applicants *is* fit for the job but neither wants to accept it.
14.	One of these students are sure to stand first.	One of these students *is* sure to stand first.
15.	Everyone of these workers want a raise.	Everyone of these workers wants a raise.
16.	None of these letters has been answered so far.	None of these letters *have* been answered so far.
17.	None of the girls were present at the party.	None of the girls *was* present at the party.
18.	Many a battle were fought on Indian soil.	Many a battle *was* fought on Indian soil.
19.	A lot of work remain to be done.	A lot of work *remains* to be done.
20.	The majority of these girls likes music.	The majority of these girls *like* music.
21.	The number of admissions are encouraging.	The number of admissions *is* encouraging.
22.	A large number of boys was present.	A large number of boys *were* present.
23.	A variety of books was on display.	A variety of books *were* on display.
24.	Variety are the spice of life.	Variety *is* the spice of life.
25.	If my estimates are correct. I will need another hundred rupees.	If my estimate is correct, I will need another hundred rupees.
26.	Mathematics *are* my favourite subject.	Mathematics *is* my favourite subject.
27.	'Gulliver's Travels' *are* written by Swift.	'Gulliver's Travels' *is* written by Swift.
28.	Ten miles *are* a long distance to cover on foot.	Ten miles *is* a long distance to cover on foot.
29.	A new pair of shoes *are* to be purchased.	A new pair of shoes *is* to be purchased.
30.	The Committee *have* issued its report.	The Committee *has* issued its report.
31.	I, who am your friend, *has* always been on your side.	I, who am your friend, *have* always been on your side.
32.	I am the person who *have* always stood by you.	I am the person who *has* always stood by you.
33.	This is one of the best novels that *has* been published this year.	This is one of the best novels that *have* been published this year.
34.	Less than half the amount *have* been wasted.	Less than half the amount *has* been wasted.
35.	A lot of people *has* turned up for the show.	A lot of people *have* turned up for the show.
36.	Much of their honour *are* un-deserved.	Much of their honour *is* un-deserved.
37.	More than a decade *have* passed since this house was built.	More than a decade *has* passed since this house was built.
38.	Either she or he *are* mistaken.	Either she or he *is* mistaken.
39.	Plenty of information *are* available on the subject.	Plenty of information *is* available on the subject.
40.	Plenty of pamphlets *is* available on the subject.	Plenty of pamphlets *are* available on the subject.

COMMON ERRORS IN USE OF WILL, SHALL, WOULD, SHOULD, MAY, MIGHT, MUST

	Incorrect	Correct
1.	When I shall see him I shall tell him this.	When I *see* him, I shall tell him this.
2.	If I should do wrong, he would punish me.	If I *did* wrong, he would punish me.
3.	Until he will have confessed his fault, he will be kept in prison.	Until he *has* confessed his fault, he will be kept in prison.
4.	She will obey me.	She *shall* obey me.
5.	You would work hard.	You *should* work hard.
6.	You shall find him in the garden.	You *will* find him in the garden.
7.	He must have died of exposure, but we cannot be certain.	He *might* have died of exposure, but we cannot be certain.
8.	You might not show disrespect to your elders.	You *must* not show disrespect to your elders.
9.	You may take exercise in order to maintain good health.	You *must* take exercise in order to maintain good health.
10.	He must be a crook for all we know.	He *may* be a crook for all we know.

COMMON ERORRS IN THE USE OF ADVERBS

(Very, Much, Too, Enough, Quite, Hardly, Scarcely, Before, Ago, Since, Yet, Still, etc.)

	Incorrect	Correct
1.	He is very much angry.	He is *very* angry.
2.	She was very good enough to help me.	She was *good enough* to help me.
3.	She runs much fast.	She runs *very* fast.
4.	She runs very faster than Seema.	She runs *much* faster than Seema.
5.	It is bitter cold today.	It is *bitterly* cold today.
6.	He is a much learned man.	He is a very learned man.
7.	She is thinking very hardly.	She is thinking very hard.
8.	To tell in brief the film was boring.	*In short* the film was boring.
9.	He told the story in details.	He told the story *in detail.*
10.	I did it anyhow.	I *managed to do* it somehow.
11.	Aeroplanes reach Europe soon.	Aeroplanes reach Europe quickly.
12.	Before long there were dinosaurs on the earth.	*Long ago,* there were dinosaurs on the earth.
13.	This book is too interesting.	This book is *very* interesting.
14.	He lives miserly.	He lives in *a miserly* way.
15.	Just I had gone when she came.	I had just gone when she came.
16.	He sings good.	He sings *well.*
17.	He sings good than I.	He sings *better* than I.

Incorrect	Correct
18. Really speaking it is cold.	*As a matter of fact* it is cold.
19. He is enough tall to reach the ceiling.	He is *tall enough* to reach the ceiling.
20. He went directly to his college.	He went *direct* to his college.
21. He is presently at Delhi	He is at Delhi *at present.*
22. Last night she returned lately.	Last night she *returned late.*
23. He was even blamed by his friends.	He was *blamed even* by his friends.
24. I only employed him for a week.	I employed him for a week only.
25. I met him four months before.	I met him four *months ago.*
26. Anil seldom ever goes to school.	Anil *seldom goes* to school.
27. I will wait here until you do not go.	I will wait here until *you go.*
28. I never remember having met her before.	I *do not remember* having met her before.
29. She has not been here too long to have many friends.	She has not *been here long* enough to have many friends.
30. Hardly I have had any rest since one week.	Hardly have *I had* any rest for a week.
31. Scarcely the water crossed the danger level, the warning signals were sounded.	Scarcely *had the* water *crossed the* danger level, when the warning signals were sounded.
32. She is neat but fairly slow.	She is *neat* but rather slow.
33. It is a rather good film.	It is a *fairly good* film.
34. We yet have time to catch the bus.	We *still have* time to catch the bus.
35. She has not still spent all her money.	She has *not yet* spent all her money.

COMMON ERRORS IN THE USE OF CONJUNCTIONS

Incorrect	Correct
1. As he is fat so he runs slowly.	As he is fat *he* runs slowly.
2. If he is fat then he will run slowly.	If he is fat, he will run slowly.
3. Though he is fat still he runs fast.	Though he is fat, *he runs* fast.
4. *As* I pulled the trigger at the sametime he shook my arm.	As I pulled the trigger, he shook my arm.
5. No sooner I had spoken than he left.	No sooner *had* I spoken than he left.
6. Not only he will go, but also he will stay there.	Not only *will he* go, but he *will also* stay there.
7. Neither he comes nor he writes.	Neither *does he* come nor *does he* write.
8. Scarcely he entered the room than the telephone rang.	Scarcely *had* he entered the room *when the* telephone rang.
9. Hardly she had left the house than it began to rain.	Hardly *had she* left the house *when* it began to rain.
10. He is the fastest runner and he comes last.	He is the fastest runner *but* he comes last.
11. She is as innocent as if she looks.	She is as innocent as she looks.

	Incorrect	Correct
12.	Until he does not try he must be punished.	He must be punished unless he tries.
13.	I want to know as to why you are late.	I want to know why you are late.
14.	I am fond of Chinese food as for example sweet and sour prawns.	I am fond of Chinese food, for example, sweet and sour prawns.
15.	He was angry therefore I ran away.	He was angry so I ran away.
16.	I was trying to work, at that time he was disturbing me.	While I was trying to work, he was disturbing me.
17.	Supposing if he is late, what will happen?	Supposing he is late (or if he is late) what will happen?
18.	He asked me that why I was late.	He asked me why I was late.
19.	Let us catch a taxi lest we should not get late.	Let us catch a taxi lest we should get late.
20.	She dresses herself like the teacher does.	She dresses herself as the teacher does.
21.	Wait while I come.	Wait *until* (or *till)* I come.
22.	Until, there is corruption in India, there can be little progress.	*As long* as there is corruption in India there can be little progress.
23.	I have never told a lie nor cheated anybody.	I have never told a lie *nor have I* cheated anybody.
24.	Both Mohan as well as Arun are responsible for this action.	Both Mohan *and* Arun are responsible for this action.
25.	Hindus and Muslims both are to blame for the riots.	*Both Hindus* and Muslims are to blame for the riots.
26.	I have bought paintings, books, records, and etc.	I have bought paintings, books *and records etc.*
27.	He as well as you is a fool.	He as well as you *are* a fool.
28.	He is so poor and he cannot save anything.	He is so *poor that* he cannot save anything.
29.	Such a book that you want is not available.	Such a book *as* you want is not available.
30.	Such was her condition as everyone was moved to pity.	Such was her condition that everyone was moved to pity.

COMMON ERRORS IN THE USE OF PREPOSITIONS

	Incorrect	Correct
1.	I will not listen him.	I will not listen *to* him.
2.	Copy this word by word.	Copy this word *for* word.
3.	He enquired from her where she lived.	He enquired *of* her where she lived.
4.	Sign here with ink.	Sign here *in* ink.
5.	Has she come in train or by foot?	Has she come *by* train or *on* foot?
6.	She said this at his face.	She said this *to* his face.
7.	Open the book on page one.	Open the book *at* page one.

Incorrect	Correct
8. I was invited for lunch.	I was *invited to* lunch.
9. I am ill since three months.	I have been *ill for* three months.
10. This paper is inferior than that.	This paper is inferior *to* that.
11. This resembles to that.	This *resembles* that.
12. My brother is superior than you in strength.	My brother is superior *to* you in strength.
13. He wrote me.	He wrote *to* me.
14. I shall explain them this.	I shall explain this *to* them.
15. Send this letter on my address.	Send this letter *to* my address.
16. He suggested me this.	He suggested this *to* me.
17. He goes *on his* work.	He goes *to his* work.
18. He *reached to* Nagpur.	He *reached* Nagpur.
19. He told *to me* to go.	He told *me* to go.
20. The term begins *from* July 1st.	The term begins *on* July 1st.
21. There are many advantages *from* this.	The advantages *of* this are many.
22. We waste much time *in* trifles.	We waste much time *on* (or *over)* trifles.
23. He sat *on* a tree.	He sat *in* a tree.
24. This is a comfortable house to *live*.	This is a comfortable house to *live in*.
25. This is the road to *go*.	This is the road to *go by*.
26. He married *with* an Indian lady.	He *married an Indian* lady.
27. He accompanied *with* his friend.	He *accompanied his* friend.
28. He went *for doing some* business.	He went away *on* business.
29. He went for *riding*.	He went *for a ride*.
30. I *pitied on* him.	I *pitied* him.
31. When this was searched it was found.	When this was searched *for* it was found.
32. I shall inform them *this*.	I shall inform them *of* this.
33. *Due to illness* I cannot go to school.	*Owing* to illness I cannot go to school.
34. He went *to the back side* of the house.	He went *behind* (or to the back of) the house.
35. I must go; there is no *help*.	I must go; there is no help *for it*.
36. I *met with your* friend there.	I *met your* friend there.
37. The First World War was fought *during* 1914-1918.	The First World War was fought *between* 1914-1918.
38. England grew prosperous *between* Queen Victoria's reign.	England grew prosperous *during* Queen Victoria's reign.
39. He asked a holiday.	He asked *for* a holiday.
40. I am obliged of you for this good turn.	I am obliged *to* you for this good turn.
41. There is no harm to try.	There is no harm *in trying*.

MISCELLANEOUS ERRORS

(Including Ambiguities and Indianisms)

	Incorrect	Correct
1.	Many *homes* are lying vacant.	Many *houses* are lying vacant.
2.	It is cool in the *shadow* of the tree.	It is cool in the *shade* of the tree.
3.	She *keeps* good health.	She *enjoys* good health.
4.	My leg is *paining*.	*I am feeling pain* in my leg.
5.	*See* this word in the dictionary.	*Look up* this word in the dictionary.
6.	The train will arrive *just now*.	The train will arrive *shortly*.
7.	They are *pulling* on well.	They are *getting* on well.
8.	The river has *over flown* its bank.	The river has *over flown* its banks.
9.	He was appointed *on* the post.	He was appointed *to* the post.
10.	Last but not *the least,* we have to discuss the problem of over population.	Last but not *least,* we have to discuss the problem of over population.
11.	*Cities* after *cities* fell.	*City* after *city* fell.
12.	What is the use Munir going there?	What is the use of Munir going there?
13.	He *did many mischief.*	He *made much mischief.*
14.	It is exact five *in* my watch.	It is exact five *by* my watch.
15.	I will dine with them on *next Sunday.*	I will dine with them *Sunday next.*
16.	Misfortunes when faced bravely and *manly* become less troublesome.	Misfortunes when faced bravely and *manfully* become less troublesome.
17.	I am *laid down* with fever.	I am *laid up* with fever.
18.	He is habituated to smoking.	He is *addicted* to smoking.
19.	*According to my opinion* he is right.	*In my opinion* (or according *to me)* he is right.
20.	Could you please *open* this knot?	Could you please *untie* this knot?

MULTIPLE CHOICE QUESTIONS

Directions: *In this section, each sentence has three parts, indicated by (A), (B) and (C). Read each sentence to find out whether there is an error. If you find an error in any one of the parts (A, B, C), indicate your response by marking the letter related to that part. If a sentence has no error, indicate this by marking '(D)' which stands for "No error". Errors may belong to grammar, usage or idiom. Ignore errors of punctuation, if any.*

1. (A) We are meeting today afternoon/(B) to discuss the matter/(C) and reach a compromise./ (D) No error.

2. (A) Either Ram or/(B) you is responsible/(C) for this action./(D) No error.

3. (A) The student flatly denied/(B) that he had copied/(C) in the examination hall./(D) No error.

4. (A) By the time you arrive tomorrow/(B) I have finished/(C) my work./(D) No error.

5. (A) The speaker stressed repeatedly on/(B) the importance of improving/(C) the condition of the slums./(D) No error.

6. (A) The captain with the members of his team/(B) are returning/(C) after a fortnight./(D) No error.

7. (A) After returning from/(B) an all-India tour/(C) I had to describe about it/(D) No error.

8. (A) The teacher asked his students/(B) if they had gone through/(C) either of the three chapters included in the prescribed text./(D) No error.

9. (A) Although they are living in the country/(B) since they were married/(C) they are now moving to the town./(D) No error.

10. (A) Do you know/(B) how old were you/(C) when you came here?/(D) No error.

11. (A) Beware of/(B) a fair-weather friend/(C) who is neither a friend in need nor a friend indeed/(D) No error.

12. (A) Copernicus proved/(B) that Earth/(C) moves round the Sun./(D) No error.

13. (A) Seldom we have been treated/(B) in such a rude manner/(C) by the police personnel./(D) No error.

14. (A) Some men are born great,/(B) some achieve greatness/(C) and some had greatness thrust on them./(D) No error.

15. (A) The property/(B) was divided/(C) among the two brothers./(D) No error.

16. (A) I am quite certain/(B) that the lady is not only greedy/(C) but miserly./(D) No error.

17. (A) The aircraft overloaded/(B) there was something wrong of the battery/(C) and the engine was making a queer noise/(D) No error.

18. (A) A thorough inquiry of the misappropriation of funds/(B) is now imperative/(C) to bring the guilty to book/(D) No error.

19. (A) The brilliant success in the examination/(B) as well as his record in sports/(C) deserves high praise/(D) No error.

20. (A) While travelling by a train/(B) on a cold winter night/(C) an argument rose between two passengers in our compartment/(D) No error.

21. (A) I cannot find/(B) where has he gone/(C) though I have tried may best/(D) No error.

22. (A) If I was/(B) the Prime Minister of India/(C) I would work wonders/(D) No error.

23. Amit's severe bout of flu/(B) debilitated him so much/(C) that he was too tired to do for work for a week./(D) No error.

24. (A) This is the crux of the entire problem;/(B) everything centres on/(C) it being resolved./(D) No error.

25. (A) One of the major aims of the Air Force/(B) was the complete demolition of all means of transportation/(C) by the bombing of rail lines and terminals./(D) No error.

26. (A) His strong voice cut over/(B) the hum of conversation/(C) like a knife through butter./(D) No error.

27. (A) Even though they weren't expecting us/(B) they managed to knock up/(C) a marvellous meal./(D) No error.

28. (A) The celebrated singer was/(B) surrounded by the usual crowd/(C) of lackeys and hanger-ons./(D) No error.

29. (A) If it weren't/(B) for you,/(C) I wouldn't be alive today./(D) No error.

30. (A) He looked like a lion/(B) baulked from/(C) its prey./(D) No error.

31. (A) Widespread flooding/(B) is effecting/(C) large areas of the villages./(D) No error.

32. (A) She regards/(B) negotiating prices with customers/(C) as her special preserve./(D) No error.

33. (A) Often in political campaigns, a point is reached at which/(B) the candidates take out their gloves./(C) and start slugging with bare fists./(D) No error.

34. (A) If we really set to/(B) we can get the whole house/(C) cleaned in an afternoon./(D) No error.

35. (A) Pieces of rock plummeted/(B) down the mountainside/(C) in the ground below./(D) No error.

36. (A) Since the two parties each won/(B) the same number of seats,/(C) the minority party holds the balance of power./(D) No error.

37. (A) It's arrogant for you/(B) to assume you'll/(C)win every time./(D) No error.

38. (A) We've paid for our travel and accommodation,/(B) so we need only to take/(C) some pocket-money with us./(D) No error.

39. (A) There's no evidence to show/(B) that information technology secrets are more/(C) vulnerable in India than Britain or the US./(D) No error.

40. (A) It is shameful that hunting/(B) is still considered sport/(C) by some unscrupulous people in the civilized world./(D) No error.

41. (A) The Prime Minister's good looks won him/(B)the election but he has still to prove/(C) that he's not a just pretty face./(D) No error.

42. (A) The two books are the same/(B) except for the fact that this/(C) has an answer in the back./(D) No error.

43. (A) He estimated his income tax bill/(B) by extrapolation over figures/(C) submitted in previous years./(D) No error.

44. (A) The modern office block/(B) sticks out like a sore thumb/(C) among the old buildings in the area./(D) No error.

45. (A) I will try to put over/(B) some feelers to gauge/(C) people's reactions to our proposal./(D) No error.

46. (A) A major contribution of Mathura sculptors/(B)of that period were the creation and popularization/(C) of the Buddha's image in human form./(D) No error.

47. (A) Amit has been deceiving Mona/(B) for many years but she/(C) has not still tumbled to it. (C)/No error. (D)

48. (A) Mahavira was an advocate of nonviolence and vegetarianism,/(B) who revived and reorganized the Jain doctrine/(C) and established rules for their monastic order. (D) No error.

49. (A) Microwaves are the principle carriers/(B) of television, telephone and data transmissions/(C)between stations on earth and between the earth and satellites./(D) No error.

50. (A) An unit is an abstract idea,/(B) defined either by reference to/(C) a randomly chosen material standard or to a natural phenomenon./(D) No error.

51. (A) With the crisis deepening,/(B) the critics sense an opportunity/(C) about putting in place a more radical strategy./(D) No error.

52. (A) The salesman gave us/(B) a big spiel about why/(C) we should buy his product./(D) No error.

53. (A) I will need several weeks/(B) to invent the lie of the land before/(C) I can make any decision about the future of the business./(D) No error.

54. (A) You should be cautious/(B) and make a few discrete enquiries about/(C) the firm before you sign anything./(D) No error.

55. (A) Your husband doesn't/(B) believe that you are older/(C) than I./(D) No error.

56. (A) There is a beautiful moon out tonight/(B) and Neeta and I are going for a stroll/(C) — would you like to come along with she and I?/ (D) No error.

57. (A) The data on/(B) the divorce case is/(C) on the judge's desk./(D) No error.

58. (A) The stood off/(B) from the crowd/(C) because of her height and flaming red hair./(D) No error.

59. (A) It's stupid to go/(B) to the expense of taking/(C) music lessons if you never practise/(D) No error.

60. (A) You will find it difficult/(B) to explain of your use/(C) of such offensive language/(D) No error.

61. (A) Because of the/(B) extenuating circumstances/(C) the court acquitted him out of the crime/(D) No error.

62. (A) The carpet was badly stained/(B) to such an extent that/(C) you couldn't tell its original colour/(D) No error.

63. (A) It is greatly to Amit's credit/(B) that he gave back the money he found/(C) his honesty does for him credit/(D) No error.

64. (A) A terrific hue and cry/(B) was raised/(C) at the new tax proposals/(D) No error.

65. (A) The former Gen̆eral was/(B) exiled of his country because of/(C) his part in the plot against the government/(D) No error.

66. (A) The company has/(B) set off itself some stiff production/(C) goals for this year/(D) No error.

67. (A) The music was so loud/(B) that we had to bellow over each/(C) other to be heard./(D) No error.

68. (A) When this beautiful girl arrived, (A) all the men in the room/(C) gravitated over her./(D) No error.

69. (A) The children are/(B) really in their element/(C) playing on the beach./(D) No error.

70. (A) The refugees are/(B) badly off for blankets,/(C) and even worse for food./(D) No error.

71. (A) From their vintage-point on the cliff,/(B) the children could watch/(C) the ships coming and going./(D) No error.

72. (A) A cogent remark/(B) compels acceptance because/(C) of their sense and logic./(D) No error.

73. (A) Credit cards have/(B) brought about a revolution/(C) in people's spending habits./(D) No error.

74. (A) In financial matters/(B) it is important to/(C) get disinterested advice./(D) No error.

75. (A) Some women admit that/(B) their principle goal in life/(C) is to marry a wealthy man./(D) No error.

76. (A) Take two spoonsful/(B) of this medicine/(C) every three hours./(D) No error.

77. (A) The film was so disjointed/(B) that I could not tell you/(C) what the story was about./(D) No error.

78. (A) He had been/(B) saved of death as if/(C) by divine intervention./(D) No error.

79. (A) I informed the principal/(B) that I was running temperature/(C) and, therefore, could not attend the meeting./(D) No error.

80. (A) The lady was broken with grief/(B) when she heard the sad news of the train disaster/(C) in which her brother was killed./(D) No error.

81. (A) The farmer is irrigating/(B) his fields/(C) since morning./(D) No error.

82. (A) I could not/(B) answer to/(C) the question./(D) No error.

83. (A) Two years passed/(B) since/(C) my cousin died./(D) No error.

84. (A) He hesitated to accept the post/(B) as he did not think/(C) that the salary would be enough for a man with a family of three (C)/ No error (D)

85. (A) Have you gone through/(B) either of these three chapters/(C) that have been included in this volume?/(D) No error.

86. (A) I am learning English/(B) for ten years/(C) without much effect/(D) No error.

87. (A) Ramesh has agreed/(B) to marry with the girl/(C) of his parent's choice (D) No error.

88. (A) The pity is that/(B) no sooner he had left the place/(C) than the fire broke out/(D) No error.

89. (A) When he was arriving/(B) the party was/(C) in full swing/(D) No error.

90. (A) The Dean wrote he constituted a committee of experts/(B) comprising of five members/(C) before the next meeting took place/(D) No error.

91. (A) Inflation and shortages/(B) have made it very difficult for him/(C) to make his both ends meet./(D) No error.

92. (A) The most studious boy/(B) in the class/(C) was made as the captain./(D) No error.

93. (A) I am participating/(B) in the two-miles race/(C) tomorrow morning./(D) No error.

94. (A) The sum and substance/(B) of his speech/ (C) were essentially anti-establishment./(D) No error.

95. (A) It has been such a wonderful evening/(B) I look forward to meet you again/(C) after the vacations./(D) No error.

96. (A) When the boy committed a mistake/(B) the teacher made him to do/(C) the sum again./ (D) No error.

97. (A) Unless the government does not revise its policy of liberalization/(B) the growth of the indigenous technology/(C) will be adversely affected./(D) No error.

98. (A) Supposing if you get/(B) a seat in the plane/(C) you will not take more than two hours to reach Mumbai./(D) No error.

99. (A) Whenever a person lost anything/(B) the poor folk around/(C) are suspected./(D) No error.

100. (A) Still impressive is that/(B) we achieve this selective attention/(C) through our latent ability to lip-read./(D) No error.

101. (A) The brakes and steering failed/(B) and the bus ran down the hill/(C) without anyone being able to control it./(D) No error.

102. (A) The polling was marred/(B) at many a place/(C) by attempts at rigging./(D) No error.

103. (A) He wanted to work all right/(B) but we saw that he was completely worn/(C) and so we persuaded him to stop./(D) No error.

104. (A) When a whale is washed ashore by the tide,/(B) the people flock together to see it./ (C) wondering how so huge an animal can swim about in the water./(D) No error.

105. (A) Few scientists changed/(B) people's ideas as much as/(C) Darwin with his Theory of Evolution./(D) No error.

106. (A) Were he/(B) to see you,/(C) he would have been surprised./(D) No error.

107. (A) The number of marks carried by each question/(B) are indicated/(C) at the end of the question./(D) No error.

108. (A) An animal/(B) can be just as unhappy in a vast area/(C) or in a small one/(D) No error.

109. (A) It is time/(B) we did something/(C) to stop road accidents./(D) No error.

110. (A) A free press is not a privilege/(B) but the organic necessity/(C) in a free society./(D) No error.

111. (A) The Indian radio./(B) which was previously controlled by the British rulers./(C) is free now from the narrow vested interests./(D) No error.

112. (A) Because of the emergency help/(B) that the patient received./(C) he would have died/ (D) No error.

113. (A) At present juncture,/(B) however, the super-computer/(C) would be a costly toy./(D) No error.

114. (A) Students should not take part/(B) in party politics and political demonstrations/(C) as they interfere in serious study./(D) No error.

115. (A) Wherever they go/(B) Indians easily adapt to/(C) local circumstances./(D) No error.

116. (A) According to the Bible/(B) it is meek and humble/(C) who shall inherit the earth./(D) No error.

117. (A) I was there/(B) many a time/(C) in the past./(D) No error.

118. (A) As much as I admire him for his sterling qualities./(B) I cannot excuse him for/(C) being unfair to his friends./(D) No error.

119. (A) Were you/(B) given a choice/(C) or you had to do it?/(D) No error.

120. (A) When he was asked what is wrong with him,/(B) he said that he was not well,/(C) and asked for leave of absence for one day./(D) No error.

121. (A) At the end of the year/(B) every student who had done adequate work/(C) was automatically promoted./(D) No error.

122. (A) Many times the news has been published/ (B) in the papers that the end of the world will be certain/(C) if a nuclear war breaks out./(D) No error.

123. (A) Happily, zoos were/(B) unwilling to cooperate/(C) in a scheme that was potentially harmful to animal welfare./(D) No error.

124. (A) We discussed about the problem so thoroughly/(B) on the eve of the examination/ (C) that I found it very easy to work it out./ (D) No errór.

125. (A) She reluctantly said that/(B) if nobody else was doing it/(C) she will do it./(D) No error.

126. (A) He will end up his work/(B) in the city/(C) by the end of the year./(D) No error.

127. (A) Though child marriage/(B) has been banned,/(C) the custom still prevailed among some groups in India./(D) No error.

128. (A) Supposing if/(B) there is no bus,/(C) how will you get there?(D) No error.

129. (A) At the moment the house/(B) was burgled the family/(C) attended a night party in the neighbourhood./(D) No error.

130. (A) On a holiday/(B) Sudha prefers reading/ (C) than going out visiting friends/(D) No error.

131. (A) Neither he/(B) nor his father is interested/ (C) in joining the party./(D) No error.

132. (A) A group of friends/(B) want to visit/(C) the new plant as early as possible./(D) No error.

133. (A) May I/(B) know who you want/(C) to see please/(D) No error.

134. (A) Myself and Gopal/(B) will take care of/(C) the function on Sunday./(D) No error.

135. (A) I could not put up in a hotel/(B) because the boarding and lodging charges/(C) were exorbitant./(D) No error.

136. (A) He is not coming tomorrow/(B) as he is having a pain in the chest/(C) and has to see a doctor./(D) No error.

137. (A) They have been/(B) very close friends/(C) until they quarrelled./(D) No error.

138. (A) Since India has gained Independence/(B) 49 years ago,/(C) much progress has been made in almost every field./(D) No error.

139. (A) The party chief made it a point to state that/(B) the Prime Minister and the Union Home Minister should also come/(C) and they see what his party men had seen./(D) No error.

140. (A) Due to me being a newcomer/(B) I was unable to get a house/(C) suitable for my wife and me./(D) No error.

141. (A) The reason why/(B) he was rejected/(C) was because he was too young./(D) No error.

142. (A) The scientist must follow/(B) his hunches and his data/(C) wherever it may lead./(D) No error.

143. (A) Firstly you should/(B) think over the meaning of the words/(C) and then use them./ (D) No error.

144. (A) Scarcely had/(B) I arrived than/(C) the train left./(D) No error.

145. (A) Unless you stop to make noise at once/(B) I will have no option but to/(C) bring the matter to the attention of the police./(D) No error.

146. (A) He couldn't but help/(B) shedding tears at the plight of the villagers/(C) rendered homeless by a devastating cyclone./(D) No error.

147. (A) Since it was his first election campaign, the candidate was confused;/(B) none could clearly understand/(C) either the principles he stood for or the benefits he promised./(D) No error.

148. (A) It is an established fact that the transcendental American poets and philosophers,/(B) who lived in the latter half of the nineteenth century,/(C) were more influenced by Indian philosophy, in particular by Upanishadic Philosophy./(D) No error.

149. (A) The crew were on board/(B) and they soon busied themselves/(C) in preparing to meet the storm./(D) No error.

150. (A) One of the members/(B) expressed doubt if/(C) the Minister was an athiest./ (D) No error.

151. (A) A body of volunteers/(B) have been organised/(C) to spread the message of the saint./(D) No error.

152. (A) If I will have the time/(B) I shall try and make it/(C) to the zoo this afternoon./(D) No error.

153. (A) To facilitate exports and improve sales in the domestic market/(B) some of the improvised fabrics and garments fabricated out from them/(C) are displayed in the main pavilion./(D) No error.

154. (A) He gave them no money/(B) nor did help them/(C) in any way./(D) No error.

155. (A) Azharuddin is one of the finest batsmen/ (B) that India have produced/(C) over the decades./(D) No error.

156. (A) An Indian ship/(B) laden with merchandise/ (C) got drowned in the Pacific./ (D) No error.

157. (A) Though senior in age,/(B) his father is junior than/(C) my father in service./(D) No error.

158. (A) If I am you/(B) I would have seen to it/(C) that I won the prize./(D) No error.

159. (A) His father died of cholera/(B) but his mother also,/(C) though very weak, is out of danger./(D) No error.

160. (A) He asked me/(B) why did I call/(C) him a rogue./(D) No error.

161. (A) I have got/(B) my M.Sc. degree/(C) in 1988./(D) No error.

162. (A) They/(B) enjoyed thoroughly/(C) at the party./(D) No error.

163. (A) After the humiliating exposure/(B) he hanged his head/(C) in shame./(D) No error.

164. (A) Kamala's fountain-pen/(B) is as expensive/(C) as Shyama./(D) No error.

165. (A) I shall certainly/(B) write you/(C) when I shall reach New Delhi./(D) No error.

166. (A) The criminal was/(B) caught, convicted the hung/(C) in a short period of time./(D) No error.

167. (A) You will get/(B) all the information/(C) if you read this booklet carefully./(D) No error.

168. (A) She sang/(B) very well/(C) isn't it?/(D) No error.

169. (A) He is working in/(B) a bank is New Delhi/ (C) for the past several months./(D) No error.

170. (A) There is no question/(B) of my failing/(C) in the examination./(D) No error.

ANSWERS

1	2	3	4	5	6	7	8	9	10
A	B	D	B	A	B	C	C	B	D
11	**12**	**13**	**14**	**15**	**16**	**17**	**18**	**19**	**20**
D	B	A	C	C	C	B	A	D	C
21	**22**	**23**	**24**	**25**	**26**	**27**	**28**	**29**	**30**
B	A	C	C	B	A	A	C	C	C
31	**32**	**33**	**34**	**35**	**36**	**37**	**38**	**39**	**40**
C	A	A	A	C	A	A	B	D	B
41	**42**	**43**	**44**	**45**	**46**	**47**	**48**	**49**	**50**
C	C	C	D	A	B	C	C	A	A
51	**52**	**53**	**54**	**55**	**56**	**57**	**58**	**59**	**60**
C	D	D	D	C	C	D	A	B	B
61	**62**	**63**	**64**	**65**	**66**	**67**	**68**	**69**	**70**
C	A	C	A	B	B	B	C	B	D

71	72	73	74	75	76	77	78	79	80
A	C	D	D	D	A	B	B	B	A
81	**82**	**83**	**84**	**85**	**86**	**87**	**88**	**89**	**90**
A	B	A	D	B	A	B	B	A	B
91	**92**	**93**	**94**	**95**	**96**	**97**	**98**	**99**	**100**
C	C	B	C	B	B	A	A	A	C
101	**102**	**103**	**104**	**105**	**106**	**107**	**108**	**109**	**110**
C	D	B	D	A	A	B	C	D	B
111	**112**	**113**	**114**	**115**	**116**	**117**	**118**	**119**	**120**
C	A	A	C	B	B	A	A	A	A
121	**122**	**123**	**124**	**125**	**126**	**127**	**128**	**129**	**130**
D	D	C	A	C	A	C	A	A	C
131	**132**	**133**	**134**	**135**	**136**	**137**	**138**	**139**	**140**
D	B	B	A	A	C	A	A	C	A
141	**142**	**143**	**144**	**145**	**146**	**147**	**148**	**149**	**150**
C	C	A	B	A	A	D	C	C	B
151	**152**	**153**	**154**	**155**	**156**	**157**	**158**	**159**	**160**
B	A	B	B	B	C	B	A	B	B
161	**162**	**163**	**164**	**165**	**166**	**167**	**168**	**169**	**170**
A	B	B	C	C	C	A	C	A	B

3

Correct Sentence Selection

One may use the same words in many ways but the best way is only one that makes the perfect usage of the words and conveys the proper meaning of the expression. Try it yourself in this exercise.

MULTIPLE CHOICE QUESTIONS

Directions: *There are four sentences in each of the following questions. One of the sentences is correct, and the rest are incorrect. You are to select the correct sentence in each question.*

1. A. She is either right nor wrong.
B. She is nor right or wrong.
C. She is neither right or wrong.
D. She is neither right nor wrong.

2. A. He went to Nepal five years ago.
B. He went to Nepal five years back.
C. He went to Nepal five years before.
D. He went to Nepal five years past.

3. A. Before leaving home, it began to rain.
B. As since I was leaving home, it began to rain.
C. As I was leaving home, it began to rain.
D. When leaving home, it began to rain.

4. A. I have given up alcoholic drinks two years before.
B. I have given up alcoholic drinks two years since.
C. I have given up alcoholic drinks two years ago.
D. I had given up alcoholic drinks two years ago.

5. A. I told to her to give me that book.
B. I said her to give me this book.
C. I said to her that to give me that book.
D. I asked her to give me that book.

6. A. My maternal grandmother said to me not go without having a cup of tea.
B. My material grandmother asked me not go without having a cup of tea.
C. My material grandmother asked me to go not without having a cup of tea.
D. My material grandmother asked me not to go without having a cup of tea.

7. A. His sister told me that he likes my new car.
B. His sister said me that she likes my new car.
C. His sister told me I like your new car.
D. His sister told me that she liked my new car.

8. A. The teacher asked me where was I going?
B. The teacher asked me where I am going.
C. The teacher asked me where I go.
D. The teacher asked me where I was going.

9. A. Your conduct admits no excuses.
B. Your conduct admit no excuse.
C. Your conduct is inexcusable.
D. Your conduct admit of no excuses.

10. A. The young woman tried on two coats and finally decided to buy the most expensive one.
B. The young woman tried on two coats and finally decided to buy the more expensive one.
C. The young woman tried on two coats and finally decided to buy the expensive one.
D. The young woman tried on coats two and finally decided to buy the very expensive one.

11. A. She is anxious about my health.
B. She is anxious of my health.
C. She is anxious for my health.
D. She is anxious with my health.

12. A. My youngest son had no difficulty with solving the problem.
B. My youngest son had no difficulty to solve the problem.
C. My youngest son had no difficulty in solving the problem.
D. My youngest son had no difficulty for solving the problem.

13. A. The plane had left before I reached the airport.
B. The plane left before I reached the airport.
C. The plane was leaving before I reached the airport.
D. The plane will leave before I reached the airport.

14. A. The four dacoits distributed the loot with themselves.
B. The four dacoits distributed the loot between themselves.
C. The four dacoits distributed the loot among themselves.
D. The four dacoits distributed the loot upon themselves.

15. A. What out country needs today is a number of selfless and competent leaders.
B. What our country need today is a number of unscrupulous leaders.
C. What our country needs today are a number of selfish leaders.
D. What our country needs today is a number of motivated leaders.

16. A. I am very sorry to learn that you lose the match yesterday.
B. I am very sorry to learn that you loosed the match yesterday.
C. I am very sorry to learn that you lost the match yesterday
D. I am very sorry to learn that you have lost the match yesterday.

17. A. It is our bounden duty to instil a sense of responsibility into people of the country.
B. It is our bounden duty to instigate a sense of responsibility into the people of the country.
C. It is our bounden duty to excite a sense of responsibility into the people of the country.
D. It is our bounden duty to incite a sense of responsibility into the people of the country.

18. A. He is over seventy years of age and are still alert and strong.
B. He is over seventy years of age but who is still alert and strong.
C. He is a man over seventy years of age but who is still alert and strong.
D. He is over seventy years of age, but is still alert and strong.

19. A. She told me that it is better to fail than pass by unfair means.
B. She told me it was better to fail than passing by unfair means.
C. She told whether it was better to fail than pass by unfair means.
D. She told me that it was better to fail than to pass by unfair means.

20. A. She asked me to name the capital of Nepal.
B. She asked me which is the capital of Nepal.
C. She asked me what is the capital of Nepal.
D. She told me in the capital of Nepal.

21. A. She heartily congratulated me about my splendid success in the examination.
B. She heartily congratulated me on my splendid success in the examination.

C. She heartily congratulated me for my splendid success in the examination.
D. She heartily congratulated me at my splendid success in the examination.

22. A. He replied that he will call on me tomorrow.
B. He replied that he would call on me tomorrow.
C. He had replied that he would have called on me tomorrow.
D. He replied that he will have called on me tomorrow.

23. A. I am sorry to say that she made me do the dirty job.
B. I am sorry to say that she made me to do the dirty job.
C. I am sorry to say that she would make me to do the dirty job.
D. I am sorry to say that she did me to do the dirty job.

24. A. Will you please excuse my dropping in at this untimely hour?
B. Will you please excuse me dropping at this untimely hour?
C. Will you please excuse my dropping at this untimely hour?
D. Will you please excuse my dropping by this untimely hour?

25. A. Now I must beg of your leave.
B. Now I must beg off your leave.
C. Now I must beg your leave.
D. Now I must beg leave of you.

26. A. When narrating the road accident, she was in tears.
B. As narrating the road accident, she was in tears.
C. In narrating the road accident, she was in tears.
D. When she was narrating the road accident, she was in tears.

27. A. A long period of ten years have passed since he has passed away.
B. A long period of ten years has passed since he passed away.
C. A long period of ten years passed since he has passed away.
D. A long period of ten years have passed since he had passed away.

28. A. Can you do it more quick than I?
B. Can you do it more quicker than I?
C. Can you do it more quickly than I?
D. Can you do it more quick than I can?

29. A. This coat is too small for her.
B. This coat is to small for her.
C. This coat is too much small for her.
D. This coat is much too small for her.

30. A. My boss was kind enough to grant me leave of absence for ten days.
B. My boss was enough kind to grant me leave of absence for ten days.
C. My boss was kindly enough to grant me leave of absence for ten days.
D. My boss was enough kind for granting me leave of absence for ten days.

31. A. You should work had lest you may fail in the examination.
B. You should work hard lest you should fail in the examination.
C. You should work hard lest you might fail in the examination.
D. You should work had lest you fail in the examination.

32. A. When entering the class-room, each of the boys kept quiet.
B. Entering the class-room, each of the boys kept quiet.
C. On entering the class-room, each of the boys kept quiet.
D. Since entering the class-room, each of the boys kept quiet.

33. A. She asked that why her son shall be punished.
B. She asked that why her son should be punished.
C. She asked why her son should be punished.
D. She asked on why her son shall be punished.

34. A. She gives me such troubles which I cannot endure them.

B. She gives me such troubles as I cannot endure them.
C. She gives on me such troubles that I cannot endure them.
D. She gives at me such troubles which I cannot endure.

35. A. I have not seen her long since.
B. I have not seen her since long.
C. I have not seen her since a long.
D. I have not seen her from a long time.

36. A. This is the same book which I lost a few weeks ago.
B. This is the same book that I lost a few weeks ago.
C. This is the same books that I lost a few weeks before.
D. This is the same book which I lost a few weeks past.

37. A. This cloth is more preferable than that.
B. This cloth is more preferable than that.
C. This cloth is more preferable to that.
D. This cloth is preferable to that.

38. A. I seldom or ever make a mistake.
B. I seldom and never make a mistake.
C. I seldom or never make a mistake.
D. I seldom that never make a mistake.

39. A. His command in the English language is very unique.
B. His command of the English language is unique.
C. His command of the English language is perfectly unique.
D. His command of the English language is totally unique.

40. A. Her speech was so halting that the stopped between each word.
B. Her speech was so halting that she stopped after each word.
C. Her speech was so halting that she has stopped each word.
D. Her speech was so halting that she was stopping between each word.

41. A. I do not know who you consider the best man of the two.
B. I do not know whom you consider to be the man of the two.
C. I do not know whom you consider better of the two.
D. I do not know who you consider as the best of the two.

42. A. Do you bathe yourself daily?
B. Do you bathe daily?
C. Do you bathe daily?
D. Do you daily bath?

43. A. Being a cold day, I did not go out to the house.
B. It being a cold day, I did not go out of the house.
C. Being a cold day, I have not gone out of the house.
D. It being a cold day, I had not gone out of the house.

44. A. One should do his duty honestly and efficiently.
B. One should do one's duty honestly and efficiently.
C. One should do his responsibility honestly and efficiently.
D. One should act his responsibility honestly and efficiently.

45. A. She is one of those girls who cannot control her anger.
B. She is one of those girls which cannot control her anger.
C. She is one of those girls that cannot control her anger.
D. She is one of those girls who cannot control their anger.

46. A. You should attentively listen what he says.
B. You should attentively listen to what he says.
C. You should attentively listen to what he say.
D. You should attentively listen to what he says.

47. A. If she will come, I shall certainly give her five hundred rupees.
B. If she will come, I shall certainly give with her five hundred rupees.

C. If she comes, I shall certainly give five hundred rupees upon her.
D. If she comes, I shall certainly give her five hundred rupees.

48. A. She asked me if I broke the mirror.
B. She asked me if I have broken the mirror.
C. She asked of me if I have broken the mirror.
D. She asked if I had broken the mirror.

49. A. Workers are prohibited to bring their cycles inside the factory premises.
B. Workers are prohibited from bringing their cycles inside the factory premises.
C. Workers are prohibited to bringing their cycles inside the factory premises.
D. Workers are prohibited from to bring their cycles inside the factory premises.

50. A. Do you remember the date of him leaving India for Japan?
B. Do you remember the date of his leaving India for Japan?
C. Do you remember the date from his leaving India for Japan?
D. Do you remember the date by his leaving India for Japan?

51. A. She expected to have passed in the examination.
B. She expected to have pass in the examination.
C. She expected in passing the examination.
D. She expected to pass the examination.

52. A. I have visited him four hours ago.
B. I have visited him four hours before.
C. I have visited him four hours since.
D. I visited him four hours ago.

53. A. I did not go out of the house after I wrote the letter.
B. I did not go out of the house since I wrote the letter.
C. I did not go out of the house after I had written the letter.
D. I did not go out of the house after I have written the letter.

54. A. The murderer was tried, convicted and hung.
B. The murderer was tried, convicted and was hung.
C. The murderer was tried, convicted and hunged.
D. The murderer was tried, convicted and hanged.

55. A. The sceneries of Kashmir are very beautiful.
B. The sceneries of Kashmir is very beautiful.
C. The scenery of Kashmir is very beautiful.
D. The scenery of Kashmir are very beautiful.

56. A. Unless you do not work hard, you will not achieve success in life.
B. Unless you work hard, you will not achieve success in life.
C. Unless you do not work hard, you will achieve success in life.
D. Unless you work hardly, you will not achieve success in life.

57. A. Every one of my children are intelligent and healthy.
B. Every one of my children is intelligent and healthy.
C. Every one of my childs are intelligent and healthy.
D. Every one of my childs is intelligent and healthy.

58. A. Neither of the two candidates are suitable for the job.
B. Neither of the two candidate is suitable for the job.
C. Neither of the two candidates is suitable for the job.
D. Neither of the two candidates is suit for the job.

59. A. As I am ill, so I shall not be able to attend the meeting.
B. As I am ill, so I shall not to be able to attend the meeting.
C. As I am ill, so I shall not be able for attending the meeting.
D. As I am ill, I shall not be able to attend the meeting.

60. A. She never has and never will disobey me.
B. She never have and never will disobey me.

C. She never has disobeyed, and never will disobey me.
D. She never have disobeyed and never will disobey me.

61. A. This is the third time he broke a cup.
B. This is the third time when he broke a cup.
C. This is the third time he had broken a cup.
D. This is the third time he has broken a cup.

62. A. Let you and I be friends again.
B. Let you and myself be friend again.
C. Let you and I become friends again.
D. Let you and me be friends again.

63. A. I have come for seeing you.
B. I have come on seeing you.
C. I have came to seeing you.
D. I have come to see you

64. A. I am true to my words.
B. I am true with my words.
C. I am true at my words.
D. I am true to my word.

65. A. She is very anxious with my health.
B. She is very anxious at my health.
C. She is very anxious about my health.
D. She is very anxious after my health.

66. A. This is one of the best books that has been published so far.
B. This is one of the best books which has been published so far.
C. This is one of the best books that have been published so far.
D. This is one of the best books which had been published so far.

67. A. She is taller than all the girls in the college.
B. She is taller then all the girls in the college.
C. She is taller than other girls in the college.
D. She is taller than all other girls in the college.

68. A. As far I am concerned, you are free to go anywhere you like.
B. As far I am concerned, you are to free go anywhere you like.
C. As far as I am concerned, you are free to go anywhere you like.
D. As far as I concerned, you are free to going anywhere you like.

69. A. He is confined to bed for about a week.
B. He was confined to bed for about a week.
C. He has been confine to bed for about a weak.
D. He has been confined to bed for about a week.

70. A. Subhash Bose was one of the greatest patriot of India.
B. Subhash Bose has been one of the greatest patriot of India.
C. Subhash Bose has been one of the greatest patriot of India.
D. Subhash Bose was one of the greatest patriots of India.

71. A. She is as good and even better than you.
B. She is as good as, or even better than, you.
C. She is as good as or even batter than you.
D. She is as good as and better than you

72. A. They said to me that the General English paper is difficult.
B. They said me that the General English paper is difficult.
C. They said to me that the General English paper was difficult.
D. They said to me that the General English paper has been difficult.

73. A. May I have some words with you?
B. May I have a few words with you?
C. Can I have words with you?
D. May I have a word with you?

74. A. Our General Manager asked me as to why I am late.
B. Our General Manager asked me as to why am I late.
C. Our General Manager asked me why I am late.
D. Our General Manager asked me why I was late.

75. A. The story should not exceed more than five hundred words.
B. The story should not exceed than five hundred words.

C. The story should not exceed five hundred words.
D. The story should not accede five hundred words.

76. A. What is the good of him trying to do that work?
B. What is the good of his trying to do that work?
C. What the good is of him trying to do that work?
D. What is the good at his trying to do that work?

77. A. He does his best to find faults with my work.
B. He does his best in finding faults with my work.
C. He does his best to find fault with my work.
D. He does his best to find faults of my work.

78. A. This is a most unique opportunity for you to go abroad.
B. This is the most unique opportunity for you to go abroad.
C. This is a unique opportunity for you to go abroad.
D. This is a unique opportunity with you to go abroad.

79. A. Will you please say my compliments to your father?
B. Will you please say my complements to your father?
C. Will you please tell my compliments to your father?
D. Will you please pay my compliments to your father?

80. A. I always have and shall be your fast friend.
B. I always have been and shall be your fast friend.
C. I always was and shall be your fast friend.
D. I always had been and shall be your fast friend.

81. A. Tell me whether she loves you or not.
B. Tell me whether she loves you or knot.
C. Tell me whether or not she loves you.
D. Tell me whether she love you or not.

82. A. Tagore was greater than any poet.
B. Tagore was great than any poet.
C. Tagore was greater then any poet.
D. Tagore was greater than any other poet.

83. A. Going up the hill, an old temple was seen.
B. Going up to the hill, an old temple was seen.
C. On our going up the hill, an old temple was seen.
D. By going up to the hill, an old temple was seen.

84. A. The reason of her failure last time was due to her negligence.
B. The reason of her failure last time is due to her negligence.
C. Her failure last time was due to her negligence.
D. Her failure last time is on account of her negligence.

85. A. Nothing is more deplorable as dishonesty of this kind.
B. Nothing is so deplorable as dishonesty of this kind.
C. Nothing is such deplorable like dishonesty of this kind.
D. Nothing is more deplorable than dishonesty of this kind.

86. A. My cousin asked me that why did I not write to him?
B. My cousin asked me why did I not write to him?
C. My cousin asked me as to why did I not write to him?
D. My cousin asked me why I did not write to him.

87. A. She has no other ambition but only to pass the examination.
B. She has no ambition but only to pass the examination.
C. She has no ambition other than to pass the examination.
D. She has no other ambition other then to pass the examination.

88. A. If I could have worked hard, I would have passed the examination.
B. If I could work hard, I would have passed the examination.
C. If I might have worked hard, I would have passed the examination.
D. If I had worked hard, I would have passed the examination.

89. A. Four men were suspected of the crime but none of them confessed their guilt.
B. Four men were suspected of the crime but none of them accepted their guilt.
C. Four men were suspected of the crime but none of them admitted their guilt.
D. Four men were suspected of the crime, but none of them confessed his guilt.

90. A. Sita is younger to Rita but senior than her (Rita) in service.
B. Sita is younger to Rita but more senior to her (Rita) in service.
C. Sita is younger than Rita, but senior to her (Rita) in service.
D. Sita is more younger than Rita but senior to her (Rita) in service.

91. A. Tell me how are you?
B. Say me how are you?
C. Tell to me how are you?
D. Tell me how you are?

92. A. He denied that he was not a dacoit.
B. He denied that he not was a dacoit.
C. He denied he was not a dacoit.
D. He denied that he was a dacoit.

93. A. She insisted to go to Kuala Lumpur.
B. She insisted for going to Kuala Lumpur.
C. She insisted on going to Kuala Lumpur.
D. She insisted at going to Kuala Lumpur.

94. A. She gave me a chair to sit.
B. She gave me a chair for sitting.
C. She gave me a chair to be seated.
D. She gave me a chair to sit on.

95. A. He is one of the wisest persons who has ever lived.
B. He is one of the wisest persons who have ever lived.
C. He is one of the wisest persons which has ever lived.
D. He is one of the wisest persons which have ever lived.

96. A. Nobody in their senses could do such a nasty work.
B. Nobody in their senses could do such a good work.
C. Nobody in his senses could do such a nasty work.
D. Nobody in their senses could do such a nasty work.

97. A. Please tell me where is the Birla Temple?
B. Please say me where is the Birla Temple?
C. Please tell to me where is the Birla Temple?
D. Please tell me where the Birla Temple is?

98. A. They have and are still doing excellent work.
B. They have and have still doing excellent work.
C. They have and have still been doing excellent work.
D. They have done and are still doing excellent work.

99. A. All our family member have gone to Calcutta.
B. All our family member has gone to Calcutta.
C. All our family member have gone to Calcutta.
D. All the members of our family have gone to Calcutta.

100. A. Although we are living in Delhi for fifty years, we have not seen the Red Fort.
B. Although we are living in Delhi for fifty years, we had not seen the Red Fort.
C. Although we have been living in Delhi for fifty years, we have not seen the Red Fort.
D. Although we live in Delhi for fifty years, we had not seen the Red Fort.

ANSWERS

1	2	3	4	5	6	7	8	9	10
D	A	C	D	D	D	D	D	C	B
11	**12**	**13**	**14**	**15**	**16**	**17**	**18**	**19**	**20**
A	C	A	C	A	C	A	D	D	A
21	**22**	**23**	**24**	**25**	**26**	**27**	**28**	**29**	**30**
B	B	A	A	D	D	B	C	D	A
31	**32**	**33**	**34**	**35**	**36**	**37**	**38**	**39**	**40**
B	C	C	B	B	B	D	C	B	B
41	**42**	**43**	**44**	**45**	**46**	**47**	**48**	**49**	**50**
C	C	B	B	D	D	D	D	B	B
51	**52**	**53**	**54**	**55**	**56**	**57**	**58**	**59**	**60**
D	D	C	D	C	B	B	C	D	C
61	**62**	**63**	**64**	**65**	**66**	**67**	**68**	**69**	**70**
D	D	D	D	C	C	D	C	D	D
71	**72**	**73**	**74**	**75**	**76**	**77**	**78**	**79**	**80**
B	C	D	D	C	B	D	C	D	B
81	**82**	**83**	**84**	**85**	**86**	**87**	**88**	**89**	**90**
C	D	C	C	D	D	C	D	D	C
91	**92**	**93**	**94**	**95**	**96**	**97**	**98**	**99**	**100**
D	D	C	D	B	C	D	D	D	C

4

Transformation of Sentences

A sentence may be written in many different ways conveying the same meaning. This is called transformation of sentences. Practise various methods of transformation given below:

REMOVING 'TOO'

By replacing 'too' with 'so that'

1. He is too weak to walk.
   He is so weak that he cannot walk.
2. The book was too tough to comprehend.
   The book was so tough that it could not be comprehended.

☛ Sentence No. 1 is in the Present Tense so in it 'cannot' has been used; Sentence No. 2 is in the Past Tense, so, in it 'could not' has been used.

INTERCHANGE OF DEGREE OF COMPARISON

Degree of Comparison of Adjectives

Read the following sentences:

1. She is as clever as a fox. (Positive)
   A fox is not cleverer than her. (Comparative)

☛ In Positive Degree as is used but in Comparative Degree a Negative sentence is used. If the negative has been used with the Positive Degree, it will be removed from the comparative degree.

2. He is not so weak as his brother. (Positive)
   He is stronger than his brother. (Comparative)
3. Shimla is the coldest tourist spot in India. (Superlative)
   Shimla is colder than any other tourist spot in India. (Comparative)
   No other tourist spot is as cold as Shimla. (Positive)
4. Rohit is one of the most intelligent boys in our class. (Superlative)
   Rohit is more intelligent than most other boys in our class. (Comparative)
   Very few boys in our class are so intelligent as Rohit. (Positive)

5. Gold is not the most expensive metal. (Superlative)
A few metals are more expensive than gold. (Comparative)
Some metals are at least as expensive as gold. (Positive)
6. Lead is the heaviest of all metals. (Superlative)
Lead is heavier than any other metal. (Comparative)
No other metal is so heavy as lead. (Positive)

CHANGING IMPERATIVE SENTENCES INTO ASSERTIVE

Read the following sentences:

1. Walk fast. (Imperative)
You are ordered to walk fast. (Affirmative)
2. Let us take a cup of tea. (Imperative)
It is proposed that we should take a cup of tea. (Affirmative)
3. Please bring me a glass of water. (Imperative)
You are requested to bring me a glass of water. (Affirmative)
4. Work hard. (Imperative)
You are advised to work hard. (Affirmative)
5. Don't smoke. (Negative imperative)
You are forbidden to smoke. (Assertive)

INTERCHANGE OF AFFIRMATIVE AND NEGATIVE SENTENCES

Read the following sentences:

1. He runs slow. (Affirmative)
He does not run fast. (Negative)
2. He loves himself the most. (Affirmative)
He does not love anybody more than himself. (Negative)
3. Mr Sharma is a busy man. (Affirmative)
Mr Sharma is not an idle man. (Negative)
4. She is as brilliant as you. (Affirmative)
You are not more brilliant than her. (Negative)
5. He spoke angrily. (Affirmative)
He did not speak calmly. (Negative)

INTERCHANGE OF INTERROGATIVE AND ASSERTIVE SENTENCES

Read the following sentences:

1. Why to speak ill of anybody? (Interrogative)
We should not speak ill of anybody. (Assertive)
2. Who can win his fate? (Interrogative)
No one can win his fate. (Assertive)
3. Where will you find such beautiful shoes? (Interrogative)
You will not find such beautiful shoes anywhere. (Assertive)

4. How can he die without paying my debt? (Interrogative)
   He cannot die without paying my debt. (Assertive)
5. When will he learn manners? (Interrogative)
   He will never learn manners. (Assertive)
6. What can be done now? (Interrogative)
   Nothing can be done now. (Assertive)

INTERCHANGE OF EXCLAMATORY AND ASSERTIVE SENTENCES

Read the following sentences:

1. What a beautiful flower it is! (Exclamatory)
   It is a very beautiful flower. (Assertive)
2. How beautiful the Taj is! (Exclamatory)
   I am surprised that the Taj is very beautiful. (Assertive)
3. O for a one-rupee coin! (Exclamatory)
   A one-rupee coin is urgently desired. (Assertive)
4. Would that I were rich! (Exclamatory)
   I wish that I were rich. (Assertive)
5. O that I were rich! (Exclamatory)
   I wish that I were rich! (Assertive)

INTERCHANGE OF PARTS OF SPEECH

Read the following sentences:

1. This way you will **minimize** the risk. (Verb)
   This way you will bring the risk to the **minimum level**. (Adjective)
2. She fought **courageously**. (Adverb)
   She showed a great **courage** in the fight. (Noun)
3. She does not speak the **truth**. (Noun)
   She is not **truthful**. (Adjective)
4. He fought **bravely**. (Adverb)
   He fought with **bravery**. (Noun)
5. He **ran** fast. (Verb)
   He ran a fast **race**. (Noun)
6. He showed **generosity** towards his opponent. (Noun)
   He was **generous** towards his opponent. (Adjective)

CHANGING OF SIMPLE SENTENCES INTO COMPOUND ONES

Read the following sentences:

1. Besides being abused he was charged with misbehaving with others. (Simple)
   He was not only abused but also charged with misbehaving with others. (Compound)
2. You must run fast to catch the bus. (Simple)
   Run fast or you may miss the bus. (Compound)

3. Having finished her kitchen work, Mrs Sharma sat against the T.V. set. (Simple)
   Mrs Sharma finished her kitchen work and sat against the T.V. set. (Compound)
4. In spite of bitter cold, they managed to climb the hill. (Simple)
   It was bitter cold, yet they managed to climb the hill. (Compound)
5. In spite of being strong, he dare not oppose his opponents. (Simple)
   He is strong but still he dare not oppose his opponents. (Compound)

CHANGING OF SIMPLE SENTENCES INTO COMPLEX ONES

Read the following sentences:

1. In spite of being on crutches, he managed to catch the thief. (Simple)
   Though he was on crutches, he caught the thief. (Complex)
2. She is too weak in mathematics to solve even a simple sum. (Simple)
   She is so weak in mathematics that she cannot solve even a simple sum. (Complex)
3. The girl in all black is my classmate. (Simple)
   The girl, who is in all black, is my classmate. (Complex)
4. Because of/Owing to his negligence he lost his credibility. (Simple)
   He lost his credibility because he was negligent. (Complex)
5. He was happy at having been able to make an impressive speech. (Simple)
   He was happy that he was able to make an impressive speech. (Complex)
6. Put the ring at the place of your finding. (Simple)
   Put the ring where you found it. (Complex)

CHANGING OF COMPOUND SENTENCES INTO COMPLEX SENTENCES

Read the following sentences:

1. He is intelligent, but he is unkind. (Compound)
   Although he is intelligent, he is unkind. (Complex)
2. Buy a ticket or you cannot go inside the hall. (Compound)
   You cannot go inside the hall unless you buy a ticket. (Complex)
3. He could not attend the meeting, for he was ill. (Compound)
   He could not attend the meeting because he was ill. (Complex)
4. Work hard or you won't be able to earn a lot. (Compound)
   If you don't work hard, you cannot earn a lot. (Complex)
5. It was fog all around, yet he managed to cross the uneven stretch of land. (Compound)
   Although it was fog all around, he managed to cross the uneven stretch of land. (Complex)

ACTIVE & PASSIVE VOICE

Sentences containing a transitive verb can usually be written in Active as well as Passive voice. When the subject acts upon the object the sentence is written in Active voice. When the subject is acted upon, the sentence is written in Passive voice.

1. Do you read a book? (Active)
   Is a book read by you? (Passive)

2. He flies an aeroplane. (Active)
An aeroplane is flown by him. (Passive)
3. She is unfolding the bed sheet. (Active)
The bed sheet is being unfolded by her. (Passive)
4. Are the boys singing songs? (Active)
Are songs being sung by the boys? (Passive)
5. Mohit has forwarded your request. (Active)
Your request has been forwarded by Mohit. (Passive)
6. Have you ever seen the Taj? (Active)
Has the Taj ever been seen by you? (Passive)
7. He freed all the slaves. (Active)
All the slaves were freed by him. (Passive)
8. Did the dog bite the stranger? (Active)
Was the stranger bitten by the dog? (Passive)
9. Ajeet was helping his relatives. (Active)
His relatives were being helped by Ajeet. (Passive)
10. Was Karan grazing the horses? (Active)
Were the horses being grazed by Karan? (Passive)
11. She had gained great flesh. (Active)
Great flesh had been gained by her. (Passive)
12. Had you gripped the knob on the door? (Active)
Had the knob on the door been gripped by you? (Passive)
13. I'll hit him hard. (Active)
He will be hit hard by me. (Passive)
14. Will you imitate your brother? (Active)
Will your brother be imitated by you? (Passive)
15. You will have opened the envelope? (Active)
The envelope will have been opened by you. (Passive)
16. Will she have printed her name on the title page? (Active)
Will her name have been printed on the title page by her? (Passive)

USE OF TIME-CLAUSES

As soon as
No sooner did .... than
Hardly had .... when
Scarcely had .... when or before

These sentences are used to express two actions taking place immediately one after the other.

1. As soon as the cat saw the dog, it started to run.
2. No sooner did the cat see the dog than it started to run.
3. Hardly had the cat seen the dog when it started to run.
4. Scarcely had the cat seen the dog when it started to run.

MULTIPLE CHOICE QUESTIONS

Directions: *In the following questions, one out of the given four alternatives is the correct transformation of the given statement, pick that one.*

1. You must be present in the meeting.
This statement can be converted into Negative as—
A. Nobody should be absent from the meeting.
B. You must not be absent from the meeting.
C. Anybody cannot be absent from the meeting.
D. You must not walk out of the meeting.

2. It is a beautiful bird.
This statement can be converted into Exclamatory as—
A. Is it a beautiful bird?
B. How is it a beautiful bird?
C. Who says it is not a beautiful bird?
D. What a beautiful bird it is!

3. It does not matter if we lose the match.
This statement can be converted into Interrogative as—
A. What does it matter if we lose the match?
B. Does it not matter if we lose the match?
C. Who says it does not matter if we lose the match?
D. How can we lose the match?

4. How happy I am!
This statement can be converted into Assertive as—
A. Am I happy?
B. I cannot say I am happy.
C. I am very happy.
D. How is it that I am happy?

5. There is none who cannot buy a bicycle.
This statement can be converted into Affirmative as—
A. Nobody can buy a bicycle.
B. Any one can buy a bicycle.
C. Some people cannot buy a bicycle.
D. It is useless to buy a bicycle.

6. You are forbidden to pluck flowers.
This statement can be converted into negative as—
A. You should not pluck flowers.
B. You are allowed to pluck flowers.
C. You are not allowed to pluck all the flowers.
D. You should give up the habit of plucking flowers.

7. He will definitely come here.
This statement can be converted into interrogative as—
A. When will he come here?
B. With whom will he come here?
C. How will he come here?
D. Will he not come here?

8. What a comfortable life he leads!
This sentence can be converted into an assertive sentence as—
A. I do not understand why he leads a comfortable life.
B. He leads a very comfortable life.
C. How does he lead a comfortable life.
D. Nobody knows how his life has become comfortable.

9. You should not absent yourself from the class any day.
This negative sentence can be converted into an affirmative one as—
A. You should be present in the class every day.
B. You should absent yourself from the class only rarely.
C. It is improper for you to be absent from the class.
D. You can come to the class any day you like.

10. What is the cause for worry?
This interrogative sentence can be converted into an assertive sentence as—
A. There is some cause for worry.
B. There is not much cause for worry.

C. There is no cause for worry.
D. Never think of a cause for worry.

11. You should give full information.
This statement can be converted into negative as—
A. Everybody should not give full information.
B. Nobody is allowed to give full information.
C. You should not hide anything.
D. You should not give full information only.

12. You dare not speak against me in public.
This statement can be converted into Interrogative as—
A. Dare you speak against me in public?
B. Is it proper for you to speak against me in public?
C. Can anybody speak against somebody in public?
D. Speaking against anybody in public is nobody's business.

13. A sailor should not be afraid of water.
This statement can be converted into Exclamatory as—
A. Should a sailor be afraid of water?
B. A sailor and afraid of water!
C. How afraid of water a sailor is!
D. A sailor cannot be afraid of water.

14. Oh! What an interesting book that was.
This statement can be converted into assertive as—
A. What an interesting book it was!
B. It was a very interesting book.
C. A very interesting book was read by me.
D. It was not an interesting book at all.

15. What can be done now?
This interrogative sentence can be converted into an assertive one as—
A. Nothing can be done now.
B. You can do everything now.
C. They can do something now.
D. Something can be done now.

16. It is useless to give any advice to an obstinate person.
This statement can be converted into negative as—
A. It is useless to ask an obstinate peson not to seek advice.
B. It is of no use giving advice to an obstinate person.
C. An obstinate person does not like the person who gives him any advice.
D. Some people do not make any use of advice given to obstinate persons.

17. Good people do not hate others.
This statement can be converted into interrogative as—
A. Do good people never hate others?
B. Why do not good people hate others?
C. When do good people say that they hate others.
D. Do good people hate others?

18. Isolation is very horrible for a child.
This statement can be converted into exclamatory as—
A. How horrible for a child isolation is !
B. How for a child isolation is horrible !
C. How horrible is for a child isolation !
D. How isolation is horrible for a child !

19. What a lame excuse !
This statement can be converted into assertive as—
A. A lame excuse it is.
B. How lame this excuse is.
C. Why do you make a lame excuse?
D. It is a very lame excuse.

20. True friends help each other not just once or twice.
This statement can be converted into affirmative as—
A. True friends help each other several times.
B. True friends help each other even unasked.
C. True friends help each other if they can.
D. True friends are helpful to each other.

Directions: *Select the correct transformation of the given sentences.*

21. She is too proud to listen to you.
A. She is very proud to listen to you.
B. She feels too proud to listen to you.
C. She is so proud listening to you.
D. She is so proud that she will not listen to you.

22. He ran so slowly that he could not catch the train.
   A. He ran so slowly to catch the train.
   B. He ran very slowly to catch the train.
   C. He ran too slowly to catch the train.
   D. He ran too slow to catch the train.

23. I like him because he is good person.
   A. He is a good person. I like him.
   B. He is a good person for which I like him.
   C. He is a good person as I like him.
   D. He is a good person for I like him.

24. In spite of working hard, he failed.
   A. He worked hard but he failed.
   B. He worked hard as he failed.
   C. He worked hard so he failed.
   D. He worked hard for which he failed.

25. Unless you work hard, you cannot pass.
   A. If you work hard, you cannot pass.
   B. Work hard if you cannot pass.
   C. You cannot pass without working hard.
   D. You should work hard, you can pass.

26. As soon as the thief saw the policeman, he started to run fast.
   A. No sooner did the thief see the policeman when he started to run fast.
   B. No sooner did the thief see the policeman than he started to run fast.
   C. No sooner did the thief saw the policeman when he started to run fast.
   D. No sooner did the thief saw the policeman than he started to run fast.

27. No sooner did I walk out of the house than it began to rain.
   A. Hardly did I walked out of the house when it began to rain.
   B. Hardly had I walked out of the house than it began to rain.
   C. Hardly had I walked out of the house then it began to rain.
   D. Hardly had I walked out of the house when it began to rain.

28. Hardly had the passenger boarded the bus when it punctured.
   A. Scarcely had the passenger boarded the bus than it punctured.
   B. Scarcely had the passenger boarded the bus then it punctured.
   C. Scarcely had the passenger boarded the bus when it punctured.
   D. Scarcely had the passenger boarded the bus but it punctured.

29. Scarcely had the ship berthed in America when it began to blow hard.
   A. No sooner did the ship berth in America than it began to blow hard.
   B. As soon as the ship berthed in America then it began to blow hard.
   C. Hardly had the ship berthed in America then it began to blow hard.
   D. Scarcely had the ship berthed in America then it began to blow hard.

30. No sooner did she alight from the train than the guard whistled.
   A. Scarcely had she alighted from the train then the guard whistled.
   B. Scarcely had she alighted from the train than the guard whistled.
   C. Scarcely had she alighted from the train when the guard whistled.
   D. Scarcely did she alight from the train when the guard whistled.

Directions: *In these questions, the sentences have been given in Active/Passive voice. From the given options, choose the one which best expresses the given sentence in Passive/Active voice.*

31. We chose him our leader.
   A. He was chosen our leader.
   B. He has been chosen our leader.
   C. He had chosen our leader.
   D. He have been chosen our leader.

32. Who made a maiden century?
   A. By whose was a maiden century made?
   B. By whom was a maiden century make?
   C. By whom was a maiden century made?
   D. By whom had a maiden century made?

33. I may help her in her project.
   A. She might be helped by me in her project.
   B. She may be helped by me in her project.
   C. She might be helped in her project by me.
   D. In her project, she may be help by me.

34. Take medicine in time.
A. Medicine should be taken in time.
B. Medicine will be taken in time.
C. Medicine will be took in time.
D. Medicine shall take in time.

35. I am solving the questions.
A. The questions are being solved by me.
B. The questions have been solved by me.
C. The questions are to be solved by me.
D. The question are solved by me.

36. May I take this pen?
A. May this pen will be taken by me?
B. May this pen shall be taken by me?
C. May this pen should be taken by me?
D. May this pen be taken by me?

37. Can we send it by air?
A. Can this be sent by air?
B. Can it be sent by air?
C. Can it go by air?
D. Can it be send by air?

38. Who wrote this book?
A. By whom was this book written?
B. By whom is this book written?
C. By whom was this book being written?
D. By whom is this book being written?

39. What did you buy?
A. What is bought by you?
B. What is being bought by you?
C. What was bought by you?
D. What was being bought by you?

40. Whom do you want?
A. Who is wanted by you?
B. Who is being wanted by you?
C. You are wanted by whom?
D. You are being wanted by whom?

ANSWERS

1	2	3	4	5	6	7	8	9	10
B	D	A	C	B	A	D	B	A	C
11	**12**	**13**	**14**	**15**	**16**	**17**	**18**	**19**	**20**
C	A	B	B	A	B	D	A	D	A
21	**22**	**23**	**24**	**25**	**26**	**27**	**28**	**29**	**30**
D	C	B	A	C	B	D	C	A	C
31	**32**	**33**	**34**	**35**	**36**	**37**	**38**	**39**	**40**
A	C	B	A	A	D	B	A	C	A

5

Narration

Direct Speech and Indirect Speech

The words spoken by a speaker are in Direct Speech.

The words spoken by somebody and expressed by someone else with some modification are known as Indirect Speech.

(*a*) Rohit says to me, "You do not understand me."

(*b*) Rohit tells me that I do not understand him.

The sentence (*a*) shows the words spoken by Rohit. So, it is a sentence of direct speech.

The sentence (*b*) shows the words spoken by Rohit and they have been reported with certain modification. So, it is a sentence of Indirect Speech.

Important Rules Regarding the change of Direct Speech into Indirect Speech

1. In a sentence of direct speech the verb outside the inverted commas is known as the Reporting Verb.
2. The words inside the inverted commas are known as Direct Speech.
3. When the sentence is indirect speech, it won't take a sign of exclamation or a sign of interrogation.
4. The Reporting Verb can be given in Present, Past or Future Tense.
5. When the Reporting Verb is in Present or Future Tense, there will be no change in the tense of direct speech while converting it into indirect speech.
6. When the Reporting Verb is in Past Tense the tense of direct speech will be changed while converting it into Indirect Speech.
7. The following adverbs and possessives should be changed as given:

(*i*) This into that

(*ii*) These into those

(*iii*) Here into there

(*iv*) Now into then

(*v*) Today into that day

(*vi*) Last night into the previous night

(*vii*) Tomorrow into the next day

(*viii*) The next day/week into the following day/week

(*ix*) Hence into thence.

Change of Tense

Reporting Verb	***Reporting Speech***	***Change of Tense***
Present Tense	Any Tense	No change
Future Tense	Any Tense	No change
Past Tense	Present/ Future Tense	Change into corresponding Past Tense
Past Tense	Past Indefinite Tense	Change into Past Perfect Tense
Past Tense	Past Continuous Tense	Change into Past Perfect Continuous Tense

Reporting Verb	*Reporting Speech*	*Change of Tense*
Past Tense	Past Pefect/ Perfect Continuous Tense	No change
Past Tense	Universal Truth	No change
Past Tense	Proverb	No change

Transformation Based on Special Rules

1. Rule Related to Interrogative Sentence

- If the answer of an interrogative sentence is possible in yes-no manner.

Illustration.

M.S. Dhoni told Rahul Dravid, "Will you help me?"

M.S. Dhoni asked Rahul Dravid whether he would help him.

☛ The answer of Reporting Verb is possible in yes-no manner.

Rule of Transformation from Direct to Indirect speech

Step I : Change R.V. into ask.

Step II : In place of comma use 'if/whether'.

Step III: Change interrogative sentence into assertive sentence.

- If the answer of an interrogative sentence is not possible in yes-no manner.

Illustration:

Rahul Dravid told Dhoni, "What do you want?"

Rahul Dravid asked Dhoni what he wanted.

☛ Only in Step II, you have to avoid comma and inverted comma and rest will be same as mentioned above.

2. Rule related to Imperative Sentence

- Imperative sentence is a sentence which shows Order/Advice/Request

Illustration:

My father said to me, "Go there".

My father ordered me to go there.

Rule of Transformation from Direct to Indirect Speech

Step I : Change R.V. as per meaning/sense of R.S. into order/request/advise.

Step II : In place of comma, use 'to'.

Step III: Rest portion will be same.

3. Rule related to Optative Sentence

- Optative sentence is a sentence which exposes the feeling of bless/curse/pray/wish.

Illustration:

Mother said to me, "May you live long!"

Mother blessed me that I might live long.

Rule of Transformation from Direct to Indirect Speech

Step I : Change R.V. as per meaning/sense of R.S. into bless/curse/pray/wish.

Step II : In place of comma, use 'that'.

Step III: Change optative sentence into assertive sentence.

4. Rule related to Exclamatory Sentence

- Exclamatory sentence is a sentence which takes note of exclamatory (!) mark in that sentence showing inner feeling.

Illustration:

She said, "Alas! I am ruined".

She exclaimed with sorrow that she was ruined.

Rule of Transformation from Direct to Indirect Speech

Step I : Change R.V. as per meaning/sense of R.S. into exclaim/exclaims/ exciaimed/will or shall exclaim + joy/sorrow/anger/surprise/applause/ contempt.

Step II : Change comma into that.

Step III: Change note of exclamation (!) into full (.)

Step IV : Change exclamatory sentence into assertive sentence.

MULTIPLE CHOICE QUESTIONS

Directions: *Each sentence in direct speech is followed by four options in indirect speech, only one is correct. Spot the correct answer.*

1. She said, ''Shall I thread the needle?''
A. She asked if she should thread the needle.
B. She asked if she shall thread the needle.
C. She requested if she should thread the needle.
D. She says that if she would thread the needle.

2. We said, ''What a place it is!''
A. We said that it was a very fine place.
B. We said that is a very fine place.
C. We said that the place is fine.
D. We exclaimed with joy that the place was very fine.

3. My father said, ''The earth is round''.
A. My father said that the earth was round.
B. My father says that the earth is round.
C. My father said that the earth is round
D. My father ordered that the earth is round.

4. The teacher said, ''Don't make a noise''.
A. The teacher says to us not to make a noise.
B. The teacher asked us not to make a noise.
C. The teacher requested us not to make a noise.
D. The teacher asked us not to made a noise.

5. He said, ''Bring a chair at once''.
A. He ordered to bring a chair at once.
B. He requested to bring a chair at once.
C. He told to bring a chair at once.
D. He says to bring a chair at once.

6. I said to my sister, "Please, give me more money".
A. I requested my sister to give me more money.
B. I ordered my sister to give me more money.
C. I advised my sister to gave me more money.
D. I requested my sister to give her more money.

7. Baby said, "I will go".
A. Baby said that she will go.
B. Baby said that she could go.
C. Baby say that she will go.
D. Baby said that she would go.

8. The teacher says, "Two and two makes four".
A. The teacher says that two and two made four.
B. The teacher wishes that two and two makes four.
C. The teacher advises that two and two makes four.
D. The teacher says that two and two makes four.

9. He told me, "Shall I go to the picture?"
A. He asked that he should go to the picture.
B. He asked me if he shall go to the picture.
C. He asked me if he should go to the picture.
D. He requested me to go to the picture.

10. I told Ravi, "Do have a cup of tea".
A. I ordered Ravi to have a cup of tea.
B. I advised Ravi to had a cup of tea.
C. I requested Ravi to have a cup of tea.
D. I said Ravi to have a cup of cold tea.

11. She said, "I am an early-riser".
A. She regretted that she was an early-riser.
B. She said that she is an early-riser.
C. She said that she was an early-riser.
D. She regretted that she is an early-riser.

12. The police officer said to the criminal, "Speak as I tell you".
A. The police officer directed the criminal to speak as he told him.
B. The police officer told the criminal to speak as he told him.
C. The police officer advised the criminal to speak as he told him.
D. The police officer requested the criminal to speak as he told him.

13. The preacher said to me, "May God help you!"
A. The preacher prayed that God might help me.

B. The preacher prayed that God might help him.
C. The preacher requested that God might help me.
D. The preacher requested the God might help them.

14. She said to me, "Happy Diwali!"
A. She blessed me a happy Diwali.
B. She wished me a happy Diwali.
C. She prayed a happy Diwali.
D. She said to me a very happy Diwali.

15. He said, "Shall I open the gate?"
A. He asked that he should open the gate.
B. He asked if he should open the gate.
C. He ordered that he should open the gate.
D. He requested that he should open the gate.

16. She said to me, "Keep quite and listen to my words".
A. She requested me to keep quite and listen to her words.
B. She ordered me to keep quite and listen to her words.
C. She entreated me to keep quite and listen to her words.
D. She told me to keep quite and listen to her words.

17. My brother said to me, "What are you doing here?"
A. My brother asked me that what I was doing there.
B. My brother asked me what I was doing there.
C. My brother asked me that what was I doing there.
D. My brother asked me what I was doing here.

18. Ravi said, "My father lived in this city two years ago."
A. Ravi said that his father had lived in that city two years before.
B. Ravi said that his father had lived in that city two years ago.
C. Ravi told that his father had lived in that city ago two years.
D. Ravi asked that his father had lived in that city before two years.

19. My brother said to me, "When I was young, I used to play cricket".
A. My brother told me that when I was young, I used to play cricket.
B. My brother told me that when I was young, I used to play cricket.
C. My brother told me that when he was young, I used to play cricket.
D. My brother told me that when he was young, he used to play cricket.

20. The student said, "Sir, I am not guilty".
A. The student said with respect that he was not guilty.
B. The student pleaded that he was not guilty.
C. The student pleaded with respect that he was not guilty.
D. The student said respectfully that he was not guilty.

21. Mohini said to me, "Trust in God."
Mohini advised me:
A. that I should trust in God.
B. should trust in God.
C. trusted in God.
D. to trust in God.

22. I said to him, "Let us go to school."
I told him:
A. we would go to school.
B. we shall go to school.
C. that we would go to school.
D. that we should go to school.

23. Rajni said, "May God bless you?"
Rajni:
A. exclaimed with wish that God might bless me.
B. expressed a wish that God might bless me.
C. asked God to bless me.
D. shouted with joy to bless me.

24. My mother said to me, "Do not have so many friends."
My mother forbade me:
A. to have so many friends.
B. not to have so many friends.

C. to have been so many friends.
D. to possess so many friends.

25. Ram said, "Pay attention to me."
Ram asked:
A. pay attention to him.
B. paid attention to him.
C. having paid attention to him.
D. to pay attention to him.

Directions (Qs. 26 to 30): *A sentence correctly changed into indirect narration is followed by four sentencs in the direct narration. Pick out from the alternative one which, when changed into indirect narration will be the same as the indirect sentence preceding the alternatives.*

26. The driver asked the mechanic if he would repair his car.
A. "Repair the car," the driver ordered the mechanic.
B. "Please repair the car," the driver asked the mechanic.
C. "O, please repair the car," the driver asked the mechanic.
D. "Will you repair my car?" the driver asked the mechanic.

27. She thanked me and asked me not to disturb her.
A. "Thank you. Do not disturb me," she said.
B. "Dear friend than you, do not disturb," she said.
C. "Disturb not, thank you," she said.
D. "Thank you, please ask not to disturb," she said.

28. In a tone of anger she asked her boy-friend why he had come.
A. "You fool, why have you come," she said.
B. "Oh, why have you come," said she.
C. "You damned! Why have you come?" she said.
D. "You, you, O you why have you come," she said.

29. Calling him a coward, the girl asked him to come out.
A. "Come out, you coward!" said the girl.
B. "Come out," said the girl to the coward.
C. The girl said, "Alas coward come."
D. The girl said, "Come out".

30. He called her a naughty girl.
A. "Oh! naughty girl," said he.
B. "You naughty girl!" said he.
C. He said, "naughty girl."
D. "Naughty," boy said to her.

ANSWERS

1	2	3	4	5	6	7	8	9	10
A	D	C	B	A	A	D	D	C	C
11	**12**	**13**	**14**	**15**	**16**	**17**	**18**	**19**	**20**
C	A	A	B	B	B	B	A	D	C
21	**22**	**23**	**24**	**25**	**26**	**27**	**28**	**29**	**30**
A	D	B	A	D	D	A	C	A	B

6
Parts of Speech

Whatever we speak or state is called speech. Speech comprises sentences which are composed of words. We can divide words into different classes called parts of speech, according to their use. The parts of speech are eight in number as shown in the table given below along with their definitions and examples.

Part of speech	*Definition or Function*	*Examples*
Noun	Name of a person, place, animal, quality or thing	Ram, boy, dog, pen, sun, Delhi, truth, honesty
Pronoun	Used in place of a noun	I, you, he she, they
Articles & Determiners	Points out indefinite and definite nouns	a, an, the, few, some
Adjective	Describes a noun or pronoun	big, honest, wooden, valuable, quiet, deep, soft, narrow
Adverb	Describes a verb, an adjective or another adverb	silently, widely, softly, quietly, very, carefully
Verb	Tells about action or state of something or someone	is, am, was, have, do, like, walk, work, make, throw, tell
Conjuction	Joins words, clauses or sentences	and, but, when, yet, while, else
Preposition	Links a noun or pronoun to another word	at, to, after, on for, under, over, with
Interjection	Expresses sudden feelings or emotions	Ah!, Alas!, oh!, ouch!, hi!, well!, Hurrah!

NOUNS

A word which denotes a person, a thing, an animal or a place is said to be a noun.

There are two noun numbers in English — the *Singular* and the *Plural*.

Singular Numbers : A noun that denotes one person or one thing, is said to be in the Singular number. For example — book, pencil, bird, dog, hen etc. are in singular number.

Plural Number : A noun that denotes more than one person or one thing is said to be in plural number. For example — boys, pens, lions, girls, men etc. are in plural number.

REMEMBER

Singular	*Plural*
Cat	Cats
Pen	Pens
Tree	Trees
Bush	Bushes
Glass	Glasses
Judge	Judges
Watch	Watches
Thief	Thieves
Scarf	Scarves
Leaf	Leaves
Half	Halves
Roof	Roofs
Gulf	Gulfs
Radio	Radios
Folio	Folios
Volcano	Volcanoes
Potato	Potatoes
Piano	Pianos
Fly	Flies
Lady	Ladies
Lady	Ladies
Monkey	Monkeys
Child	Children
Woman	Women
Axis	Axes
Foot	Feet
Englishman	Englishmen
Vertex	Vertices
Book	Books
Room	Rooms
Bus	Buses
Box	Boxes
Dish	Dishes
Tax	Taxes
Calf	Calves
Knife	Knives
Wife	Wives
Wolf	Wolves
Monarch	Monarchs
Hoof	Hoofs
Staff	Staffs
Bamboo	Bamboos

Singular	*Plural*
Hero	Heroes
Mango	Mangoes
Photo	Photos
Baby	Babies
Country	Countries
Boy	Boys
Ox	Oxen
Man	Men
Tooth	Teeth
Basis	Bases
Goose	Geese
Radius	Radii
Stimulus	Stimuli

1. Note the change in plurals of the following nouns:

Singular	*Plural*
copy	copies
baby	babies
body	bodies
family	families
fly	flies
city	cities
army	armies
bay	bays
cry	cries
duty	duties
country	countries
diary	diaries
fairy	fairies
spy	spies
storey	storeys
monkey	monkeys

2. The following nouns do not undergo any change in plural form, in general:

Singular	*Plural*
deer	deer
thousand	thousand
hundred	hundred
dozen	dozen
sheep	sheep
pair	pair
score	score
gross	gross

☛ We can write—
(*a*) thousands of men; (*b*) two pairs of shoes; (*c*) dozens of mangoes; (*d*) scores of people etc.
But—
(*a*) two thousand rupees; (*b*) three hundred men; (*c*) five dozen eggs, etc.

3. The following nouns are usually used in plural forms. They take a plural verb after them:

eatables	fetters	surroundings
riches	alms	spectacles
trousers	pants	scissors
premises	thanks	annals
congratulations	goods	shorts
tongs	pains (for troubles)	arms

4. The following are the nouns which are plural in appearance but are usually used in singular number. They are followed by a singular verb:

news	politics	physics
mathematics	economics	ethics
politics	classics	gallows
statistics	athletics	innings
mechanics	summons	mumps

5. Collective nouns often used as plurals:

public	police	cattle
audience	clergy	folk
people	poultry	nation
elite	gentry	glitterati

6. The nouns that are usually used in singular forms:

advice	hair	rice
fuel	alphabet	machinery
offspring	issue	furniture
mischief	stationery	luggage
bedding	information	abuse

7. Material nouns are always used in singular number:

gold	copper	milk
water	silk	wool

☛ They may be used in plural with a different meaning. *e.g.,* copper coins (coppers), chains or fetters (irons), cans made of tin (tins).

GENDERS

The difference in sex is denoted by Gender in grammar. The various genders are as follows:

1. **Masculine Gender :** A noun that denotes a male is said to be of the masculine gender, as man, uncle, ox, boy etc.
2. **Feminine Gender :** A noun that denotes a female is said to be of feminine gender, as woman, aunt, princess, cow etc.
3. **Common Gender :** Nouns which denote both males and females are said to be of the common gender, as friend, cousin, person, parent, baby etc.
4. **Neuter Gender :** A noun that denotes the name of object without life is said to be of neuter gender, as file, table, pencil etc.

REMEMBER

Masculine	***Feminine***
Boy	Girl
Brother	Sister
Sorcerer	Sorceress
Father-in-law	Mother-in-law
Land-lord	Land-lady
Gentleman	Lady
Earl	Countess
Sir	Madam
Emperor	Empress
Pea-cock	Pea-hen
Hero	Heroine
Mr.	Mrs.
Master	Mistress
Heir	Heiress
Lion	Lioness
Actor	Actress
Colt	Filly
Horse	Mare
Hunter	Huntress
Abbot	Abbess
Author	Authoress
Widower	Widow
He-goat	She-goat
Bridegroom	Bride
Priest	Priestess

Masculine	Feminine
Shepherd	Shepherdess
Stag	Hind
Son	Daughter
Murderer	Murderess
Son-in-law	Daughter-in-law
Man-servant	Maid-servant
Bachelor	Spinster
Monk	Nun
Lad	Lass
Duke	Dutchess
Milk-man	Milk-maid
Step-father	Step-mother
Viceroy	Vicerine
Governor	Governess
Wizard	Witch
Host	Hostess
Mayor	Mayoress
Buck	Doe
Dog	Bitch
Count	Countess
Prince	Princess
God	Goddess
Ox	Cow
Grand-father	Grand-mother
Milk-man	Milk-woman
Tiger	Tigress
Poet	Poetess
Nephew	Niece
Fox	Vixen

PRONOUNS

The repetition of a noun in a sentence or a set of sentences is really boring. So, instead of repeating the noun, we can use a word (for that noun) called the pronoun.

"A pronoun is a word that we use instead of a noun".

Example:

This is *Sachin. He* plays cricket.

☛ *He* is the pronoun used in place of *Sachin.*

Kinds of Pronouns

1. **Personal pronouns :** A pronoun which is used instead of the name of a person is known as a 'Personal Pronoun'. A list of the 'Personal pronouns' is listed below :

   I, my, mine, me, we
   (First Person)
   You, your, yours
   (Second Person)
   He, his, him, she, her, hers, it, its, they, their, theirs, them
   (Third Person)

2. **Demonstrative, Indefinite and Distributive Pronouns :**

   (a) Demonstrative Pronouns : Pronouns used to point out the objects to which they refer are called Demonstrative Pronouns.

   Examples:

   (i) *This* is a present from my uncle.
   (ii) *These* are merely excuses.
   (iii) Bembay mangoes are better than *those* of Bangaluru.

   (b) Indefinite Pronouns : All pronouns which refer to persons or things in a general way and do not refer to any particular person or thing are called Indefinite Pronouns.

   Examples:

   (i) *Somebody* has stolen my watch.
   (ii) *Few* escaped unhurt.
   (iii) Did you ask *anybody* to come?

   (c) Distributive Pronouns : Each, either, neither are called distributive pronouns because they refer to persons or things one at a time. For this reason they are always singular and followed by the verb in singular.

   Examples:

   (i) *Each* of the men received a reward.
   (ii) *These* men received *each* a reward.
   (iii) *Either* of you can go.

3. **Relative Pronouns :** A relative pronoun refers or relates to some noun going before, which is called its Antecedent.

Examples:

(*i*) I met Hari *who* used to live here.

(*ii*) I have found the pen *which* I had lost.

(*iii*) Here is the book *that* you lent me.

4. **Interrogative Pronouns :** These pronouns, are used for asking questions.

Examples:

(*i*) *Whose* book is this?

(*ii*) *What* will all the neighbours say?

(*iii*) *Which* do you prefer, tea or coffee?

☛ Interrogative pronouns can also be used in asking indirect questions. Consider the following examples:

(*i*) I asked *who* was speaking.

(*ii*) Tell me *what* you have done.

(*iii*) Say *which* you would like best.

Behaviour of the Pronouns

1. If three pronouns are used together in the same sentence they are arranged in the following order :

2	+	3	+	1
↓		↓		↓
Second Person		Third Person		First Person

Examples:

I, you and he must help *that* poor man. (Incorrect)

You, he and I must help *that* poor man. (Correct)

2. When two or more singular nouns are joined by and, the pronoun used for them should be plural.

Examples:

Mohan and Sohan are friends. *They* play football. *They* live at Lajpat Nagar.

3. But if these nouns joined by and refer to the same person or thing, the pronoun used should be singular.

Examples:

(*i*) Delhi, the beautiful city and the capital of India, is famous for *its* historical monuments.

(*ii*) The manager and owner of the firm expressed *his* views on the demands of the workers.

4. When two nouns are used with as well as, the pronoun agrees with the first subject.

Examples:

(*a*) Mohan as well as his friends is doing *his* work.

(*b*) The students as well as their teachers are doing *their* work.

5. When two singular nouns joined by 'and' are preceded by *each* or *every,* the pronoun used must be singular and should agree in gender with the second noun.

Examples:

(*a*) Every man and every woman will do *her* best for the nation.

(*b*) Each boy and each girl went to *her* house.

6. When two nouns are joined by using 'with', the pronoun agrees with the noun coming before 'with'.

Examples:

(*a*) The boy with *his* parents has gone to see a movie.

(*b*) The children with *their* parents have gone to picnic.

7. When two different nouns are joined by either.......... or; neither .... nor, the pronoun is used according to the number and gender of the second noun.

Examples:

(*a*) Either your sister or you have done *your* work.

(*b*) Neither the students nor the teacher was in *his* class.

8. The pronoun coming after '*than*' must be in the same case as that coming before '*than*'.

Examples:

(*a*) She plays better than *me.* (Incorrect)
She plays better than *I.* (Correct)

(*b*) His elder brother is more intelligent than *him.* (Incorrect)
His elder brother is more intelligent than *he.* (Correct)

9. 'Many a' always takes a singular pronoun and singular verb.

Example:

Many a soldier has met *his* death in the battle field.

10. 'Who', 'Whose', 'Whom' are used only for persons.

Examples:

(*a*) *Who* is knocking at the door?

(*b*) *Whose* pen is this?

(*c*) *What* do you want?

11. 'Which' is used for things.

Example:

Which game do you like?

MULTIPLE CHOICE QUESTIONS

Directions: *In the following questions choose the correct options to fill in the blanks.*

1. The place was so dirty that ..... wished to run away from there.
A. everybody B. anybody
C. few D. some

2. ..... was there to help me.
A. Somebody B. Anything
C. Anybody D. Nobody

3. Is there ...... to eat?
A. some B. something
C. any D. few

4. ..... of the students were making a great noise.
A. Anyone B. Somebody
C. Many D. Nobody

5. ..... of the students can solve this sum.
A. Someone B. Anybody
C. Somebody D. None

6. ...... of us should try our best to make India a heaven.
A. Any B. Somebody
C. Anybody D. All

7. ...... of us do not know the real meaning of our lives.
A. Any B. Something
C. Several D. Many

8. My .... black.
A. hairs are
B. hair is
C. hairs shall
D. hair will

9. She saw two .... on the last Sunday.
A. thiefs B. theifs
C. thieves D. theives

10. My sister is a ....
A. bacheloress B. bachelor
C. unmaried D. spinster

11. One is supposed to do ....
A. our duty B. their duty
C. one's duty D. his duty

12. Take anything .... you want.
A. that B. which
C. than D. then

13. I cannot tolerate ....
A. separated you
B. your separation
C. separation from you
D. you separated

14. He is .... faithful partner.
A. Yours B. You
C. Your D. Your's

15. Ajay is more smart than ....
A. her B. hers
C. herself D. she

16. Vivek works harder than ....
A. me B. I
C. her D. his

17. They should help ....
A. the poor people
B. the poor
C. the poor persons
D. the poor peoples

18. .... are mad.
A. All his sons
B. His all sons
C. Sons all his
D. All sons his

19. The poor fellow .... to fate.
A. resigned
B. resigned himself
C. resigned itself
D. resigned themselves

20. Nobody will help you but ....
A. I B. me
C. ours D. his

21. It is a good chance, You must avail .... this opportunity.
A. of B. yourself of
C. for D. from

22. The person who is elected .... my relative.
A. is B. he is
C. his D. him

23. He made ....
A. yours mention
B. mention of you
C. mention for you
D. mention about you

24. .... I know, he is quite faithful.
A. As far as B. So far as
C. So far this D. So far so

25. It is a duty of a person to take .... for his family.
A. pain B. pains
C. pain-killers D. pained

26. She does not love .... husband.
A. his B. her
C. its D. their

27. Let .... work together.
A. him and me B. he and I
C. he and him D. I and me

28. Copper, Silver and Gold ....
A. each will do
B. either will do
C. any one will do
D. any will do

29. Jessica and Roma are very irregular .... habits.
A. in her B. in their
C. in its D. in every

30. One likes to enjoy .... who was a great poet.
A. The sonnets of Shakespeare
B. Shakespeare's sonnets
C. Sonnets
D. Shakespeare

31. That is the boy .... everybody loves.
A. whom B. who
C. that D. whose

32. That is the girl .... won the first prize.
A. whom B. who
C. whose D. which

33. That is the man .... purse was lost.
A. who B. whom
C. whose D. their

ANSWERS

1	2	3	4	5	6	7	8	9	10
A	D	B	C	D	D	D	B	C	D
11	12	13	14	15	16	17	18	19	20
C	A	C	C	D	B	B	A	B	B
21	22	23	24	25	26	27	28	29	30
B	A	B	A	B	B	A	C	B	A
31	32	33							
A	B	C							

ARTICLES

The family of the articles has only three members. They are : A, An and The. However, they fall under two groups :

(*a*) Definite Article (*b*) Indefinite Article

'The' is known as definite article whereas 'a' and 'an' are known as indefinite articles.

Use of the Definite Article 'The'

'The' is used before:

1. The superlative degree :
   He is the ablest man of the town.
   (ablest is a superlative degree)
2. The name of states, countries etc. having a descriptive name :
   (*i*) The J & K is a small state. (J & K is a descriptive name)
   (*ii*) He lives in the U.S.A. (U.S.A. is a descriptive name)
   (But 'the Delhi' and 'the America' are wrong because neither Delhi nor America is a descriptive name)
3. The names of the scriptures :
   The Gita is a holy book. (Gita is a scripture)
4. Name of newspapers :
   The Tribune is published from Chandigarh.
5. Name of rivers, canals, seas, oceans, bays, gulfs, groups of islands etc. :
   (*i*) The Ganga is a holy river.
   (*ii*) The Indian Ocean is the deepest ocean.
   (*iii*) The Persian Gulf is a narrow gulf.
6. The name of famous buildings :
   The Taj is one of the best buildings in India.
7. The names of nationals, sects and communities:
   (*i*) The English defeated the Germans in the World War.
   (*ii*) The rich should help the poor.
   (*iii*) The Hindus believe in the caste system.
8. Proper nouns used as common nouns :
   (*i*) Kalidas is the Shakespeare of India.
   (*ii*) Delhi is the London of India.
9. Famous historical events :
   The Industrial Revolution changed the face of England.
10. The directions and the celestial bodies :
    The sun rises in the east.
11. Titles :
    Akbar, the Great was loved by his subjects.

Do not use 'the' :

1. Before languages :
   The English is an international language. (Incorrect)
   English is an international language. (Correct)
2. Before the names of games :
   The hockey is a popular game. (Incorrect)
   Hockey is a popular game. (Correct)

Use of the Indefinite Articles 'A' and 'An'

'A' is used before :

1. All singular common nouns beginning with a consonant:
   (*i*) A boy sings a song.
   (*ii*) A black and a white cow were grazing in the field.
2. If a word begins with a vowel but gives the sound of a consonant, 'a' should be used before it :
   (*i*) He was helped in his work by a European.
   (*ii*) He is a one-eyed man.
   (*iii*) It is a useful work.

'An' is used as follows:

1. All singular common nouns beginning with a vowel (*i.e.*, a, e, i, o, u) :
   (*i*) He is an artist.
   (*ii*) He is an old man.
   (*iii*) I intend to buy an umbrella.
2. If a word starts with a consonant but gives the sound of a vowel, "an" should be used before it :
   (*i*) Brutus is an honourable man.
   (*ii*) He is an honour to his profession.

(*iii*) He is an L.L.B.
(*iv*) He is an M.A.
(*v*) You will reach there in an hour.

Demonstratives, that, these and those :

1. The demonstrative adjectives and pronouns are for objects nearby the speaker:
   (*i*) This (singular) those (plural)
   and for objects far away from the speaker:
   (*ii*) That (singular) those (plural)
2. Demonstratives are the only adjectives that agree in number with their nouns.
   (*i*) That hat is nice.
   (*ii*) Those hats are nice.
3. When there is the idea of selection, the pronoun "one" (or "ones") often follows the demonstrative.
   (*i*) I want a book. I'll get this (one).
   (*ii*) If the demonstrative is followed by an adjective, "one"(or "ones") must be used.
   (*iii*) I want a book. I'll get this big one.

MULTIPLE CHOICE QUESTIONS

Directions: *In the following questions choose the correct options to fill in the blanks.*

1. .... will have to be paid for this material.
A. Half rupee B. Half a rupee
C. A half rupee D. An half rupee

2. .... is taking keen interest in India.
A. The USA B. USA
C. An USA D. A USA

3. Only .... can save our country.
A. the Hitler B. a Hitler
C. Hitler D. an Hitler

4. I can run for.......... .
A. hundred miles B. the hundred miles
C. a hundred miles D. an hundred miles.

5. .... man-eater has been killed.
A. The B. A
C. An D. Either A or B

6. What .... fine idea!
A. the B. an
C. a D. No article

7. .... earth is moving around the sun.
A. An B. A
C. The D. No article

8. This is .... first example while I got.
A. the B. a
C. an D. No article

9. This is .... house which was built during earthquake.
A. a B. an
C. the D. No article

10. .... America is a rich country.
A. The B. An
C. A D. No article

11. .... U.S.A. is a developed country.
A. A B. An
C. The D. No article

12. .... Bible is a holy book.
A. A B. The
C. An D. No article

13. .... rich should help the poor.
A. The B. A
C. An D. No article

14. .... Gold is a costly metal.
A. The B. A
C. An D. No article

15. Kalidas is .... Shakespeare of India.
A. a B. an
C. the D. No article

16. I cannot do .... difficult work.
A. a such B. the such
C. such the D. such a

17. How foolish .... plan it is!
A. a B. an
C. the D. No article

18. An ink is .... useful article.
A. an B. a
C. the D. No article

19. There are .... husband and wife.
A. a B. an
C. the D. No article

20. He is learning .... French
A. the B. a
C. an D. No article

ANSWERS

1	2	3	4	5	6	7	8	9	10
B	A	B	C	D	C	C	A	C	D
11	**12**	**13**	**14**	**15**	**16**	**17**	**18**	**19**	**20**
C	B	A	D	C	D	A	B	D	D

ADJECTIVES & ADVERBS

An Adjective is a word which adds something to the meaning of a noun or a pronoun.

Mridula is an *intelligent* girl.

He has a *black* goat.

He is a *brilliant* student.

She is a *clever* girl.

It is a *beautiful* picture.

In the sentences given above, the words in italics are adjectives.

An Adverb is a word which qualifies the meaning of a Verb, an Adjective or another Adverb.

(*i*) He talks *slowly.*

(*ii*) He is a *very* good student.

(*iii*) He talks *very* slowly.

In sentence (*i*), *slowly* qualifies the verb *talks.*

In sentence (*ii*), *very* qualifies the adjective *good.*

In sentence (*iii*), *very* qualifies the adverb *slowly.*

Adjectives have three degrees of comparison :

1. **Positive Degree :** It expresses the common form of an adjective.

Example:

Ram is a *tall* boy.

In the above sentence *tall* is an adjective and expresses the common form.

2. **Comparative Degree :** It expresses the more of the same form.

Example:

Ram is *taller* than Mahesh.

In the above sentence *taller* is an adjective that expresses the more of the common form of the adjective *tall.*

"When and How to Use" Comparative Degree?

(*a*) Comparative Degree is used when two persons or two groups of persons or things are compared.

Examples :

(*a*) He is *wiser* than his younger brother.

(*b*) This glass is *cleaner* than the other.

(*b*) When two different qualities in the same person are compared, more is used instead of 'er' to form the comparative. The formula used in this case should be :

More + Positive Degree

She is *fairer* than polite. (Incorrect)

She is *more fair* than polite. (Correct)

(*c*) When selection of one out of two persons or things is meant, the degree of comparison is followed by of and *the* is used before it.

Example:

Zia is abler of *the* two sisters.

(*d*) If two comparatives are used in the same sentence to impress upon an idea, both should be preceded by the definite article.

Examples :

(*i*) The higher you go, the cooler it is.

(*ii*) The more we get, the more we desire.

(*e*) When one person or thing is compared with another of the same kind, other is used after the comparative degree. In such sentences other is normally preceded by any or all.

Examples:

(*i*) Kalidas is greater than any dramatist. (Incorrect)

Kalidas is greater than any other dramatist. (Correct)

(*ii*) Lead is heavier than all metals. (Incorrect)

Lead is heavier than all other metals. (Correct)

(*f*) Senior, junior, superior, inferior, prior, anterior (earlier than) and posterior (later than) are always followed by 'to'.

Examples:

(*i*) Ram is senior *to* Mohan by three years.

(*ii*) That pen is inferior *to* that.

(*iii*) He is junior *to* me in rank.

(*iv*) This event was posterior *to* that.

☛ Never use *than* after the above mentioned adjectives.

Important Information

(*a*) 'Preferable' is also used as an adjective of the comparative degree. As such, it is always followed by *to* and not *a*.

Death is preferable than dishonour. (Incorrect)

Death is preferable *to* dishonour. (Correct)

(*b*) To intensify the Degree of comparison, we use *far* or *much* before the comparative.

Examples:

(*i*) This book is *far* better than that.

(*ii*) His performance was *much* better than Mohan's.

Warning: Always avoid the use of double comparatives.

Don't say: Ram is more cleverer than his younger brother.

Say: Ram is cleverer than his younger brother.

3. **Superlative Degree :** It expresses the most of the common form of an adjective.

Example:

He is the ablest man of the town.

How and when to use the Superlative Degree?

(*a*) The Superlative Degree is used when more than two persons or things are compared.

(*b*) The Superlative Degree is generally preceded by 'the' and followed by 'of' in most of the cases or otherwise.

(*c*) When an adjective of the superlative degree is preceded by a Possessive Adjective or a Noun in the Possessive case, 'the' should not be used before it.

Example:

Which is Kalidas' best play?

It will be a blunder to use 'the' before the Superlative Degree in such cases.

Don't say : Which is Kalidas' the best play.

(*d*) To intensify the degree of comparison, *by far* is used before the superlative degree.

Example:

India is *by far* the most beautiful country of the world.

☛ Always avoid the use of double superlatives.

Don't say : He is the most strongest boy in the class.

Say : He is the strongest boy in the class.

Use of some Important Adjectives

1. (*a*) '**Some**' is used as follows :

(*i*) With countable nouns where it means — a little, a small quantity.

(*ii*) In a question which shows some request.

Examples:

(*i*) There is some water in the bottle.

(*ii*) Some of the students were absent yesterday.

(iii) Will you have some milk?
(iv) Will you buy some fruit for me?

(b) **'Any'** is used as follows :
(i) In negative sentences.
(ii) In interrogative sentences.
(iii) After 'Hardly', 'Scarcely' and 'Barely'.
(iv) After 'If'.

Examples:
(i) There is not any sugar in the pot.
(ii) We haven't any rice in the house.
(iii) I have hardly any money.
(iv) There are scarcely any plants in this field.
(v) If there is any danger, blow the whistle.

2. *(a)* **Older :** Older (and oldest) are used for persons animals and things. But 'Older' and 'Oldest' refer to the persons who do not belong to the same family.

Examples:
(i) Radha is older than Shyama.
(ii) John is the oldest member of the staff.

(b) **Elder** (and **eldest**) are used in respect of the members of the same family like sons, daughters, brothers, sisters.

Examples:
(i) My elder sister is a lecturer.
(ii) Meenakshi is the eldest of the three sisters.

☛ *(i)* 'Elder' is not followed by 'than'.
(ii) 'Elder' and 'Eldest' cannot be used for things.

---

3. *(a)* **'Few'** is negative and is the opposite of 'Many'. It means 'not many'.
(b) **'A few'** is positive and means 'some at least'. It is the opposite of 'None'.
(c) **'The few'** means 'minority' and suggests 'whether there is'.

Examples:
(i) We have few holidays in school.
(ii) Only a few boys will pass in the examination.
(iii) The few poems that he wrote are very popular.

4. *(a)* **Further** means 'something additional'.
(b) **Farther** means 'a greater distance'.

Examples:
(i) Further discussion will be held in the office of the principal.
(ii) Amritsar is farther from Delhi than Ambala.

5. *(a)* **Little** is negative. It means, 'not much', or 'hardly any'.
(b) **A little** is positive. It means 'some quantity'.
(c) **The little** denotes quantity. It means, 'not much but all that is, or whatever quantity there is'.

Examples:
(i) There is little hope of his success.
(ii) He knows a little of everything.
(iii) I have spent the little money I had.
(iv) The little knowledge of Urdu proved very useful to me.

6. *(a)* **'Much'** expresses 'quantity'.
(b) **'Many'** expresses 'number'.
(c) **'Many a'**—'Singular noun' and 'Singular verb' are used with 'many a'.

Examples:
(i) There is not *much* water in the jug.
(ii) *Many* boys are absent today.
(iii) *Many* a battle has been fought on the soil of India.

7. *(a)* **'Less'** denotes 'in a small degree'.
(b) **'Fewer'** denotes 'number'.

Examples:
(i) He devotes less time to his studies.
(ii) There are no fewer than ten chairs in this room.

8. *(a)* **'Each'** is used for a single number of 'two persons' or 'things'.
(b) **'Every'** is used for a single number of 'many persons' or 'things'.

Examples:
(i) Each boy must take part in games.
(ii) There were only two poets. Each poet recited his poem.

(iii) Every man dies in this world.
(iv) Every man is expected to do his duty.

9. (a) **'Either'** means one of the two or both.
(b) **'Neither'** is negative of the either.

Examples:
(i) You may buy either of these two chairs.
(ii) Neither of them could speak on the stage.

10. (a) **'Later'** expresses 'late in time'.
(b) **'Latter'** means 'second in position or order'.

Examples:
(i) My father reached later than I expected.
(ii) The latter position was better than the former.

Use of some Important Adverbs

1. (a) **Also, too, enough:**
(i) He taught English. Also, he edited the school magazine
(ii) He is a writer and also he is a painter.
(iii) He is too obstinate to listen to any reason.
(iv) This is too difficult a piece for the junior students.
(v) Sarla was kind enough to help the poor.
(vi) He is brave enough to face the truth.

☛ 'Too' is used in a negative sense, but enough is used in a positive sense.

(b) **Fairly and rather:** Both suggest the meaning 'moderately'. But, mainly 'fairly' is used with the words that denote a positive meaning and rather is used with the words that denote a negative meaning:
(i) Rita did fairly well in that competition, but her performance was rather poor in sports.
(ii) Mona is fairly rich, but she is rather stingy.

☛ 'Rather' can also be used in a positive sense.
(i) This is a rather interesting job.
(ii) That boy is rather smart.

(c) **Hardly, barely, scarcely:** These words mostly convey the negative suggestions and are almost similar.
(i) I have hardly any strength now.
(ii) There was barely any supply to the township,
(iii) There were scarcely a hundred guests present.

☛ With slight variance in the meaning, the words given above convey the idea of 'very little', 'not enough', 'lack of quantity and number'.

(d) **Yet, Still:** These adverbs can often be used to connect the sentence units:
(i) He has been defeated many times in the contest; still he wants to be a competitor.
(ii) Mona was sick; yet she went on doing her work.

(e) **Alone:**
(i) He alone (none else) is capable of handling that fire.
(ii) He hunted all alone in the forest. (not in any company)

Special Note:

(a) Apart from their conventional positions the adverbs might be used in different positions with different meanings and angles.
(i) He had only four books.
(ii) John only contacted his friend in need.
(iii) He greeted me only.
(iv) Only he greeted me there.

(b) **Inversion:** Some adverbs can be inverted *i.e.* placed in the beginning of the sentence and then be followed by an interrogative form. The most common of these adverb are: so, seldom, never, nowhere, under no circumstances, hardly, scarcely etc.
(i) So big was the bus that it could not enter the narrow lane.
(ii) Hardly had he reached the station when he received the message.

MULTIPLE CHOICE QUESTIONS

Directions: *In the following questions choose the correct options to fill in the blanks.*

1. The girl whom you met is the .... sister of Ravi.
A. eldest B. elder
C. older D. oldest

2. The historical place is ....
A. seeing worth B. worthy of seeing
C. worth seeing D. worthy seeing

3. These flowers smell ....
A. sweet B. sweetly
C. more sweetly D. sweetest

4. .... aspirant cannot pass the entrance examination.
A. Each B. Every
C. All D. No

5. Prem Chand .... second Shakespeare.
A. is a B. is
C. is the D. is an

6. .... student in the class got prizes.
A. Each and every B. Every and each
C. Every D. Never

7. It is .... picture than the one we saw last Monday.
A. interesting B. much interesting
C. more interesting D. most interesting

8. She is clever ....
A. that her mother is
B. as her mother is
C. to her mother is
D. than her mother is

9. They will get ....
A. Red, green and black paper
B. Red, green black paper
C. Red and green and black paper
D. Red green black paper

10. Health is .... wealth.
A. preferable to
B. more preferable than
C. more preferable to
D. most preferable then

11. .... water that was in the jug evaporated.
A. Little B. The little
C. Small D. A small

12. He has not sung .... songs.
A. much B. most
C. more D. many

13. Srishti has searched .... office.
A. whole the B. the whole
C. a whole D. some whole

14. Premchand was .... best and .... famous writer.
A. a, the most B. the, a most
C. the, more D. the, the most

15. William Shakespeare is famous as ....
A. a poet and a dramatist
B. a poet and dramatist
C. the poet and the dramatist
D. a poet and the dramatist

16. What does the .... leader suggest?
A. other B. another
C. others D. anothers

17. He .... money.
A. has few B. have few
C. has little D. have little

18. The .... boys are rewarded.
A. first two B. two first
C. firsts two D. two's first

19. He is .... brave.
A. stronger than B. stronger then
C. more strong then D. more strong than

20. No sooner said ....
A. so done B. and done
C. then done D. but done

21. She returned .... than I had thought.
A. quickly B. more quicker
C. more quickly D. quicker

22. He is .... foolish person.
A. rather the
B. a rather
C. rather a
D. rather

23. This pen .... rupees.
A. costs twenty
B. twenty costs only
C. costs only twenty
D. only costs twenty

24. It is .... pride.
A. nothing else but
B. nothing else than
C. else nothing than
D. but

25. This tea is .... to drink.
A. too hot
B. very hot
C. enough hot
D. much hot

ANSWERS

1	2	3	4	5	6	7	8	9	10
A	C	A	B	A	C	C	C	A	A
11	**12**	**13**	**14**	**15**	**16**	**17**	**18**	**19**	**20**
B	D	B	D	B	A	C	A	D	C
21	**22**	**23**	**24**	**25**					
C	C	C	A	A					

DETERMINERS

Determiners are actually Adjectives. They are always followed by nouns.

Determiners are of the following kinds:

1. **Demonstrative Determiners**
this, that, these, those
2. **Possessive Determiners**
my, our, your, his, her, its, their
3. **Quantitative Determiners**
some, any, much, enough, sufficient, whole, a little, the little, little, all, both
4. **Numerical Determiners**
a few, some, few, the few, any, several, many, no, etc.
One, two, three ... (Cardinals)
First, second, third ... (Ordinals)
5. **Distributive Determiners**
either, neither
6. **Articles**
Indefinite: a, an
Definite: the

MULTIPLE CHOICE QUESTIONS

Directions: *In the following questions choose the correct options to fill in the blanks.*

1. Give me .... rice.
A. some
B. few
C. a few
D. any

2. .... sheep grazing on the slope of the hill had gone away.
A. Any
B. The few
C. This
D. Much

3. Have you got .... magazines to read?
A. all
B. much
C. some
D. little

4. I have .... money that I want to spend on shares.
A. any
B. much
C. less
D. some

5. There is .... owl on the branch of the tree.
A. a B. the
C. an D. some

6. My brother is .... MBA.
A. a B. an
C. the D. any

7. Have you got .... cheese?
A. some B. many
C. a few D. few

8. No, I have not got .... cheese.
A. many B. few
C. any D. some

9. There is only .... milk left in the bottle.
A. enough B. few
C. much D. a little

10. There is .... hope of his recovery.
A. any B. little
C. many D. few

11. .... dogs were barking at the strangers.
A. Some B. Any
C. Much D. Less

12. The girl bought her father .... juice.
A. few B. some
C. any D. many

13. You should take .... honey everyday.
A. any B. many
C. a little D. a few

14. .... boy was punished by the teacher.
A. Either B. All
C. Any D. Many

15. .... girl was asked to join the army.
A. None B. Neither
C. All D. Any

16. .... water in the jug has been drunk by Mohan.
A. The little B. The few
C. A few D. Few

17. I shall play .... piano at the party.
A. some B. any
C. the D. few

18. .... labourers were found dead in the mine.
A. Any B. Fewer
C. Many D. Less

19. Could I borrow .... umbrella?
A. our B. your
C. yours D. my

20. My brother is standing in the .... row.
A. any B. many
C. some D. first

ANSWERS

1	2	3	4	5	6	7	8	9	10
A	B	C	D	C	B	A	C	D	B
11	**12**	**13**	**14**	**15**	**16**	**17**	**18**	**19**	**20**
A	B	C	A	B	A	C	C	B	D

VERBS

A verb is a word that tells something about the action or state of or happenning to a person or thing.

A verb tells the following:

1. What a person or thing does.

Examples:

(*i*) Sachin goes to school daily.
(*ii*) The bell *rang* loudly.
(*iii*) Many birds fly in the sky.
(*iv*) She *sang* a song.

2. What a person or thing is.

Examples:

(*i*) India *is* the biggest democracy in the world.
(*ii*) Ram Mehar *is* very rich.
(*iii*) They *are* happy.

3. What is done to a person or thing.

Examples:

(*i*) You *are liked* by all.

(*ii*) Two thieves *were arrested.*

(*iii*) Four students *were punished* by the teacher.

4. What happens to a person or thing.

Examples:

(*i*) His maternal uncle *died* last week.

(*ii*) Two ships *sank* yesterday.

(*iii*) Leaves *turn* yellow in autumn.

5. What a person or thing has, had, and so on.

Examples:

(*i*) I *have* a new car.

(*ii*) He *had* a scooter last year.

(*iii*) He *has* several cows and goats.

It goes without saying that a verb is the most important part of a sentence. No sentence is complete without a Verb.

Important Information

1. If two or more singular nouns are joined by 'and' the verb used will be plural.

Example:

(*i*) He and I were going to the market.

(*ii*) Ram and Mohan are friends.

2. If two singular nouns joined by 'and' points out to the same thing or person, the verb used must be singular.

Example:

(*i*) Rice and curry is the favourite food of the Punjabis.

(*ii*) The Collector and District Magistrate is away.

3. In case two subjects are joined by 'as well as' the verb agrees with the first subject.

Example:

(*i*) Kanta as well as her children is playing.

(*ii*) Children as well as their mother are playing.

In the case of first sentence the verb (is) agrees with Kanta and in the case of second sentence the verb (are) agrees with the children.

4. 'Neither', 'Either', 'Every', 'Each', 'Everyone', and 'Many a' are followed by a singular verb.

Example:

(*i*) Either of the plans is to be adopted.

(*ii*) Neither of the two brothers is sure to pass.

(*iii*) Every student is expected to be obedient.

(*iv*) Everyone of them desires this.

(*v*) Many a person is drowned in the sea.

5. If two subjects are joined by 'Either .... or' / 'Neither .... nor', the verb agrees with the subject near to it.

Example:

(*i*) Either my brother or I am to do this work.

(*ii*) Neither he nor they are prepared to do this work.

6. 'A great many' is always followed by a 'plural noun' and a 'plural verb'. For example :
A great many students have been declared successful.

7. Similarly if two subjects are joined by 'with', 'together with', 'no less than', in addition to 'and not', etc. the verb agrees with the first subject.

Example:

(*i*) The boy with his parents has arrived.

(*ii*) He, no less than I, is to blame.

8. Nouns, plural in form, but singular in meaning, take a singular verb.

Example:

This news was broadcast from television yesterday.

MULTIPLE CHOICE QUESTIONS

Directions: *In the following questions choose the correct options to fill in the blanks.*

1. The bus with all its passengers .... lost.
A. were B. was
C. are D. would

2. You as well as I .... responsible for this work.
A. am B. are
C. was D. is

3. Raghava like all his companions .... a spoiled child.
A. are B. were
C. is D. will be

4. Pen and ink .... required for me.
A. are B. were
C. is D. has required

5. Every girl and every boy .... attended the seminar.
A. have B. has
C. is D. are

6. Not only she but all her sisters ...... been married.
A. has B. have
C. is D. are

7. There .... nothing but miseries in life.
A. is B. are
C. were D. will be

8. Neither prose nor poem .... given.
A. were B. was
C. has D. have

9. Either he or I .... wrong.
A. is B. are
C. am D. were

10. Either Sulekha or Rekha .... coming here.
A. are B. is
C. were D. have

11. .... the child or his parents to blame?
A. Is B. Are
C. Were D. Has

12. You and I .... neighbours.
A. am B. are
C. was D. has

13. The house with all its belongings ..... sold away.
A. were B. are
C. was D. must

14. Either water or juice .... required.
A. is B. are
C. were D. has

15. There were not as many tables as .... required.
A. was B. were
C. is D. are

16. They each .... a book.
A. have B. are
C. has D. is

17. He and I .... close friends.
A. is B. am
C. was D. are

18. She as well as I .... guilty.
A. is B. are
C. am D. must be

19. Purushottam .... not read more on this chapter.
A. needs
B. has been need
C. need
D. had been need

20. He came .... to his aunt.
A. run B. running
C. to run D. in run

21. She dislikes .... meat.
A. eat to B. to eat
C. eating D. to eating

22. He likes ....
A. sing to B. singing
C. to sing D. to singing

23. We are ready .... the match.
A. play to B. to playing
C. playing D. to play

24. .... is injurious to health.
A. Smoking B. To smoke
C. To smoking D. Smoke to

25. He loves .... raw vegetables.
A. eaten B. eating
C. to eating D. eat to

26. He seemed .... finished his homework.
A. have to B. to have
C. having D. to having

ANSWERS

1	2	3	4	5	6	7	8	9	10
B	B	C	C	B	B	A	B	C	B
11	**12**	**13**	**14**	**15**	**16**	**17**	**18**	**19**	**20**
A	B	C	A	B	A	D	A	C	B
21	**22**	**23**	**24**	**25**	**26**				
C	B	D	A	B	B				

CONJUNCTIONS

A conjunction is a word which connects words, clauses or sentences.

Look at the following sentences.

(*i*) He bought apples *and* mangoes.

(*ii*) God made the country *and* man made the town.

(*iii*) The door was open *but* there was no one in the house.

(*iv*) He knows that I am here *and* that I want to see him.

In the sentence (*i*), *and* connects two words—*apples* and *mangoes.*

In the sentence (*ii*), *and* connects two sentences—*God made the country* and *man made the town.*

In the sentence (*iii*), *but* connects two sentences— *The door was open* and *there was no one in the house.*

In the sentence (*iv*), *and* connects two clauses—*that I am here* and *that I want to see him.*

The main coordinating conjunctions are:

and, but, for, or, nor, also, either ..... or, neither ..... nor.

There are some conjunctions which are used in pairs. They are:

either .... or, ... neither .... nor, both .... and, though .... yet, whether .... or, not only .... but also.

Example: *Either* take it *or* leave it.

It is *neither* useful *nor* ornamental.

They *both* like *and* respect me.

Though he is suffering from high fever, *yet* he does not cry.

He does not care *whether* you go *or* stay.

He is *not only* doltish, *but also* obstinate.

The conjunctions which are used in pairs in this way, are called correlative conjunctions, or merely correlatives.

Use of Important Conjunctions

1. **As soon as:** As soon as denotes simultaneous time.

   Example: As soon as he saw his enemy, he took to his heels.

2. **No sooner .... than :**

   (*a*) 'No sooner' is always followed by 'than'.

   (*b*) Please remember that 'No sooner' is always followed by do/does/did. As such only first form of the verb should be used after the subject.

Example:
No sooner did he see his enemy than he took to his heels.

3. **Hardly:** 'Hardly' is followed by 'when'.

Examples:
(*i*) Hardly had I left the house when it started raining.
(*ii*) We had hardly come into the room when his father began chastising him.

☛ A. 'Hardly' is never followed by 'than'.
B. 'Scarcely' can also be used in the sense and manner of 'Hardly'.

4. **Lest:** Lest is used in the sense of 'so that .... not'. It is always followed by 'should'. Lest is negative in sense. Hence 'not' should never be used with it.

Example:
Work hard lest you should fail.

☛ 'Lest' is always followed by 'should' and not 'may'.

5. **Unless:** Unless expresses condition. It is also used in the negative sense. Use of 'not' is not allowed with 'unless' because 'unless' is already in the negative sense.

Example:
Unless you labour hard you will not pass.

6. **Until:** 'Until' expresses time. It means 'till not'.

Example:
Wait here until I return.

☛ Until is in the negative sense. So 'not' should not be used with it.
Example :
Wait here until I do not return. (Incorrect)
Wait here until I return. (Correct)

7. **As well as:** When two subjects are joined by 'as well as', the verb always agrees with the first subject.

Examples:
(*i*) The teacher as well as students is playing.
(*ii*) Students as well as the teacher are playing.

☛ 'Both' and 'as well as' cannot be used together in the same sentence.

Examples:
Both Sita as well as Kanta are beautiful. (Incorrect)
Sita as well as Kanta is beautiful. (Correct)
Both Sita and Kanta are beautiful. (Correct)

8. **As if:** 'As if' is used in the sense of pretension. While using 'as if' in a sentence, we should see that even the third person singular subject gets 'were'.

Example:
He talks as if he were mad.

9. **Till:** Till expresses time. Till is always used in the affirmative.

Example:
We did not come back till sunset.

10. **Rather than:** 'Rather than' is used in the sense of 'preference'. 'Rather' is always followed by 'than'.

Example:
I would rather die than submit.

11. **As long as/so long as:** Both express time during which an action or event takes place.

Example:
As long as there is life, there is hope.

12. **However:** It is both a subordinate and co-ordinate clause.

Examples:
(*a*) Mala worked hard, she however, failed.
(*b*) However hard he may work, he cannot pass.

13. **Such as:** 'Such as' gives us the sense of 'like'. Such is always followed by 'as'.

Example:
Life is such a puzzle as cannot be solved.

MULTIPLE CHOICE QUESTIONS

Directions: *In the following questions choose the correct options to fill in the blanks.*

1. Neither he .... his friend is good.
A. or B. and
C. but D. nor

2. The officer asked the peon .... why he was late.
A. that B. if
C. but D. No word needed

3. Both Ajay .... Vijay are intelligent.
A. or B. nor
C. and D. No word needed

4. No Sooner did the thief see the public .... he ran away.
A. then B. and
C. but D. than

5. Abhinav .... his brothers was going to Mumbai.
A. but B. yet
C. No word needed D. together with

6. He behaves .... he were the captain of the team.
A. as if B. as
C. No word needed D. that

7. Either Rupali .... Sonali is going to attend the meeting.
A. and B. but
C. nor D. or

8. Neither Nirmal .... Ashwinee is going to listen the speech.
A. and B. but
C. nor D. or

9. Ravi .... Prakash are going to Kolkata.
A. or B. nor
C. but D. and

10. Rice .... curry is my usual breakfast.
A. and B. but
C. then D. than

11. Hardly had he left .... his brother came.
A. then B. than
C. when D. that

12. I would rather have a copy .... a book.
A. then B. than
C. when D. that

13. He is no other .... my friend.
A. then B. than
C. when D. but

14. He saw a snake ....he awoke.
A. then B. when
C. than D. No word needed

15. Ten years have passed .... my grandmother died.
A. since B. when
C. then D. than

16. She is .... good .... bad.
A. either, not B. neither, or
C. neither, nor D. neither, than

17. The cellphone is both cheap .... best.
A. than B. and
C. then D. or

18. No sooner did the rogue see the police .... he disappeared.
A. then B. than
C. so D. because

19. Srishti will go .... Sanju goes.
A. if B. than
C. then D. although

20. She is wise .... timid.
A. and B. yet
C. but D. however

21. Make hay .... the sun shines.
A. though B. while
C. after D. before

22. He is so weak .... he cannot walk.
A. but B. that
C. then D. so

23. Although he is rich, ... he is unhappy.
A. but B. yet
C. so D. still

24. Wait here .... I come back.
A. till B. until
C. before D. after

25. He is my friend .... I shall help him.
A. so B. hence
C. that is why D. therefore

26. He must go away .... he will be beaten.
A. otherwise B. and
C. or D. else

27. God loves good men .... good men love God.
A. and B. or
C. that D. those

28. He was late .... he was not punished.
A. but B. yet
C. still D. therefore

29. Walk slowly ...., you may fall.
A. and B. or
C. so D. otherwise

30. Work hard, ... you will fail.
A. and B. or
C. otherwise D. else

ANSWERS

1	2	3	4	5	6	7	8	9	10
D	D	C	D	D	A	D	C	D	A
11	**12**	**13**	**14**	**15**	**16**	**17**	**18**	**19**	**20**
C	B	B	B	A	C	B	B	A	C
21	**22**	**23**	**24**	**25**	**26**	**27**	**28**	**29**	**30**
B	B	B	A	B	C	A	C	D	D

PREPOSITIONS

A *Preposition* is a word which is placed before a noun or a pronoun to show its relation to some other word in the sentence.

(*i*) I saw a goat *in* the field.
(*ii*) I am fond *of* hot coffee.

In sentence (*i*), the word *in* shows the relation between two things—*goat* and *field.*

In sentence (*ii*), the word *of* shows the relation between the attribute expressed by the adjective *found* and *tea.*

The words *in* and *of* are here used as prepositions.

The noun or pronoun which is used with a preposition is called its object. The noun or pronoun is in the objective case. It is governed by the preposition. Now it is absolutely clear that in sentence (*i*), the noun *field* is in the objective case. The word *field* is governed by the preposition *in.*

A preposition may have two or more objects. The road runs over *hill* and *plain.*

Here, the words *hill* and *plain* are used as objects.

Use of Important Prepositions

1. Among, Between

'**Among**' is used for more than two persons or things; '**Between**' is used only for two.

Examples:

(*i*) Distribute these sweets *among* the poor students of the class.

(*ii*) Distribute these books *between* Ram and Shyam.

2. Among, In

'**Among**' is used before collective plural nouns. '**In**' is used before collective singular nouns.

Examples:

(*i*) I found him standing *among* the crowd.

(*ii*) I saw him in the crowd.

3. Beside, Besides

'**Beside**' means 'by the side of'. '**Besides**' means 'in addition to'.

Examples:

(*i*) The daughter was sitting *beside* her mother.

(*ii*) *Besides* his relatives, he invited his friends also.

4. In, Within

'**In**' means at the expiry of a period of time in future, '**Within**' means before the expiry of a period of time in any tense.

Examples:

(*i*) She will return *in* a week.

(*ii*) I shall finish my work *within* a weak.

5. On, Upon

'**On**' is used for things at rest; '**Upon**' is used for things in motion.

Examples:

(*i*) He is sitting *on* the floor.

(*ii*) The dog sprang *upon* the table.

6. By, With

'**By**' denotes the agent or doer, '**With**' denotes the instrument with which anything is done.

Examples:

(*i*) The bird was killed *by* the hunter with an arrow.

(*ii*) He beat the dog *with* a stick.

(*iii*) I shall reach here *by* five o'clock.

7. After, In

'**After**' means at the end of a period of time in the past. '**In**' means at the end of a period of time in future.

Examples:

(*i*) I shall return your book *in* a week.

(*ii*) He returned the book *after* a week.

8. For, From, Since

'**For**' is used before a noun denoting a period of time with all the tenses. '**From**' is used before a noun or phrase denoting a point of time, it is used in all the tenses. '**Since**' is used before a noun or phrase denoting some point of time and is always produced by a verb in the perfect continuous tense or third form of a verb.

Examples:

(*i*) We have been playing cards *for* two hours.

(*ii*) She stayed with her uncle *from* the 15th of March to the 15th of May.

(*iii*) I have been reading this book *since* morning.

9. Above, Over

'**Above**' means 'higher from', **Over** is used in the following four senses:

(*i*) In the sense of 'above' :
At noon, the sun is *over* our heads.

(*ii*) In the sense of 'beyond' :
I cannot get *over* my disappointment.

(*iii*) In the sense of 'Superiority' :
God *over* all blesses for ever more.

(*iv*) In the sense of 'Conclusion' :
It is all *over* with me.

10. At, Towards

'**At**' denotes the idea of aim, '**Towards**' denotes the idea of destination.

Examples:

(*i*) He threw the stone *at* the cat.

(*ii*) He went *towards* the house.

11. At, In, On

'At' is used as follows :

(*i*) '**At**' is used with small towns and villages.

Examples :

(*a*) He was born *at* Sonepat.

(*b*) He lives *at* village Bangra. (Bangra is a village)

(*ii*) '**At**' is used before a noun denoting a definite point of time.

Example:

He called on me *at* 9 p.m. yesterday.

'In' is used as follows :

(*iii*) '**In**' is used with the names of big cities, provinces and countries.

Examples:

(*a*) His father lives *in* England.

(*b*) His younger brother lives *in* Lucknow.

(*iv*) '**In**' is used before the names of months and years.

Example:

His elder sister was born *in* 1972 *in* the month of May.

'**On**' is used with dates and names of days.

Examples :

(*a*) I joined college *on* the 26th April.

(*b*) He will leave for Kolkata *on* Wednesday next.

Important Information

1. **'In'** is also used in the following phrases : In the morning; In the evening, In winter, In summer.
2. **'In'** also denotes a place inside anything. He travelled *in* a crowded bus.
3. **'At'** is used in the following phrases : *At* home, *At* the station, *At* work, *At* play.

12. Below, Beneath

Below means 'of lower level in position, dignity and expectation' etc. *Beneath* means 'under'.

Examples:

(*i*) It is *below* my dignity to talk to her.

(*ii*) They rested *beneath* the shade of a tree.

13. In, Into, To

'In' expresses Rest or Motion inside anything. **'Into'** expresses Motion towards the inside of anything or change from one medium to another. **'To'** denotes motion from one place to another.

Examples:

(*i*) The boys are *in* the room.

(*ii*) Translate this passage from English *into* Hindi.

(*iii*) Every morning he goes *to* the temple.

14. Till, By, Of, Off

- 'Till' means upto or not earlier than.
- 'By' means not later than.
- 'Of' shows cause, source, separation, quality, contents, possession, apposition, point of reference, space in time etc.
- 'Off' shows separation at a near distance, and detached condition.

Consider the following examples:

(*i*) I shall work *till* 5 a.m.

(*ii*) Asha died *of* cancer.

(*iii*) The nib *of* the pen is made *of* gold.

(*iv*) He presented me a bottle *of* perfume.

(*v*) Our principal is a man *of* principle.

(*vi*) He lived in the house *of* his friend.

(*vii*) *By* this time tomorrow, I'll have finished my job.

(*viii*) My house is *off* the road.

(*ix*) The book fell *off* the table.

MULTIPLE CHOICE QUESTIONS

Directions: *Tick the correct preposition for the blank in each of the following sentences.*

1. He applied ...... the manager.
A. for B. to
C. with D. by

2. Trust ...... God and do the right.
A. in B. for
C. to D. with

3. She is worthy ...... a prize.
A. with B. for
C. to D. of

4. Mr. Gomes has no taste ...... music.
A. of B. for
C. with D. to

5. You are hard ...... hearing.
A. at B. of
C. with D. for

6. He is sure ...... his success
A. for B. with
C. on D. of

7. Preeti was warned ...... the danger ahead.
A. for B. at
C. of D. about

8. I am thankful ...... you for a good advice.
A. for B. with
C. to D. of

9. Deepak would not surrender .... the police.
A. with B. to
C. for D. on

10. The small plant in your lawn is very sensitive ...... touch.

A. on B. with
C. to D. about

11. Divya was sure to succeed ..... the examination.

A. for B. in
C. to D. with

12. Geeta was jealous ...... Ravina's beauty.

A. to B. with
C. for D. of

13. He was ignorant ..... what was happening there.

A. for B. of
C. to D. with

14. Your pen is inferior ...... mine.

A. than B. with
C. from D. to

15. Reenu is no match ...... Meenu.

A. to B. for
C. with D. upon

16. It is necessary ...... you to apply for this job.

A. on B. with
C. for D. to

17. Be loyal ...... your country.

A. for B. to
C. on D. with

18. Mukesh is junior ...... me.

A. than B. to
C. from D. of

19. Deepika was innocent ...... the crime.

A. of B. with
C. from D. to

20. I am desirous.... joining the Indian cricket team.

A. for B. of
C. to D. on

ANSWERS

1	2	3	4	5	6	7	8	9	10
B	A	D	B	B	D	D	D	B	D
11	12	13	14	15	16	17	18	19	20
B	D	B	D	B	D	B	B	A	B

INTERJECTIONS

An *interjection* is a word which expresses a sudden feeling for emotion. It must be borne in mind that an interjection has no grammatical relation with any other word in a sentence.

It is a convention that an interjection is followed by the exclamation mark(!).

An interjection usually expresses *joy, grief, surprise, anger, contempt, alarm, attention,* approval, disapproval , etc.

Important interjections and the emotions they express are named below:

Joy : *Hurrah! Ha! Ha!*
Grief : *Alas! Ah!*
Surprise : *Oh! What!*
Approval : *Bravo! Hear! Hear! Well done!*
Calling : *Hello! Hi! Hey!*
Contempt : *Fie! Pooh!*

Observe the following sentences

Hurrah! We have won the match.

Alas! It is a sad day for us. We have lost the game.

Hush! Don't make a noise. The baby is sleeping.

Hello! What are you doing there?
Who is there?

Oh! I got such a fright.

Ah! I should have been there. What a sorry plight.

Hark! Don't you hear a sound?

What! So early.

The following interjection phrases are in common use:

Ah me!	Good God!
For shame!	Hold on!
Well done!	Off with you!
Good Grace!	Dear me!
Good heavens!	

Other parts of speech are also sometimes used as interjections. Some examples are given below:

Noun	: A horse! A horse! My kingdom for a horse!
Pronoun	: What a lame excuse! What a beautiful sight it is!
Verb	: Would that I were young again!
Adverb	: How lovely the flowers are!
Conjunction	: If I could only see her once again!
Infinitive	: To think of him as a friend!

MULTIPLE CHOICE QUESTIONS

Directions: *Tick the correct interjection to be applied to the given sentences.*

1. .... The meeting is going on.
A. What! B. Oh!
C. Hurrah! D. Hush!

2. .... We have won the match.
A. Chi-Chi! B. Fie! Fie
C. Hurrah! D. Phew!

3. .... He is no more.
A. Hush! B. Alas!
C. Hark! D. Pooh!

4. .... How good of you.
A. Oh! B. Hush!
C. Good Heavens! D. Bravo!

5. .... You took so much trouble for us.
A. What! B. Oh!
C. Phew! D. Well!

6. .... A soldier and afraid of death.
A. Hurrah! B. Bravo!
C. Fie on you! D. Pshaw!

7. .... He didn't accept your proposal.
A. Oh! B. What!
C. Hark! D. Good Heavens!

8. .... The cuckoo is singing.
A. Hark! B. What!
C. Oh! D. Hurrah!

9. .... What do I see here?
A. Good heavens!
B. What!
C. Ha! Ha!
D. Hush!

10. .... Well done.
A. What! B. Oh!
C. Bravo! D. Hurrah!

11. .... What do you talk of him?
A. Chi! Chi! B. Alas!
C. Well! D. Hark!

12. .... What next?
A. Hush! B. Well!
C. Hurrah! D. Hark!

ANSWERS

1	2	3	4	5	6	7	8	9	10
D	C	B	A	B	C	B	A	A	C
11	**12**								
A	B								

7

Agreement of Subjects & Verbs

It is very important that the verb in a sentence should obey the subject, otherwise the sentence will be considered wrong.

1. When the Subject is a Singular Noun

A singular noun takes a singular verb.

(*i*) Mohit **makes** a noise in the class.

(*ii*) The child is **crying** for a cake.

2. When two singular nouns are joined with 'and'

When two singular nouns are joined with 'and' and they refer to two different persons, the plural verb should be used, *e.g.*,

(*i*) The novelist and the poet **were** honoured by the government.

(*ii*) The black and the white dogs **bark** at the strangers.

☛ Article 'the' is used with both the subjects.

If article is used only once, the singular verb should be used.

(*i*) The painter and singer is going abroad.

(*ii*) The white and black dog has a bushy tail.

3. When the subjects together give a single idea, singular verb is used.

(*i*) Slow and steady wins the race.

(*ii*) Rice and curry is my favourite dish.

4. A collective noun takes a singular verb when it acts as a whole, but it takes a plural verb when the individual, of which it is composed are considered separately.

(*i*) The committee was unanimous on imposing the new law.

(*ii*) The committee have given their separate opinions in the matter.

5. When the subjects are joined by neither . . . nor, either . . . or, and 'or', the verb should obey the last subject.

(*i*) Rakesh or his friends have been selected for the match.

(*ii*) His friends or Rakesh has been selected for the match.

(*iii*) Neither Rohit nor his brothers are going abroad.

(*iv*) Neither his brothers nor Rohit is going abroad.

(*v*) Either Sohan or his sisters were dancing at the function.

(*vi*) Either his sisters or Sohan was dancing at the function.

6. Either, neither, either of, neither of, take singular verb.

(*i*) Either boy was honest.

(*ii*) Neither girl was allowed to leave the premises.

(*iii*) Either of the boys was ready to help the old man.

(*iv*) Neither of the girls was asked to join the extra classes.

7. Some nouns are always used as plurals so, they take plural verbs.

(*i*) Where are your glasses?

(*ii*) His pants are attractive.

(*iii*) Cattle are grazing in the field.

(*iv*) Whose scissors are these?

8. Some nouns are always used as singulars, so, they take singular verbs.

(*i*) What is the latest news?

(*ii*) The furniture in the house is of a poor quality.

(*iii*) Mumps is not a fatal disease.

(*iv*) Physics is a tough subject.

9. Nouns formed by alongwith, as well as, together with, accompanied by, etc., take verb according to the first subject.

(*i*) I, as well as you, am to blame.

(*ii*) You, as well as I, are going to see a movie.

(*iii*) John, accompanied by his parents, is going to visit the Taj.

(*iv*) His parents, accompanied by John, are going to visit the Taj.

(*v*) His brothers, together with Vivek, are ready to whitewash the fence.

10. To indicate something hypothetical or not factually true, plural verb 'were' with *as if* is used.

(*i*) He talks as if he were a king.

(*ii*) She dresses herself as if she were a princess.

MULTIPLE CHOICE QUESTIONS

Directions: *In the following questions, a sentence is given followed by four options. Select the option that replaces the given sentence or its part correctly.*

1. Slow and steady win the race.
A. Slowly and steady wins the race.
B. Slow and steadily wins the race.
C. Slow and steady wins the race.
D. None of these.

2. These news were broadcasted on Radio BBC.
A. These news were broadcast on Radio BBC.
B. This news was broadcast on Radio BBC.
C. This news was broadcasted on Radio BBC.
D. None of these.

3. Every boy and girl were given a prize.
A. Every boy and girl were given prizes.
B. Every boy and girl was given prizes.
C. Every boy and girl was given a prize.
D. None of these.

4. Everyone of them were clapping at the performance of the clown.
A. Everyone of them were clapping at the performance of the clowns.
B. Everyone of them was clapping at the performance of the clowns.
C. Everyone of them was clapping at the performances about the clowns.
D. None of these.

5. Law and order are to be maintained at all costs.
A. Law and orders are to be maintained at all costs.
B. Law and order is to be maintained at all costs.
C. Laws and orders are to be maintained at all costs.
D. None of these.

6. Five hundred rupees are a long sum.
A. Five hundred rupee is a long sum.
B. Five hundred rupee is a big sum.
C. Five hundred rupees is a big sum.
D. None of these.

7. Mohit, not his friends are to blame.
A. Mohit, not his friends is to blame.
B. Mohit, not his friend are to blame.
C. Mohit, not his friends is on to blame.
D. None of these.

8. I as well as you are to blame.
A. I as well as you, is to blame.
B. I as well as you are to blames.
C. I, as well as you, am to blame.
D. None of these.

9. The patient died before the doctor came.
A. The patient died before the doctor had come.

B. The patient had died before the doctor came.
C. The patient had died before the doctor had come.
D. None of these.

10. I knew that he will not respect his elders.
A. I knew that he would not respect his elders.
B. I knew that he shall not respect his elders.
C. I knew that he will not be respect his elders.
D. None of these.

11. He is one of the greatest player who has participated in one day cricket matches.
A. He is one of the greatest players who has ....
B. He is one of the greatest players who have ....
C. He is one of the greatest player who have ....
D. None of these.

12. He behaves as if he is king.
A. He behaves as if he are a king.
B. He behaves as if he are kings.
C. He behaves as if he were a king.
D. None of these.

13. He laughed as if he were mad.
A. He laughed as if he was mad.
B. He laughed as if he had been mad.
C. He laughed as if he are mad.
D. None of these.

14. The white and the black dog is dead.
A. The white and black dog are dead.
B. The white and the black dog are dead.
C. The white and black dogs are dead.
D. None of these.

15. The painter and poet are dead.
A. The painter and the poet is dead.
B. The painter and poets are dead.
C. The painter and poet is dead.
D. None of these.

16. The committee has announced their decision.
A. The committees has announced their decision.
B. The committee has announced its decision.
C. The committee have announced its decision.
D. None of these.

17. I wish I am a millionaire.
A. I wish I was a millionaire.
B. I wish I are a millionaire.
C. I wish I were a millionaire.
D. None of these.

18. A large number of students is absent.
A. A large numbers of students is absent.
B. A large number of students are absent.
C. A large number of student is absent.
D. None of these.

19. Walking on the road, I met one of my old friends.
A. When I was walking on the road, I met one of my old friend.
B. When I was walking on the road, I met one of my old friends.
C. Walking on the road, I met one of my friend.
D. None of these.

20. Our only guide were the stars.
A. Our only guide were the star.
B. Our only guides was the star.
C. Our only guide was the stars.
D. None of these.

21. Renu is living in this house since 2012.
A. Renu is living in this house for 2012.
B. Renu has been living in this house for 2012.
C. Renu has been living in this house since 2012.
D. None of these.

22. Better you had not to gone there.
A. Better you had not went there.
B. Better you had not gone there.
C. Better had you not to go there.
D. None of these.

23. You did not do so, nor he did.
A. You did not do so, he nor did.
B. You did not do so, nor did he.
C. You did not do so, he did nor.
D. None of these.

24. Hardly I had opened the window when a stream of cool breeze started rushing in.
A. Hardly I had opened the window then.........

B. Hardly had I opened the window when.........
C. Hardly had I opened the window then.........
D. None of these.

25. No sooner he did open the window, when the cool breeze started rushing in.
A. No sooner did he open the window then ....
B. No sooner did he open the window when ....
C. No sooner he did open the window than ....
D. None of these.

26. Neither she laughed nor I did.
A. Neither she laughed nor did I.
B. Neither she laughed did nor I.
C. Neither she laughed I did nor.
D. None of these.

27. Deepak alongwith his aunts were present in the party.
A. Deepak alongwith his aunts were present in the parties.
B. Deepak alongwith his aunts was present in the party.
C. Deepak alongwith his aunt were present in the party.
D. None of these.

28. Many a girls have gone to see the movie.
A. Many a girl have gone to see the movie.
B. Many a girls has went to see the movies.
C. Many a girl has gone to see the movie.
D. None of these.

29. Sohan, like Mohan, are good singers.
A. Sohan, like Mohan, is a good singer.
B. Sohan, like Mohan, is a good singers.
C. Sohan, like Mohan, are a good singer.
D. None of these.

30. The train arrived before I reached the station.
A. The train arrived before I had reached the station.
B. The train arrived before I have reached the station.
C. The train had arrived before I reached the station.
D. None of these.

31. Either he or she has done his work.
A. Either he or she has done their work.
B. Either he or she has done her work.
C. Either he or she has done their work.
D. None of these.

32. A hundred miles are a high distance.
A. A hundred miles are a big distance.
B. A hundred miles are a long distance.
C. A hundred miles is a long distance.
D. None of these.

33. 'A Tale of Two Cities' were written by Charles Dickens.
A. 'A Tale of Two Cities' was written by Charles Dickens.
B. 'A Tale of Two Cities' is wrote by Charles Dickens.
C. 'A Tale of Two Cities' are wrote by Charles Dickens.
D. None of these.

34. Many a boys were playing in the garden.
A. Many a boy were playing in the garden.
B. Many a boys was playing in the garden.
C. Many a boy was playing in the garden.
D. None of these.

35. A bandit besides his gangsters were nabbed by the police.
A. A bandit besides his gangster were nabbed by the police.
B. A bandit besides his gangsters was nabbed by the police.
C. A bandits besides his gangsters was nabbed by the police.
D. None of these.

36. The bell went when I reached the school.
A. The bell went when I had reached the school.
B. The bell had gone when I have reached the school.
C. The bell had gone when I reached the school.
D. None of these.

37. My teacher told me that the earth revolved round the sun.
A. My teacher told me that the earth was revolving round the sun.

B. My teacher told me that the earth revolves round the sun.
C. My teacher told me that the earth had revolved round the sun.
D. None of these.

38. Rice and curry are the favourite food of my brother.
A. Rice and curry is the favourite food...
B. Rice and curry are the favourite foods...
C. Rice and curry is the favourite foods...
D. None of these.

39. The Principal together with his staff were on a tour to the Himalayas.
A. The Principal together with his staffs were...
B. The Principal together with his staffs was...
C. The Principal together with his staff was...
D. None of these.

40. Neither Ravi nor his friends was present in the class.
A. Neither Ravi nor his friend were present in the class.
B. Neither Ravi nor his friends was present in the classes.
C. Neither Ravi nor his friends were present in the class.
D. None of these.

41. None of the ten pens are yours.
A. None of the ten pen are yours.
B. None of the ten pens is yours.
C. None of the ten pens are your.
D. None of these.

42. The captain with all his players are in the playground.
A. The captain with all his player are in the playgrounds.
B. The captain with all his player is in the playgrounds.
C. The captain with all his players is in the playground.
D. None of these.

ANSWERS

1	2	3	4	5	6	7	8	9	10
C	B	C	B	B	C	A	C	B	A
11	**12**	**13**	**14**	**15**	**16**	**17**	**18**	**19**	**20**
B	C	B	B	C	B	C	B	B	C
21	**22**	**23**	**24**	**25**	**26**	**27**	**28**	**29**	**30**
C	B	B	B	A	A	B	C	A	C
31	**32**	**33**	**34**	**35**	**36**	**37**	**38**	**39**	**40**
B	C	A	C	B	C	B	A	C	C
41	**42**								
B	C								

EXPLANATORY ANSWERS

1. When two different nouns combine to convey one idea or are treated as a unit, a singular verb is used.

2. The forms of broadcast are broadcast, broadcast; and 'news' word is always treated as singular.

3. 'Everyboy' is treated as a singular. So, it takes a singular verb.

4. 'Everyone' is treated as a singular, so it takes a singular verb.

5. When two different nouns combine to form one idea or are treated as a unit, the verb is singular.

6. In this case the plural noun has been used as a collective noun, so it takes singular verb. The word 'long' is mostly used to express the length, not a sum.

7. In this case, when two nouns or pronouns are connected by a comma + not the verb should be used according to the first noun or pronoun used.

8. When 'as well as' is used the verb should be applied according to the first noun or pronoun used.

9. When two events or actions take place in the past tense, the event taking place first, should be shown in Past Perfect Tense.

10. If the Principal Clause, is in the Past Tense, the Subordinate Clause must also be in the Past Tense unless there is a universal truth, habitual truth.

11. We have used the sentence in the sense, "Greatest among the other greatest players", so it should take a plural verb *i.e.,* 'have'. The plural antecedent of a relative pronoun should have a plural verb.

12. 'As if' is used to express a wish. A wish should be in the past tense and in the plural form. But if the main clause *i.e.,* the Principal Clause is in the Past Indefinite Tense, it should be followed by the Past Perfect Tense.

13. When the Principal Clause is in the Past Indefinite Tense, and 'as if' has been used there, the Subordinate Clause should be in the Past Perfect Tense.

14. The term 'The White and the Black' represents two dogs *i.e.,* one of the black colour and the other of the white colour. So, it needs a plural verb.

15. The term 'painter and poet' represents a single person who has two qualities. So, it needs a singular verb.

16. The word 'committee' can be used a singular as well as plural. When it is used as a singular, the verb must agree with it, and the pronoun should also be used accordingly.

17. When one expresses a wish and the Principal Clause is in the Present Indefinite Tense, the Subordinate Clause should be in the Past Tense and should be in Plural form.

18. 'Number' is singular in structure, but mostly it is used as a plural.

19. The participle must be attached with a noun or pronoun to which it refers. In this, we have used 'One of my old friends' *i.e.,* 'One among many'.

20. A verb must agree with its subject.

21. When time has been given, use Perfect Continuous Tenses. For the point of time use 'since'.

22. After phrases like 'had better' or 'better had' etc., infinite (to) is not used.

23. The verb comes before its subject when the sentence has been introduced by 'nor'.

24. The verb comes before its subject when the sentence has been introduced by 'hardly'. Apply 'when' with hardly.

25. The verb comes before its subject when the sentence has been introduced by 'No sooner'. Apply 'than' with 'No sooner'.

26. The verb comes before its subject when the sentence has been introduced by 'neither' or 'nor'.

27. Two nouns or pronouns connected by 'alongwith' take a singular verb, if the first subject is singular.

28. 'Many' should be followed by a singular noun and a singular verb, if the first subject is singular.

29. When two nouns or pronouns are connected by the word 'like' they need a singular verb, if the first subject is singular.

30. When two events or actions take place in the past, the action or event taking place first should be shown in the Past Perfect Tense and the other one should be shown in the Past Indefinite Tense.

31. In case of 'either or' the verb agrees with the last subject and in the case that is 'she'. So,

the pronoun should also agree with the word 'she'.

32. When a plural noun is considered collectively, the verb should be singular. The word 'big' is mostly used with a sum *i.e.,* 'a big sum', 'a big amount' etc. 'high' is mostly used to express height a thing which has its basis above from the earth in the sky *i.e.,* 'a high star' etc. 'Tall' is mostly used to express the height of a thing which has its basis on the earth 'a tall building', 'a tall tower'.

33. When a plural noun is used as a proper name for some collective unit or when it denotes some specific quality, the verb should be in singular form.

34. 'Many a' needs a singular noun and a singular verb.

35. Two nouns or pronouns connected by 'besides' should take verb according to the first subject used.

36. When two actions or events take place in the past, the action or event which is taking place first should be shown in the Past Perfect Tense and the other should be in the Past Indefinite Tense.

37. In indirect speech the verb of the universal truth cannot be changed.

38. When two different nouns combine to give one idea or are treated as a unit they need a single verb.

39. When two nouns or pronouns are joined together by the word 'together' the verb should obey the first subject used.

40. In this case of 'Neither ...nor' the verb should agree with the last subject used.

41. 'None' takes a singular verb.

42. When two nouns or pronouns are joined with the word 'with' they take a verb in accordance with the first subject.

8

Tenses

1. Tense indicates a point in time or period of time in the past, present, or future tense.
2. Tense is related to the form of verb. The verb may consist of a single word, or a main verb and one or more auxiliary words. There are normally three forms of the verb, say, V_1, V_2, V_3 and for convenience a fourth form V_4 as verb+ing may be assumed.

A Comparative Chart Regarding Tenses and Verbs

Simple Present	**Simple Past**	**Simple Future**
V_1	V_2	shall/will + V_1
Present Continuous	**Past Continuous**	**Future Continuous**
is/am/are + V_4	was/were + V_4	shall/will + be + V_4
Present Perfect	**Past Perfect**	**Future Perfect**
has/have + V_3	had + V_3	shall/will + have + V_3
Present Perfect Cont.	**Past Perfect Cont.**	**Future Perfect Cont.**
has/have + been + V_4	had + been + V_4	shall/will + have been + V_4

Tenses tell us the time of actions.

There are three kinds of Tenses.

1. Present Tense
2. Past Tense
3. Future Tense

1. Present Tense

The tense which shows action in the present time is known as the present tense. It is of the following kinds :

(A) Present Indefinite Tense or Simple Present Tense
(B) Present Continuous Tense
(C) Present Perfect Tense.
(D) Present Perfect Continuous Tense.

(A) *Present Indefinite Tense or Simple Present Tense*

This tense is used:

1. To show an action in the present time without referring to its finishing time
   (*i*) I write a letter to my friend.
   (*ii*) She helps the old man lift the bag.

☛ With I, we, you, they or Plural Noun the first form of the Verb is used. But with He, She, It, or Singular Noun, first form of the verb + s/es is used.

2. To show a habit or liking or disliking in the present time
   (*i*) She hates meat.

(*ii*) We like singing and dancing.
(*iii*) I daily go out for a walk.
(*iv*) My uncle daily drinks a cup of tea after dinner.

3. To refer to a universal truth
(*i*) The sun rises in the east.
(*ii*) A bat flies better when it is dark around.
(*iii*) The stars twinkle at night.

Negative and Interrogative Sentences

With I, we, you, they or Plural Nouns: do not + 1st form of the verb is used.

In case of interrogative sentences Do + subject + 1st form of the verb + object is used.

With He, She, It, or a Singular Noun does not + 1st form of the verb is used.

In case of interrogative sentences Does + Subject + 1st form of the verb + object is used.

(*i*) He does not borrow anything from anybody.
(*ii*) I do not advise you to do this job.
(*iii*) Do they know how to write business letters?
(*iv*) Does she understand French?

(B) *Present Continuous Tense*

It is used to show the continuity of an action in the present time.

Affirmative Sentences

(*i*) I am sending a telegram to Jack.
(*ii*) You are admiring my opponent.
(*iii*) She is speaking for the manager.

☛ When 'I' is the subject of the sentence use am + present participle.

When 'we, you, they or a Plural Noun is the Subject of sentence 'are + present participle' is used. But if 'he, she, it or a Singular Noun' is the Subject of the sentence 'is + present participle' is used.

Negative and Interrogative Sentences

(*i*) I am not trying to find out errors in your essay.
(*ii*) Am I trying to find out errors in your essay?
(*iii*) He is not creating any problem to the children.
(*iv*) Is he creating any problem to the children?
(*v*) They are not decorating the room.
(*vi*) Are they decorating the room?

(C) *Present Perfect Tense*

The tense which shows the completion of an action in the present tense is known as the Present Perfect Tense

Affirmative Sentence

(*i*) I have eaten/taken breakfast.
(*ii*) She has mixed up the ingredients to bake a cake.

When the subject of the sentence is I, we, you, they or a plural noun use have + past participle.

When the subject of the sentence is 'he, she, it or a singular noun, use has + past participle.

Negative and Interrogative Sentences

(*i*) The officer has not granted leave to the clerk.
(*ii*) Has the officer granted leave to the clerk?
(*iii*) They have not shovelled snow on to the truck yet.
(*iv*) Have they shovelled snow on to the truck?

(D) *Present Perfect Continuous Tense*

The tense shows a part of an action having been completed and another part of it still being done in the Present Tense.

(*i*) He has been mending the shoes since morning.
(*ii*) We have been flying kites for three hours.

☛ Preposition 'since' is used when the point of time is given *i.e.* since 2001, since 5 o'clock, since morning, since evening, etc.

Preposition 'for' is used when the period of time is given, e.g., for two weeks, for three days, for five years, etc.

Negative and Interrogative Sentences

(*i*) The peon has not been ringing the bell for two hours.
(*ii*) Have the firemen been trying to extinguish fire since morning?

2. Past Tense

The tense which shows action in the past time is known as Past Tense. It is of the following kinds.

(A) Past Indefinite Tense or Simple Past Tense

(B) Past Continuous Tense

(C) Past Perfect Tense

(D) Past Perfect Continuous Tense

(A) *Past Indefinite or Simple Past Tense*

It is used in:

Affirmative Sentences

1. To show an action in the past time without referring to its finishing time
   (*i*) The scientist found the food contaminated with bacteria.
   (*ii*) The calves frisked in the courtyard.
   (*iii*) He typed three letters this morning.

☛ Subject + IInd form of verb + Object is used.

2. To show a habit in the past time
   (*i*) She used to go to temple daily.
   (*ii*) He daily prayed to God before going to office.
   (*iii*) They most often took a long walk in the morning.
3. To show historical truth
   (*i*) India got its freedom on 15 August, 1947.
   (*ii*) Mr. J.L. Nehru was elected the first Prime Minister of India.

Negative and Interrogative Sentences

(*i*) She did not attend the meeting.

(*ii*) We did not allow the children to play in the lawn.

(*iii*) Did he complain to the officer against you?

With 'did' first form of the verb is used.

With some Adverbs e.g. yesterday, ago, etc. Past Indefinite Tense is used.

(*i*) My father bought me a new bicycle five days ago.

(*ii*) A thief broke into my neighbour's last night.

(*iii*) We saw a movie yesterday.

(B) *Past Continuous Tense*

This tense shows the continuity of an action in the past.

Affirmative Sentences

(*i*) He was driving a car.

(*ii*) I was memorizing the lesson.

(*iii*) The workers were building the flyover.

Subject + was/were + Present Participle + object (if any)

Negative and Interrogative Sentences

(*i*) They were not planning to go to Sweden in Summer.

(*ii*) Was he advising his friends to help the poor?

(*iii*) Were the mechanics repairing the machines?

(*iv*) She was not taking any interest in houshold chores.

(C) *Past Perfect Tense*

This tense shows the completion of an action in the past time.

Affirmative Sentences

(*i*) She had finished painting the pictures.

(*ii*) We had planted the saplings of mango plants.

(*iii*) The doctor had operated upon the patient.

Subject + had + Past Participle + Object.

Negative and Interrogative Sentences

(*i*) Had she applied for the post of a clerk?

(*ii*) He had not reserved a berth in the Rajdhani Express.

(D) *Past Perfect Continuous Tense*

This tense shows the part completion of an action/work when the other part of the action/work is still continuing in the Past Tense.

Affirmative Sentences

(*i*) She had been working in that office for five years.

(*ii*) They had been living in that house since 2001.

Negative and Interrogative Sentences

(*i*) Had the gardener been watering the plants since morning?

(ii) The birds had not been chirping on the branches of the tree for three hours.

3. Future Tense

The tense which used to express the actions in future time is known as the future tense. It is of the following kinds:

(A) Future Indefinite Tense or Simple Future Tense

(B) Future Continuous Tense.

(C) Future Perfect Tense.

(D) Future Perfect Continuous Tense.

(A) *Future Indefinite Tense*

It is used to indicate the actions planned for future.

Affirmative Sentences

(i) I shall write a letter to my mother.

(ii) The maid will wash the clothes after the sunrise.

(iii) They will varnish the chairs.

Subject + Will/Shall + 1st form of the verb + Object

Negative and Interrogative Sentences

(i) He will not associate with those boys.

(ii) We shall not walk over the slippery snowy path.

(B) *Future Continuous Tense*

It is used to show a continuous action in the future time.

Affirmative Sentences

(i) She will be planning to meet the P.M. The policeman will be standing on guard at the check post.

Negative and Interrogative Sentences

(i) They will not be carrying coal to the city from the mine.

(ii) Will you be singing on radio the next month?

(C) *Future Perfect Tense*

It is used to show the completion of an action in the future.

Affirmative Sentences

(i) You will have got admission in the new school by then.

(ii) He will have joined the army by then.

Negative and Interrogative Sentences

(i) She will not have told you the story of a lion and a mouse.

(ii) Shall we have reserved two berths in the Janata Express by then?

(D) *Future Perfect Continuous Tense*

It is used to show the part completion of a work/action and the continuity of the other part in the Future Tense.

Affirmative Sentences

(i) He will have been working in the office for five years.

(ii) They will have been painting the pictures since morning.

Negative and Interrogative Sentences

(i) She will not have been discussing the matter with her friends for two hours.

(ii) Will they have been begging for food since morning?

MULTIPLE CHOICE QUESTIONS

Directions: *Choose the correct tense form of each sentence from the options given below.*

1. I speak.

A. Simple past tense

B. Simple present tense

C. Present continuous tense

D. Simple future tense

2. He is speaking.

A. Present continuous tense

B. Simple future tense

C. Future continuous tense
D. Present perfect tense

3. You are speaking.
A. Present perfect continuous tense
B. Present continuous tense
C. Past perfect continuous tense
D. Past continuous tense

4. He spoke.
A. Past perfect tense
B. Simple future tense
C. Present perfect tense
D. Simple past tense

5. You will have spoken.
A. Simple future tense
B. Future perfect tense
C. Simple past tense
D. Past perfect tense

6. He will speak.
A. Simple present tense
B. Future perfect tense
C. Simple past tense
D. Simple future tense

7. We speak.
A. Simple present tense
B. Simple past tense
C. Simple future tense
D. Present perfect tense

8. You will have been speaking.
A. Future continuous tense
B. Simple future tense
C. Future perfect continuous tense
D. Future perfect tense

9. They will have spoken.
A. Past perfect tense
B. Future perfect tense
C. Present perfect tense
D. Simple past tense

10. He has spoken.
A. Simple present tense
B. Present perfect tense
C. Simple past tense
D. Past perfect tense

11. You will be speaking.
A. Future continuous tense
B. Past continuous tense
C. Present perfect continuous
D. Present continuous tense

12. I spoke.
A. Simple present tense
B. Present perfect tense
C. Past perfect tense
D. Simple past tense

13. They were speaking.
A. Present continuous tense
B. Past continuous tense
C. Future continuous tense
D. Past perfect tense

14. I had spoken.
A. Past perfect tense
B. Future perfect tense
C. Simple present tense
D. Present perfect tense

15. They have spoken.
A. Past perfect tense
B. Future perfect tense
C. Simple present tense
D. Present perfect tense

16. They have been speaking.
A. Present continuous tense
B. Past continuous tense
C. Future continuous tense
D. Present perfect continuous tense

17. He shall/will have been speaking.
A. Future continuous tense
B. Simple future tense
C. Future perfect continuous tense
D. Future perfect tense

18. We had been speaking.
A. Past perfect tense
B. Past perfect continuous tense
C. Future perfect continuous tense
D. Simple past tense

19. You have been speaking.
A. Present perfect continuous tense
B. Present continuous tense
C. Past perfect continuous tense
D. Past continuous tense

20. We had spoken.
A. Simple past tense
B. Past perfect tense

C. Present perfect tense
D. Future perfect tense

21. They will speak.
A. Simple present tense
B. Past perfect tense
C. Simple future tense
D. Future perfect tense

22. I had been speaking.
A. Present perfect continuous tense
B. Present continuous tense
C. Past perfect continuous tense
D. Past continuous tense

23. We shall/will be speaking.
A. Past perfect tense
B. Present perfect tense
C. Past continuous tense
D. Future continuous tense

24. You were speaking.
A. Past continuous
B. Present continuous
C. Past perfect tense
D. Past perfect continuous tense

25. I shall/will have been speaking.
A. Past perfect tense
B. Present perfect continuous tense
C. Present continuous tense
D. Future perfect continuous tense

26. I have spoken.
A. Simple past tense
B. Simple present tense
C. Present perfect tense
D. Simple future tense

27. I was speaking.
A. Past continuous tense
B. Simple future tense
C. Future continuous tense
D. Present perfect tense

28. I shall/will be speaking.
A. Future continuous tense
B. Present continuous tense
C. Past perfect continuous tense
D. Past continuous tense

29. I shall/will speak.
A. Past perfect tense
B. Simple future tense
C. Present perfect tense
D. Simple past tense

30. You speak.
A. Simple present tense
B. Future perfect tense
C. Simple past tense
D. Past perfect tense

31. We speak.
A. Simple past tense
B. Simple present tense
C. Present continuous tense
D. Simple future tense

32. I shall/will have spoken.
A. Present continuous tense
B. Simple future tense
C. Future continuous tense
D. Future perfect tense

33. You had spoken.
A. Past perfect tense
B. Present continuous tense
C. Past perfect continuous tense
D. Past continuous tense

34. He has been speaking.
A. Past perfect contintuous tense
B. Simple future tense
C. Present perfect continuous tense
D. Simple past tense

35. You spoke.
A. Present perfect continuous tense
B. Past perfect contintuous tense
C. Simple past tense
D. Past perfect tense

36. They speak.
A. Simple past tense
B. Simple present tense
C. Present continuous tense
D. Simple future tense

37. I have been speaking.
A. Present continuous tense
B. Present perfect continuous tense
C. Future continuous tense
D. Past perfect continuous tense

38. He will have spoken.
A. Present perfect continuous tense

B. Present continuous tense
C. Future perfect tense
D. Past continuous tense

39. We shall/will have spoken.
A. Past perfect tense
B. Future perfect tense
C. Past perfect continuous tense
D. Future perfect continuous tense

40. He had been speaking.
A. Past perfect tense
B. Future perfect tense
C. Past perfect continuous tense
D. Future perfect continuous tense

41. They spoke.
A. Simple past tense
B. Simple present tense
C. Present continuous tense
D. Simple future tense

42. You have spoken.
A. Present continuous tense
B. Simple future tense
C. Future continuous tense
D. Present perfect tense

43. He had spoken.
A. Past perfect tense
B. Present continuous tense
C. Past perfect continuous tense
D. Past continuous tense

44. He was speaking.
A. Past perfect tense
B. Past continuous tense
C. Present continuous tense
D. Simple past tense

45. They are speaking.
A. Past perfect continuous tense
B. Past continuous tense
C. Present continuous tense
D. Simple past tense

46. I am speaking.
A. Past continuous tense
B. Simple present tense
C. Present continuous tense
D. Simple future tense

47. We have spoken.
A. Present continuous tense
B. Simple future tense
C. Future continuous tense
D. Present perfect tense

48. He will have spoken.
A. Present perfect continuous tense
B. Present continuous tense
C. Future perfect tense
D. Past continuous tense

49. You will speak.
A. Past perfect tense
B. Simple future tense
C. Present perfect tense
D. Simple past tense

50. They will be speaking.
A. Future continuous tense
B. Future perfect tense
C. Past continuous tense
D. Present continuous tense

ANSWERS

1	2	3	4	5	6	7	8	9	10
B	A	B	D	B	D	A	C	B	B
11	**12**	**13**	**14**	**15**	**16**	**17**	**18**	**19**	**20**
A	D	B	A	D	D	C	B	A	B
21	**22**	**23**	**24**	**25**	**26**	**27**	**28**	**29**	**30**
C	C	D	A	D	C	A	A	B	A
31	**32**	**33**	**34**	**35**	**36**	**37**	**38**	**39**	**40**
B	D	A	C	C	B	B	C	B	C
41	**42**	**43**	**44**	**45**	**46**	**47**	**48**	**49**	**50**
A	D	A	B	C	C	D	C	B	A

9

Synonyms and Antonyms

English is the most popular language of the world. It comprises thousands of words. No one can remember all the words and their meanings but everyone must try to read and learn the maximum number of words and their meanings. Readers must keep and use a dictionary religiously. Several important words are listed below with their synonyms and antonyms. Learn as many as you can.

ABANDON

Syn.: discard, desert, discontinue, renounce, relinquish, abnegate, forsake, surrender, give up, quit.

Ant.: retain, maintain, uphold, stay, remain.

ABATE

Syn.: lessen, decrease, diminish, subside, slacken, subside, allay, reduce, curtail.

Ant.: increase, enlarge, heighten, intensify, raise.

ABBREVIATE

Syn.: shorten, abridge, compress, curtain, condense, contract, prune, truncate, reduce.

Ant.: enlarge, expand, lengthen, extend, elongate, prolong, protract.

ABILITY

Syn.: competence, aptitude, capability, talent, intelligence, cleverness, capacity.

Ant.: inability, incompetence, incapacity, incapability, inaptitude.

ABLE

Syn.: capable, competent, intelligent, talented, efficient, skilful.

Ant.: unable, incapable, inefficient, incompetent.

ABRUPT

Syn.: sudden, curt, steep, hasty, unexpected, disconnected, disjointed, brusque, rough.

Ant.: expected, anticipated, gradual, courteous, smooth.

ABSURD

Syn.: illogical, irrational, inconsistent, silly, inane, unreasonable, funny, ridiculous, laughable, ludicrous, nonsensical, fatuous.

Ant.: logical, reasonable, rational, consistent, sensible, sound, proper, sane.

ACCURATE

Syn.: exact, precise, correct, actual, just, right, correct.

Ant.: incorrect, inexact, improper, fallacious, inaccurate, misleading, erroneous.

ADEQUATE

Syn.: ample, abundant, enough, sufficient, plentiful, copious.

Ant.: inadequate, insufficient, meagre, scant, scantly, skimpy.

AFFABLE

Syn.: urbane, polite, friendly, courteous, amiable, suave, good-tempered.

Ant.: impolite, unfriendly, discourteous, haughty.

AKIN

Syn.: kindred, similar, allied, cognate, alike, related, analogous.

Ant.: dissimilar, unrelated, unallied, unconnected, different, unlike, separate.

ALERT
Syn.: wary, vigilant, watchful, attentive, heedful, cautious, lively, fully awake.
Ant.: unwatchful, sluggish, relaxed, quiet, restful.

ABNORMAL
Syn.: unusual, irregular, anomalous, unnatural, odd, strange, erratic.
Ant.: usual, regular, natural, normal, customary.

ACTIVE
Syn.: brisk, energetic, lively, nimble, agile.
Ant.: inactive, indolent, sluggish, lazy, passive, torpid.

ACTUAL
Syn.: real, genuine, authentic, true, concrete, factual, existing.
Ant.: unreal, implied, assumed, false, imaginary, fictitious.

AMBIGUOUS
Syn.: vague, uncertain, undecided, undefined, obscure, doubtful, indistinct, dubious, perplexing.
Ant.: lucid, plain, clear, obvious, unambiguous, unmistakable, indisputable.

APT
Syn.: appropriate, apposite, suitable, fitting, pertinent, germane, relevant, congruent, harmonious, congruous.
Ant.: inapt, inappropriate, incongruous, improper, unsuitable, inapposite, irrelevant.

ARDENT
Syn.: fervid, fervent, warm, impassioned, plowing, intense, eager, earnest, passionate, hearty, cordial, enthusiastic.
Ant.: cool, indifferent, apathetic, nonchalant, unimpassioned.

ATROCIOUS
Syn.: nefarious, heinous, cruel, outrageous, beastly, horrible, horrendous.
Ant.: noble, humane, honourable, laudable, admirable, moral.

AUDACIOUS
Syn.: bold, daring, fearless, impudent, brash, rash, reckless, impertinent, madcap, insolent, brave, disrespectful, intrepid.
Ant.: cowardly, timid, fearful, meek, humble, afraid, frightened, scared, different, panicky, apprehensive, shy, mousy, timorous, fidgety.

AUTHENTIC
Syn.: genuine, real, trustworthy, true, reliable, accurate, authoritative, sound, tangible, definite, actual, precise, exact, correct, factual, veritable, sterling.
Ant.: apocryphal, unreliable, spurious, false, fictitious, fake, sham, imaginary, counterfeit, baseless, untrue.

BEAUTIFUL
Syn.: catching, prepossessing, fetching, cute, enticing, engaging, attractive, charming, fascinating, captivating, alluring, tempting, lovely, bewitching, reductive, pretty, enchanting, winning, comely.
Ant.: ugly, unattractive, unprepossessing, repulsive, gaunt, haggard, unpleasing, revolting, hideous.

BITTER
Syn.: tart, harsh, pungent, unpalatable, acrid, spiteful, cutting, stinging, sour, unpleasant, sarcastic, resentful, biting, sardonic, caustic, severe, acrimonious, poignant, distasteful.
Ant.: tasty, toothsome, tasteful, palatable, pleasant, delicious, warm.

BRIGHT
Syn.: brilliant, shining, luminous, lustrous, radiant, sparkling, quick-witted, cheerful, clever, resplendent, flashing, lucid, limpid, sagacious, keen, astute, shrewd, brainy, intelligent.
Ant.: dull, ignorant, cheerless, imbecile, murky, dark, gloomy, sullen.

BRIEF
Syn.: compendious, concise, short, terse, laconic, curt, succinct, condensed, compact, pithy.
Ant.: long, lengthy, prolonged, protracted, elongated, lengthened, extended, detailed, prolix, verbose, wordy.

BRUTAL
Syn.: atrocious, savage, beastly, brutish, fiendish, devilish, barbarous, cruel, ruthless, merciless, crude, ferocious, bestial, heinous.
Ant.: humane, gentle, civilised, merciful, polished, sympathetic, tender, liberal, considerate, good-natured.

CANDID
Syn.: frank, outspoken, sincere, impartial, honest, artless, ingenuous, straightforward.
Ant.: sly, wily, insincere, reserved, unfair, evasive.

CAPRICIOUS
Syn.: unpredictable, impulsive, fickle, changeable, inconstant, whimsical.
Ant.: constant, firm, steadfast, unswerving.

CARELESS
Syn.: heedless, inattentive, indifferent, negligent, remiss, lax, unmindful.
Ant.: cautious, vigilant, careful, mindful, attentive.

CERTAIN
Syn.: indisputable, reliable, sure, definite, undisputed, unmistakable, positive, absolute.
Ant.: uncertain, disputable, doubtful, indefinite, ambiguous, dubious, questionable.

CHEEK
Syn.: impudence, impertinence, effrontery, gall, temerity, audacity, insolence, sauce, sass.
Ant.: politeness, courtesy, humility, gentleness, respect.

☛ *Cheek* also means either side of the face below the eye.

Examples: She has healthy rosy *cheeks*.
They are dancing *cheek* to *cheek*.

CHEERFUL
Syn.: genial, happy, jolly, merry, jovial, pleasant, lively, cheery, sunny, jocund, gay.
Ant.: cheerless, joyless, dejected, unhappy, doleful, sorrowful, mournful, glum, dreary, dismal.

CHARM (Verb)
Syn.: fascinate, attract, please, delight, influence, entice, enchant, entrance, enrapture, allure, captivate, bewitch, ravish, tempt, lure, seduce, beguile, enthral, thrill.
Ant.: repel, repulse, rebuff, snub, disgust, deter, disturb, irritate, annoy, alarm, frighten, terrify.

COMFORTABLE
Syn.: cosy, snug, pleasant, pleasing, pleasurable, satisfied.
Ant.: uncomfortable, disagreeable, dissatisfied, disturbed, displeasing, irritating, miserable, wretched, troubled, cheerless.

COMPLETE (Adj)
Syn.: whole, thorough, total, entire, full, perfect, exhausive, consummate.
Ant.: incomplete, imperfect, partial, unfinished, uncompleted, unaccomplished, deficient, skimpy, sketchy.

CORDIAL
Syn.: sincere, friendly, earnest, warm, hearty, ardent, heartfelt, amiable, affable.
Ant.: unfriendly, insincere, cold, distant, formal, reserved.

COURAGE
Syn.: bravery, boldness, valour, heroism, fearlessness, intrepidity, nerve, gallantry, pluck, fortitude, daring.
Ant.: cowardice, timidity, pusillanimity, fear, funk.

CURIOUS
Syn.: inquisitive, inquiring, prying, strange, unusual, nosey, meddlesome.
Ant.: incurious, uninquiring, uninquisitive, uninterested, unconcerned, indifferent, common, usual.

CORRECT (Adj)
Syn.: accurate, proper, exact, precise, right, true, regular, perfect.
Ant.: incorrect, improper, inexact, wrong, untrue, irregular, imperfect.

DAFT
Syn.: silly, crazy, irrational, foolish, unreasonable, reckless, insane, imbecile, lumpish.
Ant.: sane, sound, sensible, deft, rational, reasonable.

DAINTY
Syn.: pretty, neat, delicate, refined, tasty, delicious, fastidious, elegant, toothsome, exquisite, cute, tasteful, palatable.
Ant.: inelegant, coarse, vulgar, rough, crude, rude, nasty, dirty.

DEEP
Syn.: abstruse, profound, intense, learned, sagacious, extreme, devious, vivid, submerged, bottomless, unfathomable, abysmal, mysterious, knotty, astute, recondite, intricate.
Ant.: shallow, apparent, familiar, artless, commonplace, ordinary, trite, naive, superficial, cursory, simple, banal.

DELIGHT

Syn.: joy, pleasure, rapture, ecstasy, enjoyment, bliss, gratification, gusto, comfort.

Ant.: displeasure, discomfort, sorrow, distress, misery, anguish, suffering, agony, woe, despair, depression.

DETRIMENTAL

Syn.: harmful, injurious, hurtful, pernicious, damaging, noxious.

Ant.: good, beneficial, valuable, useful, profitable, harmless, inoffensive, unobnoxious.

DIFFICULT

Syn.: hard, troublesome, perplexing, tough, laborious, irksome, toilsome, arduous, knotty, burdensome, uphill, herculean, enigmatic.

Ant.: easy, uncomplicated, intelligible, lucid, plain, simple, facile, manageable, tractable, elementary, rudimentary.

DILIGENT

Syn.: industrious, laborious, hard-working, attentive, assiduous, observant, mindful, vigilant, watchful, wakeful, careful.

Ant.: careless, heedless, inattentive, indifferent, unobservant, unmindful.

DISHONEST

Syn.: untrustworthy, false, fraudulent, deceitful, crooked, tricky, deceptive, treacherous, unjust, unfair, unreliable.

Ant.: trustworthy, reliable, fair, just, candid, frank, sincere, upright, truthful, veracious, honest.

DOCILE

Syn.: pliant, tractable, amenable, teachable, yielding, compliant, tame, submissive, gentle, unresisting, dutiful, passive, acquiescent, unassertive, manageable, governable, obsequious.

Ant.: obstinate, stubborn, intractable, self-willed, dogged, defiant, insolent, resistant, resisting, obdurate, disobedient, wilful, uncompromising, unyielding, refractory, recalcitrant.

DOUBTFUL

Syn.: questionable, uncertain, unsure, unlikely, improbable, disputable, debatable, dubious, controversial, fishy, moot, ambiguous.

Ant.: certain, sure, probable, indisputable, unquestionable, positive, absolute, definite, clear, unmistakable, reliable, trustworthy, undoubted, undeniable, indubitable.

DROLL

Syn.: amusing, laughable, funny, comic, sarcastic, whimsical, comical, odd, queer, farcical, ludicrous, ridiculous, absurd, diverting, rompish.

Ant.: sad, lamentable, lugubrious, tragic, painful, dolorous, hurtful, distressing, grievous, woeful, rueful, mournful, deplorable, touching.

DULL

Syn.: stupid, boring, monotonous, foolish, unintelligent, cheerless, gloomy, uninteresting, spiritless, blunt, doltish, sad, stolid, dismal, dowdy, drab, unfashionable, insensible.

Ant.: sensible, cheerful, bright, intelligent, clever, lively, animated, brilliant, sharp, talented, jolly, merry, joyful, gay, jocund, energetic, keen, active, intense, brisk, lively, trenchant, rousing.

EAGER

Syn.: ardent, earnest, zealous, keen, fervent, fervid, vehement, intent, agog, avid, excited, impatient, curious, anxious, enthusiastic, wistful, hearty, cordial, desirous.

Ant.: indifferent, disinterested, cool, loath, unconcerned, apathetic, reluctant, unwilling, disinclined.

EFFICIENT

Syn.: capable, able, competent, gifted, effective, effectual, efficacious, skilful, proficient, talented, intelligent, adept.

Ant.: inefficient, incompetent, ineffectual, unskilled, inexpert.

ELIGIBLE

Syn.: fit, suitable, desirable, worthy, qualified, acceptable, right.

Ant.: unfit, unsuitable, unworthy, unacceptable, undesirable, unqualified.

EMPHEMERAL

Syn.: short-lived, transitory, transient, fleeting, momentary, fugitive, evanescent, fugacious, temporary.

Ant.: eternal, perpetual, perennial, permanent, intransient, lifelong, everlasting, long-lived, prolonged, protracted.

ENORMOUS

Syn.: immense, gigantic, colossal, huge, vast, gargantuan, monstrous, prodigious, stupendous, plentiful, plenteous, copious.

Ant.: trivial, insignificant, ordinary, average, small, little, tiny, diminutive.

ENOUGH

Syn.: plenty, ample, sufficient, abundant, adequate.

Ant.: insufficient, inadequate, meagre, scanty, deficient, scant, jejune, skimpy.

ENTHUSIASM

Syn.: verve, ardour, zeal, fervour, fanaticism.

Ant.: apathy, indifference, detachment, ennui, unconcern, lethargy, weariness, exhaustion, lassitude, languor.

EXPERT (Adj)

Syn.: adept, skilled, adroit, proficient, skilful, deft, dexterous, versed, accomplished.

Ant.: inexpert, unskilful, unskilled, maladroit, clumsy, lungling, unqualified, raw, inexperienced, green, incompetent.

FACE (V)

Syn.: confront, oppose, defy, meet, encounter, resist.

Ant.: avoid, shun, elude, avert, eschew.

FAITHFUL

Syn.: loyal, trustworthy, conscientious, true, accurate, devoted, exact, reliable, staunch, steadfast, constant, dependable, compliant.

Ant.: disloyal, untrustworthy, inaccurate, inexact, unreliable, unfaithful, treacherous, undependable, untrue, fickle.

FICKLE

Syn.: inconstant, disloyal, unfaithful, capricious, impulsive, unpredictable, changeable, unstable, variable, vacillating, wavering, fanciful, whimsical, mutable, irresolute, erratic, unreliable, fitful.

Ant.: steady, steadfast, unchangeable, unwavering, constant, loyal, faithful, reliable, dependable, stable, immutable, invariable.

FIT (Adj)

Ant.: suitable, appropriate, proper, advantageous, sound, well, meet, becoming, fitting, qualified, apt, apposite, decent, decorous, congruent, congruous, concordant, harmonious, eligible.

Ant.: unfit, unsuitable, unbecoming, disadvantageous, unwell, indecent, indecorous, improper, inappropriate, inapt, incongruent, ineligible.

FOOLISH

Syn.: silly, stupid, unwise, ridiculous, absurd, asinine, imbecile, indiscreet, irrational, idiotic, brainless, senseless, nonsensical, witless, preposterous, inane, fatuous, imprudent, inconsistent, illogical, laughable, paradoxical, dotty.

Ant.: wise, sane, prudent, discreet, sound, sensible, rational, sagacious, judicious, sage.

FRIENDLY

Syn.: kindly, pleasantly, amicable, cordial, hearty, warm-hearted, affable, genial, well-inclined, good-tempered, amiable, favourable, pleasing, sociable, companionable, nice, neighbourly, benevolent, well-disposed.

Ant.: hostile, unsociable, unfavourable, unfriendly, adverse, inimical, antagonistic, distant, reserved, cool, ill-inclined, ill-disposed, resistant, opposed.

FUNDAMENTAL

Syn.: basic, primary, essential, cardinal, indispensable, original, rudimentary, elementary, radical, most important, prime, chief.

Ant.: secondary, subordinate, minor, inferior, resultant, second-rate, subsidiary.

FUNNY

Syn.: amusing, jocular, jocose, laughable, eccentric, absurd, droll, comical, comic, playful, ludicrous, farcical, humorous, ridiculous, odd, queer, diverting, strange.

Ant.: sad, serious, solemn, sober, sedate, staid, grave, sorrowful, mournful.

GARRULOUS

Syn.: talkative, chatty, verbose, loquacious, communicative, glib, voluble, prolix, wordy, long-winded, diffuse, profuse, discussive, rambling, circumlocutory, maundering, periphrastic.

Ant.: laconic, reticent, silent, taciturn, uncommunicative, terse, reserved, short-spoken.

GENUINE
Syn.: authentic, sound, true, real, pure, veritable, unadulterated, unalloyed, unaffected, natural, factual, actual, legitimate, undistorted, tangible, valid, sterling.
Ant.: sham, spurious, fictitious, artificial, adulterated, alloyed, impure, apocryphal, untrue, fallacious, unsound, invalid.

GIFTED
Syn.: talented, intelligent, sagacious, competent, wise, able, proficient, efficient, capable, shrewd, inventive, skilful, ingenious, experienced.
Ant.: foolish, doltish, silly, stupid, idiotic.

GLORIOUS
Syn.: famous, beautiful, splendid, magnificent, enjoyable, pleasant, grand, exalted, lofty, majestic, sublime, noble, bright, radiant, renowned.
Ant.: base, ignoble, low, ordinary, ridiculous.

GOOD (N)
Syn.: benefit, profit, advantage, virtue, boon, weal, prosperity, blessing, gain, welfare, righteousness, merit.
Ant.: harm, injury, corruption, wickedness, depravity, detriment, disadvantage, ill, calamity, loss, evil, curse.

GRACEFUL
Syn.: elegant, pleasing in style and attitude, polite, considerate, comely, beautiful, attractive, lithe, lissom, svelte, sylphlike, willowy.
Ant.: ungainly, awkward, lumbering, uncouth, ill mannered, not refined.

GRAND
Syn.: august, exalted, stately, splendid, majestic, lofty, superb, imposing, dignified, noble, princely, magnificent, big, pompous, gorgeous, sublime, impressive.
Ant.: mean, common, insignificant, secondary, inferior, unimportant, little, undignified, unimposing, petty, paltry, beggarly, lowly.

GRIM
Syn.: fearful, stern, fierce, ruthless, horrible, determined, strong-willed, horrid, repellent, frightful, ghastly, gristly, gloomy, severe, unrelenting, unpleasant, depressing, determined, repulsive, dingy, drab, savage, appalling, ferocious, ugly, sullen, hideous.
Ant.: handsome, pretty, graceful, elegant, gentle, gracious, friendly, humane, benign, mild, docile, attractive.

GRUFF
Syn.: rough, surly, blunt, harsh, rude.
Ant.: affable, courteous, mild, smooth.

HARMFUL
Syn.: detrimental, pernicious, prejudicial, deleterious, injurious, noxious, hurtful, mischievous, obnoxious, inauspicious, oppressive, baneful, baleful, menacing, malignant, unhealthful, vitiated, damaging.
Ant.: helpful, profitable, beneficial, advantageous, harmless, useful, favourable, good, salutary, healthful, inoffensive, unobnoxious.

HARMONIOUS
Syn.: congruous, concordant, uniform, proportioned, consistent, tuneful, melodious, sweet-sounding, agreeable, friendly, amicable, cordial.
Ant.: unfriendly, hostile, unfavourable, adverse, opposing, opposed, antagonistic, contrary, discordant, conflicting, inconsistent.

HARSH
Syn.: rough, stern, cruel, severe, blunt, coarse, gruff, discordant, raucous, hoarse, rugged, severe, shrill, strident, austere, acrimonious, ungenial, sharp, sour, ungracious, brutal, heartless.
Ant.: gentle, mild, smooth, soft, melodious.

HEALTHY
Syn.: robust, strong, vigorous, lusty, hearty, sound, well, hygienic, salubrious, wholesome, salutary, bracing, invigorating, harmless, healthful, hale and hearty, inoffensive, laudable, moral.
Ant.: diseased, delicate, infirm, injurious, frail, noxious, sick, ailing, ill, sick.

HEARTY
Syn.: warm, earnest, sincere, heartfelt, cordial, sound, ardent, friendly, enthusiastic, cheerful, healthy, fervent, fervid.
Ant.: cool, reserved, taciturn, insincere.

HONEST
Syn.: frank, sincere, direct, fairly earned, truthful, upright, virtuous, right, sincere, genuine, trustworthy.

Ant.: dishonest, untrustworthy, tricky, deceitful, fraudulent, insincere.

HONOUR (N)

Syn.: privilege, probity, integrity, glory, distinction, great respect, glory, dignity, reverence, grandeur, high-mindedness, eminence, renown, fame.

Ant.: dishonour, disrespect, contempt, irreverence, disgrace, degradation, slight, infamy, perfidy, treachery, improbity, scorn, disdain.

HUMOROUS

Syn.: droll, amusing, ludicrous, funny, jocular, merry, comic, jocose, waggish, farcical.

Ant.: solemn, serious, sober, grave, composed, sedate, dignified.

IDLE

Syn.: indolent, lazy, inactive, unemployed, useless, unoccupied, slothful, futile.

Ant.: active, busy, occupied, working, industrious, employed.

INDUSTRIOUS

Syn.: diligent, hard-working, laborious, assiduous, sedulous.

Ant.: lethargic, inactive, apathetic, lazy, idle, indolent, slothful, torpid, sluggish, shiftless, slack, lax, supine.

IMPORTANT

Syn.: significant, valuable, weighty, influential, momentous, prominent, material, essential, remarkable, eventful.

Ant.: insignificant, unimportant, petty, trivial, mean, secondary, minor, uninfluential, worthless, valueless, immaterial, inferior.

INGENIOUS

Syn.: adroit, clever, dexterous, quick-witted, skilful, talented, smart, bright, sharp, adept, original, inventive, expert, intelligent.

Ant.: unskilled, dull, foolish, clumsy, awkward, stupid, unskilful, inexpert, maladroit, incompetent, inexperienced, unconversant, ungainly.

INGENUOUS

Syn.: innocent, open, candid, frank, sincere, straightforward, truthful, artless, honest, naive, simple, trusting, unaffected, outspoken.

Ant.: insincere, reserved, sly, wily, contrived, disingenuous, mean, pretentious, sham, affected, priggish.

INFINITE

Syn.: boundless, endless, unlimited, unbounded, limitless, immeasurable, interminable, stupendous, eternal, immense, vast, incalculable, numberless, countless, bottomless, unfathomable, inexhaustible, indefinite, perpetual.

Ant.: finite, limited, restricted, bounded, conditioned, confined, definite, determinate, circumscribed.

INTELLIGENT

Syn.: brainy, clever, bright, brilliant, keen, sagacious, quick-witted, discerning, sharp, shrewd, astute, canny, perspicacious, perceptive, nimble, well-informed, enlightened.

Ant.: foolish, doltish, dull, stupid, unintelligent, stolid, obtuse, silly, inane.

INTEGRITY

Syn.: honesty, probity, uprightness, rectitude, truthfulness, sincerity, trustworthiness, fairness, wholeness, completeness, oneness, totality, entirety, indivisibility.

Ant.: dishonesty, duplicity, unfairness, deceit, fraud, improbity.

IRRITABLE

Syn.: peevish, touchy, irascible, testy, short-tempered, fretful, splenetic, petulant, grumpy, pettish, snappish, choleric, peppery, churlish, cantankerous, fractious, crabbed.

Ant.: calm, composed, agreeable, gracious, cheerful, genial, good-natured, blithe, jaunty, buoyant, lively, animated.

JEALOUS

Syn.: envious, invidious, suspicious, resentful, covetous, jaundiced, distrustful, apprehensive, intolerant.

Ant.: unenvious, unjealous, tolerant, liberal, genial, indifferent, unsuspecting.

JOLLY

Syn.: genial, jovial, jubilant, lively, gay, joyful, merry, mirthful, cheerful, light-hearted, jocular, jocund, blithe.

Ant.: cheerless, joyless, sad, mournful, gloomy, morose, sullen, lugubrious, sorrowful, melancholy, dismal, unhappy.

JUST

Syn.: fair, honest, proper, right, reasonable, well-founded, deserved, impartial, true, upright, exact, precise, proportioned, normal.

Ant.: unfair, unjust, improper, unreasonable, partial, untrue, inexact, abnormal, ill-proportioned, prejudiced, biased.

KEEN

Syn.: acute, sharp, penetrating, astute, clever, cunning, quick, shrewd, wily, eager, enthusiastic, intense, deep, strong, cutting, ardent, nippy, avid, fervent.

Ant.: indifferent, blunt, dull, languid, indifferent, cool, careless, half-hearted, unconcerned, lukewarm, impervious, insouciant.

KIND (Adj)

Syn.: friendly, gentle, mild, obliging, benign, lenient, helpful, sympathetic, favourable, benevolent, amiable, good-natured, cordial, courteous, gracious, warm-hearted, humane, compassionate, generous, philanthropic.

Ant.: unfriendly, unfavourable, discourteous, unkind, harsh, severe, hard, callous, cruel, inhumane.

KNOWLEDGE

Syn.: understanding, learning, information, instruction, acquaintance, cognition, cognizance, awareness, comprehension, apprehension, consciousness, familiarity, ken, enlightenment, experience, attainments, scholarship, education.

Ant.: ignorance, nescience, illiteracy, incomprehension, inexperience, unawareness.

LABORIOUS

Syn.: diligent, hard-working, industrious, toilsome, tedious, tiresome, irksome, arduous, assiduous, wearisome, strenuous, painstaking, uphill.

Ant.: easy, light, feasible, indiligent, lazy, indolent, simple, idle.

LACONIC

Syn.: curt, terse, concise, pithy, short, brief, succinct, crisp, compendious, compact.

Ant.: lengthy, prolix, wordy, circumlocutory, verbose, discursive, long-winded, rambling, roundabout, copious, diffuse.

LAX

Syn.: negligent, careless, remiss, sluggish, inattentive, neglectful, heedless, vague, desultory, unmethodical, loose, slack, relaxed.

Ant.: careful, meticulous, attentive, methodical, severe, strict, heedful, regardful, cautious, prudent, discreet.

LESSEN

Syn.: shorten, abate, curtail, decrease, reduce, diminish, abridge, mitigate, contract, deduct, subtract, shrink, allenuate.

Ant.: increase, enlarge, augment, extend, expand, grow, amplify, enhance, magnify.

LIVELY

Syn.: high-spirited, vigorous, energetic, active, animated, brisk, bright, blithe, frolicsome, merry, playful, spirited, forceful, sprightly, vivacious, joyous, joyful, gay.

Ant.: dull, listless, insipid, vapid, inactive, uninteresting, depressed, languid, torpid, apathetic, indifferent, sluggish, dejected, joyless, cheerless, unlively, spiritless.

LOGICAL

Syn.: cogent, convincing, sound, valid, effective, reasonable, natural, rational, sane, relevant.

Ant.: illogical, invalid, ineffective, unreasonable, unnatural, irrational, insane, irrelevant, fallacious.

MADDEN

Syn.: infuriate, enrage, incense, derange, craze, anger, offend, displease, embitter, exasperate, rankle, affront, irritate, provoke, nettle, inflame, annoy.

Ant.: placate, pacify, soothe, calm, assuage, appease, mollify.

MALICIOUS

Syn.: spiteful, malignant, malevolent, evil-minded, hostile, rancorous, virulent, wicked, malign, pernicious, vicious, harmful, maleficent, ill-disposed, ill-intentioned.

Ant.: benign, kind, good-natured, benevolent, cordial, unselfish, sympathetic, gracious, well-intentioned, humane, warm-hearted, affectionate.

MASTERLY

Syn.: skilful, adept, deft, dexterous, expert, skilled, consummate, perfect, masterful, dominating.

Ant.: unskilled, maladroit, clumsy, inexpert.

METHODICAL

Syn.: orderly, logical, systematic, regular, procedural, planned, arranged, tidy.

Ant.: disorderly, illogical, irregular, unsystematic, unmethodical, untidy, desultory, unarranged, disarranged, sloppy, chaotic, anarchical.

MODEST

Syn.: moderate, inexpensive, not showy or splendid in appearance, not vain or boastful, shy, bashful, humble, meek, reserved, unassuming, unpretentious, diffident, unobtrusive, coy.

Ant.: immodest, showy or splendid in appearance, vain, boastful, ostentatious, pretentious, proud, arrogant, bold, conceited, haughty, disdainful, pert, imperious, domineering, priggish, smug, self-satisfied, egotistic, self-important.

MOMENTOUS

Syn.: important, prominent, significant, weighty, material, pressing, influential, grave, consequential, serious, notable, solemn, memorable, remarkable.

Ant.: unimportant, immaterial, inconsequential, insignificant, mean, petty, trivial, slight, niggling, trifling.

NATURAL

Syn.: innate, inherent, original, normal, spontaneous, unaffected, characteristic, typical, native, unstudied, inborn, naive, ingenuous, inbred, ingrained, usual, intrinsic.

Ant.: unnatural, abnormal, artificial, affected, forced, irregular, unusual, inconsistent, fictitious.

NECESSARY

Syn.: requisite, needful, essential, inevitable, unavoidable, indispensable.

Ant.: unnecessary, optional, unessential, dispensable, voluntary, discretional, casual.

NICE

Syn.: pleasant, agreeable, friendly, kind, fine, subtle, respectable, scrupulous, dainty, attractive, fastidious, tasteful, delicate, choosy, refined, palatable, delectable, pleasing, pleasurable.

Ant.: disagreeable, coarse, unscrupulous, rough, nasty, rueful, mournful, woeful, deplorable, distressing.

NIMBLE

Syn.: agile, sharp, active, brisk, lively, spry, quick.

Ant.: slow, sluggish, clumsy, inert, lazy, indolent, awkward, slothful.

NOVICE

Syn.: beginner, tyro, neophyte, apprentice, greenhorn, learner, acolyte, rookie.

Ant.: expert, adept, master, teacher, trainer, instructor.

OBEDIENT

Syn.: observant, dutiful, complying, compliant, loyal, faithful, devoted, fractable, docile, submissive, pliable, pliant, yielding.

Ant.: disloyal, unfaithful, intractable, uncomplying, uncompliant, unruly, unsubmissive, refractory, resisting, contumacious, recalcitrant.

OBSTINATE

Syn.: stubborn, obdurate, dogged, tenacious, persistent, insistent, headstrong, pertinacious, unyielding, determined, self-willed, wilful, resolute.

Ant.: irresolute, subservient, yielding, submissive, amenable, wavering.

OFFENSIVE (Adj)

Syn.: insulting, annoying, disgusting, repulsive, aggressive, distasteful, foul, aggressive, obnoxious, nasty.

Ant.: pleasant, defensive, inoffensive, harmless, blameless, unaggressive, innocuous.

OWN (V)

Syn.: possess, confess, admit, avow, acknowledge, have, hold, concede.

Ant.: deny, disclaim, disavow, renounce, disown, abjure, abandon.

PEEVISH

Syn.: irritable, touchy, testy, tetchy, irascible, fretful, bad-tempered, crabbed, pettish, petulant, snappish, waspish, fractious, hot-headed, crabby, churlish.

Ant.: affable, genial, good-natured, good-tempered, pleasant, cordial, hearty, jolly, soft-spoken, polite, urbane.

PERFECT (Adj)
Syn.: complete, excellent, ideal, exact, precise, total, absolute, thorough, faultless, indefective, indeficient, immaculate, impeccable, sound, spotless, entire, utter, consummate.
Ant.: imperfect, incomplete, inexact, deficient, faulty, unsound, deformed, impaired, blemished, crude.

PLEASANT
Syn.: enjoyable, polite and friendly, pleasurable, agreeable, pleasing, delectable, palatable, delightful, cheerful, delicious, jocular, merry.
Ant.: unpleasant, disagreeable, unlively, lugubrious, dismal, sad, mournful, offensive, unpleasing, disgusting, obnoxious, nasty.

PLENTIFUL
Syn.: ample, abundant, copious, profuse, plenteous, prolific, bounteous, bountiful, lavish.
Ant.: scanty, meagre, limited, skimpy, insufficient, sparing, scarce, deficient, rare.

POMPOUS
Syn.: self-important, ostentatious, high-flown, bombastic, grandiose, arrogant, haughty, grand, imposing, lofty, magnificent, majestic, stately, sublime, dignified, showy, pretentious, assuming, turgid, magniloquent.
Ant.: unassuming, plain-mannered, unpretending, modest, unobtrusive, humble-minded, unpretentious, bashful, coy.

PRECISE
Syn.: exact, accurate, definite, correct, punctilious, fastidious, particular, proper.
Ant.: inexact, inaccurate, indefinite, incorrect, improper, vague, ambiguous, rough, circumlocutory.

PREPOSSESSING
Syn.: attractive, charming, taking, alluring, engaging, winning, appealing, winsome.
Ant.: unattractive, repulsive, ugly, unprepossessing, ill-looking.

PREPOSTEROUS
Syn.: outrageous, absurd, unreasonable, ridiculous, foolish, silly, stupid, inconsistent, irrational, nonsensical, laughable, idiotic, illogical, ludicrous.
Ant.: consistent, reasonable, rational, logical, sensible, sound, just, fair, right, moderate.

PRINCIPAL (Adj)
Syn.: chief, main, foremost, prime, leading, most important, pre-eminent, outstanding, excellent, conspicuous, highest, first-rate, cardinal, fundamental, primary, paramount, supreme, predominant.
Ant.: minor, inferior, subordinate, secondary, auxiliary, subsidiary.

PUSHY
Syn.: aggressive, offensive, forceful, belligerent, bold, impudent, rude, disrespectful, insolent, self-assertive.
Ant.: cowardly, timid, defensive.

QUESTIONABLE
Syn.: doubtful, uncertain, suspicious, dubious, disputable, debatable, arguable, fishy, controversial.
Ant.: certain, indisputable, obvious, evident, unquestionable, sure.

QUICKEN
Syn.: hasten, hurry, speed, accelerate, refresh, animate, rush, expedite.
Ant.: retard, slacken, moderate, curb, shorten, slow, relax, delay, impede, hinder, obstruct.

QUIET (Adj)
Syn.: calm, peaceful, serene, hushed, silent, modest, restrained, subdued, gentle, unostentatious, restful, relaxed, leisurely, unhurried, reposeful, tranquil, quiescent, unobtrusive, passive, undisturbed, motionless, still, mild, modest.
Ant.: loud, agitated, disturbed, perturbed, noisy.

QUIET (N)
Syn.: calm, calmness, hush, peace, repose, rest, silence, stillness, tranquility, serenity, quiescence, quietude.
Ant.: agitation, disturbance, uproar, noise, din, noisiness, loudness, tumult, excitement, turmoil, commotion, unrest.

RAPID
Syn.: speedy, quick, swift, fast, prompt, expeditious, hasty, hurried.
Ant.: slow, sluggish, slack, tardy, leisurely, gradual, languid.

REASONABLE
Syn.: sensible, logical, moderate, tolerable, acceptable, average, sound, fair, rational, inexpensive, sober, temperate.

Ant.: unreasonable, absurd, unfair, illogical, irrational, intolerable, immoderate, expensive, senseless, preposterous, ridiculous, silly, excessive, obstinate.

REGULAR

Syn.: proper, systematic, symmetrical, normal, usual, habitual, constant, orderly, steady, methodical, consistent.

Ant.: irregular, improper, abnormal, unusual, disorderly, inconstant, desultory, unmethodical, changeable, erratic, sporadic.

REMARKABLE

Syn.: unusual, exceptional, august, impressive, extra-ordinary, uncommon, splendid, singular, notable, noteworthy, striking, distinguished, wonderful, famous, prominent, conspicuous, imposing.

Ant.: ordinary, average, inconspicuous, normal, usual, common, customary, undistinguished.

RESPONSIBLE

Syn.: answerable, trustworthy, dependable, accountable, liable, chargeable, reliable.

Ant.: irresponsible, untrustworthy, undependable, unreliable, unaccountable, unanswerable.

RICH

Syn.: wealthy, affluent, prosperous, opulent, nourishing, abundant, ample, fruitful, fertile, luxuriant, vivid, bountiful, sumptuous, gorgeous, sonorous, well-to-do, plentiful, fecund, well-heeled, productive, wholesome, nutritious.

Ant.: poor, needy, penniless, beggarly, indigent, destitute, barren, sterile, unfruitful, unproductive, impecunious, hard up, necessitous.

SCHOOL (V)

Syn.: train, teach, direct, lead, guide, educate, instruct, control, discipline, inform, enlighten, tutor.

Ant.: misdirect, mislead, misguide, deceive, delude.

SCRUPULOUS

Syn.: absolutely honest, extremely careful and tho-rough, paying great attention to details, exact, meti-culous, punctilious, upright, moral, conscientious, veracious, truthful, right-minded, high-principled.

Ant.: dishonest, deceitful, tricky, fraudulent, unscrupulous, careless, unprincipled, conscienceless, knavish.

SILLY

Syn.: foolish, doltish, indiscreet, stupid, unwise, childish, inane, fatuous, senseless, absurd, ridiculous, idiotic, nonsensical, irrational, preposterous, outrageous, imprudent.

Ant.: wise, prudent, rational, sane, discreet, sound, intelligent, sensible, sapient, sagacious, discerning, perspicacious, brainy, brilliant, well-advised, judicious, astute, shrewd.

SLY

Syn.: foxy, wily, crafty, cunning, deceitful, secretive, furtive, roguish, mischievous, stealthy, underhand, surreptitious.

Ant.: open, frank, candid, ingenuous, sincere, artless.

SOFTEN

Syn.: mollify, soothe, ease, calm, comfort, quiet, temper, moderate, mitigate, abate, allay, alleviate, assuage, diminish, lessen, extenuate, relieve.

Ant.: harden, stiffen, augment, irritate, increase, aggravate, worsen, enhance, heighten, intensify, infuriate, indurate.

SUITABLE

Syn.: appropriate, proper, fitting, right, becoming, apposite, eligible, seemly, apt, meet, decorous, seasonable.

Ant.: unsuitable, improper, unbecoming, inapt, indecorous, unseemly, ineligible, inappropriate, inapposite.

TEDIOUS

Syn.: boring, tiresome, wearisome, irksome, monotonous, dreary, uninteresting, dull, humdrum, drab.

Ant.: interesting, amusing, entertaining, exciting, delightful, brisk.

TERRIBLE

Syn.: horrible, alarming, fearful, shocking, frightful, awesome, appalling, dreadful, terrifying, frightening, formidable, terrific, horrid, terrible, fearsome.

Ant.: pleasing, encouraging, safe, secure, joyous, informidable, unastounding.

TOLERABLE
Syn.: endurable, bearable, passable, sufferable, acceptable.
Ant.: intolerable, unbearable, unacceptable, unendurable.

TOTALLY
Syn.: fully, wholly, completely, entirely, absolutely, thoroughly, perfectly, utterly.
Ant.: partially, partly, incompletely, somewhat.

TRUE
Syn.: accurate, actual, unerring, correct, authentic, exact, real, veracious, constant, faithful, loyal, genuine, precise, veritable, reliable, rightful, sincere, factual, legitimate.
Ant.: untrue, inaccurate, incorrect, inexact, unreal, unfaithful, disloyal, unreliable, insincere, false, spurious, fictitious, erroneous, inconstant, fickle, fallacious, apocryphal.

UNASSUMING
Syn.: modest, reserved, retiring, humble, diffident, bashful, shy, coy, unpretentious, unostentatious.
Ant.: arrogant, boastful, haughty, proud, vain, immodest, pretentious, ostentatious, pert, vainglorious, imperious, smug, priggish, domineering.

URBANE
Syn.: suave, affable, polite, civil, courteous, refined, well-bred, well-mannered, accomplished, sophisticated, courtly, amiable.
Ant.: uncivil, uncouth, rude, ill-mannered, discourteous, impolite, boorish, impertinent.

UTTER (Adj)
Syn.: complete, entire, thorough, full, whole, perfect, absolute, sheer, total, downwright, consummate, arrant.
Ant.: incomplete, imperfect, partial, meagre, lacking, wanting, deficient, sketchy, skimpy.

VALID
Syn.: binding, sound, legal, logical, effective, cogent, operative, weighty, well-grounded, just.
Ant.: invalid, illegal, illogical, unjust, unsound, ineffective, null and void, inoperative.

VANITY
Syn.: pride, egotism, arrogance, conceit, immodesty, self-esteem, smugness, priggishness, vainglory, boasting, boast, bombast, bluster, brag, rodomontade.
Ant.: modesty, humility, meekness, simplicity, unostentatiousness.

VIGOROUS
Syn.: energetic, active, strong, potent, powerful, mighty, forceful, animated, lively, spirited, sprightly, brisk, vivacious, intense.
Ant.: powerless, ineffective, ineffectual, dull, feeble, unsound, impotent, flabby.

VITAL
Syn.: essential, indispensable, necessary, basic, cardinal, paramount, energetic, lively, dynamic.
Ant.: unessential, unimportant, dispensable, immaterial, insignificant.

WELCOME (Adj)
Syn.: pleasing, agreeable, acceptable, gratifying, pleasant, pleasurable.
Ant.: unwelcome, unacceptable, disagreeable, distasteful, unpleasant, offensive, repugnant, repulsive, unpalatable.

WISE
Syn.: prudent, sagacious, sage, learned, profound, well-advised, judicious, scholarly, well-informed, well-read, shrewd.
Ant.: unwise, foolish, shallow, silly, stupid, inane, fatuous, injudicious, imprudent, ill-advised, doltish, uneducated, unschooled.

WRONG (Adj)
Syn.: erroneous, incorrect, unjust, inaccurate, mistaken, faulty, untrue, unprecise, improper, bad, amiss, inappropriate, unsuitable, false, unfair, unfit.
Ant.: right, correct, true, proper, suitable, exact, just, precise, fair, accurate.

YEARLING
Syn.: youngling, colt, filly, cub, whelp, puppy.
Ant.: elder, doyen, old-timer, veteran.

YEARN
Syn.: desire, strongly, pine, long, hanker, grieve, mourn.
Ant.: hate, detest, despise, loathe, dislike, abominate.

YIELDING
Syn.: pliant, tractable, docile, submissive, compliant, flexible, soft, manageable.

Ant.: intractable, unmanageable, awkward, stubborn, obstinate, obdurate, unyielding, inflexible, hard, unruly, recalcitrant.

YOUNG

Syn.: youthful, new, fresh, inexperienced, immature, youngish, teen-age, juvenile, adolescent, green, puerile.

Ant.: old, elderly, experienced, aged, senior, mature, full-grown.

ZANY (Adj)

Syn.: ridiculous, eccentric, amusing, ludicrous, foolish, doltish, silly, inane, fatuous, stupid, droll, funny, whimsical, dull, drab.

Ant.: wise, intelligent, accomplished, well-informed, shrewd, brisk, active.

ZANY (N)

Syn.: merry-andrew, buffoon, clown, madcap, fool, comedian, jester, nitwit, dunce, dolt, nincompoop, ninny, simpleton, numbskull, oaf, loon, dullard, dunderhead, blockhead, goof, idiot, booby, bonehead, dunce, imbecile.

Ant.: sage, scholar, genius, wise person, intelligent person.

ZEAL

Syn.: enthusiasm, energy, verve, keenness, vim, vigour, heartiness, earnestness, spirit, eagerness, warmth, ardour, fervour, devotion, dash, briskness, alacrity, intensity, vehemence.

Ant.: apathy, indifference, unconcern, ennui, detachment, coldness, torpor, torpidity.

ZEALOUS

Syn.: eager, keen, enthusiastic, deep, strong, intense, earnest, passionate, spirited, ardent, warm, energetic, fervent, fervid, impassioned, vehement.

Ant.: cold, apathetic, indifferent, nonchalant, calm and casual, cool.

ZENITH

Syn.: acme, top, summit, apex, climax, vertex, culmination, peak, prime, highest point.

Ant.: nadir, lowest point or part, base, bottom, foot.

ZEST

Syn.: gusto, relish, enthusiasm, exhilaration, thrill, great enjoyment or excitement.

Ant.: distaste, disrelish, dislike, insipidity.

MULTIPLE CHOICE QUESTIONS

Directions (Qs.1 to 50): *Choose the words which are most nearly the SAME in meaning to the words given in capital letters.*

1. CARP
   A. to find fault unreasonably
   B. to hone
   C. to twist a meaning unfairly
   D. to jump to a conclusion

2. GIBE
   A. sneering remark B. praise
   C. expose D. measure

3. IMPALPABLE
   A. bad taste B. bad odour
   C. cannot be felt D. wholly false

4. DISQUISITION
   A. uncomfortable B. formal discourse
   C. deprived D. cross-examination

5. PROSCRIBE
   A. to order B. to declare
   C. to protect D. to prohibit

6. OSTRÀCIZE
   A. to expand B. to describe
   C. to exclude D. to curtail

7. INVEIGH
   A. to encroach B. to murder
   C. to hurt D. to rail

8. CONCOCT
   A. to blame
   B. to falsify
   C. to prepare or make up
   D. to make fool

9. BURGEON
   A. to sprout B. to begin
   C. to diminish D. to intrude

10. CAJOLE
A. to scold B. to ridicule
C. to wheedle D. to scorn

11. ARCHAIC
A. damaged
B. belonging to an earlier period
C. neophyte
D. lame

12. ATTENUATE
A. to support B. to pay attention
C. to brood D. to weaken

13. PERFUNCTORY
A. half-hearted B. orator
C. performer D. stern

14. INTERNECINE
A. insincere B. peaceful
C. deadly D. unreliable

15. PROLETARIAT
A. wealthy class B. trade agreement
C. intellectual class D. working class

16. PALLIDNESS
A. wanness B. obsess
C. egress D. transgress

17. IMPECUNIOUSNESS
A. habitual poverty
B. aloofness
C. impulsiveness
D. peerless

18. REPARTEE
A. irrelevant B. sarcasm
C. witty retort D. introvert

19. TENOR
A. timid B. topical
C. support D. purport

20. TERMAGANT
A. selfish B. shrewish woman
C. self-dependent D. brave

21. RELEGATE
A. retaliation B. banish
C. repeat D. bold

22. UBIQUITOUS
A. universal B. frenzied
C. omnipresent D. absent

23. UNTRAMMELLED
A. unfettered B. unwearied
C. indubitable D. unbroken

24. CHURLISH
A. sophisticated B. childish
C. rude D. polite

25. GUMPTION
A. common sense B. guilt
C. insidious D. idealistic

26. QUISLING
A. cheat B. partriot
C. traitor D. loyal

27. ARDUOUS
A. strange B. difficult
C. unique D. antique

28. DOUGHTY
A. coarse B. stupid
C. impudent D. strong and able

29. COGNIZANT
A. suitable B. aware
C. ignorant D. substitute

30. OVERTURE
A. tentative proposal B. declaration
C. exaggeration D. treaty

31. ABASH
A. lowered B. humiliate
C. embarass D. appreciate

32. ABSOLVE
A. solution B. resolve
C. confusion D. pardon

33. ACCOLADE
A. accomodation B. allotment
C. award of merit D. punishment

34. IMPUTATION
A. impending B. attribution
C. impression D. insistent

35. IMBUE
A. to force B. to attack
C. to charge D. to saturate

36. IMBROGLIO
A. complicated situation
B. climax

C. beginning
D. conclusion

37. OBFUSCATE
A. to surrender B. to confuse
C. to argue D. to punish

38. ENTHRALL
A. to exclude B. to idealize
C. to captivate D. to point out

39. EXCULPATE
A. murder
B. to sentence to death
C. to involve in crime
D. to free from blame

40. RIPOSTE
A. resignation B. re-appointment
C. commitment D. clever retort

41. RETRENCHMENT
A. forced withdrawal
B. encroachment
C. official order
D. reduction of expenses

42. SUPERCILIOUS
A. arrogant B. misbehaved
C. urbane D. sophisticated

43. MENDACITY
A. sincerity B. falsehood
C. gaiety D. consciousness

44. RETICENCE
A. cruelty B. simplicity
C. secretiveness D. honesty

45. RENDITION
A. artistic interpretation
B. summarize
C. illustration
D. elucidation

46. FEUD
A. conference B. debate
C. dual D. bitter quarrel

47. TRITE
A. unusual B. commonplace
C. widespread D. unique

48. SUPPLICATE
A. to entreat B. to provide
C. to intimate D. to affiliate

49. HIRSUTE
A. horrible B. hostile
C. humorous D. hairy

50. VICISSITUDE
A. unfortunate B. misfortune
C. change of fortune D. change of mind

Directions Directions (Qs. 51 to 100): *Choose the words which are most nearly the OPPOSITE in meaning to the words given in capital letters.*

51. ODIUM
A. affection B. hatred
C. fulfilment D. scarcity

52. COMPOSURE
A. wordiness B. tranquility
C. noisiness D. perspicuity

53. INEQUITY
A. balance B. justice
C. justified D. unequal

54. PERVERSE
A. appropriate B. exact
C. similar D. reasonable

55. EXTRINSIC
A. inherent B. extraordinary
C. god-gifted D. appreciating

56. ASSENT
A. indifferent B. descent
C. disagreement D. consent

57. FICTITIOUS
A. artificial B. illusive
C. deceiving D. real

58. DISINGENUOUS
A. sincere B. genius
C. practical D. sensible

59. ABBREVIATE
A. epitomize B. abdicate
C. amplify D. abate

60. ABHORRENCE
A. detest B. abduct
C. respect D. sympathy

61. CALUMNY
A. vituperation B. eulogy
C. obloquy D. disturbed

62. CALEFACTION
A. separation B. calid
C. cooling D. warmth

63. CARIOUS
A. careful B. putrid
C. anxious D. fresh

64. DISENCUMBER
A. burden B. free
C. discharge D. able

65. HORTATIVE
A. disappointing B. hostile
C. pleasant D. deterring

66. OBLITERATE
A. restore B. refractory
C. highly qualified D. rural

67. RETICENT
A. resonant B. relinquish
C. taciturn D. garrulous

68. VENGEANCE
A. subdued B. submissive
C. forgiveness D. forgetfulness

69. FLAUNT
A. covered B. hide
C. curtailed D. apparent

70. EXPURGATE
A. insert B. stain
C. scrutinize D. exterminate

71. DAWDLE
A. fiddle B. dally
C. hurry D. dauby

72. DISCOUNTENANCE
A. credit B. encourage
C. appreciate D. entertain

73. INSURRECTION
A. exhume B. sedition
C. surrender D. subjection

74. PERMUTATION
A. refusal B. rejection
C. transference D. sequence

75. SAUNTER
A. shelter B. linger
C. wander D. hasten

76. MOURNFUL
A. cheerful B. humorous
C. jolly D. joyous

77. DESSICATE
A. exonerate B. concenterate
C. saturate D. propagate

78. SPUNK
A. strong B. timidity
C. bold D. miser

79. PREVARICATE
A. exaggerate
B. state truthfully
C. irrelevant
D. illustrate

80. FLEDGLING
A. childish
B. energetic
C. old man
D. experienced person

81. BILK
A. small in size B. balance to pay
C. pay in full D. credit

82. CHARY
A. brash B. slow
C. lethargic D. exhausted

83. CRASS
A. refined B. garrulous
C. boastful D. introvert

84. SPLENETIC
A. distant B. cordial
C. strange D. unfamiliar

85. ADHERENT
A. oppose B. revengeful
C. rival D. opponent

86. UNASSUAGED
A. harmful B. satisfied
C. soothed D. kind

87. PULCHRITUDE
A. tranquility B. unknown
C. unsightliness D. pleasant

88. VOUCHSAFE
A. scholarship B. admit
C. permit D. prohibit

89. TESTY
A. even-tempered
B. difficult
C. puzzled
D. cheerful

90. JETTISON
A. burden
B. overloaded
C. submerge
D. salvage

91. GADFLY
A. joyous
B. thoughtful
C. nuisance
D. tranquility

92. FURORE
A. sensitive
B. discomposure
C. calmness
D. excitement

93. FRUGALITY
A. economy
B. extravagance
C. futility
D. furitive

94. GERMANE
A. apposite
B. pertinent
C. irrelevant
D. ovum

95. GRANDILOQUENT
A. simplicity
B. turgidity
C. bombastic
D. dumbness

96. GULLIBLE
A. incredulous
B. shrewdness
C. circumvent
D. beguile

97. HALCYON
A. serene
B. stormy
C. robust
D. delusion

98. HARANGUE
A. annoy
B. oration
C. mumble
D. blissful

99. INCONGRUITY
A. constant
B. convenient
C. consequent
D. consistent

100. PIQUANT
A. irritating
B. sarcastic
C. soothing
D. enviable

ANSWERS

1	2	3	4	5	6	7	8	9	10
A	A	C	B	D	C	D	C	A	C
11	12	13	14	15	16	17	18	19	20
B	D	A	C	D	A	A	C	D	B
21	22	23	24	25	26	27	28	29	30
B	C	A	C	A	C	B	D	B	A
31	32	33	34	35	36	37	38	39	40
C	D	C	B	D	A	B	C	D	D
41	42	43	44	45	46	47	48	49	50
D	A	B	C	A	D	B	A	D	C
51	52	53	54	55	56	57	58	59	60
A	C	B	D	D	C	D	A	C	D
61	62	63	64	65	66	67	68	69	70
B	C	D	A	D	A	D	C	B	B
71	72	73	74	75	76	77	78	79	80
C	B	A	D	A	D	C	B	B	D
81	82	83	84	85	86	87	88	89	90
C	A	A	B	D	C	C	D	A	D
91	92	93	94	95	96	97	98	99	100
D	C	B	C	A	A	B	C	D	C

10

One Word Substitution

There are many words in English language which can be perfectly used for a number of words. These words help in expressing ideas in a short and correct manner for the right occasion. Such words not only enhance the vocabulary but also enable you to economise in the use of words to a great extent. Here is a categorywise list of many such words.

Pertaining to Government

To give up a throne or other office of dignity	*abdicate*
Absence of government	*anarchy*
Government by Sovereign of uncontrolled authority	*autocracy, despotism*
Government by departments of states	*bureaucracy*
Government of the people, for the people and by the people	*democracy*
Government by the nobility	*aristocracy*
The right of self-government	*autonomy*
Government by a few	*oligarchy*
Government by the wealthy	*plutocracy*
Government by divine guidance	*theocracy*
To decide a political question by the direct vote of the whole electorate	*referendum*
Sweeping governmental change	*revolution*
The science of government	*politics*

Pertaining to Religion

One who believes that man can have no knowledge of God but only of natural phenomena	*agnostic*
One who renounces his religious vows or forsakes his religious principles	*apostate*
One who does not believe in existence of God	*atheist*
One intolerantly devoted to a particular creed	*bigot*
To utter profane language against God or anything holy	*blaspheme*

A breaker of church images	*iconoclast*
Worship of images or idols	*idiolatory*
One who believes in one God	*monotheist*
One who believes in many Gods	*polytheist*

Pertaining to Marriage and Children

One who marries a second wife or husband while the legal spouse is alive	*bigamist*
One vowed to a single or unmarried life	*celibate*
One engaged to be married	*fiancé, fiancee*
A child whose parents are dead	*orphan*
A hater of marriage	*misogamist*
One who has more than two wives at a time	*polygamist*

Pertaining to Death

Dead and decaying flesh (esp. of animals)	*carrion*
A monument set up for persons who are buried elsewhere	*cenotaph*
To preserve a dead body from putrefaction	*embalm*
Words inscribed on a tomb	*epitaph*
An examination of dead body	*postmortem, autopsy*
An account in the newspaper of the funeral of one deceased	*obituary*
The property left to someone by a will	*legacy*
Occurring after death	*posthumous*
The act of killing a human being	*homicide*
Murder of a new born child	*infanticide*
Murder of a brother	*fratricide*
Murder of a sister	*sororicide*
Murder of a mother	*matricide*
Murder of a father	*patricide*
Murder of a parent	*parricide*
Murder of a king	*regicide*

Pertaining to the Literary Sphere

A work whose writer is unknown	*anonymous*
A record of one's life written by oneself	*autobiography*
The history of the life of a person	*biography*
The heading or short description of a newspaper article, chapter of a book etc.	*caption*
A humorous play, having a happy ending	*comedy*
A list of books in a library	*catalogue, bibliography*
A book in which the events of each day are recorded	*diary*

A books containing the words of a language with their definitions, in alphabetical order	*dictionary*
A book of names and addresses	*directory*
A short speech by a player at the end of a play	*epilogue*
A brief summary of a book	*epitome*
A book containing information on all branches of knowledge	*encyclopaedia*
To remove the offensive portions of a book	*expurgate*
A speech delivered without earlier preparation	*extempore*
A noisy or vehement speech intended to excite passions	*harangue*
A written account, usually in book form of the interesting and memorable experiences of one's life	*memoirs*
A note to help the memory	*memorandum*
A declaration of plans and promises put forward by a candidate for election, political party or a sovereign	*manifesto*
A short speech by a player at the beginning of a play	*prologue*
Literary theft, or passing off an author's original work as one's own	*plagiarism*
Speaking aloud to oneself	*soliloquy*
A play with a sad or tragic end	*tragedy*

Pertaining to Sciences and Arts

The study of all heavenly bodies and the earth in relation to them	*astronomy*
The science of land management	*agronomics*
The study of mankind	*anthropology*
The study of physical life or living matter	*biology*
The study of plants	*botany*
The art of beautiful hand-writing	*calligraphy*
The science which deals with the varieties of human race	*ethnology*
The study of the origin and history of words	*etymology*
The study of coins	*numismatics*
The study of human face	*physiognomy*
The art of making fireworks	*pyrotechnics*
The study of birds	*ornithology*
The study of languages	*philology*
At home equally on land or in water	*amphibious*
The inside of a nut	*kernel*
The central or innermost part of fruit	*core*
The animals of a certain region	*fauna*
The plants and vegetation of a certain region	*flora*
Absence of rain for a long time	*drought*

To supply land with water by artificial means	*irrigate*
One who studies plant and animal life	*naturalist*
A cud-chewing animal, *e.g.* the cow	*ruminant*
A gnawing animal, *e.g.* the rat	*rodent*
A four-footed animal	*quadruped*
Animals which carry their young in a pouch, *e.g.* kangaroo	*marsupials*
Soil composed largely of decayed vegetable matter	*humus*
A preparation for killing insects	*insecticide*
A plant or animal growing on another	*parasite*
Living for many years	*perennial*

Pertaining to Medicine

A substance which destroys or weakens germs	*antiseptic*
Any medicine which produces insensibility	*anaesthetic*
A medicine to counteract poison	*antidote*
Want or poorness of blood	*anaemia*
A medicine which alleviates pain	*anodyne*
To cut off a person's body a part which is infected	*amputate*
One who is recovering from illness	*convalescent*
To be able to tell the nature of disease by its symptoms	*diagnose*
A disease affecting many persons at the same place and time	*epidemic*
A disease confined to a particular district or place	*endemic*
To disinfect by smoke	*fumigate*
Free or exempt from infection	*immune*
A person who is sick	*invalid*
A cure for all diseases	*panacea*
A disease widely epidemic	*pandemic*
Confinement to one place to avoid spread of infection	*quarantine*

Pertaining to War

An unprovoked attack by an enemy	*aggression*
Shells, bombs, military stores	*ammunition*
A place where naval or military weapons are made or stored	*ordnance*
An agreement between belligerents to stop fighting	*armistice*
A general pardon of offenders	*amnesty*
To reduce to nothing	*annihilate*
Nations carrying on warfare	*belligerents*
To surround a place with the intention of capturing	*besiege*
To camp in the open air without tents or covering	*bivouac*

To seize for military use	*commandeer*
A person who is forced by law to become a soldier	*conscript*
An order prohibiting ships to leave the ports	*embargo*
A number of firearms being discharged continuously	*fusillade*
To make an examination or preliminary survey of enemy territory or military objectives	*reconnoitre*

Pertaining to Professions

One who attends to the diseases of the eye	*oculist*
One who tests eyesight and sells spectacles	*optician*
One who attends to the teeth	*dentist*
One skilled in the care of hands and feet	*chiropodist*
A physician who assists women at child-birth	*obstetrician*
One who drives a motor-car	*chauffeur*
One who makes or sells candles	*chandler*
One who preserves the skins of animals and mounts them so as to resemble the living animals	*taxidermist*
One who compiles a dictionary	*lexicographer*
One who writes books	*author*
One skilled in the treatment of diseases of animals	*veterinarian*
A tradesman who manages funerals	*undertaker*
One who draws up contracts and lends money on interest	*scrivener*
One who lends money and keeps goods as security	*pawnbroker*
A teacher who travels from place to place to give instruction	*peripatetic*
One who travels from place to place selling miscellaneous articles	*hawker, pedlar*
One who collects postage stamps	*philatelist*
One who lends money at exorbitant interest	*usurer*
One who takes care of a building	*janitor*
One who sells sweets and pastries	*confectioner*
One who works in a coal-mine	*collier*
One who flies an aeroplane	*pilot, aviator*
One who studies rocks and soils	*geologist*
One who shoes horses	*farrier*
A professional rider in horses races	*jockey*
One who deals in silks, cotton, woollen, and linen goods	*mercer*
One who deals in wines	*vintner*
One who deals in fish	*fishmonger*
One who deals in iron and hardware	*ironmonger*
One who sells fruits, vegetables, etc. from a barrow	*costermonger*
One who sets type (in a printing office)	*compositor*

Pertaining to Characteristics and Actions

One who devotes his life to the welfare and interests of other people	*altruist*
One who can use both hands with equal case	*ambidexterous*
One who fishes with a rod	*angler*
One who kills secretly or by surprise	*assassin*
A person who collects things belonging to ancient times	*antiquary*
One who is always finding faults	*censorious*
One living at the same time as another	*contemporary*
One who sneers at the aims and beliefs of his fellowmen	*cynic*
One who delights in speaking about oneself	*egotist*
One who exalts his own opinion	*egoist*
One who dies for a noble cause	*martyr*
One who retires from society to live a solitary life	*recluse, hermit*
One who maliciously sets fire to buildings	*incendiary*
One who is banished from his home or his country	*exile*
One who takes refuge in a foreign country	*refugee, alien*
One who runs away from justice or the law	*fugitive*
One who walks in his sleep	*somnambulist*
One who looks on the bright side of things	*optimist*
One who looks on the dark side of things	*pessimist*
A hater of mankind	*misanthropist*
One who knows everything	*omniscient*
One who is all powerful	*omnipotent*
One who is present everywhere	*omnipresent*
One who devotes his service or wealth for the love of mankind	*philanthropist*
One new to anything	*novice, tyro, neophyte*
One who engages in any pursuit for the love of it, and not for gain	*amateur*
One who journeys to a holy place	*pilgrim*
A leader of the people who can sway his followers by his oratory	*demagogue*
One who has special skill in judging art, music, tastes, etc.	*connoisseur*
One whose reasoning is clever yet false	*sophist*
One who makes a display of his learning	*pedant*
One who is indifferent to pain or pleasure	*stoic*
One who loves his country and serves it devotedly	*patriot*
One devoted to the pleasures of eating and drinking	*epicure*
One who poses to be what he is not	*hypocrite, impostor*
One who foretells events	*prophet*
One who pretends to know a great deal about everything	*mountebank, charlatan, quack*

One versed in many languages	*linguist*
One who cannot pay one's debts	*insolvent*
One who takes over after another in office or employment	*successor*
One who has been before another in office or employment	*predecessor*
One who is opposed to intellectual progress	*obscurant*
One who abstains from alcoholic drinks	*teetotaller*
One who hides away on a ship to obtain a free passage	*stowaway*
One who spends very little	*miser*
One who spends too much	*spendthrift*

Denoting Numbers

A collection of poems	*anthology*
A number of merchant ships protected by warships (in war-time)	*convoy*
A number of stars grouped together	*constellation*
A number of hired applauders, *i.e.* persons paid to clap	*claque*
A number of people at church	*congregation*
A number of people gathered together for some common purpose	*gathering, assembly, society*
A group of people who get together to work for some cause of common interest	*coterie*
A number of workmen, prisoners, thieves	*gang*
A number of sheep	*flock*
A number of geese	*gaggle*
A number of leopards	*leap*
A number of lions, monkeys	*pride, troop*
A number of herrings, mackerel	*shoal*
A number of fish taken in a net	*catch, haul*
A number of whales, porpoises	*school, gam*
A number of oxen or horses (two or more) harnessed together	*team*
A number of ships	*fleet*

Denoting Places

A place where bees are kept	*apiary*
A place where birds are kept	*aviary*
A place where fishes are kept	*aquarium*
A dwelling-place of an animal underground	*burrow*
A squirrel's home	*drey*
A nest of a bird of prey	*eyrie, aerie*
A place where spirituous liquors are produced	*distillery*
A place where clothes are washed and ironed	*laundry*

A place where Government records are kept	*archives*
A place where treasures of art, curiosities, etc. are preserved or exhibited	*museum*
A place where fruit trees are grown	*orchard*

Miscellaneous

Loud enough to be heard	*audible*
Not distinct enough to be heard	*inaudible*
Fit for food	*edible*
Unfit for human consumption	*inedible*
Fit to be chosen or selected	*eligible*
Not having the qualities for being chosen	*ineligible*
(Writing) that is easy to read	*legible*
Writing that is difficult to decipher	*illegible*
Able to read	*literate*
Unable to read	*illiterate*
Born of married parents	*legitimate*
Born of unmarried parents	*illegitimate*
To send back a person to his own country	*repatriate*
To banish from one's country	*expatriate*
To move from one country to another	*migrate*
One who leaves his country to settle in another	*emigrant*
One who comes into a foreign country to settle there	*immigrant*
Incapable of being redeemed from evil, *i.e.* beyond correction	*incorrigible*
That which cannot be rubbed out or blotted out	*ineffaceable, indelible*
That which cannot be conquered	*invincible*
Incapable of making errors	*infallible*
That which cannot be avoided or prevented	*inevitable*
Incapable of being burnt	*incombustible*
That which easily catches fire	*inflammable, flammable*
That which cannot be seen	*invisible*
Living for ever	*immortal*
Increase the gravity of an offence	*aggravate*
Ordinary or commonplace remark	*platitude*
That which cannot be satisfied	*insatiable*
That which cannot be repaired	*irreparable*
That which cannot be imitated	*inimitable*
Persons (or efforts) that cannot be wearied	*indefatigable*
One who eats too much	*glutton*
To destroy completely	*annihilate*

A statement open to moré than one interpretation	*ambiguous*
A round about way of speaking	*circumlocution*
Cautious observation of events, etc.	*circumspection*
That which cannot be hurt	*invulnerable*

MULTIPLE CHOICE QUESTIONS

Directions: *Below are given some statements each of which is capable of being expressed by one word only. Each statement is followed by four such words of which only one is correct. Out of the given alternatives A, B, C and D choose the correct word which very closely fits each definition.*

1. One who does not believe in the existence of God:
   A. atheist B. altruist
   C. agnostic D. flippant
2. The large money paid for an early retirement:
   A. gold mine B. golden handshake
   C. gratuity D. lion's share
3. A hater of learning and knowledge:
   A. misologist B. misogynist
   C. philologist D. philanthropist
4. One who lives and acts for the welfare of others:
   A. misanthrope B. credulous
   C. altruist D. gregarious
5. Mental weariness for want of occupation:
   A. desperate B. depression
   C. fatigue D. ennui
6. That which makes it difficult to recognise the presence of real of somebody or something:
   A. cover B. mask
   C. make-up D. camouflage
7. To *bear a hand* in one's new business.
   A. partnership B. interfere
   C. assist D. join
8. One who renounces the world and practices self- discipline in order to attain salvation:
   A. devotee B. ascetic
   C. theist D. parsimonious
9. A place where gambling is practiced:
   A. hotel B. motel
   C. casino D. stadium
10. A sad song is a:
    A. dirge B. elegy
    C. ditty D. knell
11. A set of papers giving information about a person or event:
    A. editorial B. agenda
    C. dossier D. clippings
12. List and explanations of technical, difficult, etc. terms:
    A. preface B. glossary
    C. bibliography D. appendix
13. One who pays too much care to his clothes and personal appearance:
    A. conscious B. dandy
    C. cynosure D. leer
14. A child born after death of father:
    A. effeminate B. immature
    C. fatherless D. posthumous
15. A person who is hard to please:
    A. insensible B. hypocrite
    C. egoist D. fastidious
16. Complete failure in something attempted:
    A. fiasco B. vain
    C. falsies D. flop
17. A word which can be interpreted in any way:
    A. confusing B. misnomer
    C. ambiguous D. precise
18. A group of persons united by common interests:
    A. society B. class
    C. clique D. coterie
19. A person who is inexperienced and easily deceived:
    A. fool B. immature
    C. blackhorn D. greenhorn

20. Instruction by question and answer:
A. interrogatory B. catechism
C. bulletin D. alibi

21. Record of events by someone with first hand knowledge:
A. novice B. report
C. memoir D. itinerary

22. A mode of talk familiar to a particular group or profession:
A. jargon B. colloquial
C. slang D. abuses

23. Person who is crazy:
A. lackadaisical B. tarter
C. scrupulous D. loony

24. A person who readily believes others:
A. hasty B. immature
C. credulous D. credible

25. One who eats human flesh:
A. beast B. cannibal
C. maneater D. carnivorous

26. Intentional destruction of racial groups:
A. genocide B. homicide
C. fratricide D. communal riot

27. One with weakness of mind caused by old age:
A. dastard B. dotard
C. fop D. philanderer

28. Study of insects:
A. zoology B. philology
C. entomology D. etymology

29. A critical judge of any art particularly fine arts:
A. connoisseur B. veteran
C. philistine D. dilettante

30. One who introduces items of an entertainment:
A. consort B. compere
C. director D. introducer

31. A combination of business firms:
A. enterprise B. franchise
C. cartel D. autonomous

32. Freeing of suppressed emotions:
A. catastrophe B. catharsis
C. epilogue D. chagrin

33. One who believes in the power of fate:
A. optimist B. pessimist
C. fearful D. fatalist

34. The murder of brother:
A. genocide B. homicide
C. salvage D. fratricide

35. Additional to proper payment:
A. premium B. overtime
C. ex-gratia D. fringe

36. A person or thing used to tempt somebody into a position of danger:
A. decoy B. provocateur
C. jinx D. scapegoat

37. Custom of having more than one husband at the same time:
A. polygamy B. polyandry
C. bigamy D. sexagenary

38. A person of refined taste in food and drink:
A. emeritus B. epicure
C. glutton D. gourmand

39. A tombstone inscription:
A. epithet B. encomium
C. epistle D. epitaph

40. An office which has no work but high salary:
A. fortuitous B. gratuitous
C. sinecure D. ceremonial

41. One who is indifferent to pains and pleasure of life:
A. stoic B. metaphysical
C. pessimist D. sceptic

42. List of names of persons showing duties to be performed by each in turn:
A. notice B. bulletin
C. roster D. agenda

43. Long angry speech of criticism or accusation:
A. track record B. tirade
C. taut D. outburst

44. One who is in favour of never drinking alcoholic drinks:
A. idealist B. uxorious
C. teetotaller D. unalcoholic

45. Trying to win favour by flattery and charm:
A. smarmy B. shrewish
C. toady D. loquacious

46. A decision on which one cannot go back:
A. incorrigible B. irrevocable
C. rigid D. invulnerable

47. The science that studies the varieties of human race:
A. phrenology B. physiology
C. sociology D. ethnology

48. A person who hates women:
A. philogynist B. philatelist
C. misogamist D. misogynist

49. A group of people in a particular grade in an organisation:
A. colleague B. staff
C. echelon D. commission

50. Honourably discharged from service:
A. emeritus B. latitudinarian
C. infallible D. meritorious

51. Incapable of being wounded:
A. inevitable B. invulnerable
C. indomitable D. indefatigable

52. A short description of a picturesque scene or event of rural life:
A. narration B. panorama
C. idyll D. passage

53. The act of violating the sanctity of church:
A. sacrilege B. dissenter
C. immorality D. desecration

54. A dishonest dealing:
A. hanky-panky B. hocus-pocus
C. hoity-toity D. hilly-billy

55. A short and stout person:
A. lilliput B. hussy
C. humpty-dumpty D. paragon

56. Word that reads the same backwards as forwards (like did, dad, noon):
A. paradox B. palindrome
C. kowtow D. ragtag

57. Walking in sleep:
A. delusion B. somniloquism
C. somnabulism D. lethargic

58. Glamour and excitement:
A. razzle-dazzle B. razzmatazz
C. kudos D. winsome

59. Violent and bad tempered woman:
A. virago B. moll
C. concubine D. profane

60. One who pays excessive attention to preserving his health:
A. pagan B. bellicose
C. sycophant D. fop

61. Talking to one's own self:
A. pessimism B. introvert
C. soliloquy D. brooding

62. One who pretends to have more knowledge than he really has:
A. hypocrite B. charlaton
C. paragon D. lackadaisical

63. Brief biography of a person:
A. profile B. bibliography
C. synopsis D. resume

64. Very small allowance or wage:
A. lumpsum B. consolidated
C. pittance D. paltry

65. Purely spiritual love:
A. devotion B. platonic
C. passionate D. divine

66. Place where people often meet:
A. common room B. discotheque
C. roster D. rendezvous

67. A completely perfect person:
A. upright B. straightforward
C. paragon D. intellectual

68. Commencement of words with the same alphabet:
A. symmetry B. pun
C. phonetic D. alliteration

69. A person who loves everybody:
A. ascetic B. philander
C. philistine D. cosmopolitan

70. A government where the powers are concentrated in the hands of one person:
A. dictatorship B. autocracy
C. plutocracy D. anarchy

71. That which is outdated or out of use or fashion:
A. discarded B. obsolete
C. classic D. antic

72. Calendar giving information about sun, moon, stars and sometimes also the future:
A. almanac B. appendix
C. horoscope D. chronology

73. Collection in one volume of works by various authors:
A. panorama B. anthology
C. autobiography D. bibliography

74. One who takes part in a study, game, etc. for the love of it and not for professional gain:
A. apologist B. august
C. amateur D. avant-garde

75. A thing that causes annoyance:
A. bugbear B. arduous
C. anathema D. shrill

76. An allowance for support made to a wife by her husband after their legal separation:
A. alimony B. compensation
C. settlement D. ex-gratia

77. Place for hiding treasure, food, weapons, etc.:
A. store B. cache
C. stock D. armoury

78. A person who is stubborn in resisting change:
A. irresistible B. die-hard
C. dead beat D. terse

79. Able to use the left hand or the right hand equally well:
A. ambidextrous B. epicurean
C. apostle D. arbiter

80. A man who rarely speaks the truth:
A. liar B. unreliable
C. hypocrite D. bellicose

81. Partial or total loss of memory:
A. alexia B. anorexia
C. anexia D. amnesia

82. A word made by rearranging the letters of another word like eat–tea:
A. acronym B. anagram
C. byword D. dossier

83. A mass of snow and ice sliding down from a mountain:
A. avalanche B. glacier
C. icebery D. azure

84. To speak irreverently of God:
A. impious B. irreligious
C. immoral D. blasphemy

85. Sudden increase in business:
A. bonanza B. boom
C. bounce D. booze

86. Object of laughter or ridicule:
A. butt B. but
C. divert D. hurtle

87. A pioneer of a reform movement:
A. sinecure B. sycophant
C. gallant D. apostle

88. Art of handwriting:
A. cartography B. choreography
C. calligraphy D. graph

89. One who takes a low view of human nature:
A. coquette B. cynic
C. crony D. coy

90. Document that is handwritten by the author:
A. autograph B. holograph
C. editorial D. preface

91. A person who forsakes religion:
A. irreligious B. non-religious
C. fatalist D. apostle

92. Speaker or agitator who can stir the emotions of the masses:
A. demagogue B. dexterous
C. diligent D. reformist

93. Uncontrollable craving for alcohol:
A. dyspepsia B. delirium
C. edict D. dipsomania

94. A lady who remains unmarried:
A. concubine B. alien
C. spinster D. damsel

95. State payment to an unemployed person:
A. pension B. dole
C. increment D. grant in aid

96. Person slow at learning:
A. adroit B. dubious
C. dunce D. agile

97. One who has a good taste for food and enjoys it:
A. gourmet B. sensitive
C. deleterious D. debonair

98. One who is fond of gossip:
A. flippant B. flibbertigibbet
C. fuddy-duddy D. gregarious

99. A long, loud and angry speech:
A. incongruous B. hyperbole
C. hullabaloo D. harangue

100. A person chosen by the opposing parties to settle their differences:
A. mediator B. prude
C. paramour D. arbitrator

ANSWERS

1	2	3	4	5	6	7	8	9	10
A	B	A	C	D	D	C	B	C	A
11	**12**	**13**	**14**	**15**	**16**	**17**	**18**	**19**	**20**
C	B	B	D	D	A	C	C	D	B
21	**22**	**23**	**24**	**25**	**26**	**27**	**28**	**29**	**30**
C	A	D	C	B	A	B	C	A	B
31	**32**	**33**	**34**	**35**	**36**	**37**	**38**	**39**	**40**
C	B	D	D	D	A	B	B	D	C
41	**42**	**43**	**44**	**45**	**46**	**47**	**48**	**49**	**50**
A	C	B	C	A	B	D	D	C	A
51	**52**	**53**	**54**	**55**	**56**	**57**	**58**	**59**	**60**
B	C	D	A	C	B	C	B	A	A
61	**62**	**63**	**64**	**65**	**66**	**67**	**68**	**69**	**70**
C	B	A	C	B	D	C	D	D	B
71	**72**	**73**	**74**	**75**	**76**	**77**	**78**	**79**	**80**
B	A	B	C	A	A	B	B	A	C
81	**82**	**83**	**84**	**85**	**86**	**87**	**88**	**89**	**90**
D	B	A	D	B	A	D	C	B	B
91	**92**	**93**	**94**	**95**	**96**	**97**	**98**	**99**	**100**
D	A	D	C	B	C	A	B	D	D

11

Idioms & Phrases

An idiom is a group of words established by usage as having a meaning different from the individual words.

A phrase is a small group of words standing together as an idiomatic expression.

The use of idioms and phrases makes your expression more effective and powerful.

Learn and practise as many as you can.

An angel: A person who is gentle and kind to others

A devil: A particularly wicked or mischievous person

A giant: A person who is very large

A wizard: A clever and skillful person

An Adonis: A very handsome man

An Apollo: A man with a perfect physique or body shape

A Hercules: A very strong man

A Goliath: An extremely large man

A Judas: A mean traitor

A Samson: A very strong man

A Solomon: A very wise man

A dog: A worthless person; someone who is despised

A cat: A malicious, person. usually referring to females

A bear: A clumsy, rough person

A fox: A crafty, cunning person

A goose: A silly person

A lamb: An innocent harmless person

A monkey: A child who is lively and full of mischievous tricks

A mule: A very stubborn person

A wolf: A greedy and cunning person

A snake/serpent: A treacherous, dangerous person

A parrot: A person who learns things off by heart without understanding the real meaning

A pest: A troublesome person; one who annoys and pesters others

A pig: A greedy and dirty person

A shark: A greedy and cunning person; one who swindles others

A parasite: A person who lives off others and gives nothing in return

An ape: A person who foolishly imitates others

An ass/donkey: A stupid person

An elephant: A huge, clumsy, ungainly person

A wet blanket: A person who discourages others or prevents them from enjoying what they are doing

A stag party: A party where only men are allowed to be present

A hen party: A party where only women are allowed to be present

A working lunch/dinner: A meal at which the people who attend, discuss business

A working knowledge: Enough practical knowledge to do something

A willing horse: A helpful person who often gets all the work to do

A wild goose chase: A search for something which has no chance of being successful

A trend-setter: A person who starts a new fashion which becomes popular

A thick-skinned person: A person who is not easily offended

Teething troubles: Troubles and difficulties which occur during the early stages of an activity or enterprise, but which will lessen with time

A sweeping statement: A statement which is not careful or correct in its details; a generalisation

A spending spree: An outing during which one spends a lot of money

A tall order: A request which is unreasonably difficult to grant or carry out

A soft spot: A feeling of special fondness for something or someone

A sore point: A matter which irritates or hurts when it is mentioned

The small hours: The early morning hours just after midnight

A sleeping partner: A business partner who provides a share of the capital for a venture but does not take an active part in its operation

Small talk: Trivial, light conversation on unimportant topics

Second nature: Some acquired habit or skill which seems perfectly natural to someone; a very firmly fixed habit

A shady character: A person of very doubtful honesty or character

Second thoughts: A change of mind, attitude or decision after thinking about the matter

A security risk: A person who is a risk to a country's security because of his political activities; one whose loyalty is doubted

A jail bird: A man who has spent a lot of time in prison

A ladies' man: A man who likes to be with women or who likes to please them

A last fling: The last opportunity for pleasure or amusement before having to stop

An inside job: A theft committed by someone inside a building, i.e., by an employee, not a stranger

A knowing look: A look which suggests that, the person is well-informed of a matter

A hushed-up affair: An affair or matter that is kept secret by forcing silence about it

Hush money: A bribe paid to keep a matter secret from the public

A hot line: A direct telephone line between heads of governments, to be used at times of great difficulty

Hot news: Very recent, important or sensational news

High time: At the most important point of time

Fast living: A person who spends too much money in enjoying life

A fishy story: An untrue tale; an unlikely story

Half-hearted: Having no enthusiasm for a particular task

An iron will: A very strong will

Hot water: Trouble

A laughing stock: A person who is unkindly laughed at by everyone

A light-fingered person: A person who is in the habit of stealing small things

Pin money: A wife's allowance for her personal needs

Plain sailing: A plan or action that is simple and free from trouble

A pep talk: A friendly talk to give encouragement to win a game, etc. or to complete something well

A package tour: A completely planned holiday at a fixed price arranged by a company

A passing fancy: A temporary liking for something or someone

An open secret: Something supposed to be a secret but which in fact is known to everyone

A package deal: An offer or agreement which includes a number of things all of which must be taken

Plain dealing: Truthfulness and honesty, especially in business

A pet aversion: Something or someone much disliked

A sideline: Work one does apart from one's regular job

Second sight: An ability to foresee future events

A rolling stone: Person who travels around a lot without staying in any one place or job for long

A raw deal: An unjust or cruel treatment

In a rash moment: Doing something hastily without thinking of the results

A practical joke: A trick played on a person to make him look silly and to give amusement to others

A sugar daddy: An older man who has a relationship, especially sexual, with a younger woman, providing her with money and presents

Take-home pay/wages: The amount a person receives after taxes have been deducted

backstairs influence: Secret and usually unfair influence

Bad blood: Bad feelings or unfriendliness between two persons

A bad egg/a bad penny: A bad character

A false alarm: A warning of something bad, which does not happen

Elbow room: Space, in which to move and act freely

A double agent: A person who works secretly for two opposing sides without either of the sides knowing

A dead-end job: A job without prospects; a job that leads to nothing further

A dark horse: A person who competes successfully against another although little is known about him

A confirmed bachelor: A man who has no desire to marry

A burning question: A matter having to be dealt with at once; an urgent important matter

A big shot: An important person, usually someone who is wealthy and influential

A blind date: A social meeting of two persons, usually a boy and a girl who have not met before

Broken English: Imperfect, ungrammatical English

A chicken-hearted person: A timid, cowardly person

A close-fisted person : Someone who is stingy; a miser

A country cousin: A person who is simple and inexperienced and not used to city life

A close shave: A narrow escape from danger, an accident, etc.

A light sleeper: A person who is easily awakened from sleep

A cock-and-bull story: An invented story

A cold war: A serious political struggle between countries which does not actually result in fighting

A dog-eared book: A book where the corners of the pages have been turned down with use

An easy victim/mark: Somebody who can easily be cheated or treated badly

A bosom friend: A very close, trusted friend

Crocodile tears: Pretended sorrow; insincere tears

A fast colour: A colour which does not run out of the material when washed or dried

A fair copy: A neat, legible copy

An armchair critic: A person who critically judges others' work and gives advice, but who has not himself experienced doing the work

Apple-pie order: In perfect order

An absent-minded person: A forgetful, inattentive person

A flying visit: A very short visit

Forty winks: A short nap or sleep

Hard labour: Hard, manual work usually done as a punishment

Hard cash: Actual money, not a cheque, etc.

A hard drinker: A person who drinks large quantities of alcohol

A golden opportunity: A very good opportunity

A going concern: A successful, thriving business

A foregone conclusion: A result that is certain, sure

The naked eye: The eye unaided by any instrument

An odd-job man: A man who does various types of work, usually manual, for pay

Old hat: No longer fashionable

A grass widow: A wife who is alone because her husband is away temporarily

A good samaritan: A person who helps a stranger in difficulties

French leave: Absence from work that is taken without permission

The generation gap: The difficulties arising when younger and elder people do not understand each other's way of life

The happy medium: The middle course of doing something when opposite ways are suggested

A henpecked husband: A husband who is dominated and nagged by his wife

A hard and fast rule: A rule that cannot be changed; fixed, unchangeable rule

One-track mind: A person's mind that is limited and thinks of only one thing at a time

A short cut: An easier method of doing something or getting somewhere; a quicker, more direct way

A small-time business: A business limited in activity and profits

A splitting headache: A very severe and painful headache

A square deal: A fair bargain or fair treatment

A square meal: A meal with adequate good; a satisfying meal

Strong language: Angry language consisting of many swear words

Tall talk: Boastful talk

A tight spot/corner: A difficult situation

Tough luck: Bad luck; hard luck

Ready money: Money which is immediately available in coins or notes

Second best: Next to the best; second in value or importance

The writing on the wall: An indication that something bad or difficult is about to happen

A storm in a teacup: A big fuss made over a small, trivial event

The talk of the town: A person or event that is causing great excitement and is the subject of much discussion

A snake in the grass: A cunning, harmful person who pretends to be a friend; a false friend

A shot in the dark: A guess which is not supported by arguments; a wild guess

The tricks of the trade: The best and most successful ways of doing good business

The bottom of the ladder: In the least important position

A shot in the arm: Something which acts to bring back a happy state or condition

The man in the street: The ordinary, average man

The gift of the gab: A person fluent in speech; a persuasive speaker

A man about town: A man who is used to living in the city and associating with well-known fashionable people

The life and soul: The person who is the centre of attaction because he is amusing and lively

The lion's share: The greater part; an unfairly large share

The long arm of the law: The police

A bear hug: A rough, tight hug

A brain wave: A clever idea; sudden inspiration

A bone of contention: Something that causes argument

Birds of a feather: People of the same kind (often bad) who like each other's company

A feather in one's cap: A deserved honour that one is proud of

Castles in the air: Plans which cannot be carried out or which will probably not succeed

A fish out of water: A person who feels uncomfortable because he is in a strange place, or among people who are very different from himself

The ups and downs: The good and bad times, the happy and sad times

A stone's thorw: A short distance

A slip of the tongue: Something said unintentionally

A slap in the face: A rebuff

The rank and file: Ordinary people without special positions; the masses

A man of means: A rich man

A man of iron: A cruel, hard person

A jack of all trades: A person who can do many different kinds of work but who may not be good at any of them

By hook or by crook: By any means possible

By fits and starts: At irregular intervals

A pack of lies: A whole lot of untruths

A clean bill of health: A certificate or announcement that someone is healthy

A happy-go-lucky person: Someone who does not think or plan carefully

A stay-at-home person: A person who is in the habit of staying at home, and not liking to travel

A smash-and-grab robbery: A robbery done quickly, usually by breaking windows or showcases taking away valuables, and running away

A hit-and-run driver: A driver who drives away after an accident without stopping to find out about damage or injuries

A run-of the-mill job: An ordinary unexciting job

A round the-clock service: A twenty-four hour service

An out-of the way place: A place that is distant and far away from people and places

A much-talked-of affair: Something which is the subject of much discussion

A nine to six job: A job in which the working hours are from nine in the morning to six in evening

An open and shut case: A case which is easy to settle or solve

Bumper-to-bumper traffic: Cars that are very close together one after another

A hand-me-down dress: A dress used by someone after belonging to another

A well-to-do man/wom++an: A rich person

Again and again: Repeatedly; continually; very often

Back and forth/backward: Moving first in one direction and then in the opposite direction and forwards

By and by: Soon; before long

By and large: On the whole; in general; all things considered

Far and away: Very much

Far and near/far and wide: Everywhere

First and foremost: In the first place; firstly

Here and there: In various places; firstly

Here, there and everywhere: In all possible places; everywhere

In and out: Sometimes inside and sometimes outside

Up and about: On one's feet; up again after an illness

To-and fro: Backwards and forwards; from side to side

Through and through: Completely; entirely; in every way

Out and out: Complete, thorough; total

Out and away: By far

Over and over again: Again and again; repeatedly

Round and round: Repeatedly moving round

Once and for all: Finally; for the last time

On and on: Without stopping

Off and on: From time to time; occasionally

Every now and then/again: From time to time; at times

Now and again: Sometimes; occasionally; not very often

Nowadays: In these times

To backbite a person: To speak ill of someone

To back chat: To be cheeky; to talk back to someone

To be a bag of bones: To be extremely thin

To be a blockhead: To be an idiot

To be a great hand at: To be an expert

To be a sight for sore eyes: Something or someone who appears before another and is very welcome

To be all ears: To be eager to listen

To be armed to the teeth: Fully armed or protected

To be at one's wits' end: Completely puzzled

To be close-fisted: To be mean; miserly

To be double-faced: Insincere

To be down in the mouth: To feel depressed and unhappy

To be head and shoulders above someone else: To be very much better or superior

To be out of one's mind: To be mad; crazy

To be someone's blue-eyed boy: To be someone's favourite

To be the apple of someone's eye: To be someone's favourite

To bite someone's head off: To speak abruptly or sharply to another

To burn one's fingers: To get into trouble

To catch someone's eye: To suddenly exchange glances with another

To change hands: To pass from one owner to another

To dig someone in the ribs: To make unkind remarks or insinuations about another

To eat one's heart out for another: To long for someone who is unattentive

To foot the bill: To pay the bill, especially for some social outing

To get on someone's nerves: To irritate someone very greatly

To get something off one's chest: To confess to something

To get the upper hand: To gain mastery over an opponent

To give someone the cold shoulder: To ignore someone; to slight another

To give someone the sharp: To thoroughly scold another person edge of one's tongue

To go on all hands: To crawl on hands and knees

To have a chip on one's shoulder: To bear a grudge against the world/society

To have a finger in every pie: To have many business interests

To have a head like a sieve: To have a very poor memory

To have a skeleton in the cupboard: To have a guilty secret, especially a family scandal

To have at one's fingertips: To know thoroughly

To have cold feet: To be afraid

To have no backbone: To be a weak, spineless person

To have one's head screwed on: To be very sensible

To have someone under one's thumb: To dominate another

To have the upper hand: To be in command/charge; to be someone in power

To have two left hands: Someone who is clumsy

To hold one's tongue: To keep silent even though there is an urge to talk

To hold up one's head: To be able to look people in the face

To jump out of one's skin: To get a sudden fright

To keep a cool head: To keep calm, especially in an emergency

To keep a stiff upper lip: To remain calm and courageous

To keep one's fingers crossed: To hope for luck

To keep one's hair on: To keep cool and patient

To keep one's head above water: To avoid getting into debt or trouble

To keep someone at arm's length: Not too friendly with another

To knock something on the head: To suddenly stop an idea/project

To know something by heart: To be able to say something from memory

To lay hands on someone: To handle someone roughly

To lend a hand: To help

To let the grass grow under one's feet: To be inactive and uninvolved

To live from hand to mouth: To live in hardship with the barest essentials

To lose face: To lose one's reputation/honour

To lose heart: To be discouraged

To lose one's head: To be very angry; to lose control of oneself

To make a clean breast of something: To confess to something; to reveal all

To make neither head nor tail of something: To understand nothing of a particular issue

To pat someone on the back: To give praise and encouragement to another

To pay through the nose for something: To pay an excessively high price for something

To poison someone's mind: To turn someone against another person

To pull one's weight: To do one's share of work

To pull someone's leg: To play a joke on someone

To pull the wool over someone's eyes: To deceive another

To put one's back into it: To work hard

To put one's foot down: To be firm about an issue

To put one's shoulder to the wheel: To work hard and earnestly

To put someone's nose out of joint: To make someone jealous by taking his place as the centre of attraction

To rack one's brains: To try to recall or remember something

To receive with open arms: To welcome warmly

To save face: To save one's honour/reputation/name

To show a clean pair of heels: To escape by running

To snap someone's head off: To speak abruptly

To stand on one's own feet: To do things without help; to be independent

To sweep someone off his/her feet: To flatter and woo someone, usually a girl

To take matters into one's own hands: To do something independently without help

To take something to heart: To take something seriously

To take to one's heels: To run away

To throw dust in someone's eyes: To try to deceive someone

To tread in someone's foot steps: To follow the example of another, usually of talent/occupation

To tread on someone's toes: To offend another person

To try one's hand at: To try doing something for the first time

To turn a blind eye: To refuse to see

To turn a deaf ear: To refuse to hear

To turn up one's nose at something: To treat with contempt

To twist someone's arm: To force someone into doing something for you

To wash one's hands of something: To have nothing to do with a particular matter

The green-eyed monster: Jealousy

To scream blue murder: To complain loudly

Out of the blue: Suddenly; without warning

Once in a blue moon: Very rarely

To feel blue/have the blues: To be sad or depressed

A bolt from the blue: A complete surprise

Blue blood: Royal or noble blood

To blackmail someone: To threaten to reveal sorneone's misdeeds unless he pays money

In someone's black books: Out of favour with someone

A black sheep: A bad character who disgraces his family

A blacklist: A list of people groups, etc. who have done something wrong

Black and blue: Badly bruised after a beating/a fall

In black and white: In writing or print

A greengrocer: A person who sells fruit and vegetables

A greenhorn: An inexperienced person

The green light: The signal to proceed

Green with envy: Tilled with jealousy

Grey matter: Common sense; brains

In the pink of health: In excellent health

Purple with rage: So angry that the face becomes purple

To be caught red-handed: To be caught in the act of committing a crime

A red carpet welcome: A special ceremonial welcome to guest

The red flag: A flag used as a danger signal

A red-letter day: A notable, fortunate day that will be remembered

The red light: A signal to stop; a danger signal

Red tape: Official rules which cause delay in settling one's problems

To jump out of the frying-pan into the fire: To get out of one bad situation and fall into another worse situation

To see red: To lose control of oneself in anger

A white-collar job: An office job

A white elephant: A worthless possession which the owner wants to get rid of

The white flag: A sign that one accepts defeat or surrenders

To show the white feather: To show signs of cowardice

Yellow at heart: Cowardly

To be/feel off colour: To be unwell or rather ill

To come off with flying colours: To achieve great success

To have a high colour: To appear very red in the face

To show one's true colours: To show what one is really like; to show one's true character

A blue-collar job: A factory job

To act the goat: To behave foolishly

To air one's opinion: To express one's feelings in public

To be a chip off the old block: A son who is very much like his father in appearance, character, habits, etc

To be as fit as a fiddle: To be in excellent health

To be at a loose end: To have nothing to do

To be at a loss for words: Not knowing what to say; to be speechless

To be at death's door: To be so ill as to be near death

To be at sixes and sevens: To be in confusion and discord

To be at the end of one's teeter: To be at a loss as to what to do

To be born under a lucky star: To have considerable luck in whatever one does

To be born with a silver spoon in one's mouth: To be born into a rich family

To be dead beat: To be worn out by fatigue

To be in hot water: To be in serious trouble

To be in someone's bad/good books: To be out of/in favour with someone

To be in the doldrums: To be in low spirits

To be in the same boat: To have the same troubles/ circumstances

To be mad about someone: To like someone very much

To be made of money: To have plenty of money; to be well-off

To be on tenterhooks: To be in a state of suspense and anxiety

To be on the ball: To be alert, up-to-date, prepared

To be on the horns of a dilemma: Not knowing what to do from several courses of action

To be on the rocks: To be in danger of failing, collapse, especially a business, a marriage, etc

To be on top of the world: To be very happy; to be in high spirits

To be out of the woods: To be out of danger, especially a serious illness

To be quick on the uptake: To be alert and quick to do or say something

To be rolling in money: To be rich; to have plenty of money

To be scared to death: To be extremely frightened of something

To be slow on the uptake: Slow to do or say something

To be too big for one's boots: To think very highly of oneself

To bear the brunt of: To bear the main force or strain of some action

To beat about the bush: To be indecisive; not coming to the point

To blow hot and cold: To do one thing at one time and the opposite soon after

To blow one's own trumpet: To boast about one's abilities, achievements etc.

To break the ice: To take the first step; to be the first to begin, especially a conversation

To bring down the house: To cause loud and long applause through one's skill

To bring to light: To disclose, reveal

To build castles in the air: To think of things impossible to realize

To burn the candle at both ends: To use one's energy in two directions at the same time

To burn the midnight oil: To work till late at night

To call a spade a spade: To speak out bluntly and frankly

To clip one's wings: To deprive one of power and/or freedom

To cook an account: To tamper with/falsify an account

To come down on someone like a: To harshly criticise another ton of bricks

To come of age: To reach adulthood

To come to grief: To meet with danger

To come to light: To become known

To count-sheep: To try various methods to get to sleep

To cry over spilt milk: To be unhappy about something that can no longer be remedied

To curry favour: To seek/win favour by flattery or gifts

To cut off in its prime: To destroy something when it is at its best

To cut one's coat according to: To live within one's income one's cloth

To cut someone down to size: To put someone in his place especially a person who thinks too highly of himself

To do a city/the sights: To visit a city and see its well-known places

To do a thing by fits and starts: To work intermittently on something

To do a thing by hook or by crook: To do something by any means, fair or foul, direct or indirect

To do something on the spur of the moment: To suddenly decide to do something

To drop a brick: To say or do something very tactless and unexpected

To drop a hint: To make veiled and subtle suggestions

To eat like a horse: To eat a lot

To eat one's words: To take back what one has said; to apologise

To egg on: To spur on to further action

To face the music: To meet the worst; to face punishment for doing something wrong

To fall out with someone: To quarrel with someone

To fall through: To fail, especially a plan, project, etc.

To fancy someone/something: To take a great liking to someone/something

To fight shy of: To avoid

To fire someone: To dismiss someone from employment

To flog a dead horse: To try fruitlessly to revive interest in something

To follow the crowd: To follow unthinkingly; to believe or act as most people do

To follow suit : To do the same thing as another person

To gain ground: To make progress in an undertaking

To get away with something: To escape detection despite doing something wrong

To get blood out of stone: To get more than is fair out of someone

To get down to work: To start on the task in hand

To get even with someone: To take revenge of someone

To get hitched: To get married

To get into a flap: To get worried and nervous

To get into hot water: To be in/to get into trouble

To get off scot-free: To escape punishment; to be let off payment

To get out of bed on the wrong side: To start the day in a bad temper

To get the sack: To be dismissed from employment

To get wind of: To hear a rumour of

To get the wind up: To get worried and nervous; to get a fright

To give someone a telling-off: To scold someone

To give someone the slip: To manage to avoid someone who is looking for you

To give the game away: To let out a secret

To give up the ghost: To die; to cease trying

To go a long way: To excel; to go far, especially in a career

To go off at a tangent: To change suddenly to a different course of thought or action

To go like a bomb: To go fast; to function well, especially a vehicle

To go to rack and ruin: To fall into a ruined or disorganised state

To grin and bear it: To make the best of a bad job; to put up with something

To haul someone over the coals: To reprimand someone

To have a bee in one's bonnet: To be strong-minded over certain issues

To have a soft spot for: To be very fond of someone or something

To have an axe to grind: To have a selflsh motive for doing something

To have one's knife in someone: To be always finding fault with another person

To hit below the belt: To attack an opponent unfairly

To hit the nail on the head: To do or say exactly the right thing

To jog someone's memory: To remind someone of something

To keep a person in the dark: To keep something hidden from someone

To keep open house: To encourage visitors to come at any time

To keep one's pecker up: To keep one's courage up

To keep one's shirt on: To keep cool and calm in a dispute

To keep the ball rolling: To keep a conversation going

To keep up appearances: To pretend to be well-off and to live in a certain style

To kick the bucket: To die

To kid someone: To tease

To kill two birds with one stone: To accomplish two things with one action

To knock off work: To stop working

To know the ropes: To be thoroughly familiar with a particular situation

To knock someone down with a feather: To surprise someone very much

To kowtow to someone: To act in a very servile manner hoping for favour

To lay down the law: To speak in an authoritative way

To lead someone up the garden path: To deceive someone by hiding the real intention

To leave someone in the lurch: To desert someone in time of difficulties

To let bygones be bygones: To let things that are past and gone remain untouched and forgotten

To let the cat out of the bag: To reveal a secret; to expose a trick

To look like a wet week: To look miserable and depressed

To make a go of something: To try one's best to succeed in something

To make a hash/a mess of something: To fail at a task

To make believe: To pretend

To make both ends meet: To be able to manage on one's income

To make hay while sun shines: To take advantage of an opportunity

To make much ado about nothing: To make a great fuss about something unimportant

To make oneself scarce: To disappear

To nip something in the bud: To stop something before it can develop into something serious

To pass the buck: To pass on the responsibility

To pick holes in something: To find fault with

To pick to pieces: To analyse critically

To pick and choose: To make a careful selection

To play a double game: To do one thing openly and a different thing in secret

To play fast and loose: To disregard one's promises

To play second fiddle: To take a subordinate position

To pooh-pooh an idea: To express contempt for an idea

To pull strings: To use friends in influential positions, or to use one's own influence, to secure favours

To put the cart before the horse: To do the wrong thing first

To put two and two together: To arrive at a conclusion

To put a spoke in one's wheel: To hinder; to obstruct progress

To rain cats and dogs: To rain very heavily

To read between the lines: To detect the hidden meaning

To rule the roost: To domineer over others

To run in the blood: Inherited qualities

To see something through coloured spectacles: To see only the best points about a thing

To see the light: To begin to understand

To sit on the fence: To take neither side in a dispute; to remain neutral

To smell a rat: To become suspicious about something

To steer clear of: To avoid

To take French leave: To be absent from work without permission

To take someone for a ride: To deceive someone

To take the bull by the horns: To meet a difficulty with courage

To take the law into one's own hands: To punish a person, usually by force, witnout his being tried in a law court

To take with a pinch of salt: To accept what someone has said with doubt and misgiving

To talk nineteen to the dozen: To speak a lot

To talk the hind legs of a donkey: To talk a great deal at great length

To tear a strip off someone: To scold harshly

To throw cold water upon: To discourage effort

To turn over a new leaf: To give up one's bad ways, and lead a better life

To turn the tables on someone: To defeat someone who has previously defeated you

To upset the apple cart: To disturb the routine of something

MULTIPLE CHOICE QUESTIONS

Directions: *Select the options which express the correct meaning of the given Idioms/Phrases.*

1. **Cats' paw**
   A. a person who is used as a tool by another person
   B. very slowly and quietly
   C. very cleverly
   D. to share a responsibility
2. **To catch a tartar**
   A. to overcome a serious problem
   B. to attack one who turns out to be stronger than is expected
   C. to achieve the goal
   D. to struggle hard
3. **Cheek of jowl**
   A. very soft
   B. close together
   C. intimate relationship
   D. low in status
4. **A chip of the old block**
   A. a symptom of a serious disease
   B. a child of a parent
   C. a part of a whole
   D. offsprings who display characteristics of their parents
5. **To cool one's heels**
   A. to be kept waiting
   B. to give a cold response to somebody
   C. to follow somebody
   D. to answer all the queries of somebody
6. **To cleanse the Augean stables**
   A. to clean something which has not been cleaned for a long time
   B. to wind up a joint business
   C. to remove the stains of blood
   D. to remove the traces of murder
7. **A cry in wilderness**
   A. The cry of the poors
   B. a warning that goes unheeded
   C. A speech made by a less important leader
   D. A cry out of deep sorrow
8. **To cut one's coat according to one's cloth**
   A. to work according to one's capacity
   B. to allot portfolio according to one's capability
   C. to live within one's means
   D. to live as one desires
9. **Chicken hearted**
   A. coward B. brave
   C. kind D. mortal
10. **To clip one's wings**
    A. to lessen one's power
    B. to defame
    C. to dismiss
    D. to punish
11. **To come round**
    A. to agree with another's point of view
    B. to come back to the point of origin
    C. a circular movement
    D. to wander
12. **To call to order**
    A. a command
    B. to rebuke for improper or incorrect behaviour
    C. to obey an order
    D. to show superiority
13. **To cover one's tracks**
    A. to maintain the secrecy
    B. to hide one's weaknesses
    C. to carefully hide all traces of one's actions
    D. to conceal the falsity
14. **To throw up one's cards**
    A. To make a last effort
    B. to cease to struggle
    C. to end up the game
    D. to come out victorious
15. **To let the cat out of the bag**
    A. to disclose a secret
    B. to set free
    C. a person without a shelter
    D. to permit the thief to run away

16. To cave in
A. to interfere B. to prohibit
C. to find a way D. to give way

17. To chuck up
A. to abandon B. to decorate
C. to summarize D. to cut into pieces

18. A dead letter
A. a delayed report
B. a false report
C. something exaggerated
D. something which is null and void

19. To die in harness
A. to die in office
B. to die with great pain
C. a premature death
D. a cruel murder

20. At the drop of a hat
A. without fail
B. without delay
C. against the self-respect
D. against the will

21. Day in and day out
A. always
B. forever
C. to break a promise done earlier
D. to remain busy always

22. Champ at
A. to pounce at
B. be impassioned
C. be composed
D. be eager or impatient

23. Burn one's fingers
A. to get oneself into trouble
B. to commit a blunder
C. a heavy monetory loss
D. to be in great rage

24. Down in the dumps
A. in a solitary mood
B. in a bad mood
C. to be in an unfavourable situation
D. to decline

25. To beg the question
A. to beg the pardon
B. to request for some extra-time to finish the work
C. unanswerable
D. to assume in the premises somethign which is to be proved

26. To carry the day
A. to be victorious
B. an on-going discussion
C. a memorable day
D. a miserable phase of life

27. At death's door
A. on the point of expiring
B. on the point of gun
C. to show bravery
D. a gradual deterior

28. To pay the debt of nature
A. to die
B. to give birth
C. to safeguard the natural things
D. to avoid environmental pollution

29. To do up
A. to finish off B. to mend
C. to improve D. to make tidy

30. To do away with
A. to break B. to destroy
C. to get rid of D. to forget

31. To have to do with
A. to be interested in
B. to do something under compulsion
C. work done unenthusiastically
D. to complete

32. To egg on
A. just a beginning
B. to urge on
C. to develop something
D. an initial stage

33. To face the music
A. to face the consequences
B. to get filled with ecstasy
C. to be lucky
D. to lead a happy life

34. To end in smoke
A. all efforts in vain

B. the end of life
C. to come to nothing
D. to end the enmity

35. Eye to eye with
A. agree completely
B. a confrontation
C. full of anger
D. a quarrel between the two persons

36. To eat humble pie
A. to harass a humble person
B. a celebration or a treat without any cause
C. to confess that one is in the wrong
D. food provided to the needy or poor

37. Easy come easy go
A. what is gained without difficulty is spent without much thought
B. anything which is surplus
C. without any difficulty
D. to achieve something without any struggle

38. To eat out one's heart
A. to break one's heart
B. to deceive someone
C. to get deceived
D. to suffer intensely

39. To see with half an eye
A. to see with great ease
B. to dislike
C. to see stealthily
D. to feel jealous

40. A fair-weathered friend
A. A friend always eager to help
B. A friend who deserts one in times of adversity
C. a selfish friend
D. a true friend

41. A far cry
A. an unfulfilled desire
B. a very low voice
C. remote from
D. a distant place

42. To feather one's nest
A. to provide for one's own comfort
B. to be proud
C. to succeed again
D. to decorate one's house

43. To fish in troubled waters
A. to be in trouble
B. to make capital out of other's troubles
C. to be in trouble because of other's fault
D. to laugh at other's trouble

44. To follow suit
A. to follow the command
B. to obey the rules
C. to work in accordance with
D. to behave in the same manner

45. To get the hang of a thing
A. to understand the implications of something
B. to get a trace of theft
C. to find a new resource
D. to have some indications

46. To get wind of
A. to get news about something much before the event actually takes place
B. to forget the event that had taken place
C. to spread a rumour
D. to have some idea of a conspiration

47. French leave
A. a long leave
B. a small leave
C. absence from one's place of work without prior information
D. to leave the place forever

48. To steal a march upon
A. to outshine somebody
B. to rob
C. to move forward
D. to crush the enemy

49. A long face
A. a sad or mournful countenance
B. a very shameful defeat
C. a shameful act
D. an ugly face

50. To set one's face against
A. to criticise openly
B. to oppose with determination
C. a biased disapproval
D. to show disappointment

51. To fall away from
A. to decline B. to desert
C. to avoid D. to leave

52. To fall flat
A. to cause no amusement or interest
B. to lie down
C. to defeat the opponent
D. to plead

53. To have a finger in the pie
A. to be mixed up in any affair
B. to interfere in other's work
C. to have a share in the profit
D. to be a member of an organisation

54. In full cry
A. in full volume
B. in hot pursuit
C. a verbosity
D. manifestation of grief

55. To give a piece of one's mind
A. to rebuke
B. to give an idea
C. to present one's view
D. to judge one's intelligence on the basis of his work or contributions

56. Gift of the gab
A. the ability of verbosity
B. the ability of writing creatively
C. the ability to speak in an impressive manner
D. a man of versatile genius

57. To give the cold shoulder
A. to give support
B. to be indifferent
C. to express anger silently
D. to behave in a cold manner with someone

58. To give devil his due
A. to give an evil person credit for whatever good he has done
B. to punish one who has committed sin
C. an evil person meeting a tragic end
D. to give devil his share

59. To give up the ghost
A. to die
B. to sacrifice
C. to murder
D. to convert from vicious to virtuous

60. To give wide berth to
A. to give more space
B. to keep far away from
C. to appreciate more than what one deserves
D. to maintain a distance

61. To go to pieces
A. to tear
B. to feel disheartened
C. to be wrecked completely
D. to dismantle

62. To have too many irons in the fire
A. to be engaged in too many things
B. to handle more than one work at the same time
C. to have lot of energy
D. to have various plans in the mind

63. To put a spoke in one's wheel
A. to obstruct one in his work
B. to assist one in his work
C. to interfere one in his work
D. to increase the strength of a team

64. On the rack
A. in a dilemma
B. tortured by anxiety
C. highly curious
D. to be in a disadvantageous position

65. To get into hot water
A. an acute pain
B. to be in trouble
C. to face a short-tempered person
D. to be in hypertension

66. Fish and blood
A. by extreme means
B. by unlawful ways
C. human nature
D. life-like

67. From hand to mouth
A. to harm and humiliate
B. to be a bankrupt
C. to spend all that is earned
D. to feed someone

68. Hit the nail on the head
A. to take revenge openly
B. to insult on the face
C. to do a wrong thing
D. to do exactly the right thing

69. Put the cart before the horse
A. to reverse the natural order
B. to put obstruction
C. to cause problem for others
D. to stop one's advancement

70. Pay back in one's own coin
A. to save money
B. to treat in the same way as one has been treated
C. to get the return of the investment
D. to give a befitting reply

ANSWERS

1	2	3	4	5	6	7	8	9	10
A	B	B	D	A	A	B	C	A	A
11	**12**	**13**	**14**	**15**	**16**	**17**	**18**	**19**	**20**
A	B	C	B	A	D	A	D	A	B
21	**22**	**23**	**24**	**25**	**26**	**27**	**28**	**29**	**30**
A	D	A	B	D	A	A	A	D	C
31	**32**	**33**	**34**	**35**	**36**	**37**	**38**	**39**	**40**
A	B	A	C	A	C	A	D	A	B
41	**42**	**43**	**44**	**45**	**46**	**47**	**48**	**49**	**50**
C	A	B	D	A	A	C	A	A	B
51	**52**	**53**	**54**	**55**	**56**	**57**	**58**	**59**	**60**
B	A	A	B	A	C	D	A	A	B
61	**62**	**63**	**64**	**65**	**66**	**67**	**68**	**69**	**70**
C	A	A	B	B	C	C	D	A	B

12

Spelling Test

The most common errors in English are of spellings of words. Even the most learned men are sometimes confused about the correct spellings of some words. One must keep and use a dictionary religiously. Never ignore and let pass a new word casually without checking its spelling and meaning. A number of questions to test your knowledge of spellings are compiled here. Try to solve as many as you can.

MULTIPLE CHOICE QUESTIONS

Directions: *Find the correctly spelt words.*

1. A. Discriminate B. Discremineta
C. Discrimenate D. Discriminat

2. A. Juddicious B. Judiceous
C. Judicious D. Judiceus

3. A. Accompalish B. Ackmplesh
C. Acomplush D. Accomplish

4. A. Damage B. Dammage
C. Damaige D. Dammege

5. A. Lackdaisical B. Lackadaisical
C. Lckadaisicle D. Lackadisical

6. A. Efficiant B. Effecient
C. Efficient D. Eficient

7. A. Survellance B. Surveilance
C. Surveillance D. Survaillance

8. A. Schedule B. Schdule
C. Schedale D. Schedeule

9. A. Occurad B. Occurred
C. Ocurred D. Occured

10. A. Licentious B. Licontious
C. Licenttious D. Licientious

11. A. Chancelery B. Chancellery
C. Chancellary D. Chancelary

12. A. Itenerary B. Itinarery
C. Itinarary D. Itinerary

13. A. Grieff B. Grief
C. Grieef D. Grrief

14. A. Indipenseble B. Indispansible
C. Indispensable D. Indipensable

15. A. Guarantee B. Garuntee
C. Guaruntee D. Gaurantee

16. A. Meddicine B. Medicine
C. Medicene D. Medicinne

17. A. Benefeted B. Benefitted
C. Benifited D. Benefited

18. A. Kleptomonia B. Kleptemonia
C. Kleptomania D. Klaptomania

19. A. Sepalchrle B. Sepalchral
C. Sepulchrle D. Sepulchral

20. A. Acommodation B. Acomodation
C. Accomodation D. Accommodation

21. A. Teracherous B. Treacherous
C. Treacheraus D. Treachereans

22. A. Querrelsome B. Quarrelsame
C. Quarrelsome D. Querralsome

23. A. Farmament B. Farmement
C. Fermament D. Fremament

24. A. Sympathetic B. Smypathetic
C. Sympothetic D. Sympethetic

25. A. Pecification B. Pacification
C. Pecifacation D. Pecefication

26. A. Meritricious B. Merefrecious
C. Meretricious D. Merritricious

27. A. Hypocritical B. Hypocretical
C. Hypocriticel D. Hypocirticel

28. A. Vaingloriaus B. Vainglorious
C. Vainglerious D. Vaingloreus

29. A. Imprecticeability B. Impracticebility
C. Impracticibility D. Impracticability

30. A. Prograssive B. Progressive
C. Progresive D. Prograsive

31. A. Incradulous B. Incredulous
C. Incridulous D. Incredalous

32. A. Uncivilized B. Uncevilized
C. Uncivillized D. Uncevelized

33. A. Osttentatious B. Ostentetious
C. Ostentatious D. Ostenttatious

34. A. Extravagant B. Extreragent
C. Extreregant D. Extravegent

35. A. Missunderstood B. Miesunderstood
C. Misunderstood D. Misunderstod

36. A. Belligerent B. Beligirent
C. Belligarant D. Belligerrent

37. A. Pasiveness B. Passiveness
C. Passeveniss D. Passivines

38. A. Astonished B. Astronished
C. Astoneshed D. Asstonished

39. A. Obnosious B. Obnoxeous
C. Obnoxious D. Obnoseous

40. A. Polyendry B. Poliendry
C. Pollyendry D. Polyandry

41. A. Sincerely B. Sencerely
C. Sincerelly D. Sincerrely

42. A. Efflorascence B. Eflorescene
C. Effllorescence D. Efflorescence

43. A. Vulnarable B. Valnerable
C. Velnerable D. Vulnerable

44. A. Rigourous B. Rigerous
C. Rigorous D. Regerous

45. A. Omenous B. Ominous
C. Ommineous D. Omineous

46. A. Puerille B. Puerrile
C. Puerile D. Purrile

47. A. Satellite B. Sattellite
C. Satelite D. Sattelite

48. A. Pesanger B. Passenger
C. Pessenger D. Pasanger

49. A. Humurous B. Humorous
C. Humoreus D. Humorrous

50. A. Equinimity B. Equanimmity
C. Equannimity D. Equanimity

51. A. Exeggerate B. Exaggerate
C. Exadgerate D. Exagerate

52. A. Fariegn B. Forein
C. Foriegn D. Foreign

53. A. Rennaissance B. Rennaisance
C. Renaisance D. Renaissance

54. A. Excesive B. Excessive
C. Exccessive D. Exccesive

55. A. Forcaust B. Forcast
C. Forecast D. Forecaste

56. A. Valuptuous B. Volluptous
C. Voluptuous D. Volupttuous

57. A. Entrepraneur B. Entreprenuer
C. Entrapreneur D. Entrepreneur

58. A. Paralleled B. Paralelled
C. Parralleled D. Parallelled

59. A. Ocasion B. Occassion
C. Occasion D. Ocassion

60. A. Boquet B. Bouquet
C. Bouquete D. Bouquette

61. A. Loquacieous B. Lequacious
C. Loquacious D. Lequocious

62. A. Cataclysm B. Cataclism
C. Catacilysm D. Cataclesm

63. A. Chettering B. Chaterring
C. Chattering D. Chatering

64. A. Fulfilment B. Fulffilment
C. Fulfilmient D. Fullfilment

65. A. Conjectore B. Conjecture
C. Cenjecture D. Cenjectire

66. A. Endication B. Endicaltion
C. Indication D. Indicetion

67. A. Splendour B. Spllendour
C. Splandour D. Splendeur

68. A. Excllusion B. Exclussion
C. Exclusion D. Exclosion

69. A. Discourage B. Disscourage
C. Discourege D. Discaurage

70. A. Curageous B. Courageous
C. Courrageous D. Couregeous

71. A. Abandon B. Abanddon
C. Abendon D. Abbandon

72. A. Embarassment B. Emberrassement
C. Embarrassment D. Embbaresment

73. A. Veneration B. Venration
C. Venneration D. Venerration

74. A. Tacciturnity B. Taciturnity
C. Taciturrnity D. Tacitturnity

75. A. Desppoonding B. Despending
C. Desponding D. Dessponding

76. A. Bueyant B. Buoyant
C. Bueeyant D. Buoyent

77. A. Eccintric B. Eccentrie
C. Eccentric D. Eccintrie

78. A. Corrigible B. Corigible
C. Corregible D. Corrigiblle

79. A. Amandable B. Amendable
C. Amenddable D. Amendablle

80. A. Occasional B. Occassional
C. Occesional D. Occessional

81. A. Exttirpate B. Extirpete
C. Extirpate D. Exterpate

82. A. Vorecious B. Varacious
C. Voarcious D. Voracious

83. A. Insolvent B. Insolvant
C. Insollvent D. Insolvvent

84. A. Querrel B. Querral
C. Quarrel D. Quarel

85. A. Contrebution B. Contribution
C. Contributtion D. Conterbution

86. A. Desgrace B. Disgrece
C. Disgrice D. Disgrace

87. A. Harassment B. Herassment
C. Harasment D. Harassmient

88. A. Tranquilitty B. Tranquility
C. Trenquility D. Tranquillity

89. A. Imaginative B. Imeginative
C. Imagenative D. Imaginetive

90. A. Suficient B. Suficiant
C. Sufficient D. Sufficiant

91. A. Adequate B. Edequate
C. Adaquete D. Edaquete

92. A. Expairienced B. Experianced
C. Experienced D. Experrienced

93. A. Flatering B. Fletering
C. Flattering D. Fletaring

94. A. Cuttiveted B. Culltrivated
C. Cultivated D. Caltivated

95. A. Materialistic B. Materielistic
C. Meterialistic D. Matterialistic

96. A. Praiceworthy B. Peiseworthy
C. Praiseworthy D. Praisaworthy

97. A. Tranquil B. Trenquil
C. Tranquel D. Trinquil

98. A. Neggardly B. Nigardly
C. Niggerdly D. Niggardly

99. A. Magnanimity B. Megnanimity
C. Magnenimity D. Magnanimety

100. A. Darogate B. Derogate
C. Derogeta D. Deragate

101. A. Philanthropist B. Philenthropist
C. Phelanthropist D. Philanthropest

102. A. Ephameral B. Ephimeral
C. Ephemeral D. Ephemerel

103. A. Fanaticism B. Fenaticism
C. Faneticism D. Fanatecism

104. A. Profesional B. Professionel
C. Professional D. Profissional

105. A. Ameteur B. Amateur
C. Amataur D. Amateor

106. A. Philenderer B. Philandarer
C. Philanderer D. Philonderer

107. A. Honorary B. Henorary
C. Honerary D. Honorery

108. A. Darmatologist B. Dermatologist
C. Dermetologist D. Dermatologest

109. A. Compansation B. Compensetion
C. Compensotion D. Compensation

110. A. Quadruplets B. Quedruplets
C. Quadroplets D. Quadruplats

111. A. Econemist B. Economest
C. Economist D. Econimist

112. A. Catholic B. Cetholic
C. Cathelic D. Cathilic

113. A. Unfevourable B. Unfevaurable
C. Unfavourable D. Unfivourable

114. A. Bombastic B. Bombestic
C. Bombostic D. Bombastie

115. A. Posthumaus B. Posthomous
C. Posthumous D. Pasthumous

116. A. Epitaph B. Epetaph
C. Epiteph D. Epitoph

117. A. Falicitate B. Felicitate
C. Falecitate D. Falecetate

118. A. Schezophrenia B. Schizaphrenia
C. Schizophrenia D. Schizophrania

119. A. Claustrophobia B. Cloustrophobia
C. Claustraphobia D. Claustrophabia

120. A. Connoiseur B. Connaisseur
C. Connaissour D. Connoisseur

121. A. Transperency B. Transparency
C. Transpirency D. Tranporency

122. A. Superanuation B. Superennuation
C. Superannuation D. Superannuetion

123. A. Antiquated B. Antiqueted
C. Antequated D. Antiquatted

124. A. Adalescent B. Addescant
C. Adolescent D. Adolascent

125. A. Newrologist B. Neurologist
C. Neurologest D. Newrologest

126. A. Obstatrician B. Obstitrician
C. Obstetrician D. Obstetracian

127. A. Illiterate B. Iliterate
C. Illitarate D. Illiterete

128. A. Thioretical B. Theoretical
C. Theoratical D. Theoritical

129. A. Mersenary B. Marcenary
C. Marcenery D. Mercenary

130. A. Archeic B. Arcaic
C. Archeic D. Archaic

131. A. Durment B. Dorment
C. Doormant D. Dormant

132. A. Aristocracy B. Arestocracy
C. Arestocracy D. Aristocrecy

133. A. Lagislature B. Legislature
C. Lageslature D. Legesleture

134. A. Dormetory B. Dormitery
C. Dormitory D. Dermitory

135. A. Garulous B. Garrulaus
C. Gorrulous D. Garrulous

136. A. Regecide B. Regicide
C. Rigecide D. Ragicide

137. A. Epicurean B. Epecurean
C. Epicurian D. Epicorean

138. A. Commetti B. Commitee
C. Committee D. Comitte

139. A. Inemitable B. Inimitable
C. Inimetable D. Inimitabli

140. A. Pletocray B. Plitocracy
C. Plotocracy D. Plutocracy

141. A. Immortal B. Emortal
C. Immortel D. Immortol

142. A. Perrhic B. Pyrrhic
C. Pyrrhec D. Porrhec

143. A. Chauvinism B. Chouvinism
C. Chevinism D. Cauvinism

144. A. Rumenate B. Ruminote
C. Rimunote D. Ruminate

145. A. Teciturn B. Tociturn
C. Tecitorn D. Taciturn

146. A. Verteran B. Viteran
C. Veterain D. Veteran

147. A. Antitode B. Antedote
C. Antidote D. Autitote

148. A. Audeble B. Audible
C. Audcble D. Audebli

149. A. Bellicose B. Billicose
C. Bellecose D. Belicose

150. A. Pilferage B. Peliferage
C. Pilfarege D. Poliferage

151. A. Ribut B. Rebit
C. Rebut D. Rebute

152. A. Sychologist B. Psycologist
C. Psychologist D. Psychogist

153. A. Neucteus B. Neucleus
C. Nucleus D. Neocleus

154. A. Negotcate B. Negociate
C. Negotiate D. Nagotiate

155. A. Skelled B. Skilled
C. Skiled D. Skillid

156. A. Logecal B. Logical
C. Lagical D. Logicle

157. A. Effeciency B. Efficiency
C. Eficiency D. Efficency

158. A. Cumpartment B. Compartment
C. Compartant D. Comportent

159. A. Continuous B. Cuntinuous
C. Continus D. Contineuous

160. A. Valuable B. Valueable
C. Valuabel D. Valoble

161. A. Courteous B. Curteous
C. Corteous D. Courtus

162. A. Prophecy B. Phropecy
C. Propecy D. Propheci

163. A. Lonesome B. Lonsome
C. Lonesum D. Lonsum

164. A. Formedable B. Formidable
C. Formidabul D. Formdable

165. A. Inibriated B. Enibrited
C. Inebriated D. Inubrited

166. A. Guellible B. Guiellible
C. Guillibel D. Gullible

167. A. Subsequent B. Subsiquent
C. Subsequint D. Subquent

168. A. Alein B. Alien
C. Abein D. Abien

169. A. Misogynesm B. Mesogynism
C. Misogynism D. Misosogesim

170. A. Sanguini B. Sangune
C. Sangiune D. Sanguine

171. A. Exemplary B. Eximplary
C. Exemplari D. Examplary

172. A. Sycophants B. Sicophants
C. Sycopants D. Sycophints

173. A. Petchy B. Patchy
C. Patchi D. Patche

174. A. Impassi B. Impasse
C. Impase D. Inpassi

175. A. Aceelerate B. Accilerate
C. Accelerate D. Accelerati

176. A. Vendictive B. Vindective
C. Vindictive D. Vindictivi

177. A. Prudint B. Prudient
C. Prudente D. Prudent

178. A. Superfluons B. Superfleos
C. Superflous D. Superfluous

179. A. Expidite B. Expedeti
C. Expedite D. Expedit

180. A. Livity B. Levity
C. Levety D. Levite

181. A. Reluctant B. Riluctant
C. Reluctent D. Relictunt

182. A. Desparge B. Disparage
C. Disperage D. Disparege

183. A. Maegre B. Meager
C. Meagre D. Megre

184. A. Accedental B. Aceedent
C. Accidantle D. Accidental

185. A. Cheapiness B. Chaepness
C. Chepness D. Cheapness

186. A. Febulous B. Fabulus
C. Fabulous D. Fibulous

187. A. Colusion B. Collision
C. Colision D. Collison

188. A. Eradicated B. Erradicated
C. Eradecated D. Eradiceted

189. A. Ageonise B. Agonise
C. Agonice D. Agonisee

190. A. Comit B. Commiet
C. Commit D. Commite

191. A. Tasiturn B. Taciturn
C. Taceturn D. Tacitorn

192. A. Omnevorous B. Omnivorous
C. Omniverous D. Omnivarous

193. A. Feud B. Fued
C. Fiud D. Feued

194. A. Pselm B. Slam
C. Psalm D. Salm

195. A. Haphazard B. Hapahazard
C. Haphzard D. Haphazrd

196. A. Peevishness B. Pievishness
C. Peivishness D. Peeveshness

197. A. Gelactic B. Galectic
C. Galactic D. Galactec

198. A. Imbibision B. Imbision
C. Embibition D. Imbibition

199. A. Zoparasite B. Zooparaset
C. Zooparasite D. Zoprasite

200. A. Neuralgia B. Nuraliga
C. Neurolgia D. Neuraltia

ANSWERS

1	2	3	4	5	6	7	8	9	10
A	C	D	A	B	C	C	A	B	A
11	**12**	**13**	**14**	**15**	**16**	**17**	**18**	**19**	**20**
C	D	B	C	A	B	B	C	D	D
21	**22**	**23**	**24**	**25**	**26**	**27**	**28**	**29**	**30**
B	C	C	A	B	C	A	B	D	B
31	**32**	**33**	**34**	**35**	**36**	**37**	**38**	**39**	**40**
B	A	C	A	C	A	B	A	C	D
41	**42**	**43**	**44**	**45**	**46**	**47**	**48**	**49**	**50**
A	D	D	C	B	C	A	B	B	D
51	**52**	**53**	**54**	**55**	**56**	**57**	**58**	**59**	**60**
B	D	D	B	C	C	D	A	C	B
61	**62**	**63**	**64**	**65**	**66**	**67**	**68**	**69**	**70**
C	A	C	A	B	C	A	C	A	B
71	**72**	**73**	**74**	**75**	**76**	**77**	**78**	**79**	**80**
A	C	A	B	C	B	C	A	B	A

81	82	83	84	85	86	87	88	89	90
C	D	A	C	B	D	A	B	A	C
91	**92**	**93**	**94**	**95**	**96**	**97**	**98**	**99**	**100**
A	C	C	C	A	C	A	D	A	B
101	**102**	**103**	**104**	**105**	**106**	**107**	**108**	**109**	**110**
A	C	A	C	B	C	A	B	D	A
111	**112**	**113**	**114**	**115**	**116**	**117**	**118**	**119**	**120**
C	A	C	A	C	A	B	C	A	D
121	**122**	**123**	**124**	**125**	**126**	**127**	**128**	**129**	**130**
B	C	A	C	B	C	A	B	D	D
131	**132**	**133**	**134**	**135**	**136**	**137**	**138**	**139**	**140**
D	A	B	C	D	B	A	C	B	D
141	**142**	**143**	**144**	**145**	**146**	**147**	**148**	**149**	**150**
A	B	A	D	D	D	C	B	A	A
151	**152**	**153**	**154**	**155**	**156**	**157**	**158**	**159**	**160**
C	C	C	C	B	B	B	B	A	A
161	**162**	**163**	**164**	**165**	**166**	**167**	**168**	**169**	**170**
A	A	A	B	C	D	A	B	C	D
171	**172**	**173**	**174**	**175**	**176**	**177**	**178**	**179**	**180**
A	A	B	B	C	C	D	D	C	B
181	**182**	**183**	**184**	**185**	**186**	**187**	**188**	**189**	**190**
A	B	C	D	D	C	B	A	B	C
191	**192**	**193**	**194**	**195**	**196**	**197**	**198**	**199**	**200**
B	B	A	C	A	A	C	D	C	A

13

Punctuation

Punctuation Marks help us to make grammatically correct sentences.

The following pairs of sentences will bring home to you the importance of punctuation marks:

(*i*) Jack, my neighbour, is going abroad.

(*ii*) Jack, my neighbour is going abroad.

The sentence no. (*i*) means 'Jack' is my neighbour and he is going abroad. The sentence no. (*ii*) means that I'm telling Jack that my neighbour is going abroad.

The following are some most commonly used punctuation marks:

1. Full Stop
2. Note of Interrogation
3. Note of Exclamation
4. Comma
5. Inverted commas
6. Apostrophe
7. Capital Letters
8. Colon
9. Semicolon
10. Dash
11. Oblique
12. Parentheses
13. Hyphen

1. Full Stop (.)

(A) At the end of a statement or an imperative sentences the full stop is applied.

(*i*) Mohan sings a song. (Positive Statement)

(*ii*) She does not tell a lie. (Negative Statement)

(*iii*) Open the door. (Imperative Sentence)

(B) To mark abbreviations:

(*i*) M.L.A. (*ii*) M.B.B.S.

(*iii*) B.A. (*iv*) Mr R.S. Gill

☛ Now a days after Mr, Mrs, Miss, a full stop is not applied.

2. Note of Interrogation (?)

It is used to make direct questions as well as tags.

(*i*) What are you doing?

(*ii*) Where is your friend?

(*iii*) You like eggs, don't you?

(*iv*) She doesn't obey her elder brother, does she?

☛ The note of interrogation is not used after indirect questions.

(*i*) She was sure whether her brother would come there to see her or not.

(*ii*) I asked him when he would start a confectionary shop.

3. Note of Exclamation (!)

(A) It is used after an optative sentence

(*i*) May you live long!

(*ii*) May God bless you!

(B) After an exclamatory sentence

(*i*) What a beautiful butterfly it is!

(*ii*) How wonderful the rainbow is!

(C) After an Interjection

(*i*) Hurrah! We have won the match.

(*ii*) Alas! I am done.

4. Comma (,)

It is used:

(A) To separate identical words.

(*i*) Mohit is tall, thin and handsome.

(*ii*) I bought apples, bananas and guava yesterday.

(*iii*) This shopkeeper sells cakes, pastries and biscuits.

(B) In sentences of direct speech.

(*i*) She said, "I wish to be a doctor."

(*ii*) "Don't move," the man shouted.

(C) To separate pairs of words when they are joined by 'and'.

(*i*) I like rice and curry, idli and dosa.

(*ii*) In the fair were present all kinds of persons rich and poor, weak and strong, foolish and wise.

(D) To join two coordinate clauses when the latter is the consequence of the former.

(*i*) He was rejected by his friends, and he decided never to meet any of them in future.

(*ii*) He was beaten by his opponent, and he decided to leave boxing.

(E) To separate a noun or phrase in apposition.

(*i*) The Mahabharata, the longest epic, was written by Ved Vyas.

(*ii*) Hari, the tallest boy in our class, is a good player of basketball.

(F) To separate an adverbial clause from the rest of the sentences.

(*i*) If you tell me the reality, you won't be punished.

(*ii*) As soon as the thief saw the policeman, he ran away.

(*iii*) When he laughs, the dog in his house will bark.

(G) To separate a nominative of address

(*i*) Where are you, Mr Smith?

(*ii*) How are you, Seema?

(H) To separate a noun clause from the rest of the sentence.

(*i*) When she will get up, nobody knows.

(*ii*) Why he is crying so loudly, is known to his parents only.

(*iii*) What he says, no one cares.

5. Inverted Commas (" ")

Inverted commas are used in sentences of direct speech.

(*i*) She says, "I can drive a car."

(*ii*) He said to me, "I'll convey your message to your uncle."

6. Apostrophe (')

It is used:

(A) To make Genitive Case when the noun is singular

(*i*) Mohan's shirt

(*ii*) James' shoes or James's shoes.

(B) To make Genitive Case when the noun is plural

(*i*) Boys' college (*ii*) Girls' hostel

(*iii*) Men's club (*iv*) Women's hostel

(C) To make plural form of letters and figures

(*i*) H's (*ii*) A's

(*iii*) 4's (*iv*) 8's

(D) To denote the omission of letter or letters from words

(*i*) can't (*ii*) don't

(*iii*) won't

(E) To express a possessive pertaining to a period of time

(*i*) a week's holiday.

(*ii*) a year's programme.

7. Capital Letters (A, B, C,...)

Capital letters are used as under:

(A) The first word of a sentence should start with a capital letter.

(*i*) She does not know how to play the piano.

(*ii*) We are going to perform a dance in London.

(B) A proper name should be started with a capital letter.

(*i*) Mohan is my fast friend.

(*ii*) I like all students of my class but I like Ajay, Rajesh and Vinod in particular.

(*iii*) Delhi is the capital of India.

(C) The important words in the title of a book should start with a capital letter each:

(*i*) The Cat and the Mouse.

(*ii*) Love and Life.

(D) The first letter of the days of a week and the months of year should be written in capital.
- (*i*) Sunday, Monday, Tuesday.
- (*ii*) January, February, March.

(E) The names of all rivers, oceans, mountains, bays, channels, peaks, etc., should start with a capital letter.
- (*i*) The Ganga
- (*ii*) The Himalayas
- (*iii*) The Bay of Bengal
- (*iv*) Mount Everest
- (*v*) The English Channel
- (*vi*) The Indian Ocean

(F) The names of all holy books, magazines, newspapers, etc. should start with a capital letter.
- (*i*) The Gita
- (*ii*) The Bible
- (*iii*) The Tribune
- (*iv*) The Sun

8. Colon (:)

Colon represents a long pause. It is not used so frequently but in some cases it is applied.

(A) To quote the names of certain items both proper and common nouns:
- (*i*) Some of Shakespeare's plays are: Macbeth, Tempest, Julius Caesar, etc.
- (*ii*) The following items are required by our school urgently:
  - (*i*) Five Hockey Sticks
  - (*ii*) Ten Cricket Bats
  - (*iii*) Four Football
  - (*iv*) Eight Basketballs

(B) To introduce a quotation.
- (*i*) Keats says: A thing of beauty is a joy forever.
- (*ii*) Shakespeare says: All that glitters is not gold.

(C) Before some examples:
- (*i*) I know several languages:
  Hindi, Punjabi, French and English.
- (*ii*) Mohan is: honest, wise, handsome, rich and kind.

9. Semicolon (;)

It represents a pause which is longer than a comma but is of less duration than a colon. A semicolon is used:

(A) To mark off a series of clauses:
- (*i*) We love our young ones; they too in return love us.
- (*ii*) This forest is a witness to good and bad days of mankind; this is here since ancient times.

(B) To break up long sentences:
My brother reads in 10th standard; he always goes to school late; he is almost everyday punished by the teacher.

10. Dash (—)

It is used:

(A) To mark a sudden change in our thoughts
- (*i*) I think you like berries—but your brother told me that you spend no money on fruit.
- (*ii*) You must read this book—but how can you read it when you're writing a letter to your friends?

(B) To mark a sudden interruption in a sentence.
I know him—I met him five years ago—where? I can't recall.

(C) To divulge a secret in a dramatic way.
- (*i*) The most famous modern novelist is—Sydney Sheldon.
- (*ii*) The best singer is—Mohammad Rafi.

11. Oblique (/)

(A) It is used to represent abbreviations
- (*i*) D/o (Daughter of)
- (*ii*) S/o (Son of)
- (*iii*) W/o (Wife of)

(B) To represent masculine gender or feminine gender
- (*i*) He/She can join the army.
- (*ii*) I'll ask questions to him/her.

(C) To represent possibilities
- (*i*) The girl/girls should work even harder.
- (*ii*) The boy/boys cannot be given any special rights.

12. Parentheses (or Brackets) ( )

These are used:

(A) To explain something additional which is usually not of much significance.

(*i*) Manoj (a five year old boy) saved the life of his friend.

(*ii*) Meena (a girl of 5th standard) was called by the President for her remarkable paintings.

(B) To separate an after thought

(*i*) All his sons (including the eldest one, who is an addict to alcohol) are going abroad.

(*ii*) All the ingredients (excluding milk) should be put in a pan.

13. Hyphen (-)

It is shorter than a dash in length. It is most often used to make compound words or to break a word falling at the end of a line.

(*i*) maid-servant

(*ii*) self-respect

MULTIPLE CHOICE QUESTIONS

Directions: *In the questions given below, which one alternative out of four has been applied with correct punctuation marks?*

1. Hurry up the train leaves at six o'clock

A. Hurry up; the train leaves at six o'clock.
B. Hurry up, the train leaves at six O'clock.
C. Hurry up! the train leaves at six o'clock.
D. Hurry up, the train leaves at six o'clock.

2. It is a sin to waste food said the father

A. It is a sin to waste food said the father.
B. 'It is a sin to waste food' said the father.
C. "It is a sin to waste food" said the father.
D. "It is a sin to waste food," said the father.

3. This is his fathers car

A. This is his fathers' car.
B. This is his father's car.
C. This is his father's car.
D. This is his fathers' car.

4. The man asked the taxi driver will you take me to the airport

A. The man asked the taxi driver, will you take me to the airport?
B. The man asked the taxi driver, "Will you take me to the airport?"
C. The man asked the taxi driver, "Will you take me to the airport."
D. The man asked the taxi driver, "will you take me to the airport!"

5. Bring me a glass of water said the teacher I am feeling very thirsty

A. "Bring me a glass of water," said the teacher, "I am feeling very thirsty."
B. "Bring me a glass of water" said the teacher, "I am feeling very thirsty."
C. "Bring me a glass of water" said the teacher "I am feeling very thirsty."
D. "Bring me a glass of water, said the teacher, "I am feeling very thirsty."

6. Ram said I am in a hurry I cannot spare time

A. Ram said, "I am in a hurry" "I cannot spare time."
B. Ram said "I am in a hurry I cannot spare time."
C. Ram said, "I am in a hurry, I cannot spare time."
D. Ram said, "I am in a hurry I cannot spare time."

7. How have you found so much wealth asked Anil's wife

A. "How have you found so much wealth!" asked Anil's wife.
B. "How have you found so much wealth?" asked Anil's wife.
C. "How have you found so much wealth." asked Anil's wife.
D. "How have you found so much wealth?", asked Anil's wife.

8. What is the matter why are you crying he asked the child
   A. "What is the matter, why are you crying?" he asked the child.
   B. "What is the matter? why are you crying?" he asked the child
   C. "What is the matter" "why are you crying?" he asked the child.
   D. "What is the matter? Why are you crying?" he asked the child.

9. I am going to marry and I want a house to live in said the young man
   A. "I am going to marry and I want a house to live in", said the young man.
   B. "I am going to marry" and "I want a house to live in" said the young man.
   C. "I am going to marry and I want a house to live in" said the young man.
   D. "I am going to marry and I want a house to live in." said the young man.

10. What harm is there if we admit the error the lawyer said
   A. "What harm is there, if we admit the error?" the lawyer said.
   B. "What harm is there if, we admit the error?" the lawyer said.
   C. "What harm is there if we admit the error?" the lawyer said.
   D. "What harm is there? if we admit the error". the lawyer said.

11. The more we hate one another the worse it will be for everybody
   A. The more we hate one another the worse it will be for everybody.
   B. The more we hate one another, the worse it will be for everybody.
   C. The more we hate one another; the worse it will be for everybody.
   D. The more we hate one another – the worse it will be for everybody.

12. Anita's father Mr Anil Kumar is a teacher
   A. Anita's father Mr Anil Kumar is a teacher.
   B. Anita's father, Mr Anil Kumar is a teacher.
   C. Anita's father Mr Anil Kumar, is a teacher.
   D. Anita's father, Mr Anil Kumar, is a teacher.

13. Considering all aspects of the matter they decided to give up the plan.
   A. Considering all aspects of the matter, they decided to give up the plan.
   B. Considering, all aspects of the matter, they decided to give up the plan.
   C. Considering all aspects, of the matter, they decided to give up the plan.
   D. Considering all aspects of the matter they decided to give up the plan.

14. The Narmada the Ganga and the Yamuna are three of the largest Indian rivers
   A. The Narmada, the Ganga and the Yamuna are three of the largest Indian rivers
   B. The Narmada, the Ganga, and the Yamuna are three of the largest Indian rivers
   C. The Narmada, the Ganga and the Yamuna are three of the largest Indian rivers.
   D. The Narmada, the Ganga and, the Yamuna are three of the largest Indian rivers.

15. What a remarkable victory
   A. What, a remarkable victory.
   B. What a remarkable victory.
   C. What a remarkable victory?
   D. What a remarkable victory!

16. The election many people said would spring a big surprise and they were proved right
   A. The election, many people said, "would spring a big surprise and they were proved right."
   B. "The election," many people said, "would spring a big surprise and they were proved right."
   C. "The election" many people said, "Would spring a big surprise and they were proved right."
   D. "The election" many people said "would spring a big surprise and they were proved right."

17. Are you going he asked we are not I replied
   A. "Are you going?" he asked, "We are not." I replied.
   B. "Are you going?" he asked, "we are not" I replied.

C. "Are you going?" he asked. "We are not," I replied.
D. "Are you going?" he asked, "we are not" I replied.

18. Here I am master I am ready to go wherever you want me to go he said
A. "Here I am, master, I am ready to go," wherever you want me to go he said.
B. "Here I am master, I am ready to go wherever you want me to go" he said.
C. "Here I am master, I am ready to go wherever you want me to go", he said.
D. "Here I am, master, I am ready to go wherever you want me to go", he said.

19. What is your reason for refusing to marry this girl asked his mother
A. "What is your reason for refusing to marry this girl?" asked his mother.
B. "What is your reason, for refusing to marry this girl?" asked his mother.
C. "What is your reason for refusing to marry this girl?" asked his mother
D. "What is your reason for refusing to marry this girl," asked his mother.

20. He said my brother had an accident on Sunday the 28th April 2013 and is still confined to bed
A. He said "my brother had an accident on Sunday the 28th April 2013 and is still confined to bed."
B. He said "My brother had an accident on Sunday the 28th April 2013 and is still confined to bed."
C. He said, "My brother had an accident on Sunday, the 28th April 2013, and is still confined to bed."
D. He said," My brother had an accident on Sunday, the 28th April 2013 and is still confined to bed."

21. How many r's are there in referred I asked
A. How many r's are there in referred? I asked.
B. "How many r's are there, in referred" I asked.
C. "How many r's are there in referred?" I asked.
D. "How many rs' are there in referred?" I asked.

22. Friends colleagues relatives none stood by him
A. Friends, colleagues; relatives none stood by him.
B. Friends, colleagues, relatives, none stood by him.
C. Friends, colleagues, relatives, none, stood by him
D. Friends, colleagues, relatives none, stood by him.

23. He said I am sorry I could not reach in time
A. He said, "I am sorry I could not reach in time."
B. He said "I am sorry. I could not reach in time."
C. He said, "I am sorry. I could not reach in time."
D. He said "I am sorry I could not reach in time."

24. Never listen to his stories don't believe what he says and always distrust him
A. Never listen to his stories, don't believe what he says? and always distrust him.
B. Never listen to his stories, don't believe, what he says? and always distrust him.
C. Never listen to his stories, do'nt believe what he says and always distrust him.
D. Never listen to his stories, don't believe what he says and always distrust him.

25. Man proposes God disposes
A. Man proposes God disposes.
B. Man proposes, God disposes.
C. Man proposes, God disposes!
D. Man proposes God disposes!

26. He asked me what I wanted
A. He asked me, what I wanted?
B. He asked me "what I wanted."
C. He asked me what I wanted.
D. He asked me "what I wanted!"

27. He said to me lets wait for him
A. He said to me, "Let's wait for him."
B. He said to me 'Lets wait for him.'

C. He said to me, "let's wait for him."
D. he said to me, "Let's wait for him."

28. In india the ganga and the yamuna are regarded as sacred rivers
A. In India, the Ganga and the Yamuna are regarded as sacred rivers.
B. In India, the ganga and the Yamuna are regarded as sacred rivers.
C. In India, the ganga and the yamuna are regarded as sacred rivers.
D. In India, the Ganga and the yamuna are regarded as sacred rivers.

29. To err is human to forgive divine
A. To err is human to forgive divine.
B. To err is human, to forgive divine.
C. To err, is human to forgive, divine.
D. To err is human; to forgive, divine.

30. He was born on August 16, 1944 in Howrah West Bengal
A. He was born on August 16, 1944 in Howrah West Bengal.
B. He was born on August 16, 1944, in Howrah West Bengal.
C. He was born on, August 16 1944 in Howrah West Bengal.
D. He was born on August, 16 1944, in Howrah West Bengal.

31. He is to tell you the truth is a fool
A. He is, to tell you the truth, is a fool.
B. He is to tell you, the truth is a fool.
C. He is to tell you the truth, is a fool.
D. He is to tell you the truth is a fool.

32. This in brief is what he said
A. This in brief is what he said.
B. This in brief, is what he said.
C. This, in brief, is what he said.
D. This, in brief is what, he said.

33. If you need my help write to me
A. If you need my help write to me.
B. If, you need my help, write to me.
C. If you need, my help, write to me.
D. If you need my help, write to me.

34. They started running for they were getting late
A. They started running, for they were getting late.
B. They started running for they were getting late.
C. They started running for, they were getting late.
D. They started, running for, they were getting late.

35. The sun having set it became pleasant
A. The sun having set it became pleasant.
B. The sun, having set, it became pleasant.
C. The sun having set, it became pleasant.
D. The sun, having set it, became pleasant.

36. Mr Sushil please listen to me
A. Mr Sushil please listen to me.
B. Mr Sushil, please listen to me.
C. Mr Sushil please, listen to me.
D. Mr Sushil, please, listen to me.

37. Wherever you go you face the same difficulties
A. Wherever you go you face the same difficulties.
B. Wherever, you go, you face the same difficulties.
C. Wherever you go, you face, the same difficulties.
D. Wherever you go, you face the same difficulties.

38. Tell me what I can do for you
A. Tell me what I can do for you.
B. Tell me what I can do for you!
C. Tell me what I can do for you?
D. Tell me, what I can do for you?

39. May you live long
A. May you live long.
B. May you live long?
C. May you live long!
D. May, you live long!

40. May God the Greatest bless you
A. May God the Greatest bless you.
B. May God, the Greatest bless you!
C. May God, the Greatest, bless you.
D. May God, the Greatest, bless you!

41. The sun having risen the fog disappeared
A. The sun having risen the fog disappeared.
B. The sun having risen, the fog disappeared.
C. The sun having risen; the fog disappeared.
D. The sun, having risen, the fog disappeared!

42. Having done his homework he went to bed
- A. Having done his homework he went to bed.
- B. Having done, his homework he went to bed.
- C. Having done, his homework, he went to bed.
- D. Having done his homework, he went to bed.

43. He is indeed a foolish boy
- A. He is indeed, a foolish boy.
- B. He is indeed a foolish boy.
- C. He is, indeed, a foolish boy.
- D. He, is indeed, a foolish boy.

44. Naresh my younger brother has gone to Patna
- A. Naresh, my younger brother, has gone to Patna.
- B. Naresh, my younger brother has gone to Patna.
- C. Naresh my younger brother, has gone to Patna.
- D. Naresh! my younger brother has gone to Patna.

45. Well I shall look into the matter
- A. Well I shall look into the matter.
- B. Well, I shall look into the matter.
- C. Well I shall, look into the matter.
- D. Well I shall, look into, the matter.

46. All right you can go
- A. All right you can go.
- B. All right you, can go.
- C. All right, you can go.
- D. All right! you can go.

47. Carry on your work I am watching you
- A. Carry on your work I am watching you.
- B. Carry on, your work, I am watching you.
- C. Carry on, your work, I am watching you.
- D. Carry on your work, I am watching you.

48. He was a kind bold man and we all praised him.
- A. He was a kind bold man and we all praised him
- B. He was a kind, bold man and we all praised him.
- C. He was a kind bold, man and we all praised him.
- D. He was, a kind bold man, and we all praised him.

49. He said honesty is the best policy
- A. He said honesty is the best policy.
- B. He said, honesty is the best policy.
- C. He said "Honesty is the best policy."
- D. He said, "Honesty is the best policy."

50. What a beautiful flower it is
- A. What a beautiful flower it is.
- B. What a beautiful flower it is?
- C. What a beautiful flower it is!
- D. What! a beautiful flower it is.

ANSWERS

1	2	3	4	5	6	7	8	9	10
D	D	C	B	A	C	B	D	A	C
11	**12**	**13**	**14**	**15**	**16**	**17**	**18**	**19**	**20**
B	D	A	C	D	B	C	D	A	D
21	**22**	**23**	**24**	**25**	**26**	**27**	**28**	**29**	**30**
C	B	A	D	B	C	A	A	D	B
31	**32**	**33**	**34**	**35**	**36**	**37**	**38**	**39**	**40**
A	C	D	A	C	B	D	A	C	D
41	**42**	**43**	**44**	**45**	**46**	**47**	**48**	**49**	**50**
B	D	C	A	B	C	D	B	D	C

14

Figures of Speech

It is a common saying that a picture is worth a thousand words. Same goes with the figures of speech as they elaborate the meaning of words.

FIGURATIVE LANGUAGE

One meaning of "figure" is "drawing" or "image" or "picture". Figurative language creates figures (pictures) in the mind of the reader or listener. These pictures help convey the meaning faster and more vividly than words alone.

We use figures of speech in "figurative language" to add colour and interest, and to awaken the imagination. Figurative language is everywhere, from classical works like Shakespeare or the Bible, to every day speech, pop music and television commercials. It makes the reader or listener use their imagination and understand much more than the plain words.

Figurative language is the opposite of literal language. Literal language means exactly what it says. Figurative language means something different to (and usually more than) what it says on the surface. *e.g.*,

- He ran fast. (literal)
- He ran like the wind. (figurative)

In the above example "like the wind" is a figure of speech (in this case, simile). It is important to recognize the difference between literal and figurative language. There are many figures of speech that are commonly used and which you can learn by heart. At other times, writers and speakers may invent their own figures of speech. If you do not recognize them as figures of speech and think that they are literal, you will find it difficult to understand the language.

In this chapter we will discuss four common types of figures of speech :

- Simile
- Metaphor
- Hyperbole
- Oxymoron

Simile

A simile is a figure of speech that says that one thing is like another different thing. We can use similes to make descriptions more emphatic or vivid.

We often use the words *as....as* and like with similes.

Common patterns for similes, with example sentences, are :

- Something AS *adjective* AS *something*
  His skin was as cold as ice.
  It felt as hard as rock.
  She looked as gentle as a lamb.
- Something LIKE something
  My love is like a red, red rose.
  These cookies taste like garbage.
  He had a temper (that was) like a volcano.

- Something LIKE something
  He eats like a pig.
  He smokes like a chimney.
  They fought like cats and dogs.

Here are some more examples of well known similes :

AS *adjective* AS *something*	**Meaning**
as blind as a bat	completely blind
as cold as ice	very cold
as flat as a pancake	completely flat
as gentle as a lamb	very gentle
as light as a feather	very light
as old as the hills	very old
as sharp as a knife	very sharp
as strong as a bull	very strong
as white as snow	pure white
as wise as an owl	very wise

LIKE *something*	**Possible meaning (depending on context)**
like a rose	beautiful
like a volcano	explosive
like garbage	disgusting
like an animal	inhuman
like spaghetti	entangled
like dewdrops	sweet and pure
like golddust	precious
like a tip	very untidy (tip = garbage dump)
like a dream	wonderful, incredible
like stars	bright and beautiful

LIKE something	**Meaning**
to drink like a fish	to drink a lot
to eat like a bird	to eat very little
to eat like a horse	to eat a lot
to eat like a pig	to eat impolitely
to fight like cats and dogs	to fight fiercely
to sing like an angel	to sing beautifully
to sleep like a log	to sleep well and soundly
to smoke like a chimney	to smoke heavily, all the time
to soar like an eagle	to fly high and free
to work like a dog	to work very hard

Note that with the AS...AS pattern, the first AS is sometimes suppressed, for example :

His skin was cold as ice.

The above patterns of simile are the most common, but there are others made with adverbs or words such as than and as if, for example :

- He ran as fast as the wind.
- He is larger than life.
- They ran as if for their lives.

Similes can include other figures of speech. For example. "He ran like greased lightning" is a simile that includes hyperbole (greased lightning).

Similes often make use of irony or sarcasm. In such cases they may even mean the opposite of the adjective used. Look at these examples :

- His explanation was as clear as mud. (not clear at all since mud is opaque)
- The film was about as interesting watching a copy of Windows download. (long and boring)
- Watching the show was like watching paint dry. (very boring)

Similes are often found (and they sometimes originate) in poetry and other literature. Here are a few examples :

- A woman without a man is like a fish without a bicycle—Irina Dunn
- Dawn breaks open like a wound that bleeds afresh—Wilfred Owen
- Death has many times invited me : it was like the salt invisible in the waves—Pablo Neruda

- Guiltless forever, like a tree—Robert Browning
- Happy as pigs in mud—David Eddings
- How like the winter hath my absence been—William Shakespeare
- As idle as a painted ship upon a painted ocean—Samuel Taylor Coleridge
- Jubilant as a flag unfurled—Dorothy Parker
- So are you to my thoughts as food to life—William Shakespeare
- Yellow butterflies flickered along the shade like flecks of sun—William Faulkner

Metaphor

A metaphor is a figure of speech that says that one thing is another different thing. This allows us to use fewer words and forces the reader or listener to find the similarities.

The word metaphor comes from the Greek word *metapherin* (meaning "transfer").

The simplest form of metaphor is : "The [first thing] is a [second thing]."

Look at this example :

Her home was a prison.

In the above sentence, we understand immediately that her home had some of the characteristics of a prison. Mainly, we imagine, she could not leave her home. She was trapped inside. Why it was a prison we do not know, but that would be clear from the context—perhaps her husband forced her to stay at home, perhaps she was afraid of the outside. We don't know, but the rest of the story would tell us. What is important here is that in five simple words we understand a lot about her environment, how she felt and how she behaved. In this sentence, "prison" is a metaphor.

Look at another example :

George is a sheep.

What is one characteristic of sheep? They follow each other. So we can imagine that George is a follower, not a leader. In this sentence "sheep" is a metaphor.

Metaphors are very common in everyday language. But poets also like to use metaphors.

Look at these examples of metaphors with sample sentences and meanings :

Metaphor example	Metaphorical sense	Original sense
I'm not an angel, but I wouldn't a behave like that.	exemplary person	a spiritual being believed to be messenger of God
America is a melting pot.	place where different peoples, styles and cultures are mixed together	a container in which metals or other materials are melted and mixed
John is a real pig when he eats.	greedy person	a four-legged animal kept for meat (pork)
My father is a rock.	very strong or reliable person	a hard, mineral material made of stone
How could she marry a snake like that!	traitor	a long, limbless reptile (e.g., cobra, python, viper)
The policeman let him off with a yellow card.	warning	(in soccer) a yellow card that the referee shows to players when cautioning them

All the above metaphors (the simplest form) are nouns. But there are other ways of making metaphors, for example with verbs or adjectives. Here are some examples :

Metaphor example	Original sense of the word (example)
The committee **shot** ideas **down** one by one.	Anti-aircraft guns that shoot down planes.
The private detective **dug** up enough evidence to convince the police to act.	Dugs like to bury bones and dig them up later.
He **broke into** her conversation	Burglars break into buildings.
The new movie was very popular. People **flocked** to see it.	Birds flock together before they migrate.
His head was **spinning** with ideas.	Some computer hard drives spin at over 10,000 revolutions per minute.
Reading that book **kindled** my interest in branches when you kindle a camp fire.	You need to start with twigs and small politics.
Tim lost his job after a **heated** argument with his boss.	We have a heated swimming pool.
The new car's **sexy** design increased sales for the company.	Some women think that lipstick makes them look sexy.
He was dressed rather vulgarly in a **loud** checked suit.	I can't hear you because the radio is too loud.
It wasn't long before their relationship turned **sour**.	Sour food has an acid taste like lemon or vinegar.

Difference Between Metaphor and Simile

Both similes and metaphors link one thing to another. A simile usually uses "as" or "like". A metaphor is a condensed simile, a shortcut to meaning, which omits "as" or "like". A metaphor creates a relationship directly and leaves more to the imagination. With simile, A is like B. With metaphor, *A* is *B*.

Simile	Metaphor
Your eyes are like sun.	You are my the sunshine.
He eats like a pig.	He is a pig.
He lives like a pig.	He is a pig.

Dead Metaphors

In the phrase "to grasp the concept" the physical action "to grasp" is used as a metaphor for "to understand" (which is non-physical). But this phrase has been used so often that most English speakers do not have an image of the physical action in their mind. This metaphor is a "dead metaphor".

Mixed Metaphors

The awkward use of two or more different metaphors at the same time is normally best avoided. It creates conflicting images in the reader or listener's mind, reduces each metaphor's impact, and generally causes confusion. Look at this example :

America is a **melting pot** where new ideas are **kindled**.

Hyperbole

Hyperbole is a figure of speech that uses an exaggerated or extravagant to create a strong emotional response. As a figure of speech it is not intended to be taken literally. Hyperbole is frequently used for humour. Examples of hyperbole are :

- They ran like greased lightning.
- He's got tons of money.
- Her brain is the size of a pea.
- He is older than the hills.
- I will die if she asks me to dance.
- She is as big as an elephant!
- I'm so hungry I could eat a horse.
- I have told you a million times not to lie!

The media and the advertising industry often use hyperbole (which may then be described as hyper or media hype).

Oxymoron

An oxymoron is a figure of speech that deliberately uses two contradictory ideas. This contradiction creates a paradoxical image in the reader or listener's mind that generates a new concept or meaning for the whole. Some typical oxymorons are :

- a living death
- sometimes you have to be cruel to be kind
- a deafening silence
- bitter-sweet
- The Sounds of Silence (song title)
- make haste slowly
- he was conspicuous by his absence

Pseudo Oxymorons

In the standard meaning of oxymoron the contradiction is deliberate. However, in popular usage oxymoron is sometimes used to mean "contradiction in terms", where the contradiction is unintentional. Such expressions, unlike real oxymorons, are commonly used without any sense of paradox in everyday language, for example :

- anecdotal evidence
- friendly fire
- pretty ugly

A common attempt at humour is to describe a certain phrase as an oxymoron, implying that the two parts of the phrase are mutually exclusive and that consequently the phrase as a whole must be nonsensical :

- airline food
- American culture
- eco-tourism
- Microsoft security
- military intelligence

The following are the other major Figures of Speech :

1. **Personification**—In Personification inanimate objects and abstract notions are spoken of as having life or intelligence.
2. **Onomatopoeia**—Onomatopoeia is that artifice of language by which the sound of words is made to suggest or echo the sense.
3. **Apostrophe**—An Apostrophe is a direct address to the dead, to the absent, or to a personified object or idea.
4. **Alliteration**—Alliteration consists in the repetition of the same sound or syllable at the beginning of two or more words.
5. **Irony**—Irony is a mode of speech in which the real meaning is exactly the opposite of that which is literally conveyed.
6. **Pun**—This consists in a play on the various meanings of a word, and is seldom used except as a joke.
7. **Metonymy**—In Metonymy an object is designated by the name of something which is generally associated with it.
8. **Synecdoche**—In Synecdoche a part is used to designate the whole, or the whole to designate a part.
9. **Antithesis**—In Antithesis a striking opposition or contrast of words or sentiments is made in the same sentence. It is employed to secure emphasis.
10. **Transferred Epithet**—In this figure an epithet is tranferred from its proper word to another that is closely associated with it in the sentence.

MULTIPLE CHOICE QUESTIONS

Directions (Qs. 1 to 20) : *Select the correct option for each of the following questions.*

1. Recognize the figure of speech in the following statement.
He is the Newton of our class.
A. Simile B. Hyperbole
C. Metaphor D. Climax

2. Which of the following statements shows oxymoron:
A. He is leading a busy life.
B. He is leading a highly busy-idle life.
C. He is leading an idle life.
D. How happy I am!

3. Recognize the figure of speech in the following:
The Child is father of the Man.
A. alliteration B. hyperbole
C. paradox D. metaphor

4. Which of the following shows Metonymy:
A. Have you read the whole of George Eliot?
B. Which building in Delhi do you like most?
C. Whose acting do you like most among the Bollywood actors?
D. Why are day and night equal on 21 March?

5. Recognize the figure of speech in the following statement.
I wandered lonely as a cloud.
A. Simile B. Metaphor
C. Alliteration D. Hyperbole

6. Which of the following phrases shows onomatopoeia:
A. living like a king.
B. looking beyond the horizon.
C. burning the candle at both ends.
D. murmuring of innumerable bees.

7. Recognize the figure of speech in the following:
Five miles meandering in mazy motion.
A. oxymoron B. climax
C. anticlimax D. alliteration

8. Which of the following shows 'climax':
A. I walk, I jump, I dance.
B. I run, I walk, I sit.
C. He lies, runs and sits.
D. She thinks, writes and observes.

9. Recognize the figure of speech in the following:
Lightly, O lightly, they bear her along.
A. Hyperbole B. Onomatopoeia
C. Climax D. Repetition

10. Which of the following shows 'Hyperbole':
A. You will have to speak for a hundred thousand years to describe her beauty.
B. Love begets love.
C. Better alone than in bad company.
D. Nothing can be decided by war.

11. What Figure of Speech is used when a statement is made emphatic by over statement?
A. Apostrophe B. Hyperbole
C. Personification D. Antithesis

12. What Figure of Speech is used when two contradictory qualities are predicted at once of the same thing?
A. Antithesis B. Onomatopoeia
C. Oxymoron D. Hyperbole

13. In which Figure of Speech the sense is conveyed by the sound of words?
A. Metonymy B. Synecdoche
C. Alliteration D. Onomatopoeia

14. In which Figure of Speech is there a play on the various meanings of a word?
A. Pun B. Metaphor
C. Transferred Epithet D. Irony

15. Which Figure of Speech is produced when the same sound is repeated more than twice at the beginning of a word?
A. Onomatopoeia B. Alliteration
C. Metonymy D. Synecdoche

16. Which of the following is an example of Onomatopoeia?
A. Sweet-bitter tears flowed from her eyes
B. The beetle wheels his droning flight

C. A load of learning lumbering in his head
D. Fair is that fair does

17. Which of the following is an example of Oxymoron?
A. There is kind cruelty in the surgeon's knife
B. Ruin seize thee, ruthless king!
C. And Brutus is an honourable man!
D. Kalidas is the Shakespeare of India

18. Which of the following is an example of Antithesis?
A. Who is to blame but you!
B. Fair is foul, and foul is fair!
C. As you sow, so will you reap
D. Forget me not!

19. Which of the following is an example of Apostrophe?
A. Barking dogs seldom bite
B. My misfortune is your fortune
C. O Solitude! Where are thy charms?
D. I am the monarch of all I survey

20. Which of the following is an example of Alliteration?
A. Sweet are the uses of adversity!
B. Thus idly busy rolls their world away
C. He is the heir apparent
D. With beaded bubbles winking at the brim

Directions (Qs. 21 to 50) : *In each of the following sentences or verses a Figure of Speech has been used. You have to choose the correct Figure of Speech out of the four choices given under each :*

21. Rivers of blood flowed on the battlefield :
A. Simile B. Metaphor
C. Hyperbole D. Alliteration

22. Camel is the ship of the desert :
A. Metaphor B. Simile
C. Pun D. Personification

23. 'O my love's like a red, red rose, that's newly sprung in June':
A. Alliteration B. Metaphor
C. Simile D. Hyperbole

24. "Opportunity knocks at the door but once."
A. Hyperbole B. Metaphor
C. Antithesis D. Personification

25. "Death lays his icy hand on Kings" :
A. Personification B. Antithesis
C. Metaphor D. Oxymoron

26. "The murmurous haunt of flies on summer eves."
A. Hyperbole B. Alliteration
C. Onomatopoeia D. Personification

27. "Milton! thou should'st be living at this hour."
A. Personification B. Apostrophe
C. Alliteration D. Irony

28. How high his honour holds his haughty head!
A. Oxymoron B. Personification
C. Alliteration D. Irony

29. "Yet Brutus says he was ambitious. And Brutus is an honourable man."
A. Irony B. Oxymoron
C. Apostrophe D. Pun

30. Is life worth living? That depends upon the liver.
A. Pun B. Alliteration
C. Irony D. Metaphor

31. The pen is mightier than the sword.
A. Simile B. Metaphor
C. Metonymy D. Irony

32. A reeling road, a rolling road, that rambles round the shire.
A. Alliteration B. Metonymy
C. Personification D. Apostrophe

33. "The ploughman homeward plods his weary way."
A. Oxymoron
B. Synecdoche
C. Transferred Epithet
D. Pun

34. To err is human, to forgive divine :
A. Oxymoron
B. Antithesis
C. Transferred Epithet
D. Pun

35. He passed a sleepless night :
A. Transferred Epithet
B. Antithesis
C. Synecdoche
D. Oxymoron

36. The best brains assembled there :
A. Oxymoron B. Synecdoche
C. Irony D. Pun

37. I have many mouths to feed :
A. Synecdoche B. Irony
C. Pun D. Oxymoron

38. Man proposes, God disposes :
A. Synecdoche B. Antithesis
C. Pun D. Irony

39. O Death! Where is thy sting?
A. Metaphor B. Oxymoron
C. Personification D. Apostrophe

40. "Life is a tale told by an idiot,
Full of sound and fury ...."
A. Simile B. Personification
C. Metaphor D. Apostrophe

41. "Thy soul was like a star, and dwelt apart."
A. Metaphor B. Personification
C. Simile D. Onomatopoeia

42. He can devour mountains of food, and drink rivers of whisky.
A. Onomatopoeia B. Hyperbole
C. Metaphor D. Personification

43. "There Honour comes a pilgrim grey" :
A. Metaphor
B. Apostrophe
C. Personification
D. Onomatopoeia

44. An ambassador is a man who lies abroad for the good of his country :
A. Metonymy B. Personification
C. Pun D. Irony

45. "Husbands had she five on the holy altar" :
A. Hyperbole B. Metaphor
C. Irony D. Pun

46. His honour rooted in dishonour stood :
A. Antithesis B. Oxymoron
C. Irony D. Personification

47. "Sceptre and crown must tumble down."
A. Metonymy B. Antithesis
C. Irony D. Oxymoron

48. A lie has no legs :
A. Apostrophe B. Pun
C. Personification D. Irony

49. Youth is full of pleasure; Age is full of care :
A. Antithesis B. Pun
C. Metaphor D. Personification

50. The righteous shall flourish as the palm trees :
A. Simile
B. Transferred Epithet
C. Antithesis
D. Synecdoche

ANSWERS

1	2	3	4	5	6	7	8	9	10
C	B	C	A	A	D	D	A	D	A
11	**12**	**13**	**14**	**15**	**16**	**17**	**18**	**19**	**20**
B	C	D	A	B	B	A	B	C	D
21	**22**	**23**	**24**	**25**	**26**	**27**	**28**	**29**	**30**
C	A	C	D	A	C	B	C	A	A
31	**32**	**33**	**34**	**35**	**36**	**37**	**38**	**39**	**40**
C	A	C	B	A	B	A	B	D	C
41	**42**	**43**	**44**	**45**	**46**	**47**	**48**	**49**	**50**
C	B	C	C	C	B	A	C	A	A

15

Word Analogy

Like different people words also have different relationships with each other in comparison to each other. This is called word analogy. Try and master it in the following questions.

MULTIPLE CHOICE QUESTIONS

Directions: *Each question below consists of two words which have a certain relationship to each other followed by four pairs of related words. Select the pair which has the same relationship as in the given pair of words.*

1. Lunatic : Asylum

A. The poor : Palace
B. Soldiers : Barracks
C. Flowers : Fields
D. Crops : Garden

2. Soldier : Rifle

A. Blacksmith : Anvil
B. Thief : Ladder
C. Watchman : Uniform
D. Barber : Hair

3. Frog : Tadpoles

A. Man : Sons
B. Woman : Daughters
C. Cat : Kids
D. Elephant : Calves

4. Lizards : Reptiles

A. Frogs : Amphibians
B. Tree : Fruit
C. Earth : Moon
D. Man : Woman

5. Earthworm : Segments

A. Tree : Wood
B. Crocodiles : Scales
C. Apple : Juice
D. Earth : Moisture

6. Mosquito : Malaria

A. Rabid dog : Rabies
B. House fly : AIDS
C. Cockroach : Influenza
D. Virus : Diabetes

7. Fish : Water

A. Man : Air
B. Cat : Mouse
C. Lion : Flesh
D. Tree : Roots

8. Impulsive : Cautious

A. Liberty : Bondage
B. Tyrant : Bully
C. Tremble : Quake
D. Vulgar : Indecent

9. Weighty : Voluminous

A. Jolly : Dismal
B. Loyalty : Perfidy
C. Wealth : Opulence
D. Odd : Normal

10. Innocent : Guilty
A. Kill : Produce
B. Suspect : Doubt
C. Depress : Discourage
D. Contract : Condense

11. Useless : Cheap
A. Late : Unpunctual
B. Real : Illusive
C. Just : Unfair
D. Humble : Proud

12. Loyal : Faithful
A. Treacherous : Devoted
B. Just : Fair
C. Yield : Suppress
D. Uncertain : Sure

13. Cancel : Confirm
A. Certain : Ambiguous
B. Vulgar : Crude
C. Reliable : Trustworthy
D. Obscure : Anonymous

14. Gloomy : Bright
A. Pleasant : Delightful
B. Funny : Comic
C. Condemn : Blame
D. Hard : Flexible

15. Modern : Ancient
A. Happy : Joyful
B. Service : Slavery
C. Mild : Harsh
D. Assumed : Unreal

16. Dexterous : Clumsy
A. Cheap : Worthless
B. Usual : Common
C. Zenith : Acme
D. True : False

17. Luscious : Sweet
A. Above : Below
B. Absolve : Penalise
C. Lucrative : Profitable
D. Adopt : Abandon

18. Fraud : Duplicity
A. Inferior : Cheap
B. Delicious : Abhorrent
C. Desire : Detest
D. Diligent : Lackadiasical

19. Weired : Ordinary
A. Vacant : Void
B. Vivid : Clear
C. Vivid : Dim
D. Wicked : Unvirtuous

20. Build : Demolish
A. Abide : Persist
B. Compel : Coax
C. Odious : Hateful
D. Claim : Demand

21. Passionate : Impassive
A. Deter : Discourage
B. Folly : Stupidity
C. Polite : Rude
D. Fanciful : Whimsical

22. Gauche : Attractive
A. True : Exact
B. Tough : Hard
C. Tasteful : Palatable
D. Insipid : Delicious

23. Existence : Life
A. Silence : Noise
B. Risk : Shield
C. Enormous : Immense
D. Rural : Urban

24. Belief : Suspicion
A. Unravel : Unweave
B. Profuse : Insufficient
C. Urge : Spur
D. Use : Occupy

25. Violent : Calm
A. Tranquil : Peaceful
B. Reticent : Quiet
C. Even : Smooth
D. Disdain : Reverence

26. Lawyer : Court
A. Businessman : Market
B. Chemist : Laboratory
C. Labourer : Factory
D. Athlete : Olympics

27. Corporeal : Spirtual

A. Mesa : Plateau
B. Moron : Savant
C. Foreigner : Ummigrant
D. Pedagogue : Teacher

28. Ten : Decimal

A. Seven : Septet
B. Four : Quartet
C. Two : Binary
D. Five : Quince

29. Grain : Salt

A. Shard : Pottery
B. Shred : Wood
C. Blades : Grass
D. Chip : Glass

30. Fish : Shoal

A. Audience : Theatre
B. Elephant : Flock
C. Whale : Herd
D. Shark : School

31. Wan : Colour

A. Copulent : Weight
B. Insipid : Flavour
C. Pallid : Complexion
D. Enigmatic : Puzzle

32. Thrust : Spear

A. Mangle : Iron
B. Scabbard : Sword
C. Bow : Arrow
D. Fence : Epee

33. Indigent : Wealthy

A. Angry : Rich
B. Native : Affluent
C. Gauche : Graceful
D. Scholarly : Erudite

34. Diva : Opera

A. Producer : Theatre
B. Director : Drama
C. Conductor : Bus
D. Thespian : Play

35. Army : Logistics

A. Business : Strategy
B. Soldiers : Students
C. War : Logic
D. Team : Individual

36. Distance : Mile

A. Liquid : Litre
B. Bushel : Corn
C. Weight : Scale
D. Fame : Television

37. After : Before

A. First : Second
B. Present : Past
C. Contemporary : Historic
D. Successor : Predecessor

38. Mundane : Spiritual

A. Common : Ghostly
B. Worldly : Unworldly
C. Routine : Novel
D. Secular : Clerical

39. Filter : Water

A. Curtail : Activity
B. Expurge : Book
C. Edit : Text
D. Censor : Play

40. Pork : Pig

A. Rooster : Chicken
B. Mutton : Sheep
C. Steer : Beef
D. Lobster : Crustacean

41. Pain : Sedative

A. Comfort : Stimulant
B. Grief : Consolation
C. Trance : Narcotic
D. Ache : Extraction

42. Hope : Aspires

A. Love : Elevates
B. Film : Flam
C. Fib : Lie
D. Fake : Ordinary

43. Gravity : Pull

A. Iron : Metal
B. North pole : Directions
C. Magnetism : Attraction
D. Dust : Desert

44. Light : Blind
A. Speech : Dumb
B. Language : Deaf
C. Tongue : Sound
D. Voice : Vibration

45. Symphony : Composer
A. Leonardo : Music
B. Fresco : Painter
C. Colours : Pallet
D. Art : Appreciation

46. Astringent : Pucker
A. Car : Engine
B. Spark : Ignition
C. Quell : Allay
D. Sophisticated : Rural

47. Saga : Heroic
A. Epigram : Pithy
B. Tragedy : Comedy
C. Editorial : Newspaper
D. Picture : Book

48. Obdurate : Flexibility
A. Stagger : Amaze
B. Adamant : Submissiveness
C. Semite : Jew
D. Redicule : Scorn

49. Percept : Instructive
A. Ribald : Decent
B. Metaphor : Figurative
C. Institution : Study
D. Library : Calmness

50. Hermit : Gregarious
A. Sanguine : Optimistic
B. Repose : Rest
C. Ruthless : Merciless
D. Ascetic : Hedonostic

51. Braggart : Modesty
A. Profound : Intelligence
B. Opinionated : Over confident
C. Buffoon : Dignity
D. Arrogant : Acuity

52. Posthumous : Death
A. Selection : Nomination
B. Product : Factory
C. Clay : Mould
D. Cloudy : Sunny

53. Prophet : Foreteller
A. Precursor : Forerunner
B. Pretentious : Ambitious
C. Prodigy : Wonderful
D. Teacher : Intelleclual

54. Indigent : Wealth
A. Yelp : Cry
B. Yearn : Disire
C. Wrangle : Argue
D. Emaciated : Nourishment

55. Senorita : Woman
A. Sophisticated : Self-assured
B. Monologue : Discourse
C. Semite : Jew
D. General : Military

56. Yeoman : Farming
A. Clerk : Office
B. Waiter : Restaurant
C. Hawker : Business
D. Apprentice : Engineer

57. Genuine : Authentic
A. Light : Reflection
B. Image : Shadow
C. Mirage : Illusion
D. Vaccum : Transparency

58. Colour : Bleach
A. Buzz : Hum
B. Echo : Sound
C. Paper : Burn
D. Blush : Faint

59. Labour : Wages
A. Capital : Interest
B. Doctor : Medicine
C. Ink : Writing
D. Agree : Oppose

60. Brusque : Unceremoniousness
A. Apparatus : Experiment
B. Auditor : Lecture
C. Malaria : Relapse
D. Obstinate : Intractability

61. Mature : Regressed
A. Intruder : Privacy
B. Varied : Monotonous
C. Sufficiency : Adequacy
D. Train : Compartment

62. Celerity : Snail
A. Curosity : Cat
B. Cunning : Crow
C. Humility : Peacock
D. Obstinacy : Mule

63. Dilatory : Expeditious
A. Direct : Circuitous
B. Skirmish : Mar
C. Language : Grammar
D. Ice : Coolness

64. Molt : Feathers
A. Flutter : Wings
B. Slough : Skin
C. Sharpen : Talons
D. Bare : Fangs

65. Jeopardy : Peril
A. Plead : Insist
B. Promote : Reward
C. Rely : Support
D. Jealousy : Envy

66. Surfeit : Appetite
A. Refine : Taste
B. Sniff : Nose
C. Cloy : Palate
D. Cling : Touch

67. Aeroplane : Cockpit
A. Train : Engine
B. Train : Compartment
C. Train : Coach
D. Train : Wagon

68. Rider : Bill
A. Meter : Electricity
B. Endorsement : Policy
C. Purchase : Receipt
D. Violation : Law

69. Wax : Wane
A. Earth : Orbit
B. Depth : Shallow
C. Fall : Bottom
D. Zenith : Nadir

70. Painting : Artist
A. Wood : Furniture
B. Analysis : Critic
C. Symphony : Composer
D. Symphony : Poet

71. Windfall : Jubilation
A. Grief : Sorrow
B. Pratfall : Embarrassment
C. Bravery : Courageous
D. Calm : Melancholy

72. Foresight : Anticipation
A. Insomnia : Sleeplessness
B. Intuition : Happening
C. Indolent : Incredible
D. Impromptu : Preparation

73. Novice : Learner
A. Voters : Politicians
B. Gigolo : Dance
C. Harbinger : Forerunner
D. Roster : Duty

74. Life : Autobiography
A. Witness : Truth
B. Witness : Documents
C. Culprit : Punishment
D. Jailor : Prison

75. Grieve : Sorrow
A. Wallow : Misery
B. Smart : Pain
C. Weaken : Strength
D. Afflict : Torment

76. Cloud : Scud
A. Fog : Disperse
B. Blood : Clot
C. Mist : Fall
D. Water : Race

77. Fire : Ashes
A. Heart : Breath
B. School : Education
C. Explosion : Debris
D. Alma mater : Certificate

78. Ocean : Water
A. Mountain : Peak
B. Cave : Hollow
C. Glacier : Ice
D. River : Current

79. Unctuous : Sincerity
A. Urban : Society
B. Pleasant : Jovial
C. Wrest : Amusing
D. Sardonic : Sympathy

80. Audible : Hear
A. Fascinating : See
B. Palpable : Touch
C. Distinctive : Smell
D. Unique : Personality

81. Article : Newspaper
A. Scene : Play
B. Food : Diet
C. Account : Diary
D. Maize : Field

82. Beginning : Culmination
A. Tragedy : Catastrophe
B. Language : Grammar
C. Stanza : Poetry
D. Prologue : Denouement

83. Ballerina : Ballet
A. Stage : Performance
B. Protagonist : Play
C. Grief : Tragedy
D. Ballad : Poem

84. Bellicose : Quarrelsome
A. Boost : Boom
B. Bonny : Unhealthy
C. Babel : Babble
D. Bane : Ruin

85. Annihilation : Fire
A. Ordinance : Parliament
B. Emergency : Failure
C. Cataclysm : Flood
D. Cataclysm : Earthquake

ANSWERS

1	2	3	4	5	6	7	8	9	10
B	A	D	A	B	A	A	A	C	A
11	**12**	**13**	**14**	**15**	**16**	**17**	**18**	**19**	**20**
A	B	A	D	C	D	C	A	C	B
21	**22**	**23**	**24**	**25**	**26**	**27**	**28**	**29**	**30**
C	D	C	B	D	A	B	C	D	D
31	**32**	**33**	**34**	**35**	**36**	**37**	**38**	**39**	**40**
C	D	C	D	A	A	D	B	D	B
41	**42**	**43**	**44**	**45**	**46**	**47**	**48**	**49**	**50**
B	C	C	A	B	B	A	B	B	D
51	**52**	**53**	**54**	**55**	**56**	**57**	**58**	**59**	**60**
C	A	A	D	B	C	C	D	A	D
61	**62**	**63**	**64**	**65**	**66**	**67**	**68**	**69**	**70**
B	C	A	B	D	C	A	B	D	C
71	**72**	**73**	**74**	**75**	**76**	**77**	**78**	**79**	**80**
B	A	C	A	B	D	C	C	D	B
81	**82**	**83**	**84**	**85**					
A	D	B	D	C					

ENGLISH LITERATURE

1

Introduction to Literature

Literature plays a very significant role in human life. It is considered to be the mirror of the society which reflects the image of the time in which it was created. It is a medium of expressing thoughts and ideas for the writer. It is one of the most ancient forms of entertainment in the history of mankind. At the beginning when there was no written form of language, literature was composed in the form of poetry and preserved through the words of mouth. In the history of literature, poetry is the most ancient form of literature. Then it developed into various other forms like drama, novel, and short story.

CLASSIFICATION & FORMS

Literature can be classified and sub-classified in various forms as:

1. Drama
2. Non-fiction or prose
3. Poetry
4. Novel

Drama

The following are the Major Forms of Drama :

1. Miracles & Mystery Plays, Morality Plays and Interludes
2. Heroic, Revenge, Shakespearean, Sentimental, Tragedies & Melodramas
3. Comedies
   - Classical Comedies
   - Tragi-Comedies
   - Romantic Comedies
   - Comedy of Humour
   - Comedy of Manners
   - The Farce
   - The Masque
4. The Poetic Play
5. The Dramatic Monologue
6. The Problem Play
7. The One-Act Play

Non-Fiction or Prose

The following are the Major Forms of Prose :

1. Long Prose-Works
2. The Essay
3. The Periodical Journals
4. The Biography
5. The Autobiography
6. The Memoirs

Poetry

Poetry and its Major Forms are these :

1. The Epic
2. The Mock Epic
3. The Sonnet
4. The Ode
5. The Lyric
6. The Idyll
7. The Pastoral
8. The Elegy
9. The Pastoral Elegy
10. The Ballad
11. The Satire

Novel

The following are the Major Forms of the Novel :

1. The Prose Romances
2. The Travelogues
3. The Gothic Novel
4. The Picaresque Novel
5. The Epistolary Novel
6. The Domestic Novel
7. The Historical Novel
8. The Regional Novel
9. The Prophetic Novel
10. The Psychological Novel
11. The Short Story

DRAMA

The term 'drama' originates from Greek language, which means 'to do'. In a drama, we come across objective representation of the conflicts, actions, events and crisis from the lives of the concerned characters. Drama is the specific mode of fiction represented in performance. It is primarily a performing art. It is the most powerful literary expression as action is presented on the stage, engaging the audio-visual faculties of the audience.

Drama is an ancient form of literature having a long history of more than 2500 years. Historically speaking following are the stages in the development of drama:

STAGES IN THE DEVELOPMENT OF DRAMA

Greek Drama

History of literature shows the origin of drama in Greece in 6th century B.C. In ancient Greece dramatic competitions were held to celebrate the festival of God Dionysus. The dramatists participating in this competition were required to present a tetralogy of plays consisting of three tragedies and a satyr play. The plays performed in this period were tragedy, comedy and the satyr play. Aeschylus, Sophocles, Euripides, Aristophanes and Menander are the best-known dramatists of Ancient times.

Roman Drama

Greek drama came in contact with the Romans after the Roman Empire expanded into Greece territories in the 3rd century B.C. Roman dramatists of this period like Andronicus and Naevius took drama all over Europe. During the 2nd century B.C. it had become one of the chief means of entertainment with many men of letters practicing it. The comedies written by Plautus and Terence became very popular, many of which have survived. The Roman tragedian, Seneca popularized tragedy so much so that it is called Senecan tragedy.

Medieval Drama

The drama of the Middle Ages dealt with Bible stories and allegorical mysteries. It was being written in the regional languages of the times. To help the laymen understand the teachings of the religion, the clergymen used to perform the incidents from Bible in dramatic form. The plays of this period are called Mystery and Miracle plays.

Elizabethan Drama

With the construction of Globe Theatre in London, drama as a major form of literature flourished in England. The main practitioners of this form in 16th and 17th century are Ben Jonson, Shakespeare and Christopher Marlowe. The plays of this period were written on the themes like ancient history and Greek and Roman mythology, and contemporary socio-political issues.

Modern Drama

Henrik Ibsen and Bertolt Brecht dominate the modern drama of 19th and 20th Century respectively. Ibsen started a new kind of drama by making an ordinary housewife as the heroine of his play, 'A Doll's House'. Anton Chekhov, Eugene O'Neill, Luigi Pirandello, Samuel Beckett, Harold Pinter, John Osborne and George Bernard Shaw are the important dramatists of this period.

Indian Classical Drama

Indian Classical drama originated from the Rig-Veda. The plots of these plays were based on the stories taken from the great Sanskrit epics, *The Ramayana* and *The Mahabharata*. Our ancient writer, Bharata penned the theory of writing a play in his book '*Natya Shastra*'. Bhasa, Kalidasa, Sudraka, Asvaghosa and Harsha are the famous Sanskrit playwrights.

ELEMENTS OF DRAMA

Aristotle, in his book entitled 'The Poetics' has discussed theoretical aspects of drama. Here he has given emphasis on tragedy and its elements. These elements are plot, theme, character, diction, music and spectacle.

Plot

According to Aristotle's theory of drama in 'Poetics', plot is the most important element of drama. He equals the plot of a play with the soul in human body. The plot can be either simple or complex. Simple plot is straight-forward, with continuous movements, whereas the complex plot has peripeity and Anagnorisis. Peripeteia means the opposite results produced by the human actions. In such a plot the character goes on acting naively in certain way without realizing the effects of his actions. But these actions ultimately lead it to its doom. Anagnorisis means the realization of truth. The simple plot has only one story in it whereas the complex plot can have more than one story or episodes in it. The skill of the dramatist lies in knitting all these episodes in a single whole to create a singular effect on the audience.

An ideal plot can be divided into three parts—beginning, middle and an end. A good beginning is that which is not dependent on some previous incident or knowledge. A good middle is the outcome of the events which have taken place in the beginning and leads those events to their satisfactory conclusion. A good ending is the result of whatever has happened before the end. It is the natural conclusion of the events gone before.

Character

Drama is the representation of the conflicts of human life. And so it requires some characters in the happenings of life. As the dramatist represents a story, it is but natural that there should be some characters on whose life the story is based. The characters in a play are selected from the host of people according to the need of the plot. As the play has a limited canvas, he does not make his play over crowded with too many characters. There is no scope for a full length character study in a drama. So the writer selects only those incidents from the life of his protagonist that are necessary for the action of the play.

The characters are of two types—flat characters and round characters. A flat character does not grow with the development of the plot. It remains static from the beginning to the end of the play. On the other hand, round character grows with the action of the play. Another type of character is the stock character, a character that reappears again and again in various plays with the same attributes each time. Such characters are also called stereotypes or the stock characters.

While developing his characters, the dramatist uses the following methods: one method is to develop his characters by the help of the dialogues which the character speaks; the other method is to expose the character by through the speeches of the other characters; and the third method is the combination of the earlier two methods, i.e. developing the character partly through his/her own speeches and partly by what others say about him/her. Actually the last method is more convincing and so used by the greater number of writers.

One more aspect of the characters in a play is the selection of the hero or the heroine. The dramatist has to be very careful regarding this aspect because the success of the play is dependent on the proper selection of the characters. So the dramatist follows certain well-defined principles for this purpose. The Greek philosopher, Aristotle has laid down some rules for the proper choice of characters. According to Aristotelian canon the hero of a tragedy should be a 'good' person. It means the hero of a play should be of an intermediate type of person. He should neither be 'too good' nor 'too bad'. Similarly, the heroine of a play should also be selected as per the demands of the plot. The hero and the heroine should belong to the royal families or to the upper strata of the society because the fall of such a person from happiness to misery would create the cathartic effect on the minds of the audience.

Diction

As is mentioned earlier that there should be a proper selection of the characters, similarly there should be a proper choice of the language to be used in a play. Language or the diction is *'the choice of words made by the playwright and enunciation of the actors delivering these words'*. The dramatist represents only the selected incidents and events from the lives of the characters in the form of dialogue and action. Therefore the language used in the play should be decorative, stylistic and becoming to the specific class to which the character belongs. It means a king should speak like a king and a clown should speak like a clown. Otherwise the audience will not believe in whatever is happening on the stage. Shakespeare has closely followed this principle in his plays. The characters belonging to the upper strata of the society in his plays mostly speak in verse and the characters from lower classes use prose. As every word in a play helps the playwright to further the action so the diction is very important substance of the play.

Subject or the Theme

The various events of the plot are held together by some central idea. This central idea is called the 'subject' or 'theme' of the play. If the theme of a play is noble and dignified, it will make the play great and successful. A great work of art comes into existence if the theme is noble and worthy of artistic treatment. And so the dramatist must deal with noble and dignified action. It is possible that some plays with a good plot may be having a little or no theme in them. Such plays may become temporarily successful with the audience. This success is short-lived as the audiences forget about the play after coming out of the theatre. Therefore along with a well-constructed plot, there should be a good theme in a play to make it universal.

Music

The dramatist is relied on music to create a specific effect on the audiences. Music means the sound, rhythm and melody of the speeches. The history of dramaturgy shows that the performances of the plays were accompanied by music produced by the musicians. But with the development in the field of science and technology, modern theatre has introduced the use of recorded sounds. The dramatist is now able to make the play more realistic by the use of a variety of recorded sounds like the sounds of animals, wind, storm, rain and lightning.

Spectacle

The element of spectacle is also enriched in the modern times. Spectacle means the visual elements of the production of a play. It includes the stage, furniture, scenery, costumes and curtains.

A costume means the different things which the actors use on their body. A costume includes clothing, wigs, and masks and make up. Costumes help the audience to understand about the time and the place of the action. A mask is a special element of costume. Though mask is rarely used in modern theatre, it was indispensable in ancient India. Makeup is sometimes used to exaggerate and distort facial features. It also helps to conceal the signs of age or the colour of face. The scenery is a special element of stage properties. Its elements are balcony, trapdoors, elevators, and gallery. In modern theatre, lighting is used very effectively. It helps the dramatist to control the focus of the audience and create specific mood.

MAJOR FORMS OF DRAMA

1. Miracles & Mystery Plays, Morality Plays and Interludes
2. Heroic, Revenge, Shakespearean & Sentimental Tragedies & Melodramas
3. Comedies
   - Classical Comedies
   - Tragi-Comedies
   - Romantic Comedies
   - Comedy of Humour
   - Comedy of Manners
   - The Farce
   - The Masque
4. The Poetic Play
5. The Dramatic Monologue
6. The Problem Play
7. The One-Act Play

MIRACLE & MYSTERY PLAYS, MORALITY PLAYS AND INTERLUDES

These are all types of late-medieval drama, written in a variety of verse forms.

Miracle & Mystery Plays

The miracle play had as its subject either a story from the Bible, or else the life and martyrdom of a saint. In the usage of some historians, however, "miracle play" denotes only dramas based on saints' lives, and the term mystery play is applied to dramas based on the Bible.

"Mystery" is used in the archaic sense (probably derived from the Latin *ministerium*, "work," "occupation") of the "trade" conducted by each of the medieval guilds which sponsored these plays.

The plays representing biblical narratives originated within the church in about the tenth century, in dramatizations of brief parts of the Latin liturgical service, called tropes, especially the "*Quem quaeritis*" ("Whom are you seeking") trope portraying the visit of the three Marys to the tomb of Christ. Gradually these evolved into complete plays which were written in English instead of in Latin, produced under the auspices of the various trade guilds, and acted on stages set outside the church. The miracle plays written in England are unknown authorship. In the fourteenth century there developed in cities such as York and Chester the practice, on the feast of Corpus Christi (sixty days after Easter), of putting on great "cycles" of such plays, representing crucial events in the biblical history of mankind from the Creation and Fall of man, through the Nativity, Crucifixion, and Resurrection of Christ, to the Last Judgement. The precise way that the plays were staged is a matter of scholarly debate, but it is widely agreed that each scene was played on a separate "pageant wagon" which was drawn, in sequence, to one after another fixed station in a city, at each of which some parts of the cycle were enacted. The biblical texts were greatly expanded in these plays, and the unknown authors added scenes, comic as well as serious, of their own invention. For examples of the variety, vitality, and power of these dramas, see the Wakefield "Noah" and "Second Shepherd's Play," and the Brome "Abraham and Isaac."

Morality Plays

Morality plays were dramatized *allegories* of a representative Christian life in the plot form of a quest for salvation, in which the crucial events are temptations, sinning, and the climactic confrontation with death. The usual protagonist represents Mankind, or Everyman; among the other characters are personifications of virtues, vices, and Death, as well as angles and demons who contest for the prize of the soul of Mankind. A character known as the Vice often played the role of the tempter in a fashion both sinister and comic; he is regarded by some literary historians as a precursor both of the cynical, ironic villain and of some of the comic figures in Elizabethan drama, including Shakespeare's *Falstaff*. The best-known morality play is the fifteenth-century *Everyman*, which is still given an occasional performance; other notable examples, written in the same century, are *The Castle of Perseverance and Mankind*.

Interludes

Interlude (Latin, "between the play") is a term applied to a variety of short stage entertainments, such as secular farces and witty dialogues with a religious or political point. In the late fifteenth and early sixteenth centuries, these little dramas were performed by bands of professional actors; it is believed that they were often put on between the courses of a feast or between the acts of a longer play. Among the better-known interludes are John Heywood's farces of the first half of the sixteenth century, especially The Four PP (that is, the Palmer, the Pardoner, the 'Pothecary, and the Peddler, who engage in a lying contest), and *Johan the Husband, Tyb His Wife, and Sir John the Priest*.

Until the middle of the twentieth century, concern with medieval drama was scholarly rather than critical. Since that time a number of studies have dealt with the relationships of the texts to the religious and secular culture of medieval Europe, and have stressed the artistic excellence and power of the plays themselves.

THE TRAGEDY

The history of drama shows that tragedy originated in religious festival of the Greek God, Dionysus in 6th century B.C. Etymologically the word 'tragedy' is derived from Greek word 'tragodi' meaning 'a goat song' It came to be used for plays probably because of the practice of sacrificing a goat during the festival of Dionysus. The other reason may be that the winner of the dramatic contest was given a goat as the award. To participate in the dramatic contest, the contestants were required to present a tetralogy of plays consisting of three tragedies and a satyr play. In ancient Greek literature the concept of tragedy is different from the modern concept. The modern tragedy is usually considered to as a play with unhappy ending. However, many of the Greek tragedies end on a happy note.

Tragedy is defined as "the imitation of an action, serious, complete and of a certain magnitude, in a language beautified in different parts with different kinds of embellishment, through action and not narration, and through scenes of pity and fear bringing about the catharsis of these or such like emotions".

Plato considers 'imitation' to be an act of mimicry. But Aristotle has given a new meaning to this term. For him imitation does not mean servile copying but an imaginative recreation. Aristotle says that imitation is the basic principle of all fine arts. Tragedy is distinguished from other fine arts according to the object, medium and manner of imitation. On the basis of objects of imitation, tragedy is distinguished from comedy. Tragedy imitates serious actions whereas comedy imitates the non-serious. So far as the medium of imitation is concerned, tragedy is distinguished from the lyric, as tragedy uses several kinds of embellishments. Tragedy is differentiated from epic on the basis of its manner of imitation, as tragedy represents through action whereas epic narrates.

Aristotle has used the term 'magnitude' for the length of the action of a tragedy. In this respect, usually the tragedy is compared with the human body. As too short or too tall human body does not look beautiful, similarly, too short or too long tragedy is not good. As a tragedy is performed on the stage within two or three hours, the dramatic action should not be too long as the audience will forget about the beginning before the dramatic action reaches to its end. It should not also be too short as it would not allow the writer to develop the essential aspects of the plot and characters.

Any dramatic action must have a beginning, middle and an end. A good beginning is the one which is not dependent on any of the previous situation and from which further action flows out. A good middle arises out of the events which have gone before and leads the action towards its logical and convincing conclusion. A good end is the natural outcome of whatever has gone before without leading the action any further.

The function of tragedy, like any other work of literature, is to 'delight' or to 'please'. While speaking about the function of a tragedy, Aristotle has used the term 'catharses'. But Aristotle has not defined 'catharsis' and so there are endless debates on the exact meaning of the term. Some scholars consider that 'catharsis' means purgation. According to the theory of purgation, the spectators in the theatre are relieved or cleansed or purged of the harmful emotions of pity and fear. According to the other group of scholars Catharsis is the resolution of dramatic tension, within the plot. It means in his play, the dramatist represents the incidents which arouse the emotions of pity and fear for the fate of the protagonist. During the course of the action, the dramatist resolves the conflicts which help him to take the action to its logical conclusion along with creating the emotions of pity and fear.

TYPES OF TRAGEDY

1. Heroic Tragedy
2. Revenge Tragedy
3. Shakespearean Tragedy
4. Sentimental Tragedy
5. Melodrama

Heroic Tragedy

The Heroic Tragedy is also known as the Restoration Tragedy. The influence of French romance and drama produced its first important result in the form of the heroic play.

The Heroic Tragedy is artificial. Its emotions are unreal. It mainly deals with conflict between love and honour.

John Dryden was the principal writer of the Heroic Tragedy. His famous tragedies are *Tyannic Love, Conquest of Granada* and *All for Love.* In Dryden's heroic plays we find a hero of superhuman powers and with superhuman ideals; there is a heroine of unsurpassed beauty and constancy; there is an inner conflict in the minds of several characters between love and honour; and there is a striving story of fighting and martial enthusiasm, filled with intense dramatic interest. *All For Love* is the finest tragedy of this period.

Another playwright was Thomas Otway. He wrote *Alcibiades, Don Carlos, The Orphan* and *Venice Preserved.*

Revenge Tragedy

The Revenge Tragedy genre of English literature generally refers to a body of dramatic works written from the mid-1580s to the early 1640s, from the Elizabethan to the Caroline period. Typically, these works feature such themes and devices as a wronged revenge-seeker, ghosts, madness, delay, sinister intrigue, a play-within-the-play, torture, multiple murders, and the realistic depiction of bloody violence on stage. Nearly all of the major playwrights of the time contributed to this class of drama, including Thomas Kyd, William Shakespeare, John Marston, George Chapman, Cyril Tourneur, Thomas Middleton, John Webster, James Shirley, and John Ford. Most literary scholars have credited Kyd with initiating the dramatic archetype with his *The Spanish Tragedy* (1585–90) and the so-called *Ur-Hamlet*—a drama no longer extant but which is believed to have been written before 1589, and upon which Shakespeare likely based his great tragedy—and have credited Shakespeare with bringing the genre to its artistic maturity with *Hamlet* (c. 1600-01). Critics have maintained that revenge tragedy was a markedly dynamic genre, observing that while Kyd invented the basic formula, his successors added ingenious new layers of dramatic suspense, characterization, symbolism, and ideological representation to the theatrical form.

Shakespearean Tragedy

Shakespeare wrote tragedies from the beginning of his career. One of his earliest plays was the Roman tragedy *Titus Andronicus*, which he followed a few years later with *Romeo and Juliet.* However, his most admired tragedies were written in a seven-year period between 1601 and 1608. These includes his four major tragedies *Hamlet, Othello, King Lear* and *Macbeth*, along with *Antony & Cleopatra, Coriolanus, Cymbeline, Julius Caesar* and the lesser-known *Timon of Athens* and *Troilus* and *Cressida.*

Shakespearean Tragedy is fundamentally serious, involving the downfall of a heroic figure. The themes are lofty: passion *(Romeo and Juliet),* revenge *(Hamlet),* ambition *(Macbeth)* and jealousy *(Othello).*

Unique elements of tragedy are the tragic hero who is an articulate, social authority, someone who is "important" within his society, this hero has at least one weakness or fault—a tragic flaw—which during the course of the drama grows until it overcomes his virtues and leads to his downfall and the destruction of his world; and chorus borrowed from Greek tragedy in which dancers/singers appear at intervals within the play to comment on the action—express objective judgement on the proceedings.

Sentimental Tragedy

While sentiment, in its modern sense, may be found in all forms of drama and theatre, Sentimental Drama was a specifically 18th century European form in which, as Oliver Goldsmith put it, "the virtues of private life are exhibited, rather than the vices exposed". "Sentiment" at this period meant "feeling" or "sensibility". While many of the plays were nominally comic, the characters tended to be dull and priggish, the plots bathetic and the language stilted. Despite this, it was popular with the rising middle-class audience, especially in Germany, France and Britain, because it tended to treat them seriously in ways which neither comedy nor tragedy did. For all its dramatic ineptness (at least from today's perspective) it is important in theatre-historical terms, as it marks an important stage in the development of serious prose drama.

In the English language, the most famous and most successful tragedies are those by William Shakespeare and his Elizabethan contemporaries.

A contemporary of Shakespeare, Christopher Marlowe, also wrote examples of tragedy in English, notably:

The Tragical History of Doctor Faustus; and *Tamburlaine*

John Webster also wrote famous plays of the genre: *The Duchess of Malfi* and *The White Devil.*

The Melodrama

Though the term "melodrama" is sometimes applied to the dramatic productions of a certain period, it also often designates a certain kind of literary structure.

Melodrama is the fantasy of a world that operates according to our heart's desires in contrast to the other formula types that are fantasies of particular actions or states of being that counter some of our deepest fears or concentrate on particular wishes for victory or love or knowledge. Therefore, melodrama can contain all the other fantasies and often does. In fact, its chief characteristic is the combination of a number of actions and settings in order to build up the sense of a whole world bearing out the audience's traditional patterns of right and wrong, good and evil.

One thing possessed in common by these otherwise very different sorts of stories is the quality that has traditionally been understood as the hallmark of melodrama: the drama of intensified effects (i.e., music, "melos") added to the play to increase its emotional power and intensify its hold on the audience. Therefore, the idea of melodrama has come to be associated with violence and sensationalism— "the plot revolves around malevolent intrigue and violent action, while credibility both of character and plot is sacrificed for violent effect and emotional opportunism." This is undoubtedly one major characteristic of melodrama, but the quest for intensified narrative or dramatic effects is characteristic of the entire range of formulaic types. Particular formulas come into existence and flourish at least in part because they invent heightened narrative or dramatic patterns. In this sense all formulaic stories are melodramatic, and we might look at the various formulaic types—adventure, romance, and mystery—as simply specialized forms of melodrama. Indeed, many of the modern specialized formulas such as the classical detective story, the spy story, the hard-boiled detective story, and the gothic romance did evolve historically from the broader melodramatic forms of the early nineteenth century.

The specific formulas that depend on the basic moral fantasy of melodrama are many and various. Some of the more important contemporary examples are the best-selling panoramic social novel such as those written by Irving Wallace, Harold Robbins, and Jacqueline Susann, the historical spectacle such as *Gone with the Wind,* the soap opera, the gangster saga, the professional drama such as the doctor, lawyer, or teacher story, and many others. Though extremely various in the cultural materials they employ, all these formulas are shaped by the basic qualities of melodrama: the heightening of feeling and moral conflict and multiple lines of action that work together to create a sense of the rightness of the world order.

Some important examples of melodramas are:

John Fletcher's *The Maid's Tragedy;* John Webster's *The White Devil;* John Ford's *The Broken Heart;* Thomas Heywood's *A Woman Killed with Kindness;* Francis Beaumont's *A King and No King.*

THE COMEDY

Comedy may be considered to be a representation of the character of a lower type. Here 'lower' means 'ridiculous.' By presenting the character in a ridiculous manner, the writer of a comedy aims at producing laughter. Though the genre of comedy is practiced since the ancient times with the practitioners like Aristophanes and Plautus, the scholars have not paid enough attention towards the serious study of its nature and function. While speaking about the function of comedy, George Meredith says that comedy appeals to the intelligence pure and simple and aims not at our ribs or armpits but at our heads. It means, it is the business of a comedy writer to look on what ails the world. He observes his environment minutely and fids out its follies and exposes them. But while exposing those follies, the purpose of the writer is to 'correct' or 'reform' those follies. Some scholars are of the opinion that the function of a comedy is not 'to reform' or 'to correct' the follies of the world bur to provide light-hearted mirth. But while creating mirth, the comedian encourages the audience to laugh with not laugh at the follies of the world. Such kind of play is purely meant for the entertainment of the audience.

Comedies are of following types:

1. Classical Comedies
2. Tragi-Comedies
3. Romantic Comedies
4. Comedy of Humour
5. Comedy of Manners
6. The Farce
7. The Masque

The Classical Comedy

This type of comedy is written as per the rules laid down by the ancient Greek and Roman masters. The function of such a comedy is 'corrective' or 'reformative'. In this comedy some human folly is exposed and ridiculed. It follows the rules of three unities—unity of time, place and action. The writer of this comedy strictly avoids the mingling of comic with tragic.

The Tragi-Comedy

In understanding about tragi-comedy, one finds oneself in the position of the proverbial blind philosophers attempting to identify an elephant. The individual who gets hold of its trunk thinks it is a snake, he who grasps its tail supposes it a rope, while she who clasps one of its legs believes it to be a tree. A.E. Housman commented in the essay "the legitimate meanings of the word poetry were themselves so many as to embarrass the discussion of its nature." The same is true to a lesser degree of the word *tragi-comedy*. The nature of tragicomedy is difficult to define because its name has been used so variously since Plautus first coined the term as a joke in his *Amphitryon* and because the dramatic genre tragi-comedy can comprise so many different modes (romantic, satiric, pastoral, melodramatic, and so on, as well as, indispensably, tragic and comic).

This play is a combination of the elements of both the comedy and the tragedy. Naturally, the play ends on a happy note for some characters and on a sad note for the others. Shakespeare is a famous practitioner of this kind of play. Though Aristotle had opposed the mingling of the tragic with the comic, scholars like John Dryden and Dr. Samuel Johnson have defended this type of play by saying that it is nearer to the human life. These critics argue that as the life itself is a combination of happy and sad events there is no harm in combining them in plays. Shakespeare's well-known tragi-comedies are *The Winter's Tale, The Merchant of Venice* and *The Tempest*.

The study of genre, despite recurring critical objections, continues to be indispensable to the study of drama in particular. Genre is not simply a matter of definition or classification. Rather, genre communicates; genre enables comprehension and conditions response. As Tzvetan Todorov explains, "It is because genres exist as an institution that they function as 'horizons of expectation' for readers and as 'models of writing' for authors." And Marco De Marinis, writing of performance, similarly observes, "By supplying the receiver with intertextual schemas and systems of expectation, *genre* (in its widely accepted analytical and descriptive meaning as a 'class of texts with specific co-textual and/or contextual traits in common') plays a crucial role in the process of textual comprehension and interpretation."

Dramatic genres in particular are modes of perception, conveying attitudes to human experience, as much as they are formal categories.

Although tragi-comedy is an especially slippery genre, there is actually a good deal of critical agreement (among those critics who recognize it as a genre at all) as to which plays constitute its major achievements. Differences of opinion arise inevitably and properly at the edges of the genre. The familiar central examples of the genre range from *Il Pastor Fido, The Malcontent, Measure for Measure, The Winter's Tale, A King and No King,* and *A Wife for a Month* to *The Wild Duck, The Cherry Orchard, The Playboy of the Western World, The Killer, Waiting for Godot, and No Man's Land*. Within each of these two groups, however, the plays seem in many respects quite unlike one another, and the modern tragi-comedies appear superficially to have little in common with those written in the sixteenth and early seventeenth centuries.

The Romantic Comedy

Romantic comedy is a popular genre that depicts burgeoning romance in human terms, and focuses on the foibles of those who are falling in love.

Comedy as a whole has rarely been seen as being as critically respectable as other genres; perhaps it is rather a self-defeating paradox to ask for it to be taken seriously. Even Shakespeare's comedies seem to be critically overshadowed by the tragedies, perhaps diminished by the foregrounding of characters who are not heroic or noble, and themes that concern issues that can be found in everyday life, such as love and relationships, rather than elemental issues of life, death, good and evil. The most respected romcoms are those associated with artistic figures that are respected as auteurs.

Romantic comedy has proved to be one of the most enduring genres. It has certainly undergone some ebbs and flows in its popularity, but, as with all the major genres, it proves perennially resilient. Audiences still enjoy the blueprint of the romantic comedy, with all its traditional ingredients. Every year sees the release of new romantic comedies, which are strongly in the mould of the earliest examples in history. We want to see the same characters, the same situations, the same narrative trajectory, the same settings and dialogue, with new stars that speak to new generations, yet tell the same story.

Romantic comedy does not follow the rules of writing a comedy laid down by the ancient classical writers. The writer freely mingles the comic with the tragic. The unities of time, place and action are modified as per the requirements of the plot. The aim of such a comedy is 'to produce innocent, good-natured laughter, thereby entertaining the audience without trying to teach anything.

Shakespearean Comedy

Shakespeare is a great writer of comedies. His comedies are called romantic or sunny comedies. With the help of his creative imagination, Shakespeare creates a brilliant world of romance which is far away from the drab realities of the everyday life. These comedies are usually set in some distant, far-off places, where the inhabitants have no other business but that of love-making. The lovers of a Shakespearean comedy fall in love at first sight and get married at the end. But the course of their love is always full of difficulties. There are made a lot of misunderstandings, family feuds, tears and sighs. Shakespeare forces his lovers to face these difficulties in order to test their love for each other. But ultimately, these lovers are helped to overcome these difficulties but the intervention of Goddess Fortune. Then comes the Goddess Marriage who unites the lovers in the bond of marriage followed by music, dance and merry-making.

The Comedy of Humours

A type of comedy developed by Ben Jonson, the Elizabethan playwright, based on the ancient physiological theory of the "four humours" that was still current in Jonson's time. The humours were held to be the four primary fluids—blood, phlegm, choler (or yellow bile), and melancholy (or black bile)—whose "temperament" (mixture) was held to determine a person's both physical condition and type of character. An imbalance of one or another humour in a temperament was said to produce four kinds of disposition, whose names have survived the underlying theory: sanguine (from the Latin "sanguis," blood), phlegmatic, choleric, and melancholic. In Jonshon's comedy of humours each of the major characters has a preponderant humour that gives him a characteristic distortion or eccentricity of disposition. Jonson expounds his theory in the "induction" to his play *Every Man in His Humour* (1598) and exemplifies the mode in his later comedies; often he identifies the ruling disposition of a humours character by his or her name: "Zeal-of-the-land Busy," "Dame Purecraft," "Wellbred." The Jonsonian type of humours character appears in plays by other Elizabethans, and remained influential in the *comedies of manners* by William Wycherley, Sir George Etheredge, William Congreve, and other dramatists of the English Restoration, 1660–1700.

The characters in a Comedy of Humour represent some 'humour'. The actions and behaviour of the characters are governed by some kind of passion. As the characters represent some typical trait, there is a lack of individuality in them. Rather they become stereotypes. Generally, these characters are taken from low life. The purpose of the writer of such a comedy is to satirize the follies of the characters and correct them.

The Comedy of Manners

A kind of comedy representing the complex and sophisticated code of behaviour current in fashionable circles of society, where appearances count for more than true moral character. Its plot usually revolves around intrigues of lust and greed, the self-interested cynicism of the characters being masked by decorous pretence. Unlike satire, the comedy of manners tends to reward its cleverly unscrupulous characters rather than punish their immorality. Its humour relies chiefly upon elegant verbal wit and repartee. In England, the comedy of manners flourished as the dominant form of Restoration comedy in the works of Sir George Etherege, William Wycherley (notably *The Country Wife*, 1675), and William Congreve; it was revived in a more subdued form in the 1770s by Goldsmith and Sheridan, and later by Oscar Wilde. Modern examples of the comedy of manners include Noël Coward's Design for living (1932) and Joe Orton's *Loot* (1965).

The Comedy of Manners is also called Restoration Comedy. It focuses upon the mannerism of the upper classes of the society. The characters of this comedy belong to the upper class. Here the dramatist represents a fashionable men and women, with their manners, love-intrigues, scandals and affectations. These comedies attempt to imitate everything refined. So anything coarse or low is strictly avoided.

The language of such a comedy is very witty and refined. The focus of the dramatist is not on the 'individuality' of the character but on its manners, so the characters become lifeless. This type of comedy was very famous during the Restoration period with the writers like William Congreve, William Wycherley and Oliver Goldsmith practicing it.

The Farce

This was another popular form of theatre in France (and England) in the 19th century. Farce consists of unsubtle physical and verbal comedy. It flourishes in a moral community because it is anarchical, relying on overturning widely accepted values. The chief characteristics of farce are sexual misadventure, flirtation, verbal abuse and comic despair, which frequently lead to instant decisions and spontaneous action.

The most prolific and famous French farce writers were Feydeau (1862–1921) and Labiche (1815–1888). Labiche wrote nearly sixty plays and helped write about 100 others. Not surprisingly, the plays lack originality and concentrate on reworking old jokes. His most famous is *An Italian Straw Hat* (1851).

Feydeau was the originator of bedroom farces, the descendants of which can still be seen occasionally in London today.

Feydeau's middle period plays are the archetype of French farce. The principal characters are Parisian bourgeois, their major driving force is extra-connubial lust, and the basic source of the humour is their ever more desperate attempts to avoid being found out. Although no respectable married woman is ever seduced by her husband's best friend, it is not for want of trying on either side. The plots seem to have been constructed by a mad watchmaker, but the status quo is always restored at the end.

A farce is a comedy that focuses on physical humour. The dramatist aims at creating hilarious laughter by representing absurd characters and situations on the stage. To create his characters and situations, the dramatist makes use of exaggeration and extravagance. Exaggerated characters and situations, improbable coincidences, mistaken identities and miscommunication are the common techniques used by the writers to make his plot more complicated. All these instruments enable the dramatist to entertain his audience in the most direct way.

The Masque

Form of dramatic entertainment popular with the French and English aristocracy of the sixteenth and seventeenth centuries. Developed in Renaissance Italy, the masque was probably an evolution of primitive folk rituals. When adopted by court circles, it became a lavish spectacle, usually based on a mythological theme and involving elaborate costumes and stage machinery. Essentially it was a theatrical performance by a group of disguised guests (hence the name) who, arriving at a banquet, offered the host an entertainment of dances, poetry and music.

The characters in a masque wear some masks on their faces. Initially, a masque was a series of dances, illustrating some story, but afterwards it developed into a play. The writer of a masque chooses his characters and story from mythology. These masques were written to be performed on some private occasions by a limited number of characters. There is abundant use of music, dance, costly costumes and elaborate scenery.

The masque first appeared in the fifteenth century when Lorenzo de' Medici adapted the seasonal revels of the Florentines into sophisticated displays of art and poetry for the delight of his guests. In the French court these displays evolved into the *ballet de cour* and *the mascarade*. A form of the masque was brought to England in 1512 by Henry VIII, who liked to disguise himself as a player and pretend to be an uninvited guest at his own parties. Henry's daughter Elizabeth added the spoken introduction, which, with the inclusion of speeches and elements of court drama, was developed into a unified dramatic performance in the hands of Ben Jonson, who became court poet of the Stuarts in 1603. Until his time the main feature of the masque was the dance and revel, which the audience was invited to join. Under Jonson's influence the masque became a literary form, a dramatic poem of classical scholarship. Jonson also introduced the antimasque, so called because it preceded the main masque and because it included grotesque or comic elements in contrast, yet relevant, to the serious main masque. Jonson's influence was eventually eclipsed by his sometime collaborator and rival Inigo Jones, the architect and scenic designer, to whom theatrical spectacle was more important than literary content. It was Jones who thought of placing the layers on a raised stage and who eventually, by his attentions to spectacle rather than content, effected the deterioration of the masque as a dramatic form.

A courtly rather than a popular entertainment, the masque disappeared with the Puritan revolution of the 1640s. When the theatres reopened in 1660, however, scenic designers, playwrights, and actors took their principal inspiration not from the Elizabethan stage but from the masques of the court festivals.

THE POETIC PLAY

Poetic drama is not merely a drama which is written in verse, because prose may also be its effective medium. It is, in fact, a blending of the poetic and dramatic elements in a fruitful union. Here poetry is an integral part of the play, twined with plot, character and their interplay, not an element of isolated beauty or lyricism for its own sake, as is the case with splendid lyricism in some parts of Marlowe's *Dr. Faustus*, for example. At the same time the dramatic elements must be capable of sustaining the poetic grace and intensity. It means its themes and characters should be poetically convinced and should be larger than the average humanity and humdrum monotony of daily life, the passions and emotions permeating them should be naturally productive of the poetic expression, calculated to lift the mind of the spectator above the sphere of our ordinary joys and sorrows and send the penetrating gaze of his inner vision far down below the surface of life to the very springs of human action and human drives. Moreover, drama being so intimately bound up with the stage condition and the historic skill its practitioner must combine mastery over the poetic resources, with a real understanding of the peculiar needs and modes of the dramatic representation in the theatre. The history of the poetic drama in England is littered with the frozen anatomies of poetic plays written by the distinguished poets of the nineteenth century who failed to subordinate poetry to the general dramatic spirit and adapt the plays to the conditions and requirements of the stage.

Poetic drama reached its glorious peak in Elizabethan England when the general conditions of society and richness of language combined with the whole nation's insatiable craving for amusement and edification and the writer's intimacy with the theater to make the stage a national institution. But the glory did not last long and its decline was precipitated by the victory of the puritan fanaticism which sounded its death-knell. When it was revived again in the Restoration era, the conditions had changed and the heroic tragedy in rhyming couplet was simply the fury and the violence of its ghost. A sort of artificial respiration was given to it is the blank-verse tragedies which followed. They, however, failed to sustain its life and with one flash of life in Otway's *Venice Preserved* it gave up the ghost.

The nineteenth century efforts by the great poets were splendid failures on the big commercial stage, for which the writers themselves were partly to blame because they could not rise above the slavish imitation and adaptation of the Elizabethan blank-verse tragedy to re-orient the poetic drama to changed conditions of society and the taste and sensibility of the spectators. This was the condition when the present century opened with the prospect of a great dramatic Renaissance.

THE DRAMATIC MONOLOGUE

In theatre, a monologue (or monolog) is a speech presented by a single character, most often to express their thoughts aloud, though sometimes also to directly address another character or the audience. Monologues are common across the range of dramatic media (plays, films, etc.) as well as in non-dramatic media such as poetry. Monologues share much in common with several other literary devices including soliloquies, apostrophes, and asides. There are, however, distinctions between each of these devices.

One of the most important influences on the development of the dramatic monologue is the Romantic poets. The long, personal lyrics typical of the Romantic period are not dramatic monologues, in the sense that they do not, for the most part, imply a concentrated narrative. However, poems such as William Wordsworth's *Tintern Abbey* and Percy Bysshe Shelley's Mont Blanc, to name two famous examples, offered a model of close psychological observation and philosophical or pseudo-philosophical inquiry described in a specific setting.

The novel and plays have also been important influences on the dramatic monologue, particularly as a means of characterization. Dramatic monologues are a way of expressing the views of a character and offering the audience greater insight into that character's feelings. Dramatic monologues can also be used in novels to tell stories, as in Mary Shelley's Frankenstein, and to implicate the audience in moral judgments, as in Albert Camus' *The Fall* and Mohsin Hamid's *The Reluctant Fundamentalist.*

Monologues are also linked with soliliquys—such as in *Macbeth,* when Lady Macbeth reads a letter to herself and then speaks her thoughts as though she is thinking.

The Victorian Period

The Victorian period represented the high point of the dramatic monologue in English poetry.

Alfred, Lord Tennyson's *Ulysses,* published in 1842, has been called the first true dramatic monologue. After *Ulysses,* Tennyson's most famous efforts in this vein are Tithonus, *The Lotos-Eaters*, and St. Simon Stylites, all from the 1842 poems; later monologues appear in other volumes, notably *Idylls of the King*.

Matthew Arnold's *Dover Beach* and Stanzas from the *Grand Chartreuse* are famous, semi-autobiographical monologues. The former, usually regarded as the supreme expression of the growing skepticism of the mid-Victorian period, was published along with the later in 1867's New Poems.

Robert Browning is usually credited with perfecting the form; certainly, Browning is the poet who, above all, produced his finest and most famous work in this form. While *My Last Duchess* is the most famous of his monologues, the form dominated his writing career. Fra Lippo Lippi, Caliban upon Setebos, Soliloquy of the Spanish Cloister and Porphyria's Lover, as well as the other poems in *Men and Women* are just a handful of Browning's monologues.

Other Victorian poets also used the form. Dante Gabriel Rossetti wrote several, including *Jenny* and *The Blessed Damozel;* Christina Rossetti wrote a number, including *The Convent Threshold.* Algernon Charles Swinburne's *Hymn to Proserpine* has been called a dramatic monologue vaguely reminiscent of Browning's work.

THE PROBLEM PLAY

The "problem play" idea has sometimes helpfully, sometimes dubiously informed discussion of Shakespeare's plays, and though, along with much genre criticism, it has gone out of fashion now, it has figured periodically in the scholarship that helps us understand how the plays work technically. Problem play as a term has aroused debate because in some ways it may seem to solve nothing: it leaves us with only a question about a play's genre, not with even a tentative guideline for reading such as we get from calling a work comedy or tragedy.

As Harold Goddard wrote, we can find "nothing to indicate that Shakespeare's imagination ever allowed itself to be shackled by such prescriptions or definitions"; one of the few points that caused audiences of his own time to question his skills, his freedom with respect to Classical "rules" or transgressing genre expectations, allowed him to create plays that beg irresolution and thus continued meditation from his audiences.

The term problem play comes from F.S. Boas in Shakespeare and His Predecessors in 1896 (printed in the U.S. in New York by Charles Scribner's Sons, 1900): Boas used it to label those plays (such as *Measure for Measure, All's Well That Ends Well,* and *The Merchant of Venice*) that foreground perhaps unsolvable moral problems. More recently critics have used the term to indicate plays that defy easy categorization by genre, or literary type. Genre, a term that applies largely to the form and partly to the content of an artistic work (as in comedy, tragedy, epic, or novel), has much to do with how we read or view a work: if we attend a comedy or tragedy, we go with expectations about how we will find the work presented and how it will end. So criticism had already problematized problem play itself, since different critics have used it with different notions in mind. But it remains useful, because it directs our attention to an immediate interpretive difficulty that we experience as soon as we study particular plays. The idea of the problem play applies to nearly all of Shakespeare's plays: what we call them does make a difference in how we read and interpret and play them, since labels (like titles) guide audience expectations and invoke interpretive strategies.

THE ONE-ACT PLAY

In October 1909, when Strindberg wrote a brief preface to then unpublished *Författaren* (The Author), the fourth volume of his autobiography *Tjänstekvinnans son* (1886), he listed among his most important (viktigaste) works the one-act plays of the early 1890s as "one-actors out of cynical life." The item included The First Warning, Debit and Credit, Facing Death, Mother Love, Playing with Fire, and The Bond. He might just as well have included three one-act plays from the late 1880s: *The Stronger, Pariah,* and *Simoon.* All nine are short, stageworthy one-act plays; all were designed for production in experimental theaters; and all are interpretations of human situations from a cynical point of view.

Strindberg's hope of having a theater in which his plays would be produced seemed to have a chance of realization in the late 1880s in Copenhagen but did not materialize until the Intimate Theater opened in Stockholm in 1907. He had written his great plays—*The Father* (1887), *Lady Julie* (1888), and *Creditors* (1888)—deliberately as what might very well be segments of actual life with increasing emphasis on universal themes, avoidance of distracting factors such as intermissions, and simplification of staging. The one-act plays listed above are essentially further extensions of his "attempts to transform drama into a form suitable for the time". They deal, moreover, with universal and timeless themes. The very brevity of these plays precludes examination in appreciable depth as in the longer plays of 1887 and 1888, but they have enough detail to provide audience and reader with material for creative participation and involvement. In each there is enough irritating matter to arouse reaction and to stimulate discussion.

The human situations presented are surely typical: people's willingness to claim credit for a fellow human being's success, a mother's manipulation of her daughter's life, a wife's indifference to her mate except when others obviously want him, denigration of a mate for one's own purposes, indifference to and rationalization of one's sins, playing with one's own and other's emotions, and the unhesitating destruction of a fellow human being at least partly in the name of religion.

NON-FICTION OR PROSE

Non-Fiction is prose writing that presents and explains ideas or that tells about real people, places, objects, or events. It is an account or representation of a subject which is presented as fact. This presentation may be accurate or not; that is, it can give either a true or a false account of the subject in question. However, it is generally assumed that the authors of such accounts believe them to be truthful at the time of their composition. Autobiographies biographies, essays, reports, letters, memos, and newspaper articles are all types of non-fiction.

Characteristics of Non-Fiction (Prose)

Works of non-fiction differ from works of fiction in several ways.

- The people, events, places, and ideas presented in nonfiction are real, not invented.
- Non-fiction is narrated by an author who is a real person.
- It presents facts, describes true-life experience, or discusses ideas.
- Non-fiction is written for a specific audience, or group of readers. In addition, it addresses a clear purpose, or reason for writing. The audience and purpose influence the type of information a writer includes.
- Tone, the author's attitude toward the subject or reader, is displayed through the writer's word choice and style.

The writer contributes more than informal to non-fiction.

- Style is the particular way in which a writer uses language. Style reflects an author's personality. Factors that contribute to an author's style include level of formality, use of figurative language, diction or word choice, sentence patterns, and methods of organization.
- Tone is the author's attitude toward both the subject and readers or listeners. In conversations, you can hear a speaker's tone in the way words and phrases are spoken. When reading, you can "hear" tone in an author's choice of words and details. The tone of a literary work can often be described with a single word such as: pompous, playful, serious, personal, sarcastic, or friendly.
- Perspective is the viewpoint or opinion an author expresses about the subject, either directly or indirectly. Bias occurs when a writer makes a one-sided presentation (for example, by ignoring relevant facts or by using emotional language that unfairly sways readers' or listeners' feelings).
- Purpose is the author's reason for writing. Common purposes are to inform, to persuade, to honour, to entertain, to explain, and to warn.

Types of Non-Fiction (Prose)

There are four main types, or modes, of non-fiction that are defined by their purposes.

- Narrative non-fiction tells stories of real-life events. Examples include autobiographies and memoirs. Some narrative non-fiction is reflective writing, which shares the writer's thoughts and feelings about a personal experience, an idea, or a concern. Examples include reflective essays, personal essays, and journals.
- Expository non-fiction informs or explains. Examples include analytical essays and research reports.
- Persuasive non-fiction presents reasons and evidence to convince the reader to act or think in a certain way. Examples include editorials and political speeches.
- Descriptive non-fiction uses details related to the senses to create mental images for the reader. Examples include character sketches and scientific observations.

NON-FICTION OR PROSE AND ITS MAJOR FORMS

The following are the Major Forms of Prose :

1. Long Prose-Works
2. The Essay
3. The Periodical Journals
4. The Biography
5. The Autobiography
6. The Memoirs

LONG PROSE-WORKS

In its ordinary and practical sense, Prose is the sustained use of language as we ordinary speak it. Prose is different from verse in the sense that it is not split up into meter or stanza forms like the verse. However, the lack of meter does not mean that prose has no art or aesthetic sense. The writing of distinguished prose has as much art as the writing of distinguished verse. In all literatures, written prose developed much later than written verse. Good prose has high aesthetic value, and it can fully make use of all figures of speech. Good prose can also have high poetic cadence too, as the prose of the Bible.

Many forms of literature are normally written in prose only. They include long social, religious, scientific, or metaphysical treatises, essays, prose romances, novels, short stories, biographies, autobiographies, memoirs, travelogues, adventures and literary criticism.

Many great authors wrote long prose-works even before the Age of Chaucer. They included long religious, metaphysical, political, and biographical treatises and prose-romances. The trend has come down ever since to the present day.

Some Examples of the great prose-works are:

Chaucer's : *The Treatise on the Astrolabe,*

Wyclif's : *The Bible,*

and Walter Pater's : *Renaissance*

THE ESSAY

An essay is generally a short piece of writing written from an author's personal point of view, but the definition is vague, overlapping with those of an article, a pamphlet and a short story.

Essays can consist of a number of elements, including: literary criticism, political manifestos, learned arguments, observations of daily life, recollections, and reflections of the author. Almost all modern essays are written in prose, but works in verse have been dubbed essays (e.g. Alexander Pope's *An Essay on Criticism* and *An Essay on Man*). While brevity usually defines an essay, voluminous works like John Locke's *An Essay Concerning Human Understanding* and Thomas Malthus's *An Essay on the Principle of Population* are counter examples.

THE PERIODICAL JOURNALS

A journal has several related meanings: a daily record of events or business; a private journal is usually referred to as a diary, a newspaper or other periodical, in the literal sense of one published each day many publications issued at stated intervals, such as magazines, or scholarly journals, academic journals, or the record of the transactions of a society, are often called journals. Although journal is sometimes used as a synonym for "magazine" in academic use, a journal refers to a serious, scholarly publication that is peer-reviewed. A non-scholarly magazine written for an educated audience about an industry or an area of professional activity is usually called a professional magazine.

The word "journalist", for one whose business is writing for the public press and nowadays also other media, has been in use since the end of the 17th century.

THE BIOGRAPHY

A biography or simply bio is a detailed description or account of a person's life. It entails more than basic facts like education, work, relationships, and death—a biography also portrays a subject's experience of these events. Unlike a profile or curriculum vitae (résumé), a biography presents a subject's life story, highlighting various aspects of his or her life, including intimate details of experience, and may include an analysis of the subject's personality.

Biographical works are usually non-fiction, but fiction can also be used to portray a person's life. One in-depth form of biographical coverage is called legacy writing. Works in diverse media—from literature to film—form the genre known as biography.

An authorized biography is written with the permission, cooperation, and at times, participation of a subject or a subject's heirs.

THE AUTOBIOGRAPHY

An autobiography is a written account of the life of a person written by that person. An autobiography is written by the person themselves or sometimes with the assistance of a collaborator or ghostwriter.

THE MEMOIRS

Memoir (from French: *mémoire: memoria*, meaning memory or reminiscence), is a literary non-fiction genre. More specifically, it is a collection of memories that an individual writes about moments or events, both public or private that took place in the author's life. The assertions made in the work are understood to be factual. While memoir has historically been defined as a subcategory of autobiography since the late 20th century, the genre is differentiated in form, presenting a narrowed focus. Like most autobiographies, memoirs are written from the first-person point of view. An autobiography tells the story of a life, while memoir tells a story from a life, such as touchstone events and turning points from the author's life. The author of a memoir may be referred to as a memoirist.

POETRY

A poem is a literary composition that is given intensity by particular attention to diction (sometimes involving rhyme), rhythm, and imagery. Poems, collectively are called poetry.

As writing poetry is an art, reading poetry also is an art. We cannot enjoy reading anything without understanding it. And understanding poetry requires a special taste and aesthetic sense. Poetry is the language of heart. It flows from heart to heart.

POETRY AND ITS MAJOR FORMS

Poetry and its Major Forms are these :

1. The Epic
2. The Mock Epic
3. The Sonnet
4. The Ode
5. The Lyric
6. The Idyll
7. The Pastoral
8. The Elegy
9. The Pastoral Elegy
10. The Ballad
11. The Satire

THE EPIC

An epic (from the Ancient Greek adjective "word, story, poem" is a lengthy narrative poem, ordinarily concerning a serious subject containing details of heroic deeds and events significant to a culture or nation. Oral poetry may qualify as an epic, and Albert Lord and Milman Parry have argued that classical epics were fundamentally an oral poetic form. Nonetheless, epics have been written down at least since the works of Virgil, Dante Alighieri, and John Milton. Many probably would not have survived if not written down. The first epics are known as primary, or original, epics. One such epic is the Old English story Beowulf. Epics that attempt to imitate these like Milton's *Paradise Lost* are known as literary, or secondary, epics. Another type of epic poetry is epyllion (plural: epyllia), which is a brief narrative poem with a romantic or mythological theme. The term, which means 'little epic', came into use in the nineteenth century. It refers primarily to the erudite, shorter hexameter poems of the Hellenistic period and the similar works composed at Rome from the age of the neoterics; to a lesser degree, the term includes some poems of the English Renaissance, particularly those influenced by Ovid. The most famous example of classical epyllion is perhaps *Catullus 64*.

In the East, the most famous works of epic poetry are the *Ramayana* and *Mahabharata*, with the *Iliad* and the *Odyssey*, which form part of the Western canon, fulfilling the same function in the Western world.

Oral epics or world folk epics

The first epics were products of preliterate societies and oral poetic traditions. In these traditions, poetry is transmitted to the audience and from performer to performer by purely oral means.

Early twentieth-century study of living oral epic traditions in the Balkans by Milman Parry and Albert Lord demonstrated the paratactic model used for composing these poems. What they demonstrated was that oral epics tend to be constructed in short episodes, each of equal status, interest and importance. This facilitates memorization, as the poet is recalling each episode in turn and using the completed episodes to recreate the entire epic as he performs it.

THE MOCK EPIC

A poem which deals with slight and trivial subjects but employs the elevated and dignified conventions of epic poetry. Thus, such a poem becomes a satire, a mockery, a burlesque at the inconsistency of the subject to its representation. The characteristic conventions of the epic poetry, such as invocations, epic similes, grand and elevated language, battles and supernatural machinery, are comically used in mock-epic, which make the trivial subject ridiculous. A few well-known examples are Alexander Pope's *Rape of the Lock*, Jonathan Swift's *Battle of the Books*, Pope's *The Dunciad*, Chaucer's *The Nun's Priest's Tale* and Boileau's" *Le Lutrin* (French).

THE SONNET

A sonnet is a form of poetry that originated in Europe, mainly Italy: the Sicilian poet Giacomo da Lentini is credited with its invention. They commonly contain 14 lines. The term "sonnet" derives only from the Occitan word *sonet* and the Italian word *sonetto*, both meaning "little song" or "little sound". By the thirteenth century, it signified a poem of fourteen lines that follows a strict rhyme scheme and specific structure. Conventions associated with the sonnet have evolved over its history. Writers of sonnets are sometimes called "sonneteers," although the term can be used derisively. One of the best-known sonnet writers is William Shakespeare, who wrote 154 of them (not including those that appear in his plays). A Shakespearean, or English sonnet consists of 14 lines, each line containing ten syllables and written in iambic pentameter, in which a pattern of an unstressed syllable followed by a stressed syllable is repeated five times. The rhyme scheme in a Shakespearean sonnet is a-b-a-b, c-d-c-d, e-f-e-f, g-g; the last two lines are a rhyming couplet.

Traditionally, English poets employ iambic pentameter when writing sonnets, but not all English sonnets have the same metrical structure: the first sonnet in Sir Philip Sidney's sequence *Astrophel and Stella*, for example, has 12 syllables: it is iambic hexameters, albeit with a turned first foot in several lines. In the Romance languages, the hendecasyllable and Alexandrine are the most widely used metres.

THE ODE

Ode (from the Ancient Greek is a type of lyrical verse. A classic ode is structured in three major parts: the strophe, the antistrophe, and the epode. Different forms such as the homostrophic ode and the irregular ode also exist. It is an elaborately structured poem praising or glorifying an event or individual, describing nature intellectually as well as emotionally.

Greek odes were originally poetic pieces accompanied by symphonic orchestras. As time passed on, they gradually became known as personal lyrical compositions whether sung (with or without musical instruments) or merely recited (always with accompaniment). For some, the primary instrument of choice was either the aulos or the lyre (the latter of which was the most revered instrument to the Ancient Greeks). The written ode, as it was practiced by the Romans, returned to the lyrical form of the Lesbian lyricists.

There are three typical forms of odes: the Pindaric, Horatian, and irregular. Pindaric odes follow the form and style of Pindar. Horatian odes follow conventions of Horace; the odes of Horace deliberately imitated the Greek lyricists such as Alcaeus and Anacreon. Odes by Catullus, as well as other poetry of Catullus, was particularly inspired by Sappho. Irregular odes are rhyming, but they do not employ the three-part form of the Pindaric ode nor the two- or four-line stanza of the Horatian ode.

English ode

An ode is typically a lyrical verse written in praise of, or dedicated to someone or something which captures the poet's interest or serves as an inspiration for the ode.

The initial model for English odes was Horace, who used the form to write meditative lyrics on various themes. The earliest odes in the English language, using the word in its strict form, were the Epithalamium and Prothalamium of Edmund Spenser.

In the 17th century the most important original odes in English are those of Abraham Cowley and Andrew Marvell. Marvell, in his Horatian Ode upon Cromwell's Return from Ireland uses a regular form (two four-foot lines followed by two three-foot lines) modelled on Horace, while Cowley wrote *"Pindarique"* odes which had irregular patterns of line lengths and rhyme schemes, though they were iambic. The principle of Cowley's *Pindariques* was based on a misunderstanding of Pindar's metrical practice but was widely imitated nonetheless, with notable success by John Dryden. With Pindar's metre being better understood in the 18th century, the fashion for Pindaric odes faded, though there are notable actual Pindaric odes by Thomas Gray, *The Progress of Poesy* and *The Bard.*

The Pindarick of Cowley was revived around 1800 by William Wordsworth for one of his very finest poems, the Intimations of Immortality ode; irregular odes were also written by Samuel Taylor Coleridge, John Keats, and Percy Bysshe Shelley who wrote odes with regular stanza patterns. Shelley's *Ode to the West Wind*, written in fourteen line terza rima stanzas, is a major poem in the form, but perhaps the greatest odes of the 19th century were Keats's *Five Great Odes* of 1819 which included *Ode to a Nightingale, Ode on Melancholy, Ode on a Grecian Urn, Ode to Psyche*, and *To Autumn.* After Keats, there have been comparatively few major odes in English. One major exception is the fourth verse of the poem *For the Fallen* by Laurence Binyon which is often known as *"The Ode to the Fallen"* or more simply as *"The Ode"*.

W.H. Auden also wrote *'Ode'*, one of his most popular poems from his earlier career when based in London, in opposition to people's ignorance over the reality of war. In interview Auden once stated that he had intended to title the poem *My Silver Age* in mockery of the supposedly imperial Golden age, however chose *'Ode'* as it seemed to provide a more sensitive exploration of warfare.

The English ode's most common rhyme scheme is ABABCDECDE.

THE LYRIC

Is a genre of poetry that expresses personal and emotional feelings. In the ancient world, lyric poems were sung, accompanied by a lyre a musical instrument. Lyric poems do not have to rhyme, and today do not need to be set to music or a beat. Aristotle, in *Poetics*, mentions lyric poetry (kitharistike played to the cithara, a type of lyre) along with drama, epic poetry, dancing, painting and other forms of mimesis. The lyric poem, dating from the Romantic era, does have some thematic antecedents in ancient Greek and Roman verse, but the ancient definition was based on metrical criteria, and in archaic and classical Greek culture presupposed live performance accompanied by a stringed instrument.

Although arguably the most popular form of lyric poetry in the Western tradition is the 14-line sonnet, either in its Petrarchan or its Shakespearean form, lyric poetry appears in a variety of forms. Other forms of the lyric include ballades, villanelles, odes, pastourelle and canzone.

Ancient Hebrew poetry relied on repetition, alliteration, and chiasmus for many of its effects. Ancient Greek and Roman lyric poetry was composed in strophes. Pindar's epinician odes, where strophe and antistrophe are followed by an epode, represent an expansion of the same basic principle. The Greeks distinguished, however, between lyric monody (e.g. Sappho, Anacreon) and choral lyric (e.g. Pindar, Bacchylides). In all such poetry the fundamental formal feature is the repetition of a metrical pattern larger than a verse or distich. In some cases (although not in antiquity), form and theme are wed in the conception of a genre, as in the medieval alva or aubade, a dawn song in which lovers must part after a night of love, often with the watchman's refrain telling them it is time to go. A common feature of some lyric forms is the refrain of one or more verses that end each strophe. The refrain is repeated throughout the poem, either exactly or with variation. In the medieval Galician-Portuguese *cantigas de amigo*, thought to reflect an old oral tradition, 90% of the texts have a refrain.

Lyric in European literature of the medieval or Renaissance period means a poem written so that it could be set to music—whether or not it is. A poem's particular structure, function or theme is not specified by the term. The lyric poetry of Europe in this period was created largely without reference to the classical past, by the pioneers of courtly poetry and courtly love. The troubadours, travelling composers and performers of songs, began to flourish towards the end of the 11th century and were often imitated in successive centuries. Trouveres were poet-composers who were roughly contemporary with and influenced by the troubadours but who composed their works in the northern dialects of France. The first known trouvere was Chretien de Troyes (1160s-80s). The dominant form of German lyric poetry in the period was the Minnesang, "a love lyric based essentially on a fictitious relationship between a knight and his high-born lady". Initially imitating the lyrics of the French troubadours and trouveres, Minnesang soon established a distinctive tradition. There is also a large body of medieval Galician-Portuguese lyric. Hebrew singer-poets of the Middle Ages include: Yehuda Halevi, Solomon ibn Gabirol and Abraham ibn Ezra.

In Italy, Petrarch developed the sonnet form pioneered by Giacomo da Lentini, which Dante used in his Vita Nuova. In 1327, according to the poet, the sight of a woman called Laura in the church of Sainte-Claire d'Avignon awoke in him a lasting passion, celebrated in the Rime sparse ("Scattered rhymes"). Later, Renaissance poets who copied Petrarch's style named this collection of 366 poems Il Canzoniere ("Song Book"). Laura is in many ways both the culmination of medieval courtly love poetry and the beginning of Renaissance love lyric.

The eighteenth and early nineteenth centuries constitute the period of the rise of Russian lyric poetry, exemplified by Aleksandr Pushkin. The Swedish "Phosphorists" were influenced by the Romantic movement and their chief poet, Per Daniel Amadeus Atterbom produced many lyric poems. Italian lyric poets of the period include Ugo Foscolo,

Giacomo Leopardi, Giovanni Pascoli and Gabriele D'Annunzio. Japanese lyric poets include Taneda Santoka, Masaoka Shiki and Ishikawa Takuboku. Spanish lyric poets include Gustavo Adolfo Becquer, Rosalia de Castro and Jose de Espronceda.

THE IDYLL

A composition in verse or prose which describes scenes and incidents of country life which are simple, charming and appealing due to their idealised innocence and contentment. An idyll is a pastoral poem, and an ancient example is *Theocritus's Idylls* (in 3rd century B.C.) which describes the country life, and the charming rustic life of the Sicilians. John G. Whittler's *Maud Muller* is yet another example of an idyll.

THE PASTORAL

The originator of the pastoral was the Greek poet Theocritus, who in the third century BC wrote poems representing the life of Sicilian shepherds. ("Pastor" is Latin for "shepherd.") Virgil later imitated Theocritus in his Latin *Edogues*, and in doing so established the enduring model for the traditional pastoral a deliberately conventional poem expressing an urban poet's nostalgic image of the supposed peace and simplicity of the life of shepherds and other rural folk in an idealized natural setting. The conventions that hundreds of later poets imitated from Virgil's imitations of Theocritus include a shepherd reclining under a spreading beech tree and meditating on the rural muse, or piping as though he would ne'er grow old, or engaging in a friendly singing contest, or expressing his good or bad fortune in a love affair, or grieving over the death of a fellow shepherd. From this last type developed the pastoral elegy, which persisted long after the other traditional types had lost their popularity. Other terms often used synonymously with pastoral are idyll, from the title of Theocritus' pastorals; eclogue (literally, "a selection"), from the title of Virgil's pastorals; and bucolic poetry, from the Greek word for "herdsman."

Classical poets often described the pastoral life as possessing features of the mythical golden age. Christian pastoralists conjoined the golden age of pagan fable with the Garden of Eden in the Bible, and also exploited the religious symbolism of "shepherd" (applied to the ecclesiastical or parish "pastor," and to the figure of Christ as the Good Shepherd) to give many pastoral poems a Christian range of reference. In the Renaissance the traditional pastoral was also adapted to diverse satirical and allegorical uses. Edmund Spenser's *Shepherd's Calendar* (1579), which popularized the mode in English poetry, included most of the varieties of pastoral poems current in that period.

Such was the attraction of the pastoral dream that Renaissance writers incorporated it into various other literary forms. Sir Philip Sidney's *Arcadia* (1581–84) was a long pastoral romance written in an elaborately artful prose. (*Arcadia* was a mountainous region of Greece which Virgil substituted for Theocritus' Sicily as his idealized pastoral milieu.) There was also the pastoral lyric (Christopher Marlowe's *"The Passionate Shepherd to His Love"*), and the pastoral drama. John Fletcher's *The Faithful Shepherdess* is an example of this last type, and Shakespeare's *As You Like It*, based on the contemporary pastoral romance *Rosalynde* by Thomas Lodge, is set in the forest of Arden, a green refuge from the troubles and complications of ordinary life where enmities are reconciled, problems resolved, and the course of true love made to run smooth.

The last important series of traditional pastorals, and an extreme instance of their calculated and graceful display of high artifice, was Alexander Pope's *Pastorals* (1709). Five years later John Gay, in his Shepherd's Week, wrote a parody of the type by applying its elegant formulas to the crudity of actual rustic manners and language; by doing so, he inadvertently showed later poets the way to the seriously realistic treatment of rural life. In 1783 George Crabbe published *The Village* specifically in order to paint the cot. *As Truth* will paint it and as bards will not.

How far the term then lost its traditional application to a poetry of aristocratic artifice is indicated by Wordsworth's title for his realistic rendering of a rural tragedy in 1800: *"Michael, A Pastoral Poem"*.

THE ELEGY

A lament or a meditative poem, often written on the occasion of a death or other solemn event or theme. Although an elegy may appear as a discrete section in a larger work (as in the oration at the funeral of Beowulf), it is usually a complete poem in a formal style. A famous example is Thomas Gray's *"Elegy Written in a Country Churchyard"* (1751), whose thirty-two stanzas ruminate upon the passing of time and souls:

Can storied urn or animated bust
Back to its mansion call the fleeting breath?
Can Honor's voice provoke the silent dust,
Or Flattery soothe the dull cold ear of Death?

Perhaps in this neglected spot is laid
Some heart once pregnant with celestial fire;
Hands that the rod of empire might have swayed,
Or waked to ecstasy the living lyre.

THE PASTORAL ELEGY

One kind of elegy that is especially important in English literary history is the pastoral elegy, whose highlights include John Milton's *"Lycidas"* (1637) and Percy Bysshe Shelley's *"Adonais"* (an elegy for the dead John Keats, 1821). Pastoral elegies combine pastoral themes and images—nature deities, seasonal vegetation—with a memorialization of a deceased friend or comrade.

THE BALLAD

A ballad is a form of verse, often a narrative set to music. Ballads were particularly characteristic of the popular poetry and song of the British Isles from the later medieval period until the 19th century and used extensively across Europe and later the Americas, Australia and North Africa. Many ballads were written and sold as single sheet broadsides. The form was often used by poets and composers from the 18th century onwards to produce lyrical ballads. In the later 19th century it took on the meaning of a slow form of popular love song and the term is now often used as synonymous with any love song, particularly the pop or rock power ballad.

Most northern and west European ballads are written in ballad stanzas or quatrains (four-line stanzas) of alternating lines of iambic (an unstressed followed by a stressed syllable) tetrameter (eight syllables) and iambic trimeter (six syllables), known as ballad meter. Usually, only the second and fourth line of a quatrain are rhymed (in the scheme a, b, c, b), which has been taken to suggest that, originally, ballads consisted of couplets (two lines) of rhymed verse, each of 14 syllables. As can be seen in this stanza from *'Lord Thomas and Fair Annet'*:

The horse| fair Ann|et rode| upon|
He amb|led like| the wind|,
With sil|ver he| was shod| before,
With burn|ing gold| behind|.

However, there is considerable variation on this pattern in almost every respect, including length, number of lines and rhyming scheme, making the strict definition of a ballad extremely difficult. In southern and eastern Europe, and in countries that derive their tradition from them, ballad structure differs significantly, like Spanish romances, which are octosyllabic and use consonance rather than rhyme.

In all traditions most ballads are narrative in nature, with a self-contained story, often concise and relying on imagery, rather than description, which can be tragic, historical, romantic or comic. Another common feature of ballads is repetition, sometimes of fourth lines in succeeding stanzas, as a refrain, sometimes of third and fourth lines of a stanza and sometimes of entire stanzas.

THE SATIRE

Satire can be described as the literary art of diminishing or derogating a subject by making it ridiculous and evoking toward it attitudes of amusement, contempt, scorn, or indignation. It differs from the *comic* in that comedy evokes laughter mainly as an end in itself, while satire derides; that is, it uses laughter as a weapon, and against a butt that exists outside the work itself.

That butt may be an individual (in "personal satire"), or a type of person, a class, an institution, a nation, or even (as in the Earl of Rochester's *"A Satyr against Mankind,"* 1675, and much of Jonathan Swift's *Gulliver's Travels*, 1726, especially Book IV) the entire human race. The distinction between the comic and the satiric, however, is sharp only at its extremes. Shakespeare's *Falstaff* is mainly a comic creation, presented primarily for our enjoyment; the puritanical Malvolio in Shakespeare's *Twelfth Night* is for the most part comic but has aspects of satire directed against the type of the fatuous and hypocritical Puritan; Ben Jonson's *Volpone* (1607) clearly satirizes the type of person whose cleverness—or stupidity—is put at the service of his cupidity; and John Dryden's *MacFlecknoe* (1682), while representing a permanent type of the pretentious poetaster, satirized specifically the living author Thomas Shadwell.

Satire has usually been justified, by those who practice it, as a corrective of human vice and folly; Alexander Pope, for example, remarked that "those who are ashamed of nothing else are so of being ridiculous." Its frequent claim (not always borne out in the practice) has been to ridicule the failing rather than the individual, and to limit its ridicule to corrigible faults, excluding those for which a person is not responsible. As Swift said, speaking of himself in his ironic *"Verses on the Death of Dr. Swift"* (1739):

> Yet malice never was his aim;
> He lashed the vice, but spared the name....
> His satire points at no defect,
> But what all mortals may correct....
> He spared a hump, or crooked nose,
> Whose owners set not up for beaux.

Satire occurs as an incidental element within many works whose overall mode is not satiric—in a certain character or situation, or in an interpolated passage of ironic commentary on some aspect of the human condition or of contemporary society. But for some literary writings, verse or prose, the attempt to diminish a subject by ridicule is the organizing principle of the whole, and these works constitute the formal genre labeled.

NOVEL

A novel is a book of long narrative in literary prose. The genre has historical roots both in the fields of the medieval and early modern romance and in the tradition of the novella. The latter supplied the present generic term in the late 18th century.

Further definition of the genre is historically difficult. The construction of the narrative, the plot, the way reality is created in the works of fiction, the fascination of the character study, and the use of language are usually discussed to show a novel's artistic merits. Most of these requirements were introduced in the 16th and 17th centuries, in order to give fiction a justification outside the field of factual history. The individualism of the presentation makes the personal memoir and the autobiography the two closest relatives among the genres of modern histories.

NOVEL AND ITS MAJOR FORMS

The following are the Major Forms of the Novel :

1. The Prose Romances
2. The Travelogues
3. The Gothic Novel
4. The Picaresque Novel
5. The Epistolary Novel
6. The Domestic Novel
7. The Historical Novel
8. The Regional Novel
9. The Prophetic Novel
10. The Psychological Novel
11. The Short Story

THE PROSE ROMANCES

Romances in verse were written much earlier than the Romances in prose. Prose Romances are the earliest form of the novel. They are simply fantasies in which the authors make the fullest use of their imagination and fancy and create an ideal world which bears little or no semblance with real life. The earliest of them is the famous *Morte d' Arthur*, the legends retold by Sir Thomas Malory in prose. This takes us back to the legendary world of knighthood and chivalry. The other sixteenth century prose romances are Lyly's *Euphues* in two parts and Sidney's *Arcadia*, a pastoral romance, conceiving a dream-land of pre fancy. Lodge's *Rosalynde* is a love-romance, so is also Robert Greene's *Pandosto*, Bacon's *The New Atlantis* is also a prose romance.

THE TRAVELOGUES

The novel proper started in a limited sense with Travelogues. The travelogues are travel-stories relating the adventures of the travelers or voyagers in unknown and unchartered seas. They often land on uninhabited islands or some islands inhabited by strange creatures. The earliest of them is Daniel Defoe's *Robinson Crusoe*. Robinson Crusoe lands on an uninhabited island and somehow managers to live there for several years, until he is rescued from there by a lucky chance by a passing ship of his own country. Another famous travelogue is Jonathan Swift's *Gulliver's Travels*. In this romance Gulliver lands on several islands inhabited by such strange creatures as the Lilliputians, Houynhnms, Brobdingnags, and Yahoos. However, Swift's episodes in these adventures have very pungent satire on contemporary political situations.

THE GOTHIC NOVEL

Derived from the word 'Goths' used for a Germanic tribe, the Gothic novel has supernatural elements like ghosts, haunted houses, etc. which induces horror, apprehension and insecurity. Examples – Horace Walpole's *Castle of Otranto, a Gothic Story*, Ann Radcliff's *The Mysteries of Udolpho*, etc.

THE PICARESQUE NOVEL

The picaresque novel (Spanish: "picaresca," from "piçaro," for "rogue" or "rascal") is a popular sub-genre of prose fiction which is usually satirical and depicts, in realistic and often humorous detail, the adventures of a roguish hero of low social class who lives by his wits in a corrupt society. This style of novel originated in sixteenth century Spain and flourished throughout Europe in the seventeenth and eighteenth centuries. It continues to influence modern literature.

The word picaro starts to first appear in Spain with the current meaning in 1545. The word picaro does not appear in *Lazarillo de Tormes* (1554), the novella credited with founding the genre. The expression picaresque novel was coined in 1810.

The character type of Lazarillo, which determines the story and the so-called picaresque novel genre, has been shaped from characterization elements already present in Roman literature. With Petronius' *Satyricon*, Lazarillo takes some of the traits of the central figure of Encolpius, a former gladiator. but it is unlikely that the author had access to Petronius' work; from the comedies of Plautus, it borrows from the figure of the parasite and the supple slave; other traits are taken from Apuleius's *The Golden Ass*. *The Golden Ass* and *Satyricon* were particularly revived and widely read in renaissance Europe, and are rare surviving samples of a mostly lost genre, which was highly popular in the classical world, known as *"Milesian tales"*.

Arabic literature, which was read widely in Spain in the time of Al-Andalus and possessed a literary tradition with similar themes, is another possible formative influence on the picaresque style. *Al-Hamadhani* (d.1008) of Hamadhan (Iran) is credited with inventing the literary genre of maqamat in which a wandering vagabond makes his living on the gifts his listeners give him following his extemporaneous displays of rhetoric, erudition, or verse, often done with a trickster's touch *Ibn al-Astarkuwi* or *al-Ashtarkuni* (d.1134) also wrote in the genre maqamat, comparable to later European picaresque novels. While elements of Chaucer and Boccaccio have a picaresque feel and are likely to have contributed to the style, the modern picaresque begins with Lazarillo de Tormes, which was published anonymously in Antwerp and Spain in 1554. It is variously considered either the first picaresque novel or at least the antecedent of the genre. The title character, Lazarillo, is a picaro who must live by his wits in an impoverished country full of hypocrisy.

The autobiography of Benvenuto Cellini, written in Florence beginning in 1558, also has much in common with the picaresque. Another early example is Mateo Aleman's *Guzman de Alfarache* (1599), characterized by religiosity.

Francisco de Quevedo's *El buscon* (1604 according to Francisco Rico; the exact date is uncertain, yet it was certainly a very early work) is considered the masterpiece of the subgenre by A.A. Parker, because of his baroque style and the study of the delinquent psychology. However, a more recent school of thought, led by Francisco Rico, rejects Parker's view, contending instead that the protagonist, Pablos, is a highly unrealistic character, simply a means for Quevedo to launch classist, racist and sexist attacks. Moreover, argues Rico, the structure of the novel is radically different from previous works of the picaresque genre: Quevedo uses the conventions of the picaresque as a mere vehicle to show off his abilities with conceit and rhetoric, rather than to construct a satirical critique of Spanish Golden Age society.

Indeed, in order to understand the historical context that led to the development of these paradigmatic picaresque novels in Spain during the sixteenth and seventeenth centuries, it is essential to take into consideration the circumstances surrounding the lives of conversos, whose ancestors had been Jewish, and whose New Christian faith was subjected to close scrutiny and mistrust. In other European countries, these Spanish novels were read and imitated. In Germany, Grimmelshausen wrote *Simplicius Simplicissimus* (1669), the most important of non-Spanish picaresque novels. It describes the devastation caused by the Thirty Years' War. In Le Sage's *Gil Blas* (1715) is a classic example of the genre, which in France had declined into an aristocratic adventure. In Britain, the body of Tobias Smollett's work, and Daniel Defoe's *Moll Flanders* (1722) are considered picaresque, but they lack the sense of religious redemption of delinquency that was very important in Spanish and German novels. The triumph of *Moll Flanders* is more economic than moral.

The classic Chinese novel *Journey to the West* is considered to have considerable picaresque elements. Having been written in 1590, it is contemporary with much of the above - but is unlikely to have been directly influenced by the European genre.

THE EPISTOLARY NOVEL

An epistolary novel is a novel written as a series of documents. The usual form is letters, although diary entries, newspaper clippings and other documents are sometimes used. Recently, electronic "documents" such as recordings and radio, blogs, and e-mails have also come into use. The word epistolary is derived through Latin from the Greek word *epistole*, meaning a letter.

The epistolary form can add greater realism to a story, because it mimics the workings of real life. It is thus able to demonstrate differing points of view without recourse to the device of an omniscient narrator.

There are two theories on the genesis of the epistolary novel. The first claims that the genre originated from novels with inserted letters, in which the portion containing the third person narrative in between the letters was gradually reduced. The other theory claims that the epistolary novel arose from miscellanies of letters and poetry: some of the letters were tied together into a (mostly amorous) plot. Both claims have some validity. The first truly epistolary novel, the Spanish *"Prison of Love" (Carcel de amor)* (c.1485) by Diego de San Pedro, belongs to a tradition of novels in which a large number of inserted letters already dominated the narrative. Other well-known examples of early epistolary novels are closely related to the tradition of letter-books and miscellanies of letters. Within the successive editions of Edme Boursault's *Letters of Respect, Gratitude and Love (Lettres de respect, d'obligation et d 'amour)* (1669), a group of letters written to a girl named Babet was expanded and became more and more distinct from the other letters, until it formed a small epistolary novel entitled *Letters to Babet (Lettres a Babet)*. The immensely famous Letters of a Portuguese Nun *(Lettres portugaises)* (1669) generally attributed to Gabriel-

Joseph de La Vergne, comte de Guilleragues, though a small minority still regard Marianna Alcoforado as the author, is claimed to be intended to be part of a miscellany of Guilleragues prose and poetry. The founder of the epistolary novel in English is said by many to be James Howell (1594–1666) with *"Familiar Letters"*, who writes of prison, foreign adventure, and the love of women.

The first novel to expose the complex play that the genre allows was Aphra Behn's *Love-Letters Between a Nobleman and His Sister* (1684), which appeared in three successive volumes in 1684, 1685, and 1687. The novel shows the genre's results of changing perspectives: individual points were presented by the individual characters, and the central voice of the author and moral evaluation disappeared (at least in the first volume; her further volumes introduced a narrator). Behn furthermore explored a realm of intrigue with letters that fall into the wrong hands, with faked letters, with letters withheld by protagonists, and even more complex interaction.

The epistolary novel as a genre became popular in the 18th century in the works of such authors as Samuel Richardson, with his immensely successful novels *Pamela* (1740) and *Clarissa* (1749). In France, there was *Lettres persanes* (1721) by Montesquieu, followed by *Julie, ou la nouvelle Heloise* (1761) by Jean-Jacques Rousseau, and Laclos' *Les Liaisons dangereuses* (1782), which used the epistolary form to great dramatic effect, because the sequence of events was not always related directly or explicitly. In Germany, there was Johann Wolfgang von Goethe's *Die Leiden des jungen Werthers* (1774) *(The Sorrows of Young Werther)* and Friedrich Holderlin's *Hyperion*. The first North American novel, *The History of Emily Montague* (1769) by Frances Brooke was written in epistolary form.

Starting in the 18th century, the epistolary form was subject to much ridicule, resulting in a number of savage burlesques. The most notable example of these was Henry Fielding's *Shamela* (1741), written as a parody of Pamela. In it, the female narrator can be found wielding a pen and scribbling her diary entries under the most dramatic and unlikely of circumstances.

The epistolary novel slowly fell out of use in the late 18th century. Although Jane Austen tried her hand at the epistolary in juvenile writings and her novella *Lady Susan*, she abandoned this structure for her later work. It is thought that her lost novel *"First Impressions"*, which was redrafted to become *Pride and Prejudice*, may have been epistolary: *Pride and Prejudice* contains an unusual number of letters quoted in full and some play a critical role in the plot.

The epistolary form nonetheless saw continued use, surviving in exceptions or in fragments in nineteenth-century novels. In Honore de Balzac's novel *Letters of Two Brides*, two women who became friends during their education at a convent correspond over a 17 year period, exchanging letters describing their lives. Mary Shelley employs the epistolary form in her novel *Frankenstein* (1818). Shelley uses the letters as one of a variety of framing devices, as the story is presented through the letters of a sea captain and scientific explorer attempting to reach the north pole who encounters Victor Frankenstein and records the dying man's narrative and confessions. In the late 19th century, Bram Stoker released one of the most widely recognized and successful novels in the epistolary form to date, *Dracula*. Printed in 1897, the novel is compiled entirely of letters, diary entries, newspaper clippings, telegrams, doctor's notes, ship's logs, and the like, which Stoker adroitly employs to balance believability and dramatic tension.

There are three types of epistolary novels: monologic (giving the letters of only one character, like *Letters of a Portuguese Nun*), dialogic (giving the letters of two characters, like *Mme Marie Jeanne Riccoboni's Letters of Fanni Butlerd* (1757), and polylogic (with three or more letter-writing characters). In addition, a crucial element in polylogic epistolary novels like *Clarissa*, and *Dangerous Liaisons* is the dramatic device of 'discrepant awareness': the simultaneous but separate correspondences of the heroines and the villains creating dramatic tension.

THE DOMESTIC NOVEL

The Domestic Novels as their title suggests, present the day-to-day life of the average of middle-class families. The life-patterns of the members of a family and their relations with their friends and neighbours are artistically presented in these novels. The festivals and festivities, functions and celebrations, birthdays, nuptials, and marriages are graphically described in these novels. Jane Austen is the most important writer of the domestic novels. Her *Pride and Prejudice, Sense and Sensibility* and *Emma* are the best examples of domestic novels.

THE HISTORICAL NOVEL

A novel that has as its setting a usually significant period of history and that attempts to convey the spirit, manners, and social conditions of a past age with realistic detail and fidelity (which is in some cases only apparent fidelity) to historical fact. The work may deal with actual historical personages...or it may contain a mixture of fictional and historical characters.

An early example of historical prose fiction is Luo Guanzhong's *14th century Romance of the Three Kingdoms*, which covers one of the most important periods of Chinese history and left a lasting impact on Chinese culture.

The historical novel was further popularized in the 19th century by writers classified as Romantics. Many regard Sir Walter Scott as the first to write historical novels. Gyorgy Lukacs, in his *The Historical Novel*, argues that Scott is the first fiction writer who saw history not just as a convenient frame in which to stage a contemporary narrative, but rather as a distinct social and cultural setting. His novels of Scottish history such as *Waverley* (1814) and *Rob Roy* (1817) focus upon a middling character who sits at the intersection of various social groups in order to explore the development of society through conflict. His *Ivanhoe* (1820) gains credit for renewing interest in the Middle Ages. Victor Hugo's *The Hunchback of Notre Dame* (1831) furnishes another 19th century example of the romantic-historical novel as does Leo Tolstoy's *War and Peace*. In the United States, James Fenimore Cooper was a prominent author of historical novels. In French literature, the most prominent inheritor of Scott's style of the historical novel was *Balzac*.

Though the genre has evolved since its inception, the historical novel remains popular with authors and readers to this day; bestsellers include Patrick O'Brian's *Aubrey–Maturin* series, Ken Follett's *Pillars of the Earth*, and Neal Stephenson's *Baroque Cycle*. A striking development in British/ Irish writing in the past 25 years has been the renewed interest in the First World War. Works include William Boyd's *An Ice-Cream War*; Sebastian Faulks' *Birdsong* and *The Girl at the Lion d'Or* (concerned with the War's consequences); Pat Barker's *Regeneration Trilogy* and Sebastian Barry's *A Long Long Way*.

Many early historical novels played an important role in the rise of European popular interest in the history of the Middle Ages. Hugo's *Hunchback* often receives credit for fueling the movement to preserve the Gothic architecture of France, leading to the establishment of the Monuments historiques, the French governmental authority for historic preservation.

The genre of the historical novel has also permitted some authors, such as the Polish novelist Boleslaw Prus in his sole historical novel, *Pharaoh*, to distance themselves from their own time and place to gain perspective on society and on the human condition, or to escape the depredations of the censor.

In some historical novels, major historic events take place mostly off-stage, while the fictional characters inhabit the world where those events occur. Robert Louis Stevenson's *Kidnapped* recounts mostly private adventures set against the backdrop of the Jacobite troubles in Scotland. Charles Dickens's *Barnaby Rudge* is set amid the Gordon Riots, and *A Tale of Two Cities* in the French Revolution.

In some works, the accuracy of the historical elements has been questioned, as in Alexandre Dumas' *Queen Margot*. Postmodern novelists such as John Barth and Thomas Pynchon operate with even more freedom, mixing historical characters and settings with invented history and fantasy, as in the novels *The Sot-Weed Factor* and *Mason & Dixon* respectively. A few writers create historical fiction without fictional characters. One example is *I, Claudius*, by 20th century writer Robert Graves; another is the *Masters of Rome* series by Colleen McCullough.

THE REGIONAL NOVEL

This type of novel is set in a particular geographical section and deals with the living and culture of that area. Examples are: Thomas Hardy's *Wessex*, R.K.Narayan's *Malgudi*, etc.

These are the common types of novel. Apart from these there are many more varieties that excel in creating the literature of the time and making the essence of novel more dedicated and authentic in the present scenario.

THE PROPHETIC NOVEL

The Prophetic novels try to forecast what the future would be like. These novels do not claim to be absolutely correct or authentic. They only give us a tentative picture of the future on the basis of the tendencies prevailing in the present. Aidous Huxley in the Brave New World envisaged in 1932 a future in which the entire populace would be mentally conditioned by the totalitarian despots.

THE PSYCHOLOGICAL NOVEL

A Psychological fiction is a specific sub-genre of the wide ranging thriller genre. This genre often incorporates elements from the mystery genre in addition to the typical traits of the thriller genre. Usually thrillers focus on plot over fictional characters, emphasizing on intense physical action over the character's psyche. Psychological thrillers tend to reverse this formula to a certain degree, emphasizing the characters just as much if not more so than the plot. psychological novel, also called psychological realism, is a work of prose fiction which places more than the usual amount of emphasis on interior characterization, and on the motives, circumstances, and internal action which springs from, and develops, external action. The psychological novel is not content to state what happens but goes on to explain the motivation of this action. In this type of writing character and characterization are more than usually important, and they often delve deeper into the mind of a character than novels of other genres. The psychological novel can be called a novel of the "inner man," so to say. In some cases, the stream of consciousness technique, as well as interior monologues, may be employed to better illustrate the inner workings of the human mind at work. Flashbacks may also be featured. While these three textual techniques are also prevalent in "modernism," there is no deliberate effort to fragment the prose or compel the reader to interpret the text.

The Tale of Genji, written in 11th century Japan, has often been considered the first psychological novel. In the west, the origins of the psychological novel can be traced as far back as Giovanni Boccaccio's 1344 *Elegia di Madonna Fiammetta;* that is before the term psychology was coined.

THE SHORT STORY

A short story is a work of fiction that is usually written in prose, often in narrative format. A short story usually deals with a few characters and often concentrates on the creation of the mood rather than the plot.

The short story format tends to be more pointed than longer works of fiction, such as novellas (in the 20th and 21st century sense) and novels. Short story definitions based on length differ somewhat, even among professional writers, in part because of the fragmentation of the medium into genres. Since the short story format includes a wide range of genres and styles, the actual length is determined by the individual author's preference (or the story's actual needs in terms of creative trajectory or story arc) and the submission guidelines relevant to the story's actual market. Guidelines vary greatly among publishers.

Many short story writers define their work through a combination of creative, personal expression, and artistic integrity. They attempt to resist categorization by genre as well as definition by numbers, finding such approaches limiting and counter-intuitive to artistic form and reasoning. As a result, definitions of the short story based on length splinter even more when the writing process is taken into consideration.

A short story is often judged by its ability to provide a complete or satisfying treatment of its characters and subject. Fiction, such as novellas (in the 20th and 21st century sense) and novels. Short story definitions based on length differ somewhat, even among professional writers, in part because of the fragmentation of the medium into genres. Since the short story format includes a wide range of genres and styles, the actual length is determined by the individual author's preference (or the story's actual needs in terms of creative trajectory or story arc) and the submission guidelines relevant to the story's actual market. Guidelines vary greatly among publishers.

Many short story writers define their work through a combination of creative, personal expression, and artistic integrity. They attempt to resist categorization by genre as well as definition by numbers, finding such approaches limiting and counter-intuitive to artistic form and reasoning. As a result, definitions of the short story based on length splinter even more when the writing process is taken into consideration.

MULTIPLE CHOICE QUESTIONS

1. Which of the following is the oldest form of literature?
A. Drama B. Novel
C. Poetry D. Prose

2. The term 'drama' originates from which language?
A. English B. Arabic
C. Sanskrit D. Greek

3. 'Drama' originated in ______.
A. Greece B. Rome
C. London D. India

4. Which one of these is not a type of drama?
A. The Tragedy B. The Farce
C. The Masque D. The Ballad

5. Which one of these is a type of drama?
A. The Epic B. The Ode
C. The Farce D. The Satire

6. Which one is a prose work?
A. The Epic B. The Memoirs
C. The Idyll D. The Elegy

7. Which one of the following is not a prose work?
A. The Farce
B. The Essay
C. The Biography
D. The Memoirs

8. Which one is a major poetry form?
A. The Farce B. The Gothic
C. The Pastoral D. The Masque

9. Which one of the following is not a poetic form?
A. The Epic B. The Lyric
C. The Idyll D. The Farce

10. Which one is a major novel form?
A. The Melodrama B. The Tragedy
C. The Pastoral D. The Travelogues

11. Which one is not a major form of novel?
A. The Travelogue B. Gothic
C. Picaresque D. The Tragedy

12. Interlude is a type of ______.
A. Novel B. Poetry form
C. Prose form D. Drama

13. A sonnet is a form of ______.
A. Poetry B. Drama
C. Novel D. Prose

14 Shakespearan sonnet contains ______ lines.
A. four B. six
C. twelve D. fourteen

15. An ode is a ______.
A. Drama B. Novel
C. Poetry D. Prose

16. A ballad is a form of ______.
A. Prose B. Poetry
C. Novel D. Drama

17. A satire is a form of ______.
A. Poetry B. Prose
C. Drama D. Novel

18. Which one is a form of novel?
A. The Prophetic B. The Farce
C. The Masque D. The Elegy

19. Which one is not a form of novel?
A. Epistolary B. Regional
C. Pastoral D. Psychological

20. The elegy is a form of ______.
A. Drama B. Prose
C. Poetry D. Novel

21. Why were the *Interludes* introduced?
A. They pleased the common class of the spectators
B. They provided comic relief
C. They had better theatrical effect
D. They dealt with the real problems of life

22. The *Mystery Plays* deal with—
A. Heaven and Hell
B. Moral values
C. Biblical Themes
D. The life and deeds of the saints

23. Who is the author of *The Spanish Tragedy*?
A. Christopher Marlowe
B. Thomas Kyd
C. Robert Greene
D. George Peele

24. Which of the following plays is written by George Peele?
A. *Titus Andronicus*
B. *Jocasta*
C. *The Spanish Tragedy*
D. *The Wounds of Civil War*

25. What is the function of the *Chorus* in a play?
A. The Chorus is a band of singers who sing
B. The Chorus comes to declare the ending of an Act
C. The Chorus explains the past and the future events in the play
D. The Chorus represents the views of the dramatist

26. John Heywood's *Interlude* entitled 4PP (or 4P's) caricatures four professionals whose professions begins with P. In the four professionals listed below, which one is wrong?
A. The Piper B. The Palmer
C. The Pedlar D. The Pardoner

27. How many Dramatic Unities were recommended by the Greeks?
A. One central unity
B. No number fixed
C. Three dramatic unities
D. Two dramatic unities

28. In which one of the following plays the *Epilogue* appears?
A. *Dr. Faustus*
B. *Midsummer Night's Dream*
C. *Hamlet*
D. *As You Like it*

29. The *Miracle Plays* principally deal with the miracles performed by—
A. Supernatural powers
B. Personified Vices and Virtues
C. Saints and Sages
D. Magic

30. Virtues and Vices are personified in—
A. The Moralities B. The Miracles
C. The Interludes D. The Mysteries

31. Which is supposed to be the first regular tragedy in English?
A. *Morte de Arthur*
B. *Gorboduc*
C. *Troylus and Cryseyde*
D. *Roister Doister*

32. The first tragedy *Gorboduc* was later given the title—
A. *Corpus Christi*
B. *Ferrex and Porrex*
C. *Gammer Gurton's Needle*
D. *Endymion*

33. What is meant by 'Catastrophe'?
A. The ending of a tragi-comedy
B. The ending of a tragedy
C. The ending of a farce
D. The ending of a comedy

34. Which one of the following types of the plays is not meant for acting?
A. A Closet play B. A Chronicle play
C. A Masque D. A Romance

35. The *Resurrection of Lazarus* was a very popular play in the fifteenth century. It was a—
A. Morality Play B. Mystery Play
C. Miracle Play D. An Interlude

36. One of the following dramatists has written only tragedies. He is—
A. Ben Jonson B. John Webster
C. Marlowe D. John Ford

37. How many constituent parts are there in a Tragedy according to Aristotle?
A. Five B. Six
C. Four D. Three

38. At what stage of the plot in a play does the Epilogue appear?
A. At the end of the play
B. At any stage where its presence is felt necessary
C. In the beginning of the play
D. At the end of the third act

39. There were four famous theatrical Cycles enacting the Morality Plays. Which one of the following four names given below is wrong?
A. Towneley Cycle B. Chester Cycle
C. York Cycle D. Charles Cycle

40. Biblical themes were enacted in—
A. The Miracle plays B. The Mystery plays
C. The Interludes D. The Morality plays

41. In which year was the *Globe Theatre* built?
A. 1588 B. 1594
C. 1598 D. 1599

42. Who is the author of *The Spanish Tragedy*?
A. Thomas Lodge B. Thomas Kyd
C. George Peele D. Robert Greene

43. A *'Soliloquy'* is defined as the 'loud thinking' of a character. Who can hear this 'loud thinking'?
A. The heroine of the play
B. The whole audience
C. The character himself
D. The characters present on the stage

44. What is meant by *'Denouement'*?
A. The ending of a comedy
B. The ending of a romance
C. The ending of a tragedy
D. The ending of a historical play

45. What is the most significant feature of the *Morality Plays*?
A. They present biblical figures
B. They symbolise Christian moral values
C. They present saints and sages
D. They present Vices and Virtues as personified figures

ANSWERS

1	2	3	4	5	6	7	8	9	10
C	D	A	D	C	B	A	C	D	D
11	12	13	14	15	16	17	18	19	20
D	D	A	D	C	B	A	A	C	C
21	22	23	24	25	26	27	28	29	30
B	C	B	A	C	A	C	D	C	A
31	32	33	34	35	36	37	38	39	40
B	B	B	A	C	C	B	A	D	B
41	42	43	44	45					
D	B	B	A	D					

2

Authors & Their Works

WILLIAM SHAKESPEARE (1564–1616)

Life

William Shakespeare was born on 23rd April 1564 at Stratford-on-Avon. His father was a grain-dealer. His business deteriorated when William was yet a child and so William could not study more than a few years in the local grammar school and left it at the age of about 13 to help out in his family's business. He married at the age of 18 to Anne Hathaway, who was eight years his senior. They had three children, but the marriage was not happy. According to tradition, William was caught poaching deer and rabbits in Thomas Lucy's park at Charlecote. He was lynched and ran away from home, gradually reaching London. There he got a job as a holder of visitors' horses at a theatre. He later on got a job as an actor and is supposed to have done the roles of the type of Ghost in *Hamlet* and Adam in *As You Like it.* Shakespeare very soon got the hang of the theatre and began revising plays or writing plays based on English translations of Greek and Latin stories. These plays were very successful with audiences and provoked the jealousy of rivals like Greene who denounces Shakespeare in a pamphlet entitled *A Groatsworth of Wit* (1592). Greene describes him as "an upstart crow beautified with our feathers, that with his Tyger's heart wrapped in a player's hide ....".

From then on there was no stopping of Shakespeare's upward rise in career. He was attached to and wrote his plays for the Earl of Leicester's Players. In 1595, his name appears on the Payroll of the Lord Chamberlain's and finally of the King's Servants. These companies performed at The Rose, The Curtain and The Theatre. The company finally bought the Globe and Shakespeare, growing prosperous, became a partner of the Globe Theatre and later of the Blackfriars.

Shakespeare wrote and published for twenty years from 1591 to 1611. During this period he wrote 37 plays and more than 154 sonnets. The first 126 of the sonnets are addressed to a man Mr. W.H., the Earl of Southampton, who introduced him to the important courtiers, and the remainder to a "dark lady". He grew prosperous day by day, acquired estate, got his father to apply for a coat of arms and became a gentleman by inheritance. He bought New Place, the largest house at Stratford and retired there after 1611. After a drinking bout in 1616, he fell sick and died untimely.

Works

Shakespeare wrote the famous love poems, *Venus and Adonis* (1593) and *The Rape of Lucrece* (1594) dedicated to the Earl of Southampton. These poems in themselves entitle him to a place among the immortals. But he was destined to become famous and known to posterity as England's greatest dramatist. He began, as was the custom of the times, by collaborating with Marlowe and Kyd in revising and touching up old plays like *Titus Andronicus,*

Henry VI and *Richard III.* The exact sequence of dates in which his plays came out is not known, but only sixteen were published in quarto form during his life-time. There were copyright laws at the time and unscrupulous writer 'pirates' took down bits of the plays as they were enacted and published them in different editions. In 1623, seven years after his death, two of Shakespeare's friends and fellow-actors, Heminge and Condell, published all his plays as the first folio in memory of their worthy friend. This folio contains all the plays except *Pericles.* There are references to Shakespeare's plays in *Palladis Tamia, Wit's Treasury* (1593) by Francis Meres. The date of composition is guessed by topical and contemporary allusions in the plays and the tone and metre used.

In the earlier plays there is in general a youthful exuberance, a lot of verbal wit, strange conceits and light-heartedness. The blank verse used is end-stopped (the sense ends with each line) and rhyming couplets are used. As the plays grow in maturity and Shakespeare's art advances he uses run-on lines in which the sense of one line carries on to the next. This allows the verse to express a greater range of emotions. Still later on, feminine endings are used, that is, a number of unstressed syllables are added at the ends of lines. In the last plays, rhyme completely disappears.

Shakespeare's plays were written in three periods. Although their date of writing is based on conjecture, the periods give a clue to the gradual development of his art.

Early Period (1590-1596)

Henry VI (three plays), *Richard III, Richard II, Love's Labour Lost, A Midsummer Night's Dream, Romeo and Juliet.*

Middle Period (1596-1608)

Herry IV (two plays), *The Merchant of Venice, As You Like It, Julius Caesar, Hamlet, Othello, Macbeth, Twelfth Night King Lear, Antony and Cleopatra,* etc.

Late Period (1608-1613)

Cymbeline, The Tempest, Pericles, The Winter's Tale, etc.

The above are some of the 37 plays he wrote. An analysis of the plays reveals some common characteristics of the different categories like comedies and tragedies. The comedies are boisterous and farcical. They show Shakespeare's immature period. *The Merchant of Venice* (1596) is one of his most popular comedies with several episodes woven together. In those days when the Christians hated the Jews, Shakespeare's portrayal of Shylock in sympathetic tones caused a stir. *A Midsummer Night's Dream* (1595), the one play for which Shakespeare did not borrow the story, takes us to a wonderland of fairies, the impish Puck Goodfellow and Bottom whose scenes are the most hilarious in all Shakespeare. In this play, Theseus says *"The lunatic, the lover, and the poet/Are of imagination all compact."* This line refers to Shakespeare's own weird fancies as he creates them in his plays. *The Merry Wives of Windsor* (1600) was written on the behest of Queen Elizabeth. The character Falstaff is one of Shakespeare's best creations. According to the critic Hazlitt, Falstaff is all laughter and merriment, "laughing 3 inches below the skin". *Much Ado about Nothing* (1598) contains bracing wit-combats between Benedick and Beatrice. *As You Like It* (1600) provides glimpses of an emotionally rich life in the forest of Arden. *Twelfth Night* (1601) is a hilarious comedy. Through Malvolio, Shakespeare satirizes Puritanism.

Histories like *Richard III* (1593) and *Richard II* (1596) show the influence of Marlowe on Shakespeare. He wrote the three parts of *Henry VI* (1591-92) in collaboration with Marlowe. Most of these histories show the patriotic victory of kings.

The tragedies show Shakespeare's maturity in character delineation. *Titus Andronicus* (1594) is a horror play. *Romeo and Juliet* (1594) is a romantic tragedy which has become immortal. The four great tragedies of Shakespeare are psychological plays which show how a man of high rank falls from grace, becomes a plaything of destiny and ends up wretchedly all because of a "fatal flaw" in his character. In Greek tragedy, man was a complete puppet whose destiny was in the hands of the gods. Shakespeare often alludes to this: *"As flies to wanton boys are we to the gods/They kill us for their sport"*. But he gives his tragic characters "will-power". The tragic flaw in their characters, however, becomes the cause of their undoing. Thus with *Julius Caesar* (1599), it is his inordinate ambition; with *King Lear* (1605) it is dotedness and bad temper; with *Hamlet* (1601), it is over-refinement of thought leading to indecision; and with *Othello* (1604), it is simplicity causing suspicion. *Timon of Athens* (1607) is the tragedy of a misanthrope. *Coriolanus* (1606) depicts how pride leads to downfall. The last plays — *Pericles* (1608), *Cymbeline* (1609), *The Winter's Tale* (1610) and *The Tempest* (1611) have happy endings. With *The tempest* Shakespeare bid farewell to the theatre just as Prospero in the play puts away his wand and magic books.

To estimate the complete contribution of Shakespeare to English literature and the literature of the world is a difficult task. Thousands of books have been written on Shakespeare by scholars from all over the world and his plays have been translated into all the major languages. They are enacted everywhere and the Russians even claim he was a Slav! Even after 400 years his fame is on the rise. In *Julius Caesar,* Brutus says, *"How many times will this scene of ours be acted over/In states unborn and accents yet unknown"*. This indeed was a prophetic statement about his own plays.

Dryden stated that Shakespeare had 'a universal mind' and Ben Jonson said, "Shakespeare was not of an age but for all times." Indeed Shakespeare's characters — a gallery of 800 — are types of characters that have inhabited this planet throughout the human history. Shakespeare could enter into his characters and present them so vividly that they are more real than life itself. Master of the whole keyboard of emotions and expressions, the subtlest feelings are expressed in his plays. No wonder we quote him the most after the Bible.

Another aspect of his genius is that he excelled many of his contemporaries in whatever they invented. Thus he took Marlowe's 'mighty line' or the blank verse and made it a supple instrument for expressing many intense feelings. Ben Jonson described the 'humours' or human moods in his plays; Shakespeare bettered him in the description of greed, vice, folly and virtue.

Many have expressed doubt about his claim to the authorship of 37 plays in just 20 years. Yet there is no cause for doubt here. After all, he borrowed the stories from Latin and Greek translations and enlivened them with his genius. One of the sources of his Roman histories like *Julius Caesar,* for example, was Plutarch's *Lives of the Noble Romans* translated by North.

Shakespeare undoubtedly had many demerits, but these are overwhelmed and eclipsed by his outstanding gifts. Shakespeare, not being educated more than a few years in grammar school, was thrown upon his own resources. He observed Nature and human behaviour very keenly and had rare intuition and imagination. So he was trained in the school of life. His faults of grammar so prevalent in his plays are glossed off as poetic licence. In fact, he created his own grammar, using nouns as adjectives and inventing syntax. These have become expressions so apt, it is impossible to change or correct them without reducing the impact.

What was Shakespeare's philosophy? Was he a Christian? Shakespeare's ideas as expressed through his noble characters show universal virtue free from dogma and any religious denomination. They are virtues in the human spirit. He was capable of seeing good in all people.

> *"There is a soul of goodness*
> *In things evil*
> *Distil it if we may".*

His advocacy of the cause of Shylock, the Jew, in the days when rank hatred existed for them among the Christians, shows the truth of the above lines. It reinforces the view that Shylock was a man *"more sinned against than sinning"*. Portia's speech on mercy and forgiveness in *The Merchant of Venice* is one of the most beautiful passages of his plays: *"The quality of mercy is not strained/It droppeth like the gentle rain from above/This mightiest in the mightiests".*

The great range and variety of human behaviour treated by Shakespeare gives his plays an everlasting interest. We may ascribe to the Bard what he himself makes Enobarbus say of Cleopatra:

> *"Age cannot wither her*
> *Nor custom state her infinite variety".*

SUMMARY AND MAIN POINTS

Life

1. He was born on or about 23 April, 1564 at Stratford-on-Avon, Warwickshire.
2. His father was a prosperous tradesman.
3. He was sent to a Grammar school where he learnt "small Latin and less Greek."
4. Later misfortunes overtook the family.
5. In his 19th year, he married Anne Hathaway, who was eight years his senior.
6. His marriage seems to have been an unhappy one.
7. (*i*) There are several anecdotes why he left for London, but we need not study them here.
   (*ii*) It is almost certain that he went to London in or about 1587 to seek fortunes there.
8. It was the time when drama was being popularized by the University Wits.
9. (*i*) There are again several stories how he came on the stage, but what we are concerned here is that soon he gained popularity and appeared on the stage as an actor.
   For example, he acted in Ben Jonson's "Everyman in His Humour."
   (*ii*) Soon alongwith being an actor, he became a playwright also.
10. It is certain from the deathbed words of Greene who called him an "upstart" that by 1592, Shakespeare had quite established himself as a playwright.
11. Soon he became a shareholder in prestigious theatres such as the Globe and the Blackfriars.
12. (*i*) He also purchased property in London and Stratford.
    (*ii*) It is clear that he had become sufficiently prosperous.
13. However, misfortunes were not late in visiting him :
    (*i*) His only son died in 1596.
    (*ii*) His father died in 1601.
    (*iii*) His mother died in 1608.
14. Still, financially he was sound.
15. Between 1610 and 1612 he retired to his hometown, Stratford, where he bought the largest house in the town named the New Place.
16. As his health broke down, he died on 23rd April, 1616.

Works

In all, he wrote :

(*i*) 37 plays
(*ii*) Two narrative poems:
  (*a*) Venus and Adonis
  (*b*) Lucrece
(*iii*) 154 sonnets:
  (*a*) 126 addressed to a man—a patron or friend.
  (*b*) the rest 28 addressed to a dark lady.

His dramatic work is generally divided in four periods:

1. **The First Period (1588-93) :** It was the period of apprenticeship and experiment. It included:
   (*i*) Revision of old plays such as:
     (*a*) Henry VI
     (*b*) Titus Andronicus,
   (*ii*) the first comedies such as :
     (*a*) Love's Labour's Lost
     (*b*) Two Gentlemen of Verona
     (*c*) The Comedy of Errors, and
     (*d*) A Midsummer Night's Dream, and
   (*iii*) the first attempt at writing a tragedy—Romeo and Juliet.
2. **The Second Period (1594-1600) :** It was the period of the great Comedies and Chronicle Plays, such as
   (*a*) Richard II
   (*b*) King John

(*c*) The Merchant of Venice
(*d*) Henry IV Part I
(*e*) Henry IV Part II
(*f*) Henry V
(*g*) The Taming of the Shrew
(*h*) The Merry Wives of Windsor
(*i*) Much Ado About Nothing
(*j*) As You Like It, and
(*k*) Twelfth Night

3. **The Third Period (1601-08):** This was the period of his great tragedies and sombre comedies, such as
   (*i*) Julius Caesar
   (*ii*) Hamlet
   (*iii*) All's Well That Ends Well
   (*iv*) Measure for Measure
   (*v*) Troilus and Cressida
   (*vi*) Othello
   (*vii*) King Lear
   (*viii*) Macbeth
   (*ix*) Antony and Cleopatra
   (*x*) Coriolanus
   (*xi*) Timon of Athens
4. **The Fourth Period (1608-12):** This was the period of later comedies or what are known as "Dramatic Romances"—
   (*a*) (*i*) Cymbeline
   (*ii*) The Tempest
   (*iii*) Winter's Tale
   (*b*) There are two other plays of this period which are only partly written by Shakespeare
   (*i*) Pericles
   (*ii*) Henry VIII

☛ Henry VIII was completed by his friend, Fletcher (1579-1625) after his death.

Characteristics

1. No single writer has contributed to literature as much literary work as Shakespeare has done.
2. There is "infinite variety" in his work.
3. He was indisputably a versatile genius—a deft master both at prose and verse of all kinds:
   (*i*) blank verse
   (*ii*) rhyme
   (*iii*) dramatic verse
   (*iv*) narrative verse, etc.
4. He is the most often quoted among all the English writers.
5. He is one of the greatest poets and dramatists of the world, probably the greatest.
6. It is said that he is the only man in the history of mankind who has said all that is worth-saying.
7. He himself might not be a great thinker, but he could reproduce the borrowed matter in an original form such as none else perhaps could do.
8. No other writer, not even Dickens, has been able to produce so many living and throbbing characters as he has done.
9. It is estimated that he coined more than 15000 (some say, about 18000) words which he contributed to the English language.
10. He is the single writer who has given such a solid footing to the English language that its undying endurance over the centuries can hardly ever be doubted.
11. Needless to say his command over the language he uses is unrivalled.
12. Though a romantic writer, he is all the same the master of realism.
13. He steered the drama clear of stiff classical rules based on ancient masters, and made it a national movement.
14. With all the brutalities as shown by him like other dramatists, unlike them, he upheld the moral law such that truth triumphs in the long run, though poetic justice is not essentially done.
15. Thus his dramas are true to life and human nature.
16. There is a mixture of tragedy and comedy in his dramas as in life.
17. He is the master of true humour and has genuine sympathy with mankind.

Shakespeare's Faults

Like everyone he too is not without faults. Here are listed some of his faults:

1. The feeling of hastiness is evident at places in his works.
2. At places, he uses claptrap methods and means to cater to the 'groundlings', thus sacrificing some of the essential elements of genuine drama, consistency of character and propriety.
3. At places his psychology is hopelessly crude and unconvincing; his style vicious; his wit forced and poor; his tragic language bombastic.
4. At some places there are factual errors in his dramas such that the story, plot, scenes and characters start seeing unreal, *e.g.*
   (*i*) The modern Switzerland in 'Winter's Tale' is shown as having a sea-coast.
   (*ii*) There are trees of coconut and palm-dates side by side in 'As You Like It'.
   (*iii*) Sometimes, the "mistaken identity" scenes as in 'The Merchant of Venice' and 'Twelfth Night' seem unreal.

JOHN MILTON (1608–1674)

Life

John Milton was born on December 9, 1608 in London. His father was a lawyer-cum-banker. Although a Puritan, he loved art and literature and was known as a musician. Milton was trained in music and inherited a love for music. He was charming and aloof. After his education at St. Paul's School he joined Christs' College, Cambridge. But he was rusticated from college for protesting against the curriculum.

Even while he was at Cambridge, he wrote Latin and Italian poems. The best one was *Ode on the Morning of Christ's Nativity* written at the age of twenty-one. In this poem he celebrates the end of paganism and "the death of Pan". The style is rich with Elizabethan devices.

He refused ordination as minister or taking holy orders under the Church of England because this would have fettered his liberated conscience. He settled at Horton near London and devoted himself to writing poems. *L' Allegro* and *Il Penseroso* and two masques *Arcades* and *Comus* and the famous elegy, *Lycidas,* are the works of this period.

In 1638 he left for a tour of the Continent. He won many friends in Italy because of his interest in and mastery of Latin and Italian. But before he could go to Greece, he heard of the conflict between the King and the Parliament and hurried back to England to support the latter. He also taught for a time at a school and wrote a tract on education.

Between 1640 and 1660 he wrote prose pamphlets and some sonnets. When the Commonwealth was established, he was appointed Latin Secretary to the department of foreign affairs. He married Mary Powell in 1643. The marriage was an unhappy one. The daughter of a Cavalier Royalist, she could not tolerate Milton's puritanical ways and left him after marriage. He was much aggrieved and wrote tract pleading for a change in divorce laws. Mary returned to him after two years and he had three daughters by her.

Milton turned fully blind in 1653. Andrew Marvell and others assisted him in his work of writing. He accepted his blindness as the will of God in his beautiful sonnet *On His Blindness: "They also serve who only stand and wait".*

He married Catherine Woodcock after his first wife died. But Catherine also expired within fifteen months. When monarchy was restored, Milton lost his post and was arrested. He was soon released. He lost some of his property. Now Milton set himself to writing the work that was to make him immortal. In 1667, he completed the *Paradise Lost.* During this period he married for the third time. He finished *Paradise Regained* and *Samson Agonistes* in 1671. He died on November 8, 1674.

Milton was a tolerant Puritan. That is why he got along well with a Royalist father-in-law and a Catholic brother. In later life he became an Arian and did not accept Christ as the divine son. He kept away from wine and women in order to concentrate on higher goals. An unshakeable idealist, he could not understand man completely. His desire to reform mankind was too ambitious and failed. His poetry is remembered today for its magnificent grandeur rather than for any message.

Works

There are four clear-cut periods in Milton's career as a poet: (1) At Cambridge till 1632, (2) At Horton from 1632 to 1638, (3) The period of journalism from 1640 to 1660, (4) The final period of his masterpieces.

The period of his youth produced the famous *Ode on the Morning of Christ's Nativity* (1629). The poem is marred by exaggeration and metaphysical conceits in describing his devotion to the infant Jesus. He also wrote a number of Latin and Italian poems which have been translated into English.

In 1632, he wrote the exquisite *"L' Allegro"* and *Il Penseroso.* The titles only are in Italian. The poems and their spirit are quite English. The first one describes the poet's thoughts in a gay mood and *Il Penseroso* describes the gloomy side of his thinking. The poems are written in octosyllabic couplets and have a haunting music. *L'Allegro* means *'the cheerful man'* and describes his revels, his delight in a castle or a theatre and *Il Penseroso,* his pensive thoughts. Dr. Johnson is said to have admired these poems very much. The poems depict not so much natural scenes as moods of the mind. Milton seeks pure pleasure. In *L'Allegro*, it is Mirth, fresh, rosy and vigorous, dancing on tiptoe. In *Il Penseroso,* divine Melancholy is presented as a pensive nun *"devout and pure .... with even step and musing gait"*.

Milton's inner conflict, the moral problem before him, is the theme in the masques *Arcades* and *Comus.* Although these are Renaissance in form, the spirit is grave, austere and Miltonic. *Comus* (1634) is a paean to chastity. It is obviously didactic and lacks any dramatic power to thrill. A young, immaculate heroine is confronted by the magician, Comus, who is drunk and sensual. He tries to have her beautiful virginity, but she is successful in warding him off. The poem is full of discourses and learned reminiscences of the classics and lyrical grace. The morality is high and only the select few could appreciate it.

In *Lycidas* (1637) Milton laments the death of a friend by drowning. The elegy asks the question that if a young man full of promise is carried away in the prime of youth then what avails in this life? Pleasure, therefore, calls him to *"sport with Amaryllis in the shade, Or with the tangles of Neaera's hair"*. But another voice, that of fame, calls him away to a life of virtue.

Milton wrote in prose for twenty years. He also composed some exquisite sonnets including the one *On His Blindness* where he regrets he might be incapable of performing God's wish on earth because of his impairment, but consoles himself that even through poetry he can fulfill his life:

"And that one talent which is death to hide
Lodged with me useless
But Patience to prevent that murmur soon replies
They also serve who only stand and wait".

The Restoration of 1660 deprived him of his post for sometime. Poverty, blindness and leisure brought forth his best works: *Paradise Lost* (1667), *Paradise Regained* and *Samson Agonistes* (1671). Here we read in magniloquent lines through great biblical allegories of his personal unhappiness and a nation's agony. He is Beelzebub Satan and Samson in rebellion. Thrown out of Heaven by God, Satan exhorts:

"What though the field be lost
All is not lost
The unconquerable will to survive".

He wrote in blank verse only and used choruses in *Samson Agonistes. Paradise Lost* is his magnum opus, a Puritan's meditation of the Bible or his interpretation of it. The story of Adam and Eve becomes the drama of conscience, the exposure to temptation. The Bible has the ingredients of his own life. *Paradise Regained* is a reply to *Paradise Lost.* This poem is an allegory based on the story of Christ's fast for forty days where he resists the three temptations of Satan and destroys the latter's reign on earth. Christ is seen not as divine incarnation, but as a superman. In fact, Milton himself is Christ, like in that he resists the great temptation for worldly fame by mastering Greek culture and becoming a poet. Literature, philosophy and art are all vain compared to the true wisdom of the Bible.

In *Samson Agonistes,* we again see Milton. He is Samson betrayed by Delilah. He is alone and isolated, blind and helpless, the last of the Republicans among the triumphant Royalists. He lashes out against woman, as the inferior of the human race, deceitful and untrustworthy. The poem is like a Hellenic drama, but lacks movement. There is unending dialectics and reasoning.

SUMMARY AND MAIN POINTS

Life

1. Milton got a very good education and this, combined with his matchless genius, enabled him to achieve things never attempted, much less achieved, by any poet so far.
2. (*i*) His father became a puritan and Milton inherited all the qualities of virtue, purity, discipline and austerity from him.
   (*ii*) However, Milton by natural bent of mind was a great lover of art, music and literature. Hence the qualities of Hebraism and Hellenism blended in him in equal measure.
3. Thus Milton was :
   (*i*) a religious man
   (*ii*) a great scholar
   (*iii*) a lover of music, if not a musician
   (*iv*) a great epic poet
   (*v*) a politician
   (*vi*) a radical in thought
   (*vii*) a lover and crusader of liberty and freedom, particularly that of the press and the soul.
   (*viii*) a reformer
   (*ix*) a lover of beauty in man and nature
   (*x*) He had spirit of devotion and dedication to cause and duty.
4. Milton imbibed the love of religion, art, music and literature and even politics from his father and those of generosity and charity from his mother.
5. From 1632 onwards, Milton withdrew to the country home of his father in Horton where he led an almost solitary life studying deeply the classics in various languages such as :
   (*i*) Greek (*ii*) Latin
   (*iii*) Hebrew (*iv*) French
   (*v*) Italian (*vi*) Spanish
   (*vii*) English, etc.
6. Not only this, Milton also got a mastery over such disparate subjects as:
   (*i*) music (*ii*) science
   (*iii*) mathematics (*iv*) theology, etc.
7. (*i*) Thereafter, Milton went on a continental tour.
   He visited France, Switzerland and Italy.
   (*ii*) He met Grotius, the Dutch scholar in Paris, and Galileo in Florence where he was serving a jail term.
8. As Civil War broke out in England, Milton hurried back to England.
9. In His "Tenure of Kings and Magistrates," Milton asserted the divine right of the people to take the action necessary for their self-defence and protection, as against the Divine Right of the King asserted earlier by James I and now by Charles I.
10. (*i*) Milton was married in 1643 to Mary Powell.
    (*ii*) She was not a woman of high calibre and, moreover, she was fond of a luxurious life.
    (*iii*) To cap it all, she belonged to a Royalist family.
11. (*i*) Just a month after their marriage, the girl deserted Milton.
    (*ii*) It was then that Milton wrote :
    (*a*) "Doctrine and Discipline of Divorce," and
    (*b*) "Tetrachordon"
    (*iii*) This he did to justify the repudiation of marriage from his side.
    (*iv*) Milton's arguments were not taken with pleasant approval by the people of England.

12. (*i*) After the death of his wife he married the second time.
 (*ii*) After her death he wrote his famous sonnet: "Methought I saw my late espoused saint."
 (*iii*) He married the third time in 1663.
 (*iv*) Now, Milton had been stone blind since 1652 and his third wife was like a nurse to him.
13. (*i*) He wrote "Defensio pro Populo Anglicano"—a controversial work but containing powerful prose.
 (*ii*) However, his best prose work is "Areopagitica" in which he fights the cause of freedom of press like a true crusader.

Works

Early works : Among his early works, we have :

1. On the Morning of Christ's Nativity
2. L'Allegro
3. Il Penseroso
4. The Masque of Comus (1634)
5. Lycidas
6. Sonnets

Characteristics

1. **On the Morning of Christ's Nativity:** Long points out, "In his early work Milton appears as the inheritor of all that was best in Elizabethan literature, and his first work, the ode "On the Morning of Christ's Nativity" approaches the high-water mark of lyric poetry in England."
2. **L'Allegro and Il Penseroso:**
 (*i*) These poems belong to Milton's Horton period.
 (*ii*) The former is about the happy man, and the latter about the sad man.
 (*iii*) Long writes on **L'Allegro:**
 "The air is sweet; birds are singing; multitude of sights, sounds, fragrances, fill all the senses; and to this appeal of nature the soul of man responds by being happy, seeing in every flower and hearing in every harmony some exquisite symbol of human life."
 (*iv*) **In Il Penseroso,** we have inter alia:
 (*a*) a scene of twilight and the appearance of the moon.
 (*b*) "a quiet thoughtfulness.... which is not sad, though like all quiet moods, it is akin to sadness, and which sounds the deeps of human emotion in the presence of nature." (Long)
3. **Comus**
 (*i*) According to Long, it "is in many respects the most perfect of Milton's poems".
 (*ii*) In Comus, we have inter alia:
 (*a*) dance and music
 (*b*) gorgeous visual scenery
 (*c*) the hoary past moral purpose but so consummately delineated by Milton—
 The Triumph of Virtue over vice.
4. **Lycidas**
 (*i*) It is an elegy written by Milton on the death of his college friend, Edward King.
 (*ii*) It is a blend of "high moral purpose with the noblest poetry." (Long)
 (*iii*) There is abundance of supernatural element in the poem in the form of nymphs, fauns, satyrs, etc.
 (*iv*) So, the poem is an unrivalled example of "Pagan Renaissance."
5. **Sonnets**
 (*i*) Milton made use of the form which is known as Miltonic, Italian or Petrarchan in his sonnets instead of the Shakespearean form.
 (*ii*) Instead of love, Milton directed his sonnets towards such subjects as:
 (*a*) fulfilment of duty
 (*b*) unflinching patriotism
 (*c*) music and harmony
 (*d*) undying love for political struggle
 (*e*) undeterrable faith in God and His creation.
 (*f*) justification of ways of God to man which he later endeavoured most vehemently, elaborately and consummately in Paradise Lost.

(*iii*) That is why Wordsworth says of him:

"Thy soul was like a star and dwelt apart;
Thou hadst a voice whose sound was like the sea—
Pure as the naked heavens, majestic, free."

(*iv*) Some of his famous sonnets are:
(*a*) On Arriving at the Age of Twenty Three
(*b*) On His Deceased Wife
(*c*) The Massacre in Piedmont
(*d*) On His Blindness

(*v*) Unlike Wordsworth who wrote 500 or more sonnets, Milton did not write many sonnets.

6. **Paradise Lost**

(*i*) Its theme is the Fall of Man.
(*ii*) In it Milton wanted to justify the ways of God to man.
(*iii*) No doubt, it is Milton's greatest and best work which has made him immortal.
(*iv*) According to Lamartine, it is "the dream of a Puritan fallen asleep over his Bible."
(*v*) It was composed by Milton when he had fully lost his eye-sight.
(*vi*) Paradise Lost has 12 books like any true epic.

Book I: It contains *inter alia*:
(*i*) A noble invocation
(*ii*) A description of Satan and his legions,
(*iii*) The description of the rebel angels' plot to wife out the state of innocence of Adam and Eve, our first parents, as created by God.

Book II: It contains *inter alia*:
(*i*) The great meeting of the devils
(*ii*) The start of Satan's journey to cause temptation of Adam and Eve.

Book III: It contains *inter alia*:
(*i*) God's despatch of Raphael to undertake the warning of Adam and Eve about the impending danger.
(*ii*) The Son of God's offer of personal sacrifice to take upon himself the punishment to man for disobedience to God.
(*iii*) Satan is also seen again.

Book IV: It contains *inter alia*:
(*i*) The scene of Paradise
(*ii*) Satan is caught while tempting Eve in a dream, but is not punished.

Book V, VI: It contains *inter alia*:
(*i*) Eve's narration of her dream to Adam.
(*ii*) Scenes of their daily routine
(*iii*) Arrival of Raphael, etc.

Book VII: It contains the story of creation as told by Raphael.

Book VIII: It contains Adam's narration of his own story, etc.

Book IX: It describes Satan's temptation of Eve, etc.

Book X: It contains *inter alia*:
(*i*) God's judgement upon Adam and Eve.
(*ii*) Their repentance
(*iii*) Satan and his followers' changing into hissing serpents.

Book XI: It describes :
(*i*) God's acceptance of Adam's repentance, but His ordering of his banishment from Eden.
(*ii*) Michael's departure to execute God's orders.

Book XII: It describes *inter alia* :
(*i*) Adam and Eve's having the assurance regarding their future redemption.
(*ii*) Man's first ancestors' being turned out of paradise "hand in hand."

Comments: The poem is :
(*i*) a triumph of Milton's most artistic blank verse.
(*ii*) a triumph of the Epic art.
(*iii*) an assertion of the Puritan view-point.
(*iv*) a perfect expression of Milton's own love of music, liberty, justice, etc.
(*v*) a triumph of sublimity and what is called "the grand style."
(*vi*) a justification of man's ways to God, instead of God's ways to man, as Milton claimed to assert.
(*vii*) the unrivalled character of Satan which resembles Milton's own in many respects.
(*viii*) a triumph of Hebraism.

(*ix*) a triumph of the subjective art.

(*x*) a triumph of the Elizabethan wonder, which earned Milton the title : "A belated Elizabethan".

7. **Paradise Regained**

(*i*) It is a bare poem as compared to Paradise Lost in the matter of style, as is shorn of ornate prosody.

(*ii*) It has wonderful lines and passages showing Milton's :

(*a*) purity and loftiness of mind

(*b*) most exquisite scenery and imagery

(*iii*) Here, Christ, who spurns the tempter, is, in fact, Milton himself as 'In Paradise Lost' Milton is often identified with Satan, who loves liberty above anything else, at least in the first two books.

(*iv*) The theme of the poem is "Christ's temptation in the wilderness."

8. **Samson Agonistes**

(*i*) Samson was an Israeli wrestler who was blind and much maligned.

(*ii*) He was a champion of liberty.

(*iii*) Milton can indisputably be identified with him.

(*iv*) The poem is "a pure tragedy, with all the passion and restraint which marked the old Greek dramas." (Long)

(*v*) The climax is reached when Samson chained with the central pillar of a dome where his tormentors are making merry, brings down the whole structure which destroys all.

WILLIAM WORDSWORTH (1770–1850)

Life

William Wordsworth was born on April 7, 1770 at Cockermouth in the cumberland highlands. His father was a lawyer and land agent. He lost both the parents by the age of fourteen. His school days at Hawkeshead was full of joy, spent in games and reading. He joined St John's College, Cambridge when he was seventeen and went on a walking tour of France during one of his vacations. Taking his degree in 1791 he went to France to stay. The cause of the French Revolution — liberty and equality — attracted him much. He spent 1797-98 mostly with Coleridge and published *Lyrical Ballads* in collaboration with him. After this he visited Germany with his sister Dorothy. Finally he returned to Grasmere in the Lake district of England. Here he published the second volume of the *Lyrical Ballads* and married his cousin Mary Hutchinson.

Wordsworth's life was spent in quiet contempiation and meditation in the beautiful Lake district. Here nature inspired him to write his poetry. He also visited Wales, Scotland and Ireland. He was left a legacy of money by a kind man and got a job as sinecure — distributor of stamps. A man of simple living and high thinking, he could lead a comfortable life and devote himself to poetry. In 1842, the Government provided him a pension of £ 300 a year.

Earlier Wordsworth's poetry received no recognition. In fact, there was adverse criticism of it. But during the last two decades of his life, recognition came to him. He received an honorary degree from the Universities of Durham and Oxford. In 1843 he was appointed poet-laureate. He died in 1850.

Wordsworth was of hardy north-country stock. In austerity he reminds us of Milton. Wordsworth's egotism came in the way of appreciation of the poetry of others.

Works

Most of Wordsworth's voluminous work is dull and prosaic. Only a few works like *The Prelude* and *The Excursion* make him worthy of the recognition he received as poet-laureate. First and foremost, Wordsworth was the High Priest of Nature. While Cowper, Burns, Blake, Byron, Shelley and Keats all loved Nature 'it was only the external forms'. To

Wordsworth Nature was where the Spirit of the Supreme Being dwelt. Nature revealed God's peace and mystery. He had a mystic understanding of Nature. Nature showed the bonds that united all forms of life together — birds, animals and humans. To love all was the message of Nature, Nature was a great teacher. In his own words:

"One impulse from a vernal wood
May teach you more of man,
Of moral evil and of good,
Than all the sages can".

To be able to learn such lessons, Wordsworth advocated a receptive heart. If one bared oneself to the influence of Nature one received wisdom, health, beauty, grace and peace of mind. In one of his *Lucy* poems he says:

"And beauty born of murmuring sound
Shall pass into her face".

When England went to war with France, his mind was in conflict between patriotic loyalty and his love and admiration for the Revolution. War shattered all hopes. He returned to Nature to restore his faith in divine providence and found Nature a great healer.

Nature was a teacher of morals. *"Stern Daughter of the voice of God,"* he called her. His attitude to Nature developed in stages. First, he saw the visionary gleams of childhood in the *Ode on the Intimations of Childhood.*

"There was a time when valley, rock and hill
Seem'd apparelled in celestial light".

Later he developed a passion for Nature which gave him *"aching joys."* Finally, Nature in all its manifestations gave him a lesson in living: *"the meanest flower that blows"* gave him *"thoughts that do often lie too deep for tears".*

Once when Wordsworth was returning home from Cambridge, he passed through a very beautiful landscape of mountains and the sea and that moment of enchantment with Nature was a flash of illumination. He realized that his mission of life was to teach mankind. He wished to bring mankind back to Nature for healing and morals. He set out to write the long poem *The Recluse,* consisting of two parts *The Prelude* (1850) and *The Excursion* (1814). He could not finish the work. Wordsworth claimed that his work as a poet was to teach and this is what he does. The poem is marred by too much moralizing.

Wordsworth felt that the real characters for his poetry must be common, noble men, not Lords and Ladies. He, therefore, wrote a number of poems like *The Idiot Boy, Harry Gill* and *Peter Bell* (1819) in which metre is ignored and common everyday speech is used. The effect is prosaic poetry — dull and ineffective. The real great poetry of Wordsworth is that which springs from his genius, not his poetic beliefs. Wordsworth's great poetry shows spiritual depths of calm reflection. As he writes in *Laodamia,* his classical poem, *"For the Gods approve / The depth and not the tumult of the soul".*

Wordsworth wrote a great variety of poems — odes, lyrics and almost 400 sonnets of which *Upon Westminster Bridge, On Milton* and *The World is too much with Us* are famous.

According to Wordsworth, poetry was "emotion recollected in transquillity". *The Solitary Reaper, To a Highland Girl, The Daffodils, Tintern Abbey* and the *Immortality Ode* were written after sometime had elapsed from the event described. These events were moments of perception and when the time had passed the emotions stirred by those moments surfaced clearly. These emotions are then put into words.

SUMMARY AND MAIN POINTS

Life

1. He was born at Cockermouth, Cumberland. (A poet/critic has called him "the gander of Cockermouth").
2. He got education at Hawkeshead School, Lancashire, and Cambridge.
3. He paid two visits to France :
   (*i*) The first time in 1790
   (*ii*) The second time in 1791-92.

   Long divides his life into four periods :
   (*i*) *1770-87:* It belongs to his childhood and youth-Cumberland.

(*ii*) *1787-97:* This period covers :

(*a*) his life at Cambridge

(*b*) his travels abroad which enabled him to be influenced by the revolutionary ideas.

☛ We know that his revolutionary enthusiasm died soon with :

(*i*) the excesses of the Revolution including what is called "The Reign of Terror,"

(*ii*) the rise of tyrannical Napoleon

(*iii*) 1797-99: This period was very significant as it enabled him to understand his own abilities and take full advantage of them.

(*iv*) 1799-1850: It was practically a period of retirement in the lake region of his birth and childhood and to remain in direct touch with nature.

Works

1. His "Lyrical Ballads"—a book which is often considered the start of the Revival of Romanticism in England appeared in 1798.
2. His Preface to the Lyrical Ballads is considered important in the history of Criticism of English literature.
3. (*i*) He intended to write a single great poem under the caption "The Recluse."

   (*ii*) The poem was intended to give a comprehensive treatment of: (*a*) nature, (*b*) man and (c) society.

   (*iii*) His intention was that his "The Prelude"—the Growth of a Poet's Mind—should introduce the Recluse.

   (*iv*) (*a*) The first book of The Recluse "The Home at Grasmere" was published posthumously in 1888.

   (*b*) The name of the second book was 'The Excursion.'

   (*c*) The third was never completed by the poet.

His most famous poems are :

1. The Prelude
2. Tintern Abbey
3. Ode on Intimations of Immortality.
4. Ode to Duty or Education of Nature
5. The Rainbow
6. The Solitary Reaper
7. Michael
8. To a Skylark
9. Yarrow Revisited
10. Lucy Gray
11. She Dwelt Among the Untrodden Ways
12. Daffodils

He also wrote a large number of sonnets such as :

1. On Milton
2. On Westminster Bridge
3. The World is Too Much With Us, etc.

Characteristics

1. He was a great lover of nature.
2. He felt the presence of a spirit in nature, that is, the spirit of nature.
3. He believed in pantheism.
4. He believed that nature could bestow peace, sympathy, love, joy and other virtues on man.
5. He did not like to depict nature "red in tooth and claw."
6. He believed that nature gave purity to man and ennobled his heart.
7. He was a great lover of the common man and the rustic and rural life.
8. He loved the child and thought that because of its innocence, purity of thought and nearness to God, childhood was the golden period of human life.
9. He loved all creation and all kinds of creatures, including the smallest and most insignificant animals and insects.
10. He believed that "nature never did betray the heart that loved her."
11. He himself practised what he preached and spent most of his time in the company of nature.
12. His poetry is full of :

    (*i*) vivid descriptions of scenes of nature.

    (*ii*) simple human affections.

    (*iii*) fervent adulations of childhood and love of animals.

(*iv*) depictions of country and village life.
(*v*) sweet and haunting music.
(*vi*) personal reminiscences and memories
(*vii*) autobiographical tones
(*viii*) adulation of simplicity and homeliness.
(*ix*) tones of true theism and fervent faith in greatness, goodness and benignity of nature.

13. Although much of his later poetry is dull and interesting, yet it contains flashes of imaginative lines and good poetry.

JOHN GALSWORTHY (1867–1933)

John Galsworthy was an English novelist and playwright. His notable works include *The Forsyte Saga* (1906–1921) and its sequels, *A Modern Comedy* and *End of the Chapter*. He won the Nobel Prize in Literature in 1932.

Life

John Galsworthy was born on 14 August 1867 at Kingston Hill in Surrey, England, the son of John and Blanche Bailey (nee Bartleet) Galsworthy. His family was wealthy and well established, with a large estate in Kingston upon Thames that is now the site of three schools: Marymount International School, Rokeby Preparatory School, and Holy Cross. He attended Harrow and New College, Oxford, training as a barrister, and was called to the bar in 1890. However, he was not keen to begin practising law and instead travelled abroad to look after the family's shipping business. During these travels he met Joseph Conrad, then the first mate of a sailing-ship moored in the harbour of Adelaide, Australia, and the two future novelists became close friends. In 1895 Galsworthy began an affair with Ada Nemesis Pearson Cooper (1864–1956), the wife of his cousin Major Arthur Galsworthy. After her divorce ten years later, they married 23 September 1905 and stayed together until his death in 1933. Before their marriage, they often stayed clandestinely in a farmhouse called Wingstone in the village of Manaton on Dartmoor, Devon. From 1908 he took out a long lease on part of the building and made it their regular second home until 1923.

From the Four Winds, a collection of short stories, was Galsworthy's first published work in 1897. These and several subsequent works were published under the pen name John Sinjohn, and it would not be until *The Island Pharisees* (1904) that he would begin publishing under his own name, probably owing to the death of his father. His first full-length novel, *Jocelyn* was published in an edition of 750 under the name of *John Sinjohn* – he later refused to have it republished. His first play, *The Silver Box* (1906), – in which the theft of a prostitute's purse by a rich 'young man of good family' is placed beside the theft of a silver cigarette case from the rich man's father's house by 'a poor devil', with very different repercussions – became a success, and he followed it up with *The Man of Property* (1906), the first in the Forsyte trilogy. Although he continued writing both plays and novels, it was as a playwright that he was mainly appreciated at the time. Along with those of other writers of the time, such as George Bernard Shaw, his plays addressed the class system and social issues, two of the best known being *Strife* (1909) and *The Skin Game* (1920).

He is now far better known for his novels, particularly *The Forsyte Saga,* his trilogy about the eponymous family and connected lives. These books, as with many of his other works, deal with social class, upper-middle class lives in particular. Although sympathetic to his characters, he highlights their insular, snobbish, and acquisitive attitudes and their suffocating moral codes. He is viewed as one of the first writers of the Edwardian era who challenged some of the ideals of society depicted in the preceding literature of Victorian Eng'and. The depiction of a woman in an unhappy marriage furnishes another recurring theme in his work. The character of Irene in *The Forsyte Saga* is drawn from Ada Pearson, though her previous marriage was not as miserable as that of the character.

Through his writings he campaigned for a variety of causes, including prison reform, women's rights, animal welfare, and the opposition of censorship. During World War I he worked in a hospital in France as an orderly after being passed over for military service. He was elected as the first president of the PEN International literary club in 1921, was appointed to the Order of Merit in 1929 — after earlier turning down a knighthood — and was awarded the Nobel Prize in 1932. He was too ill to attend the Nobel awards ceremony, and died six weeks later on 31 January 1933 of a stroke at his London home.

John Galsworthy lived for the final seven years of his life at Bury in West Sussex. In accordance with his will he was cremated at Woking with his ashes then being scattered over the South Downs from an aeroplane, but there are also memorials in High gate 'New' Cemetery and in the cloisters of New College, Oxford (the latter cut and placed in the cloisters by Eric Gill). The popularity of his fiction waned quickly after his death but the hugely successful adaptation of *The Forsyte Saga* in 1967 renewed interest in his work.

A number of John Galsworthy's letters and papers are held at the University of Birmingham Special Collections.

In 2007, Kingston University, London opened a new building named in recognition of his local birth. Galsworthy Road in Kingston, location of Kingston Hospital, is also named for him.

Works

- *From the Four Winds,* 1897 (as John Sinjohn)
- *Jocelyn,* 1898 (as John Sinjohn)
- *Villa Rubein,* 1900 (as John Sinjohn)
- *A Man of Devon,* 1901 (as John Sinjohn)
- *The Island Pharisees,* 1904
- *The Silver Box,* 1906 (his first play
- *The Man of Property,* 1906 – first book of *The Forsyte Saga* (1922)
- *The Country House,* 1907
- *A Commentary,* 1908
- *Fraternity,* 1909
- *A Justification for the Censorship of Plays,* 1909
- *Strife,* 1909
- *Fraternity,* 1909
- *Joy,* 1909
- *Justice,* 1910
- *A Motley,* 1910
- *The Spirit of Punishment,* 1910
- *Horses in Mines,* 1910
- *The Patrician,* 1911
- *The Pigeon,* 1912
- *The Eidest Son,* 1912
- *Quality,* 1912
- *Moods, Songs, and Doggerels,* 1912
- *For Love of Beasts,* 1912
- *The Inn of Tranquillity,* 1912
- *The Dark Flower,* 1913
- *The Fugitive,* 1913
- *The Mob,* 1914
- *The Freelands,* 1915
- *The Little Man,* 1915
- *A Bit's Love,* 1915
- *A Sheaf,* 1916
- *The Apple Tree,* 1916
- *Beyond,* 1917
- *Five Tales,* 1918
- *Indian Summer of a Forsyte,* 1918 – first interlude of *The Forsyte Saga*
- *Saint's Progress,* 1919
- *Addresses in America,* 1912
- *The Foundations,* 1920
- *In Chancery,* 1920 – second book of *The Forsyte Saga*
- *Awakening,* 1920 – second interlude of *The Forsyte Saga*
- *Awakening,* 1920 – second interlude of *The Forsyte Saga*
- *The Skin Game,* 1920
- *To Let,* 1921 – third book of *The Forsyte Saga*
- *A Family Man,* 1922
- *The Little Man,* 1922

- *Loyalties,* 1922
- *Windows,* 1922
- *Captures,* 1923
- *Abracadabra,* 1924
- *The Forest,* 1924
- *Old English,* 1924
- *The White Monkey,* 1924 – first book of *A Modern Comedy* (1929)
- *The Show,* (1925
- *Escape,* 1926
- *The Silver Spoon,* 1926 – second book of *A Modern Comedy*
- *Verses New and Old,* 1926
- *Castles in Spain,* 1927
- *A Silent Wooing,* 1927 – first Interlude of *A Modern Comedy*
- *Passers By,* 1927 – second Interlude of *A Modern Comedy*
- *Swan Song,* 1928 – third book of *A Modern Comedy*
- *The Manaton Edition,* 1923–26 (collection, 30 vols.)
- *Exiled,* 1929
- *The Roof,* 1929
- *On Forsyte Change,* 1930
- *Two Essays on Conrad,* 1930
- *Soames and the Flag,* 1930
- *The Creation of Character in Literature,* 1931 (The Romanes Lecture for (1931).
- *Maid in Waiting,* 1931 – first book of *End of the Chapter* (1934)
- *Forty Poems,* 1932
- *Flowering Wilderness,* 1932
- *Over the River,* 1933
- *Autobiographical Letters of Galsworthy: A Corres-pondence with Frank Harris,* 1933
- *The Grove Edition,* 1927–34 (collection, 27 Vols.)
- *Collected Poems,* 1934
- *Flowering Wilderness,* 1932 – second book of *End of the Chapter*
- *One More River* (originally *Over the River*), 1933 – third book of *End of the Chapter*
- *Punch and Go,* 1935
- *The Life and Letters,* 1935
- *The Winter Garden,* 1935
- *Forsytes, Pendyces and Others,* 1935
- *Selected Short Stories,* 1935
- *Glimpses and Reflections,* 1937
- *Galsworthy's Letters to Leon Lion,* 1968
- *Letters from John Galsworthy* 1900–1932, 1970

SUMMARY AND MAIN POINTS

1. Galsworthy's early works which were written over the pseudonym "John Sinjohn" were all rejected by the publishers.
2. (*i*) His first work which made him widely known was 'The Man of Property' (a novel).
   (*ii*) It deals with middle-class Victorian society.
3. In 1904 he published his play "Island Pharisees", which reappeared as "The Pigeon" in 1922.
4. The same year (1922) was published "The Forsyte Saga.
5. In all, he wrote about thirty works of fiction. According to Long, the best among them all is "Indian Summer of a Forsyte."
6. Galsworthy is better known as a play-wright than a fiction writer.
7. His plays are what now we know as "Problem Plays."
8. His most famous plays among his thirty plays are :
   (*i*) Strife (For this work he received the Nobel Prize for Literature)
   (*ii*) Justice (1910)
   (*iii*) Loyalties (1922)
   (*iv*) The Silver Box (1909)
   (*v*) Escape (1926)

The Skin Game was adapted and directed by Alfred Hitchocock in 1931. It starred C.V. France, Helen Haye, Jill Esmond, Edmoud Gwenn, and John Longden.

Escape was filmed in 1930 and 1948. The latter was directed by Joseph L. Mankiewicz, starring Rex Harrison, Peggy Cummins, and William Hartnell. The screenplay was by Philip Dunne.

One More River (a film version of Galsworthy's *Over the River*) was filmed by James Whale in 1934. The film starred Frank Lawton, Colin Clive (one of Whale's most frequently used actors), Diana Wynyard, and featured Mrs. Patrick Campbell in a rare sound film appearance.

The First and the Last, as short play, was adapted as *21 Days*, starring Vivien Leigh and Laurence Olivier.

Galsworthy's short story *The Apple Tree* was adapted into a radio play for Orson Welles's *Lady Esther Almanac* radio series on CBS, first broadcast on 12 January 1942; the play was again produced by Welles for CBS on *The Mercury Summer Theatre* of 6 September 1946. The 1988 film *A Summer Story* was also based on *The Apple Tree.*

The Patrician was broadcast on NBC University Theater of the Air radio show on 24 February 1950.

Characteristics

In the works of **John Galsworthy (1867-1933)** we find an artistic conscience. Like Wells, he also attacked the concept of property and commercialism in his novels. He too exposed and criticized national prejudices, especially those existing among his own class, the landed gentry. He was widely read in Continental Literature and was especially influenced by France and Russia. Turgenev with his noble realism was his ideal. He is a detached and impartial observer of his country's decadent values. He advocates a fearless search for truth. *In The Island Pharisees* (1904) he exposes the stagnation of thought among English privileged classes. A similar theme is touched in other novels like *The Country House* (1907), *The Patrician* (1911) and *The Dark Flower* (1913) where country squires, aristocracy and artists are critically studied. *The Forsyte Saga* (1922) is his masterpiece. It is a natural history of the rich upper-middle class family. He describes their attitude to events like the Great War, the growth of socialism, unemployment and the coal strike.

MULTIPLE CHOICE QUESTIONS

1. Shakespeare was born at:
A. London B. Stratford-on-Avon
C. Leicester D. Edinburgh

2. Shakespeare married:
A. Portia B. Imogen
C. Anne Hathaway D. Lucy

3. Shakespeare's first job in a London theatre was:
A. acting as a ghost
B. translating plays
C. to write plays
D. holding visitor's horses

4. Shakespeare first wrote his plays for:
A. Earl of Leicester's Players
B. The Globe
C. The King's Players
D. The Shakespeare Society

5. Shakespeare wrote:
A. 20 plays B. 35 plays
C. 24 plays D. 37 plays

6. His sonnets are mostly addressed to:
A. Queen Elizabeth
B. Ben Jonson
C. The Earl of Southampton
D. The Duke of Edinburgh

7. *Venus* and *Adonis* is a poem of:
A. Two Sisters B. Victory
C. Love D. Greek art

8. The play written in collaboration with Marlowe was:
A. Winter's Tale
B. Merchant of Venice
C. Titus Andronicus
D. Hamlet

9. Portia is a character in the Shakespearean play:
A. Merchant of Venice
B. Twelfth Night
C. The Tempest
D. Romeo and Juliet

10. The Shakespearean play which describes the assassination of a Roman general is:
A. Macbeth B. Julius Caesar
C. Othello D. Richard II

11. The first folio of all of Shakespeare's plays were published in:
A. 1616 B. 1638
C. 1640 D. 1623

12. The only play missing from the first folio is:
A. The Winter's Tale
B. The Merry Wives of Windsor
C. Pericles
D. A Midsummer Night's Dream

13. Shakespeare wrote his plays in:
A. Rhyming couplets
B. Blank verse
C. Quatrains
D. lambic metre

14. The Jew with whom Shakespeare showed sympathy in one of his plays is:
A. Morose B. Barabbas
C. Nicodemus D. Shylock

15. Puck Goodfellow in *A Midsummer Night's Dream* is a/an:
A. impish fairy B. courtier
C. moneylender D. soldier

16. The downfall of Shakespeare's tragic characters is owing to:
A. the Will of God
B. a fatal flaw in character
C. destiny
D. evil advisers

17. Shakespeare got the plot of most of his plays from:
A. Existing plays
B. Ben Jonson
C. The original classics
D. Translations of Greek, Roman and other European stories.

18. Although Macbeth is a murderer, he is still the hero because:
A. he wants to become the king
B. his life ends tragically
C. he shows uncommon intelligence and vitality
D. he refuses to surrender

19. The part of a play where all the major themes and characters are introduced is known as:
A. Revelation B. Exposition
C. Chorus D. Introduction

20. Among Shakespeare's 37 plays, *Macbeth* was .... in order of being published.
A. 28th B. 26th
C. 30th D. 35th

21. In tragedy, human beings are shown coming to terms with forces larger and greater than themselves. These forces are:
A. Devils B. Fate or Death
C. Circumstances D. Natural calamities

22. The cause of the downfall of a Shakespearean hero is:
A. *hubris* or pride
B. God's will
C. a bad woman
D. some wrong decision

23. The book which influenced Shakespeare the most in introducing witches in *Macbeth* was:
A. Demonology
B. Chronicles of Scotland
C. Discovery of Witchcraft
D. Written by King James I

24. Shakespeare's Macbeth is an important source of information about the history of:
A. Scotland
B. England of his own times
C. Ireland
D. The world

25. The belief in Elizabethan times that the King was God's representative or image on earth led to the theory of the:
A. Divine Right of Kings
B. Great Chain of Being
C. Natural Order
D. Witchcraft

26. According to the Elizabethans anything that went contrary to the natural order was:
A. good B. strange
C. revolutionary D. evil

27. In Tudor England, women's role in society was:
A. more important than men
B. that of a slave
C. equal to men
D. secondary to men

28. Widows could not protect their property, and if they showed bold ideas, they were accused of being:
A. thieves B. wrongful owners
C. witches D. greedy

29. In the beginning of *Macbeth*, the three witches meet:
A. in a health
B. in a ruined building
C. in a forest
D. in a barn

30. What title do the witches use to hail Macbeth?
A. General B. Victor
C. Glamis D. King

31. The fourth witch is the name usually given to:
A. One of Duncan's royal maids
B. An invisible spirit
C. Macduff's wife
D. Lady Macbeth

32. The witches prophesy that Macbeth cannot be killed till a forest comes moving down towards him. This forest is:
A. Dunsinane B. The Black Forest
C. Brinam Wood D. The Scottish Forest

33. Duncan wants to make which one of these his successor to the throne?
A. Malcolm, his own son
B. Macbeth
C. Banquo
D. Fleance

34. In the beginning of the play, Macbeth is shown returning from:
A. a tour B. a holiday
C. battle D. an expedition

35. Lady Macbeth is described as:
A. masculine B. frail as any woman
C. kind-hearted D. dull and powerless

36. Lady Macbeth does not wish to kill the sleeping Duncan because:
A. he resembles her father
B. it is not proper for a woman
C. her husband is the one who will succeed him
D. it is not proper to kill the enemy in sleep

37. Duncan is a guest of the Macbeths at:
A. Edinburgh Castle B. Dunsinane
C. Buckingham D. Inverness Castle

38. A speech in which an actor reveals his innermost thoughts is called a:
A. Soliloquy B. Aside
C. Chorus D. Loud thinking

39. The dagger that Macbeth sees in the air is:
A. his own dagger held by a spirit
B. a projection of his imagination signifying the murder of his conscience and peace
C. some other object resembling a dagger
D. suspended from a thread

40. Who says "I have supped too much with horrors/And know the taste of blood"?
A. Banquo B. Duncan
C. Macbeth D. Lady Macbeth

41. Who says that all the sweet scents of Arabia cannot remove the stench of blood and all the seven seas cannot wash off the blood of Duncan from the hands?
A. Lady Macbeth B. Malcolm
C. The Witches D. Macbeth

42. No man of woman born will be able to kill Macbeth. So the witches prophesied. But Macduff succeeds in killing him because he was born from:
A. a goddess
B. a miracle
C. a Caesarean operation
D. a test-tube

43. Lady Macbeth's sleep-walking is a result of her:
A. deep sense of guilt
B. overactive brain

C. dreams
D. pretence

44. Which of these plays by Shakespeare does *not* use 'cross-dressing' as a device?
A. *As You Like It*
B. *Julius Caeser*
C. *Cymbeline*
D. *Two Gentlemen of Verona*

45. The etymological meaning of the word "trope" is
A. gesture B. turning
C. mirror D. desire

46. In the late seventeenth century a "Battle of Books" erupted between which two groups?
A. Cavaliers and Roundheads
B. Abolitionists and Enthusiasts for slaves
C. Champions of Ancient and Modern Learning
D. The Welsh and the Scots

47. Shakespeare's sonnets:
A. do not carry a dedication.
B. are dedicated to James I of England.
C. are dedicated to Mary Arden.
D. are dedicated to an unknown "Mr. W.H."

48. Which of the following poems uses *terza rima*?
A. John Keats's "Ode to a Nightingale"
B. P.B. Shelley's "Ode to the West Wind"
C. William Wordsworth's "The Solitary Reaper"
D. Alfred Tennyson's "Ulysses"

49. When one says that "someone is no more" or that "someone has breathed his/ her last", the speaker is resorting to
A. euphism B. euphony
C. understatement D. euphemism

50. Which of the following are "companion poems"?
A. "Gypsy songs" and "Songs and Sonnets"
B. "L'Allegro" and "II Penseroso"
C. "The Good Morrow" and "The Sun Rising"
D. "Full Fathom Five" and "Hark, Hark! the Lark"

51. *'Fluency'* in language is the same as:
A. the ability to put oneself across comfortably in speech and/or writing
B. the ability to command language rather than language commanding the user
C. glibness
D. accuracy

52. What is a mock-heroic poem? A mock-heroic poem
A. mocks at heroic pretensions in poets and critics
B. mocks heroism, an exaggerated virtue in all epics
C. uses a heroic style to deride airs and affectations
D. uses a mocking style to deride heroes and hero-worship

53. In drama, an aside is addressed…
A. to an audience by an actor; the words so spoken are not meant to be heard by other actors on the stage.
B. to other actors on the stage; the words so spoken are not meant to be heard by the audience.
C. by the playwright to the audience.
D. by the protagonist to his/her antagonist

54. Which of the following is not a revenge tragedy?
A. *Hamlet*
B. *The Duchess of Malfi*
C. *Volpone*
D. *Gorboduc*

55. "The pen is mightier than the sword" is an example of
A. simile B. image
C. conceit D. metonymy

56. An epilogue is
A. prefixed to a text which it introduces.
B. suffixed to a text which it sums up or extends.
C. a piece of writing or speech that formally begins a book.
D. a piece of writing or speech that bears no relation to the text at hand.

57. Items in a published book appear in the following order:
A. Index, Copyright Page, Bibliography, Footnotes
B. Copyright Page, Bibliography, Index, Footnotes
C. Copyright Page, Footnotes, Bibliography, Index
D. Bibliography, Copyright Page, Index, Footnotes

58. Which of the following statements on The Prelude by William Wordsworth is/are not true?
1. *The Prelude* was published posthumously.
2. In this poem, Wordsworth records his development as a poet.
3. The poem runs to 14 books; at crucial stages the poet celebrates the sublime natural scenery in developing his spiritual, moral and imaginative nature.
4. Poems like "Michael", "The Old Cumberland Beggar", "She dwelt among the untrodden ways", "Nutting" etc. are the highlights of this volume.

A. 1 to 4 are true B. 1 is not true
C. 4 is not true D. Only 3 is true

59. One of the following *Canterbury Tales* is in prose, identify.
A. *The Pardoner's Tale*
B. *The Parson's Tale*
C. *The Monk's Tale*
D. *The Knight's Tale*

60. A 'curtal sonnet' consists of
A. 11 lines B. 12 lines
C. 13 lines D. 14 lines

61. The expression "murderous innocence" is an example of
A. Oxymoron B. Zeugma
C. Chiasmus D. Pun

62. Which of the following works of John Milton is an elegy?
A. *Lycidas* B. *L'Allegro*
C. *Camus* D. *Paradise Lost*

63. The rhyme scheme of the Spenserian sonnet is
A. abab bcbc cdcd ee
B. abab cdcd efef gg
C. abba cddc effe gg
D. abba abba cde cde

64. A monosyllabic rhyme on the final stressed syllable of two lines of verse is called
A. monorhyme B. feminine rhyme
C. masculine rhyme D. eye rhyme

65. A sequence of repeated consonantal sounds in a stretch of language is
A. alliteration B. acrostic
C. assent D. syllable

66. English Iambic Pentameter was brought to its first maturity in
A. sonnet B. dramatic verse
C. lyric D. elegy

67. The Restoration comedy has been criticized mainly for its
A. excessive wit and humour
B. bitter satire and cynicism
C. indecency and permissiveness
D. superficial reflection of society

68. Sexual possessiveness is a theme of Shakespeare's
A. *Coriolanus*
B. *Julius Caesar*
C. *Henry IV Part–I*
D. *A Midsummer Night's Dream*

69. Johnson's *Dictionary of the English Language* was published in the year
A. 1710 B. 1755
C. 1739 D. 1759

70. The first complete printed English Bible was produced by
A. William Tyndale B. William Caxton
C. Miles Coverdale D. Roger Ascham

71. Arrange the following in ascending order in terms of size:
1. epic 2. epigram
3. stanza 4. sonnet

A. 1 2 3 4 B. 2 1 3 4
C. 2 3 4 1 D. 1 3 4 2

72. Hyperbole is
1. an extravagant exaggeration
2. a racist slur
3. a metrical skill
4. a figure of speech

A. 1 is correct
B. 1 and 4 are correct
C. 1 and 3 are correct
D. 3 is correct

73. The poetry of Wordsworth and Coleridge was notably influenced by...
A. The Napoleonic Wars
B. The Glorious Revolution
C. The French Revolution
D. Poor Laws

74. "He's not the brightest man in the world" is an example of :
A. Chiasmus B. Hyperbole
C. Litotes D. Simile

75. *Prosody studies*:
A. Line endings B. Meanings of words
C. Patterns of prose D. Metrics

76. *"Formal Criticism"* relates to the structure of:
A. Literary devices B. Myths
C. Content D. Form

77. A *"Foot"* in prosody is a basic unit of :
A. rhyme
B. length
C. rhythmic measurement
D. height

78. "Iambus" is a metrical foot consisting of :
A. two syllables B. three syllables
C. four syllables D. one syllable

79. An "Idyll" is usually a poem about a :
A. picturesque city life
B. panoramic view of nature
C. picture of industrial society
D. picturesque country life

80. The rhyme scheme of the Shakespearean sonnet is :
A. abab, cdcd, efef, gg
B. abba, cddc, effe, gg
C. abab, cdcd, efef, gh
D. aabb, ccdd, eeff, gg

81. A poem that captures the essence of a moment in a simple image is:
A. Lyric B. Ballad
C. Ode D. Haiku

82. The word 'nature' in the eighteenth century literature stands for :
A. Nature of writing B. External nature
C. Human nature D. The Universe

83. Who is given credit for first using the term "romantic"?
A. Friedrich Schlegel B. Kant
C. Coleridge D. Schiller

84. Heroic Couplet is a pair of :
A. Rhyming iambic pentameter lines
B. Unrhyming iambic pentameter lines
C. Rhyming iambic hexameter
D. Unrhyming iambic hexameter

85. Heroic quatrain is :
A. a stanza in blank verse
B. eight line stanza in iambic hexameter
C. four line stanza in iambic pentameter
D. six line stanza in iambic pentameter

86. Victorian Age witnessed a clash between:
A. faith and reason
B. tradition and modernity
C. oriental and occidental civilization
D. romanticism and neo romanticism

87. The historical novel began in:
A. Restoration Period
B. Augustan Age
C. Victorian Period
D. Romantic Period

88. Internal rhyme is :
A. the basic rhythmic structure of a poem
B. rhyming of two words in alternative lines
C. rhyming of two or more words in the same line of poetry
D. all the lines of a poem ending with the same line pattern

89. "Fancy" deals with:
A. "Fixities and definities"
B. "Imagination and Reason"
C. "Judgement and Memory"
D. "Structure and Superstructure"

90. The early religious drama is associated with:
A. Superstitions and beliefs
B. Mysteries and histories
C. Interludes and mysteries
D. Miracles and morality

91. Feminine ending refers to :
A. a stressed final syllable in a line of verse
B. the ending of a poem in a stressed syllable
C. the ending of a poem in an unstressed syllable
D. an unstressed final syllable in a line of verse

92. Johnson's edition of Shakespeare appeared in:
A. 1752 B. 1765
C. 1791 D. 1760

93. After Shakespeare made his debut as a London playwright, he was described as an 'upstart crow' by :
A. Robert Greene
B. Thomas Lodge
C. Christopher Marlowe
D. John Lyly

94. The term 'metaphysical poets', was first used by:
A. Ben Jonson B. Dr. Johnson
C. Helen Gardner D. Dryden

95. Which are the figures of speech used in the following lines by Blake?
"Tyger, tyger, burning bright
In the forest of the night,
What immortal hand or eye
Could frame thy fearful symmetry?"
A. simile and personification
B. irony and synecdoche
C. apostrophe and synecdoche
D. metonymy and apostrophe

96. More's Latin Masterpiece *Utopia* was translated into English in :
A. 1551 B. 1498
C. 1516 D. 1532

97. The Gutenberg Bible was first published in:
A. 1456 B. 1516
C. 1449 D. 1498

98. Restoration Comedy marks the restoration of :
A. women's rights B. democracy
C. monarchy D. human rights

99. "Hamartia" means :
A. reversal of fortunes
B. purgation of emotions
C. depravity
D. error of judgement

100. The term "gothic", a category of fiction, also applies to:
A. architecture B. painting
C. music D. theater

101. Miracle plays are based on the lives of :
A. Knights B. Crusaders
C. Pilgrims D. Saints

102. A metrical foot consisting of an unstressed syllable followed by a stressed syllable is:
A. dactyl B. trochee
C. iamb D. anapaest

103. Using "the Bench" for the judiciary is an example of :
A. metaphor B. irony
C. synecdoche D. metonymy

104. Four feet, comprising a monosyllable, trochee, dactyl and first paeon is often called:
A. running rhythm B. sprung rhythm
C. blank verse D. rhymed verse

105. "Essays of Elia" are:
A. political ideology
B. economic disparity
C. literary criticism
D. personal impressions

106. "Peripetia" means :
A. purgation of emotion
B. tragic flaw
C. reversal of fortune
D. recognition of error

107. "Gynocriticism" focuses on :
A. Criticism on women
B. Criticism by women
C. Criticism of male writers by women writers
D. Women as writers

108. Pre-Raphaelite poetry is mainly concerned with:
A. narrative and style
B. narrative and nature
C. form and design
D. form and value

109. Who among the Victorians is called "the prophet of modern society"?
A. Ruskin B. Carlyle
C. Macaulay D. Arnold

110. The mystery plays deal with:
A. the life of Christ
B. the New Testament
C. Psalms
D. Apocrypha

111. Pope's "Essay on Criticism" sums up the art of poetry as taught first by:
A. Aristotle B. Horace
C. Longinus D. Plato

112. A particle is:
A. a patchwork of words, sentences, passages
B. a satirical poem
C. a love song
D. a collection of lines from different poems

113. "Careless she is with artful Care/Affecting to seem unaffected" is an example of:
A. irony B. paradox
C. simile D. metaphor

114. A metrical foot containing a stressed, followed by an unstressed, syllable is:
A. anapaest B. iamb
C. trochee D. dactyl

115. The rhyme scheme of a Spenserian sonnet is:
A. abba, cbcb, cdcd, ee
B. abab, bccb, ccdd, ee
C. aabb, bcbc, ccdd, ee
D. abab, bcbc, cdcd, ee

116. Using the expression "Crown" for the monarchy is an example of:
A. Metonymy B. Synecdoche
C. Irony D. Metaphor

117. Dr. Johnson's *A Dictionary of the English Language* was published in:
A. 1755 B. 1756
C. 1757 D. 1758

118. A figure of speech in which two terms opposite in meaning are placed side-by-side in one phrase is known as:
A. paradox B. oxymoron
C. sarcasm D. antithesis

119. A stanza of eight iambic pentametres on the pattern of ab, ab, ab, cc is known as:
A. Rhyme royal
B. Ottava rima
C. Tennysonian stanza
D. Spenserian stanza

120. In the assertion "Four out of five people suffer from *dreaded* pyorrhoea", the writer wants to arouse the feeling of:
A. Sympathy B. Fear
C. Hatred D. Ill-will

121. "John is six feet tall and 240 lb" is an assertion of:
A. a fact B. a judgement
C. an opinion D. an inference

122. What is the pseudonym of John Galsworthy?
A. John Gals B. Elia
C. John Sinjohn D. Boz

123. "I wandered lonely as a cloud" makes an assertion that:
A. The poet travelled with the cloud
B. The poet moved aimlessly with the cloud
C. Both the poet and the cloud were lonely
D. The poet moved as aimlessly as the cloud

124. Which was Galsworthy's first published novel?
A. Jocelyn
B. A Man of Devon
C. Villa Rubcin
D. The Science

125. The First Folio of Shakespeare's plays appeared in:
A. 1664 B. 1631
C. 1623 D. 1650

126. Restoration comedy begins with:
A. Congreve B. Sheridan
C. Dryden D. Etherege

127. The soul of tragedy, according to Aristotle is:
A. Thought B. Character
C. Plot D. Spectacle

128. "United we stand, divided we fall" is an example of:
A. Antithesis B. Bathos
C. Tautology D. Litotes

129. A metre in which an unaccented syllable precedes the accented is called:
A. anapaestic B. dactylic
C. catalectic D. iambic

130. Which play analyses the impact of modern publicity on private domestic tragedy?
A. The Show B. Escape
C. Jocelyn D. None of these

131. According to Galsworthy, which play made a great sensation, especially in Parliamentary and official circles?
A. The Mob B. Justice
C. The Skin Game D. The Eldest Son

132. John Galsworthy was awarded the Nobel Prize for literature in
A. 1942 B. 1932
C. 1922 D. 1912

133. The masterpiece of Galsworthy is
A. The Forsyte Saga B. The Freelands
C. Fraternity D. The Patrician

134. Galsworthy deals with the inadequacy of the administration of justice and the attitude of different types of people towards and escaped prisoner in the play
A. Escape B. The Show
C. Jocelyn D. None of these

135. Which universities awarded D. Litt to Galsworthy?
A. Oxford and Princeton University
B. Cambridge and Sheffiled University
C. Oxford and Cambridge
D. None of the above

136. Which novel of Galsworthy illustrates the breaking down of inhibitions and barriers as the result of war?
A. Saint's Progress B. Fraternity
C. Jocelyn D. None of these

137. What is "The White Monkey"?
A. A pet B. A book
C. A poem D. A painting

138. D. Litt was conferred upon Galsworthy in the year
A. 1929 B. 1930
C. 1940 D. None of these

139. The Forsyte Saga includes two interludes. Name the interludes.
A. Indian Autumn of Forsyte Tales and Awakening
B. Indian Winter of Forstye Tales and Awakening
C. Indian Summer of Forsyte Tales and Awakening
D. None of these

140. Galsworthy's Forsyte Saga is said to be an English parallel to
A. Milton's Paradise Lost
B. Thomas Mann's Buddenbrooks
C. Seth's A Suitable Boy
D. Shakespeare's Hamlet

141. Which novel earned Galsworthy the reputation of a novelist?
A. Jocelyn
B. Country Mouse
C. The Island Pharisees
D. Fraternity

142. In 1929, which honour was conferred upon Galsworthy?
A. Order of merit B. Order of demerit
C. Booker Prize D. All of the above

143. Which play of Galsworthy is a study in social pride and social convention?
A. The Mob B. The Skin Game
C. The Loyalties D. The Silver Box

144. Which play made Galsworthy famous as a dramatist?
A. Justice B. The Silver Box
C. Loyalties D. None of these

145. What is the title of Galsworthy's collection of essays?
A. The Inn of Tranquility
B. The River of Tranquility
C. The Ocean of Tranquility
D. None of the above

146. Which play of Galsworthy dramatizes strike?
A. Mob B. Justice
C. Strife D. None of these

147. What is the name of Galsworthy's first play?
A. Loyalties B. Joy
C. Justice D. Silver Box

148. The Essays and Stories—The White Monkey, The Silver Spark, Swan Song, A Slient Wooing and Passers by were collected together as
A. awakening B. a modern tragedy
C. a modern comedy D. None of these

149. In 1931, Oxford University and Princeton University conferred upon Galsworthy
A. Knighthood
B. Honorary Doctorate
C. Both A and B
D. None of these

150. Galsworthy is the chief exponent of
A. romantic tales B. adventures tales
C. problem plays D. None of these

ANSWERS

1	**2**	**3**	**4**	**5**	**6**	**7**	**8**	**9**	**10**
B	C	D	A	D	C	C	C	A	B
11	**12**	**13**	**14**	**15**	**16**	**17**	**18**	**19**	**20**
D	C	B	D	A	B	D	C	B	A
21	**22**	**23**	**24**	**25**	**26**	**27**	**28**	**29**	**30**
B	A	D	B	A	D	D	C	A	C
31	**32**	**33**	**34**	**35**	**36**	**37**	**38**	**39**	**40**
D	C	A	A	C	A	A	A	B	C
41	**42**	**43**	**44**	**45**	**46**	**47**	**48**	**49**	**50**
A	C	A	B	B	C	D	B	D	B
51	**52**	**53**	**54**	**55**	**56**	**57**	**58**	**59**	**60**
A	C	A	C	D	B	C	C	B	A
61	**62**	**63**	**64**	**65**	**66**	**67**	**68**	**69**	**70**
A	A	A	C	A	A	C	D	B	C
71	**72**	**73**	**74**	**75**	**76**	**77**	**78**	**79**	**80**
C	B	C	C	D	A	C	A	D	A
81	**82**	**83**	**84**	**85**	**86**	**87**	**88**	**89**	**90**
D	C	A	A	C	A	B	C	B	A
91	**92**	**93**	**94**	**95**	**96**	**97**	**98**	**99**	**100**
C	B	A	B	D	A	A	C	D	A
101	**102**	**103**	**104**	**105**	**106**	**107**	**108**	**109**	**110**
D	C	C	B	D	C	D	B	A	B
111	**112**	**113**	**114**	**115**	116	117	118	119	120
A	A	B	C	D	B	A	B	B	B
121	**122**	**123**	**124**	**125**	**126**	**127**	**128**	**129**	**130**
A	C	D	A	C	A	C	A	B	A
131	**132**	**133**	**134**	**135**	**136**	**137**	**138**	**139**	**140**
B	B	A	A	B	A	B	B	C	B
141	**142**	**143**	**144**	**145**	**146**	**147**	**148**	**149**	**150**
C	A	C	B	A	C	D	C	B	C

3

English Literature At A Glance

THE OLD ENGLISH PERIOD

ANGLO-SAXON PERIOD (450-1050)

Beowulf is probably the oldest epic of the Teutonic world. It is believed to be belonging to the first half of the sixth century.

Some important works of the Anglo-Saxon period (Pre-Christian Era).

Some important works of the Anglo-Saxon period are: *The Ruined Burg, The Lover's Message. The Maiden's Complaint, The Wanderer* and *the Seafarer.*

'*The Wanderer* is also known as '*Widsith*'. The work is based on the wandering life of the gleeman.

Belonging to this period, we also have *"Deor's Lament"*, which, according to Long is, "much more poetic than '*Widsith,*' and is the one perfect lyric of the Anglo-Saxon period."

In the *Seafarer*, we have glimpses of hard sea life along with the call of the sea, which we, in our times, find more pronouncedly, but perhaps less picturesquely, in Masefield's *"Sea-Fever"*.

Some Christian writers of the Anglo-Saxon period.

Whereas the pagan literature of the Anglo-Saxon period was chiefly in the form of oral legends which they had brought with them from the foreign lands which they previously inhabited, the Christian writing mainly came into existence as a result of the teachings of the monks who had come under the influence of two schools—the Augustinian School (from Rome) and Northumbrian School (from Ireland).

While the former, did not produce much lasting works, the latter produced a number of good and great writers, *e.g.,* **The Venerable Bede (673-735), Caedmon (seventh century)** and **Cynewulf (eighth century)**.

Besides the poets mentioned above, we have **Alfred (848-90)** who is chiefly known as a translator.

ANGLO-NORMAN PERIOD (1066-1350)

Some important works of the Anglo-Norman period.

One important work of this period is *Geoffrey's "Historic Regum Britanniae"* (1137) commonly known as *"History"*. Geoffrey is believed to have died in 1154.

Geoffrey's work which became immensely popular in his own life, is a mixture of pagan and Christian legends and is based more on lies than on real historical events.

However, the said work has its literary value for its poetry and romance pertaining to king Arthur and his Knights, and hence, it became a source of inspiration and scintillating subject matter for such illustrious authors as Malory, Shakespeare and Tennyson.

Geoffrey's work was in Latin verse. Thereafter appeared *"Layman's Brut"* (c. 1200) which has its main interest in giving Arthur's legends in (Anglo-Saxon) English itself.

Then there appeared what are known as *"Metrical Romances"* which were based on the "matter" of France, Rome and Britain.

While in the *Matter of France,* **Charlemagne's** exploits dominated and in the *Matter of Rome* Alexander's adventures and the war of Troy were the main subjects, in the *Matter of Britain*, exploits of Arthur and his knights of the Round Table were chief subject matter. There were a number of cycles pertaining to the knights of Arthur, among them being **Sir Gawain (1350)** *Quest of the Holy Grail, Death of Arthur, Merlin, etc.*

Besides the above, other works of the period included ballads, lyrics and such poems as the *Owl and the Nightingale, Ormulum, Cursor Mundi* (*1320*)*, The Pearl, Patience, Cleanness, etc.* Also **Roger Bacon's** *"Opus Majus"* appeared in 1267.

THE AGE OF CHAUCER (1340-1400)

The Hundred years war between England and France had already started in 1338 when **Chaucer** was born in **1340**.

In the earlier years of the war, England was all-powerful and under Edward III it won victories over France at Sluys in 1340 and Crecy in 1346, culminating in the capture of Calais in 1347.

Another thumping victory was won by the Black Prince, Edward III's son in 1356 by defeating the French at Poitiers.

As a result of the English victories, the English foreign trade began to flourish, particularly in the export of wool to Flanders, which filled the coffers of the English king and the people also became richer, as we notice conspicuously in **Chaucer's** *Canterbury Tales* when we consider the lot of so many acters, particularly those belonging to landed aristocracy.

This picture is also graphically depicted in **Trevelyan's** *British History of Six Centuries.*

It was unfortunate for England that in the moment of its glory it was overtaken by plague, the Black Death which took a heavy toll of life all over Europe in 1348-49.

As a result of the Black Death, most of the labourers who escaped death, left the country, and this caused an intense scarcity of the availability of essential commodities at cheap rates. To meet this menace, the Parliament tried to force the labourers to accept the same wages as they were getting before the Black Death, and it all finally precipitated into the well-known Peasants' Revolt during the reign of Richard II.

In spite of the passage of certain statutes purported to safeguard the English clergy against the undue domination of the Pope, the low simmering of wrath among the clergymen for several reasons, there emerged in the "Lollards Movement" under the leadership of the redoubtable Wyclif.

Another prominent feature, this one in the literary world, was the slow advent of the spirit of New Learning from Italy and drastic changes in the structure of the English language which had already been continuing as the inevitable outcome of the Norman conquest at Hastings in 1066.

These were the general conditions in which the most significant writers of the age—**Chaucer, Langland, Dunbar,** etc. lived and flourished, thus heralding a new age slowly, but boldly and surely.

MAJOR AUTHORS AND THEIR WORKS OF CHAUCER'S AGE

Sir Thomas More (1478-1535)

Utopia (*English Version*)

William Tyndale (1485-1536)

New Testament

Geoffrey Chaucer (1340-1400)

The Boke of the Duchesse

The Romaunt of the Rose

The House of Fame

Troylus Cryseyde

The Canterbury Tales
Legends of Good Women
The Parliament of Fouls
Wyclif (1320-1384)
The Bible

John Heywood (1564-1627)
Four P's
Thomas Sackville and Thomas Norton : (1536-1608) (1532-1584)
Gorboduc

THE SEVENTEENTH CENTURY

THE RENAISSANCE (1578-1625)

The Renaissance of English Literature coincides with the Age of Queen Elizabeth I. Hence, in the history of English literature, this period is also called as the *Elizabethan Age*. The inspiration for the great works of this period came from the prolific translations into English of works of ancient Rome and Greece. Thus, **Plutarch's** *Lives* was translated by **Sir Thomas North (1579)** from the French version. Montaigne's Essays was translated by **John Florio (1603)**. In verse, **Ovid's** *Metamorphoses* was translated by **Arthur Golding (1565, 1567)**. Among other works of foreign origin translated into English were Ariosto's *Orlando Furioso* by **Harrington (1591)**, and Homer's *Iliad* by **George Chapman (1598)**.

The rising English stage and the English novel borrowed from Boccaccio, Cinthio, Bandello and Straparola — the Italians. Attracted though England was to Italian art, it resisted the evil influences of debauchery, crime and passions that the Italian spirit represented. Yet, the time was ripe in England for the full development of every art and literary form. Renaissance means *a flowering again of art and culture*. It inculcated a sense of wonder in things. England also wanted to rival Spain, France and Portugal in her navigational triumphs. Thus in 1578, Sir Francis Drake circumnavigated the world, and in 1588, the English navy destroyed the Armada. The same spirit of adventure moved literature. In *Apologie for Poetrie*, Sidney described the poet — of all sciences 'the monarch'. Poets were encouraged to innovate new styles and rhythms.

Poetry

Three great men of letters led the Renaissance in England — Spenser, Sidney and Lyly.

Edmund Spenser (1552-1599) wrote the *Shepheardes Calendar* (1579)—an allegory. The union of line and metre is varied and rich. In *Hymnes In honour of Love and Beautie*, he sets forth his philosophy, the conflict in his mind between paganism and Christianity. He also wrote a satire named, *Mother Hubberd's Tale* to denounce the neglect of arts and letters. His pastoral, *Colin Clout's Come Home Again* describes his stay in London in 1589. His *Amoretti* (1595) are sonnets on love and his *Epithalamion* is an ode, but his masterpiece is the *Faerie Queene* (1589, 1595), an allegory in which characters represent virtues and vices. In it his lyrical quality and colour-effects are at their best. The *Faerie Queene* is Queen Elizabeth. The nine-line stanza he used is now called the *Spenserian stanza*.

Sir Philip Sidney (1554-1586) was a scholar, knight and courtier. In 1580 he wrote *Arcadia* which has a blend of pastoral and heroic elements. It is a romance of chivalry and love. The language is characterized by *pathetic fallacy* — endowing inanimate objects with feelings and sensations. William Shakespeare borrowed from this style. His other poem, *Astrophel and Stella* (1591) describes his lost love for the daughter of an Earl. His *Apologie for Poetrie* (1595) written in an unaffected prose, is a plea for poetry.

John Lyly (1554-1606) invented an artistic, flowery style called *euphuism* through his famous romance, *Euphues, the Anatomy of Wit* (1579). This style was adopted by the refined people of the Court. The style is characterized by the use of alliteration and antithesis, fantastic metaphors and similes based on mythology, and natural history of flora and fauna.

The works of these three trail-blazed many poets and sonneteers like Samuel Daniel, Michael Drayton, Thomas Watson, Henry Constable and Thomas Lodge. Notable works from 1590 to 1603 were **Samuel Daniel's (1562-1619)** *The Civil Wars* (1595) describing the *War of the Roses*, **Michael Drayton's (1563-1631)** *Idea, the Shepherd's Garland, The Baron's Wars, England's Heroicall Epistles* (1603) and *Poly-Olbion*, a long description of England in 15,000 alexandrines or lines of twelve syllables. England came to be known as *"a nest of singing birds"* because of the great number of lyrics and poems written in this period. **Thomas Campion (1567-1620)** published an anthology called *Two Books of Ayres* (1612). Many of the best poems are found in plays by Ben Jonson, Thomas Dekker, Beaumont and Fletcher, and Webster. But those of William Shakespeare are probably the most beautiful. In his *Sonnets*, he describes his love for a married woman who betrays him. Other poems of this period are Marlowe's Hero and Leander (1598), Shakespeare's *Venus and Adonis* (1593) and *The Rape of Lucrece* (1594).

After Elizabeth's reign, in James I rule, poetry became religious and didactic. The Protestant spirit dominated the literary works. The poems of George Wither, William Browne, the Fletcher brothers and William Drummond show the influence of Spenser still.

Ben Jonson (1573-1637) was the greatest humanist of the time. He was mainly a playwright but wrote poems also. His poetry is found in collections like *Epigrams* and *The Forest* (1616) and *The Underwoods* (1640). He was a satirist and neo-classicist being influenced by the Latin classics.

John Donne's (1573-1631) poetry is revolutionary. He disobeys the laws of rhythm and uses a device called the metaphysical conceit in which strangely opposite ideas are juxtaposed.

Prose

Much of the prose of the period is poetical, influenced by euphuism. Robert Greene, Thomas Lodge, Thomas Nashe, Thomas Deloney, and Thomas Dekker are the major writers. **Robert Greene's (1558-1592)** works include *Mamilia* and *Menaphon* and **Thomas Lodge's (1558-1625)** include *Rosalynde: Euphues Golden Legacie* (1590). **Thomas Nashe (1567-1601)** wrote pamphlets like The *Anatomie of Absurdities* and *The Terrors of the Night*. **Thomas Dekker's (1572-1632)** *The Gils Horne booke* is famous for its picturesque prose. Most of the poets and prose writers of this period were also dramatists. Shakespeare used prose for homely and humorous scenes and verse for tragic ones.

Many writers of the English Renaissance were inspired by the literary criticism of the Continent to write some themselves. Stephen Gosson's *The Schoole of Abuse* (1579) and *Sidney's Apologie for Poetrie* are good examples. Sidney eulogizes the poet as a law-giver. The period also saw works of religious prose. **Richard Hooker's (1554-1600)** pamphlet on the Marlin Marprelate controversy is a famous one. Hooker's *Of the Laws of Ecclesiastical Polity* (1594) is a masterpiece of English prose. The most seminal work of the period is the authorized version of the Bible published in 1611. The work was commissioned by James I. A beautiful prose minus archaism is used by the revisers. The diction was to influence the English language very deeply. It is the language of daily speech, yet fresh and lofty.

Side by side with religious literature, secular and philosophical literature, mostly written by **Francis Bacon (1561-1626)**, came out. He had taken all knowledge as his province and elaborated his doctrines in his *Novum Organum* (1620). His ideas influenced the formation of *The Royal Society for Improving Natural Knowledge* in 1645. His most popular work is his *Essays* written on diverse topics in a terse, epigrammatic style. The English writers quote copiously from Bacon today. His sentences are household terms. Take for example, "*He that hath wife and children hath given hostages to* *fortune*". "*Some books are to be tasted, others to be swallowed and some few to be chewed and digested*".

Another great prose-writer of the period was **Robert Burton (1577-1640)** whose *The Anatomy of Melancholy* (1621) is full of pedantry. He borrowed from numerous sources and is full of melancholy and jests; his style abounds in synonyms and epithets.

Drama

Drama thrived in the Renaissance. Foreign influence, especially of Italy, predominated. Plays were written so that the public would enjoy them and applaud the stage. There was a great variety of plays written — pure tragedy, tragi-comedy, historical drama, romantic comedy, comedy of errors, farce, pastoral, etc. The stage was a simple structure, circular in form with a courtyard open to the sky. A platform projected into the courtyard. Boys played the female roles. The public consisted of groundlings and courtiers on galleries. The unities of time, place and action were disregarded. Farce and tragedy were found in succession.

Several mythological allegories were acted before the court. **John Lyly's** euphuistic romances like *Campaspe* (1584), *Sapho and Phao, Endymion* (1592), *Midas* were praises of the queen. **George Peele (1558-1598)** wrote *The Araygnement of Paris* (1584) and *The Old Wives' Tale*. There were violent plays like **Thomas Kyd's (1558-1594)** The *Spanish Tragedie* (1585) and **Christopher Marlowe's (1564-1593)** *Tamburlaine, the Great* (1587) and *Doctor Faustus* (1592). *Doctor Faustus* is an allegory on the Renaissance love of power. It shows how Doctor Faustus, the scientist, sells his soul to the devil for twenty-four years of full power to satisfy every desire. In the end his agony increases as the devil approaches to claim his soul. Marlowe also wrote *The Jew of Malta*, which shows the unbridled love for wealth, and the historical play Edward II. Marlowe crafted the blank verse (mighty line as Shakespeare called it and used). This was suited to the fiery speeches of his characters.

The towering genius of the age was certainly **William Shakespeare (1564-1616)**. He was versatile and wrote about 36 plays and 144 sonnets. "Shakespeare was not of an age but for all times" and "Poets are born not made", wrote Ben Jonson about him. He created a gallery of nearly 800 characters who typify personalities found through human history. Julius Caesar's pride and ambition, Macbeth's unbridled ambition, King Lear's dotedness, and Othello's susceptibility to suspicion against his wife — are tragic flaws that govern men even today.

Shakespeare was not educated except for a few years at a grammar school. He had 'little Latin and less Greek' and read books in translation from Latin and Greek. He adapted the stories into a World entirely his own, instinct with life and vibrancy. Shakespeare began his career by acting for the stage. Then he wrote plays and staged them, mainly to seek court patronage. His great success made him the envy of his contemporaries like Robert Greene. In his tragedies he depicts the fall of great men owing to a tragic flaw in their character. Although they had the will to change their destiny, a fate controlled them. He used the beliefs of his time like the supernatural powers and phenomena to capture the interest of his audience. Some of his historical plays are *Richard II* (1596) and *King John* (1595). Among the romantic comedies *As You Like It* (1600), *The Merchant of Venice* (1596) and *Twelfth Night* (1601) are popular. *A Midsummer Night's Dream* (1595) is a fairy play. *Romeo and Juliet* (1594) is a tragicomedy. He used prose and blank verse.

His *Henry IV* (I & 2) (1597, 1598) contain much more blank verse than his other plays. In depth of psychological insight, and power of style *Hamlet* (1601), one of Shakespeare's great tragedies, stands supreme. *The Tempest* (161I) is one of his last plays which shows the dramatist's mellowed maturity.

Even after 400 years, Shakespeare's plays are very popular, being translated into almost every important language. *"Age cannot wither her nor custom stale her infinite variety"*; Shakespeare described Cleopatra in these words. The same may be said about his plays also.

Ben Jonson was Shakespeare's antithesis. He borrowed the style of the classics and was very erudite. He carefully studied society and wrote about it. He took the different 'humours' or dominating characteristics of men and satirized them in *Every Man in his Humour* (1598) and *Every Man out of his Humour* (1599), *Volpone, or the Fox* (1605) and *The Alchemist* (1605). He also wrote the historical tragedies, *Sejanus His Fall* (1603) and *Catiline His Conspiracy* (1611). The plays are very true to history. John Marston, Thomas Dekker, Thomas Heywood and Middleton were other playwrights of the age. John Webster (1580-1625) is famous for horror plays like *The White Devil* (1609-1612) and *The Duchess of Malfi* (1613-1614).

MAJOR AUTHORS AND THEIR WORKS

Edmund Spenser (1552-1599)

The Faerie Queene
The Shepheardes Calendar
Amoretti
Epithalamion
Prothalamion
Mother Hubberd's Tale
The Ruins of Time
The Tears of the Muses
Astrophel

Phillip Sidney (1554-1586)

Arcadia
Astrophel and Stella
An Apologie for Poetrie

Ben Jonson (1573-1637)

Every Man in His Humour
Every Man Out of His Humour
Volpone Or the Fox
Cynthia's Revels
The Alchemist
Bartholomew Fayre
Epicaene or the Silent Women
Sejanus His Fall
Catline His Conspiracy
The Poetaster
The Devil as an Ass
The Masque of Beauty

Samuel Daniel (1562-1619)

Delia
Civil Wars between the Two Houses of Lancaster and York

Michael Drayton (1563-1631)

The Battle of Agincourt
England's heroic Epistles
The Barons' Wars
Polyolbion

William Shakespeare (1564-1616)

The Two Gentlement of Verona
The Merry Wives of Windsor
Measure for Measure
The Comedy of Errors
Love's Labour's Lost
The Taming of the Shrew
All's Well that Ends Well
A Midsummer Night's Dream
The Merchant of Venice
Much Ado About Nothing
As You Like it
Twelfth Night
Romeo and Juliet
Macbeth
Hamlet
King Lear
Othello
Antony and Cleopatra
Julius Caesar
Timon of Athens
Coriolanus
Titus Andronicus
Troilus and Cressida
King John
King Richard the Second
King Henry the Fourth-Part First
King Henry the Fourth-Second Part
King Henry the Fifth
King Henry the Sixth-First Part
King Henry the Sixth-Second Part
King Henry the Sixth-Third Part

King Richard the Third
King Henry the Eighth
Cymbeline
Pericles
The Winter's Tale
The Tempest
Venus and Adonis and Rape of Lucrece (Narrative Poems)
Sonnets (154 in number).

Christopher Marlowe (1564-1593)
Tamburlaine the Great
Edward II
Doctor Faustus
The Jew of Malta
The Tragedy of Dido, Queen of Carthage.

George Peele (1558-1597)
The Araygnement of Paris
The Famous Chronicle of King Edward I

Robert Greene (1560-1592)
Frier Bacon and Frier Bungey
Orlando Furioso
Pandosto

Thomas Nashe (1567-1601)
The Unfortunate Traveller Or The Life of Jack Wilton

Thomas Lodge (1558-1625)
The Wounds of Civil War
Rosalynde

Thomas Kyd (1557-1595)
The Spanish Tragedy

John Lyly (1554-1606)
Euphues, The Anatomy of Wit
Euphues and His England
Endymion

Francis Bacon (1561-1626)
Essays
The Advancement of Learning
The New Atlantis
Novum Organum

John Webster (1580-1625)
The White Devil
The Duchess of Malfi
The Devil's Law Case.

Thomas Heywood (1575-1650)
A Woman Killed with Kindness
The English Traveller
The Captives

Robert Burton (1577-1640)
The Anatomy of Melancholy

Sir Thomas Browne (1605-1682)
Religio Medici
Vulgar Errors
Hydrotaphia or Urne Burriale
Christian Morals

Thomas Hobbes (1588-1679)
Leviathan

Jeremy Taylor (1613-1667)
The Liberty of Prophesying
Holy Living
Holy Dying

END OF THE RENAISSANCE (1625-1660)

Prose

Puritanism set the trend for the literature during the reign of Charles I. The Bible was the guiding spirit which may be best seen in Milton's works. The zealous Calvinists enforced Presbyterianism. The passionate curiosity for life which characterized the Renaissance gave place to a search for salvation. **Sir Thomas Browne (1605-1682)** was a scientist, but in his *Pseudodoxia Epidemica or Vulgar Errors* (1646), we see his belief in miracles. His *Religio Medici* (1642) speaks of the vanity of earthly life. **George Herbert's (1596-1633)** *The Country Parson* and **Jeremy Taylor's (1613-1667)** *Holy Living* (1650) and *Holy Dying* (1651) are sermons championing religious freedom. **John Milton (1608-1674)**, who is famous as a poet, wrote numerous pamphlets in favour of divorce which are models of beautiful prose. His *Areopagitica* (1644) is a speech for the liberty of unlicensed writing.

Another great prose-writer was **Thomas Hobbes (1588-1679)** whose *Leviathan* (1651) is a famous work. He was an empiricist and realist and believed that sensations and ideas are caused by physical reasons. Numerous works of ethics, sociology and history were written. *The History of the Rebellion and Civil Wars in England* was written by **Edward Hyde (1609-1674). Izaac Walton (1593-1683)** wrote the biographies of John Donne and George Herbert. *The Compleat Angler* (1653) is his famous work on the post-Civil War scene and contains descriptions of the English countryside.

Poetry

Two types of poets existed then — the Cavaliers, who were the Royalists, and the religious or Metaphysical poets. Thomas Carew, Sir John Suckling, John Cleveland, Robert Herrick were Cavalier poets who displayed epicurean tastes. Imagination and sensuous imagery predominate their poems. Among the religious poets, Herbert, Crashaw, Vaughan and Marvell stand out. They were mystics. **George Herbert's (1593-1633)** style is simple and expresses Christian piety in his anthology The Temple (1633). His poems *The Pulley and Love* are very popular. **Richard Crashaw (1613-1649)** used fantastic conceits; e.g. he describes the maudlin St Mary Magdalene's eyes as "walking baths, compedious oceans", **Henry Vaughan (1622-1695)** was a mystic and his poem The Retreat is a nostalgic longing for the blissful heavenly state of childhood.

John Milton's greatest achievement was his *Paradise Lost* (1667). In theme it deals with the fall of man. In form, it follows the strict unity of the classical epic. His other poems are *L'Allegro* (1632), *Il Penseroso* (1632), *Comus* (1634), *Lycidas* (1637), *Samson Agonistes* (1671), etc.

RESTORATION LITERATURE (1620-1734)

Prose

In 1660, Charles II returned to the throne and the Puritan republic ended. The year is also marked as the beginning of the modern literature. **John Bunyan's (1628-1688)** works, *Grace Abounding* (1666) and *The Pilgrim's Progress* (1678) are the last surviving works of Puritan faith. The Pilgrim's Progress is an allegory describing the trials and tribulations on the way to salvation as faced by a Christian. Bunyan's prose is a blend of common speech and the grandeur of the revised Bible.

The scientific spirit took over the reign. The Royal Society of London for the Improvement of Natural Knowledge, to which Bacon and William Harvey (who discovered the circulation of blood) had contributed, now had many learned men. **Sir Isaac Newton** published Principia in 1687. He discovered the laws of gravity, of the diffraction of white light and the theory of fluxions.

John Locke (1632-1704) propounded a new philosophy of commonsense and intelligent reasoning in his *An Essay Concerning Human Understanding* (1690). It lays stress on development of character. It was to influence the English thought. Voltaire was one of his French disciples.

Poetry

Restoration literature was derived from pre-Commonwealth national literature and was a reaction against Puritan oppression. It rejected severe moral codes of conduct and was chiefly satiric in nature. **Samuel Butler's (1612-1680)** poem, *Hudibras* published in three parts (1663, 1664 & 1678), is a typical work of this period. It is inspired by *Don Quixote*. He satirizes Sir Hudibras as a grotesque Presbyterian with a squire called Ralpho. It lays bare all the human follies in octosyllabic couplets. Many court poets like **Andrew Marvell (1621-1678)** and **John Oldham (1653-1683)** were veterans of the Republican era and satirize the follies of the new age.

The great poet of the period was **John Dryden (1631-1700)**. He excelled in almost every kind of composition. He wrote a series of heroic stanzas in honour of Cromwell on his death. He was a disciple of the metaphysical poets displaying their far-fetched images and conceits. In *Astraea Redux* (1660), he celebrated the return of Charles II and in *Annus Mirabilis* (1667) he commemorated the Grea‘

Fire of London and the war with Holland. He was a staunch Tory and his famous satires are *Absalom and Achitophel* (1681), *The Medal and Mac-Flecknoe*. In this last work he satirizes Shadwell, the Whig poet. *The Hind and the Panther* (1687) is an allegory on Catholicism and Anglicanism. Dryden also translated the classics, chiefly Persuis and Juvenal. He turned Virgil's *Aeneid* into brilliant couplets. His *Alexander's Feast* is an ode in honour of St. Cecilia.

Drama

The dramatic works of the Restoration were licentious and full of cynicism. They regarded the moral code of the Puritans as a matter of ridicule. Scenery now played an important part on the stage and actresses, not boys, played the female roles. The theatre was regarded as a place of vice and evil. Shakespeare's plays were rewritten and his tragedies like *Romeo and Juliet* given happy endings. French influence dominated and extraordinary superhuman feats were described. Heroes were presented as ideals and were made to give pompous speeches.

Dryden wrote many plays like *Aureng-zebe* or *The Great Mogul* (1675) and The Conquest of Granada (1669, 1670) which abound in rhetoric.

The tragedians were **Thomas Otway (1651-1685)**, Nathaniel Lee (1653-1692) and **Nicholas Rowe (1674-1718)**. The comedy of this period reflects the gay intrigues of the society. Caricature and farce were used and obscenity also touched it. The main aim was to amuse. **Sir George Etheredge (1635-1691)** was an innovator and **William Wycherley (1640-1715)** was a moralist playwright. **William Congreve (1670-1729)** wrote a series of masterpieces including *The Way of the World* (1700). **John Vanbrugh** (1664-1726) and **George Farquhar (1678-1707)** were other comedy writers of the period.

Criticism

Dryden was the first English critic. *The Essay of Dramatick Poesie* (1668) is his longest single prose work and a major piece of English literary criticism. It is in the form of a discussion between four characters, one of whom is Dryden himself. It deals with topics related to theatre and evaluates the works of the Elizabethan dramatists, especially of Shakespeare.

The Diarists of the Restoration Period

One of the sources of information and genres of prose writing during the Restoration were diaries. The important names are those of John Evelyn, Samuel Pepys and Roger North. **John Evelyn (1620-1706)** was a rich man who had cultured tastes. He was a member of the Royal Society and had wide interests in diverse fields like gardening, forestry, navigation and architecture. His *Diary* which was written almost throughout his lifetime throws a floodlight on the major social and national events of the time like the Galley Slaves and the Great Fire. It is written in a plain, graphic style. **Samuel Pepys (1633-1703)** had a chequered career. Coming from the middle classes, he joined the civil services and rose to be the secretary of the Admiralty. He also became the President of the Royal Society and a member of Parliament. His famous *Diary*, covering a period of ten years, is in the form of confessions. It was written in laconic sentences like the messages of a telegram and was in a sort of code which was deciphered only in 1825. The diary shows him to be a man of versatile interests like music, science and literature. But the most controversial aspect is the detailed confessions of his life. Nobody seemed to guess he was a libertine, a morally debauched character who could stoop to low means. When we read the diary, it seems he is writing of another person. **Roger North** belonged to an elite family. He was a Tory gentleman and was engaged in the politics of the times. His famous work is *North's Lives of the Norths* containing biographies of three relatives and an autobiography. His pen pictures and anecdotes are in colloquial style.

MAJOR AUTHORS AND THEIR WORKS

Robert Herrick (1591-1574)

Noble Numbers

Hesperides

Thomas Carew (1598-1639)

Poems

'He that loves a rosy cheek'

Sir John Suckling (1660-1642)

'Ballad upon a Wedding'

'Why so pale and wan, Fond Lover'?

Andrew Marvell (1621-1678)

'To His Coy Mistress'

'The Rehearsal Transprosed'

'Ode upon Cromwell's Return from Ireland'

New Letters (a Prose Work)

George Herbert (1593-1633)

The Temple

Affliction

Easter Wings

The Collar

Man

Richard Crashaw (1613-1649)

Carmen Deo Nostro

The Infant Morturs

Steps to the Temple

John Milton (1608-1674)

Paradise Lost (in twelve Books)

Paradise Regained

Comus

Lycidas

Samson Agonistes

L'Allegro

Ill Penseroso

Areopagitica (Prose Work)

Ode on the Morning of Christ's Nativity

Sonnets (including) :

'On His Blindness'

'On the Late Massacre in Piedmont'

'When the Assault was Intended to the City'

'On His Having Arrived at the Age of Twenty-three'

A large number of Tracts and Pamphlets in support of the Parliament

John Donne (1573-1631)

Songs and Sonnets

Aires and Angels

A Nocturnall upon Lucies Day

A Valediction : Forbidding Mourning

The Extasie

Devotions (Sermon in Prose)

Ignatius His Enclave (a Prose Work)

Of the Progress of the Soul

Death's Duell

Abraham Cowley (1618-1667)

Pyramus and Thisbe

The Mistress

The Davideis

Pindarique Odes

Constantia and Philetus

Discourse by Way of Vision

Concerning the Government of Cromwell (a Prose Work)

Henry Vaughan (1622-1695)

Poems

Regeneration

The Retreat

Olor Iscanus

Thalia Redivia

Silex Scintillans

John Dryden (1631-1700)

(*i*) *Heroic Stanzas on the Death of Oliver Cromwell*

Astraea Redux (on the Restoration of Charles II)

Absalom and Achitophel

Religio Laici

The Hind and the Panther

The Fables

Annus Mirabilis

The Medal

Mac Flecknoe

Alexander's Feast

Prefaces to His Plays (in Prose)

An Essay of Dramatic Poesy

(*ii*) *Dryden's Plays*

Tyrannic Love

Conquest of Granada

All for love
The Rival Ladies
The Indian Emperor
Aureng-Zeb
Don Sebastian
Cleomenes
Love Triumphant

John Vanbrugh (1664-1726)
The Relapse
The Provoked Wife
The Confederacy

George Farquhar (1678-1707)
The Recruiting Officer
The Beaux Stratagem

Thomas Otway (1652-1685)
Orphan
Venice Preserved
Don Carlos
Alcibiades

Nathaniel Lee (1653-1692)
Nero
The Rival Queens
Sophonisba

John Bunyan (1628-1688)
The Pilgrim's Progress
Grace Abounding
The Life and Death of Mr. Badman
The Holy War

John Locke (1632-1704)
Essay on the Human Understanding
Treatise on Government
Thoughts on Education

John Evelyn (1620-1706)
Diary

Samuel Pepys (1633-1703)
Diary

MULTIPLE CHOICE QUESTIONS

1. Who wrote the *Faerie Queene?*
A. John Lyly
B. Edmund Spenser
C. Ben Jonson
D. Shakespeare

2. What is the nine-line stanza used in the *Faerie Queene* called?
A. Alexandrine B. Shakespearean
C. Spenserian D. Petrarchan

3. *The Anatomy of Melancholy* is written by:
A. Robert Burton B. John Dryden
C. Thomas Dekker D. Milton

4. *Doctor Faustus* is a story of:
A. a scientist
B. revenge
C. the Renaissance love of power
D. a greedy Jew

5. Marlowe invented:
A. sprung rhythm B. sonnet
C. allegory D. blank verse

6. *Romeo and Juliet* is a:
A. tragedy B. comedy
C. tragi-comedy D. history

7. *Every Man in His Humour* is written by:
A. Ben Jonson B. Dryden
C. John Donne D. Marston

8. Dryden wrote:
A. *Sejanus*
B. *The Compleat Angler*
C. *Aureng-zebe*
D. *Principia*

9. The song *Drink to me only with thine eyes* is written by:
A. Lyly
B. Ben Jonson
C. Shakespeare
D. Spenser

10. The Puritan Parliament closed the theatres in:
A. 1638 B. 1632
B. 1606 D. 1642

11. *The Shoemaker's Holiday* is a play written by:
A. Shakespeare B. Marlowe
C. Thomas Dekker D. Marston

12. Ben Jonson's *The Poetaster* is a satire on:
A. Marston and Dekker
B. Marlowe
C. Kyd
D. Greene

13. The main theme of Webster's plays is his:
A. humour
B. satire
C. preoccupation with death
D. social life

14. Marlowe, Kyd, Lyly and Greene were known as:
A. Humorists
B. University Wits
C. The Rivals of Shakespeare
D. The Decadents

15. The person who collaborated with Beaumont for many plays was:
A. Fletcher B. Shakespeare
C. Marston D. Greene

16. Herrick, Carew, Suckling and Lovelace were collectively called:
A. Metaphysical Poets
B. Religious Poets
C. Puritans
D. Cavalier Poets

17. The *Horatian Ode* by Andrew Marvel is addressed to:
A. Cromwell B. Charles II
C. Queen Elizabeth D. Shakespeare

18. *Comus* by Milton is a/an:
A. masque B. ode
C. epic D. lyric

19. *Lycidas* is an elegy by Milton on:
A. Arthur Hallam B. Edward King
C. Cromwell D. Ben Jonson

20. *The Compleat Angler* is written by:
A. Milton B. Robert Burton
C. Izaak Walton D. Thomas Fuller

21. *Leviathan* is written by:
A. Milton B. Marvel
C. Thomas Hobbes D. Farquhar

22. *The Pilgrim's Progress* by John Bunyan is a/an:
A. book of philosophy
B. treatise on education
C. masque
D. allegory

23. Samuel Butler's satire on Puritanism is:
A. *Hudibras* B. *Way of the World*
C. *Utopia* D. *Paradise Lost*

24. John Evelyn's *Diary* is famous for:
A. describing major social events of his times
B. describing personal experiences
C. scholarly research
D. noting facts and figures

25. Samuel Pepys' *Diary* is mainly:
A. social B. confessional
C. descriptive D. argumentative

ANSWERS

1	2	3	4	5	6	7	8	9	10
B	C	A	C	D	C	A	C	B	D
11	**12**	**13**	**14**	**15**	**16**	**17**	**18**	**19**	**20**
C	A	C	B	A	D	A	A	B	C
21	**22**	**23**	**24**	**25**					
C	D	A	A	B					

THE EIGHTEENTH CENTURY

THE AUGUSTAN AGE (1700-1740)

In general, the eighteenth century was the age of understanding and enlightenment. The emphasis was on the advancement of the human mind. Sensibility was the guiding principle. This age borrowed the humour and poetic technique of the previous century.

This age is generally called *The Augustan Age* or *The Age of Queen Anne* because the queen patronized the men of letters. The period is also known as the Classical Age. It was an age of tolerance and harmony and was guided by reason. Dryden still wrote and was a contemporary of French authors Corneille, Racine and Moliere. Many English works were translated by the French. Poetry was still for aristocrats and the courts, but prose spread among the common public. People demanded instructions and information and practical hints for living. This led writers to use a simple style to be comprehensible to all.

Poetry

Matthew Prior (1664-1721) began by writing a parody of The Hind and the Panther in which he expounded his opinions on politics. **Sir Samuel Garth (1661-1791)** and **Joseph Addison (1672-1719)** used the heroic couplet of Dryden. Addison described Marlborough's victory at Blenheim in his poem *The Campaign* (1704). But the poetical luminary of the period was **Alexander Pope (1688-1744)**. He polished Dryden's couplet and used it as a weapon of satire, like in the famous *An Essay on Man* (1732-1734). His *An Essay on Criticism* (1711) and *The Rape of the Lock* (1712, 1714) are other great works. The latter is in mock-heroic style and describes the anger of a lady whose lock of hair had been cut off. Pope also translated the Iliad. He wrote *The Dunciad* (1728) to castigate bad poets. His *Imitations of Horace* (1733-1737) is highly admired even today.

Jonathan Swift, usually known as a prose writer, also showed a gift or versification like in his poem *On the Death of Dr. Swift*. **John Gay (1685-1732)** was popular for his fables like *The Hare with Many Friends* and his songs in *The Beggar's Opera.* **Edward Young's (1683-1765)** *The Commaint, or Night Thoughts on Life, Death, and Immortality* (1742), is a poet's delight in meditation underlining the vanity of all earthly glory.

Prose

This period saw an increasing demand for the circulation of facts and ideas among the public. **Daniel Defoe (1659-1731)** was a trail-blazer as a Journalist and his popular works are *The True-Born Englishman* (1701) and *The Shortest Way with the Dissenters* (1702). Defoe wrote the first English novel *Robinson Crusoe* (1719), which is a children's classic or collection of adventure stories. He cultivated the art of reporting and presented his stories as historical narratives which are precise and practical.

Steele, Addison, Swift, Arbuthnot were the other great prose-writers of the time. They introduced a style adorned by figures of speech. The periodicals of Steele and Addison contain essays which deal with practical moral questions and reflect the morals of the time.

Richard Steele (1672-1729) led a dissipated life and was full of remorse for it. He extols the Bible as a guide in life in his work *The Christian Hero*. He launched the journal *The Tatler* in 1709. **Joseph Addison** propagated rational and moderate ideas. He collaborated with Steele on *The Tatler.* Steele then founded *The Spectator* in 1711 and Addison again collaborated. Here they were merely the spectators of the society and its foibles. It epitomizes the whole nation. The character of Sir Roger de Coverley is a masterpiece, a comic personality with eccentricities. Other characters, Sir Andrew Freeport. Will Honeycomb, Captain Sentry capture the imagination of the readers.

Jonathan Swift (1667-1745) enjoyed ridicule rather than correction. He lays bare all the vices of man as something that are beyond correction. He ridiculed the modern authors in his The *Battle of the Books* (1704) and attacked the Papists and Presbyterians in *The Tale of a Tub* (1704). His most popular work is a children's classic, *Gulliver's Travels* (1726), which is also a satire on politics, religions, science and nature of man.

John Arbuthnot (1667-1735) was another humanist and man of wit and is known for his *The History of John Bull* (1712), an amusing allegory on the politics of the time.

During this period a number of deists like Locke, Collins and Tindal propounded a philosophy advocating reasoning rather than superstitious beliefs as advocated by orthodox Christians. Earl of Shaftesbury (1671-1713), Lord Bolingbroke (1678-1751) and Mandeville were other rationalists of the time who wrote many prose works.

THE AGE OF TRANSITION (1740-1800)

Like all other periods of transition, this age was also disturbed and confused. Two movements can be clearly observed in the writings of the time: (*i*) the allegiance to the old order of classicism, and (*ii*) the search after the new order of Romanticism. The period was marked by new learning, new philosophy, growth of historical research and new realism.

This period is also known as the *Age of Johnson* because **Samuel Johnson (1709-1784)**, the greatest English man of letters, flourished during this period. Samuel Johnson was a versatile man of letters translator, journalist, commentator, critic, novelist, biographer and poet. He created two satirical poems, *London* (1738) and *The Vanity of Human Wishes* (1749). He had a supple style and describes his personal reflections in his essays *The Rambler* (1750-1752) and *The Idler* (1758-1760). His *Dictionary of English Language* (1747-1755) shows remarkable precision in definition and a feeling for the correct use of words. Besides the novel *Rasselas, Prince of Abyssinia* (1759) his best works are biographical and literary studies and his edition of *Shakespeare* (1765). His *Lives of the Poets* (1777-1781) is a biographical work. His admirer James Boswell's famous biography of Johnson has made him immortal. He is described here in candid details. His prejudices, excellences and demerits are all laid bare.

Poetry

Poetry showed the influence of Dryden and Pope. It was mainly didactic and satirical and the couplet still was the major form.

Oliver Goldsmith's (1728-1774) *Deserted Village* (1770) is a masterpiece of the period. **James Thomson's (1700-1748)** *The Seasons* (1730) is a praise of the beauties of Nature in all her diversity. Other noteworthy poems of the period are **William Collins' (1721-1759)** *Ode to Evening*, a delightful lyric, and **Thomas Gray's (1716-1771)** *Elegy Written in a Country Churchyard* (1751).

A general belief in human liberty was seen as the French Revolution proceeded. **William Cowper** (1731-1800) who wrote *The Ballad of John Gilpin*, **George Crabbe (1754-1832)**, the Scotsman **Robert Burns (1759-1796)** and the mystic **William Blake (1757-1827)** echoed the sentiments of the period. Burns was a farmer and wrote in original racy dialect thus causing a break from convention. Blake was a visionary and his poems are collected in *Songs of Innocence* (1789) and *Songs of Experience* (1794). In *The Tyger,* he uses the Lamb as a symbol of innocence and of Jesus, and the Tiger as the symbol of evil in the world, of the evil seen in the French Revolution where thousands were sent to the guillotine.

Novel

The period saw the development of the novel. A series of masterpieces came out. In the novel, the author could describe events in detail. Defoe's novels so far were based on strange subjects. Now they concentrated on commonplace events of family life and society. Adventure of earlier novels gave place to character portrayal. The novels were very long and filled with minute details. **Samuel Richardson (1689-1761)** wrote *Pamela, or Virtue Rewarded* (1740) and *Clarissa Harlowe* (1747-1748). **Henry Fielding (1707-1754)** is famous for *Joseph Andrews* (1742) and *Tom Jones* (1749), **Tobias Smollet (1721-1771)** wrote *The Adventures* *of Roderick Random* (1748) and *The Expedition of Humphry Clinker* (1771), **Laurence Sterne (1713-1768)** wrote *Tristram Shandy* (1760), and **Oliver Goldsmith** *The Vicar of Wakefield* (1766).

Letter

There were famous letter writers also, like **Lord Chesterfield (1694-1773). Horace Walpole (1719-1797), Thomas Gray and Richardson**. Frequently, a series of letters was bound into book-form. Collections of this kind were the letters of **Lady Mary Wortley Montagu (1689-1762)**, written to Pope from Constantinople, and of Thomas Gray, from the Lake District. Chesterfield's letters to his son contain comments on political and social matters. Richardson's *Pamela* is entirely in letter-form.

Drama

The century was the age of the great novels. Drama lost originality and talent. People saw Shakespeare's plays enacted, but what attracted them was the genius of the actors. However, there were a few good plays written. For instance, Johnson's *Irene* (1749), Fielding's *The Miser*, Goldsmith's anti-sentimental comedy *She Stoops to Conquer* (1773), and Sheridan's *The School for Scandal* (1777) and *The Rivals* (1775).

Historical Work

Towards the last part of the century the history of England was rocked by many revolutionary changes the impact of which were felt in English literature. Till the mid-18th century Victorian England reigned supreme. She was mistress of the seas and her imperial rule covered many colonies. In 1776, America declared her independence and the British Parliament was divided on the issue. Many Britishers favoured the American claims. In 1789, the French Revolution broke out and here too the Britishers were divided into two camps. Inspired by the writings of Rousseau, many believed the Revolution was being fought for the right causes. The Parliament resounded with the speeches of the famous. Some even accused Warren Hastings for his extortion policies in India and some others were against slave-trade.

Treatises on philosophy by **David Hume (1711-1776)** and histories by **William Robertson (1721-1793)** and political economy (*Wealth of Nations*) by **Adam Smith (1723-1790)** came out.

Edmund Burke (1729-1797) read law and began writing to propound his views on human feelings and emotions. His language is as oratorical in Parliament at the trial of Warren Hastings as in his famous writing *A Philosophical Inquiry into the Origin of our Ideas of the Sublime and the Beautiful* (1756).

Other orators who expressed themselves in writing were Tom Paine, Godwin and Jeremy Bentham. **William Godwin (1756-1836)** advocated the elimination of government in *Enquiry Concerning Political Justice* (1793). He proscribed law, marriage, gratitude, everything that limited liberty. His monumental work is *The Decline and Fall of the Roman Empire* (1776-1788) in which he describes the growth of Christianity and his belief in reason rather than the divine. At the same time **William Paley (1743-1805)** wrote *A View of the Evidences of Christianity* (1794) to prove the existence of miracles by logic.

MAJOR AUTHORS AND THEIR WORKS

Alexander Pope (1688-1744)

Pastorals

An Essay on Criticism

Windsor Forest

The Rape of the Lock

Dunciad

Translation of Iliad and Odyssey

To Lord Bathrust

On the Use of the Riches

An Essay on Man

Epistle to Dr. Arbuthnot

Of the Knowledge and Characters of Men

Of the Characters of Women

The Messiah

Satires and Epistles of Horace Imitated

Matthew Prior (1664-1721)

Solomon on the Vanity of the World

Alma : or the Progress of the Mind

The Town and Country Mouse

John Gay (1685-1732)

Fables

The Shepherd's Week

The Rural Sports

Trivia

The Beggar's Opera

The Streets of London

Edward Young (1683-1765)

Night Thoughts

Dr. Samuel Johnson (1709-1784)

The Vanity of Human Wishes

London

The Lives of the Poets

Preface to Shakespeare

Dictionary of the English Language

A Journey to the Western Islands of Scotland

The Rambler

Rasselas

Prince of Abyssinia

The Life of Savage

The Adventurer

The Idler

Daniel Defoe (1661-1731)

Robinson Crusoe

Mall Flanders

Colonel Jack

The Memoirs of a Cavalier

Captain Singleton

Journal of the Plague Year

Roxana

Jonathan Swift (1667-1745)

The Battle of the Books

A Tale of a Tub

Gulliver's Travels

Journal to Stella

The Drapier's Letters

Cadenus and Vanessa

Joseph Addison (1672-1719)

The Spectator

The Campaign

Public Credit

The Vision of Mirza

Cato

Rosamond

The Drummer

Richard Steele (1672-1729)

The Tatler

The Guardian

The Funeral

The Lying Lover

The Tender Husband

The Conscious Lover

Thomas Gray (1716-1771)

Elegy Written in a Country Churchyard

On a Distant Prospect of Eton College

On the Death of a Favourite Cat

The Bard

The Progress of Poesy

The Fatal Sisters

The Descent of Odin

MULTIPLE CHOICE QUESTIONS

1. *The Hind and the Panther* is a parody about:

A. religion

B. society

C. politics

D. human beings in general

2. Which poem is in mock-heroic style?

A. *The Rape of the Lock*

B. *The Christian Hero*

C. *On the Death of Dr. Swift*

D. *The Hare with Many Friends*

3. Who was the first journalist of the age?
A. Dryden B. Daniel Defoe
C. Swift D. Arbuthnot

4. Who wrote the first English dictionary?
A. Goldsmith B. Boswell
C. Webster D. Samuel Johnson

5. Lord Chesterfield is famous as a:
A. Novelist B. Letter-writer
C. Playwright D. Poet

6. The novel written in epistolary or letter form is:
A. *Joseph Andrews*
B. *Pamela*
C. *Vicar of Wakefield*
D. *Tom Jones*

7. Johnson's biographer was:
A. Boswell B. Irene
C. Swift D. Edmund Burke

8. A play which describes heroes as virtues personified and is full of pompous speeches is:
A. Heroic play
B. Sentimental Comedy
C. Anti-Sentimental Comedy
D. Tragi-Comedy

9. Edmund Burke was:
A. poet and scholar B. playwright
C. orator and writer D. lexicographer

10. *The Decline and Pall of the Roman Empire* is written by:
A. Paley B. Smith
C. Johnson D. Godwin

11. The main reason why papers came out in Queen Anne's time was:
A. People were hungry for information about current events
B. People wanted to contact businessmen
C. People wanted to improve their writing style
D. People liked sensational fiction stories

12. The characters Sir Andrew Freeport, Captain Sentry and Sir Roger are featured in:
A. *The Tatler*
B. *The London Gazette*
C. *The Spectator*
D. *The Review*

13. The countries that influenced British literature and art in the 18th century were:
A. Germany and Holland
B. Sweden and Norway
C. Austria and France
D. France and Italy

14. The religious revival of the 18th century started by John and Charles Weslay was known as:
A. Methodism B. Deism
C. Presbyterianism D. Evangelism

15. *The Hind and the Panther Transvers'd to the Story of the Country and City Mouse* is a poem by:
A. Dryden B. Matthew Prior
C. Pope D. John Gay

16. John Gay is famous for a musical drama named:
A. *The Beggar's Opera*B. *Polly*
C. *The Secretary* D. *Fables*

17. *The Ballad of John Gilpin* is written by:
A. Thomas Gray B. William Cowper
C. William Blake D. Robert Burns

18. The son of a British Prime Minister is famous for his letters and *The Castle of Otranto*, a gruesome play. His (the son's) name was:
A. Robert Walpole B. Horace Walpole
C. William Pitt D. Churchill

19. *Wealth of Nations* is written by:
A. Joshua Reynolds B. Adam Smith
C. Godwin D. David Hume

20. Sheridan was a:
A. poet B. dramatist
C. novelist D. musician

21. *The Rivals* is a play by:
A. Sheridan B. Goldsmith
C. Johnson D. David Garrick

22. *Origin of our Ideas of the Sublime and the Beautiful* is an essay by:
A. Edmund Burke B. Godwin
C. Thomas Paine D. Hume

23. The greatest Scottish poet of the 18th century is:
A. Robert Burns B. Walter Scott
C. William Cowper D. John Gay

24. The lines, *"O My luve's like a red, red rose,/That's newly sprung in June;...."* are attributed to:
A. William Blake B. Fergusson
C. Robert Burns D. Macpherson

25. Who was known as the "Man of Feeling" after his sentimental novel *The Man of Feeling*?
A. Francis Burney B. Ann Rediliffe
C. Matthew Lewis D. Henry Mackenzie

ANSWERS

1	2	3	4	5	6	7	8	9	10
C	A	B	D	B	B	A	B	C	D
11	**12**	**13**	**14**	**15**	**16**	**17**	**18**	**19**	**20**
A	C	D	A	B	A	B	B	B	B
21	**22**	**23**	**24**	**25**					
A	A	A	C	D					

THE NINETEENTH CENTURY

THE ROMANTIC AGE (1798-1830)

The eighteenth century literature of England was inspired by reason, but the nineteenth century was the age of imagination. The Preface to the *Lyrical Ballads* by William Wordsworth and Samuel Taylor Coleridge in 1798, heralds the period of English Romanticism. The authors of this work were disgusted with the excesses of the French Revolution, they condemned the Rationalist Movement. England turned away from the literature of France and transferred her sympathies to Germany. The philosophical doctrine of Romanticism was inspired by Germany. Romanticism was essentially poetic. Although poles apart in their political beliefs, Wordsworth and Shelley both considered the poet as the guide, prophet and seer of mankind.

Poetry

For the great Romantics — Wordsworth, Shelley, Keats, Byron — the study of the wondrous world of feelings, senses, instincts, of Man' relation to Nature, were of prime importance. Romanticism is shot with *metaphysics*. As M. Lanson puts it, *tout traverse de frissons metaphysique* Alexander Pope had used poetry to depict the thoughts of the philosophers in his *Essay on Man*. The Romantics, dedicated to Romantic imagination — *the esemplastic imagination* as Coleridge called it — were convinced that what was revealed to their poetic intuitions, was right, the Truth. Mysterious forces divine in origin moved the earth, not cold rationalist cause and effect. Pope's couplet was dull and too precise governed by convention. The Romantics sought a lyrical form using unusual images and association of words. They found models for these in the Renaissance and the old popular poetry.

William Wordsworth (1770-1850) is aptly called the "High Priest of Nature". He saw Nature as the *'Stern Daughter of the voice of God'*, man's conscience whose balmy presence never disappointed. He was born in 1770 in the picturesque Lake District of England. Here he spent happy years of his childhood in communion with God and Nature. After study at Cambridge, he went to France in 1791 and was enthused by the cause of the Revolution. But when the Reign of Terror came and thousands died at the guillotine, his fine sensibilities, his search for human equality and peace received a rude shock. He engaged himself in the philosophy of William Godwin for sometime. Finding no solution to the problem of human pain, he finally turned to the study of Nature. In the poems of the Lyrical Ballads he describes the mundane happenings of country life, the activities of humble people. He used their common dialect with its flawed grammar as his style. He decries the coming of the industrial era which mechanized English life. With no ornament, his poetry draws its power from the intensity of his feelings and imagination, In The Prelude (1805), a long poem, Wordsworth set out to look back and retrospect on his life. He follows the growth, the turnings of his poetic genius since childhood, ruminates on his errors and recalls the corrective lessons of Nature. In his great moral poem, The Excursion (1814), he uses a philosophy to refute the pessimism that the Revolution had brought.

Samuel Taylor Coleridge (1772-1834) was Wordsworth's "Spirits Brother". He was guided by the same philosophy of the imagination. While Wordsworth's imagination gave him a special vision of the common things of rustic life, Coleridge stirred up the supernatural. To appreciate his poetry peopled with strange, translunary beings like *The Ancient Mariner,* one needs *'that willing suspension of disbelief that constitutes poetic faith'*. In *The Rime of the Ancient Mariner,* Coleridge describes the strange adventures of a sailor in a ship. Having killed an albatross, the mariner suffers from hallucinations. The poem, with strange rhythm and cadences, creates a wondrous world. Coleridge was a master of lyrical style. His other famous poems are *Christabel* (1816), and *Kubla Khan* (1816). *Kubla Khan* was written as a result of an opium dream and described the wonderful, strange palace of the Chinese king, Kubla Khan. Coleridge certainly fulfils the meaning of *'Renaissance'* as *'a renascence of wonder'*.

Robert Southey (1774-1843) wrote poetry based on outlandish settings and myths like *Thalaba, the Destroyer* (1801), *The Curse of Kehama* (1810), and *Roderick, the Last of the Goths* (1814). His descriptions are rich and graphic and he uses a great variety of verse forms. He wrote a number of poems in ballad form.

Walter Scott (1771-1832) also had an interest in ballad poetry. He translated the *Lenore* from German (1796). His *The Minstrelsy of the Scottish Border* (1802) shows a great romantic interest in the Middle Ages and the days of chivalry.

The second generation of great Romantic poets include Shelley, Keats and Byron.

Percy Bysshe Shelley (1792-1822) gave up his title and wealth to write poetry. His aim was to awaken mankind to the millenium, the coming future, which would remove human anguish and sorrow. His famous ode, *Ode to the West Wind* is an impassioned exhortation — *Make me thy lyre eu'n as the forest is ...... If Winter comes, can Spring be far behind?* He came under the influence of William Godwin, the philosopher. He proclaimed himself an atheist at the age of 21. His works include *Queen Mab* (1813), *Prometheus Unbound* (1818-1819), which shows human revolt against false gods, *To a Skylark, Adonais* (1821), which is an elegy to Keats, and The Cenci (1819). Shelley's style is a mixture of abstractions and visual images.

John Keats (1795-1821) was the most sensuous of the great Romantic poets. As we read his poems, richly laden with imagery and associations, all the senses are stirred up the visual, olfactory, auditory and tactile. It is said he tasted pepper in wine to describe certain lines. His famous odes are *To a Nightingale, To Autumn* and *On a Grecian Urn.*

Lord George Gordon Byron (1788-1824) was a wealthy nobleman who shunned the popular beliefs of his times. He was notorious as a dilletante. At the age of 19, he wrote Hours of Idleness (1807). With the publication of *Childe Harold's Pilgrimage* (1812) he became famous. Childe Harold was Byron himself, the figure of the disillusioned man, the hero fed up of pleasures and debauches. He lives an outlawed life and is rebellious in spirit. He took on more incarnations in his poems, *The Giaour* (1813), *The Corsair* (1814), *The Siege of Corinth* (1815). In these he displayed his own passions and eccentricities. In 1816, divorced from his wife, he retired to Switzerland and then to Italy. He wrote a number of plays — *Manfred* (1817), *Cain* (1821) and *The Deformed Transformed* (1824). The crowning work was his lyrical, satirical *Don Juan* (1819-1823). He went to Greece to fight for its independence, but died of illness. His satire is political, against England and also against English hypocrisy and cant. His licentious descriptions caused scandals. Don Juan, his magnum opus, is written in ottava rima or eight-line stanzas and is full of wit and mockery.

Thomas Moore (1779-1852), Thomas Campbell (1777-1844), Samuel Rogers (1763-1855), James Hogg (1770-1835), Walter Savage Landor (1775-1864) and **Leigh Hunt (1784-1859)** were other poets of the time.

Novel

Novels of terror and mystery prospered from 1800 to 1830. **Matthew Gregory Lewis** (1775-1818) wrote *Tales of Terror* (1800) and *Tales of Wonder* (1801). **Charles Lamb's (1775-1834)** *Tales from Shakespeare* (1807) is very popular even today. *Mrs Shelley,* the poet's wife, wrote the classic *Frankenstein* in which a scientist creates a monster that turns on its creator and destroys his most beloved ones. It is a novel of prophetic fear. **Miss Mary Mitford** wrote on country life and **Maria Edgeworth (1767-1849)** brought out educational novels like Belinda (1801) and *Tales of Fashionable Life* — novels for children.

Jane Austen (1775-1817) produced half a dozen novels which are drawing-room comedies of life. They study the passion and distress of young ladies and the life of country-folk. The novels — *Pride and Prejudice* (1813), *Sense and Sensibility* (1811), *Emma* (1816), *Persuasion* (1818), *Mansfield Park* (1814), *Northanger Abbey* (1818) — are realistic and witty, full of bracing dialogue.

Walter Scott was Scotland's greatest novelist recreating the past of his country's myths and ballads with rich humour. *Waverly* (1814), *Guy Mannering* (1815), *The Heart of Midlothian* (1818) contain history and direct observation. In *Ivanhoe* (1820), he describes the history of England in the days of the legendary Richard, the Lion Heart. *Kenilworth* (1821), *Quentin Dunward* (1823) were his other famous historical novels. He imbued the Romantic era with a love for the Middle Ages.

Prose/Criticism

The Romantic Age saw a number of reviewers and critics like **Jeremy Bentham (1748-1832)**, who expounded utilitarian doctrines, **Sydney Smith (1771-1845)**, and **William Cobbett (1762-1835)**. Coleridge, the poet, interpreted the doctrines of Kant and Schelling which show the distinction between pure reason and practical reason.

Lamb, Hazlitt, De Quincey and Leigh Hunt were Romantic critics of literature. **Charles Lamb's** essays on Shakespeare's tragedies state that we cannot do justice to them by staging them since the passions which are to be felt in their intensity are torn to tatters by the gimmickry of the actors. **William Hazlitt's (1778-1830)** criticism of some of Shakespeare's characters like Falstaff — *he laughs three inches below the flesh* — is a masterpiece. Coleridge's famous work of criticism, *Biographia Literaria* (1817), marvellously analyses Wordsworth's poetry. The Romantics believed that Shakespeare's art was organic like a work of Nature and *"esemplastic"* — able to blend different elements by imagination. **Thomas De Quincey's (1785-1859)** style is penetrating and incisive when criticizing the poets in *The Confessions of an English Opium Eater* (1821).

MAJOR AUTHORS AND THEIR WORKS

William Wordsworth (1770-1850)

The Lyrical Ballads
The Prelude
The Excursion
Tintern Abbey
Ode on Intimations of Immortality
Michael
The Solitary Reaper
Loadamia
Ode to Duty
To Milton
The Leech-Gatherer
Upon Westminster Abbey
The Rainbow

We Are Seven
The World Is Too Much with Us
To the Cuckoo
The Daffodils
Lucy Gray
Simon Lee
Early Spring
Strange Fits of Passion Have I Known

Walter Scott (1771-1832)

The Bride of Lammermoor
Ivanhoe
Quentin Durward
The Heart of midlothian
Old Mortality
The Antiquity
Guy Mannering
Waverly
Rob Roy
Kenilworth
Red Gauntlet
The Black Dwarf
The Monastery
The Abbot
The Pirate
The Fortunes of Night
The Betrothed
The Talisman
Woodstock
Lives of the Novelists
Life of Napoleon
Tales of Grandfather
The Lay of the Last Minstrel
The Minstrelsy of the Scottish Border
Marmion
The Lady of the Lake
Rockeby

Robert Southey (1774-1843)

Joan of Arc
Wat Tyler
After Blenheim
The Holly Tree
The Scholar
A Vision of Judgement
Madoc
Life of Nelson
Thalaba the Destroyer
Roderick
The Curse of Kehama

S.T. Coleridge (1772-1834)

Biographia Literaria
Table Talk
Aids to Reflection
Christabel
Kubla Khan
The Rime of the Ancient Mariner
France : An Ode
Destiny of Nations
Frost at Midnight
Dejection : An Ode
Youth and Age
Religious Musings

Lord Byron (1788-1824)

Childe Harold's Pilgrimage
Don Juan
The Bride of Abydos
Manfred
The Giaour
Hours of Idleness
The Vision of Judgement
The Prisoner of Chillon
Lara
Marino Faliero
English Bards and Scotch Reviewers
The Siege of Corinth
The Corsair
Cain

P.B. Shelley (1792-1822)

On the Necessity of Atheism
The Revolt of Islam
Prometheus Unbound
The Mask of Anarchy
Hellas

The Cenci
The Witch of Atlas
The Indian Serenade
Ozymandias of Egypt
Epipsychidion
Alaster
Queen Mab
Adonais
Ode to the West Wind
The Cloud
Ode to a Skylark
O World! O Life! O Time!
Defence of Poetry (a Prose Work)
To Night
The Sensitive Plant
A Lament

John Keats (1795-1821)

Endymion
Lamia
Hyperion
The Eve of St. Agnes
Isabella
The Eve of St. Mark
La Belle Dame Sans Merci
Ode to a Nightingale
Ode to Autumn
Ode On a Grecian Urn
Ode to Psyche
On Melancholy
On First Looking into Chapman's Homer
Bright Star

Jane Austen (1775-1871)

Sense and Sensibility
Pride and Prejudice
Mansfield Park
Emma
Persuasion
Northanger Abbey

Charles Lamb (1775-1834)

Essays of Elia
The Last Essays of Elia
John Woodvil
Tales from Shakespeare
Specimens of English Dramatic Poets
The English Comic Writers
The Old Familiar Faces

William Hazlitt (1778-1830)

Characters of Shakespeare's Plays
The English Poets
The English Comic Writers
The Dramatic Literature of the Age of Elizabeth
The Round Table : A Collection of Essays
Table Talk on Men and Manners
The Spirit of the Age

Thomas De Quincey (1785-1859)

Confessions of an English Opium Eater
Joan of Arc
English Mail Coach
Dream Fugue
Murder Considered as One of the Fine Arts
Suspiria de Profundis

Samuel Rogers (1763-1855)

Pleasures of Memory
Italy

James Hogg (1770-1835)

Kilmeny
The Queen's Wake

Thomas Campbell

Pleasures of Hope
Theodoric
Gertrude of Wyoming
Lachiel
Lord Ullin's Daughter
The Last Man
Ye Mariners of England
Hohenlinden
The Battle of Baltic

Thomas Moore (1779-1852)

Lalla Rookh
Irish Melodies

Leigh Hunt (1784-1859)

Story of Rimini
Autobiography
Walter Savage Landor (1775-1864)
Gebir
Hellenics
Imaginary Conversations
The Citations of William Shakespeare
Pericles and Aspasia

THE VICTORIAN ERA (1830-1880)

During this era, the conflict between religion and science, mysticism and rationalism, became intense. There were those who, influenced by Darwin's theory of evolution as expounded in his *On the Origin of Species,* lost their faith in the biblical explanation of man's descent from Adam and Eve. They wanted to shun dogma and accept the scientific spirit. Others lamented the loss of faith and the rising consumer values. Mathew Arnold in his poem *Dover Beach* writes:

"The Sea of Faith was once too at the full.....
But now I only hear its long withdrawing melancholy roar......"

Prose

Carlyle and Ruskin echoed the prophecies of the Romantic era in their prose works. **Thomas Carlyle (1795-1881)**, the Scotsman, abandoned orthodoxy and came under the influence of the German writers Schiller, Novalis, Richter and Goethe. His work *Sartor Resartus* (1833-1834) is a sort of allegory based on a German professor who has written a treatise on clothes. He penetrates through the clothes to the essence of the man's being. Carlyle was also a historian. His historical works are *The French Revolution* (1837) and *The History of Frederich II of Prussia, called frederik the Great* (1858-1865). These are satirical and prophetic, expounding how man and society are organized. He was against materialism and praised the Magi and prophets of the past. He advocates strength and power.

John Ruskin (1819-1900) was indignant about the ugliness of existence brought in by industrialism and the machine. *Unto This Last* (1860), which influenced Gandhiji's economic theories, describes his disgust for soulless labour. He was a student of arts. *Modern Painters* (1843, 1860) is about landscape painters like Turner. He also wrote *The Seven Lamps of Architecture* (1849) and *The Stones of Venice* (1851-1853), praising Gothic art.

Matthew Arnold (1822-1888), the poet, wanted his countrymen to inculcate classical qualities to become harmonious in morals and in creative works. The English must break away from their insular moorings by imbibing the teachings of Greece and the French. He is *the detector-general of the intellectual failings of his own nation.* Poetry, according to him, is important in character formation, and culture is *"the minister of the sweetness and light essential to the perfect character"*. His works include *On translating Homer, The Study of Celtic Literature and Essays in Criticism* (1865, 1889). He wrote St. Paul and Protestantism advocating that dogma should be removed from Christianity and it should adjust itself to the findings of science.

A number of philosophers, historians and scholars wrote in this period. Charles Darwin's theory of evolution dramatically affected human thought. **John Stuart Mill (1806-1873)** expounded the processes of logic and political economy. **Herbert Spencer (1820-1903)** and **Thomas Henry Huxley (1825-1895)** were scientists. **Thomas Babington Macaulay (1800-1859)** was a poet, essayist and historian who advocated English education in India. The Oxford Movement gave rise to religious writers like **John Keble (1792-1866)** and **John Henry Newman (1801-1890)**. Newman's famous work is *Apologia pro Vita Sua* (1864) in which he explains why he had converted to the Roman Church.

Novel

The transition from Walter Scott's novels to Charles Dicken's first novel in 1836 is a great one. When Queen Victoria ascended the throne, **Frederick Marryat (1792-1848)** produced sea-stories; **Edward Bulwer Lytton (1803-1873)** wrote about Byronic heroes, attractive criminals and historical novels like *The Last Days of Pompeii* (1834);

Benjamin Disraeli (1804-1881), the Prime Minister of England, wrote *Coningsby: or The New Generation* (1844) and *Sybil: or The Two Nations* (1845) to show that the aristocrats of the society had a duty towards the unfortunate ones. In Disraeli's novels, one finds the politics of Queen Victoria's reign.

Perhaps the greatest Victorian novelist is **Charles Dickens (1812-1870)**, whose identification with the underdog in society was unmatched by any writer. One reason for this is his own troubled childhood led in penury under the shadow of a father who was in debtor's prison. The part of his life comes through vividly in his novel *David Copperfield* (1849-1850) which is also an indictment of the cruel, unimaginative schools of his times. He was a master craftsman in character delineation. A host of characters and their dialogues have become household in the English-speaking world. Thus the incorrigible optimist Micawber, Geakle, Pickwick, Fagin and others are types of characters that may be seen all around us anywhere. Dickens had a forgiving sense of humour. He never let bitterness creep into his recreations of painful events of the past. Among his famous novels are: *Pickwick Papers* (1836; in the picaresque style), *Barnaby Rudge* (1841) and *A Tale of Two Cities* (1859; based on the French Revolution), *Oliver Twist* (1837) and *Hard Times* (1854); novels exposing social conditions. He has a picturesque style and concrete imagination.

William Makepeace Thackeray (1811-1863) made a penetrating analysis of upper middle class and aristocratic society. He was a master of irony. In *The Book of Snobs* (1849), he ridicules the tendency to fawn on nobility and to imitate their manners. *Vanity Fair* (1847-1848), *History of Pendennis* (1848-1850), *The Newcomes* (1853-1855), *The History of Henry Esmond* (1852) and *The Virginians* (1857-1859) are pictures of contemporary life in which he depicts human eccentricities and follies. He was adept at reproducing jargon and idiolects.

The Romantic spirit was still alive in the works of the Bronte sisters. **Charlotte Bronte (1816-1855)** wrote *Jane Eyre* (1847), the story of a governess in a terrifying house. Her sister **Emily Bronte (1818-1848)** wrote *The Wuthering Heights* (1847), set in a wild landscape. Powerful passions and characters have made this one of the greatest novels of all times.

George Eliot (1819-1880), a pen-name for Mary Ann Evans, wrote Adam Bede (1859), the story of a girl who was forced to murder her own baby. *The Mill on the Floss* (1860) and *Romola* (1863) are other novels by her. In *Middlemarch, a Study of Provincial Life* (1871-1872), the novelist builds up, from the lives of a great number of deeply studied characters, the complex picture of the life of a small town.

Poetry

The poetry of this period still shows the influence of the Romantic Era. **Alfred, Lord Tennyson (1809-1892)** was an eclectic, selecting the best of his forerunners. He was first interested in style and metre, but later on ideas started interesting him. A great many poems by him are flawlessly beautiful. If *The Lotus Eaters* is softly languorous, *Ulysses* has a striking severity. Tennyson also experienced the intellectual crisis of his times and shared its anxieties. For instance, *The Princess* (1847) is occupied with the question of feminism. *In Memoriam* (1850) is one of his most beautiful poems. It is an elegy on the premature death of his friend Arthur Hallam. It concerns itself with the belief in immortality, the conflict between the hopes of Christianity and the rationalism of science. It is composed of octosyllabic quatrains. He shows a type of Byronic revolt in Locksley Hall (1886) and Maud (1855). In *Idylls of the King* (1859, 1869, 1889) he took Arthurian legends as his theme.

Robert Browning (1812-1889) was famous for using the technique of dramatic monologue in his poems. Through the protagonists of his poems he gives vent to his feelings, passions and aspirations. Thus in *Paracelsus* (1835), he describes the highly ambitious hero who wanted to transform man's life. We find here Browning's views on truth and philosophy. His other poems include *Sordello* (1840), *Pippa Passes* (1841), *My Last Duchess, Porphyria's Lover* and his masterpiece, *The Ring* *and the Book* (1868-1869). In his works we find an excess of thought and a rare vocabulary. He uses blank verse dexterously. His brusque speech, broken syntax and uneven rhythm are in contrast to Tennyson's. As Pound and Eliot have said, Browning brought verse nearer to modern colloquial speech. Browning's characters are remote in time and culture. Some of these are Rabbi Ben Ezra, Fra Lippo Lippi and Andrea del Sarto. In *The Ring and the Book* he takes as his subject an Italian crime and explores the minds of all his characters. He strikes a note of hope in his poems. The lines *"God's in his heaven/ And all's well with the world"* lay bare his beliefs. But in general, Browning is considered a difficult poet.

Matthew Arnold (1822-1888) was a reflective poet with a melancholic bent. A deep brooding pensiveness informs his poetry. Dover Beach shows his concern with the loss of faith in a world of science. His epic poem *Sohrab and Rustum, Tristram and Iseult, The Scholar Gypsy* are other famous works.

Dante Gabriel Rossetti, William Morris and Algernon Charles Swinburne together are known as the Pre-Raphaelite poets. They affected Raphael, the Renaissance painter, in their desire to paint sonorous wordpictures which may not have much content to conveyor any philosophy to reveal. It was in accordance with the aestheticism of Ruskin. In fact Rossetti and Morris were painters as well as poets. They worshipped beauty like John Keats did. Robert Buchanan attacked these poets as belonging to *the fleshly school of poetry*.

Dante Gabriel Rossetti (1828-1882) translated the Italian poet Dante's *Vita Nuova*. His *The Blessed Damozel* is an exquisite poem and his best sonnets are contained in *The House of Life* in which he extols his young and beautiful wife. They are full of rich sounds and images and mystic symbols. Rossetti was inspired by the ballads of the Middle Ages. Like the primitive Italian painters, he uses rich colours and depicts warm sensuous feelings.

William Morris (1834-1896) was enchanted by Gothic art of the Middle Ages. His poems drew inspiration from those of Froissart, Chaucer and Malory. He borrowed stories from Scandinavia and Iceland. His poems are like frescoes and are very lyrical in quality. The famous ones are *The Earthly Paradise* (1868-1870) and *The Life and Death of Jason* (1867). These works show rhythm and use of archaism. He strove to bring civilization back to art from the utilitarian industrialization.

Algernon Charles Swinburne (1837-1909) was a prodigy. He was a musician, and a sonority of rhymes filled his poetry. He took romantic themes like revolt against society, hatred of monarchy and struggle against traditional morality. His *Atalanta in Calydon* (l865) is his masterpiece and is known for its choral passages.

To these poets of the Victorian Age must be added the name of **Edward Fitzgerald (1809-1883)** whose **The Rubaiyat of Omar Khayyam (1859)** is a classic.

MAJOR AUTHORS AND THEIR WORKS

Alfred Lord Tennyson (1809-1892)

The Princess
In Memoriam
Maud
Enoch Arden
Idylls of the King
Queen Mary
Harold
Backet
Akbar's Tomb
Crossing the Bar
Locksley Hall
Locksley Hall Sixty Years After
Dora
Poems by Two Brothers
The Falcon
The Cup
Poems Chiefly Lyrical
Ulysses
Poems Chiefly Lyrical
Ulysses
The Lotos-Eaters
The Death of Oenone and Other Poems

Robert Browning (1812-1889)

Pauline

Paracelsus

Strafford

Sordello

Bells and Pomegranates

Christmas Eve and Easter Day

Men and Women

Dramatis Personae

The King and the Book

Asolando

Pippa Passes

Fra Lippo Lippi

Andrea del Sarto

King Victor and King Charles

Dramatic Lyrics

Dramatic Romances and Lyrics

Matthew Arnold (1822-1888)

Sohrab and Rustum

Tristram and Iseult

Balder Dead

Empedocles on Etna

Stanzas from the Grande Chartreuse

The Strayed Reveller and Other Poems

Dover Beach

Thyrsis

Scholar Gypsy

On Translating Homer

New Poems

On the Study of Celtic Literature

Essays in Criticism

Culture and Anarchy

Literature and Dogma

Mixed Essays

Friendship's Garland

God and the Bible

D.G. Rossetti (1828-1882)

The Blessed Damozel

World's Worth

Ave

The White Ship

Sister Helen

Eden Bower

The House of Life

Ballads and Sonnets

Christina Georgina Rossetti (1830-1894)

The Goblin Market

The Prince's Market

A Pageant and Other Poems

William Morris (1834-1896)

The Defence of Guenevere

The Life and Death of Jason

The Earthly Paradise

A Dream of John Bull

News from Nowhere

A Tale of the House of the Wolfings

The Roots of the Mountains

The Story of the Glittering Plain

The Sundering Flood

Hope and Fears for Art

Signs of Change

A.C. Swinburne (1837-1909)

Atalanta in Calydon

Erechtheus

Tristram of Lyonesse

Chasteland

Bathwell

Mary Stuart

William Blake : A Critique

A Study of Shakespeare

A Study of Ben Jonson

Songs Before Sunrise

Edward Fitzgerald (1809-1883)

Euphranor : A Dialogue on Youth

Translation of Rubaiat

Thomas Carlyle (1795-1881)

Sartor Resartus

The French Revolution

Heroes and Hero-Worship

Past and Present

The Letters and Speeches of Oliver Cromwell

Latter-day Pamphlets
Life of John Sterling
History of Frederick the Great
Chartism

John Ruskin (1819-1900)

The Modern Painters
Salsette and Elephanta
The Seven Lamps of Architecture
The Stones of Venice
The Two Paths
Unto This Last
Munera Pulveris
Time and Tide by Wear and Tyne
Fors Clavigera
Sesame and Lilies
The Crown of Wild Olive

T.B. Macaulay (1800-1859)

History of England from the Accession of James II
Lays of Ancient Rome

Charles Dickens (1812-1870)

Pickwick Papers
Nicholas Nickleby
Martin Chuzzlewit
Dombey and Son
David Copperfield
Bleak House
A Tale of Two Cities
Great Expectations
Our Mutual Friend
Edwin Drood
Oliver Twist
Little Dorrit
Baraby Rudge
The Uncommercial Traveller
A Christmas Carol
Hard Times
Old Curiosity Shop

William Makepeace Thackeray (1811-1863)

Vanity Fair
Barry Lyndon
Pendennis
Henry Esmond
The New Comes
The Virginians
Adventures of Philip
The Book of Snobs
The History of Pendennis
Lovel the Widower
The Round about Papers
The English Humorists of the Eighteenth Century
The Four Georges
Rebecca and Rowena
The Rose and The Ring
Ivanhoe—the Legend of the Rhine

George Meredith (1828-1909)

The Ordeal of Richard Feveral
Evan Harrington
Emilia in England
Rhoda Fleming
Vittoria
The Adventures of Harry Richmond
Diana of the Crossways
One of Our Conquerous
The Amazing Marriage
The Egoist
Beauchamp's Career
The Tragic Comedians

Charlotte Bronte (1816-1855)

Jane Eyre
Shirley
The Professor
Villette

Emily Bronte (1818-1848)

Wuthering Heights

George Eliot (1810-1880)
(Mary Ann Evans)

Adam Bede
The Mill on the Floss
Silas Marner
Scenes of Clerical Life
Life of Jesus

Romola
Fleix Holt the Radical
Daniel Deronda
Middlemarch

Benjamin Disraeli (1804-1881)
Vivian Gray
Sybil : Or the Two Nations
The Voyage of Captain Popavilla
Henrietta Temple
Coningsby : or the New Generation
Tancred : or the New Crusade
The Wondrous Tale of Alroy and the Rise of Iskander
Contarini Fleming : A Psychological Autobiography

R.L. Stevenson (1850-1894)
Travels with a Donkey in the Cevennes
An Inland Voyage
Virginibus Pueresque
New Arabian Nights
Treasure Island
The Strange Case of Dr. Jackyll and Mr. Hyde
Kidnapped
The Black Arrow
The Master of Ballantrae
Catriona
Underwords
A Child's Garden of Verses

Thomas Hardy (1840-1828)
Under the Greenwood Tree
Desperate Remedies
A Pair of Blue Eyes
Two on a Tower
Far From the Madding Crowd
The Return of the Native
The Mayor of Casterbridge
Tess of the D'Urbervilles
Jude the Obscure
The Hand of Ethelberta
The Trumpet Major
The Woodlanders
The Well-beloved
A Laodicean
A Group of Noble Dames
Life's Little Ironies
Wessex Poems
The Dynasts
A Changed Man
Winter Words
The Waiting Supper and Other Tales

MULTIPLE CHOICE QUESTIONS

1. *"Bliss was it in that dawn to be alive, But to be young was very heaven!"* These lines have been attributed to:
A. Wordsworth B. Shelley
C. Keats D. Byron

2. *The Essays of Elia* is written by
A. De Quincey B. Charles Lambs
C. Hazlitt D. Cobbett

3. The publication of Wordsworth's Lyrical Ballads coincides with the
A. French Revolution
B. War for American Independence
C. Industrial Revolution
D. Invention of the steam engine

4. The poem Coleridge wrote as a result of an opium-induced dream was:
A. *The Solitary Reaper*
B. *Christabel*
C. *Rime of the Ancient Mariner*
D. *Kubla Khan*

5. Byron's poem, *The Vision of Judgment,* is an attack on the works of:
A. Coleridge B. Keats
C. Shelley D. Southey

6. *Childe Harold* is a poem by:
A. Coleridge C. Southey
B. Byron D. Shelley

7. *Prometheus Unbound* is written by:
A. Browning B. Tennyson
C. Shelley D. Spenser

8. *Adonais* is an elegy on:
A. Keats B. Arthur Hallam
C. Byron D. Shakespeare

9. John Keats is famous for his:
A. odes B. plays
C. blank verse D. masques

10. *Tales from Shakespeare* was written by:
A. Coleridge
B. Lamb and his sister Mary
C. Wordsworth
D. Byron

11. *Confessions of an English Opium Eater* is written by:
A. De Quincey B. Coleridge
C. Byron D. Leigh Hunt

12. William Godwin was a:
A. Psychologist B. Statesman
C. Scotsman D. Philosopher

13. *Don Juan* by Byron is written in:
A. blank verse B. rhyming couplets
C. ottava rima D. quatrains

14. The educational novel written by Maria Edgeworth is:
A. *Waverly* B. *Belinda*
C. *Ivanhoe* D. *Northanger Abbey*

15. Coleridge's *Biographia Literaria* critically analyzes the works of:
A. Byron B. Wordsworth
C. Keats D. Shelley

16. *The Stones of Venice* is a book about:
A. History of Venice
B. Landscapes
C. Romantic Literature
D. Gothic Art

17. Hopkins and Patmore were:
A. religious poets B. nature poets
C. war poets D. critics

18. Swinburne, Rossetti and Morris together were known as the:
A. Decadent poets
B. Pre-Raphaelite poets
C. War poets
D. Absurd poets

19. Christina Rossetti's work containing poems for children is:
A. *The Earthly Paradise*
B. *Scholar Gypsy*
C. *Goblin Market*
D. *The House of Life*

20. Swinburne's masterpiece known for its choral passages is:
A. *Atalanta in Calydon*
B. *Cain*
C. *Sohrab and Rustam*
D. *Queen Mab*

ANSWERS

1	2	3	4	5	6	7	8	9	10
A	B	C	D	D	B	C	A	A	B
11	12	13	14	15	16	17	18	19	20
A	D	C	B	B	D	A	B	C	A

THE MODERN AGE (1880-ONWARDS)

As the 20th century dawned, new values replaced the old ones and shaped the literature of Great Britain. England fast lost its imperial image as her colonies revolted and fought for independence. Industrialization progressed by leaps and bounds and the two World Wars brought economic depression. All this affected the content of literature. Writers sought new vehicles of expression. The findings of **Sigmund Freud** in the realms of psychology took novelists to the subconscious mind. A great number of writers who became famous men of letters in English came from Ireland **(G.B. Shaw, W.B. Yeats, James Joyce and Samuel Beckett)** and from America **(T.S. Eliot and Ezra Pound)**. Socialism became a practising creed and feminism raised her head. Dogmatic Christianity was more or less ignored. Although great strides were made in scientific inventions, science could not provide suitable answers to the deep questioning of the human mind resulting in ethical philosophy. The age saw the end of feudalism. Victorian reticence and prudery gave way to decadence in literature. English writers came under the influence of the French Parnassians and Symbolists. Scandinavia and Russia represented by **Ibsen** and **Tolstoy** also influenced the British men of letters. Many a poet wished to fight free from the fixed rules of versification and wrote in free verse. Many imitated the American poet **Walt Whitman**. English literature became more expansive in its concerns. The life and culture of foreign lands were depicted. Although **Kipling** was an imperialist, his works go beyond England. Being born in India, his works give a graphic view of the country. The great Celtic Revival under Yeats brought a new strain to English literature. Finally, the theatre, lying dormant for a century, now woke up with renewed vigour.

Criticism

The Age began with scholarly works in literary history. **Leslie Stephen (1832-1904)** wrote biographical and critical essays. He produced *The English Utilitarians and the Dictionary of National Biography*. He was an agnostic and rationalist. **A.C. Bradley (1851-1935), H.J.C. Grierson (1866-1960)** and **Edward Dowden (1843-1913)** were other famous critics. Bradley is famous for his critical work on Shakespeare's tragedies.

Walter Horatio Pater (1839-1894) propounded the literary doctrine *Art for Art's Sake* which was a quest for the most refined pleasure. The exquisite in art came from a reflection of the past. He eulogized the accomplishments of the Renaissance. His prose style was rich, musical and classical. His works include *Studies in the History of the Renaissance* (1873) and *Marius the Epicurean* (1885).

John Addington Symonds (1840-1893) was another admirer of the Renaissance. **Oscar Wilde (1856-1900)**, more known as a novelist and dramatist, gave a wider dimension to the theory of Art for Art's Sake by spicing it with wit and paradox. **George Saintsbury (1845-1933)** and **Sir Walter Raleigh (1861-1922)** were other famous critics.

Poetry

Most of the poetry written in this period are the works of those more renowned as novelists: Robert Louis Stevenson, Rudyard Kipling and Thomas Hardy. William Butler Yeats, who pioneered the Celtic Revival, Thomas Steams Eliot, whose *Wasteland* is a watershed leading to modern poetry, Gerard Manley Hopkins, the Catholic poet, are the famous poets of this period.

Rudyard Kipling (1865-1936) wrote on imperialist themes in *Barrack Room Ballads* (1892), *The Seven Seas* (1896) and *Five Nations* (1903). These poems were aimed by their rugged music to rouse people to protest. He combined folk-music with music-hall chorus. It had the sound of drum beats and bugle-calls and even the refinements of chamber music. The poetry of imperialism, heroism of national policy, contained slang and even biblical allusions. In fact, his popularity was that of Walt Whitman, the national poet of America. Many of his subjects were from India, like the poem *Gunga Din*.

W.E. Henley (1849-1903) also wrote poetry which praised Britain's colonial power. *The Song of the Sword, For England's Sake* and *London Voluntaries* are some of his better-known poems.

There were also a group of poets called the Decadents. They were aesthetes and their doctrine was *'Art for Art's Sake'*. **Oscar Wilde** was the leading poet of the group. *The Ballad of Reading Gaol* (1898) is his famous work inspired by his crime and imprisonment.

A group of poets had a pessimistic view of life. **John Davidson (1857-1909), Ernest Dawson (1867-1900)** and **A.E. Housman (1859-1936)** are some of these poets. But the leading pessimist of the age was **Thomas Hardy (1840-1928)**, better known as a novelist. He published *Wessex Poems* (1898) after the novel *Jude the Obscure* failed to receive public acclaim. His poetry was musical and highly individual. He had a disillusioned view of life. From 1903 to 1908, he produced the vast poetical work *The Dynasts*, written under the background of Napoleon's struggle against Europe combining real history with symbolic flashes. His poem, *To an Unborn Pauper Child,* reveals his utter dejection with life: *'Breathe : hid heart'*, it begins.

Francis Thompson (1859-1907) and **Gerard Manley Hopkins (1844-1889)** were religious poets of the beginning of the twentieth century. Thompson's poem, *The Hound of Heaven* is a masterpiece. It describes God as a Heavenly Hound chasing man to capture his soul and man fleeing Him in the pleasures of life. The Jesuit, Hopkins invented a new type of verse called *'sprung rhythm'*. It was filled with strange word coinages and is difficult for the ordinary reader to understand. His poetry reflects the conflict within him between his attraction to Roman Catholicism and his joy for the beautiful creation. He wrote a number of religious poems of which *The Wreck of the "Deutschland"* is one of the best. It describes the death of five Franciscan nuns on board the ship, *Deutschland.*

Irish, English and Continental influences met in **W.B. Yeats (1865-1939)**. He was born in Ireland but came to live in London. He was influenced by the strange mystical visions of William Blake, by pre-Raphaelite refinement and even the mysticism and occultism of the Orient, especially of India. His poetry is an attempt to revive Celtic mysticism and Irish mythology. Apparently it was Yeats who introduced Rabindra Nath Tagore to the West. He also came under the influence of Verlaine, a French symbolist poet. His best poetry is in *The Wild Swans at Coole* (1919), *The Tower* (1928) and *The Winding Stair* (1933). Some of his well-known poems are: *Easter* (1916), *The Second Coming, Byzantium, A Prayer for my Daughter, Leda and Swan, Sailing to Byzantium, Meru, Lapis Lazudili, Among School Children,* etc. His progress as a poet can be assessed by comparing the beautiful but simple *Lake Isle of Innisfree* with the beautiful and profound *Byzantium.*

The towering poet of the 20th century is **Thomas Steams Eliot (1888-1965)**. Eliot came on to the scene when the West was passing through tremendous upheavals — belief in religion, especially of the Church was fading, democracy was the new experiment in politics, and many modernist trends were noticeable in literature. Eliot proclaimed himself "a royalist in politics, an Anglo-Catholic in religion and a classicist in literature". Tradition, according to him, was not the dead past but the past living in the present. In his essay *Tradition and the Individual Talent*, he states that "the talent of an artist shows itself not where he differs from the ancients but where, in his work, they assert their immortality". Eliot's poetry shows metaphysical, symbolist and imagist strains, but his individual talent shines forth unmistakeably. An eclectic philosophy, borrowed from his own Christianity and Buddhism and the Upanishads informs his poetry. His poetry, especially *The Wasteland* (1922) is a poem that describes the zeitgeist (spirit of the times) and the *angoisse metaphysique* (metaphysical anguish) of life in post-World War Europe. It begins with the sentence *"April is a cruel month"* and this sets the strain for the whole poem. A brooding sense of futility and human inanity pervades modern life. Eliot achieves this effect by a combination of literary allusions to the past which stirs associations, and by what is called as the *objective correlative*. This last technique means that images are described which call up an emotion or a feeling. His other poems are *The Lave Song of J. Alfred Prufrock* and *Four Quartets* (1944). These lines from the *Four Quartets* may sum up the disillusionment of the times: *"Footfalls echo in the memory/Down the passage one could not take / To the door one could not open"*. Eliot was a poet of spiritual regeneration.

As the century proceeds, a host of poets make their mark **Stephen Spender (1909-1995), W.H. Auden (1907-1973), C. Day Lewis (1904-1972), Louis MacNeice (1907-1963)** — all of them wrote with a Social awareness, exposing the horror of the bourgeois culture and capitalist exploitation and the terror of totalitarianism.

We cannot end this section of the early modern twentieth century without a reference to **Rupert Brooke (1887-1915), Wilfred Owen (1893-1918)** and **Siegfried Sassoon (1886-1967)** popularly known as the "War poets". They had served the Armed Forces in the First World War, and after 1918, disillusioned by the horrors they had witnessed took their pens to write against the war. The poem *The Soldier* is one of the finest lyrics in the English language. It describes the poet's sense of impending death in battle and his love for his country: *"If I should die/Think only this of me/That there is a part of England/Buried in some foreign land".* Another poem is Sassoon's *Everyone Sang,* which describes the exultation felt by the soldiers returning home after the General Armistice was signed. They are described as *freed birds.*

Novel

Just like poetry, the novel of this century reflects the great passions and strivings of the age. The discoveries of **Sigmund Freud (1856-1939)** revealed the relationship of man's behaviour to his subconscious mind. The subconscious contains impressions of past experiences which influence a person's attitudes and behaviour. These discoveries led not only to new methods of psychiatric treatment but also to new dramatic techniques in the art of the novel. The stream-of-consciousness method used by James Joyce and Virginia Woolf spring from these discoveries. The modern novel is more and more concerned with an analysis of human behaviour. The focus shifts from a description of the external atmosphere to the thoughts of the characters.

Thomas Hardy's works are tinged with a gloomy pessimism reminiscent of Schopenhauer, and an analogy may be found in his works to Flaubert and Zola from France. Hardy's country Dorsetshire and the surroundings become the 'Wessex' of his novels. His work is full of realistic descriptions of the countryside. The places, full of pre-historic and Roman remains, heaths, have a character, and influence the people living there. The pre-historic past presses on the life of today. He is adept at delineating rustic characters. Man is a puppet of fate and an uncontrollable destiny drives him along life. A bitter helplessness pervades his novels *Far from the Madding Crowd* (1874), *The Return of the Native* (1878), *The Mayor of Casterbridge* (1886), and *Jude the Obscure* (1895). His success reached a climax with *Tess of the d'Urbervilles* (1891). His *Tess of the D'UrberviUes* and *Jude the Obscure,* because of their frank handling of sex and religion, aroused the hostility of the reading public. These two books, however, present Hardy's most moving indictments of the human situation.

The works of George Robert Gissing (1857-1903) produce a sense of absolute dejection. He worked as an ill-paid hack in the poor districts of London and described these places vividly in his books. Although impressed by Charles Dickens, his writings show none of Dickens' humour. One bitter, wretched world, a miserable London, exists in his works. Thus *Demos, a Story of English Socialism* (1886) describes the futility of socialist agitation, *The Nether World* (1889), the wretchedness of the London slums, *New Grub Street* (1891), the hopeless lot of a penniless writer, and *The Odd Women* (1893), the plight of unmarried women. His style is as bare and unaffected as his ideas.

Robert Louis Stevenson (1850-1894) stands in contrast to Hardy and Gissing in his recreation of the life of action and adventure. Although he suffered from an incurable malady, he did not lose faith in himself. He brought out *An Inland Voyage* (1878), *Travels with a Donkey in the Cevennes* (1879), *The Silverado Squatters, Treasure Island* (1833), *Kidnapped* and *The Master of Ballantrae* (1889) among others. The last three are very popular among children the world over. He also wrote children's adventure classics like *The Treasure Island* (1883), *Dr Jekyll and Mr. Hyde* (1886) and *Kidnapped* (1886). In *Dr. Jekyll and Mr Hyde* he touches upon the dual nature of man his good and evil aspects. His style is vivid and full of interesting details.

Another great novelist was the Pole, **Joseph Conrad (1857-1924)**, who perfected his knowledge of English and wrote in a vivid style with a strong foreign accent. His experience of sailing life and work in the English merchant service gave him the ideas to write masterpieces like *The Nigger of the Narcissus* (1897), and *Lord Jim: A Tale* (1900). Like the Slavs he was preoccupied with the problem of human misery. *Lord Jim* and *The Heart of Darkness* (1902) show his anger at what the white man had done to exploit Africa and other nations. A trait of his narrative technique is the gradual picture of his character formed from fragmentary descriptions of witnesses. He has a rich, sensuous prose style full of striking imagery.

Rudyard Kipling wrote stories about Indian life: *Plain Tales from the Hills* (1888) and *Soldiers Three* (1888). *Plain Tales from the Hills* depicts an Englishman's encounter with the strange East. Kipling was born in Bombay and spent his early life in India. He knew the land and its customs, its people and languages. His best book is *Kim* (1901), the story of a half-Irish boy, who speaks the language of the rustics of India and accompanies a Buddhist Lama on his search for "Nirvana" or Salvation. Kipling is adept at describing the sights and smells of India and its colourful people with their racy dialects. He also wrote two animal epics entitled, *The Jungle Book* (1894) and a series of short stories for children like *Captains Courageous* (1897), *Just So Stories* (1902) and *Puck of Pook's Hill* (1906). Kipling was influenced by Carlyle's doctrine of energy. As a spokesman of the Imperialist theme he believed that it was ideal for a person to sacrifice himself for his tribe. He believed that especially the white man was ordained to rule and lead nations. His works praise Britain's hegemony over her colonies.

Shortly after Kipling, came H. G. Wells and John Galsworthy who were Socialists and criticized the English society. **H.G. Wells** (1866-1946) began by writing stories with a semi-scientific flavour like *The Time Machine* (1895), *The Island of Dr Moreau* (1896), *The Invisible Man* (1897) and *The War of the Worlds* (1898). The stories are ingenuously plotted and thrill and disturb the readers. Later on Wells' interest shifted to social problems. He became a member of the Fabian Society. He wrote *Mankind in the Making* (1903) describing how society would look like when reformed by socialism. He also satirized the society in *Love and Mr Lewisham* (1900), *Kipps* (1905). *Tono-Bungay* (1909) and *Marriage* (1912). He does not glorify Britain's past and he scorns the existing institutions of his country. He wrote a number of remarkable books after the outbreak of World War I in 1914. These show his restless self-examining spirit. Some of these are *Mr Britling Sees it through* (1916) and *The Undying Fire* (1919).

In the works of **John Galsworthy (1867-1933)** we find an artistic conscience. Like Wells, he also attacked the concept of property and commercialism in his novels. He too exposed and criticized national prejudices, especially those existing among his own class, the landed gentry. He was widely read in Continental Literature and was especially influenced by France and Russia. Turgenev with his noble realism was his ideal. He is a detached and impartial observer of his country's decadent values. He advocates a fearless search for truth. *In The Island Pharisees* (1904) he exposes the stagnation of thought among English privileged classes. A similar theme is touched in other novels like *The Country House* (1907), *The Patrician* (1911) and *The Dark Flower* (1913) where country squires, aristocracy and artists are critically studied. *The Forsyte Saga* (1922) is his masterpiece. It is a natural history of the rich upper-middle class family. He describes their attitude to events like the Great War, the growth of socialism, unemployment and the coal strike.

Enoch Arnold Bennett (1867-1931) wrote a number of different types of novels presenting a detailed picture of an industrial district in the provinces. He is a realist like the French nationalists. His masterpiece is *The Old Wives' Tale* (1908).

G.K. Chesterton (1874-1936) was a champion of tradition and he refuted and opposed the attacks of his contemporaries against English society in *Orthodoxy* (1908), *The Napoleon of Notting Hill* (1904). He believed in tradition sanctified by ages of experience and even in the religious bond between men. His style is effective with the use of imagery and comparison and he spices it with plenty of humour.

James Joyce (1882-1941) pioneered a new type of novel with the *stream-of-consciousness* technique. Characters in *Ulysses* (1922) unreel themselves by a sort of interior monologue. Speech is mimicked and styles are parodied. *Ulysses* is modelled on the *Odyssey* of Homer and set in the slums of Dublin. The thousand pages of this novel cover just one day in the life of Leopold Bloom and Stephen Dedalus. Joyce coined words from several languages and was a master craftsman with wit and conceits. His other famous work is the autobiographical *A Portrait of the Artist as a Young Man* (1916) which describes his adolescence and sensuous tendencies.

Virginia Woolf (1882-1941) continued the stream-of-consciousness technique. Her works *To the Lighthouse* (1927) and *Mrs Dallaway* (1925) reveal the hidden inner life of her characters.

E.M. Forster (1879-1970) was the novelist of cultural relations. In **A Passage to India** (1924) he studies the conflict between the west and the east and takes a favourable stand for the latter. *Where Angels Fear to Tread* (1905) studies how the cultural divide between an Italian girl and her English husband leads to the ruination of their marriage and life.

D.H. Lawrence (1885-1930) was a prolific writer. His outspoken views on sexual relations raised much hue and cry. He considered sex the religion of the blood. His novels were dubbed pornographic. He believed in the free expression of human personality, in being guided by unrestrained primitive instincts. In *Sons and Lovers* (1913) he studies the relationship of son and mother and the social disparity of a father, a coalminer and a mother, a teacher. The novel is autobiographical. Other works by him are *The Rainbow* (1915), *Women in Love* (1921), and *The Plumed Serpent* (1926). *The Rainbow,* suppressed as obscene, treats the conflict between man and woman. *Lady Chatterley's Lover* (1928) was canned for being obscene.

George Orwell (1903-1950) wrote novels which were an indictment of totalitarian government: *Animal Farm* (1945) and *Nineteen Eighty-Four* (1949). **Aldous Huxley's** *Brave New World* (1932) is a prophetic book about the future of civilization in the context of scientific advancement.

Drama

After Shakespeare, **George Bernard Shaw (1856-1950)** is the great playwright whose works enlivened the British stage. Shaw, like Ibsen, believed in drama as a vehicle for ideas. He had a rich Irish sense of humour and his plays are satires on various social and philosophical themes. His general technique was to discuss the problem of his play first in its preface. Often this preface is longer than the play itself. *Widowers' Houses* (1892) was his first play. In this he discusses the problem of Housing. In *Mrs Warren's Profession* (1894) he lays bare the profession of a prostitute. In *Arms and the Man* (1894) the theme is the chocolate-cream soldier. Shaw was an iconoclast breaking well-established idols or myths. Thus this play disillusions us of the romantic image of a soldier. He is not one who is willing to die for his country, but one who loves his life. When the enemy is weak, he attacks, but withdraws and takes to his heels if the enemy is strong. George Bernard Shaw had a keen interest in the English language and formulated a standard pronunciation for it. He studies the theme of how language can influence one's rise in the social ladder. Professor Higgins succeeds in teaching a flower-girl to rid herself of a cockney accent and to speak well enough to pass for royalty! In *Man and Superman* we see Shaw as a master conversationalist. Ideas are discussed without much action taking place in the play. *The Apple Cart* (1929) shows the weaknesses of democracy. Although an Irish man, Shaw did not write on Irish themes as such.

Oscar Wilde reminds one of the Restoration playwrights Sheridan and Congreve in his comedy of manners. His style is full of paradox and verbal wit. Some of his famous plays are *Lady Windermere's Fan* (1892), *A Woman of No Importance* (1893) and *The Importance of Being Ernest* (1895).

John Galsworthy's plays *Strife* (1909), *Justice* (1910) and *Loyalties* (1922) were based on the theme of class exploitation.

W.B. Yeats contributed to the Irish drama. His Celtic theme comes through in *The Countess Cathleen* (1892) and *The Land of Heart's Desire*

(1894). **Sean O'Casey** (1884-1964) and **J. M. Synge** (1871-1909) were other noted Irish playwrights. The latter's plays, *The Playboy of the Western World* (1907) and *Riders to the Sea* (1904) are famous.

T.S. Eliot's contribution to the modern theatre were religious and moral plays. He uses the Greek "chorus" style in *Murder in the Cathedral* (1935) to heighten the dramatic effect of the murder of Thomas Becket by the Archbishop of Canterbury's men. *The Family Reunion* (1939) is a play about sin and expiation. Eliot pruned verse to sound like prose. This is done dexterously in *The Cocktail Party* (1949) and *The Confidential Clerk* (1953) where characters speak verse which sounds like prose.

A group of playwrights came to be known as the "Angry Young Men". **John Osborne (1929-1994)** was the most prominent of them. His play *Look Back in Anger* (1956) catches the mood of the frustrated youth in post-War England. In his plays, he exposes the wretchedness of the working class.

Harold Pinter (1930-2008) mixes comedy and horror in his plays like *The Birthday Party* (1958).

Another group of dramatists drew their inspiration from France. *The Absurd Theatre*, as it was called, began in France with Albert Camus, Jean Genet and Ionesco as its pioneers. In England, **Samuel Beckett (1906-1989)** was the Irish dramatist of this school. His plays *Endgame* (1955), *Krapp's Last Tape* (1958) and *Waiting For Godot* (1906) show the meaninglessness of human action and the unrelieved gloom of existence.

MAJOR AUTHORS AND THEIR WORKS

George Bernard Shaw (1856-1950)

Widowers' Houses
Candida
You Never Can Tell
Man and Superman
Back to Methuselah
Saint Joan
Heartbreak House
The Philanderer
Mrs. Warren's Profession
Caesar and Cleopatra
John Bull's Other Island
Major Barbara
The Doctor's Dilemma
Getting Married
The Apple Cart
Pygmalion
The Dark Lady of the Sonnets
Plays Pleasant and Unpleasant
The Millionaire
The Intelligent Woman's Guide to Socialism
Everybody's Political What is What
Cashel Byron's Profession
Love Among the Artists
Androcles and the Lion
The Devil's Disciple
The Man of Destiny

W.B. Yeats (1865-1939)

The Land of Heart's Desire
The Countess Cathleen
The Shadowy Waters
The Hour-glass
The Resurrection
The King's Threshold
On Baile's Strand
The Cat and the Moon
Ideas of Good and Evil
Discoveries
The Wind among the Reeds
The Wanderings of Oisin
The Tower
The Winding Stair and Other Poems
Lake Isle of Innisfree
Byzantium

John Galsworthy (1867-1933)

The Silver Box
Strife
The Skin Game
The Man of Property
Justice

Loyalties
Escape
The Inn of Tranquility
The Forsyte Saga
The Country House
Fraternity
The Patrician
The Dark Flower
Saint's Progress
Maid in Waiting
Flower Wilderness

Rudyard Kipling (1865-1936)

Kim
The Jungle Book
Barrack-room Ballads
Departmental Ditties
The Seven Seas
The Five Nations
Tales from the Hills
Soldiers Three
Life's Handicap
The Phantom Rickshaw
Many Inventions
The Day's Work
Just-so Stories for Little Children
Rewards and Fairies
Debits and Credits

H.G. Wells (1866-1946)

The Time Machine
Love and Mr. Levisham
Kipps
The History of Mr. Polly
Mr. Britling Sees It Through
Christina Albertas Father
The Wonderful Visit
The Island of Dr. Moreau
The Invisible Man
The War of the Worlds
The First Men in the Moon
The Food of the Gods
Marriage
Experiment in Autobiography
The Contemporary Novel

Joseph Conrad (1857-1924)

The Nigger of the 'Narcissus'
Typhoon
Lord Jim
Victory
Almayer's Folly
An Outcast of the Islands
Youth
Heart of Darkness
The Secret Agent
The Shadow of Line
Suspense-A Napoleonic Novel

Arnold Bennett (1867-1931)

The Old Wives' Tale
Clayhanger
Riceyman Steps
Buried Alive
Hilda Lessways
These Twain
Sacred and Profane Love
The Pretty Lady
The Love Match
The Author's Craft

Walter de la Mare (1873-1956)

Peacock Pie
Memoirs of a Midget
Songs of Childhood
Bells and Grass
The Traveller
Early the Morning
Love

T.S. Eliot (1888-1965)

The Waste Land
Prufrock and Other Observations
Gerontion
The Hollow Men
Ash Wednesday
Four Quartets
Sweeney Agonistes

Murder in the Cathedral
The Rock
The Family Reunion
The Cocktail Party
The Confidential Clerk
The Sacred Wood
After Strange Gods
The Elder Statesman
The Idea of a Christian Society
What is a Classic?
For Lancelot Andrews
The Use of Poetry and the Use of Criticism
Elizabethan Essays
Points of View

Virginia Woolf (1882-1941)

The Voyage Out
Jacob's Room
Mrs. Dalloway
To The Light House
The Waves
Flush
Orlando : A Biography
The Common Reader
Roger Fry
The Death of the Moth
Mr. Bennett and Mrs. Brown
A Room of One's Own
Between the Acts (Unfinished)

E.M. Forster (1879-1970)

Abinger Harvest
Two Cheers for Democracy
A Passage to India
Howard's End
The Hill of Devi
The Celestial Omnibus
Collected Short Stories
Where Angels Fear to Tread
The Longest Journey
The Story of the Siren
A Room with a View
The Eternal Moment

James Joyce (1882-1941)

Ulysses
Portrait of the Artist as a Young Man
Finnegans Wake
Dubliners

D.H. Lawrence (1885-1930)

Sons and Lovers
Woman in Love
Lady Chatterly's Lover
The Rainbow
The White Peacock
Kangaroo
The Plumed Serpent

Aldous Huxley (1894-1963)

Point Counter Point
The Burning Wheel
Those Barren Leaves
Brave New World
After Many a Summer
Eyeless in Gaza
Antic Hay
Time Must Have a Stop
Crome Yellow
The Defeat of Youth
The Perennial Philosophy
The Devils of Loudun

George Orwell (1903-1950)

The Animal Farm
The Road to Wigan Pier
Nineteen Eighty-Four
Burmese Days
Keep the Aspidistra Flying

Oscar Wilde (1854-1900)

The Sphinx
The Ballad of Reeding Gaol
The Canterville Ghost
De Profundis
The Duchess of Padua
The Importance of Being Earnest
An Ideal Husband

Lady Windermere's Fan
Salome
The Picture of Dorian Gray
The Happy Prince and the Other Tales

Harold Pinter (1930-2008)

The Birthday Party
The Dumb Waiter
The Care Taker
A Night Out
The Home Coming
Old Times
Silence

MULTIPLE CHOICE QUESTIONS

1. The Celtic Revival was begun by:
A. George Bernard Shaw
B. W.B. Yeats
C. J.M. Synge
D. James Joyce

2. *The Wasteland* is written by:
A. T.S. Eliot B. John Galsworthy
C. Thomas Hardy D. Virginia Woolf

3. Hardy is famous for his poem:
A. *The Hound of Heaven*
B. *The Dynasts*
C. *Four Quartets*
D. *Wild Swans of Coole*

4. The Irish dramatist, who wrote absurd plays, was
A. W.B. Yeats B. Samuel Beckett
C. Sean O'Casey D. J.M. Synge

5. *Everyone Sang* is a poem about:
A. socialism B. music
C. war D. death

6. *The Old Wives'* Tale is written by:
A. Robert Gissing B. Galsworthy
C. H.G. Wells D. Arnold Bennet

7. Robert Louis Stevenson wrote stories about:
A. adventure B. human nature
C. war D. nature and man

8. *The Invisible Man* is written by:
A. D.H. Lawrence B. H.G. Wells
C. Kipling D. Dickens

9. *Nigger of the Narcissus* is written by:
A. Hardy B. Eliot
C. Lawrence D. Conrad

10. Sex was considered the religion of the blood by:
A. D.H. Lawrence B. Ibsen
C. G.B. Shaw D. Oscar Wilde

11. The British novelist and poet who described India best was:
A. Virginia Woolf B. Graham Greene
C. Rudyard Kipling D. Aldous Huxley

12. Rupert Brooke, Wilfred Owen and Siegfried Sassoon are together known as:
A. Flower Poets B. War Poets
C. Poets of Revolt D. Patriotic Poets

13. Walt Whitman was the national poet of:
A. England B. Poland
C. America D. France

14. *The Wreck of the Deutschland* is a:
A. war poem B. historical poem
C. romantic poem D. religious poem

15. *Sprung rhythm* was invented by:
A. Gerard Manley Hopkins
B. T.S. Eliot
C. Auden
D. Yeats

16. *The Family Reunion* — a play, is written by:
A. W.B. Yeats B. T.S. Eliot
C. Cecil Day Lewis D. Louis MacNiece

17. Gissing's *The Odd Women* is a work on:
A. plight of unmarried women
B. poverty of slum-dwellers
C. war and love
D. the life force

18. *Ulysses* is written by:
A. Virginia Woolf B. George Orwell
C. Arnold Bennett D. James Joyce

19. *The Patrician* is written by:
A. Kipling B. H.G. Wells
C. Henry James D. Galsworthy

20. *Look Back in Anger* is written by:
A. A. J. Cronin B. Aldous Huxley
C. D. H. Lawrence D. John Osborne

ANSWERS

1	2	3	4	5	6	7	8	9	10
B	A	B	B	B	D	A	B	D	A
11	**12**	**13**	**14**	**15**	**16**	**17**	**18**	**19**	**20**
C	B	C	D	A	B	A	D	D	D

INDIAN WRITING IN ENGLISH

ANAND, MULKRAJ (1905-2004)

He was greatly influenced by Premchand on the one hand and Tagore on the other.
Some of his famous novels are :

1. The Village (1939)
2. Across the Black Waters (1940)
3. The Sword and the Sickle (1942)
4. Untouchable (1933) (his first novel)
5. Seven Summers (1951)
6. Private Life of an Indian Prince (1953)
7. The Big Heart (1945)
8. Coolie (1936) (It was recast in seventies)
9. Two Leaves and a Bud (1937)
10. The Old Woman and the Cow (1960)
11. The Road (1961)
12. Death of a Hero (1963)
13. Confession of a Lover (1976)
14. Morning Face (1968)

AUROBINDO, GHOSE (1872-1950)

- He was known as the "firebrand" of India.
- He was a poet, a saint, a philosopher, statesman, yogi and a prophet.
- He is one of the pre-Independence Titanic trio of Indian poets—Tagore, Aurobindo and Sarojini Naidu.
- He is chiefly known for his
  - (*i*) Savitri (1953) a poetic epic on a grand scale.
  - (*ii*) The Life Divine (1939-40)
  - (*iii*) Essays on Gita
- He is a great exponent and proponent of ancient Indian thought.
- According to R. K. Singh, "Aurobindo is sympathetic to the modernist trends in writing and study of poetry and, in fact, himself adopts some of the methods followed by the modern poets."
- To quote Mr. Singh again, "In Aurobindo's literary order, poetry is a means of spiritual expression that helps to open the consciousness..."

CHATTERJEE, BANKIM CHANDRA (1838-94)

- He is generally called 'The Father of Bengali fiction.'
- Today he is most known for his patriotic bent of mind.
- In all he wrote 14 novels.
  - (*i*) Some of them are historical.
  - (*ii*) Others are social.
  - (*iii*) Still others are philosophical with stress on renunciation and non-attachment.
- Some of his novels are :
  - (*i*) *The Poison Tree* (*1884*): It is a story of Hindu life in Bengal of the period
  - (*ii*) Kapalkundala (1885)

(*iii*) Durgeshnandini (1890)
(*iv*) Krishnakanta's Will (1895)
(*v*) The Two Rings (1897)
(*vi*) Rajmohan's Wife (1904) (published posthumously)
(*vii*) Anand Math (1884)

CHAUDHURI, NIRAD, C. (1897-1999)

- He came into limelight with the publication of his "The Autobiography of an Unknown Indian." (1951).
- His other important works are:
  (*i*) A Passage to India (1959)
  (*ii*) Continent of Circe (1966)
  (He received the Duff Cooper Memorial Prize).
  (*iii*) The Intellectual in India (1967)
  (*iv*) To Live or Not to Live (1970)
- He is known for his most correct and chaste prose for which he has earned much acclaim from the scholars and critics, including Khushwant Singh.

DESAI, ANITA (Born-1937)

- She is a renowned novelist and short story writer.
- Some of her famous novels are :
  (*i*) Cry, the Peacock (1963)
  (*ii*) Voices in the City (1965)
  (*iii*) Bye-Bye, Blackbird (1971)
  (*iv*) Fire on the Mountain (1977)
  (*v*) Clear Light of Day (1980)
- Her collection of short stories is captioned "Games at Twilight" (1978)

GANDHI, M.K. (1869-1948)

1. His famous work in English is "My Experiments with Truth."
2. The work is an important autobiographical writing which is held in high esteem for its truthfulness, frankness, simplicity and directness of expression in non-ornamental effective English.

MARKANDAYA, KAMALA (1924-2004)

1. She is one of the modern novelists and is known for her:
   (*i*) Nectar in a Sieve (her first novel) (It is a novel on miserable rural life).
   (*ii*) Some Inner Fury (1955)
   (It is a novel of violence and destruction)
   (*iii*) A Silence of Desire (1960)
   (It is a novel urging the readers to speak out frankly to unburden their hearts).
   (*iv*) Possession (1963)
   (The problem of possession is discussed in this novel).
   (*v*) A Handful of Rice (1966)
   (It depicts the life of the poor classes in Madras).
   (*vi*) The Coffer Danus (1969)
   (*vii*) The Nowhere Man (1972)
   (*viii*) Two Virgins (1973)
   (*ix*) The Golden Honeycomb (1977)
   (*x*) Pleasure City (1982).

KHUSHWANT SINGH (Born-1915)

- He is known for his novels :
  (*i*) Train to Pakistan (his masterpiece)
  (*ii*) I Shall Not Hear the Nightingale (1959). (It describes the social life of a Sikh family during the pre-Independence period).
- "The Mark of Vishnu" is another of his well-known works.
- Some of his known stories
  (*a*) Karma
  (*b*) When Sikh Meets Sikh
  (*c*) The Rape, etc.
- He is also known for his:
  (*i*) A History of the Sikhs
  (*ii*) Translation of Japji Sahib, etc.
- His regular columns appear weekly in some dailies, *e.g.* :
  (*i*) 'With Malice Towards One And All'—The Hindustan Times.
  (*ii*) 'This Above All'—The Tribune.

- Mulk Raj Anand is stated to have said that Khushwant Singh's "Train to Pakistan" is likely to last, while about his other creative literary work, one may have some doubts.
- Among his latest work is "Truth, Love and Little Malice."

MULLER, MAX (1823-1900)

- He was a famous Indologist, German orientalist and linguist, who unearthed a lot of ancient Indian history and Sanskrit scriptures, the Rig Veda, in particular, of which he published six colossal volumes, for which he had got an assignment from the East India Company in 1847.
- Actually he was a student of Sanskrit, who started comparative study of languages and "Avesta" (in 1845) which is the renowned sacred book of the Zoroastrians.
- He gave seven lectures on Indian and ancient Indian philosophy at Cambridge University, which have now been published by Rupa & Co. under the caption: "India : What Can it Teach Us?"
- He distnguishes the highest wisdom of Greece and India by using the terms "to know ourselves" and "to know our self", respectively.
- Muller makes very appreciative comments on the Rig Veda and the Vedic Religion.

NAIDU, SAROJINI (1879-1946)

- She is a well-known Indian English poet who started writing poetry at a very early age and she was inspired by Edmund Gosse to choose Indian themes and scenery rather than imitating the English classics.
- She is now known as 'The Nightingale of India.'
- She took a keen interest in India's struggle for freedom.

Some of her works are :

1. The Golden Threshold (1905)
2. The Bird of Time (1912)
3. The Broken Wing (1917)
4. The Sceptred Flute (1946)
5. The Feather of the Dawn (1961) (It appeared posthumously)

Some of her famous poems are :

1. The Queen's Rival
2. Palanquin Bearers
3. To My Fairy Fancies
4. The Pardah Nashin
5. Awake
6. Village Song
7. The Soul's Prayer
8. Fishermen of Coromondel
9. It You Call Me
10. Caprice
11. Summer Woods
12. Songs of Radha
13. The Bird Sanctuary, etc.

NANDY, PRITISH (Born-1947)

- He was the editor of the 'Illustrated Weekly of India' and has now Telecast a T.V. serial over the Doordarshan: "Hungama Unlimited."
- (*i*) He is a prolific poet, though he is still not considered one of the best.

  (*ii*) Most of his poetry has been dismissed by critics as mere experimental gimmickry. Such was Saleem Peeradina.

  (*iii*) Even Nissim Ezekiel dubbed him to be a poetaster.
- Some of his works are :

  (*i*) Gods and Olives (1967)

  (*ii*) On Either Side of Arrogance (1968)

  (*iii*) From the Outer Bank of the Brahmputra (1969)

  (*iv*) Riding the Midnight River (1975)

  (*v*) In secret Anarchy (1979), etc.
- He has written a number of anthologies and translated a number of poets including Agyeya, Amrita Pritam, Kaifi Azmi etc.
- He has also written some short stories and a verse play.

NARAYAN, R.K. (1906-2001)

- Of the three great novelists, Narayan, Anand and Rao, it is Narayan who has won the maximum accolade both in India and abroad.
- One of his great achievements is his creation of the famous town of Malgudi like Hardy's Wessex.
- Narayan is the true master of humour, irony, realism, romance and artistry.
- Most of his novels and stories depict the life of people of South India.
- It is sometimes held that Narayan lacks true pathos, genuine depth of feeling, realistic description of poverty and misery, the elements which go in for making a novelist a great one.
- However, he has earned much popularity as a novelist, and within the range of his own art, he cannot be taken except with due regard and attention.

Some of his famous novels are :

1. Swami and Friends (1935)
2. Bachelor of Arts
3. The English Teacher
4. The Financial Expert
5. Mr. Sampath (1949)
6. The Guide (1958)
7. The Man-eater of Malgudi
8. The Dark Room (1939)
9. Waiting for the Mahatma
10. The Vendor of Sweets
11. The Painter of Signs (1976)

(He won the Sahitya Akademi Award for 'Guide' in 1961)

R.K. NARAYAN (as a short story writer)

- Some of his stories have appeared in the following collections:
  (*i*) Malgudi Days
  (*ii*) Dodu and Other Stories
  (*iii*) Cyclone and Other Stories
  (*iv*) Gods, Demons and Others

Narayan has written a few hundred stories, most of them quite interesting and highly readable:

Some of his famous short stories are :

1. The Golden
2. A Career
3. The Snake Song
4. Man Hunt
5. A Willing Slave
6. An Astrologer's Day
7. The Doctor's word
8. God of Troubles, etc.

NEHRU, JAWAHARLAL (1889-1964)

- He needs no introduction as a freedom fighter, statesman and first Prime Minister of India.
- Some of his literary works are :
  (*i*) An Autobiography (1936)
  (*ii*) Glimpses of World History (1939)
  (*iii*) Discovery of India (1946)
- Children enjoy reading his "Letters from Father to His Daughter."
- He is known for his simple, chaste, poetic English which is a model of natural style.

PRITAM, AMRITA (1919-2005)

- She is the most famous Punjabi Author.
- She won the Jnanpith Award for her "Kagaj Te Kenvas" in 1981.
- Her best known autobiographical work which appeared in the seventies is "Rasidi Ticket."
- (*i*) Her "Shadows of words : An Auto-biography" (a transcreation of the Hindi original by Jyoti Sabharwal) has been published by Macmillan in 2002.

  (*ii*) The book presents "an inner journey down the memory lane" presented by the author, who considers old age the best part of her life, like the last sips of tea, which are "usually the sweetest."

RADHAKRISHAN, SARVAPALLI (1888-1975)

- He is known as an outstanding educationist and a philosopher who presented the Hindu/Indian viewpoint to the world.
- His works include
  - (*i*) An Idealist View of Life (Lectures)
  - (*ii*) Indian Philosophy (1923, 1927)
  - (*iii*) The Hindu View of Life (1932)
  - (*iv*) An Idealist View of Life (1932)
  - (*v*) Eastern Religious and Western Thought (1939)
- He wrote in a very simple, intelligible prose-style.

RAO, RAJA (1908-2006)

- His famous works are:
  - (*i*) The Serpent and the Rope (1960)
  - (*ii*) Kanthapura (1938)
  - (*iii*) The Cat and Shakespeare (1965-66)
- (*i*) He was awarded the Sahitya Akademi Award for his 'The Serpent and the Rope' in 1964.
  (*ii*) He was also decorated with Padma Bhushan in 1969.

Raja Rao as a short story writer

- He is also a well-known short story writer.
- His first collection of short stories was "Jauni" which was published in France in 1930.
- The collection: "The Cow of the Barricades" was published in 1947

  Some of his famous short stories are :
  1. Akkayya
  2. The Little Gram-shop
  3. Kanaka Pal
  4. Narsiga

ROY, ARUNDHATI (Born-1961)

She made her debut with her novel: "The God of Small Things" which won her the Booker Prize in 1997, besides a handful amount running into crores as royalty for less than four hundred pages which comprise the said novel.

DE, SHOBHA (Born-1948)

- She is a renowned contemporary Indian English novelist and T.V. serial script writer.
- Some of her novels are prescribed in universities in England and Australias.
- Her T.V. serial "Swabhiman" which ran into numerous episodes was telecast over the Doordarshan.
- (*i*) She has become even more popular with her serial "Kittie Party" telecast over the Zee T.V.
  (*ii*) According to the Tribune, it "is a clever insight into the mind of today's urban Indian women poised at the crossroads of modernity and tradition."

TAGORE, RABINDRANATH (1861-1941)

Tagore was a versatile genius. He was a :

(*i*) poet
(*ii*) novelist
(*iii*) short story writer
(*iv*) dramatist
(*v*) musician
(*vi*) actor (in dramas)
(*vii*) painter
(*viii*) statesman and a host of other things.

Some of his famous novels are :

1. The House and the World (1919)
2. The Wreck (1921)
3. Gora (1923)

VIVEKANANDA, SWAMI (1863-1902)

He is a well-known Indian seer, prophet, recluse preacher, lecturer and poet, who:

(*i*) made the ancient Indian philosophy known to the whole world at the Parliament of Religious in Chicago, USA.
(*ii*) Brought about a wave of resurgence among the Indian masses through his stirring spiritually inspired speeches which were also full of:
  (*a*) patriotic fervour
  (*b*) love for universal brotherhood.
  (*c*) spirit of social uplight, etc.

SOME LITERARY MASTERPIECES

CANTERBURY TALES

by Chaucer

'Canterbury Tales' is a collection of stories in verse by Chaucer. These tales are told by twenty-nine pilgrims who are going on a visit to the shrine of St. Thomas-a-Becket at Canterbury.

Each tale is a complete unit in itself without being intended to be linked with other tales. But, in the narration which is fictional in essence, we have head-links which are actually connecting passages. The headlinks are descriptions of the pilgrims as well as the events that take place in the course of the journey besides valuable digressions.

In those days, the people were very fond of pilgrimages for the sake of religious devotion and fun and they generally travelled in groups to face the dangers of the journey. The tales are written and descriptions of pilgrims given as if Chaucer himself had met such characters and had some experiences like those given.

The pilgrims meet at the Tabard Inn in Southwark on the eve of their departure and there they plan the journey. Chaucer himself is one of the pilgrims and the host of the Inn, Harry Bailly, not only gives a hearty welcome to the pilgrims but also accompanies them to the shrine.

Since the journey is quite tedious, each pilgrim is required to tell two tales on the journey towards the shrine and two during the return journey. But, Chaucer could complete only twenty four tales during his life time and in this sense, the Canterbury Tales is only a fragment.

An important aspect of the tales which brings Chaucer near to a dramatist and a novelist is that the tales differ in character as widely as do those by whom they are told.

The Knight tells, a chivalrous tale, the Clerk a devotional tale while the Miller's and the Reeve's tales are coarse and farcical in complete harmony with their own characters.

UTOPIA

by Thomas More

The period when Renaissance was in full bloom, Utopia was written by Sir Thomas More who lived from 1478-1535. He was imbued with the spirit of humanism.

The Greek word "Utopia" means "nowhere". Hence, it is in this light that Sir More tried to present an imaginary ideal republic of his dreams, which was of course, impossible to be achieved on this earth.

Utopia was originally written in Latin and was published in 1516. Later, it was translated into Italian and French. It was much later, after death of More, that its English translation appeared.

The Important characters in the book are :

1. The writer himself.
2. Peter Giles—writers's friend
3. Raphael Hythloday—a Portuguese traveller.

The book comprises two parts. In part one the protagonist (Hythloday) describes his voyaging with the explorer, Amerigo Vespucci.

In part two Hythloday describes the country of Utopia.

COMMENTS :

Utopia Glorifies

1. A democratic society.
2. A socialistic society with public control over wealth.
3. Religious tolerance
4. Economic equality
5. Peace and prosperity (upto a limit)
6. Love of this world.
7. Love of nature and natural way of living.
8. Love of beauty.
9. Love of the common man.
10. Love of human dignity.

Utopia Condemns

1. Aristocracy
2. Elitism
3. Asceticism and stoicism
4. Other worldliness

5. Fanaticism and bigotry.
6. False Chivalry
7. A Luxurious way of life
8. Scholasticism
9. Narrow-mindedness
10. War, Jingoism and Chauvinism.

GORBODUC

by Thomas Norton & Thomas Sackville

The other name of Gorboduc is Ferrex and Porrex. It is known for being the first regular English tragedy. It was written by Thomas Norton and Thomas Sackville and was first staged in 1562, that is, two years before the birth of Shakespeare. The work became a model for the Renaissance dramatists. It is, in essence, a Senecan tragedy of revenge.

The important characters in this tragedy are :

1. Gorboduc, The king of England
2. Ferrex—Gorboduc's elder son
3. Porrex—Gorboduc's younger son
4. Videna—The Queen
5. The murderers of the king and the queen
6. The nobles
7. The common people, etc.

The story in a nutshell: After the king divides his kingdom between his two sons, the latter begin to quarrel as a result of which Porrex kills Ferrex. The latter is so much loved by the queen that she kills Porrex. The people rise in revolt and kill the king and the queen. The nobles thereafter kill the murderers of the royal couple. This leads to a bloody civil war. There is chaos and anarchy as the question of success remains unsolved.

Senecan Features

1. Division into five acts.
2. Revenge as the chief motive.
3. A chain of murders—one murder leading to the other.
4. A ghost as one of the characters.
5. Lack of humour and any comic relief.
6. All-pervading seriousness and blood and thunder.
7. Avoidance of bloodshed on the stage, as it is reported by the characters through dialogues and monologues.
8. A plethora of rhetorical speeches by the characters.
9. Appearance of the chorus at the end of each act.

The use of blank verse in a drama was for the first time made in Gorboduc.

ASTROPHEL AND STELLA

by Philip Sidney

Astrophel and Stella is a sonnet series written by Sir Philip Sidney, Sidney is known more as a critic for his 'Apologie for Poetry' than as a poet, though his poetic claim is not altogether rejectable. His chief position as a poet rests on Astrophel and Stella.

Significance

1. The work is significant in the sense that it is perhaps the first work in English literature written in the white heat of passion, arising out of a personal and intimate experience.
2. In spite of artificiality of certain sonnets and general Petrarchan extravagance in the series, the work, having arisen out of real experience and genuine feelings, does not altogether look unreal.
3. It sounds real in several respects as in the apostrophe to the moon, in minute, vivid details and descriptions, etc.
4. Though the excessive use of conceits, hyperboles and embellishments mars the series in certain respects, yet its overall significance for the English literature cannot be underestimated.
5. Sidney was, no doubt, influenced by Petrarch. Yet he tries to assert himself every now and then by following a rhyme scheme other than the Petrarchan.
6. His most frequently used rhyme scheme is abba, abba, cdcd, ee. In other words, his sonnets end with a couplet in the Shakespearean style.

DOCTOR FAUSTUS

by Christopher Marlowe

The play opens with the chorus which announces the theme of the play i.e., the story of a scholarly doctor who has his end because of excessive lust for knowledge in the fields of magic and necromancy.

At the start Faustus looks at several fields of study such as Logic, Medicine, Law, Divinity, etc. But he finally settles at Magic. Then appear the Good Angel and the Evil Angel. The former warns Faustus against studying Magic book. He asks him to study the holy books. But the latter encourages him to study the Magic book.

The End of Faustus: His end is as tragic as it can be. He has not indulged or little indulged in sensual pleasures. What makes his sin more serious in theological circles in his association with Satan and the Satanic forces-demons, ghosts, devils etc. So, he gets no forgiveness and relief of any kind despite all his wailings and is taken away to hell by the Devils.

THE WINTER'S TALE

by Robert Green

Robert Greene's prose novel 'Pandosto' or 'The Triumph of Time' was published in 1588 and reprinted in 1607. This became the source for Shakespeare's *The Winter's Tale* which seems to have been composed in 1610 or 1611.

The title signifies an old wives' tale told to the curious children before they go to bed. Hence, such a tale can contain fairy-tale, exaggerative or legendary elements which may be far from reality because of some romantic, imaginary, unreal, absurd persons, incidents and situations.

Characters

Polixenes—the King of Bohemia, Leontes—the King of Sicilia, Hermione—Leontes's wife, Mamillus—Son of Leontes, Camillo—a Gicilian Lord, Cleomenes & Dion—courtiers, Paulina—Antigonus's wife, Emilia—the queen's lady, Florizel—the son of the king of Bohemia, Florizel—known as Doricles, Paulina.

BARTHOLOMEW FAIR

by Johnson

It is one of the most famous of Jonson's comedies which pleases all but hurts none. It is an authentic picture of the London of Queen Elizabeth's times. It was first staged in 1624, in manuscript form. It was published later in 1631.

There is a broad spectrum of humanity in the work at all levels, chiefly low level. Thus we have in the play gallants, gulls, cutpurses and bawds, lovers, squires, servants and justices of peace, etc.

Important Characters

1. **Bartholomew Cokes:** He is a foolish young squire.
2. **Waspe:** He is servant to Cokes who accompanies him to the fair.
3. **Grace Wellborn:** She is the fiancee of Waspe
4. **Edgeworth:** He is a cutpurse.
5. **Nightingale:** A ballad singer and companion and accomplice of Edgeworth.
6. **Adam Overdo:** A justice of peace.
7. **Zeal-of-the Land Busy:** He is a Puritan who becomes an object of mockery.
8. **Dame Purecraft:** She is a rich widow.
9. **Winwife:** He is a London gallant who is Busy' rival in wooing Purecraft.
10. **Quarlous:** He is a gamester but he is guised as a madman. He is Busy's friend, with whom he finds himself in a quarrel. He at last win the hand of Purecraft.

Plot: There is virtually no plot in the play but only a presentation of a plethora of incidents and episodes which are mostly left undeveloped. Jonson's chief aim is to hold a mirror to the London life of his times.

The main incidents are

1. Cokes being relieved of purse, sword, cloak and marriage licence at the hands of Edgeworth.
2. Overdo being taken for a pickpocket and put in the stocks.
3. Waspe and Busy being put in the stocks for fighting and creating nuisance.
4. Overdo's escape from the stocks.
5. Quarlous's disclosing to Overdo the real face of Edgeworth.
6. Overdo's invitation to all to dinner.
7. Quarlous's winning of the hand of Purecraft

Thus, the play proves Jonson to be a gentle satirist who has an ocean of sympathy with his characters of all kinds.

PARADISE LOST

by John Milton

Needless to say that the said Epic is the greatest heroic poem in English literature and one of the greatest of its kind in world literature.

A true epic on classical lines though with several diversional elements, as it is, it has twelve books.

A bookwise "Argument of Paradise Lost" is given by W.J. Long, which may be summarised as under :

Book I

It contains *inter alia*,

(*i*) a statement of the subject, the Fall of Man, and

(*ii*) a noble invocation for light and divine guidance.

Thereafter, in it, we have—

(*i*) description of Satan and the rebel agents. Satan's physical size, his gigantic shield, etc. are on supernatural lines, as can be visualised for a devil of his kind, as in a true epic in particular.
Satan's great power of oratory is also there before us.

(*ii*) the ouster of the rebel angels from heaven by the Almighty.

(*iii*) the diabolical plot of the rebel angels to wreak their vengeance on God by beguiling Adam and Eve, God's children and first parents of mankind, from their state of innocence by bringing about their fall by eating the forbidden fruit in the Eden.

(*iv*) a description of the sulphurous hell-fire and the eternal agonies undergone by the damned spirits there.

(*v*) the raising of Satan's palace, Pandemonium.

Book II

It contains, *inter alia*,

(*i*) a description of the council of devils in the Pandemonium.

(*ii*) Satan's desire to take up the task of beguiling Adam and Eve upon himself.

(*iii*) his journey to the gates of hell, guarded by Sin and Death.

Book III

It contains *inter alia*—

(*i*) God's behest to Raphael to warn Adam and Eve of the imminent danger of disobedience to them.

(*ii*) Son of God's offer to take upon himself the sin of the impending disobedience of man.

(*iii*) Satan's meeting with Uriel, the Angel of the sun, for the purpose of learning the way to earth, the abode of God's new creation.

(*iv*) Satan's journey to the earth in the guise of an angel of light.

Book IV

It contains, *inter alia*—

(*i*) The scenes of Paradise and of Adam and Eve being in the state of innocence.

(*ii*) Eden being guarded by an angel.

(*iii*) The arrest of Satan when he is trying to tempt Eve in a dream.

(*iv*) the setting free of Satan in an unconvincing way.

Book V

It contains, *inter alia*—

(*i*) the description by Eve of her dream to Adam.

(*ii*) Adam and Eve's routine life.

(*iii*) Raphael's visit to Eden.

(*iv*) Raphael's description of the revolt of the fallen angels.

Book VI

It contains, *inter alia*—

a continuation of Raphael's description of the revolt of the fallen angels.

Book VII

It contains a description of the story of creation by Raphael.

Book VIII

It contains Adam's description to Raphael of himself and his meeting with Eve.

Book IX

It contains an account of Satan's temptation of Eve.

Book X

It contains, *inter alia*—

(*i*) God's judgement on Adam and Eve.
(*ii*) Sin and Death's construction of a highway through chaos to the earth.
(*iii*) Satan's return to Pandemonium.
(*iv*) Adam and Eve's repentance.
(*v*) the turning of fallen angels into serpents.

Book XI

(*i*) Acceptance of Adam's repentance by God.
(*ii*) Michael's departure to bring into effect Adam and Eve's banishment from Eden.
(*iii*) Michael's prophecy regarding the destiny of man.

Book XII

It contains *inter alia*—

(*i*) Continuation of Michael's prophecy.
(*ii*) Learning by Adam and Eve of future redemption of mankind.
(*iii*) Adam and Eve's departure out of Eden.

Given below are some extracts from Book I:

The lines given below state the theme: The Fall of Man and present an Invocation to the Muse and the Holy spirit (*i.e.* the spirit of God):

THE WAY OF THE WORLD

by Congreve

As the play opens, we find two men Mirabell and Fainall talking to each other in a Chocolate House.

We learn that Fainall is married to Lady Wishfort's daughter, Arabella who is referred to as Mrs Fainall in the play. We also learn, that Mirabell loves Lady Wishfort's niece, Millament. Lady Wishfort is not only Millament's aunt but also her guardian.

It is learnt that Mirabell often went to Wishfort's house ostensibly to court her but actually to meet Millament. This pretence of Mirabell is at last exposed by Mrs. Marwood.

An enigmatic situation is now created for Millament. Since Lady Wishfort has learnt about Mirabell's sham, she forbids any meeting between him and Millament, Further, in order to inherit the lady's wealth, she has to marry according to her wish. This means that if she marries Mirabell against her wishes, she is likely to be deprived of the fortune of the lady who is fifty-five.

Mirabell has his own plot. He arranges marriage between his servant, Waitwell and Lady Wishfort's maid servant, Foible. The purpose of this marriage is that Waitwell is presented by Mirabell as his (imaginary) uncle, named Sir Rowland.

As Foible has been taken into confidence, she would impress upon Lady Wishfort that Sir Rowland, a wealthy man, has in his heart a deep love and wants to marry her. Through this plan Mirabell wanted to cause embarrassment to Lady Wishfort by revealing the identify of Sir Rowland later and thus compelling her to allow Millament to marry him.

A hindrance is created in the execution of the plot when Mrs. Marwood, Fainall's mistress comes to know about the plan, and she makes her lover aware of it. Besides, not only Millament but also Mrs. Fainall know about this plot.

Mrs. Fainall had once been Mirabell's mistress and in her heart of hearts, she still loves him. Hence, she also does not want that Mirabell should marry Millament, as her heart is burning with the fire of jealousy.

Mr. Fainall is a mean fellow, and he finds it an easy opportunity to blackmail Lady Wishfort. For this, he threatens to divorce Mrs. Fainall. It is further another proof of his avaricious nature that in a deed which is in his possession, he has already arranged the settlement of major part of Mrs. Fainall's estate in his own favour.

It is at the most critical moment when Sir Rowland and Lady Wishfort are busy in constructive prospects and Mirabell and Millament have agreed to marry each other, that Fainall makes his appearance.

Thus Mirabell's apple-cart is disturbed. However, Foible reveals the secret of Fainall's love affair with Mrs. Marwood. However, Fainall, rising on the crest of the situation sets forth certain conditions to remain silent. The conditions concern the fortunes of Mrs. Fainall and Millament and the marriage of Lady Wishfort.

Just then Waitwell presents a deed which is executed by Mrs. Fainall before her marriage with Fainall. In it, she has conferred her then estate on

Mirabell. Thus the deed with Fainall becomes infructuous.

The net result of this *deus ex machina* is that Mirabell and Millament now have no obstacle in tying the nuptial knot to each other.

SENSE AND SENSIBILITY AND PRIDE AND PREJUDICE

by Jane Austen

In essence, the novel *Sense and Sensibility* is a satire on sentimentalism. Elinor represents sense, while sensibility is represented by her sister Marianne. The story, like all stories of Jane Austen, is very simple, but interesting.

Mrs. Henry Dashwood with her three daughters Elinor, Marianne and Margaret, is left in a very straitened situation on the death of her husband. They have to retire to Devonshire where they begin to live in a very humble cottage.

Edward Ferrars is the brother of Mr. John Dashwood. John is the step son of Mr. Henry Dashwood. He had been entrusted by the latter to take care of his wife and daughter after his death. But he does not discharge his responsibilities in this respect.

Edward and Elinor fall in love with each other. Marianne falls in love with a poor, unscrupulous young man, John Willoughby.

Willoughby suddenly leaves for London. Marianne and Elinor go after him. But Willoughby says that he is going to be married to a rich heiress. Elinor also learns that even her lover, Edward, has been untrue to her, as he is already engaged to Lucy Steel who is the niece of Edward.

Edward's mother is not happy with his engagement to Lucy, and settles her property on his younger brother, Robert, who is a fool of the first water. Then Robert and Lucy are married, while Edward stands rejected. Then Edward marries Elinor. Marianna who has been wooed by Colonel Brandon, marries him.

Immature style of Jane Austen is evident in this novel, but her future greatness and maturity is also visible here in seed form. The novel was completed in 1797, though it was published in 1813.

The story of Pride and Prejudice which is regarded as her best work and was published in 1813 is well-known to all scholars and need not be given here. It is in this novel that all the plot and stylistic perfection of Jane Austen comes into play. It is here that the dialogues are most lively, characters life like and her humour at its best.

Whereas in Sense and Sensibility, her characters such as Mrs. Jennings, her stupid daughter, her uncouth son-in-law and Mr. Palmer are some of the humorous characters they are no match for Mr. Collins, Mrs. Bennet, Catherina de Borough and others of Pride and Prejudice.

DAVID COPPERFIELD (1849-50)

by Charles Dickens (1812-70)

David Copperfield is perhaps the most popular novel of Dickens. It is an autobiographical novel in which Dickens's power of characterization, depicting humorous and pathetic situations and characters is perhaps the best brought out. The novel is told in the first person.

THE MAYOR OF CASTERBRIDGE

by Thomas Hardy

It was published serially in 1886. It is the story of a man who brings doom upon himself.

THE MILL ON THE FLOSS (1860)

by George Eliot (1819-80)

The Mill on the Floss is the most popular novel of George Eliot. It is also perhaps her most auto-biographical novel. The story represents the typical Victorian problem of morality and a moral order which spares nobody.

The Mill mentioned in the title of the novel is the imaginary mill 'Dorlcote Mill' owned by Mr. Tulliver. The mill is situated on the river Floss.

The two main characters in the novel are:

(*i*) Tom Tulliver, and

(*ii*) Maggie Tulliver.

THE WASTELAND

by T.S. Eliot

When the Wasteland was published in book form in 1922, it was soon realized to be the beginning of the emergence of the Modernist Poetry.

Earlier the Georgians and the Imagists had appeared and disappeared but their effect, particularly that of the latter, had been retained in the inner recesses of the minds of the writers, poets included, even though superficially the movement of Imagism had all but spent itself.

It was because Ezra Pound who had occupied a pivotal position in the movement which had such protagonists as Hilda Doolittle and Aldington, also was instrumental in giving the final shape, as were now have, to Eliot's poem.

The Wasteland depicts the collapsing civilization of Europe and, connotatively, the fall of values in the modern world. The poem is highly realistic in this sense, but it promises vaguely some possibility of redemption through some everlasting philosophies such as that of the Buddha and the Upanishadas.

It cannot be disputed that the overwhelming picture of pessimism, death and desolation in the poem is to a great extent the result of the annihilation and mayhem which was witnessed in the First World War that ended in 1917. Then there emerged a particularly distressing mood in the twenties and this mood of depression of the entire period all over the world is very deftly brought about in the poem.

The poem's merit does not lie just in depicting a particular mood, but in its employment of complex symbolism and references to mythology, history, culture, religion and literature from varied sources in modern and medieval world and even the remote ancient times.

SAINT JOAN

by G.B. Shaw

It is one of the most famous plays of G.B. Shaw. It is this play which won him the Nobel Prize. The play was first produced in 1923.

Historical Background to Saint Joan: Saint Joan is a historical play which is based on the life and career of a real character, Joan of Arc. She was a common country girl, who was born in 1412. As a girl, she heard divine voices and had divine visions. But she was sent to the stake on the charges of heresy in 1431.

Social, political and religious conditions of the period are closely related to the story of Joan of Arc.

It was in 1415 that the English forces under the leadership of their young king, Henry V defeated Charles VI, the French King at Agincourt—a decisive battle which aroused waves of nationalism in England.

As a result of this humiliating defeat, the French king had to accept certain most unpleasant terms such as :

1. He had to sign a treaty with the English King in 1420.
2. According to it, he had to :
   (*i*) disown his own son, the Dauphin, declaring him as illegitimate.
   (*ii*) marry his infant daughter to the English king.
   (*iii*) allow the English to keep with them large area of France which they had conquered.

It is to be noted that at that time, France was not one united country. It consisted of a number of estates which were under the control of different feudal lords or barons.

TO THE LIGHT HOUSE

by Virginia Woolf

Virginia Woolf's most famous novel, Mrs. Dalloway was published in 1925. Two years later, another masterpiece of hers was published in 1927.

It is the only novel of Mrs. Woolf which has a Three Part Structure :

(*i*) Part I: The Window
(*ii*) Part II: Time Passes
(*iii*) Part III: The Lighthouse.

The main characters in the novel are:

1. **Mrs. Ramsay:** She is a middle-aged charming woman, a mother of eight children. She is the central figure in the novel.
2. **Mr. Ramsay:** He a scholar and philosopher of great repute and has won several academic honours.
3. **Charles Tansley:** He is an intelligent young student of Mr. Ramsay.

4. **Minta Doyle:** He is a young man who loves Paul Rayley.
5. **Paul Rayley:** She loves Doyle.
6. **Augustus Carmichael:** He is an old man and poet.
7. **Lily Briscoe:** She is a painter.
8. **William Bankes:** He is an old friend of Mr. Ramsay's.
9. **James Ramsay:** He is six year old child of Ramsays.
10. **Cam :** Janes's sister.

The scene is laid in the island of Skye in the Hebrides.

The story is autobiographical in nature in the sense that:

(*i*) Mr. and Mrs. Ramsay resemble Mrs. Woolf's parents.

(*ii*) Lily Briscoe greatly resembles Mrs. Woolf herself.

The novel whether more artistic than Mrs. Dalloway or not, has earned as much if not more popularity than Mrs. Woolf's other masterpiece.

The novel is written on the stream-of-consciousness technique:

(*i*) In the *Window,* not only the personality of Mrs. Ramsay is revealed, but also we have the personality of Mr. Ramsay before us which is laid bare through the eyes of Lily Briscoe, Charles Tansley, William Bankes, etc.

(*ii*) In *Time Passes*, we learn more about Mrs. Ramsay and others through the memory of the Charwoman, Mrs. Mc Nab.

(*iii*) In *Lighthouse* we have another focus on Mrs. Ramsay through the memory of Lily Briscoe.

The novel is poetic, as usually all of Mrs. Woolf's novels are

ADVENTURES OF HUCKLEBERRY FINN

by Mark Twain

The novel opens with a warning to the reader:

"Persons attempting to find a moral in it will be banished; persons attempting to find a plot in it will be shot."

Although Mark Twain wrote this novel as a companion to Tom Sawyer, yet it is much more than that. However, a link with the earlier novel is established in the first chapter.

Huck is adopted by the widow Douglas to "civilize" him. The money which is found at the end of Tom Sawyer is put by Judge Thatcher on interest and it fetches a dollar to each boy 'all the year round.'

Huck is not much interested in Douglas' prescriptions of a strict disciplined moral life. Twain attains a technical tour de force by shifting narrative to the first person. This enables Twain to establish *point of view*. Huck is the model of *radical innocence* and *instinctive knowledge*.

SONS AND LOVERS

by D. H. Lawrence

The family of Morels lived in the mining village of Betswood. Mrs. Morel who has had a puritan nourishment, still upholds the values of refinement and nobility. She gets enamoured of Morel's rich ruddy face and merry laughter as well as wavy black hair. Mr. Morel is also captivated by her. The two get married.

The two have an antithetical nature and temperament. Whereas Mrs. Morel is a puritan lady, Mr. Morel is fond of a sensuous, luxurious life. He tries to domineer over his wife. But she rebels against this and the result is that even the children dislike Mr. Morel.

The estrangement between the couple becomes intense when one day, out of jealousy, Mr. Morel clips off the curls of the young William, whom his mother loves so such.

Mrs. Morel does not give up her efforts to reform her husband. But he rather goes more and more astray in his fondness for drinking, etc.

The couple had two more children. Morel tries to entertain the children, but often, the more Mrs. Morel instigates them against him, the more he teases them.

Mrs. Morel is frightened of her estranged relationship with her husband and focuses all her attention on her sons. She wants to possess her first child William whose love affair with Lily she condemns. But the boy dies of pneumonia.

Then Paul Morel, the third child, and the hero of the novel, falls ill. He is suffering from bronchitis. She nurses him tenderly and virtually treats him as her lover. This is how the famous Oedipus complex gets manifested in the novel.

Paul has relationship with three women, that is, his mother, Miriam and Clara. Among these, Miriam is his beloved.

The relationship between Paul and Miriam develops as Paul goes to the Willey Farm with his mother. He offers to teach her French and algebra and thus a friendship develops between the two. But, as Lawrence himself points out, their friendship is "chaste" and purely spiritual.

This relationship between Paul and Miriam cannot become an everlasting one since Mrs. Morel is afraid that Miriam is going to suck Paul's soul and she herself can ill-afford to lose her son. Paul too realises that as long as his mother is alive, his relationship with any woman cannot be permanent.

Paul is interested not only in a spiritual relationship with Miriam. He wants to have with her a physical contact also, but this she denies to him.

Since Paul cannot get physical satisfaction from Miriam, he enters into physical union with a married woman, Clara, who lives separately from her husband. But, the problem is that the woman is unable to satisfy Paul spiritually. The result is that Paul is thrashed by Clara's husband to his complete discomfiture.

Since Paul feels that his failure with both the women, Miriam and Clara, has been because of his mother's possessive nature towards his soul, he begins to hate her. But, when she falls ill with cancer, he tries to arrange the best medical treatment for her.

Being no longer able to witness the agonising misery of his mother, he ends the story of her life by administering morphia to her.

Now, it was impossible for Paul to establish relationship with any woman. He had to be lonely, and there was no escape for him from this state of affairs.

HAMLET

by Shakespeare

Introduction: The king of Denmark has recently died. On his death, his son, Hamlet, the Prince of Denmark, who is a student at the University of Wittenberg, is summoned to the Danish Court.

Hamlet feels miserable that his father's throne has been seized by his uncle, Claudius and his mother has married him.

Ophelia: Another shock comes to Hamlet when his beloved, Ophelia, rejects his suit on the advice of his father, Polonius.

The Ghost: Hamlet learns from his friend, Horatio, and two officers that they have sighted his father's ghost. As Hamlet himself encounters the ghost, the latter tells him the reality that his father had been poisoned by his uncle. The ghost also burdens Hamlet with the responsibility of avenging his death.

The spies: Claudius appoints two spies, Rosencrantz and Guildenstern to keep a watch on Hamlet. The latter arranges the staging of a play "The Murder of Gonzago" to which the king is also invited. The king's abnormal behaviour while watching the play (in which the murder of a king in a manner similar to that in which Hamlet's father is killed is staged) convinces Hamlet of Claudius's guilt.

Having been convinced of Claudius's and his mother's collusion in the murder of his father, Hamlet scolds his mother in a closed room. But as he hears an echo from behind the curtain, he thrusts his rapier at the person hidden. This is how Polonius who was eavesdropping gets killed.

Cause of Hamlet's Madness: Claudius tries his best to know the real cause of Hamlet's "madness," "ecstasy" or distraction, but having failed in his effort, he decides to send him out to England.

In the Ship: In the ship with the two spies, Rosencrantz and Guildenstern, Hamlet opens the sealed letter which contains the orders for his execution on his reaching England. He cleverly replaces these orders for the execution of the spies who lose their life in the venture.

Ophelia's Madness and Death: On learning about the death of her father, Ophelia goes mad, while her brother Laertes burns with the desire for revenge which is sharpened by Claudius.

The Duel: As Ophelia's dead body is being lowered in the grave, Hamlet grapples with Laertes. The two have a bloody duel in which both of them are badly wounded.

Claudius's end: When the two fighters are dying the villainy of Claudius is divulged by Laertes and Gertrude, the Queen. Hamlet kills Claudius with his poisoned rapier and soon Fortinbras arrives to be the next ruler of Denmark.

A Dialogue between the ghost and Hamlet

There are several extremely interesting scenes in Hamlet. Hamlet's dialogue with the ghost of his father is one of them. Here are the following lines which need no explanation.

MACBETH

by Shakespeare

Macbeth was the Lord of Glamis. He was related to Duncan, the king of Scotland. As the play begins, he returns with another general, Banquo, after crushing the rebellion of the Lord of Cawdor.

The Three Witches: When the two generals were returning, they met three witches, one of whom addressed Macbeth as the Lord of Cawdor. Macbeth felt greatly excited as he heard the witches' prophecies that he would soon be king and Banquo's descendants would also be kings. Thereafter, they disappeared.

Macbeth's Promotion: Soon thereafter, Macbeth was informed by two nobles that he had been made Lord of Cawdor by the king. This further thrilled Macbeth as he realized that the prophecy of the witches had come out true. He was so curious and enthusiastic that he wanted that the second prophecy of the witches that he would become the king should also turn true as early as possible.

Duncan's visit to Macbeth's Castle: The king Duncan wanted to visit Macbeth's castle to honour him. Meanwhile, Macbeth informed his wife through a letter regarding the witches' prophecies.

Lady Macbeth's Ambition: Lady Macbeth was even more ambitious than Macbeth and wanted to see him king. As Macbeth reached home, at the earliest, she incited her husband to murder Duncan to make the prophecy come out true. Macbeth was hesitant in accepting this advice.

Duncan was warmly welcomed by the Macbeth couple. He loved the peaceful atmosphere of the castle and went to sleep peacefully and without an iota of suspicion in his mind.

Lady Macbeth continued inciting her husband and even called him a coward when he expressed hesitation and his feeling of non-propriety in killing a guest who was also one of their kins.

The couple drugged the guards and they went into a sound sleep. Then Lady Macbeth herself went to kill Duncan, but now the king's face seemed to her as that of her father. So, she could not execute her plan.

The Bloody Dagger: Thereafter, Macbeth went into the king's room, but as he saw the vision of a bloody dagger, he changed his mind. Yet again, he took courage and struck a dagger into Duncan's heart and killed him.

The Voice: As Macbeth told his wife about the deed, he heard a voice: "Macbeth shall sleep no more." As Macbeth was now terribly overtaken by fear and madness, Lady Macbeth, showing greater courage, put the blood-covered dagger by the side of the guards and stained their clothes with blood to put the blame on them.

The Porter: Soon, the gate knocked. As the porter opened the gate, two of Duncan's nobles entered and went into the king's room where they found him dead.

Duncan's sons: As the news of the king's murder was conveyed to Macbeth, he killed the two guards. Meanwhile, as the news reached Scotland, the king's sons began to run for safety. The elder one, Malcom fled to England. Macbeth was then proclaimed king of Scotland.

Banquo: Macbeth was satisfied that the witches' second prophecy had also turned out to be true, but he feared Banquo. It was because the witches had also prophesied that Banquo's descendants would be kings. Hence, to perpetuate his kingdom Macbeth made up his mind to kill not only Banquo but also his son, Fleance.

The Banquet: Macbeth hit upon a plan. He invited all the nobles to a banquet. As Banquo and his son were on their way to Macbeth's castle, two assassins hired by Macbeth waylaid Banquo and his son. In the attempt, Banquo was killed but his son escaped.

Banquo's Ghost: Macbeth saw Banquo's ghost seated in a chair at the banquet. He even heard the ghost's whispers. Those present there were surprised to note Macbeth's strange behaviour.

For a brief period, the ghost disappeared, but soon it appeared again. Macbeth began to tremble and cry wildly. His such behaviour made him a suspect in the eyes of the guests.

The Witches Again: Macbeth went to consult the witches again. As he saw them, they called three ghosts. Macbeth was told the following three prophecies in turn :

(*i*) Macbeth should beware of Macduff.

(*ii*) No man born of woman could harm Macbeth.

(*iii*) Macbeth could never be defeated until Birnam Wood came to Dunsinane hill.

Lady Macbeth's mental state: Lady Macbeth was in an extremely depressed mood. As such she committed suicide. Macduff had run away to England. It was reported to Macbeth that the Birnam wood was marching towards Dunsinane hill. Macbeth felt puzzled. Soon, it was known that the green branches of the wood were being carried by Malcom's soldiers who were marching towards Macbeth.

Macbeth and Macduff: A fight started between Macbeth and Macduff face to face besides their soldiers fighting with their opposites. As Macduff told Macbeth that he was taken from his mother's womb, Macbeth felt so much discouraged that he got killed without a fight. The witches' prophecies had come full circle on Macbeth, as all his ambition was finally dashed to the ground with true poetic justice meeting out to him, which is perhaps not present in any other of Shakespeare's plays.

Macbeth is a great poet and *inter alia,* Macbeth is a wonderful piece of lyrical and dramatic poetry.

ARMS AND THE MAN

by G. B. Shaw

The young, romantic Raina is standing in her balcony to enjoy the beauty of the night in that month of November in 1885. She has all the romantic ideas of heroism of her lover Major Sergius Saranoff who is out taking part in the war between the Bulgarians and the Serbs.

Suddenly, there comes an intruder. He is a Swiss officer, Captain Bluntschli. He threatens Raina with his pistol and orders her to keep quiet.

Soon, a Russian army officer enters Raina's room to search for the fugitive. Raina hides Bluntschli behind the curtain. She tells the officer that nobody has entered her room.

As the officer goes away, Raina offers some chocolate cream to the fugitive. He tells her that he always carries chocolates to the war in place of cartridges. Then he goes to sleep.

It is the 6th of March, 1886. As Major Petkoff, Raina's father returns from the war, he is welcomed by Raina and her mother, Catherine. Major Sergius also comes. He has resigned from the army as he has not been given promotion.

The two family servants, Nicola, the man-servant and Louka, the maid-servent are already engaged. But when Sergius and Louka are alone, Sergius embraces Louka. She tells him that Raina loves a Swiss officer and would marry him.

Bluntschli comes to return the coat lent to him by Raina and Catherine. Major Petkoff instructs Bluntschli to prepare papers for sending three regiments. The papers are then delivered to the messengers.

Raina has already learnt from Bluntschli about non-heroic part of Sergius in the army. Sergius thinks that she is no longer loyal to him.

At last Raina is married to Bluntschli to which both Petkoff and his wife agree. Louka gets married to Serguis.

In this way, the myth of both the heroism of a soldier and the romance of love is exploded by Shaw in his own inimitable, interesting and simple way.

THE PORTRAIT OF A LADY

by Henry James

It is perhaps Henry James' most important novel which was written in 1881. James believed in images rather than in a story. Yet, if the novel is to be studied as a story, it can be said to be the psychological study of Isabel Archer a young American girl who leaves America with her aunt Mrs. Touchett and goes to Europe in a sort of what may be called her spiritual odyssey.

☛ 1. While portraying Isabel, Henry James had the model of his cousin Mary Temple called "Minny" in his mind. The young girl died in 1870 when she was only 24.
2. The European tour is arranged as once dreamed by Minny, though she got no opportunity to fulfil her dream.
3. Minny had died of T.B.; here we find Ralph dying of the same disease.
4. Gardencourt is a 16th Century English mansion– the kind of architecture Henry cherished.
5. Henry was particularly fond of painting and architecture.
6. Isabel's European odyssey comprises a visit to several countries, *e.g.* England, Italy, France, Greece, Turkey and Egypt.
7. It is to be noted that Henry James had a high regard for the European culture with its vast history, but he had no fondness for his native, American culture which had no history except that worth the name.
8. Isabel is shown as having fondness for Browning and George Eliot, as Minny also had. Besides she is also interested in the German philosophy.

THE GUIDE

by R.K. Narayan

Written in 1958, The Guide which won R.K. Narayan the Sahitya Akademi Award is one of his best novels and a masterpiece giving ample proof of his *tour de force* in the matter of artistic technique.

There are two distinct aspects of the story of The Guide. One half of it is supposed to be told by Raju, the hero, to one of his followers (as he turns from a tourist guide to a saint). The entire life story of Raju is however put in a flashback and told as such by the author. This technical achievement is a rare triumph in the modern artistic style.

Again, to understand more clearly, the story of Raju as saint forms the objective aspect and that of Raju as a tourist guide the autobiographical aspect. This artistic pattern is woven in the entire novel and this is what makes it artistically unique.

Simply speaking, it is the story of Raju's life and death. Raju has to indulge in several vocations and avocations, such as:

(*i*) as a food vendor at the railway station.
(*ii*) as a tourist guide.
(*iii*) as a sentimental adulterer.
(*iv*) as a manager to a dancing girl, Rosy.
(*v*) as a prisoner.
(*vi*) as a reluctantly holy martyred saint.

The setting is, as usual with Narayan, Malgudi town. It is at the newly set up railway station that Raj becomes a vendor. As a tourist guide also, he is quite successful.

One day Rosy, the dancer, and Marco, her husband, an archaeologist, engaged Raju as their guide. There were often quarrels between the husband and the wife.

Raju fell in love with Rosy and spent most of his time with her. He wanted to make her a famous dancer. Rosy's husband at last left her and she now lived with Raju. She was his 'snake-girl'.

Raju who was too ambitious, crossed the limit of propriety. He got addicted to habits such as gambling, drinking, etc. But when he forged the signature of Rosy on an important document, he was caught by Rosy's husband. He had to spend two years in jail. Then Rosy parted ways with him.

After completing his jail term, Raju went to a village, Mangal. There the people mistook him for a saint. Raju, depending on the art of simulation and dissimulation, found it a golden opportunity to be something, and if still dilly-dallying, he willy-nilly took it upon himself to be a holy man.

It was Raju's misfortune that his test was too near and too hard and it was beyond his imagination and comprehension. As usual, the villages were a superstitious lot, and as the famine hit the village, they expected of Raju to do some miracle to appease the rain God.

Raju had no grounding in such machinations of the so-called holy men and he had to go on a fast into death to cause the rain god to show his mercy. Once started, it was now impossible to give up the fast, as the whole area had been converted into a hubbub of pilgrims, tourists, visitors and mediamen who were reporting every now and then on Raju's determination and condition.

The days passed by and yet there was no sign of a cloud. It was the twelfth day of his fast. Raju was too weak to walk or even talk. Somehow he managed to reach the bank of the river, the venue of his prayer for rain. He collapsed uttering the words, "Velan, it's raining in the hills. I can feel it coming up under my feet, up my legs."

GORA

by R.N. Tagore

Written in 1923, it is perhaps the most famous novel of Tagore. It is a patriotic novel which expresses the voice of Resurgent India which is arousing to shake up the shackles of slavery. The novel expresses true secularism and a fusion of the oriental and the occidental. Even Gourmohan, the hero, the son of an English lady is brought up in a Hindu household and stands for that universal blend of ideologies and cultures which is so characteristic of Tagore.

MULTIPLE CHOICE QUESTIONS

1. Who wrote *Don Juan*?
A. Shakespeare B. Tennyson
C. Byron D. T.S. Eliot

2. Who wrote *The Life of Johnson*?
A. Boswell
B. Macaulay
C. Churchill
D. Sir Walter Raleigh

3. *Priest's Nun's Tale* was written by
A. Spenser B. Charles Lamb
C. Tennyson D. Chaucer

4. Who is said to have first used the term "Metaphysics"?
A. Matthew Arnold B. Sidney
C. Donne D. Dr. Johnson

5. The writer of *Volpone* is
A. Johnson B. Milton
C. Jonson D. Shelley

6. Which is the correct chronological sequence?
A. Spenser—Chaucer—Milton—Donne
B. Spenser—Wordsworth—Tennyson—T.S. Eliot
C. Milton—Shakespeare—Philip Larkin—Keats
D. Auden—Eliot—Shelley—Keats

7. *Pilgrim's Progress* was written by
A. Milton B. Shelley
C. Swinburne D. John Bunyan

8. The writer of the line : *"Stone walls do not a prison make"* is
A. Lovelace B. Milton
C. W.B. Yeats D. T.S. Eliot

9. *"Monkey's Paw"* is a
A. Poem B. Drama
C. Short story D. Novel

10. Lyrical Ballads appeared in
A. 1690 B. 1798
C. 1802 D. 1800

11. The writer of *'A Pair of Blue Eyes'* is
A. Thackeray B. Dickens
C. George Eliot D. Thomas Hardy

12. *Hard Times* was written by
A. Thackeray B. Dickens
C. Trollope D. Marquese

13. Which of the following poets was most impressed by the German philosophy?
A. Chaucer B. Wordsworth
C. Coleridge D. Southey

14. The two cities referred to in *"A Tale of Two Cities"* are
A. London and Paris B. London and Rome
C. Rome and Paris D. Moscow and Rome

15. *The Peasant's Bread* is a story by
A. Maupassant B. Tagore
C. R.K. Narayan D. Tolstoy

16. *The Financial Express* was written by
A. Raja Rao B. R.K. Narayan
C. Tagore D. Mulk Raj Anand

17. *"Negative Capability"* is a term associated with
A. Tagore B. Shelley
C. Keats D. Coleridge

18. The most impressive treatment of "imagination" has been given by
A. Coleridge B. Shelley
C. Eliot D. Yeats

19. *Lady Chatterley's Lover* was banned because it was considered
A. obscene B. revolutionary
C. obscurantist D. None of these

20. *For Whom The Bell Tolls* was written by
A. Marquese B. Hemingway
C. Hawthorne D. None of these

21. The writer of : *"A Pair of Mustachios"* is
A. Anand B. Tagore
C. Raja Rao D. Anita Desai

22. The writer of *Scarlet Letter* is
A. Henry James B. James Joyce
C. Hawthorne D. None of these

23. Rousseau is associated with
A. French Revolution
B. American War of Independence
C. Russian (Bolshevik) Revolution
D. None of these

24. Who wrote *'Train to Pakistan'*?
A. Narayan
B. Manohar Malgaon
C. Khushwant Singh
D. Anand

25. Who is the writer of *Azadi*?
A. R.K. Narayan B. Khushwant Singh
C. Tagore D. Chaman Nahal

26. *"The God of Small Things"* is written by
A. R.K. Narayan B. Hemingway
C. Graham Greene D. Arundhati Roy

27. Who wrote the poem *"Listeners"*?
A. Tennyson B. Thomas Hood
C. Goldsmith D. Walter de la Mare

28. In writing *"Canterbury Tales"* Chaucer was influenced by
A. Decameron
B. The Divine Comedy
C. The Holy Bible
D. None of these

29. *'Animal Farm'* was written by
A. James Joyce B. Virginia Woolf
C. George Orwell D. Hemingway

30. Shobha De is a
A. poet B. dramatist
C. novelist D. an actress

31. Dunciad was written by
A. Dryden B. Pope
C. Tennyson D. Shelley

32. Bernard Shaw got the Nobel Prize for
A. Pygmalion
B. Man and Superman
C. Saint Joan
D. None of these

33. The Victorian Period is marked by
A. Great political upheavals
B. Great social security
C. Great wars
D. Economic deprivation

34. Swift is known mainly as
A. an essayist B. a poet
C. a satirist D. a short story writer

35. Who is the writer of the novel *"The Village"*?
A. Khushwant Singh B. Anita Desai
C. Mulk Raj Anand D. R.K. Narayan

36. The most famous writer of the heroic couplet is
A. Dryden B. Chaucer
C. Spenser D. Pope

37. *Macflecknoe* is a poem written by
A. Dryden B. Pope
C. Tennyson D. Yeats

38. Who wrote *'Everyman in His Humour'*?
A. Shakespeare B. Jonson
C. Milton D. Keats

39. *'Indian Jugglers'* is an essay by
A. De Quincey B. Gardiner
C. Hazlitt D. Lamb

40. Who wrote *'The Gropes of Wrath'*?
A. Pearl Buck B. Hemingway
C. Virginia Woolf D. John Steinbeck

41. Who rendered into English the ancient Greek tragedy *"Atlanta in Calydon"*?
A. Swinburne
B. Shelley
C. Tennyson
D. Arthur Hugh Clough

42. *The Deserted Village* was written by
A. Cowper B. Goldsmith
C. Keats D. Johnson

43. *'Savitri'* is an epic written by
A. Tagore
B. Prem Chand
C. Aurobindo
D. Bankim Chandra Chatterjee

44. The anthem *"Vande Mataram"* occurs in
A. Godan B. Anand Math
C. Gora D. Train to Pakistan

45. *'All Fool's Day'* is an essay written by
A. Charles Lamb B. Hazlitt
C. A.G. Gardiner D. R.C. Stevenson

46. The drama *Tamburlaine* is written by
A. Shakespeare B. Marlowe
C. Lyly D. Green

47. The book *"Appreciations"* was written by
A. Morris B. Arnold
C. Walter Pater D. Christina Rossetti

48. *"The Admirable Crichton"* was written by
A. Steinbeck B. T.S. Eliot
C. Trollope D. James Barrie

49. *"The Death of a Salesman"* was written by
A. James Barrie B. Eugene O'Neill
C. Arthur Miller D. None of these

50. The Restoration period is said to have started from
A. 1660 B. 1676
C. 1625 D. 1645

51. Who wrote *"The Lady's Not for Burning"*?
A. Barrie B. Christopher Fry
C. Robert Bridges D. T.S. Eliot

52. Who wrote the poem *"Brahma"*?
A. T.S Eliot B. Emerson
C. Whitman D. Frost

53. The writer of *Walden* is
A. Tennyson B. Whitman
C. Thoreau D. Frost

54. In *'Sons and Lovers'* Lawrence has depicted the life of
A. factory workers B. miners
C. farmers D. animals

55. Who wrote *Kim*?
A. Kipling B. Tagore
C. Lawrence D. Narayan

56. *'The Hairy Ape'* is a famous play by
A. Barrie B. Eugene O'Neill
C. Christopher Fry D. T.S. Eliot

57. Who is the writer of *Frankenstein*?
A. George Eliot B. Jane Austen
C. Mary Shelley D. Emile Bronte

58. Who wrote the *'Cries of Children'*?
A. Robert Browning B. Elizabeth Barrett
C. Thomas Hood D. Cowper

59. Which poet is known as poet's poet?
A. Shakespeare B. Milton
C. Spenser D. Shelley

60. Who wrote the maximum number of sonnets?
A. Shakespeare B. Milton
C. Sidney D. Wordsworth

61. *Adonais* is the eulogy written on the death of
A. Coleridge B. Byron
C. Keats D. Wordsworth

62. Who wrote *Mother*?
A. Tolstoy B. Maxim Gorky
C. Chekhov D. Hardy

63. Who is associated with *Malgudi*?
A. Narayan
B. Anand
C. Manohar Malgonkar
D. Anita Desai

64. The author of *Beowulf* is
A. Bede B. Cynewulf
C. Chaucer D. Unknown

65. The Anglo-Saxon period is often said to be from 450 to ......
A. 900 B. 1000
C. 1050 D. 1100

66. *"To a Mountain Daisy"* is a poem by
A. Wordsworth B. Shelley
C. Keats D. Burns

67. Who wrote: *"The Devil's Disciple"*?
A. Galsworthy B. Barrie
C. Shaw D. Fry

68. Who wrote *"The Decline and Fall of the Roman Empire"*?
A. Walter Raleigh B. Trollope
C. Smollett D. Edward Gibbon

69. Richard Hooker was a prose writer of the
A. Victorian period
B. Romantic period
C. Elizabethan period
D. Chaucerian age

70. Alexander Dumas was
A. an English writer B. an American writer
C. a French writer D. a German writer

71. Which one was not one of the Lake poets?
A. Shelley B. Wordsworth
C. Southey D. Coleridge

72. *The Theory of Catharsis* is associated with
A. Plato B. Dryden
C. Aristotle D. Sidney

73. Who wrote *'In Defence of Poetry'*?
A. T.S. Eliot B. Yeats
C. Keats D. Shelley

74. *'The Playboy of the Western World'* is a play by
A. Barrie B. Synge
C. Fry D. Eliot

75. *'Silent Woman'* is a play by
A. Marlowe B. Shakespeare
C. Ben Jonson D. Lyly

76. The Scene of *Beowulf* is laid in
A. England B. France
C. Spain D. None of these

77. *"Kidnapped"* was written by
A. Dickens B. Thackeray
C. Hardy D. R.L. Stevenson

78. *'The Prisoner of Zenda'* was written by
A. Sterne B. Trollope
C. Anthony Hope D. George Eliot

79. What was the full name of Cervantes?
A. Jim Cervantes
B. John Cervantes
C. Miguel de Cervantes
D. Sir Roger Cervantes

80. Besides being a poet, Chaucer was
A. a trader B. a manufacturer
C. a teacher D. a diplomat

81. The name of William Golding's first novel is
A. The Inheritors B. Lord of the Flies
C. Pincher Martin D. The Pyramid

82. The author of *Erewhon* is
A. Hardy B. Marquese
C. Samuel Butler D. Cervantes

83. Which of the following is a *Comedy of Manners*?
A. The Way of the World
B. The Duchess of Malfi
C. The Lady's Not for Burning
D. The Hairy Ape

84. Which one among the following is not a pessimist?
A. Gissing B. Browning
C. Hardy D. Thomson

85. Charles Reade's drama *"Drink"* was adapted from a work of
A. Goethe B. Zola
C. Mallarwe D. Tennyson

86. Which one among the following was not a utilitarian?
A. Rousseau B. James Mill
C. Ricardo D. Bentham

87. *'The Praise of Folly'* was written by
A. Walter Raleigh B. Thomas Moore
C. Charles Lamb D. Ruskin

88. Who wrote: *"In Praise of Idleness"*?
A. Bertrand Russell B. Thomas More
C. Charles Lamb D. Hazlitt

89. The real name of Saki is
A. H.H. Munro B. Samuel Butler
C. George Orwell D. The Duke

90. Who started: *"The Tatler"*?
A. Addison B. Swift
C. Steele D. Stevenson

91. The poem *'The Song of the Shirt'* was written by
A. Mrs. Browning B. Pope
C. Shelley D. Thomas Hood

92. *Sir Roger* was originally the creation of
A. Addison B. Dryden
C. Steele D. Milton

93. Who wrote: *"Areopagitica"*?
A. Charles Lamb B. Hazlitt
C. De Quincey D. Milton

94. *'The Selfish Giant'* is a story written by
A. Tagore B. Oscar Wilde
C. Maupassant D. Tolstoy

95. Who wrote : *"Four Quartets"*?
A. T.S. Eliot B. W.B. Yeats
C. W.H. Auden D. Philip Larkins

96. Who wrote : *"Look Back in Anger"*?
A. Steinbeck B. Christopher Fry
C. John Osborne D. Barrie

97. Who wrote : *"The Devils of Loundun"*?
A. Bertrand Russell B. Aldous Huxley
C. J.B. Priestley D. Hazlitt

98. Who wrote : *"Principles of Human Knowledge"*?
A. Milton B. John Bunyan
C. Nash D. George Berkeley

99. Who wrote : *"Liber Amoris"*?
A. Lamb B. Hazlitt
C. Byron D. Wordsworth

100. *"A Railway Clerk"* is a poem by
A. Keki N. Daruwallah
B. Nissim Ezekiel
C. Shiv K. Kumar
D. Jayanta Mahapatra

101. Who won The Booker of Bookers?
A. Arundhati Roy B. Khushwant Singh
C. Mulk Raj Anand D. Salman Rushdie

102. Who wrote: *"The Battle of Books"*?
A. Bacon B. Hazlitt
C. Swift D. None of these

103. Who wrote: *"Nectar in a Sieve"*?
A. Mulk Raj Anand
B. Manohar Malgonkar
C. Kamala Markandaya
D. Pearl S. Buck

104. *'The Good Earth'* was written by
A. Raja Rao
B. R.K. Narayan
C. Pearl S. Buck
D. Kamala Markandaya

105. The writer of *'The Dove Found No Rest'* is
A. Pearl S Buck B. Hemingway
C. Raja Rao D. Dennis Stoll

106. Who wrote: *"So Many Hungers"*?
A. Bhabani Bhattacharya
B. Kamala Markandaya
C. Manohar Malgonkar
D. Chaman Nahal

107. Who is the writer of *"The Middleman and Other Stories"*?
A. Mulk Raj Anand B. Bharati Mukherjee
C. Tagore D. Prem Chand

108. Cicero was a Roman
A. philologist B. physician
C. orator D. None of these

109. Who is the writer of *"Gita Rahasya"*?
A. Tulsi Das B. Vivekananda
C. Shivananda D. B.G. Tilak

110. *'The Rubaiyat of Omar Khayyam'* was translated into English by
A. Robert Browning B. Tennyson
C. Fitz Gerald D. Hopkins

111. Mayakovsky was the famous poet of
A. France B. Italy
C. Austria D. Russia

112. Marquese originally wrote his *"One Hundred Years of Solitude"* in
A. French B. German
C. Spanish D. Italian

113. Identify Emile Bronte's novel in the following
A. Persuasion
B. Wuthering Heights
C. Jane Eyre
D. Middlemarch

114. Which one is believed to be the first English tragedy?
A. Gorboduc
B. The Spanish Tragedy
C. Dr. Faustus
D. The Jew of Malta

115. Which of the following works is not by Milton?
A. Paradise Lost B. Il Penseroso
C. Lycidas D. Maud

116. *'Music At Night'* is a book of essays by
A. A.G. Gardiner B. Bertrand Russell
C. Aldous Huxley D. Chesterton

117. The character of Sherlock Holmes was created by
A. Arthur Conan DoyleB. Hazlitt
C. I.A. Richards D. Agatha Christie

118. Who wrote the Preface to the *Gitanjali*?
A. W.B. Yeats B. T.S. Eliot
C. Auden D. Philip Larkin

119. What can be said to be the tragic flaw in *Hamlet*?
A. Revenge B. Indecisiveness
C. Hastiness D. Suspicion

120. Who wrote *'The Spanish Tragedy'*?
A. Shakespeare B. Thomas Kyd
C. Marlowe D. Lyly

121. Name the author of *"1984"*
A. George Orwell B. Graham Greene
C. Naipaul D. James Joyce

122. Who is the creator of *Wessex*?
A. Dickens B. Smollett
C. Meredith D. Hardy

123. Whose novel *"The Foundation Pit?"* was discovered only a few years ago?
A. Andrey Platanov . B. Cherneshevysky
C. Jane Austen D. George Eliot

124. The novel *"We"* was written by
A. Andrey Platanov B. Tolstoy
C. Maxim Gorky D. Zamayatin

125. Name the writer of *"What Is To Be Done"*
A. Zamayatin B. Gorky
C. Cherneshevysky D. Chekhov

126. Name the writer of the novel *"Les Miserables"*
A. Virginia Woolf B. Mrs. Radcliffe
C. Victor Hugo D. James Joyce

127. Which of the following novels is not by Salman Rushdie?
A. Midnight's Children
B. Grimus
C. The Moor's Last Sigh
D. The Lighthouse

128. A sonnet comprises
A. 16 lines B. 14 lines
C. 12 lines D. 20 lines

129. Who is renowned for his outstanding work *"Holy Sonnets"*?
A. Donne B. Herrick
C. Milton D. Pope

130. Which of the following is not written by Hugo Charteris?
A. Pictures in the Wall
B. A Piece of String
C. The Old Boys
D. The Boarding House

131. Which of the following works is by H.G. Wells?
A. All in a Garden Fair
B. The Invisible Man
C. A Child of the Jago
D. Point Counter Point

132. Who wrote : *"The Ideal of a Christian Church"*?
A. John Keble
B. Newman
C. Nash
D. William George Ward

133. Which of the following odes is not by Keats?
A. Ode on Intimations of Immortality
B. Ode to a Nightingale
C. Ode on a Grecian Urn
D. Ode to Autumn

134. Which of the following works is not that of David Hume?
A. Treatise of Human Nature
B. The Rise and Fall of the Roman Empire
C. Political Discourses
D. History of Great Britain

135. Who is the writer of *'The School for Scandal'*?
A. Ben Jonson B. R.B. Sheridan
C. Congreve D. Webster

136. Who is the writer of the poem *"The Canonization"*?
A. Milton B. Dryden
C. Donne D. Chaucer

137. Name the writer of the poem *"Wind Hour"*?
A. Hopkins B. Eliot
C. Dryden D. Yeats

138. Who is the writer of the poem *"Adam's Course"*?
A. Eliot B. Tagore
C. Yeats D. Shelley

139. Who wrote the poem: *"Lay Your Sleeping Head"*?
A. Auden B. Yeats
C. Stephen Spender D. Ted Hughes

140. The play *"The Birthday Party"* is written by
A. G.B. Shaw B. Galsworthy
C. Harold Pinter D. Osborne

141. Who is believed to be the writer of *"On the Sublime"*?
A. Aristotle B. Longinus
C. Plato D. M. Arnold

142. Name the author of *"An Essay on Dramatic Poesie"*
A. Dryden B. Sidney
C. Shelley D. Arnold

143. Who is the writer of *"Culture and Society"*?
A. Cleanth Brooks
B. Eliot
C. Bertrand Russell
D. Raymond Williams

144. The writer of the *'Mirror and the Lamp'* is
A. Hume B. Lionel Trilling
C. M.H. Abrams D. Sean Lucy

145. The writer of *"Provide Provide"* is
A. Whitman B. Frost
C. Yeats D. Auden

146. Who wrote *"Desire Under the Elms"*?
A. Arthur Miller B. Osborne
C. Eugene O'Neill D. Shaw

147. Who is the writer of *"A Severed Head"*?
A. Iris Murdoch B. Paul Scott
C. Goldwing D. Huxley

148. *'Das Kapital'* is written by
A. Engel B. Freud
C. Marx D. Lawrence

149. *"Waiting for Godot"* is written by
A. Samuel Beckett B. Ibsen
C. Brecht D. Chekhov

150. Who is the writer of *"A House for Mr. Biswas"*?
A. Salman Rushdie B. V.S. Naipaul
C. Vikram Seth D. R.K. Narayan

151. Name which is not the work of Marlowe
A. Richard I B. Tambarlaine
C. The Jew of Malta D. Dr. Faustus

152. Name the writer of the poem *"The Weary Blues"*
A. Longfellow B. Whitman
C. Frost D. Langston Hughes

153. Which of the following poems is not written by Robert Lowell?
A. In the Cage B. Dolphin
C. Good Morning D. The Old Flame

154. Which of the following poems is written by Wallace Stevens?
A. Red Sun Blues B. Sunday Morning
C. From Survivor D. "Going"

155. Which of the following poems is not written by Philip Larkin?
A. Art Grass B. Sad Steps
C. Traveller D. Church going

156. *Oedipus Rex* was written by
A. Sophocles B. Homer
C. Seneca D. Aeschylus

157. Flaubert's famous work is
A. Odysseus B. Madame Bovary
C. The Trial D. The Outsider

158. Northrop Fry is basically a
A. Dramatist B. Novelist
C. Poet D. Critic

159. The writer of *"The Beauty in a State"* is
A. Raja Rao
B. Tagore
C. Shelley
D. Ananda Coomaraswami

160. The most important work of K.R. Srinivas Iyengar is
A. Indian Way of Writing

B. Indians Under the Foreign Rule
C. Indian Writing in English
D. Indian Literary Scene

161. The writer of *"The Swan and the Eagle"* is
A. M.K. Naik
B. C.D. Narasimhaiah
C. Bruce King
D. V.K. Gokak

162. Who wrote the poem: *"The Lake Isle of Innisfree"*?
A. Yeats B. Eliot
C. Spender D. Auden

163. Who wrote : *"The Lives of the Poets"*?
A. Boswell B. Hazlitt
C. Macaulay D. Dr. Johnson

164. Who wrote: *"The Interpretation of Dreams"*?
A. Marx B. Jung
C. Freud D. Darwin

165. Who wrote : *"Principles of Literary Criticism"* (in 1924)?
A. T.R. Leavis B. Kenneth Brooke
C. I.A. Richards D. A.G. Gardiner

166. Whose book "Language" (1933) is considered *"The Bible of American Linguistics"*?
A. Robert A. Hall B. Bloomfield
C. Bernard Bloch D. Edward Sapir

167. Which of the following poems is not by Frost?
A. Design B. Birches
C. Reluctance D. Michael

168. The famous soliloquy *"To be or not to be"* occurs in
A. Macbeth B. King Lear
C. Hamlet D. Othello

169. Which is the *'Odd man out'* in the following?
A. Paradise Lost B. The Ramayana
C. Essay on Man D. Iliad

170. Which Italian poet is most famous for his sonnets?
A. Petrarch B. Dante
C. Ovid D. None of these

171. What figure of speech has been used in the following line?

"Milton! thou shouldn't be living with us at this hour."

—Wordsworth

A. Hyperbole B. Simile
C. Metaphor D. Apostrophe

172. Which figure of speech has been used in the term : *"immemorial elms"*?
A. Allegory B. Rhyme
C. Alliteration D. Oxymoron

173. Which play of Shaw is also sometimes called *"The Chocolate Soldier"*?
A. Arms and the Man
B. Candida
C. Pygmalion
D. Saint Joan

174. Which one among the following cannot be deemed to be a writer of the *"Problem Play"*?
A. G.B. Shaw
B. Galsworthy
C. Harley Granville-Barker
D. Eliot

175. Who is the writer of *"Metamorphoses"*?
A. Ovid B. Dante
C. Petrarch D. Virgil

176. The book *"Euphues"* was written by
A. Greene B. Jonson
C. Dryden D. John Lyly

177. Who can be said to be the greatest writer of the *Comedy of Humours*?
A. Dryden B. Ben Jonson
C. Congreve D. Etherege

178. Which one among the following is not a play by Ben Johnson?
A. Volpone
B. Alchemist
C. Every man out of His Honour
D. The Way of the World

179. Who is the writer of the book *"Prince"*?
A. Ovid B. Boccaccio
C. Machiavelli D. Montaigne

180. Who is the writer of the essay *"Simulation and Dissimulation"*?
A. Montaigne B. Lamb
C. De Quincey D. Bacon

181. Name the figure of speech for which Lyly is chiefly remembered
A. Malapropism B. Euphuism
C. Melodramaticism D. None of these

182. *Utopia* was written by
A. Walter Raleigh B. Sir Thomas Moore
C. Daniel Defoe D. None of these

183. The other name for *Euphues* is
A. The Anatomy of Melancholy
B. The Anatomy of Joy
C. The Anatomy of Wit
D. None of these

184. *Ferrex and Porrex* is the other name for
A. The Spanish Tragedy
B. Dr. Faustus
C. Goboduc
D. None of these

185. Which one among the following belongs to the group known as University Wits?
A. Shakespeare B. Congreve
C. Dryden D. Marlowe

186. *Astrophel and Stella* is a
A. play B. novel
C. sonnet sequence D. short story

187. What is the Greek meaning of *'Utopia'*?
A. An ideal place
B. A healthy place
C. A lovely place
D. Not a place (=*ou*=not; *topos*=a place)

188. The word "Volksgeist" means
A. The spirit of the age
B. (As per) tradition, custom and consensus
C. The essence of something
D. None of these

189. Which one of the following was a contemporary of Chaucer?
A. Spenser B. Herrick
C. Robert Graves D. John Gower

190. The famous work of Boccaccio is
A. Decameron
B. Divine Comedy
C. Essays
D. A collection of sonnets

191. What is meant by *"Grub Street"*?
A. The literary scene of hacks' crowds during Pope's period.
B. Unhygienic streets of London
C. Streets full of worms
D. Plague-infested streets

192. Who wrote: *"Idylls of the King"*?
A. Tennyson B. Browning
C. Spenser D. Keats

193. What could be another name for Renaissance?
A. The New Learning
B. The Reformation
C. The Prostantism
D. Humanism

194. Who wrote: *'Hudibras'*?
A. Butler B. Addison
C. Steele D. Goldsmith

195. *"London"* by Dr. Johnson is
A. An epic B. A verse satire
C. A prose satire D. A critical work

196. Who wrote *Moll Flanders*?
A. Richardson B. Fielding
C. Smollett D. Defoe

197. *The Gothic novel* was primarily a novel of
A. Pity
B. Terror
C. Love
D. Description of nature

198. *'Unto This Last'* is a work by
A. Carlyle B. Pater
C. Oscar Wilde D. John Ruskin

199. Who is the writer of *"The Blessed Damozel"*?
A. Christina Rossetti B. Emile Bronte
C. D.G. Rossetti D. W.B. Yeats

200. Who among the following was not a critic?
A. M. Arnold B. Ruskin
C. Dryden D. Tennyson

201. Which one among the following was not a contemporary or predecessor of Shakespeare?
A. Marlowe B. Kyd
C. Fry D. Greene

202. Who among the following was not a prose writer?
A. Ascham B. Coleridge
C. Hooker D. Raleigh

203. Who among the following was not a character writer?
A. Wordsworth
B. Joseph Hall
C. John Earle
D. Sir Thomas Overbury

204. Who among the following was not an essayist of the seventeenth century?
A. Halifax
B. Sir Thomas Browne
C. Hazlitt
D. Sir William Temple

205. About whom has it been said :
"He knew small Latin and less Greek"
A. Ben Jonson B. Shakespeare
C. Milton D. Aristotle

206. Who said about Shakespeare:
"He was not of age but of ages"?
A. Jonson B. Johnson
C. Dryden D. Arnold

207. Who wrote: *'Modern Painters'*?
A. Rossetti B. Reynolds
C. Hazlitt D. Ruskin

208. Which one of the following is not the work of Lamb?
A. Of Style B. All Fools' Day
C. Dream Children D. Grace Before Meat

209. Who is stated to have said :
"veni, vidi, vici"?
A. Julius Caesar B. Alexander
C. Napoleon D. Homer

210. Who wrote : *"The Advancement of Learning"*?
A. Pope B. Tennyson
C. Bacon D. Eliot

211. Who wrote: *"We are hollow men"*?
A. Eliot B. Yeats
C. Tagore D. Ezekiel

212. By which character is the following line in Shakespeare's Julius Caesar spoken?
"I'm well-armed in honesty"?
A. Caesar B. Cassius
C. Brutus D. Cicero

213. *'The Way of All Flesh'* was written by
A. Swift B. Congreve
C. Butler D. Addison

214. Who is the writer of *"The Good Companions"*?
A. A.G. Gardiner B. Chatterton
C. Hazlitt D. J.B. Priestley

215. Who is the writer of the poem *'Vagabond'*?
A. MacNeice
B. Masefield
C. Sir Henry Newbolt
D. Rupert Brooke

216. *"Gallathea"* in written by
A. Spenser B. Herbert
C. Lyly D. Shelley

217. Who wrote: *"The Harp of India"*?
A. Govind Chunder Dutt
B. Michael Madhusudan Dutt
C. Henry L.V. Derozio
D. V.K. Gokak

218. *"King Porus—A Legend of Old"* is written by
A. Henry Derozio
B. Toru Dutt
C. Sarojini Naidu
D. Michael Madhusudan

219. Who is the writer of the poem *"The Dance of the Eunuchs"*?
A. Nissim Ezekiel B. Kamala Das
C. Daruwallah D. A.K. Ramanujan

220. Which Indian poet wrote the poem *"The Trojan War"*?
A. Vikram Seth B. Keki N. Daruwalla
C. Sri Aurbindo D. Tagore

ANSWERS

1	2	3	4	5	6	7	8	9	10
C	A	D	D	C	B	D	A	C	B
11	**12**	**13**	**14**	**15**	**16**	**17**	**18**	**19**	**20**
D	B	C	A	D	B	C	A	A	B

21	22	23	24	25	26	27	28	29	30
A	C	A	C	D	D	D	A	C	C
31	32	33	34	35	36	37	38	39	40
B	C	A	C	C	D	A	B	C	D
41	42	43	44	45	46	47	48	49	50
A	B	C	B	A	B	C	D	C	A
51	52	53	54	55	56	57	58	59	60
B	B	C	B	A	B	C	B	C	D
61	62	63	64	65	66	67	68	69	70
C	B	A	D	C	D	C	D	C	C
71	72	73	74	75	76	77	78	79	80
A	C	D	B	C	D	D	C	C	D
81	82	83	84	85	86	87	88	89	90
B	C	A	B	B	A	B	A	A	C
91	92	93	94	95	96	97	98	99	100
D	C	D	B	A	C	B	D	B	B
101	102	103	104	105	106	107	108	109	110
D	C	C	C	D	A	B	C	D	C
111	112	113	114	115	116	117	118	119	120
D	C	B	A	D	C	A	A	B	B
121	122	123	124	125	126	127	128	129	130
A	D	A	D	D	C	D	B	A	B
131	132	133	134	135	136	137	138	139	140
B	D	A	C	B	C	A	C	A	C
141	142	143	144	145	146	147	148	149	150
B	A	D	C	B	C	A	C	A	B
151	152	153	154	155	156	157	158	159	160
A	D	C	B	C	A	B	D	D	C
161	162	163	164	165	166	167	168	169	170
B	A	D	C	C	B	D	C	C	A
171	172	173	174	175	176	177	178	179	180
D	C	A	D	A	D	B	D	C	C
181	182	183	184	185	186	187	188	189	190
B	B	C	C	D	C	D	B	D	A
191	192	193	194	195	196	197	198	199	200
A	A	A	A	B	D	B	D	C	D
201	202	203	204	205	206	207	208	209	210
C	B	A	C	B	A	D	A	A	C
211	212	213	214	215	216	217	218	219	220
A	C	C	D	B	C	C	D	B	C

4

Literary General Knowledge

HISTORY OF ENGLISH LITERATURE TIMELINE

Given below is the History of English Literature timeline.

- **Old Literature (858-1100)**
  Anglo Saxon
  Norman Conquest (A landmark)
- **Middle Ages (1100-1500)**
- **Renassaince (1500-1660)**
  Tudor (1485-1603)
  Elizabethan (1558-1603)
  Jacobian (1603-1625)
  Caroline (1625-1649)
  Late Renaissance (Puritans) (1625-1660)
- **Neo-Classical Age (1660-1798)**
  Restoration Age (1660-1700)
  Augustan Literature
  Age of Sensibility
- **19th Century Literature**
  Romanticism (1798-1837)
  Victorian Age (1837-1901)
  Edwardian Age
- **English Literature Since 1901**
  Modernism (1901-1939)
  Post Modernism (1940-21st Century)

Old Literature (858-1100)

People communicated the poems and literary works orally during the period under consideration. Writing was not given much importance.

The Anglo-Saxons were made up of three tribes who came to England through the North Sea route - the Angles, Saxons, and Jutes. The Anglo-Saxon age comprises about 600 years.

Beowoulf is one of the most important works of that age. It is an epic poem which throws light on a young warrior in Geatland who fought for his people. It's all about the heroic deeds of the German Warrior which happened apparently in 5th & 6th centuries. Beowoulf is a 300 line poem and it was probably written 300 years later when 'written texts' came into existence. It was probably completed in the 8th Century.

Norman Conquest: Invasion of the Normans in England in the year 1066. The army consisted of the Norman, Breton and the French which was led by William the Conqueror. They brought the French language to England. French was adopted as the new language for the parliament.

These people were initially sea rovers who inhabited Scandinavia, who later invaded the northern part of France which is until present day known as Normandy. Later they also picked up the French language.

Middle Ages (1100-1500)

The most respected and famed writer of the middle age was Geoffrey Chaucer. He is known as the father-figure in English literature. In the 13th century, the English literature prospered at a distinguished rate. Chaucer introduced the Iambic Pentameter. His greatest works are mostly narratives like The Canterbury Tales, The House of Fame etc.

Medieval theatre included Mysteries, Miracle and Morality plays. We will be discussing the Miracle and Morality plays only because these two are the ones which are widely discussed upon.

(A) Miracle plays: They are also known as Saints play as they present a real or fictitious account of their life. They are the principal kind of vernacular drama of European Middle Ages. By the 13th century, they became vernacularized.

In miracle plays, the actual story revolves around the main characters and on the other hand, the other characters were short reckoned or undervalued. Comic scenes were also a part of Miracle plays. Moreover, there were devil characters present in those plays. The structure of the play is basically unpleasant.

It is based on the biblical story of the life of the religious persons. The Miracle plays were banned in England because of the teachings of the Roman Catholic. The language of the play shifted to English because that made the play less religious. Moreover, they were performing in town festivals. Most plays were about Saint Nicolas and Virgin Marry.

(B) Morality Plays: In morality plays, the protagonist of the play generally meets various moral attributes through personification. The other characters in the play signify moral qualities and the hero of the play represents mankind and humanity. Supporting characters in the play are personifications of either good or bad. So, moral lessons can be learned from these plays. The hero or the protagonist shows the difference between good and bad.

These type of plays were developed at the later 14th c. It gained more popularity in the 15th c.

Renassaince (1500-1660)

The word Renaissance implies the rebirth of culture and learning. Renassaince was initially started at Italy in the late 14th century. The European scholars and writers found that Renassaince was doing good at Italy. So, at around 1500 they brought the Renassaince literature in England. This age is one of the most important in the History of English Literature.

There are several factors for the coming of Renassaince literature in England. The first primary factor is the introduction of the printing press. It made it possible for the writers to produce written works. Secondly, the 'plague' in England has passed and the hundred years' wars were over. The productivity of people at that time had increased as people lived longer because they weren't dying or fighting. Moreover, for a century and a half, after Chaucer passed away the English literature became stagnant in England. The standard of literature became low. So, people have to adopt Renaissance which was doing really great in Italy.

Talking about the famous writers, the first person to come on the list is William Shakespeare. Besides him, there are few other writers who gained popularity due to their writings like, Christopher Marlowe, Ben Jonson etc. Shakespeare coined a lot of words by his own. According to scholars, he is responsible for coining around 1700 words. His works are said to be universal for which it got more prevalent. He made the English vocabulary damn rich. A word which we use widely, 'beautiful' was coined by Shakespeare. It's hard to imagine such an indispensable word not being used before him. He also came up with a genre called, 'Tragi-Comedy' which implies the merging through two micro niches, tragedy and comedy. His famous plays are Julius Caesar, Romeo and Juliet, Hamlet, Macbeth, Merchant of Venice etc.

According to some scholars, Marlowe and Shakespeare were rivals in this field. People also suspected Marlowe to be a secret agent of Queen Elizabeth. One of his most famous work is 'Dr. Faustus', where he talks about the tragical history of the life and death of Doctor Faustus. He also wrote 'The Jew of Malta' which got popular during that period. He died when he was 29. The third popular dramatist or playwright was Ben Jonson. He is well known for his satirical plays. Some of the famous works of him are Volpone, The Alchemist etc.

Elizabethan Era (1558-1603): This era was the period of new ideas and new thinking. Various other works like fine arts endured support and assistance from the Queen. Due to the Queen's support and patron, the works of that time came to be known as 'Elizabethan'. This period is generally regarded as the greatest in the history of English literature. The age saw a great flourishment in literature. The poetries and dramas were prospered more, in particular. Three most important and remarkable writers of that period are William Shakespeare, Christopher Marlowe, and Ben Jonson.

There were three types of Sonnet - Shakespearean Sonnet, Petrarchan Sonnet, and Spenserian Sonnet. Sir Wyatt brought Sonnet from Italy which was later popularized in England. Later, they gave a different style to the sonnets. It was being changed by Shakespeare. He divided the Sonnet into 3 quatrains summed by a couplet. Shakespeare, in his career, wrote 154 sonnets. He dedicated 126 of them to a young man and the others to a woman.

Even though this age produced a lot of prose works, essentially it was an age of poetry. Moreover, the theatre became central to the Elizabethan era. During that era, drama shifted from religious to secular.

The first English comedy was 'Gammer Gurton's Needle' and the first tragedy was 'Gorboduc'. They came in this period. One of the biggest comedy play written at that time was 'Every Man in his Humour'.

Some of the characteristics or features of play are:

- Plays were presented quickly. The actors use their voice, bodies expressively to convey feeling and meaning.
- Plays were generally performed at the time of the afternoon. It is because there were no light facilities available. Special effects were a part of the show.
- Women were not allowed to perform as there was the existence of gender inequality. The males only played as females.
- The Wealthy people bought the best seats. Sometimes they even sat on the stage itself.
- Even the illiterates could understand the play.
- The theatre is also seen as a good mode of business in that period.

Jacobian Era (1603-1625): Jacobian Era comes just after the Elizabethan era. The two primary contribution of this age in English literature is the Revenge play and Metaphysical poetry. Revenge play signifies the plays where the victim is retaliated or avenged. These type of plays often results in the death of both the murderer and the avenger. These type of plays were extremely popular during the Elizabethan and the Jacobean era. Some of the best writers of plays of this kind are Thomas Kyd, Shakespeare etc.

Secondly, there was the wide popularity of metaphysical poetry. The term 'metaphysical poetry' was coined by Samuel Johnson. This type of poetry is witty and ingenious. They are also highly philosophical. Some of the topics on which metaphysical poems are written are love, existence, life etc. Similie, metaphors, imagery and other literary elements are used in writing these poems.

One of the greatest lyricists of that era was John Donne. He was famous for his unconventional and metaphysical style of poetry. He wrote short sonnets and love poems. Two of his most popular poems are - The Sun Rising and The Canonization.

Caroline Era (1625-1649): This era coincided with the age of Charles I (1625-1642). During that time, a civil war was fought between the supporters of the king (Cavaliers) and the supporters of the parliament (Roundheads).

Some of the prominent writers of that era are George Herbert, Henry Vaughan, Katherine Philips, John Donne etc.

Puritan Age (1625-1660): The half-century between the years 1625 and 1675 is known as the Puritan age. The age is named 'Puritan Age' because of the Puritan dominance in England for the first time. Furthermore, the greatest literary figures of that time were Puritans. One remarkable figure was John Milton. Some of his popular works are:

- Paradise Lost (1667)
- Paradise Regained (1671)

- On Shakespeare (1632)
- Doctrine and Discipline of Divorce (1643) etc.

Milton became most famous for the poem, Paradise Lost. It was a poem with religious beliefs.

The Puritans closed the Theatre which was given much importance in the Elizabethan era. There was a Civil war during that period. One group of people supported the King (Cavaliers) and the other supported the Parliament (Roundheads). The ones supporting parliament won. So, as a result, Charles I was removed and Oliver Cromwell came into power. To sum up in one line, 'The Puritan age starts with Charles I beheaded and Oliver Cromwell into the rule'. Cromwell built a commonwealth of members which didn't last long. After him, Charles II from France came into power and Restoration began.

Neo-Classical Age (1660-1798)

The word 'Neo-Classical' is merged with the two words 'Neo' and 'Classical'. Neo implies 'new' and classical denotes the 'Roman and Greek classics'.

This era is also known as the era of enlightenment. People in England would meet at the coffee house and talk about productive things. It started the British tradition of 'afternoon tea'. Popular types of literature include parody, letters, essays, and satire.

People were interested in appearance, not in the being genuine. Having good manners and doing the right thing to the public was essential.

This age is divided into three parts:

- Restoration Period
- Augustan Literature &
- Age of Sensibility

Restoration Period (1660-1700): The restoration age begins in 1660. In the restoration period, James II was restored to the throne. There was a complete rejection of ideas. People had a different way of living as compared to the other ages. A lot of changes took place during that period.

Monarchy was restored in England. James II, brother of Charles I who was defeated and beheaded returned to England from France. He became the king there.

Most importantly, the Theatre closed down by the Puritans was restored. John Dryden, greatest of all the poets of this age, established heroic couplet in English Poetry. He developed a new prose style that was suited to the practical needs of the age.

Charles II and his followers enjoyed a gay life in France during the exile. Later, when he came to England, he demanded that drama should follow the French style of writing. Establishment of Royal Society, Development of science.

John Dryden's text, 'Absalom and Achitophel' talks about the religious and political conflict. The religious quarrel between the Protestants and the Catholics are also portrayed in his book.

There was the rise of the two political parties - the Whigs and the Tories. The Tories supported the king and the Whigs opposed it. Here are some of the chief characteristics of this period. This age was the beginning of modern prose.

Charles II wanted to establish Catholicism in the country. As the entire country was Protestant it leads to a conflict between the two. Charles II became infamous for this act. As a consequence, this led to a revolution which is known as the 'Bloodless Revolution'. It took place in 1688.

Augustan Literature: The Augustan age was a Roman Empire age. King Augustus was the emperor of that time. Some of the most famous Augustan writers are Virgil, Horace etc. Major poets of that age are Pope and Dryden. And on the other hand, Jonathan Swift was famous for his prose works.

This age is also known as classical age. The first half of the 18th century was marked by the preparation of Industrial revolution. The main social classes were merchants, landowners, and manufacturers. The condition of women was not satisfactory. Sexual harassment, abduction of women, forced marriage took place in the period. The politicians were corrupt too. This is the age of material greed.

John Dryden lived between the Restoration and Augustan age. He wrote various comedies. But the attribute for which he was highly admired was his verse satires. His followers and other small poets valued this writing style.

Alexander Pope was the biggest name of this period. He basically wrote on harmony. The heroic couplet is famous in his poems. One of his famous work is The Canterbury Tales.

Age of Sensibility (1750-1798): The age of Sensibility is also known as the age of Johnson. Two most famous writers of this period are Richard Brinsley Sheridan and Oliver Goldsmith. Sheridan was a love poet. Most of the literary works of this age talk about human feelings, classicism and Romantic revival.

19th Century Literature (1799 to 1900)

The 19th-century literature is merged with three ages. They are:

- Romanticism (1798-1837)
- Victorian Age (1837-1901)
- Edwardian Age (1901-1910)

Romanticism (1798-1837): This period was mainly a reaction against the philosophy of Enlightenment period that dominated much of European Philosophy. Individual achievements are highly valued. Many of the Romantic writers believed that people regardless of wealth or social class must be able to appreciate art and literature.

Some of the most famous poets of the period are - John Keats, William Blake, William Wordsworth, Thomas Grey etc. The works were basically on the depiction of nature. They used personification frequently in the poems. The poets basically tried to bring out their inner feelings.

Victorian Age (1837-1901): The Victorian era was one of the most important eras in the History of English Literature. Queen Victoria, at the age of 18 ruled England continuously for 64 years until her death. It is one of the longest reigns in the history of England. Many important social and historical changes altered the structure of the nation. The population of the country almost doubled. The British empire expanded exponentially. Technology and industrial progress helped Britain to be one of the most dominant countries in the world.

The Victorian age was a time of great prosperity in the History of English Literature. This period made a lot of changes amongst people. The lowerclass became more self-conscious but on the other hand, the middle-class people got more power in them. The rich became vulnerable in the society. Just like the Elizabethan England, The Victorian England saw a great expansion of prosperity, prestige, and culture. Some of the most trending topics of that time are the democracy, feminism, unionization of workers, Marxism, socialism etc.

Due to the industrial revolution, the country saw progress and growth. But along with that poverty and exploitation was also a part of it. The poor were hired for industrial labor at a very low rate.

The Victorian period was a time of contradiction, often referred to as the Victorian Compromise. There were differences between science and religion. Various conflicts arose due to this differences. Secondly, the gap between the rich and the poor widened drastically. The poor starting becoming poorer and the rich started becoming more richer. The wealthy or the rich people hired the labors at a very cheap rate.

The Victorian novels depicted almost every perspective of nineteenth-century Victorian life. Though poetry and prose were unquestionably brilliant, it was the novel that conclusively proved to be the Victorians special literary success. Charles Dickens, Great Expectations, and David Copperfield are some of the most prominent authors.

Charles Darwin wrote Origin of the Species which caused full-scale controversy in Europe. Darwin in his book wrote that the species survive and evolve by natural selection, or in other words, it's the survival of the fittest. This led to a debate among the Victorian people which also led to the alteration of their intellectual and religious life. Another most popular author of the period under consideration was Lord Alfred Tennyson. He wrote In Memoriam which talks about the reflection on the death of his friend.

The Edwardian Age (1901-1910): After the death of Queen Victoria, Edward VII came into the throne. His throne at England is known as the

Edwardian age. It lasted less than a decade. Even though Queen Victoria, a lady was on the throne for the last 64 years, she was unable to do something for the upliftment of women. But in this era, the women status in the society seem to increase. Science and technology were also developed. Wright brothers invented the first airplane during that time.

H.G. Wells, Beatrix Potter, Lucy Maud Montgomery, Edith Nesbit were some of the renowned writers of the age.

English Literature Since 1901

Modernism (1901-1939): Literature from various parts of the world started spreading. New writers were tried to impersonate the glory of British writers. Women at the time were suppressed in the literary sense. They were not allowed to write freely.

Post-Modernism (1940-21st Century) - In post-modernism, basically the history of English Literature of 5 geo-locations are being studied. They are - African, Australian, Canadian, Caribbean and Indian Literature.

FAMOUS BOOKS AND AUTHORS

Book	*Author*
A Secular Agenda	Arun Shourie
A Suitable Boy	Vikram Seth
Accession of Extinction	D.R. Mankekar
Adam Beda	George Eliot
Adhe Adhure	Mohan Rakesh
Adonis	P.B. Shelley
Adventures of Huckleberry Finn	Mark Twain
Adventures of Sherlock Holmes	Arthur Conan Doyle
Adventures of Tom Sawyer	Mark Twain
Advise and Consent	Allen Drury
Affluent Society	J.K. Galbraith
After the Dark Night	S.M. Ali
Age of Reason	Jean Paul Sartre
Agni Pariksha	Acharya Tulsi
Agni Veena	Kazi Nazrul Islam
The Agony and the Ecstasy	Irving Stone
Ain-i-Akbari	Abul Fazal
Airport	Arthur Hailey
Ajat Shatru	Jai Shankar Prasad
Akbarnama	Abul Fazal
Alchemist, The	Ben Jonson
Alice in Wonderland	Lewis Carroll
All is Well that Ends Well	William Shakespeare
All Quite on the Western Front	Erich Maria Remarque
All the President's Men	Carl Bernestin and Bob Woodward
All the Prime Minister's Men	Janardhan Thakur
All things Bright and Beautiful	James Herroit
Amar Kosh	Amar Singh
Ambassador's Journal	J.K. Galbraith
Ambassador's Report	Chester Bowles
An American Tragedy	Theodore Drieser
An Autobiography	Jawaharlal Nehru
An Eye to China	David Selbourne

Book	*Author*
An Idealist View of Life	Dr. S. Radhakrishnan
An Unknown Indian	Nirad C. Choudhury
Anandmath	Bankim Chandra Chatterjee
Ancient Mariner	Samuel Taylor Coleridge
And Quiet Flows the Don	Mikhail Sholokhov
Androcles and the Lion	George Bernard Shaw
Animal Farm, The	George Orwell
Anna Karenina	Count Leo Tolstoy
Another Life	Derek Walcott
Answer of History	Mohammed Raza Pahlavi
Antony and Cleopatra	William Shakespeare
Ape and Essence	A. Huxley
Apple Cart	George Bernard Shaw
Arabian Nights	Sir Richard Burton
Area of Darkness	V.S. Naipaul
Arms and the Man	George Bernard Shaw
Around the World in Eighty days	Jules Verne
Arrangement, The	Elia Kazan
Arrival and Departure	Arthur Koestler
Arrowsmith	Sinclair Lewis
Arthashastra	Kautilya
As You Like It	William Shakespeare
Ascent of the Everest	Sir John Hunt
Ashtadhyayi	Panini
Asian Drama	Gunnar Myrdal
Asia and Western Dominance	K.M. Panikkar
Atoms of Hope	Mohan Sundara Rajan
August 1914	Alexander Solzhenitsyn
August Coup, The	Mikhail S. Gorbachev
Autumn Leaves	O. Pulla Reddi
Avanti Sundari	Dandi
Babur Nama	Zaheeruddin Mohammed Babur
Babbit	Sinclair Lewis
Back of Methuselah	George Bernard Shaw
Backward Place, A	Ruth P. Jhabwala
Bandicoot Run	Manohar Malgonkar
Bang-i-Dara	Mohammed Iqbal
Bangla Desh The Unfinished Revolution	Lawrence Liftschultz
Banyan Tree, The	Hugh Tinker
Beast and Man	Murry Midgely
Beginning of the Beginning	Acharya Rajneesh
Betrayal of Pearl Harbour	James Rusbridge and Eric Nave
Bend in the Ganges, A	Manohar Malgonkar
Ben Hur	Lewis Wallace
Bermuda Triangle	Charles Berlitz
Berry Patches	Yevgeny Yevtushenko
Best and the Brightest, The	David Halberstan

Book	*Author*
Between the Lines	Kuldip Nayar
Beyond Modernisation, Beyond Self	Sisir Kumar Ghose
Bharat Bharati	Maithili Sharan Gupta
Bharatiya Parampara Ke Mool Swar	Govind Chandra Pande
Big Breach, The	Richard Tomlinson
Big Fisherman, The	Lloyd C. Douglas
Biographia Literaria	Samuel Taylor Coleridge
Bisarjan	Rabindra Nath Tagore
Birth and Death of Sun	George Gamow
Bitter Sweet	Noel Coward
Black Arrow, The	Robert Louis Stevenson
Blind Ambitions	John Dean
Blind Beauty	Boris Pasternak
Blind Men of Hindustan ! Indo-Pak Nuclear War	General K.S. Sundarji
Bliss was it in that Dawn	Minoo Masani
Bloodline	Sidney Sheldon
Blue Bird	Maurice Macterlink
Bone People, The	Kerl Hulme
Born Free	Joy Adamson
Bread, Beauty and Revolution	Khwaja Ahmed Abbas
Breakthrough	Gen. Moshe Dayan
Bride for the Sahib and other Stories, A	Khushwant Singh
Bride's Book of Beauty, The	Mulk Raj Anand
Broken Wings	Sarojini Naidu
Brothers Karamazhov	Fyodor Dostoevsky
Bubble, The	Mulk Raj Anand
Bhudha Charitam	Ashvaghosha
Bunch of Old Letters, A	Jawaharlal Nehru
Butterfield-8	John O' Hara
By Love Possessed	James Cozzens
Caesar and Cleopatra	George Bernard Shaw
Cancer Ward	Alexander Solzhenitsyn
Candida	George Bernard Shaw
Candide	Voltaire
Canterbury Tales	Geoffery Chaucer
Cardinal, The	Henry M. Robinson
Centennial	James Michener
Chandalika	Rabindra Nath Tagore
Chemmeen	Thakazhi Sivasankar Pillai
Cherry Orchard	Anton Chekov
Chesaplake	James A. Michener
Chidambara	Sumitra Nandan Pant
Chikaveera Rajendra	Masti Venkatesh Iyengar
Children of Gebelawi	Naguib Mahfouz
Childe Herolds Pilgrimage	Lord Byron
China Passage, A	J.K. Galbraith

Book	*Author*
China's Watergate	Leo Goodstadt
Chinese Betrayal	B.N. Mullick
Chitra	Rabindra Nath Tagore
Chittirappaval	P.V. Akilandam
Chomas Drum	K. Shivaram Karnath
Chronicle of a Death Foretold	Gabrel Garcia Marquez
Class, The	Eric Segal
Climate of Treason	Andrew Boyle
Comedy of Errors	William Shakespeare
Common Sense	Thomas Paine
Comus	John Milton
Communist Manifesto	Karl Marx
Confessions	J.J. Rousseau
Confessions of a Lover	Mulk Raj Anand
Confessions of an Opium Eater, The	Thomas Dequicey
Confidential Clerk	T.S. Eliot
Conquest of Self	M.K. Gandhi
Conservationist, The	Ms. Nadine Gordimer
Continent of Circle	Nirad C. Choudhury
Coolie	Mulk Raj Anand
Coup, The	John Updike
Count of Monte Cristo	Alexander Dumas
Court Dancer	Rabindra Nath Tagore
Covertly Papers	Joseph Addison
Cresent Moon	Rabindra Nath Tagore
Crescent over Kashmir	Anil Maheshwari
Crime and Punishment	Fyodor Dostoevsky
Crisis into Chaos	E.M.S. Namboodiripad
Crisis in India, The	Ronald Segal
Critique of Pure Reason, A	Immanuel Kant
Crown and the Loincloth, The	Chaman Nahal
Crown of Wild Olive, The	John Ruskin
Cry My Beloved Country	Alan Patan
Culture in the Vanity Bag	Nirad C. Choudhury
Curtain Raisers	K. Natwar Singh
Dangerous Summer, The	Ernest Hemingway
Darkness at Noon	Arthur Keostler
Dark Room, The	R.K. Narayan
Dashkumar Charitam	Dandi
Das Kapital	Karl Marx
Daughter of the East	Benazir Bhutto
David Copperfield	Charles Dickens
Day in Shadow, The	Nayantara Sehgal
Days of His Grace	Eyvind Johnson
Dean's December	Saul Below
Death of a City	Amrita Pritam
Death of a Patriot	R.E. Harrington

Book	Author
Death of a President	William Manchester
Death, The Supreme Friend	Kakasaheb Kalelkar
Debacle	Emile Zola
Decameron	Giovanni Boccaccio
Decline and Fall of the Roman Empire	Edward Gibbon
Decline and Fall of Indira Gandhi	D.R. Mankekar and Kamala Mankekar
Decline of the West	O Spengier
Deewan-i-Ghalib	Mirza Ghalib
Delhi	Khushwant Singh
Democracy Means Bread and Freedom	Piloo Mody
Democracy Redeemed	V.K. Narsimhan
Descent of Man	Charles Darwin
Deserted Village	Oliver Goldsmith
Devdas	Sharat Chandra Chatterjee
Die Blendung	Elias Canetti
Dilemma of our Time	Harold Joseph Laski
Diplomacy in Peace and War	J.N. Kaul
Discovery of India	Jawaharlal Nehru
Distant Drums	Manohar Malgonkar
Distant Neighbours	Kuldip Nayar
Divine Comedy	A. Dante
Divine Life	Swami Sivananda
Doctor's Dilemma	George Bernard Shaw
Dolls's House, A	Ibsen
Don Juan	Lord Byron
Don Quixote	Saavedra Miguel de Cervantes
Double Helix, The	J.D. Watson
Dragon's Teeth	U.B. Sinclair
Dream in Hawaii, A	Bhabani Bhattacharya
Dream of Fair to Middling Women	Samuel Beckett
Dreams Roses and Fire	Eyvind Johnson
Dr. Jekyll and Mr. Hyde	Robert Louis Stevenson
Durgesh Nandini	Bankim Chandra Chatterjee
Dynamics of Social Change	Chandra Shekhar
Earth	Emile Zola
Earth Mother, The	Pupul Jayakar
Economic Planning of India	Ashok Mehta
Economics of the Third World	S.K. Ray
Education of Public Man	Hubert Humphery
Eight Lives	Raj Mohan Gandhi
Elegy Written in a Country Church Yard	Thomas Grey
Emile	J.J. Rousseau
Emma	Jane Austen
End of Era	C.S. Pandit
Ends and Means	Aldous Huxley
Envoy to Nehru	Escott Reid
Essays for Poor to the Rich	John Kenneth Galbraith

Book	Author
Essays of Elia	Charles Lamb
Essays on Gita	Sri Aurobindo Ghosh
Eternal Himalayas	Major H.P.S. Ahluwalia
Eternal India	Indira Gandhi
Executioner's Song	Norman Mailer
Expanding Universe	Arthur Stanley Eddington
Eye of the Storm, The	Patric White
Face to Face	Lasse & Mrs. Lisa Berg
Faces of Everest	Maj. H.P.S. Ahluwalia
Facts are Facts	Khan Abdul Wali Khan
Fall of a Sparrow, The	Salim Ali
Family Reunion	T.S. Eliot
Far From the Madding Crowd	Thomas Hardy
Far Pavilions, The	M.M. Kaye
Faraway Music, The	Svetlana Allilueva
Farewell the Trumpets	James Morris
Farewell to Arms, A	Ernest Hemingway
Farm House	George Orwell
Father and Sons	Ivan Turgenev
Faust	J.W. Von Goethe
Fidelio	L. Beethoven
Fifth Horseman, The	Larry Collins and Dominique Lapierre
Final Days, The	Bob Woodward and Carl Bernstein
Finding a Voice-Asian Women in Britain	Amrit Wilson
Fire Next Time, The	James Balbwin
First Circle	Alexander Solzhenitsyn
Flames form the Ashes	P.D. Tandon
Flounder, The	Gunter Grass
Food Nutrition and Poverty in India	V.K.R.V. Rao
For Whom the Bell Tolls	Ernest Hemingway
Forbidden Sea, The	Tar Ali Baig
Forsyte Saga	John Galsworthy
Forty Nine Days	Amrita Pritam
Freedom At Midnight	Larry Collins and Dominique Lapierre
French Revolution	Thomas Carlyle
Friends and Foes	Sheikh Mujibur Rehman
Friends not Masters	Ayyub Khan
From Here to Eternity	James Jones
From India to America	L. S. Chandrashekhar
From Raj to Rajiv	Mark Tully & Zaheer Masani
Ganadevata	Tara Shanker Bandopadhyay
Gandhi and Stalin	Louis Fisher
Gardener	Rabindra Nath Tagore
Gathering Storm	Winston Churchill
Geeta Govinda	Jaya Dev
Ghasiram Kotwal	Vijay Tendulkar
Gita Rahasya	Bal Gangadhar Tilak

Book	*Author*
Glimpses of World History	Jawaharlal Nehru
Godan	Munshi Prem Chand
Godfather, The	Mario Puzzo
God of Small Things, The	Arundhati Roy
Gold Bat, The	P.G. Wodehouse
Golden Gate	Vikram Seth
Golden Threshold, The	Sarojini Naidu
Gone with the Wind	Margaret Mitchel
Good Earth	Pearl S. Buck
Gora	Rabindra Nath Tagore
Grammar of Politics	Harold Joseph Laski
Grapes of Wrath	John Steinbeck
Great Challenge, The	Louis Fishcer
Great Depression of 1990, The	Ravi Batra
Great Expectations	Charles Dickens
Great Gatsby	F. Scott Fitzgerald
Great Illusion	Norman Angel
Great Tragedy	Z.A. Bhutto
Guide, The	R.K. Narayan
Gulag Archipelago	Alexander Solzhenitsyn
Gul-i-Naghma	Raghupati Sahai (Firaq) Gorakhpuri
Gulistan and Bostan	Sheikh Saadi
Gulliver's Travels	Jonathan Swift
Gurusagaram	O.P. Vijayan
Hamlet	William Shakespeare
Handful of Dust, A	Evelyn Waugh
Harry Potter	J.K. Rowling
Harsha Charita	Ban Bhatt
Heat and Dust	Ruth P. Jhabwala
Heir Apparent	Dr. Karan Singh
Henderson, the Rain King	Saul Below
Henry Esmond	William Thackeray
Hero of our Times	Richard Hough
Heroes and Hero Worship	Thomas Carlyle
Higher than Hope	Fatima Meer
Himalayan Blunder	Brigadier J.P. Dalvi
Hindu Civilization	J.M. Barrier
Hinduism	Nirad C. Choudhury
Hindu View of Life	Dr. S. Radhakrishnan
Hounds of Baskervilles, The	Arthur Conan Doyle
House Divided	Pearl S. Buck
House for Mr. Biswas, A	V.S. Naipaul
Huckieberry Finn	Mark Twain
Human Factor	Graham Greene
Humboldt's Gift, The	Saul Bellow
Humour	Ben Johnson
Hunchback of Notre Dame	Victor Hugo

Book	Author
Hungary Stones	Rabindra Nath Tagore
I Am Not an Island	K.A. Abbas
I Follow the Mahatma	K.M. Munshi
Idiot, The	Fyodor Dostoevsky
Idols	Sunil Gavaskar
Idylls of the King	Alfred Tennyson
If I am Assassinated	Z.A. Bhutto
Illiad	Homer
Importance of Being Earnest	Oscar Wilde
In Afghanistan's Shadow	Salig S. Harrison
In Evil Hour	Gabriel Garcia Marquez
In a Free State	V.S. Naipaul
In Memorium	Alfred Lord Tennyson
In Search of Gandhi	Richard Attenbrough
In Search of Identity	Anwar-al-Sadat
India A Wounded Civilization	V.S. Naipaul
India Changes	Taya Zinkin
India Discovered	John Keay
India Divided	Rajendra Prasad
India from Curzon to Nehru and After	Durga Das
India Remembered	Percival and Margaret Spear
India of Our Dreams	M.V. Kamath
India, The Critical Years	Kuldip Nayar
India Today	Rajni Palme Dutt
India We Left	Humphry Trevelyan
India Wins Freedom	Maulana Abul Kalam Azad
Indian Home Rule	M.K. Gandhi
Indian Muslims	Mohammed Mujeeb
Indian Muslims The Need For a Positive Outlook	Wahiduddin Khan
Indian Philosophy	Dr. S. Radhakrishnan
Indian War of Independence	V.D. Savarkar
India's China War	Neville Maxwell
India's Priceless Heritage	N.A. Palkhivala
India	Magasthenes
Indira's India	S. Nihal Singh
Indira Gandhi's Emergence and Style	Nayantara Sehgal
Inheritance of Loss, The	Kiran Desai
Inner Circle, The	Jonathan Frost
Inside Asia (also, Inside Europe and Inside Africa)	John Gunter
Inside Third Reich	Albert Spencer
Intimacy	Jean Paul Sartre
Invisible Man	H.G. Wells
Iron in the Soul	Jean Paul Sartre
Isabella	John Keats
Islamic Bomb	Stev Weissman and Herbert Krounsney

Book	Author
Island in the Steams	Ernest Hemingway
Is Paris Burning	Larry Collins and Dominique Lapierre
Ivanhoe	Sir Walter Scott
Jane Eyre	Charlotte Bronte
Jazz	Toni Morison
Jean Christopher	Roman Rolland
Jinnah-India-Partition Independence	Jaswant Singh
Jobs for Millions	V.V. Giri
Judgement, The	Kuldip Nayar
Judge's Miscellany, A	M. Hidayatullah
Jullius Caesar	William Shakespeare
Jungle Book	Rudyard Kipling
Justice of Peace Ke Aansu	Janardan Prasad Singh
Kadambari	Bana Bhatt
Kagaz te Kanwas	Amrita Pritam
Kali Aandhi	Kamleshwar
Kamayani	Jai Shanker Prasad
Kamasutra	S.J. Vatsyayan
Kanthapura	Raja Rao
Kapal Kundala	Bankim Chandra Chatterjee
Kashmir-Behind the Vale	M.J. Akbar
Kaya Kalp	Munshi Prem Chand
Kayar	Thakazhi Sivasankara Pillai
Ken Attendant Godot	Samuel Backett
Kenilworth	Sir Walter Scott
Khak-i-Dil	Jan Nissar Akhtar
Kidnapped	Robert Louis Stevenson
Killer Angels	Michael Shaara
Kim	Rudyard Kipling
King of Dark Chamber	Rabindra Nath Tagore
King Lear	William Shakespeare
Kipps	H. G. Wells
Kissinger Years, The	T.N. Kaul
Kitni Navon Main Kitni Bar	S.H. Vatsyayan
Kore Kagaz	Amrita Pritam
Kublai Khan	Samuel Taylor Coleridge
Kulliyat-i-Iqbal	M. Iqbal
Kumar Sambhava	Kalidas
L'Allegro	John Milton
La Divine Comedia	A. Dante
Lady Chatterley's Lover	D.H. Lawrence
Lady of the Lake	Sir Walter Scott
Lajja	Ms. Taslima Nasreen
Last Days of Pompeii	Edward George Lytton
Last Maharaja, The	Jean Louis Nou and Jacques Pouchepadass
Last Thing	C.P. Snow
Laws Versus Justice	V.R. Krishna Iyer

Book	Author
Lead Kindly Light	Vincent Shean
Le Contract Social (The Social Contract)	J.J. Rousseau
Leaders	Richard Nixon
Leaves of Grass	Walt Whiteman
Letters from the Field	Margaret Mead
Les Miserables	Victor Hugo
Leviathan	Thomas Hobbes
Life Divine	Aurbindo Ghosh
Life of Dr. Johnson	James Boswell
Light that Failed	Rudyard Kipling
Lines of Fate	Marek Kharitonov
Lipika	Rabindra Nath Tagore
Living Room	Graham Greene
Lolita	V. Nabokov
Long Walk to Freedom	Nelson Mandela
Look Back in Anger	John Osborne
Lord of the Files	William Golding
Lost Child	Mulk Raj Anand
Lost Honour	John Dena
Lotus Eaters	A Tennyson
Love Story	Eric Segal
Lycidas	John Milton
Macbeth	William Shakespeare
Magic Mountain	Maharishi Ved Vyas
Main Street	Sinclair Lewis
Major Barbara	George Bernard Shaw
Making of a Midsummer Night's Dream, The	David Selbourne
Malgudi Days	R.K. Narayan
Malti Madhav	Bhavabhuti
Malavikagnimitra	Kalidas
Man and Superman	George Bernard Shaw
Man Eaters of Kumaon	Jim Corbett
Man of Destiny	George Bernard Shaw
Mankind and Mother Earth	Arnold Toynbee
Man, The Unknown	Lewis Carroll
Man for All Seasons, A	Robert Bolt
Man for Moscow	G. Wynne
Many Worlds	K.P.S. Menon
Marriage and Morals	Bertrand Russel
Masters, The	C.P. Snow
Mati Matal	Gopinath Mohanty
Maurice	E.M. Forster
Mayor of Casterbridge	Thomas Hardy
Meghdoot	Kalidas
Mein Kampf	Adolf Hitler
Memories of Hope	Charles de Gaulle
Memories of Malgudi	R.K. Narayan

Book	Author
Men who Kept the Secrets	Thomas Powers
Men who Killed Gandhi, The	Manohar Malgonkar
Merchant of Venice	William Shakespeare
Middle Ground, The	Margaret Drabble
Middle March	George Eliot
Midnight's Children	Salman Rushdie
Midsummer Night's Dream, A	William Shakespeare
Mill on the Floss	George Eliot
Miser, The	Moliere
Mistaken Identify	Nayantara Sehgal
Moby Dick	Hermann Melville
Modern Painters	John Ruskin
Moon and Six Pence	W. Somerset Maugham
Moonlight Sonata	L Beethoven
Mookhajiva Kanasugalu	K. Shivram Karnath
Mother	Maxim Gorky
Mother India	Katherine Mayo
Mountbatten and Independent India	Larry Collins & Dominique Lapierre
Mountbatten and The Partition of India	Larry Collins & Dominique Lapierre
Mrinalini	Bankim Chandra Chatterjee
Mrs. Gandhi's Second Reign	Arun Shourie
Much Ado About Nothing	William Shakespeare
Mudra Rakshasa	Vishakhadatta
Murder in the Cathedral	V.S. Eliot
Muslim Dilemma in India	M. K. A. Baig
My Days	R.K. Narayana
My Early Life	M.K. Gandhi
My Experiments with Truth	M.K. Gandhi
My India	S. Nihal Singh
My Life and Times	V.V. Giri
My Music, My Love	Ravi Shankar
My Own Boswell	M. Hidayatullah
My Presidential Years	R.Venkata Raman
My Struggles	E.K. Nayanar
My Truth	Indira Gandhi
Mysterious Universe	James Jens
Naked Came the Stranger	Penelope Ashe
Naked Face, The	Sidney Sheldon
Naked Triangle, The	Balwant Gargi
Naku Thanthi	D.R. Bendre
Nana	Emile Zola
Nature of Mass Poverty, The	J.K. Galbraith
Natya Shastra	Bharat Muni
Neela Chand	Shiv Prasad Singh
Nehru Family and Sikhs	Harbans Singh
Netaji Dead or Alive	Samar Guha
New Dimensions of India's Foreign Policy	Atal Behari Vajpayee

Book	*Author*
Nine Days' Wonder	John Mansfield
Nineteen Eighty-four	George Orwell
1999-Victory Without War	Richard Nixon
Nisheeth	Uma Shanker Joshi
Niti-Sataka	Bharatrihari
Nixon in White House	Seymour M. Hersh
Non-Violence in Peace and War	M.K. Gandhi
Nuclear India	G.G. Mirchandani and P.K.S. Namboodari
O'Jerusalem	Larry Collins and Dominique Lapierre
Occasion for Loving	Nadine Gordimer
Oddakkuzal	G. Shankara Kurup
Odyssey	Homer
Of Human Bondage	W. Somerset Maugham
Old Man and the Sea	Ernest Hemingway
Oliver Twist	Charles Dickens
Omeros	Derek Walcott
One Day on the Life of Ivan Denisovich	Alexander Solzhenitsyn
One Hundred Years of Solitude	Gabriel Marquez
One World	Wendell Wilkie
One World to Share	Sridath Ramphal
Origin of Species	Charles Darwin
Oru Desattinte Katha	S.K. Pottekkatt
Oscar and Lucinda	Peter Carey
Othello	William Shakespeare
Other Side of Midnight, The	Sidney Sheldon
Our Films, Their Films	Satyajit Ray
Paddy Clarke Ha Ha Ha	Roddy Doyle
Pakistan Papers	Mani Shankar Aiyer
Painted Veil	W. Somerset Maugham
Painter of Signs	R.K. Narayan
Pair of Blue Eyes, A	Thomas Hardy
Pakistan Crisis	David Loshak
Pakistan Cut to Size	D.R. Mankekar
Pakistan, The Gathering Storm	Benazir Bhutto
Panchatantra	Vishnu Sharma
Paradise Lost	John Milton
Paradise Regained	John Milton
Passage to England, A	Nirad C. Choudhury
Passage to India, A	E.M. Forster
Past and Present	Thomas Carlyle
Pather Panchali	Bibhuti Bhushan Bandhopadhayaya
Patriot, The	Pearl S. Buck
Personal Adventure, A	Theodore H. White
Peter Pan	J. M. Berrie
Pickwick Papers	Charles Dickens
Pilgrim's Progress	John Bunyan
Pinjar	Amrita Pritam

Book	Author
Plans for Departure	Nayantara Sehgal
Portrait of India	Ved Mehta
Post Office	Rabindra Nath Tagore
Power and Glory	Graham Greene
Power That Be	David Halberstan
Pratham Pratishruti	Ashapurna Devi
Prelude	William Wordsworth
Prem Pachisi	Munshi Prem Chand
Premonitions	P.N. Haksar
Price of Power	Kissinger
Pride and Prejudice	Jane Austen
Prince	Nicolo Machiaveli
Principla	Issac Newton
Prison and Chocolate Cake	Nayantara Sehgal
Prison Diary	Jaya Prakash Narayan
Prisoner of Zenda	Anthony Hope
Prisoner's Scrapbook, A	L.K. Advani
Prithviraj Raso	Chanda Bardai
Professor, The	Charlotte Bronte
Promises to Keep	Chester Bowels
Pygmalion	George Bernard Shaw
Pyramids of Sacrifice	Peter L. Berger
Radharani	Bankim Chandra Chatterjee
Rage of Angels	Sidney Sheldon
Raghuvamsha	Kalidas
Ragtime	E.L. Doctorow
Rainbow, The	Pearl S. Buck
Rains Came	Louis Bromefield
Rajtarangini	Kalhana
Ram Charita Manas	Tulsidas
Ramayana	Maharishi Valmiki
Rangbhoomi	Munshi Prem Chand
Rang-i-Shairi	Raghupati Sahai (Firaq Gorakhpuri)
Rape of Bangladesh	Anthony Mascarenhas
Rape of the Lock	Alexander Pope
Ratnavali	Harsh Vardhan
Razor's Edge	W. Somerset Maugham
Rebel, The	Albert Camus
Rebirth	Leonid Brezhnev
Red and Black, The	Stendhal
Red Badge of Courage	Stephan Crane
Red Star over China	Edgar Snow
Reflections of the French Revolution	Edmund Burke
Reminiscences of the Nehru Age	M.O. Mathai
Reprieve	Jean Paul Sartre
Republic	Plato
Resurrection	Count Leo Tolstoy
Return of the Native, The	Thomas Hardy
Returning to the Source	Acharya Shree Rajneesh

Book	*Author*
Revenue Stamps, The	Amrita Pritam
Rich Like Us	Nayantara Sehgal
Riding the Storm	Harold MacMillan
Rights of Man	Thomas Paine
Rise and Fall of the Great Powers	Paul Kennedy
Ritu Samhara	Kalidas
Rivals, The	R.B. Shridan
Road to Folly	Leslie Ford
Robe, The	Lloyd C. Douglas
Robinson Crusoe	Daniel Defoe
Romeo and Julliet	William Shakespeare
Rubaiyat	Omar Khayyam
Rubaiyat-i-Omar Khayyam	Edward Fitzgerald
Sadar-i-Riyasat	Karan Singh
Saket	Maithili Sharan Gupta
Sakha Ram Binder	Vijay Tendulkar
Samler's Planet	Saul Bellow
Sands of Time	Sidney Sheldon
Satanic Verses	Salman Rushdie
Sanctuary	William Faulkner
Satyartha Prakash	Swami Dayanand
Savitri	Sri Aurobindo Ghosh
Scarlet Letter	Nathaniel Hawthorne
Scarlet Pimpernal	Baroness Orczy
Sceptred Flute	Sarojini Naidu
Scholar Extraordinary	Nirad C. Choudhury
School for Scandal, The	R.B. Sheridan
Scope of Happiness, The	Vijayalakshmi Pandit
Search for Home, A	Sasthi Brata
Sense and Sensibility	Jane Austen
Sense of Time, A	H.S. Vatsyayan
Sesame and Lilies	John Ruskin
Seven Lamps of Architecture	John Ruskin
Seven Summers	Mulk Raj Anand
Shadow from Ladakh	Bhabani Bhattacharya
Shahnama	Firdausi
Shakuntala	Kalidas
Shalimar	Manohar Malgonkar
Shall We Tell the President	Jeffrey Archer
Shape of Things to Come	H.G Wells
Shame	Salman Rushdie
She Stoops to Conquer	Oliver Goldsmith
Ship of Fools	Katherine Anne Porter
Shivaji, The Great Patriot	Lala Lajpat Rai
Shoes of the Fisherman, The	Morris West
Silas Marner	George Eliot
Six Characters in Search of an Author	Lugi Pirandello
Slave, The	Issac Bashevis Singer
Small Land	Leonid Brezhnev

Book	*Author*
Sohrab and Rustam	Matthew Arnold
Song of India, The	Sarojini Naidu
Sonnets, The	William Shakespeare
Sons and Lovers	D.H. Lawrence
Sound and the Fury, The	William Faulkner
Soz-i-Watan	Munshi Prem Chand
Spaniard in the Works, A	John Lennon
Spirit of the Age	William Hazlitt
Spy Catcher	Peter Wright
St. John	George Bernard Shaw
Story of My Life	Moshe Dayan
Story of Real Man	Nikolayev Polevol
Strangers and Brothers Omnibus	C.P. Snow
Sunny Days	Sunil Gavaskar
Study of History, A	Arnold Toynbee
Swami and Friends	R.K. Narayan
Swapnavasvadatta	Bhasa
Sword and the Sickle	Mulk Raj Anand
Tale of a Tub, A	Jonathan Swift
Tale of Two Cities, A	Charles Dickens
Tales from Shakespeare	Charles Lamb
Talisman	Sir Walter Scott
Tamas	Bhisham Sahni
Tarzan of the Apes	Edger Rice Burroughs
Tears of D'Urberviles	Thoms Huardy
Tempest, The	William Shakespeare
Thank You, Jeeves	P.G. Wodehouse
The Garden of Life	Naveen Patnaik
The White Tiger	Arvind Adiga
Thieves in the Night	Arthur Koestler
Thirteenth Sun	Amrita Pritam
Three Musketeers	Alexander Dumas
Thorn Birds	Colleen McCollough
Thousand Days, A	Arthur M. Shlesinger
Through the Indian Looking Glass	David Selbourne
Through the Looking Glass	Lewis Carroll
Times Machine	H.G. Wells
Time to be Happy	Nayantara Sehgal
To Live or not to Live	Nirad C. Choudhury
Tom Jones	Henry Fielding
Train to Pakistan	Khushwant Singh
Traveller, The	Olive Goldsmith
Treasure Island	Robert Louis Stevenson
Trial, The	Franz Kafka
Trinity	Leon Uris
Triumph	John Kenneth Galbraith
Tropic of Cancer	Henry Miller
Tryst with Destiny	L. S. Gopalan
Twelfth Night	William Shakespeare

Book	Author
Twenty Years After	Alexander Dumas
Two Leaves and a Bud	Mulk Raj Anand
Two Women	Alberto Moravia
Ulysses	James Joyce
Uncle Tom's Cabin	H.B. Stowe
Unhappy India	Lala Lajpat Rai
Universe Around Us	James Jeans
Unto this Last	John Ruskin
Untold Story	General B.M. Kaul
Upturned Soil, The	Mikhail Sholokhov
Urvashi	Ramdhari Singh Dinkar
Utopia	Thomas Moore
Uttar Ramcharita	Bhava Bhuti
Valley of Dolls	Jacqueline Susann
Vanity Fair	William Thackeray
Vendor of Sweets, The	R.K. Narayan
Vicar of Wakefield	Oliver Goldsmith
Victim, The	Saul Bellow
View From Delhi, A	Chester Bowles
View From the UN	U. Thant
Village by the Sea, A	Anita Desai
Village, The	Mulk Raj Anand
Vinay Patrika	Tulsidas
Virangana	Maithili Sharan Gupta
Virginians, The	William Thackeray
Vish Vriksha	Bankim Chandra Chatterjee
Voice of Conscience	V.V. Giri
Voice of Freedom , A	Nayantara Sehgal
Voice of the Voiceless	Ruth Harring
Waiting for Godot	Thomas Becket
Wake up India	Annie Besant
Walls of Glass, The	K.A. Abbas
War and Peace	Count Leo Tolstoy
War of the Worlds, The	H.G. Wells
Waste Land	T.S. Eliot
Way to all Flesh	Samuel Butler
Way of the World, The	William Congreve
Wealth of Nations	Adam Smith
Week with Gandhi, A	Louis Fisher
We Indians	Khushwant Singh
We, the People	N.A. Palkivala
Where the Grass is Greener	David M. Smith
White House Years	Henry Kissinger
Wings of Fire	A.P.J. Abdul Kalam
Willhelm Meister	J.W. Von Goethe
Without Fear or Favour	Neelam Sanjiva Reddy
Witness to an Era	Frank Moraes
Woman's Life, A	Guy de Maupassant
Wonder That Was India, The	A.L. Basham

Book	Author
Worthy it is	Odysseus Elytis
Wreck , The	Rabindra Nath Tagore
Wuthering Heights	Emile Bronte
Yajnaseni	Pratibha Roy
Yama	Mahadevi Verma
Yashodhara	Maithili Sharan Gupta
Yayati	V.S. Khandekar
Year of the Upheaval	Henry Kissinger
Year of the Vulture, The	Amita Malik
Yesterday and Today	K.P.S. Menon
Zhivago, Dr.	Boris Pasternak
Zulfi, My Friend	Piloo Mody

FAMOUS AUTHORS IN DIFFERENT LANGUAGES

English	William Shakespeare, John Milton, Chaucer, Spenser, Lord Byron, P.B. Shelley, John Keats, Francis Bacon, T.S. Eliot, Cecil Dlay Lewis, Alduous Huxley, W.B. Yeats Bunyan, Dryden, Dr. Johnson, Alexander Pope, Robert Browning, Charles Lamb, Charles Dickens, Thomas Hardy, W.M. Thackeray, George Eliot, Alfred Tennyson, Robert Bridges, George Bernard Shaw, D.H. Lawrence, Oliver Goldsmith, Sheridan, Walter Scott, William Wordsworth, S.T. Coleridge, Henry Fielding, Somerset Maugham, J.K. Rowling.
French	Imile Zola, Gustave Flaubert, Moliere, Proudhon, Jean Paul Sartre, Le Sage, Victor Hugo, Alexander Dumas, Balzac.
German	Goethe, Hoffman, Lessing, Schelling, Schaupenhuer, Heinrich Heine, Guenter Grass
Russian	Tolstoy, Mikhail Solokhov, Turgenev, Dostoevsky, Maxim Gorky, Techov, Alexander Salzhenitsyn, Boris Pasternak
Greek	Homer, Aesop, Aristophanes, Euripedes, Herodotus, Hesoid, Theocritus, Xenophon, Aeschylus, Sophocles
Latin	Dante, Boccacio, Terence, Virgil, Ovid, Horace, Seneca
Norwegian	John Bojer, Ibsen
Persian	Ghalib, Umar Khyyam, Abul Fazal, Amir Khusro, Faiz, Firdausi, Mohd. Iqbal Saddi
Spanish	Juan Valera, Lope De Vega, Cervantes

FAMOUS CHARACTERS AND THEIR CREATORS

Character	Creator	Character	Creator
Adam	Milton	Bassomio	William Shakespeare
Alice	Lewis Carroll	Bertie Wooster	P.G. Wodehouse
Ancient Mariner	Coleridge	Brutus	William Shakespeare
Ariel	William Shakespeare	Beatrix	Thackery
Antonio	William Shakespeare	Beatrice	William Shakespeare
Anna Karenina	Leo Tolstoy	Christian	John Bunyan

Character	Creator	Character	Creator
Cordelia	William Shakespeare	King Arthur	Tennyson
Cleopatra	William Shakespeare	Kim	Rudyard Kipling
Clare	Thomas Hardy	Long John Silver	R.L. Stevenson
Claudius	William Shakespeare	Macbeth	William Shakespeare
David Copperfield	Charles Dickens	Micawber	Charles Dickens
Dushyanta	Kalidas	Miranda	William Shakespeare
Don Quixote	Cervantes	Mephistopheles	J.W. Von Goethe
Eliza Doolittle	George Bernard Shaw	Mellors	D.H. Lawrence
Estella	Charles Dickens	Malaprop	Sheridian
Faust	J.W. Von Goethe	Oliver Twist	Charles Dickens
Gora	Rabindranath Tagore	Peggotty	Charles Dickens
Hamlet	William Shakespeare	Priyangbada	Kalidas
Harry Potter	J.K. Rowling	Portia	William Shakespeare
Hyde	R.L. Stevenson	Pip	Charles Dickens
Hercule Poirot	Agatha Christie	Perry Mason	Erle Stanley Gardner
Hawkins	R.L. Stevenson	Pickwick	Charles Dickens
Hector	Homer	Rip Van Winkle	Washington Irving
Ivanhoe	Sir Walter Scott	Sam Weller	Charles Dickens
Iago	William Shakespeare	Surpanakha	Valmiki
James Bond	Ian Fleming	Shylock	William Shakespeare
Juliet	William Shakespeare	Sherlock Halmes	Arthur Conan Doyle
Jessica	William Shakespeare	Shakuntala	Kalidas
Jean Valjin	Victor Hugo	Sancho Panza	Cervantes Saavedra
Jacques	William Shakespeare	Tess	Thomas Hardy
Jeeves	P.G. Wodehouse	Watson	Arthur Conan Doyle
		Zhivago	Boris Pasternak

GREAT POETS

Language	Poet
Hindi	Surdas, Tulsidas, Keshav
Sanskrit	Valmiki, Vedvyas, Kalidas
Bengali	Rabindra Nath Tagore
Urdu	Mirza Ghalib
Persian	Sheikh Saadi
Latin	Virgil
Greek	Homer
English	Shakespeare
German	Goethe
Italian	Dante
French	Sully Proudhone
Punjabi	Waris Shah

GREAT INDIAN AUTHORS AND POETS IN ENGLISH

Kamala Das; Manohar Malgonkar; R.K. Narayan; Raja Rao; Mulk Raj Anand; Bhabani Bhatacharya; Sasthi Brata; Arun Joshi; Chaman Nahal; K.A. Abbas; Anita Desai; R. Prawer Jhabwala; Kamla Markandaya; Khushwant Singh; Manoj Dass.

WELL KNOWN QUOTATIONS

1. A thing of beauty is a joy for ever; Its loveliness increases; It will never pass into nothingness. *— Keats: Endymion*
2. A little knowledge is a dangerous thing *— Pope*

3. Beauty is truth, truth beauty that is all. Ye know on earth, all all ye need to know
— *Keats: Ode on a Grecian urn*

4. All the world is a stage and all the man and women merely players
— *Shakespeare: As you like it*

5. Some books are to be tested, others to be swallowed and some few to be chewed and digested — *Bacon*

6. Better to reign in hell than serve in heaven
— *Milton: Paradise lost*

7. The child is father of the man
— *Wordsworth: My heart leaps up*

8. A single step for man — a giant leap for mankind — *Neil Armstrong*

9. Dilli Chalo— *Netaji Subhash Chandra Bose*

10. To be or not to be — that is the question.
— *Shakespeare: Hamlet*

11. Only free men negotiate. I shall never negotiate while I am still a prisoner
— *Nelson Mandela*

12. Truth and non-violence are my God
— *Mahatma Gandhi*

13. Let a hundred flowers bloom and let a thousand schools of thought contend
— *Mao Tse-tung*

14. Jai Jawan, Jai Kisan— *Lal Bahadur Shastri*

15. Eureka! Eureka! — *Archimedes*

16. Some are born great, some achieve greatness and some have greatness thrust upon them
— *Shakespeare*

17. Where wealth accumulates, men decay
— *Goldsmith*

18. Power tends to corrupt and absolute power corrupts absolutely — *Lord Acton*

19. Man is by nature a political animal
— *Aristotle*

20. I have nothing to offer but blood, toil, tears and sweat — *Winston Churchill*

21. I came, I saw, I conquered — *Julius Ceaser*

22. For fools rush in where angels fear to tread
— *Pope*

23. Generations to come, it may, will scarce believe that such a one as this ever in flesh and blood walked upon this earth — *Einstein*

24. Government of the people, by the people, for the people — *Lincoln*

25. East is east and west is west and never the twain shall meet — *Kipling*

26. Swaraj is my birth right
— *Bal Gangadhar Tilak*

27. Cowards die many times before their death: The valiant never taste of death but once
— *Shakespeare: Julius Ceaser*

28. Where ignorance is bliss, It is folly to be wise
— *Grey*

29. I know nothing except the fact of my ignorance — *Socrates*

30. We are such stuff as dreams are made of and our little life is rounded with a sleep
— *Shakespeare: The Tempest*

31. What's in a name? That which we call a rose By any other name would smell as sweet
— *Shakespeare: Merchant of Venice*

32. Patriotism is the best refuge of a scoundrel
— *Samuel Johnson*

33. Reading maketh a full man; conference a ready man; and writing an exact man
— *Francis Bacon*

34. It is excellent to love a giant's strength but it is tyrannous to use it like a giant
— *Shakespeare: Measure to Measure*

35. Water, water everywhere
Not any drop to drink
— *S.T. Coleridge: The Ancient Mainer*

36. It is strange but true, for truth is always strange
— *Byron: Don Juan*

37. Virtue is its own reward
— *Cicero: De Fintibus*

38. Frailty, thy name is woman
— *Shakespeare: Hamlet*

39. We don't fear to negotiate, but we do not negotiate out of fear — *J.F. Kennedy*

40. Give us good mothers and I shall give you good nation — *Napoleon*

41. The woods are lovely, dark and deep
But I have promises to keep
And miles to go before I sleep
— *Robert Frost*

42. We have made a tryst with destiny — *Pt. Nehru*

43. Eli, Eli, Lamma Sabcathani (My God, my God, why last thou forsaken me) — *Jesus Christ at the Cross*

44. If winter comes can spring be for behind — *Shelley*

45. Man does not live by bread alone — *Bible*

46. Nothing is good or bad, thinking makes it so — *Shakespeare: Hamlet*

47. Garibi hatao — *Indira Gandhi*

48. Aram haram hai — *Jawaharlal Nehru*

49. Quit India — *Mahatma Gandhi*

50. Jai Jawan, Jai Kisan, Jai Vigyan — *Atal Behari Vajpayee*

MULTIPLE TYPE QUESTIONS

1. Who are the authors of following works?
A. *Hidden Love*
B. *My Book of Human Rights*
C. *Devil May Care*
D. *A Prisoner of Birth*

2. Who was the first English writer to win Nobel Prize for Literature?

3. Whose autobiography is titled *Freedom in Exile*?

4. Who wrote *The Dream of the Red Chamber,* China's greatest novel?

5. Name the author of following Books—
A. *Reconciliation, Islam, Democracy and the West;*
B. *My Country: My Life* (Autobiography);
C. *Good-bye Shahzadi: A Political Biography of Benazir Bhutto.*

6. Which Indian freedom-fighter and staunch nationalist's work is *India Wins Freedom*?

7. Who has written the Tales Of The Future?

8. Which American historian wrote the 10-volume *History of the United States*?

9. *Songs of Innocence* is the work of which English poet, philosopher and artist?

10. Who is the author of *'The Enchantress of Florence'*?

11. Name the sister of forceful novelist Charlotte Bronte who wrote *Wuthering Heights.*

12. Which Libyan leader and military dictator wrote *The Green Book*?

13. Which former British Prime Minister's autobiography is titled *Full circle*?

14. Which is the longest biography in publishing history?

15. Who is the author of best sold series of Harry Potter?

16. What is the pen name of K.K. Nair, who wrote a 10 volume *History of Literature*?

17. Who is the author of *'The Kalam Effect – My Years with the President'*?

18. Which is the longest single-volume novel of the 20th century?

19. Which Pakistani Prime Minister's autobiography is titled *Daughter of the East?*

20. Name the Russian-American novelist, poet, and an authority on butterflies, whose *Lolita* is world famous.

21. Which Indian diplomat and author's work is *The Flying Troika*?

22. Name the Indian author and journalist, settled in New York, who became blind at the age of 3, and is a writer for *New Yorker.*

23. Who is credited to have authored the first modern Indian novel in English, *Rajmohan's Wife*?
24. Which British Prime Minister (1951-55), won Nobel Prize for literature?
25. Name the Indian writer and social critic, whose work includes *Autobiography of an Unknown Indian*.
26. Which English satirist's work is *Gulliver's Travels?*
27. Which India-born British writer's controversial book *The Satanic Verses* made Iran's spiritual leader Ayatollah Khomeini sentence him to death?
28. Which French novelist and dramatist's works include *Jean-Christophe* (a ten-volume novel), biographies of Mahatma Gandhi and Vivekananda?
29. Which Indian president authored the *Hindu View of Life?*
30. Which Hindi writer's real name was Dhanpat Rai?
31. Which Greek Philosopher and educator's work, *Dialogues,* includes the *Republic,* the longest and one of the most celebrated works?
32. What do you call the art of compiling dictionaries?
33. What was the pseudonym of Lewis Carroll?
34. Give the title of the book Jim Corbett wrote on animals.
35. Who is called the Father of English poetry?
36. What is the term for 'the fear of books'?
37. Which former Indian Prime Minister's autobiography is titled *The Insider*?
38. What is the title of famous Musician Pt. Ravi Shankar's autobiography?
39. A. Which book is considered China's greatest novel?
    B. Who wrote it?
40. A. Who wrote *Mahatma Gandhi and his Apostles*?
    B. What was the title of the book on Mahatma Gandhi by Romain Rolland?
41. Name the German poet who wrote a poem appreciating Kalidasa's *Shakuntala*.
42. Who created the character 'Tarzon'?
43. In Arthur Conan Doyle's novels, who narrates the Sherlock Holmes stories?
44. Which English novelist and playwright wrote detective thrillers including *The Four Just Men* and *The Ringer*?
45. This 19th century Irish author and dramatist authored *An Ideal Husband*. Who was he?
46. Who wrote the following books:
    A. Confessions
    B. Confessions of a Lover
    C. Confessions of an English Opium Eater
47. Who wrote the following two books :
    A. *A Passage to England*
    B. *A Passage to India*
48. Which famous character, created by Jonathan Swift, found himself lying on the island of Laputa?
49. Name the British jounalist and author of best-sellers like *Day of the jackal, The Odessa File* and *The Dogs of War*.
50. Which German philosopher wrote *Critique of Pure Reason*?
51. Name the Hungarian author of *Darkness at Noon*.
52. Name the ghost who narrates the stories to king Vikramaditya.
53. Who wrote the famous sea-story *The Cruel Sea*?
54. Which country is the setting for the famous story of *Alibaba and the Forty Thieves*?
55. Name the authors of the following books:
    A. *Making Peace with Partition*
    B. *The Grapes of Wrath*
56. Who wrote the book *Pather Panchali*?
57. Which staunch socialist leader of India wrote *Prison Diary*?
58. Who wrote *Small is Beautiful: A study of Economics as if people Mattered*?
59. Who is considered the Father of comedy?
60. Who wrote the book *Somnium*, regarded by

some people as the first science fiction to be written?

61. Who wrote the book *The Great Indian Novel*?

62. Who wrote the famous sea-story *The Rover*?

63. Dr. Samuel Johnson's biography was written by ....

64. Name the Sanskrit writer who wrote the famous *Kamasutra*.

65. Which English author is known for his works like *The Time Machine, Kipps* and *The Outline of History*?

66. Which English writer developed the stream-of-consciousness technique and is known for works like *To the Lighthouse, Mrs. Dalloway* and *Orlando*?

67. Which Indian authored *Bread, Beauty and Revolution*?

68. A business tycoon of world fame, authored *Business @ the Speed of Thought*. Name him.

69. Who wrote the following books:
A. *Conquest of Self*
B. *Devdas*

70. Give the names of the authors of following books:
A. *The Book of Negroes*
B. *The God of Small Things*
C. *Hungary Stones*
D. *The Water Babies*

71. Name the British historian who authored the adage "power tends to corrupt and absolute power corrupts absolutely".

72. Which Indian Sanskrit scholar and poet wrote *Kadambari* and *Harsha Charita*?

73. Which Italian author and humanist, also called the Father of the Novel, wrote *Life of Dante*?

74. Who said it— "All the world is a stage And all the man and women merely players"?

75. Name the French educationist, who as a (blind) teacher of the blind, devised the touch system of reading and writing for blind.
(**Clue:** She died in the year 2000.)

76. Name the authentic book on statecraft by Chanakya (Kautilya) (4th century B.C.).

77. Which English poet wrote *The Canterbury Tales*?

78. Who wrote the following books:
A. Secrets of the World's Inspirational Women (Westland);
B. Gandhi : A Political and Spiritual Life
C. *Brushes with History : Autobiography of Dr. K.K. Birla*

79. Which football player's autobiography, released in 2007, is titled 'Moments'?

80. Along which famous road is Rudyard Kipling's novel *Kim* set?

81. In *Alice in Wonderland,* a fictional work of Lewis Caroll, to which animal does Alice first speak in French?

82. In which book of the Old Testament were the Ten Commandments first listed?

83. Name the musical maestro whose work is *'The Secret of My Life'*.

84. Name the author of the following works.
A. My Truth B. India Divided

85. Name the Indian aristocrat whose work is 'India– *From Midnight to the Mellenium*'.

86. Who is the author of *'The Post American World'*?

87. Name the Indian-born American who authored the prize winner book 'The Namesake'?

88. Who is the author of the prize winner book 'The White Tiger'?

ANSWERS

1. A. Angshumita Deka.
B. Jaya-shree Gupta.
C. Sebastian Faulks.
D. Jeffrey Archer.

2. Rudyard Kipling, in 1907.

3. Dalai Lama.

4. Cao Chan (he wrote 80 of the 120 chapters). Following his death in 1763, Kao Eh finished it.

5. A. Mrs. Benazir Bhutto;
B. Lal Krishna Advani;
C. Shyam Bhatia.

6. Abul Kalam Azad (1888-1958).

7. Jayant Narlikar.

8. George Bancroft (1800-1891).

9. William Blake (1757-1827).

10. Salman Rushdie.

11. Emily Bronte (1818-48).

12. Col. Muammar al Gaddafi (1924-2011). (He took power in a coup in 1969 and became President in 1977).

13. Sir Anthony Eden.

14. The ongoing biography of Sir Winston Churchill, coauthored by his son Randolph and the historian Martin Gilbert (both UK).

15. J.K. Rowling.

16. Krishna Chaitanya.

17. P.M. Nair.

18. *A Suitable Boy* (p. 1349) by Vikram Seth.

19. Benazir Bhutto.

20. Vladimir Nabokov (1899-1977).

21. Kumara Padmanabha Shivashankar Menon (1898-1982).

22. Ved Mehta (b. 1934).

23. Bankim Chandra Chattopadhyaya (1834-94). He is often called the 'Father of the Indian novel'.

24. Sir Winston Churchill (1874-1965).

25. Nirad C. Chaudhary (1897-1999).

26. Jonathan Swift (1667-1745).

27. Salman Rushdie (b. 1946).

28. Romain Rolland (1866-1944).

29. Dr. Sarvepalli Radhakrishnan (1888-1975).

30. Munshi Premchand (1880-1936).

31. Plato (427-347 B.C.). He was a pupil of legendary Socrates and teacher of Aristotle.

32. Lexicography.

33. Charles Lutwidge Dodgson.

34. *Man-eaters of Kumaon*.

35. Geoffery Chaucer.

36. Bibliophobia.

37. P.V. Narasimha Rao.

38. *My Music and My Life*.

39. A. *The Dream of the Red Chamber*.
B. Cao Chan wrote 80 of the 120 chapters of the book. Following his death in 1763, Kao Eh finished it.

40. A. Ved Mehta.
B. *Mahatma Gandhi*.

41. J.W. Von Goethe.

42. Edgar Rice Burroughs.

43. Dr. Watson.

44. Edgar Wallace (1875-1932).

45. Oscar Wilde (1854-1900).

46. A. J.J. Rousseau.
B. Mulk Raj Anand.
C. Thomas De Quincey.

47. A. Nirad C. Choudhuri.
B. E.M. Forster.

48. Gulliver.

49. Fredrick Forsyth (b.1939).

50. Immanuel Kant (1724-1804).

51. Arthur Koestler (1905-83).

52. Betaal.

53. Nicholas Monsarrat.

54. Persia.

55. A. Radha Kumar.
B. John Steinbeck.

56. Bibhuti Bhushan.

57. Jayaprakash Narayan.

58. Ernst Schumacher.

59. Aristophanes.

60. Johannes Kepler.

61. Shashi Tharoor.

62. Joseph Conrad.

63. James Boswell.

64. Vatsyayana (5th century A.D.).

65. Herbert George Wells (1866-1946).

66. Virginia Woolf (1882-1941).

67. Khwaja Ahmad Abbas.

68. Bill Gates.

69. A. Mahatma Gandhi.
B. Sarat Chandra.

70. A. Lawrence Hill.
B. Arundhati Roy.
C. Rabindranath Tagore.
D. Charles Kingsley.

71. John Acton (1834-1902).

72. Banabhatta (7th Century).

73. Giovanni Boccaccio.

74. Shakespeare.

75. Louis Braille (1809-52).

76. *Artha Shastra.*

77. Geoffrey Chaucer.

78. A. Zerbanoo Gifford.
B. Kathryn Tidrick.
C. Sonia Gandhi.

79. Christiano Ronaldo.

80. Grand Trunk Road.

81. The Mouse.

82. Exodus.

83. Zubin Mehta.

84. A. Smt. Indira Gandhi.
B. Dr. Rajendra Prasad.

85. Shashi Tharoor.

86. Farid Zakaria.

87. Jhumpa Lahiri.

88. Arvind Adiga.

5

Glossary of Literary Terms

ABRIDGED EDITION: Condensed or shortened version of a work.

ABSENCE: It is a modern term which is used to explain a work of art on the basis of aspects which are absent rather than those which are manifestly present in the work.

ACRONYM:

1. A word formed from the initial letters of other words, *e.g.*
   NOIDA for New Okhla Industrial Development Authority.
2. The word may be considered synonymous to 'acrostic'.

ACROSTIC: It is a form of literary exercise in which the first letters of each line in a poem form a word as we read downwards. *e.g.*

"Wait, O little child, wait!
In the wind lies thy message,
Not in the hubbub of the worldly;
Else you may repent, says the sage."
(The word formed is "WINE")

ACT: Major division in a dramatic work.

ADAGEL: Maxim or proverb.

ADDENDUM: Addition or appendix to a book.

AESTHETIC REALISM:

1. According to Hudson, "Esther Waters" by George Moore was a landmark in this movement toward aesthetic realism.
2. This movement was the vehicle of the new realists of which Moore and Gissing were representatives.
3. According to Hudson, "they mistook mere ugliness for frankness and "seeing life steadily and seeing it whole."

ALEXANDRINE:

1. It is a line of six iambic feet instead of five.
2. It is not known for certain how this line originated.
3. It appears that it was evolved by Spenser by adding the Alexandrine to the eight-line stave (a b a b b c b c) of Chaucer that he used in *the Monkeys Tale*.

ALIENATION EFFECT: It was a term devised by the famous German playwright, Bartolt Brecht, who wanted to bring home the need, for realization of a kind of 'alienation' of the audience and the actors from the stage during the performance of a play, as the play being a play and not a part of real life.

ALLEGORY: When the abstract or spiritual ideas are presented through living images, the result is the allegory.

Examples of Allegorical Works

(*i*) The Pilgrim Progress
(*ii*) The Scarlet Letter
(*iii*) The Faerie Queene
(*iv*) Morality Plays, such as "Everyman".
(*v*) Seven Deadly Sins in Dr. Faustus, etc.

ALLITERATION: It signifies the repetition of initial consonant sounds, *e.g.* The furrow followed free.

ALLUSION: Allusion is a reference to a well-known person, place, event, literary work, or work of art. Writers often make allusions to stories from the Bible, the Mahabharata, Greek or Roman mythology, plays by Shakespeare, famous quotes by historical figures such as Mahatma Gandhi, political and historical events, and to other materials with which they can expect their readers to be familiar. By using allusions, writers can bring to mind complex ideas simply and easily. Gandhi used an allusion to the writings of the Bible when he said, "An eye for an eye turns the whole world blind."

ALMANAC: Book or table comprising a calendar of days, weeks and months indicating special occasions or events.

ANAGNORISIS: It means Discovery or Reversal in a Tragedy.

ANAGRAM: Letters or word or phrase which, when re-arranged, form a new word.

ANAPAEST: It comprises two unaccented syllables followed by an accented one:

(*i*) Redeploy
(*ii*) Introduce
(*iii*) Camouflage

ANDROCENTRISM: The term implies the predominance of man in all social and intellectual activities.

ANECDOTE: Brief account or story about an individual.

ANGRY YOUNG MEN: It was a movement which came into existence in the second half of the twentieth century, mainly as a result of Osborn's play: "Look Back In Anger."

ANNOTATION: Textual comment on a book.

ANTAGONIST: Antagonist is a character or force in conflict with a main character, or protagonist. In the Harry Potter series, for example, Voldemort is the antagonist. Not all stories contain antagonists; however, in many stories the conflict between the antagonist and the protagonist is the basis for the plot.

ANTHOLOGY: Collection of poetry or prose from diverse sources.

ANTITHESIS:

1. It signifies the setting of one thing against another, often of opposite sense *e.g.*

   'A *friend never* betrays, an *enemy always* does.'
2. 'Antithesis' can be expressed in literature also by presenting two aspects (of life) side by side, *e.g.* the real and the marvellous.

APHORISM: Short statement of a truth or dogma couched in memorable terms.

APHORISTIC ESSAY: Aphoristic Essays are impersonal essays. They are pithy and short essays packful of the author's knowledge, wisdom and philosophy of life. They are rugged and abrupt and difficult to understand on account of their depth of thought.

APOSTROPHE: It implies an exclamatory address to a person. (usually a dead one), some inanimate object or an abstract idea, *e.g.* "Milton! thou shouldn't be living with us at this hour..."

ARCHAISM: It is a word or phrase which is no longer in use, *e.g.* loon, quoth, yclept, eftsoon(s), etc.

ARCHETYPAL APPROACH TO CRITICISM:

1. This Approach is also called Mythological, Ritualistic or Totemic Approach.
2. It endeavours to study literature on the basis of myth.

AREOPAGITICA: This is the name of Milton's famous prose pamphlet, pleading for freedom, freedom of the press, in particular.

ARGOT: Slang or coarse vernacular language.

ASIDE:

1. It is a kind of device similar to "soliloquy" (being probably comparatively brief) when a character speaks to himself.
2. The best example of an "aside" may be Shylock's words : "How like a fawning publican he looks" in Act, I sc. 3 of The Merchant of Venice.

ASSONANCE: Unlike the alliteration (which signifies the repetition of consonant sounds), it signifies the repetition of vowel sounds, *e.g.*
I *hear* him *bear* the mark of a *seer* on his head.

AUTOBIOGRAPHY: A form of nonfiction in which a person tells his or her own life story. Notable examples of autobiographies include Gandhi's My Experiments with Truthand Nehru's Towards Freedom. A memoir is a first-person account of personally or historically significant events in which the writer was a participant or an eyewitness and is a particular kind of autobiography.

AUTO SUGGESTIVE TEXT: The texts of certain very ancient books are not found in their authentic forms. Different editors or publishers modify them in their own way. Efforts should be made to discover their real or authentic form.

AVANT-GARDE: Without going into historical aspects of the word, one can say that it implies those (persons) who support or create the newest ideas, fashions (generally literary or artistic), techniques, styles, etc. in an art, piece of literature, etc.

BALLAD: The word 'Ballad' literally means 'a dance-song'. They generally sang of the brave deeds and heroic exploits of historical or legendary heroes and knights.

BATHOS:

1. It is a term to denote anticlimax.
2. It is generally used when there is sudden descent or fall from the sublime to the trite or ridiculous, *e.g.*

Delay not thine departure hence,
For thou mightst have a hot pudding,
Awaiting thee.

BELLES LETTERS: Essays on literary studies and the aesthetics of literature.

BIBLIOGRAPHY: List of works on a particular subject or author.

BIOGRAPHY: An account of a person's life.

BLANK VERSE: Poetry with unrhymed line endings (usually written in iambic pentameters).

BLURB: These are the words of praise or description of a book in a nutshell, inserted usually by the publisher on the cover page or jacket of the book, to attract the reader's eye.

BOUND VERSE: Verse based on metrical pattern.

BURLESQUE: Burlesque is defined as 'an incongruous imitation'. It imitates the matter or manner of a serious literary work, or literary genre, but makes the imitations funny and amusing by a ridiculous disparity.

BOWDLERIZE: To 'cleanse' a work by omitting or cutting out indecent passages, phrases or words.

CACOPHONY: When the excessive use of high sounding words is made such that the meaning is lost or diminished in value in the sound, the result is cacophony instead of euphony.

CADENCE: Rhythm and phrasing of language.

CAESURA:

1. In classical prosody, 'Caesura' means "break between words within a metrical foot." (Concise Oxford).
2. In English prosody, it means "pause about middle of line." (ibid.).
3. A Caesura "which does not immediately follow the ictus" is known as 'Feminine Caesura" (Chambers 20th century).

☛ In modern connotation, Caesura implies natural pause in a line of verse and not an unnatural or forced one.

CAMPUS NOVEL: The Campus Novels deal with the life and problems of students in colleges and universities. They highlight the problems of education and careers of students during this formative period.

CANON: Collection of works established as genuine.

CANTO: Division of an epic or narrative poem.

CAPTION: Short description accompanying an illustration.

CARICATURE: The chief characteristics of characters are sometimes so exaggerated by the author that the characters look like some humorous or even funny creatures. The result is the creation of caricatures. This is what Dickens (more than any other author) has done.

CATASTROPHE: The final end of the tragedy is called catastrophe. At this point the hero or the heroine or both meet their tragic death. The tragic end comes through Hamartia and Perpheteia. It signifies the complete (often sudden) devastation of the fortunes of a character (often the hero and/or the heroine) in a play or piece of fiction.

CATALOGUE: List of books or works.

CATHARSIS: This is the term used for the ousting of the emotions of pity and fear in the tragedy.

CAVALIER POETS: The Cavalier Poets were associated with the Court of Charles I. They wrote witty and polished lyrics of live and gallantry. The group included Richard Lovelace, John Suckling, Thomas Carew and Robert Herrick.

CHARACTER: Character is a person or an animal that takes part in the action of a literary work. The following are some terms used to describe various types of characters:

- main character is the one on whom the work focuses
- major characters include the main character and any other characters who play significant roles
- minor character is one who does not play a significant role
- round character is one who is complex and multifaceted, like a real person
- flat character is one who is one-dimensional
- dynamic character is one who changes in the course of a work
- static character is one who does not change in the course of a work
- protagonist is the leading character or main character in a drama, movie, novel or other fictional work
- antagonist is a character or a force which actively opposes or is hostile to the main character or protagonist

CHARACTERIZATION: Characterization the act of creating and developing a character. There are two primary methods of characterization: direct and indirect. In direct characterization, a writer simply states a character's traits, as when F. Scott Fitzgerald writes in his story "Winter Dreams," "He wanted not association with glittering things and glittering people—he wanted the glittering things themselves." In indirect characterization, character is revealed by one of the following means:

1. the words, thoughts or actions of the character
2. descriptions of the character's appearance or background
3. what other characters say about the character
4. the ways in which other characters react to the character

CHORUS: The term Chorus is taken from Greek drama. In English drama it is applied to a character who speaks the Prologue and Epilogue and also communicates to the audience the exposition, setting and offstage events in the play.

CHRONICLE OR HISTORICAL PLAY: A Chronicle or Historical play deals with the life of a king or with some important historical event. However, the dramatist weaves an imaginative or highly emotional garb around it to make it appealing to the spectators sitting in the theatre.

CIPHER: Writing that employs substitution or transposition of letters.

CLASSIC:

1. A classic (in reality, any book) is "the expression of man" as an individual.
2. It is also the expression of his mindset and the stance taken by him.

CLICHE: Any word, phrase or expression that has lost its real effect for having been too frequently used by authors or laymen is called a cliche which may otherwise be quite lovable, *e.g.*

(*i*) The news is too good to be true.
(*ii*) The sorrow was too deep for tears.
(*iii*) Thanking you in anticipation, etc.

CLIMAX:

1. It is the main point of interest in a play or novel which is reached usually in the third act (or sometimes 4th or a 5th act of a play) or towards the end.
2. The resolution often takes place after the Climax or the forces for it start working or increase their intensity after it.

COLLOQUIAL:

1. In speech, the use of certain words and phrases which are not acceptable in standard speech.
2. Such colloquial expressions should be avoided in all formal speech or writing.

COLONIALISM: The term differs from 'colonization' as the term may imply political or economic control of policies in a political unit without real annexation of land.

COLONISATION: Literarily, the most significant modernist theories in the matter of

(*i*) colonisation
(*ii*) post-colonisation
(*iii*) decolonisation, and
(*iv*) neo-colonisation have been provided and practised by—
    (*a*) Ngugiwa Thiong'o
    (*b*) Soyinka
    (*c*) Achebe Chinua, etc.

COMEDY: Comedy, in general, is a play of love, romance and marriage, joy and delight, wit and humour, light satire and irony exposing the follies and foibles of man good-humouredly. It deals with the light and trivial occurrences of life which are treated in such a manner that the ludicrous and comic element predominates.

COMEDY OF HUMOURS: Ben Jonson was the principal exponent of the Comedy of Humours. The Comedy of Humours was actually satirical comedy based on the classical concept of humours.

COMEDY OF MANNERS: The Comedy of Manners exhibited the artificial manners and low moral values of the high class society of the Restoration Age. They largely displayed the intrigues, witty remarks, sparkling dialogues and verbal fencings between gentleman and sophisticated ladies.

COMIC RELIEF: It is the name given to the brief light or comic dramatic action within the performance of a regular serious play to bring about a relief to the spectators to regain their real selves, for a short while to relax their strained nerves and prepare for further action, often more serious and culminating into breath-taking, gasping climax before denouement.

CONCEIT:

1. A conceit is a far-fetched or highly complex and even obscure or unintelligible comparison between two, often dissimilar, persons or objects.
2. It was commonly used by the Elizabethans particularly the Metaphysical poets, especially Donne.

CONCORDANCE: Alphabetical index of words in a work, or works by a single author.

CONFIDANT/CONFIDANTE:

1. In a play when a character takes upon himself/herself the task of some secret or information characteristic about a character to another, the character indulging in such an activity is

known as a "confidant" (mas.) or "confidante" (fem.)

2. Such information or secret is generally in the matter of love.
3. A good example of a 'confidante' is Nerissa in the Merchant of Venice.

CONFLICT: Conflict a struggle between opposing forces. Sometimes this struggle is internal, or within a character; at other times this struggle is external, or between a character and an outside force. Conflict is one of the primary elements of narrative literature because most plots develop from conflicts

CONNOTATION:

1. It signifies the suggested or implied meaning of word as against the transparent or literary meaning.
2. Connotative devices are brought into play by the artists, poets in particular to enhance pleasure and acceptability conveyed by words and other expressions.
3. Poets like Keats and T.S. Eliot frequently resort to the device of suggestiveness which is akin to connotation.

CONSONANCE: Consonance the repetition of similar final consonant sounds at the ends of words or accented syllables. Emily Dickinson uses consonance in the following lines:

But if he ask where you are hid
Until tomorrow–happy letter!
Gesture, coquette, and shake your head!

CONSUMMATION:

1. When a work achieves complete satisfaction on all counts—literary as well as artistic, it is consummation that results.
2. An artist who has the knack, calibre or skill to make this achievement, is a consummate artist.

COPYRIGHT: Protective law to prevent pirating or plagiarism of an author's work.

COUPLET: Two successive rhyming lines in poetry.

COURT COMEDY: It is opposed to the Domestic Comedy in the sense that instead of domestic scenes it contains other elements which attract a different kind of audience, *e.g.*

(*i*) endless play of words
(*ii*) elaborate dialogues
(*iii*) repartees, jests, retorts, etc.

CYCLE: Group of works united by an overall theme.

DACTYL: Dactyl means one accented syllable followed by two unaccented ones, *e.g.*

(*i*) Lazily
(*ii*) Separate
(*iii*) Unspoken.

DEISM: A "deist" is a theist who believes in the existence of God but rejects the idea of a revealed religion.

DENOTATION: Denotation the objective meaning of a word, independent of other associations that the word brings to mind.

DENOUEMENT: The conclusion of a comedy is called denouement. Here all the obstacles and tangles that came in the path of true love are resolved and the lovers get happily married.

DESCRIPTION: Description a portrayal, in words, of something that can be perceived by the senses. Writers create descriptions by using images. Description is one of the major forms of discourse and appears quite often in literary works of all genres.

DESCRIPTIVE CRITICISM OR PRACTICAL CRITICISM: Descriptive Criticism is a study or evaluation of individual works or authors. The critic evaluates their aims, methods and effects, and brings out their aesthetic beauty, emotional effect and literary significance by whatever criteria he deems fit.

DETONATION: When a word refers to its literal meaning independent of the meaning which the author may intend to convey, it is the device of "Detonation" which is at play.

DIABOLUS EX MACHINA:

1. The term literally means "devil out of the machine".

2. When all of a sudden a person or an event spoils the whole good game, causing unmitigated misery, it is the work of "Diabolus Ex Machina".
3. Thus, the term signifies sudden, unexpected turn of events for a plightful situation.

DIALECT: Manner of speaking pertaining to a particular class or geographical region.

DIALECTIC:

1. It was used originally to refer to the nature of a logical argument.
2. Later, it began to be linked to Kant, Hegel and Marx in varying forms.
3. The three generally accepted aspects of 'dialectic' are:
   (*i*) *Thesis:* It is akin to the (original) idea.
   (*ii*) *Antithesis:* It implies the inherent opposition in the thesis, which may operate after some time.
   (*iii*) *Synthesis:* It implies the resolution of the conflict to evolve a higher (or final) truth.

DIALOGUE:

1. Dialogue is something very important in any poetic or prose play or a piece of prose fictions.
2. (*i*) The nature of the dialogue, including its language depends upon the kind of the play—a tragedy, comedy, romance, etc. or the kind of the scene prevailing there at the time and place of the dialogue.
   (*ii*) Much also depends upon the taste of the spectators or audience which again is related to the spirit of the age.

A DIALOGICAL NOVEL: It is a kind of novel in which a number of voices, interactive in the scheme, operate in work, resulting in a kind of dialogue (or series of dialogues) as against the Monologic Presentation.

DIARY: Sequential private record of personal and other events kept by an individual.

DICTION:

1. It refers to the selection, arrangement and order of words.
2. The term which has become more popular in literary world is "Poetic Diction" to which a lot of space has been devoted by Wordsworth in his "Preface to Lyrical Ballads."

DICTIONARY: Book containing the words of a language, and their definitions, alphabetically; two-language dictionaries contain the corresponding words of both languages and their meanings, also alphabetically; any book that gives words and phrases about a particular subject, arranged alphabetically.

DIDACTIC: A work is didactic in nature when it undertakes to teach a moral, *e.g.* much of Wordsworth's poetry.

DIDACTIC LITERATURE: Didactic Literature is that form of literature that directly seeks to teach some moral or religious lesson. Allegorical works like Spenser's *Faerie Queene* or Bunyan's *Pilgrim's Progress* are didactic literature. Most of the eighteenth-century literature is didactic.

DIGEST: Publication where works are abridged.

DIGRESSION:

1. When a writer, instead of carrying on the main plot or incident, starts indulging in a side story, dialogue or descriptive narration, it is digression that results.
2. Digression gives extraneous pleasure which is not inherent in or indispensable to the main story.
3. Digression can sometimes enhance the value of a work but more often it mars its spirit.

DOCUMENTARY: Form of fiction or drama based on documentary evidence provided by newspapers, recent historical reports or other contemporary or recent factual evidence.

DOGGEREL: Rough, ill-constructed verse.

DOMESTIC COMEDY:

1. One of the earliest examples of the Domestic Comedies is "Gammer Gurton's Needle" (Cir. 1562)

2. It presents realistic life of the peasant class of its times.
3. It is full of fun and coarse humour.

DOUBLE ENTENDRE: Ambiguity in a word or expression, one of whose meanings is usually bawdy or frivolous.

DOMESTIC NOVEL: The domestic novels present the day-to-day domestic life of the middle-class families and their friends and relations. The festivals and festivities, functions and celebrations, birthdays and marriage are graphically described in them.

DRAMA: Drama is a long literary composition in prose or verse, developed through dialogues and action to be presented on the stage. While every other form of literature is complete in itself; drama remains incomplete without a stage.

DRAMATIC IRONY: It is a device occurring in a drama when a character on the stage is unaware of a fact which the audience know and understand.

DRAMATIC MONOLOGUE: 'Monologue' literally means 'Dialogue with the self'. In the Dramatic Monologue there is only one character who expresses out his own innermost feelings and thoughts through a long poetic speech. It offers a psychological analysis of the solo-speaker.

DRAMATIS PERSONAE: Characters in a play.

DUOLOGUE: Conversation between two characters in a play, story or poem.

EDITION: Total number of copies of a book printed from unchanged set of type.

ELECTICISM: The term implies the gleaning of facts or ideas from different sources instead of depending on just one source (or a few sources).

ELEGY: Serious meditative poem; often lamenting death.

EMPATHY: In a play or novel, when the reader or spectator begins to feel like the hero/heroine or some particular character as if he/she were that character, it is "empathy" which is at play.

EMPIRICISM: Empiricism implies the importance of experiment and experience in the matter of gaining knowledge.

ENCYCLOPAEDIA: Comprehensive work encompassing and describing many aspects of knowledge; specialist work covering comprehensively a subject or discipline.

EPIC: The Epic is the greatest and most sublime form of poetry. The Epic is a long poem, divided into several books, celebrating the life, heroic deeds and achievements of a national hero, whether historical or legendary.

EPIC STYLE:

1. It is a style which is dignified and exalted (as grand style is), as:
   (*i*) *Paradise Lost* by Milton
   (*ii*) *Aeneid* by Virgil
   (*iii*) *Iliad* by Homer
   (*iv*) *Hyperion* by Keats, etc.
2. Sometimes, it is, also referred to as 'heroic' style.'

EPIGRAM: A brief, pointed statement, in prose or in verse, often characterized by use of some rhetorical device or figure of speech.

EPILOGUE: It is the last item in a work of art (as in a drama) which often declares or comments upon the conclusion of the work.

EPIPHANY: Epiphany a sudden revelation or flash of insight.

EPISTLE: Direct address to another person, a 'letter' in the form of verse.

EPISTOLARY NOVEL: The Epistolary Novel is a novel of which the plot develops through the medium of letters. The characters exchange their thoughts and views through letters. There is very little dialogue face to face.

EPITAPH: Valediction to dead person or persons; inscription on a tomb or grave.

EPITHET: It comprises a word or group of words to describe the chief characteristics of a person, *e.g.*

(*i*) Alexander the Great

(*ii*) The Holy Bible.

EPONYMOUS: Person whose name becomes the title of the work.

ERASTIANISM:

1. It implies the doctrine that the state should have supremacy over the church in ecclesiastical matters.
2. Erastianism was one of the doctrines which was vehemently opposed by the followers of the Oxford Movement
3. The doctrine is probably wrongly ascribed to Erastus.

ESSAY: Short composition, usually in prose, discussing a topic or variety of topics.

EUPHEMISM: When an unpleasant expression has to be made in a comparatively pleasant or less harsh way, the mellowed or toned down words which are used express euphemism, *e.g.*

(*i*) Instead of saying about a person "He acted foolishly, we can say, "He should have acted more wisely."

(*ii*) Instead of saying about a person that he has died, we sometimes say, "God Almighty has called him" or "He has left for his heavenly abode."

EUPHONY:

1. It signifies the pleasant combination of words which create desirable rhythms and tonal effects without interfering with the intended meaning.
2. An excessive use of such devices can lead to tautology or bombasticism and sound superficial or facile.
3. The generally accepted antonym of euphony is "Cacophony".

EUPHUISM: An ornate, floral style of writing popularized by Lyly.

EXPOSITION: It signifies a way of writing where explanations are not withheld or suppressed but manifestly made clear to the reader for immediate response based on clarity.

FABLE: A short narrative in prose or verse, often with animals, that points a moral.

FICTION: General term for an imaginative work, usually in prose.

FIGURATIVE LANGUAGE: writing or speech not meant to be taken literally. Writers use figurative language to explain ideas in vivid and imaginative ways.

For example, Emily Dickinson begins one poem with this description:

It sifts from leaden sieves,
It powders all the wood.

By describing the snow as if it were flour, Dickinson renders a precise and compelling picture of it.

FIGURE OF SPEECH (OR OF RHETORIC): It signifies the unusual use of words to heighten their effect.

FIRST PERSON: Style of novel, etc., in which narrator is a character.

FLASHBACK:

1. When a writer while presenting a situation suddenly refers to a past situation or event, it is the device of "flashback" that he exploits.
2. Browning, T.S, Eliot and Stream of consciousness novelists, in particular, take advantage of this device.

FOIL: Foil is a character who provides a contrast to another character. In the Arthur Conan Doyle detective stories, Dr. Watson provides a foil to Sherlock Holmes.

FOLK TALE: Story handed down by word of mouth from generation to generation.

FOOT: In poetry, rhythmic unit of two or three syllables.

FORESHADOWING:

1. It is a device in which the author himself prepares the spectators (or readers) for the catastrophe or some important event which may be on the cards.
2. Such a device checks the readers, etc. from suffering from the malady of disbelief.
3. Shakespeare is probably one of the greatest masters of this device, and it is sometimes believed that one of the main reasons of Shakespeare's grand success was his convincing mastery over the technique of foreshadowing.

FOREWORD: Short introduction to a work.

FREE VERSE (VERS LIBRE): Poetry free from mechanical restrictions such as metre and rhyme, cadenced according to meaningful stress.

FUSTIAN: It means the use of pompous, ornate, Euphuist or bombastic language.

GAZETTEER: Geographical dictionary or index.

GENRE: Genre a division or type, of literature. Literature is commonly divided into three major genres: poetry, prose and drama. Each major genre can in turn be divided into smaller genres. Poetry can be divided into lyric, concrete, dramatic, narrative, and epic poetry. Prose can be divided into fiction (novels and short stories) and nonfiction (biography, autobiography, letters, essays, and reports.) Drama can be divided into serious drama, tragedy, comic drama, melodrama, and farce.

GHOST WRITER: Person who undertakes literary work for another who takes the credit.

GLOSSARY: Alphabetical list of unfamiliar or uncommon words, usually appended to work in which they appear.

GOTHIC: Gothic the use of primitive, medieval, wild, or mysterious elements in literature. Gothic novels feature places like mysterious and gloomy castles, where horrifying, supernatural events take place.

GROTESQUE: Grotesque the use of bizarre, absurd, or fantastic elements in literature. The grotesque is generally characterized by distortions or striking incongruities.

HAIKU: A Haiku is a Japanese poem of seventeen syllables, in three lines of five, seven and five traditionally evoking images of the natural world.

HAMARTIA: Hamartia is the 'tragic flaw' in the character of the tragic hero who is basically a good and great man. This 'tragic flaw' becomes the cause of his fall, doom and death.

HAPLOLOGY: Omission in utterance of a sound resembling neighbouring sounds.

HAPLOGRAPHY: The inadvertent writing once of what should have been written twice.

HEROIC COUPLET: A couplet written in iambic pentametre is known as a 'heroic couplet'.

HEROIC DRAMA: Heroic drama was mainly written in the Restoration Age principally by Dryden. It tried to emulate the dimensions of Epic or Heroic poetry. Its hero was a great warrior whose fate affected the fate of an empire, such as Dryden's *All For Love*.

HEROIC VERSE: A poem written in heroic couplets is known as 'heroic verse,' *e.g.* Pope's poems such as:

(*i*) Essay Man
(*ii*) Essay in Criticism
(*iii*) The Rape of the Lock, etc.

HISTORICAL NOVEL: The Historical Novel draws its theme from some important historical event. But around this historical event the novelist weaves some imaginative and artistic environment to make it an interesting and arresting theme for a novel.

HOMILY:

1. It is a term pertaining to a work which instead of laying stress on artistic or aesthetic standards, undertakes to urge the readers on to a high moral life.
2. It is just like a sermon in a church.
3. Such are the most of the poems of Longfellow.

HOMOGRAPH: It implies a word which has the same spelling and pronunciation as another, but is different in meaning and origin from the other, *e.g.* :

(*i*) bear (*n*) an animal
(*ii*) bear (*v*) (to) tolerate
(*iii*) bear (*v*) (to) carry

HOMONYM:

1. It is "a word having the same sound and perhaps the same spelling as another, but a different meaning and origin"
2. Hence, *Homonymous* means: " having the same name : having different *significations* and origin but the same sound." (ibid.)

HYPERBOLE: It is a figure of speech which expresses an exaggerated statement to heighten the effect of a rhetorical statement, *e.g.*

(*i*) O child, may you never die!
(*ii*) Child is Father of the Man

IAMBIC PENTAMETER: Iambic Pentameter a line of poetry with five iambic feet, each containing one unstressed syllable followed by one stressed syllable. Iambic pentameter may be rhymed or unrhymed. Unrhymed iambic pentameter is called blank verse, which Shakespeare often used in his plays.

IDIOM: Form of expression of phrase peculiar to its language and possessing a meaning other than its literal one.

IDOLATRY: It means the worship of an image which is believed to be the abode of a superhuman being.

IDYLL: The origin of Idyll may be traced back to the Greek poet Theocritus, Idylls are small lyrical poems generally describing the scenes and pleasures of rural countryside. They depict country life as realistically and pictorically as possible.

IMAGE: Image is a word or phrase that appeals to one or more of the five senses—sight, hearing, touch, taste, smell.

IMAGERY: Imagery is the descriptive or figurative language used in literature to create word pictures for the reader. These pictures or images are created by details of sight, sound, taste, touch, smell, or movement. The following stanza, from Kuangchi C. Chang's "Garden of My Childhood," shows how a poet can use imagery to appeal to several sense:

I ran past the old maple by the terraced hall
And the singing crickets under the latticed wall.
And I kept on running down the walk
Paved with pebbles of memory big and small
Without turning to look until I as out of the gate
Through which there be no return at all.

IMAGISM: School of poetry (early 1900s) concerned with precise language, direct treatment, and freedom of form.

IMPERIALISM: It means the state policy for a country (as of England and certain other European countries, in particular during certain periods of history) to expand its area by annexing foreign lands and subduing the natives.

IMPERSONALITY: It means that the author himself should not be palpably visible in a piece of literature, in other words, the work should be done on highly objective lines.

IMPRESSIONISTIC CRITICISM: Impressionistic Criticism is that branch of criticism in which the critic evaluates a work by the impressions it makes upon his own mind. He expresses the attitudes and feelingful responses the work evokes in him as an individual.

INDIANISM: When an expression is commonly used in India but is not used by the English, it is called an "Indianism," *e.g.*

(*i*) 'demise' instead of 'death'
(*ii*) 'bearer' instead of 'waiter'
(*iii*) 'left for his heavenly abode' instead of 'died,' etc.

INTERIOR MONOLOGUE:

1. It is a device, as used by James Joyce in *Ulysses*, to express the thoughts, feelings and emotions of a character on usually more than one levels of consciousness.

2. It is a sort of inner debate which may or may not be conflict in essence.

INTERLUDES: The interludes were generally short entertainments inserted within a longer play or amidst some other festivities or festivals. Their primary function was to entertain the audience by humour or even by farce.

INTRODUCTION: Essay stating author's intention to reader.

INVERSION: It is the figure of speech (much used by Milton but ridiculed by many modern critics) in which words are presented in their unnatural order, *e.g.*

O God's glory I sing,
And to His Mercy I pray.

IRONY: It is a device used to convey a meaning which is the opposite of the apparent meaning, *e.g.* What a brave son of India Jai Chand was!

JINGLE: Verse or verses with strong rhyme and rhythm.

JOURNAL: Paper, periodical or magazine.

JUDICIAL CRITICISM:

1. It is the kind of criticism which is a sort of judgement on a writer or his work of art.
2. Such kind of best example is Pope's *"Essay on Criticism"*.

LEGEND: Story about a particular person containing myth and historical fact; explanation of symbols on a map or chart.

LETTER: Letter is a written message or communication addressed to a reader or readers and generally sent by mail. Letters may be private or public, depending on their intended audience. Letters to the editor are a common form of public letter.

LEXICON: Dictionary, especially for Classical and Middle Eastern languages.

LIMERICK:

1. It is a kind of humorous verse written in five jingling lines.
2. The form seems to have derived "from a refrain formerly used, referring to 'Limerick' in Ireland."

LINGUISTICS: The scientific study of language.

LITOTES:

1. It is akin to "understatement" which is sometimes used by writers to emphasise the desired meaning, *e.g.* India is not lagging in Information Technology.
2. However, more often it is an "understatement used ironically, especially using a negative to express the category as :
   'I shan't be sorry when it's over' meaning 'I shall be very glad', or 'It was no easy matter' for 'It was very difficult.'

LOCAL COLOR: Local Color a literary work of characters and details unique to a particular geographic area. Local color can be created by the use of dialect and by descriptions of customs, clothing, manners, attitudes, scenery, and landscape.

LYRIC: A Lyric is a short musical composition meant to be sung to the accompaniment of a lyre by a single singer. Now the term is used for any short non-narrative poem expressing a single thought or feeling of the poet.

LYRIC POEM: Lyric Poem a melodic poem that expresses the observations and feelings of a single speaker. Unlike a narrative poem, a lyric poem focus on producing a single, unified effect. Types of lyric poems include the elegy, the ode, and the sonnet.

MANUSCRIPT: Book or work written by hand.

MAXIM: Short statement or even sentence containing a general truth about human conduct and human nature.

MELODRAMA:

1. It was a crude form of drama which appealed to the groundings who were not much interested in the artistic minuteness such as the plot, characterization, etc.

2. They wanted only entertainment through striking scenes and absorbing movement of incidents and situations.

METAPHOR: A figure of speech in which one thing is spoken of as though it were something else. The identification suggests a comparison between the two things that are identified as in "death as a long sleep" or "the sleeping dead." A mixed metaphor occurs when two metaphors are jumbled together. For example, thorns and rain are illogically mixed in "the thorns of life rained down on him." A dead metaphor is one that has been overused and has become a common expression, such as "the arm of the chair" or "nightfall." Metaphors are used to make writing more vivid and meaningful.

METAPHYSICAL: The term 'metaphysical' was first used by Dryden in his assessment of the poetry of John Donne. The metaphysical poets were men of learning, and to show their learning was their whole endeavour.

METAPHYSICAL SCHOOL OF POETRY: The term 'Metaphysical' was first used by Dryden and further extended by Dr Johnson. It refers to a group of seventeenth-century poets who employed far-fetched imagery, abstruse arguments, scholastic philosophical terms, and subtle logic.

METRE: The rhythmical pattern if a poem. The pattern is determined by the number and types of stresses or beats in each line. To describe the meter of a poem, scan the lines. Scanning involves marking the stressed and unstressed syllables as follows, with the stressed syllables in bold and the unstressed syllables in italics:

"*Me* **thinks** *the* **la***dy* **doth** *pro***test** *too* **much**"
(Shakespeare's *Macbeth*)

The weak and strong stresses are then divided by vertical lines (/) into groups called feet. The following types of feet are common in poetry written in English:

1. Iamb: a foot with one unstressed syllable followed by one stressed syllable, as in the word: a**round**.
2. Troche: a foot with one stressed syllable followed by one unstressed syllable, as in the word: **bro**ken
3. Anapest: a foot with two unstressed syllables followed by one stressed syllable, as in the phrase: in a**flash**
4. Dactyl: a foot with one stressed syllable followed by two unstressed syllables, as in the word: **ar**gument

Lines of poetry are often described as iambic, trochaic, anapestic or dactylic. Lines are also described in terms of the number of feet that occur in them, as follows:

1. *Monometre :* It means a line (or verse) with a single iamb (foot)
2. *Dimetre:* It means a line with two iambs.
3. *Trimetre:* It means a line with three iambs.
4. *Tetrametre:* It means a line with four iambs.
5. *Penta metre:* It means a line with five iambs.
6. *Hexta metre:* It means a line with six iambs.
7. *Hepta metre:* It means a line with seven iambs.

METONYMY:

1. It implies the use of the name of some person or thing for another person or thing, *e.g.*
   - (*i*) Have you studied 'Milton'? (Milton here means Milton's works).
   - (*ii*) In the 'light' of these remarks: ('light' here means in view of....)
   - (*iii*) Sceptre and Crown (i.e. monarchy) Must tumble down.

MIRACLE PLAY: A Miracle play is basically a religious play. They deal with the lives of saints and the miracles performed by them. The life and martyrdom of a saint formed the central theme of a Miracle play.

MOCK HEROIC: When an apparent epic is presented in a light vein, it is known as a "mock heroic" poem piece of fiction, etc., *e.g. The Rape of the Lock.*

MODERNISM: Towards the close of the 20th century, a movement against such modes as realism and naturalism started in all forms of literature and art such as poetry, drama, novel, music, painting, architecture, sculpture, etc. which continued unabated during the first world war period and partly upto the middle of the century.

MODULATION:

1. Of necessity, poetry is musical.
2. As in music, to avoid poetry from falling into "monotony," there is the system of "modulation" which here means, changing the key or tone, to introduce the element of variety to give or enhance pleasure.

MONOLOGUE: Single person addressing an audience alone, in drama, verse or prose. *Interior monologue*: unspoken but thought speech in verse or prose.

MOOD: Mood is the feeling created in the reader by a literary work or passage. Elements that can influence the mood of a work include its settling, tone, and events.

MORALITY PLAY: Morality Plays are allegorical plays. They present on the stage, personified Virtues and Vices. Everyman is presented as the Hero. Satan personified as Vice, God or Christ as Virtue, and Death as the Reward of Sin.

MOTIVATION: Motivation is a reason that explains a character's thoughts, feelings, actions, or speech. Characters are motivated by their values and by their wants, desires, dreams, wishes, and needs. Sometimes the reasons for a character's actions are stated directly, but other times the motives are implied or stated indirectly.

MYSTERY PLAY: The Mystery Plays basically deal with the themes taken from the Bible. They present in chronological order major events from the creation and fall of man through Nativity, Crucifixion, Resurrection of Christ to The Last Judgement.

MYTH: A fictional tale that explains the actions of gods or heroes or the causes of natural phenomena. Myths that explain the origins of earthly life, as does the Book of Genesis in the Bible and the Rig Veda, are known as origin myths. Other myths express the central values of the people who created them.

NARRATIVE: A story told in fiction, nonfiction, poetry or drama. Narratives are often classified by their content or purpose. An exploration narrative is a firsthand account of an explorer's travels in a new land. A historical narrative is a narrative account of significant historical events. Narrative poems also tell a story in verse form. Three traditional types of narrative verse are ballads, songlike poems that tell stories; epics, long poems about the deeds of gods or heroes, and metrical romances, poems that tell tales of love and chivalry.

NATURALISM: Naturalism was a literary movement among novelists at the end of the nineteenth century and during the early decades of the twentieth century. The Naturalists tended to view people as hapless victims of immutable natural laws. Authors include Jack London and Stephen Crane. Naturalism is a form of realism.

NARRATOLOGY: It means the study of different forms and structures of a narrative work in the matter of its various syntactical, literary and grammatical frameworks.

NEOCLASSICISM: Movement of late 17th and 18th century reviving classical values in English literature, emphasizing discipline, reason and clarity.

NEOLOGISM: Newly-coined word.

NEW WAVE (LA NOUVELLE VAGUE): Movement in literature and cinema originating in France in late 1950s that attempted to eschew fixed values, revealing a character by the way he experienced objects and events, which were often meticulously described.

NOM DE PLUME: Term used to indicate a fictitious name used by a writer to represent his work.

NON-FICTION: Nonfiction prose writing that presents and explains ideas or that tells about real people, places, objects or events. Essays, biographies, autobiographies, journals, and reports are all examples of non-fiction.

NOVEL: A long work of fiction. A novel often has a complicated plot, many major and minor characters, significant theme, and several varied settings. Novels can be classified in many ways, based on the historical periods in which they are written, on the subjects and themes that they treat, on the techniques that are used in them, and on the literary movements that inspired them.

NOVELETTE: Long short-story of some 15,000 words.

NOVELLA: Prose fiction longer than a short story, shorter than a novel (about 30,000 words), concentrating upon a single event. A novella is not as long as a novel but is longer than a short story. Ernest Hemingway's *The Old Man and the Sea* is a novella.

OBSCURITY: When a writer's language is not (or not easily) intelligible to the reader, the work concerned is termed as obscure.

ODE: An Ode is a long lyrical poem, serious in subject, elevated in style and elaborate in its stanzaic structure. It is in the form of an address to the object or the person about whom it is written.

OMNISCIENT AUTHOR: It is a device used by some outstanding modern novelists to move freely from the objective narrative to the internal or subjective psyche of a character or characters and then comment freely and apparently unattached on the significance, possibility or outcome of any or some events.

ONOMATOPOEIA: The use of words that imitate sounds. Examples of such words are buzz, hiss, murmur, and rustle. Isabella Gardner uses onomatopoeia in "Summer Remembered":

Sounds sum and summon the remembering of summers
The humming of the sun
The mumbling in the honey-suckle vine
The whirring in the clovered grass
The pizzicato plinkle of ice in an auburn uncle's amber glass

ORAL TRADITION: the passing of songs, stories and poems from generation to generation by word of mouth.

ORATORY: public speaking that is formal, persuasive, and emotionally appealing.

OXYMORON: It is a figure of speech in which two apparently contradictory words or terms are used to convey, a paradoxical sense, e.g.

(*i*) 'busy-idle days' (Lamb in *Dream children*)
(*ii*) Life in Death (Coleridge in *'Rime.....'*).

PANTOMIME:

1. A Pantomime is a dramatic representation pertaining to some myth, legend or traditional tale (or it may have some fairy element in it).
2. Pantomimes became popular in England particularly in the first quarter of the 18th century.

PARABLE: A story which conveys a moral lesson is known as a parable, as for instance, the biblical parables.

PARADOX: It is a figure of speech in which a truth is brought home through the use of self-contradictory statement, *e.g.*

(*i*) Cowards die many a time before their death.
(*ii*) Discretion is the better part of valour.
(*iii*) After death, we awake into an eternal life.

PARALLELISM:

1. It is a rhetorical device where balancing sentences, phrases or words are used to enhance effect, e.g.

   What is important is not what you say, but what is important is what you mean.
2. Excessive use of this device leads to monotony and superficiality.

PARODY: Comic imitation of serious words, style, sense, subject of a writer to make them appear ridiculous.

PASTORAL: Literature depicting idealized rural life.

PASTORAL ELEGY: It is an elegy cast into the conventional pastoral form. It is presumed that the poet is a shepherd mourning the death of a fellow shepherd. The whole image of goats, sheep, pastures and pastoral gods and goddesses is drawn into it.

PATHETIC FALLACY: When nature is shown as sympathising with human lot, the device used is called "pathetic fallacy," *e.g.*

(*i*) Byron's description of the battle of Waterloo in Childe Harold's Pilgrimage.

(*ii*) The behaviour of slow-moving nature in Tennyson's "Lotos-eaters".

PEDANTRY: The term refers to the excessive display of knowledge such as:

(*i*) Foreign words and phrases

(*ii*) Allusions

(*iii*) Archaic words

(*iv*) High sounding and sesquipedalian words

(*v*) Cataloguing, etc.

when these are not strictly needed within the context of the work.

PERIODIC SENTENCE: A sentence in which the Principal clause occurs at the end when it is preceded by one or more subordinate clauses, such that the sense is clear only when the whole sentence is read, is known as a 'periodic sentence'.

PERIODICAL: Magazine or journal published regularly.

PERIPETEIA: Peripeteia means sudden change in the fortune or position of the hero from good to bad, or high to low. This reversal of fortue happens due to Hamartia in the character of the hero.

PERIPHRASIS:

1. It means a round about way of saying a thing, *e.g.* An idle singer of an empty day, etc.
2. The term is close to circumlocution and euphemism in sense and effect.

PERSONAL ESSAY: According to Hudson, true essay is essentially personal. Montaigne says, "I am myself the subject of my book". In the Personal essay the author gives his own experiences, impressions of reactions about the subjects taken up for writing his essays.

PERSONIFICATION: A figure of speech in which a non-human subject is given human characteristics. In "April Rain Song," Langston Hughes personifies the rain:

Let the rain kiss you
Let the rain sing you a lullaby.

Effective personification of things or ideas makes them seem vital and alive, as if they were human.

PERSUASION: Writing or speech that attempts to convince a reader to think or act in a particular way. Persuasion is used in political arguments as well as in advertising, editorials and sermons.

PESSIMISTS: Although in English literature, we have a number of pessimist poets or a good number of poets expressing at times pessimistic ideas or writing sometimes in a pessimistic mood, yet two of the poets are known in particular, as "Pessimists." They are:

(*i*) Thomas Hardy

(*ii*) A.E. Housman

PHILOLOGY: Study of literature, language and linguistics.

PICARESQUE: Chronicle of adventures of a rogue; originated in 16-century Spain.

PINDARIC ODE: The Pindaric Odes are written on the model of the odes written by Pindar, the great Greak poet. They are choric in character and designed to be sung by a troupe of dancers in churches or public halls.

PLAGIARISM: Wrongful appropriation and publication of another's work as one's own.

PLATITUDE: It means a truth or generalization which is too well-known mainly because of its overuse, *e.g.*

Truth is evergreen.

PLEONASM:

1. It means the use of words more than those which are absolutely necessary, *e.g.*
   (*i*) He sat *down* on the ground.
   (*ii*) He looked up *high* towards the sky.
   (*iii*) He has got *sole* monopoly over such kind of business.
2. In essence, it is akin to Tautology or circumlocution.

PLOT: The plan or sequence of events in a literary work. In most novels, dramas, short stories, and narrative poems, the plot involves both characters and a central conflict. The plot usually begins with an exposition that introduces the setting, the characters, and the basic situation. This is followed by the inciting incident, which introduces the central conflict. The conflict then increases during the development until it reaches a high point of interest or suspense, the climax. The climax is followed by the end, or resolution, of the central conflict. Any events that occur after the resolution make up the denouement. The events that lead up to the climax comprise the rising action. The events that follow the climax comprise the falling action.

POEM: Literary work which may be in rhyme, blank verse or a combination of the two.

POETIC DICTION:

1. Diction stands chiefly for choice of words.
2. In poetry, poetic diction is unavoidable as mere metre is not enough to make a poem a literary piece of work.
3. In other words, mere versification or combination of words in rhyme or any other verse form does not make poetry.
4. The poets resort to several devices in this regard, some of which are :
   (*i*) Use of similes, metaphors, symbols, inversions, and other figures of speech as such as hyperbole, irony, antithesis, personification, etc.
   (*ii*) Omission of some parts of speech or grammatical rules.
   (*iii*) Use of archaic or uncommon words.
   (*iv*) Change in order of words, etc.
   (*v*) Use of picturesque phrases and expressions
   (*vi*) Use of other ornamental devices such as epithets
   (*vii*) Use of highly musical lies, fanciful flights etc.

POETIC JUSTICE: The term 'Poetic Justice' was coined by Thomas Rhymer. It means exact reward or punishment given to a character according to his good or bad deeds. This exactness of justice is possible only in the world of poetry.

POETIC LICENCE: By 'Poetic Licence' it is meant a certain amount of liberty enjoyed by the poets in the use of grammar, word-order or coinage of words in order to produce greater poetic effects.

POETRY: One of the three major types of literature, in which form and content are closely connected, like the two faces of a single coin. Poems are often divided into lines and stanzas and often employ regular rhythmical patterns, or meters. Most poems make use of highly concise, musical, and emotionally charged language. Many also make use of imagery, figurative language, and special devices such as rhyme.

POINT OF VIEW: The perspective or vantage point from which a story is told. Three commonly used points of view are first person, omniscient third person, and limited third person.

In *first person point of view*, the narrator is a character in the story and refers to himself or herself with the first-person pronoun "I."

The two kinds of *third-person point of view*, *limited* and *omniscient*, are called "third person" because the narrator uses third-person pronouns such as "he" and "she" to refer to the characters. There is no "I" telling the story.

In stories told from the *omniscient third person point of view*, the narrator knows and tells about what each character feels and thinks.

In stories told from the *limited third-person point of view*, the narrator relates the inner thoughts and feelings of only one character; and everything is viewed from this character's perspective. The *Harry Potter* series by J.K. Rowlings is told from the limited third-person point of view.

PORNOGRAPHY: Work in which there is a deliberate emphasis on the sexual behaviour of characters, in order to arouse sexual excitement.

POTBOILER: Work written essentially to gain the author a livelihood.

PRECIS: Concise statement; short summary of a work.

PREFACE: Introduction to a work.

PRE-RAPHAELITE SCHOOL OF POETS: A group of painter-poets led by D.G. Rossetti founded the Pre-Raphaelite School of poetry. Other poets of this school were Christina Rosetti, Swinburne, and William Morris. They wrote highly sensuous, pictorial and symbolical poems which could be painted with equal effect.

PROLOGUE: It is often the original statement by the writer (as in a drama) which highlights the chief aim of the work which is going to be unfolded or staged.

PROPAGANDA: Work devoted to the dissemination of an idea or belief, usually biased.

PROPHETIC NOVEL: The Prophetic Novels try to forecast what the future would be like. They do not claim to be absolutely correct. They only give a tentative picture of the future on the basis of the tendencies prevailing in the present.

PROSE: The ordinary form of written language. Most writing that is not poetry, drama or song is considered prose. It occurs in fiction and nonfiction.

(MODERN) PROSE STYLE:

1. The English prose style started by Bacon, flourished in the hands of Addison and Steele and numerous essayists and prose stylists that followed.
2. As a fine example of the latest modern prose style, Naipaul who won the Nobel Prize for Literature in 2001 deserves to be mentioned.

PROSODY: Study of the handling of language in poetry.

PROSOPOPAEIA: This figure of speech is used when:

(*i*) The past (called the Historic Present) is written in the present tense:
Sohrab and Rustam clash with their full might.

(*ii*) The (anticipated) future is written in the present tense:
Here, we go to our new house tomorrow with all our belongings carried in a lorry and then tucked in elegant mahogany almirahs.

PSEUDONYM: Name other than the true one used by an author to represent his work.

PSYCHOLOGICAL NOVEL: The Psychological Novels are also known as the "Stream of Consciousness Novels'. These novels probe into the working of human psychology at the conscious, subconscious and unconscious levels.

PSYCHOLOGICAL PROCESS: It is the process applied to the study of a piece of literature to penetrate another's mind and to study the activities, utterances, etc. of various characters, as, for instance, to arrive at the exact nature of Hamlet's madness whether there was "method" in it or not.

PUN:

1. When a word gives several meanings (often for fun) as in a play, it is the "pun" that is used.
2. Shakespeare is a great master of this device.
3. **Example :**
   (*i*) This is the *book*.
   (*ii*) It means
      (*a*) any book
      (*b*) a holy book, often the Bible.

REALISM: Literature that attempts to depict life objectively and faithfully.

REFORMATION: Reformation was a religious Movement led by Martin Luther in the fifteenth century. It protested against the practices of the Roman Catholic Church. It advocated complete faith in the Bible and in one's own soul for salvation.

REFRAIN: Phrase, line or lines repeated at intervals or at the end of a stanza in poetry.

REGIONAL NOVEL: The Regional Novel is a novel which describes the social and family life, customs and manners, language and dress, occupations and professions of the people of a particular region. The entire novel is woven around these factors of the region.

RENAISSANCE: The term Renaissance literally means re-birth on revival. In Art and Literature it meant the rebirth or revival of Greek art, literature, culture and pattern of life which had been partly or largely destroyed by the repeated invasions of the Turks.

REVIEW: Notice or critical article on musical, artistic or literary work.

REVUE: Theatrical entertainment made up of sketches, dances, songs, recitals and improvised pieces, usually humorous, satirical or topical.

RHETORIC: Art of using language, in speaking or writing, to persuade. The persuasive style (rather than the content) of a work.

RHYTHM:

1. It signifies the measured regular beat or movement of sounded words in language.
2. Rhythm is a must in poetry as well as prose, as it introduces or enhances the element of pleasure, interest and curiosity.

RHYME: Echoing sound or audible similarity in two or more words, especially at endings. Device used to construct much poetry.

RIDDLE: Puzzle, question or enigma; conundrum.

ROMAN A CLEF: Novel based upon actual people under disguised names.

ROMANCE: Tale of chivalry, originally written in verse (Medieval times); term applied now to any wonderful or mysterious tale far removed from reality.

ROMANCE LANGUAGES: Languages which have emerged straightaway from Latin and/or Greek, are called Romance Languages.

ROMANTICISM: Romanticism has been variously defined by various critics and scholars. According to Walter Peter, "Romanticism is the addition of curiosity to the desire of beauty.

ROMANTIC COMEDY: The Romantic Comedy is basically a love comedy. There is usually a story of triangular love with two heroes and one heroine, or two heroines and one hero, but finally the play ends in happy marriage.

SAGA: Lengthy prose work, sometimes in several parts, describing the history and events surrounding medieval kings, warrriors and, recently, fictitious families.

SATIRE: Dryden defines the Satire as "a literary composition whose principal aim is to ridicule folly or vice. The true end of Satire is the amendment of vices by correction." A healthy satire good-humouredly exposes one's folly or vice.

SCIENCE FICTION: Literature based on scientific fact or fantasy, on earth or on other worlds in space, often set in periods in the distant future.

SEMANTICS: Branch of linguistics dealing with meaning, and the change of meaning, in words.

SEMIOLOGY: General study or science of signs with which humans communicate with each other (including words and their use in every context).

SERMON: Verbal instruction of some length, usually religious.

SHORT STORY: Work of fiction usually revolving around single event.

SIC: Included in brackets after a printed word or quoted passage to indicate that it is quoted accurately, however actually incorrect.

SIMILE:

1. When we draw comparison between two persons by using (usually 'like', as-so or as) it is the 'simile' that we make use of, *e.g.*
   (*i*) As red as a rose
   (*ii*) As happy as a lark
   (*iii*) She looked like a violet, half-hidden behind the rock.
2. *An Exaggerated Simile:* It is a simile in which the sense is clearly exaggerated, *e.g.*
   (*i*) He ran as fast as lightning
   (*ii*) He has in himself the force as much as there is in ten horses.

SLANG: Colourful and vernacular language of the street, marketplace, barrackroom, workplace, sportsplace and playground.

SOLILOQUY: Kind of monologue in which a stage character expresses his thoughts and feelings.

SONG: Poem or verse set to music.

SONNET: 14-line poem of set rhyme-scheme; Elizabethan (Shakespearean) *ababcdcdefefgg*, Italian *abbaabba cdcdcd* (or *cdecde*).

STANZA: A group of lines in a poem that are considered to be a unit. Many poems are divided into stanzas that are separated by spaces. Stanzas often function just like paragraphs in prose. Each stanza states and develops a single main idea.

STREAM OF CONSCIOUSNESS: A narrative technique that presents thoughts as if they were coming directly from a character's mind. Instead of being arranged in chronological order, the events of the story are presented from the character's point of view, mixed in with the character's feelings and memories just as they might spontaneously occur in the mind of a real person. Stream-of-consciousness writing reveals a character's complex psychology and presents it in realistic detail.

STROPHE AND ANTI STROPHE:

1. Strophe is "the song sung by the chorus (in a Greek play) as it moved towards one side, answered by an exact counterpart."
2. Anti-Strophe is the term for the Strophe, "as it returned : part of any ode thus answered..."

STYLE: A writer's typical way of writing. Style includes word choice, tone, degree of formality, figurative language, rhythm, grammatical structure, sentence length, organization-in short, every feature of a writer's use of language. Ernest Hemingway in The Old Man and the Sea and Aravind Ardiga in The White Tiger, for example, use a simple or informal prose style that contrasts with V. S. Naipaul's more formal style of writing.

STOCK MATERIAL: Material necessary for a writer to write.

STOCK CHARACTERS: Characters that are commonly found in most of pieces of dramas or fiction.

STOCK SITUATIONS: Situations which are frequently presented by authors in their works.

SUSPENSE: A feeling of growing uncertainty about the outcome of events in a literary work. Writers create suspense by raising questions in the minds of the readers. Suspense builds until the climax of the plot, at which point the suspense reaches its peak.

SYMBOL: Anything that stands for or represents something else. A conventional symbol is one that is widely known and accepted, such as a voyage symbolizing life or a skull symbolizing death. A personal symbol is one developed for a particular work by a particular author. Examples include Melville's white whale in *Moby Dick.*

SYNTHESIS, POETRY OF: The term "Poetry of Synthesis" is referred to by I.A. Richards, and it has been thus explained by Cleanth Brooks—

"... a poetry which does not leave out what is apparently hostile to its dominant tone, and which, because it is able to fuse the irrelevant and disordant, has come to terms with itself and invulnerable to irony."

STRUCTURE: The structure meant is a structure of meaning, evaluations and interpretations; and the principle of unity which informs it seems to one of balancing and harmonizing connotations, attitudes and meanings.

SUBLIMITY: It is a term which is used to describe inexplicable beauty which is beyond any rules to describe or measure.

SYMBOLISM: French poetic movement of late 19th century that developed as revolt against realism, concentrating on evoking emotions by use of indirect suggestion (symbol and metaphor); flourished in Russia at turn of century as literary movement, and later in British novel.

SYNECDOCHE:

1. This figure of speech is used when the understanding of one thing by means of another is employed.
2. This can be done in several ways, some of which are mentioned below :
   (*i*) When a part stands for a whole or genus, e.g.
   We have fifty *hands* in our factory.
   (hands = workers)
   (*ii*) When a whole or genus stands for a part, e.g. He belongs to a different *world* from yors (world = category, social set-up, economic status, etc.)
   (*iii*) When an individual represents a class, *e.g.* He is the *Nestor* of our village.
   (Nestor = the oldest man)

SYNTAX: It means:

(*i*) The way a sentence is constructed
(*ii*) Arrangement of words in writing (or in speech) according to the rules of grammar
(*iii*) Rules pertaining to this system or arrangement.

SYNONYM: A word similar in meaning to another.

SYNOPSIS: Outline of the main points of a work; a summary.

TALE: Spoken or written narrative.

TAUTOLOGY: Overuse of synonyms or repetition of ideas in sentence.

THEME: A central message or insight into life revealed by a literary work. An essay's theme is often directly stated in its thesis statement. In most works of fiction, the theme is only indirectly stated: a story, poem, or play most often has an implied theme. In some forms of didactic literature, which is intended to be morally instructive, such as a fable or a parable, the theme can be stated outright at the end as the "moral of the story." In some modern literature, the theme can be very subtle and abstract.

THESIS: Long essay or treatise on a subject, usually expository; work presented to examiners for academic qualification.

THIRD PERSON: Style of novel, etc., in which narrator is outside action.

TONE: The writer's attitude towards his or her subject, characters, or audience. A writer's tone may be formal or informal, friendly or distant, personal or pompous.

TRACT: Short printed treatise on religious or political subject.

TRAGEDY: The Tragedy is the tragic story of a good and great man who, on account of a slight flaw in his character, passes through a harrowing emotional and spiritual crisis, and finally meets his doom and death.

TRAGEDY OF BLOOD (AND THUNDER):

1. It was basically a melodramatic presentation of horrible, gory scenes.
2. The first famous tragedy of this kind is Kyd's "Spanish Tragedy".

TRAGIC-COMEDY: A Tragic-Comedy is an artistic combination of both tragedy and comedy. It develops as a tragedy to the point of climax, and then takes a happy turn and finally ends into a happy denouement.

TRAGIC FLAW: In Shakespeare's tragedies, in particular, we often find a particular flaw in the character of the hero which ultimately leads to the fall of his destiny, along with the fall of his state or estate.

TRANSFERRED EPITHET: When an epithet is transferred from a person to a thing, it is known as a 'transferred epithet', *e.g.*

(*i*) It is a *foolish* idea

(*ii*) Let *happy* days come.

TRANSLATION: Rendering of a work into another language.

TREATISE: Formal work examining a subject and the principles underlying it.

TROCHAIC LINE METRE:

1. A line in verse is known as a *"trochaic" line* when the first, third and other odd syllables in it are accented (as in the 'Iambic metre') irrespective of the length of the line.
2. A poem comprising such lines is known as having been written in the "Trochaic" metre.

UNDERSTATEMENT: It is practically the opposite of hyperbole and is sometimes used by the writers to emphasise indirectly the desired meaning.

VADE MECUM: Manual or handbook carried for frequent reference.

VERISIMILITUDE: It is the likeness of truth presented in a work of art that makes it similar to the characteristics or situation in real life and that enables the readers to accept it ungrudgingly as truth (and may be, sometimes, more than real happening in life).

VERNACULAR: Domestic or native language.

VERSIFICATION: Study of how traditional verse is constructed.

WIT: Dryden defines (in "Annus Mirabilis") wit as "delightful imagining of persons, actions, passions or things."

YARN: Story or tale, sometimes improbable and far-fetched.